BVR Guide to Ancillary Healthcare Services Valuation

Mark O. Dietrich
Editor

BVR
What It's Worth
1000 SW Broadway, Suite 1200, Portland, OR 97205
(503) 291-7963 • www.bvresources.com

BVR
What It's Worth

Publisher: Sarah Andersen

Managing Editor: Monique Nijhout-Rowe

Senior Copy Editor: David Solomon

Chair and CEO: David Foster

President: Lucretia Lyons

Chief Revenue Officer: Lisa McInturff

Customer Service Manager: Retta Dodge

Print ISBN: 978-1-62150-092-6

EPUB ISBN: 978-1-62150-093-3

Library of Congress Control Number: 2016961782

Table of Contents

About the Authors

ABOUT THE EDITOR

Mark O. Dietrich, CPA/ABV, is editor, technical editor, and contributing author to the *Business Valuation Resources (BVR)/American Health Lawyers' Association (AHLA) Guide to Healthcare Valuation,* 4th edition (2016); editor and principal author of Business Valuation Resources' *Guide to Physician Practice Valuation,* 3rd edition (2016); co-editor and contributing author of the *BVR/AHLA Guide to Healthcare Industry Compensation and Valuation,* 2nd edition (2016); and co-author with Gregory Anderson, CPA, CVA, of The Financial Professional's *Guide to Healthcare Reform,* published by John Wiley & Sons. Mark is also author of the *Medical Practice Valuation Guidebook* and co-author of *PPC's Guide to Healthcare Consulting,* along with more than 100 articles on valuation, taxation, managed care, and the healthcare regulatory environment. He serves as Of Counsel to Meyers, Harrison & Pia. Mark's career experience includes serving as partner-in-charge of the annual audit of an 80-physician tax-exempt faculty group practice, representation of tax-exempt and taxable entities in Internal Revenue Service field audits, participation in the development of a 250-physician independent network and negotiation of its managed care and Medicare Advantage contracts, and more than 400 valuation engagements in the healthcare industry.

A regular speaker at national conferences on healthcare valuation and other topics, Mark also has lectured in the United Kingdom during 2009, 2011, 2012, and 2014 on managed care, healthcare valuation, and valuation of medical practices to Her Majesty's Revenue and Customs. He is a member of the editorial board of *Financial Valuation and Litigation Expert* and chaired the AICPA's National Healthcare Industry Conference Committee in 2012 and 2013. Mark has also served on the AICPA's ABV Credential Committee and ABV Exam Review Course Task Force.

CONTRIBUTING AUTHORS

G. Don Barbo, CPA/ABV, is a managing director with VMG Health. Don has extensive experience in healthcare valuation engagements involving mergers and acquisitions, divestitures, partnership transactions, leasing arrangements, divorces, and commercial damages. His healthcare valuation experience includes hospitals, ambulatory surgery centers, imaging centers, cardiac catheter centers, and physician practices. He has also served as the chief financial officer for a physician practice management company. Don has published numerous articles and is a frequent speaker regarding the valuation of healthcare businesses. He also serves on the Panel of Experts for the Healthcare Section of the Financial Valuation and Litigation Expert's newsletter. He holds an undergraduate degree in accounting from Texas Tech University and an MBA from the SMU Cox School of Business.

Carol W. Carden, CPA/ABV, ASA, CFE, is a principal with PYA and provides business valuation and related consulting services to a wide variety of business organizations, primarily in the healthcare industry. Ms. Carden's primary areas of expertise are in finance, valuation, managed care, and revenue cycle operations for healthcare organizations. She has performed appraisals of businesses and securities for a wide variety of purposes such as mergers, acquisitions, joint ventures, management service agreements, and other intangible assets. She is also a nationally recognized speaker and writer on healthcare valuation topics. She is the chair of the Business Valuation Committee for the AICPA, was chair of the 2010 National AICPA Business Valuation Conference, and was on the planning committee for the 2011 AICPA National Healthcare Conference.

Darcy Devine, ASA, CVA, specializes in the valuation of healthcare assets and services. For 20 years, she has assisted hospitals, health systems, investors, physicians, and other providers with business and equipment appraisals, fair market value opinions, compensation assessments, and valuation report reviews. She holds a Bachelor of Business Administration with a concentration in finance from the Goizueta Business School at Emory University and a Master of Business Administration from the University of Georgia.

Alice G. Gosfield, Esq., is the principal of Alice G. Gosfield & Associates, P.C. in Philadelphia. Her legal career has been restricted to health law with an emphasis on representation of physicians and their group configurations and a focus on noninstitutional reimbursement including Medicare, managed care, fraud and abuse compliance and avoidance, medical staff issues and utilization management, and quality issues. Ms. Gosfield served as chairman of the board of directors of the National Committee for Quality Assurance and on four committees of the Institute of Medicine of the National Academy of Sciences. She is the first chairman of the board of PROMETHEUS Payment Inc. and served as president of the American Health Lawyers Association and chaired its Physician and Physician Organizations Institute. She is a graduate of Barnard College and New York University School of Law.

Alyssa C. James, Esq., works with clients in numerous aspects of healthcare law. Her work involves counsel regarding hospital/physician contracting matters, fraud and abuse/Stark analyses, hospital and health system matters, regulatory and compliance issues, organization governance, corporate transactions, and hospital/physician alignment. James has made several presentations in the area of fraud and abuse, including for the Healthcare Financial Management Association and Indianapolis Bar Association. She received her law degree and graduate certificate in health law from Indiana University Robert H. McKinney School of Law.

Matthew D. Jenkins, JD, is a partner in the Richmond, Va., office of Hunton & Williams LLP and heads the firm's Health Law Group. He has worked extensively with hospitals and multi-hospital systems on regulatory, corporate, governance, and transactional matters. He has led a number of nonprofit entities through conversion transactions resulting in the creation of substantial community foundations. His work also involves legislative matters and practice before administrative agencies. Mr. Jenkins is a member of the American Bar Association's Health Law Section, where he serves as a vice-chair of the Transactional & Business Interest Group. He served two terms as a governor's appointee on the Special Advisory Commission on Mandated Health Insurance Benefits for the Commonwealth of Virginia. He is a past chair of the Health Law Section of the Virginia State Bar. Mr. Jenkins earned his J.D. in 1984 from the University of Virginia.

Elliott Jeter, CFA, CPA/ABV is a managing director at VMG Health. He specializes in providing valuation, transaction advisory, strategic, and operational consulting services to the firm's clients. He has extensive experience working closely with ambulatory surgery centers, hospital systems, physician groups, and other healthcare providers. Jeter is a graduate of Texas A&M University and also earned a Masters of Business Administration from the University of Texas at Austin. He is a frequent speaker at healthcare trade association meetings and has written numerous articles on healthcare valuation issues that have been published in industry magazines and journals.

Karin Chernoff Kaplan, MBA, CVA is a director at Veralon, a national healthcare strategy and valuation firm. She is an expert in healthcare valuation and has extensive experience in healthcare strategy, finance, and operations, having spent more than 30 years as a consultant and healthcare management professional. Kaplan works with health systems, community and teaching hospitals, physicians, and other healthcare providers on a wide range of matters. She holds a certification from the National Association of Certified Valuators and Analysts and is a frequent speaker on physician-hospital alignment, compensation design, and business valuation topics at the national level.

Robert M. Mundy, CPA, ABV, CVA, is consulting principal at Pershing Yoakley & Associates P.C. (PYA). He has a broad background in business valuations with extensive experience in healthcare valuation engagements involving mergers and acquisitions, financial reporting, joint ventures, divestitures, partnership transactions, leasing arrangements, and divorce settlements. His healthcare valuation experience includes general acute care and specialty hospitals, diagnostic imaging centers, ambulatory surgery centers, skilled nursing facilities, assisted living centers, cancer treatment centers, cardiac catheter labs, and a variety of physician practices. He has also held business valuation and auditing positions at a regional public accounting firm.

Aaron Murski, CVA is a managing director at VMG Health where he focuses on developing client relationships and providing valuation, transaction advisory, and operational consulting services in the healthcare services industry. Specifically, he has significant experience with the acute care and specialty hospital, physician practice, inpatient rehabilitation, cancer treatment, ambulatory surgery center, and diagnostic imaging segments. In addition to the extensive valuation experience for transaction planning and financial reporting purposes, he has consulted on numerous development, feasibility, and recapitalization analyses for joint venture, restructuring, and de novo business development purposes. Murski received a Bachelor of Business Administration in finance from the Mays Business School at Texas A&M University.

Kenneth W. Patton, ASA, is managing director of ComStock Advisors and specializes in providing business valuation and ESOP-related services. He is the author or co-author of approximately 30 articles on business valuation. He has made numerous speeches on business valuation topics. Patton acted as expert witness in many state and federal courts on matters that reached the stage of deposition and trial testimony. He has a bachelor's degree in economics from the University of Tennessee and a master's degree in finance from Rhodes College.

James M. Pinna, Esq., is a partner in the Richmond, Va., office of Hunton & Williams LLP and practices with the firm's Health Law Group. He works primarily with hospitals, multihospital systems, and other healthcare providers on regulatory, transactional, corporate governance, and compliance matters. He is a vice chair of the Business & Transactions Interest Group of the American Bar Association's Health Law Section and a member of the American Health Lawyers Association. Previously, he worked in business development for National Nephrology Associates, a privately held dialysis company based in Nashville. Mr. Pinna earned his J.D. from the University of Virginia.

Robert F. Reilly, MBA, CPA, CMA, CFA, ASA, CBA, is a managing director of Willamette Management Associates. Robert has been the principal analyst on over 2,000 valuations of businesses, business interests, and intellectual properties in virtually every industry and business sector. Robert holds an MBA in finance from Columbia University. He is a member of the American Economic Association, National Association of Business Economists, American Society of Appraisers, Institute of Business Appraisers, American Bankruptcy Institute, Institute of Property Taxation, and several other professional organizations. He is a co-author of the following six textbooks: *Valuing a Business: The Analysis and Appraisal of Closely Held Companies, The Handbook of Advanced Business Valuation, Valuing Intangible Assets, Valuing Small Businesses and Professional Practices, Valuing Accounting Practices,* and *Valuing Professional Practices: A Practitioners Approach.*

Stuart J. Schaff, CVA, CHFP is a manager at Veralon, a national healthcare strategy and valuation firm. He advises healthcare organizations on a wide range of physician-hospital alignment matters including conducting valuations for healthcare businesses including medical practices and ambulatory surgery centers, determining the fair market value of hospital-physician compensation arrangements, designing physician compensation models for practices from a single physician to large groups with multiple specialties, and facilitating the formation of clinically integrated networks and accountable care organizations. Schaff is designated as a certified valuation analyst by the National Association of Certified Valuators and Analysts and a certified healthcare financial professional by the Healthcare Financial Management Association. He frequently presents on healthcare finance and physician alignment topics.

Alan B. Simons, CPA/ABV, CFF, CMPE, DABFA, is the principal-in-charge of LarsonAllen's national health care valuation practice and the business valuation and litigation support practice for the Philadelphia office. He is an active member of the Healthcare Financial Management Association (HFMA), the Medical Group Management Association (MGMA), the American Health Lawyers Association (AHLA), the American Society of Appraisers (ASA candidate), the Institute of Business Appraisers (IBA), the American Institute of Certified Public Accountants (AICPA), the Pennsylvania Institute of Certified Public Accountants (PICPA), and the Forensic and Valuation Services Division of the AICPA.

Douglas G. Smith is managing partner of strategic positioning and consulting services at Integrated Medical Partners. He is experienced with strategic action planning, operations profit improvement, physician leadership development, and radiology group governance and management. Smith is a frequent speaker on a variety of topics for the diagnostic imaging services sector.

Todd J. Sorensen, MBA, CVA, is managing director of VMG Health. He specializes in providing valuation and transaction advisory services to the firm's healthcare clients. He has acted as financial advisor in transactions with physician groups, acute care hospitals, health maintenance organizations, preferred provider organizations, diagnostic centers, ambulatory surgery centers, home health agencies, physical and operational therapy centers, institutional pharmacies, retail pharmacies and rural health clinics. Mr. Sorensen received his MBA from Baylor University.

Jessica E. Stack, MBA is a manager at Veralon, a national healthcare strategy and valuation firm. She advises clients on a wide range of physician-hospital alignment, compensation, financial planning, and valuation matters. Stack has worked with nonprofit and for-profit hospitals, health systems, physician organizations, and healthcare attorneys across the United States. In addition to her healthcare valuation experience, Stack has managed valuations of AIG's central region entities located in the Middle East and Africa and provided services to organizations in a variety of industries for M&A planning and reporting, ASC 805 purchase price allocations, ESOPs, strategic business and financial planning, startup venture feasibility, and tax and estate planning.

Kathie L. Wilson, CPA, CVA, maintains a consulting practice, assisting accountants and attorneys in the areas of medical practice accounting and valuation and family law litigation in the San Francisco Bay Area. She holds a Masters in Taxation from Bentley College and a B.A. in business administration from the University of Washington.

Joseph N. Wolfe, Esq., is a partner with Hall Render, the largest healthcare-focused law firm in the country, now with offices nationwide. He provides advice and counsel to some of the nation's largest health systems, hospitals, and medical groups on a broad range of regulatory, operational, and strategic matters. He regularly counsels clients on a national basis regarding compliance-focused physician compensation strategies. He is a frequent speaker on issues related to the physician self-referral statute (Stark Law), hospital-physician transactions, physician compensation, and healthcare valuation issues. Before attending law school at the University of Wisconsin, he served as a combat engineer in the United States Army.

Introduction

I am pleased to release the first edition of the *BVR Guide to Ancillary Healthcare Services Valuation*, the successor to my first book, *The Medical Practice Valuation Guidebook*, which was published back in 1999.

The Contents

This new guide, which focuses specifically on ancillary healthcare services, opens with an analysis of the healthcare market and how the market share of insurers and relative negotiating strength of ancillary service providers affects value. This is followed by a chapter, "Factors in Estimating Cost of Capital and Forecasting Cash Flow in Healthcare," that focuses more on finance and expanded examples of cash flow forecasting anomalies in the industry.

Separate chapters address various aspects of the regulatory environment, the knowledge of which is critical to a defensible valuation conclusion. Robert Reilly contributes a comprehensive chapter titled "Valuation Issues Affecting Tax-Exempt Healthcare Organizations." He includes an important discussion subtitled "Analyst Common Misconceptions Regarding Healthcare Property and Services Valuations." I encourage you to read that section in particular and, notably, the context of Robert's statement that "the analyst should consider if there are several contracts being entered into as part of the healthcare property transfer.... And the analyst should consider whether there are employment agreements, noncompete agreements, intellectual property licensees, lease transfers, or other agreements that are part of the overall transaction. If so, the analyst should assess the fair market value of the total (multicontract) transaction."

"Converting Physician Practices to Tax-Exempt Status" is included in the guide since hospitals often employ this strategy with their physician practices.

As editor and contributor to the guide, I developed a new chapter, "Patient Medical Records, HIPAA and State Medical Records Law in Valuation and Litigation." I am most grateful to reviewer and technical contributor Lara B. Winn, Esq., of Ankner and Levy in Boston for her work on this chapter. The focus of this chapter is threefold: (1) to provide knowledge of the law; (2) to identify circumstances in which valuation analysts and experts become subject to HIPAA's privacy and security rules; and (3) to explore how HIPAA, state law, contract law, and technology in the form of electronic health records have combined to end the appropriateness of conventional application of the cost approach to value medical records. More often than not, it is likely that the liability for secure storage and retrieval of medical records, especially paper records that will soon be functionally obsolete, exceeds the potential value of those records.

To address the explosion in qui tam case litigation and settlements involving valuation issues, I have contributed a chapter analyzing key cases, including *DaVita* (a dialysis company), *Citizen's Medical* (a hospital), *Meridian* (a surgery center operator), and *North Broward* (a hospital). The chapter looks at issues involving business valuation techniques and analyzes expert testimony and expert reports. Readers should find a wealth of insight and warnings here, regardless of whether one accepts or rejects the position of the relators. Joseph Wolfe and Alyssa James of Hall Render provide an in-depth review of the Stark law and regulations' volume or value of referrals prohibition that can serve as a useful guide in evaluating the qui tam cases.

The "Valuation of Healthcare Industry Enterprises" section of the guide contains nine chapters. Elliott Jeter of healthcare valuation firm VMG contributes one on urgent care, a rising phenomenon in the post-ACA era that has attracted much attention and equity capital. Darcy Devine has added a chapter on the valuation of pathology labs. Karin Chernoff Kaplan, Stuart J. Schaff, and Jessica E. Stack (Veralon) contribute "Valuing CINs, ACOs, PHOs, and IPAs," an in-depth look at the mechanics of valuing common forms of clinical integration arrangements between physicians and hospitals.

Carol Carden (PYA) provides two chapters from her depth of expertise, including one on valuing dialysis clinics that is an important read given the focus of regulators on this industry segment. She also wrote "Valuing Joint Ventures and Other Physician Alignment Initiatives," a topic that is critical for hospital integration strategies with physicians.

Don Barbo (Deloitte) and Robbie Mundy (Ankura) provide a comprehensive chapter on valuing hospitals in the post-ACA era. Doug Smith of Integrated Medical, a leading imaging industry consultant, offers a complete chapter on revenue forecasting in the imaging sector, and Alan Simons (CliftonLarsonAllen) updates the home health chapter. Finally, Todd Sorensen (VMG) contributes a comprehensive chapter on valuing ambulatory surgery centers, including the nuances of control versus noncontrol transactions.

Closing

As an industry, the government and by extension the public, as well as our clients, rely upon us to exercise professional judgment in a sound and reasoned manner that reflects not only technical knowledge of finance and valuation, but also a profound respect for the law and regulations. I hope readers of this new guide will find herein technical knowledge that is also practical and tempered with respect for the law.

Acknowledgements

I am deeply indebted to all of the contributing authors for taking the time out of their business and personal lives to provide content for the guide. With an unprecedented volume of work in healthcare appraisal and transactions, this is a considerable commitment to the profession's body of knowledge.

As editor and technical editor for this first edition of the *guide,* and on behalf of Business Valuation Resources, our thanks to all the contributors.

Mark O. Dietrich, CPA/ABV

Part I.
The Healthcare Marketplace

Chapter 1.
Healthcare Market Structure and Its Implication for Valuation of Privately Held Provider Entities—An Empirical Analysis

CONTENTS

Chapter 1.
Healthcare Market Structure and Its Implication for Valuation of Privately Held Provider Entities—An Empirical Analysis

By Mark O. Dietrich, CPA/ABV

Author's note: I originally conducted this study in early 2008 to see if I could confirm my hypothesis and experience that there were underlying structural reasons that existed in local markets that would explain—and convince my colleagues of—the vast differences in reimbursement, profitability, and market participants that I had encountered in my appraisal and consulting practice and seminar presentations. As the research demonstrated, there were long-standing, historical reasons for these differences. The results first appeared in the Summer 2008 edition of Business Valuation Review *and the information is reprinted with permission.*

Subsequent to my research, a variety of other studies appeared, including one by the Government Accountability Office (GAO), another in the journal Health Affairs, one by the Center for Studying Health System Change, and one by KQED National Public Radio reporter Sarah Varney.[1] A series of annual studies titled "National Insurer Report Card" by the American Medical Association of concentration of insurer market share also bears out the findings in this article.

The GAO report *Nonprofit Hospitals: Variation in Standards and Guidance Limits Comparison of How Hospitals Meet Community Benefit Requirements* was released in September 2008. Exhibit 1 is taken from that report and shows a concentration of nonprofit hospitals consistent with my research.

1 www.npr.org/2010/11/18/131410569/big-hospital-chains-use-clout-to-dictate-premiums, November 2010.

Exhibit 1. Geographic Distributions of Nonprofit Hospitals in 2006

Sources: GAO analysis of 2006 CMS data; Map Resources (map).

Note: Hospitals include nonfederal, acute care, general hospitals.

The *Health Affairs* study "The Increased Concentration of Health Plan Markets Can Benefit Consumers Through Lower Hospital Price"[2] found that markets in which insurers held the upper hand in terms of market power had lower hospital prices by approximately 12%, while most markets had high concentrations of hospital market power and this latter condition led to higher hospital prices.

Research Brief No. 16 from the Center for Studying Health System Change, "Wide Variation in Hospital and Physician Payment Rates Evidence of Provider Market Power," looked at eight specific healthcare markets—Cleveland; Indianapolis; Los Angeles; Miami; Milwaukee; Richmond, Va.; San Francisco; and rural Wisconsin—and found dramatic differences in inpatient hospital rates consistent with local market power of insurers and providers.

Greg Anderson and I documented much of my earlier work as well as our joint work elsewhere herein ("Evaluating RVU-Based Compensation Arrangements") in our 2012 book *The Financial Professional's Guide to Healthcare Reform.* Timothy Smith's work in the third edition of the *Healthcare Guide* expands on and emphasizes Greg's and my seminal work on market differences in RVU

2 Glenn A. Melnick, Yu-Chu Shen and Vivian Yaling Wu, *Health Affairs*, 30, no.9 (2011):1728-1733.

payment rates and the resultant limitations on generic market data. The aggregate of this research led to the new chapter in the guide's 4th edition titled "Using Work RVUs and 'Particular Market' Rates to Establish Fair Market Value Physician Compensation."

In December 2014, the GAO released a study titled "Private Health Insurance: Concentration of Enrollees Among Individual, Small Group, and Large Group Insurers From 2010 Through 2013,"[3] updating similar studies it had conducted in the past. The 2014 study is significant because it reflects certain post-ACA changes in the insurance market. Here are some of the notable observations that are consistent with my own research and that have significantly influenced my approach to local-market-specific valuation.

> *While states may have* ***multiple local markets*** *with differing concentrations of enrollees among health insurers,* the data we used to measure this concentration by type of market segment are only available at the state level. Therefore, to make comparisons between state and local level estimates of concentration, we also analyzed a recent study by the American Medical Association (AMA). Although the AMA study does not report concentration by type of market segment, it does report concentration for Metropolitan Statistical Areas (MSA) within each state (emphasis added).
>
> We found that, while several insurers participated in each state's individual, small group, and large group health insurance markets in 2013, enrollment was concentrated among the three largest insurers in most states. Specifically, in each of the three market segments, the three largest insurers had at least 80 percent of the total enrollment in at least 37 states.
>
> Further, these three market segments remained concentrated in most states from 2010 through 2013. Specifically, for each of these market segments, there were at least 30 states for which the three largest insurers had at least 80 percent of the total enrollment in each of the four years.[4]

There are three market segments in health insurance as noted above, individual, small group, and large group. Not described is the self-insured segment, which is the largest segment. The maps in Exhibit 2 show state-by-state concentration in each of the three insured markets.

3 www.gao.gov/products/GAO-15-101R.

4 www.gao.gov/products/GAO-15-101R.

Exhibit 2. Enrollment Share for Three Largest Health Insurers in the Individual Market

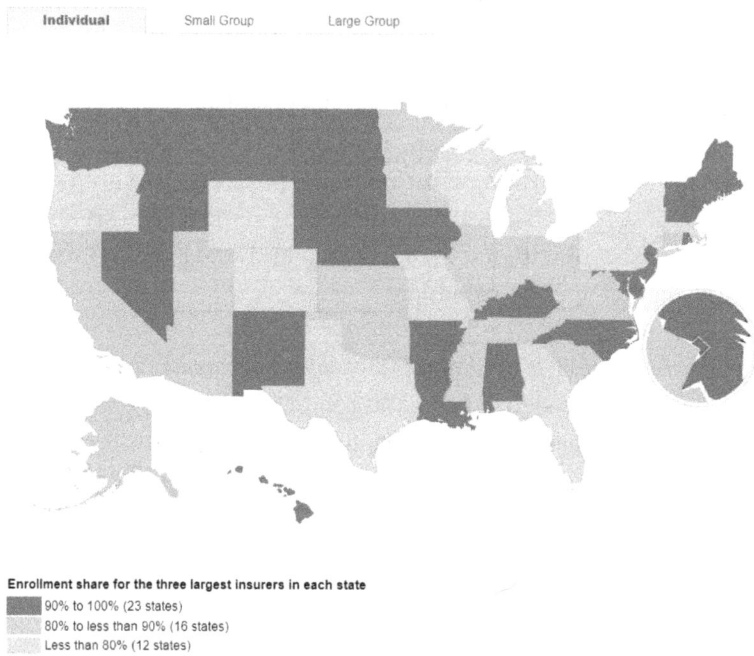

Exhibit 3. Enrollment Share for Three Largest Health Insurers in the Small-Group Market

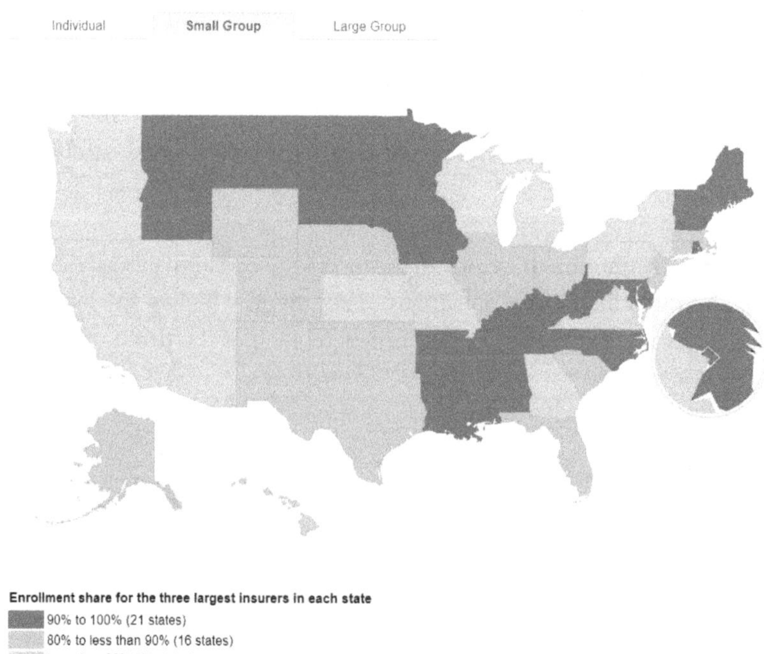

Exhibit 4. Enrollment Share for Three Largest Health Insurers in the Large-Group Market

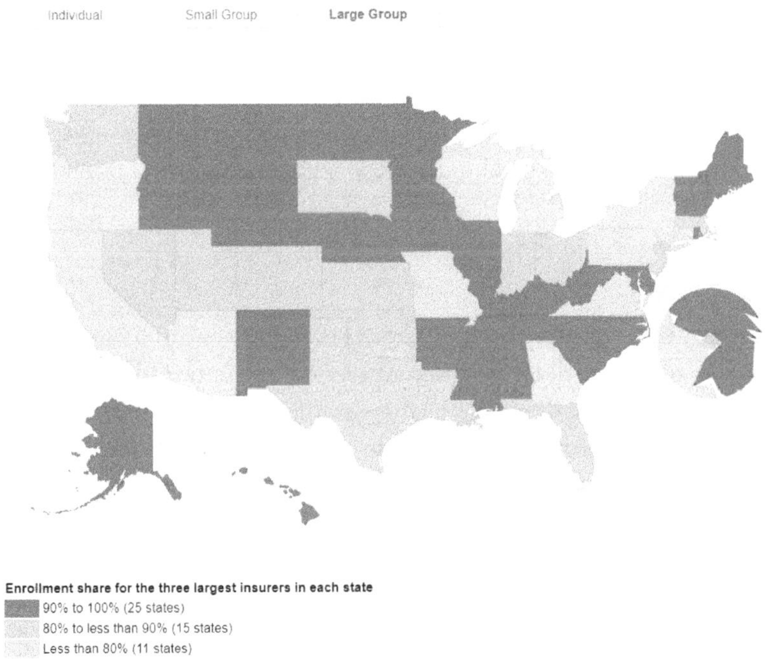

All healthcare is still local five years after the passage of the ACA.

1.0 Results of Original Study

The explosion in healthcare transactions after a 10-year hiatus has created a booming market for appraisal and valuation services. One of the peculiar aspects of the healthcare industry is that many if not most transactions must be supported by an independent appraisal due to governmental regulatory concerns. As such, failure of appraisers or valuation analysts to understand healthcare markets and government regulations can lead to transactions taking place at prices inconsistent with both economic reality and, as discussed later herein, regulatory parameters. These transactions can then find their way into databases relied upon by other appraisers resulting in further transactions based upon suspect opinions of value.

The degree of revenue and profit for healthcare provider entities varies significantly from state to state and even within different regions of individual states. As a threshold matter, areas with high healthcare spending and particularly high Medicare[5] spending tend to offer the greatest opportunity for profit. The elderly, of course, receive the bulk of medical care. Given that high localized spending is the primary driver of profit, what other factors contribute to the pattern of location of larger for-profit providers?

5 Medicare is a federal program primarily for the elderly and is distinct from Medicaid, a state-determined program for the poor that is funded 50% by federal funds and 50% by state funds.

- The presence and market strength of Blue Cross plans;
- The degree of market strength of local nonprofit hospitals versus for-profit hospitals;
- The degree of market strength of local nonprofit health insurers versus for-profit health insurers;
- Certificate of need laws; and
- Other local demographic and economic factors.

As discussed later herein with respect to Blue Cross plans and nonprofit hospitals, these primary indicators reflect prevailing attitudes in different areas of the nation about the appropriateness of "profit" motivation in the provision of health care. In turn, the presence or lack thereof of these larger for-profit providers and insurers has a substantial impact on the acquisition and sales value of provider entities. This impact can be traced to at least two specific factors: the likelihood that for-profit entities will be acquirers of providers in a given area and the revenue and profit growth potential inherent in such acquisitions.

Growth potential in the form of acquisition growth is typically only available to publicly traded companies whose stock prices are in large part driven by expected growth rates. High growth rates typically result in high valuation multiples due to low capitalization rates. Economies of scale from acquisitions that affect future "same store" profit growth also contribute to localized valuation differences. As such, all things being equal, a growth-driven public company is able to pay a higher value for a given business because the stock market rewards growth.[6]

The Stark laws contain restrictions on the use of "comparable" market data, much of which are pegged to local market conditions. As far back as 1994, published statements of the Internal Revenue Service focused on local factors that determined the character of a market. The factors discussed in this chapter suggest that the government agencies' views of fair market value should be seriously considered by appraisers and analysts in their own opinions of fair market value.

This study offers appraisers and valuation analysts a foundation for comparing market conditions in different areas of the country. In turn, it provides a basis for determining whether market data in the form of merged and acquired companies or guideline companies is comparable to a given subject company that is being valuated.

2.0 Data Sources and Impact on Analysis

Sources of data utilized in this study include that maintained by The Kaiser Family Foundation (KFF). KFF maintains data on the breakdown of for-profit and not-for-profit hospitals for each

6 See "Understanding the Difference Between Strategic Value and Fair Market Value in Consolidating Industries" *Business Valuation Review*, June 2002, by the author.

of the 50 states, along with Medicare and Medicaid enrollment, spending, length of stay, and other detailed statistical data, some of which are described and utilized in this chapter. Detail of the market share of each state's health maintenance organization (HMO) and preferred provider organization (PPO) enrollment is available from each state's division or department of insurance or, for example, from Lehman Brothers' *Managed Care Guidebook*.[7] Often states will provide detail at the county level as well. Data on local Medicare spending from the Centers for Medicare and Medicaid (CMS) were also utilized, along with information taken directly from the Securities and Exchange Commission (SEC) filings of the public companies discussed.

Local market conditions can lead to dramatic differences in provider revenue, profitability, and related acquisition demand. This affects both the relevance of transaction data in determining fair market value as well as the perceived risk of provider entities in a given market area, which in turn affects the discount rate and value determined under the income approach.

As will be seen from the analysis throughout this chapter, for-profit public companies engaged in the healthcare industry tend to concentrate their activities in certain states, notably Texas and Florida, which have specific characteristics discernible from the data sources. The analysis considers presence and dominance of the following companies and certain of their competitors:

- Ambulatory surgery: AmSurg (AMSG);
- Hospitals: HCA, Tenet, HMA, Vanguard;
- Health insurers: United Healthcare (United), as well as Aetna, Cigna, Humana and Health Net, collectively referred to later as "other public"; and
- Imaging: Radnet.

3.0 Public Healthcare Insurers

One key to understanding the strategy of provider entities such as AMSG discussed later is to examine the presence of the for-profit health insurers in a given state as well as the concentration of market power by those companies along with Blue Cross plans and local HMOs. The more concentrated a market is in terms of health insurers, the less likely a healthcare services provider will be able to negotiate favorable contracts. This is because market control over pricing is then held by those few insurers.[8] That, of course, leads to an expectation of lower profits.

A number of large publicly traded companies are engaged in providing health insurance, primarily in a managed-care format. These include United Healthcare, Aetna, Cigna, Humana, and Health Net.[9] There has been a spate of consolidation in the industry stemming back to the

7 Used in this study's market analysis.
8 The Federal Trade Commission and Department of Justice Anti-Trust Division favor insurers over providers.
9 Wellpoint is a large public company; however, it owns Blue Cross plans, including Anthem, which are

late 1990s, when a number of smaller entities got burned at the bottom of the so-called "underwriting cycle."[10] Aggressive setting of premiums over multiyear contracts to build market share resulted in bankruptcy or near-bankruptcy for such companies as Oxford when the costs increased more rapidly than expected. The consolidation trend continues today, driven in part by Medicare Advantage contracts as reflected in the acquisition of PacifiCare—the originator of Secure Horizons, the oldest Medicare HMO in the country—by United. Given the present backlash against managed care, Medicare HMOs are the principal source of growth for these public health insurers.

For purpose of this analysis, using data from Lehman Brothers' *2007 Managed Care Guidebook*, the market shares of each of the 50 states were divided into subgroupings based upon: (1) Blue Cross plans; (2) United (the largest public health insurer); (3) Aetna, Cigna, Health Net, and Humana; and (4) local HMOs with strong market presence, e.g., Harvard Pilgrim and Tufts in Massachusetts. After eliminating states[11] where for-profit insurers had small market share, where for-profit providers had little or no market presence, and rural states, 35 states were left in the sample.

The remaining states were then ranked by the concentration of market power in the hands of those insurers as well as by the number of insurers[12] operating in each market. Concentration percentages were as high as 98% in Alaska, where the Blue Cross plan had a 49% share and the named public companies collectively had a 49% share as well. Rhode Island's market consolidation ratio was 97%, with 58% in the Blue Cross plan and 26% in United. The lowest concentrations were in Wisconsin and Kansas. The latter market is highly stratified, however, as described later herein.

4.0 Market Share

Exhibits 5, 6, and 7 summarize the analysis for eight states, divided into those where public for-profit providers are principally present (Florida, Texas, California, and Tennessee) [13] and those where they have little or no presence (New York, North Carolina, Massachusetts, and Michigan). Market concentration is defined here as the total market share of the Blue Cross plans, public health insurers, and large local health insurers. Average is the market concentration divided by the number of insurers included in the market concentration total. Blue Cross Plans are discussed in the next section.

otherwise addressed.

10 This is the business cycle for the insurance industry and refers generally to the annual gap between premium increases and cost increases and the medical loss ratio, that portion of the premium expended on medical costs.

11 Hawaii, Idaho, Iowa, Maine, Montana, Nebraska, Nevada, New Mexico, North Dakota, Oklahoma, South Dakota, Utah, Vermont, West Virginia.

12 For example, New York has multiple Blue Cross plans.

13 According to the Kaiser Family Foundation using 2013 data, Florida, Texas, and Tennessee are ranked second, fifth, and third in terms of the *percentage* of their hospitals that are for-profit. California ranks 19th by percentage, but third by *count*, with Texas, Florida and Tennessee first, second, and fourth. //kff.org/other/state-indicator/hospitals-by-ownership/, viewed July 23, 2015.

Exhibit 5 lists the above larger states where for profit providers are prevalent. Although market concentration varies, these states generally have smaller Blue Cross plans and a large market presence of for-profit health insurers (shown as United and other public). Tennessee is the only state in the top half of market concentration[14] where for-profit providers are prevalent—and it is the location of the headquarters of many of those companies.

Exhibit 5. Insurance Market Concentration In States Where For-Profit Providers Are Prevalent

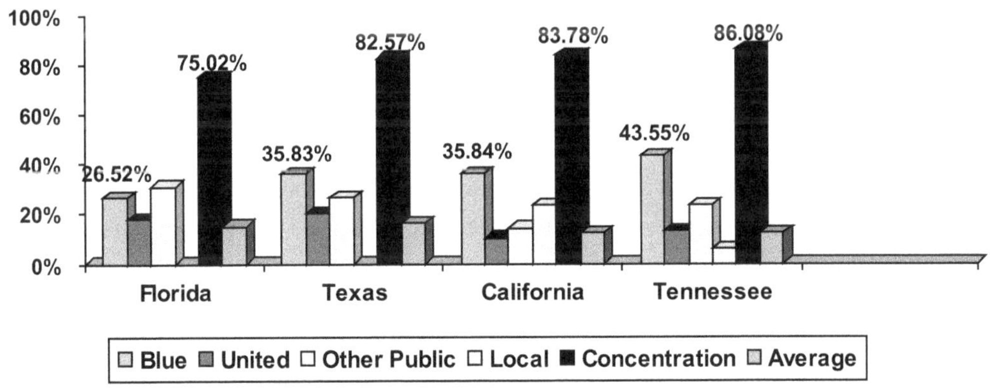

Exhibit 6 is of representative larger states where for profit providers are not prevalent. Although market concentration again varies, these states generally have very large Blue Cross plans and a small market presence of for-profit health insurers.

Exhibit 6. Insurance Market Concentration States Where For-Profit Providers Are Not Prevalent

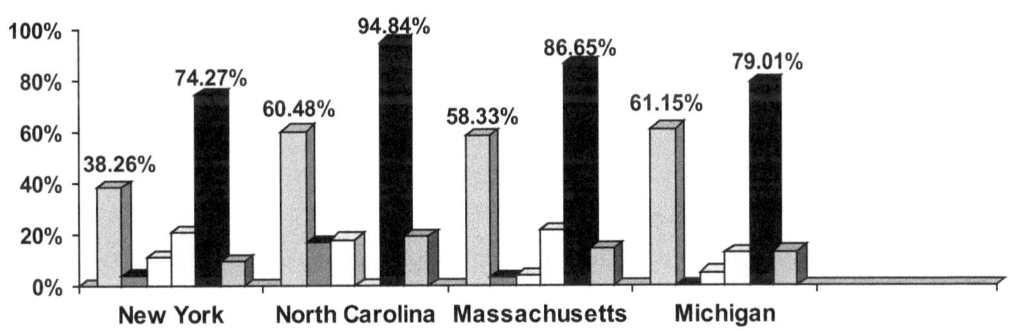

5.0 History of Blue Cross Plans

The history of Blue Cross plans plays an important part in the structure of today's health insurance and provider markets. Blue Cross plans expanded rapidly during the Second World War's period of wage and price controls as union sought enhanced benefits to supplement

14 The median is 85% versus 86% for Tennessee.

their members' limited incomes. At one point, there were more than 100 Blue Cross plans, the majority of which were located in the industrialized states primarily north of the Mason-Dixon Line in what is sometimes called the Rust Belt. Certain plans refused to contract with for-profit hospitals, thus serving as an effective barrier to market entry. Blue Cross plans also enjoyed a tax-exempt status[15] for many years and protection from anti-trust action in many states.

As will be seen below, this type of insurance market analysis is one critical element in understanding why public healthcare companies locate in some states and not others. In turn, the acquisition transactions of those public companies are likely only relevant in such states. Further, if an analyst or appraiser is considering the guideline publicly traded company method, it is likely only relevant in those states where the purported guideline companies are active.

Exhibit 7 combines the earlier two charts to compare Blue Cross, for-profit (the combined United and other public companies' share), and market concentration. In markets where for-profit insurers are prevalent (Florida, Texas, California, and Tennessee), Blue Cross plans are less so and for-profit hospitals also tend to be more prevalent, as seen in the next section.

Exhibit 7. Comparative Insurance Market Consolidation

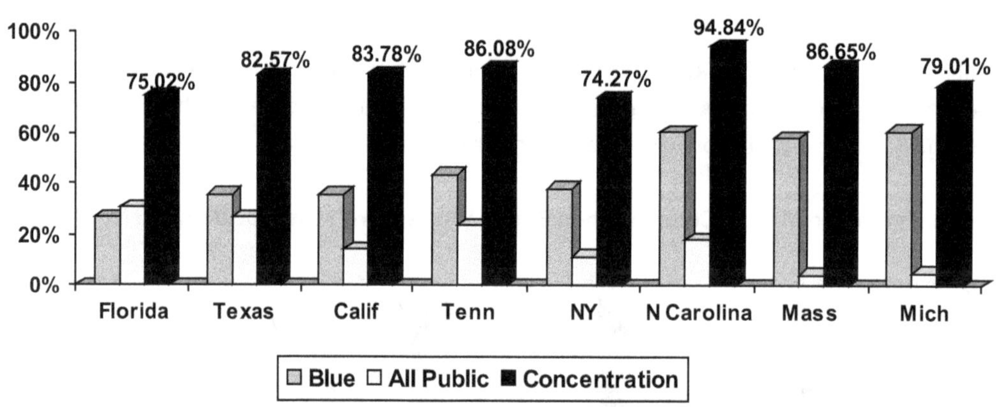

6.0 Public Hospital Companies

As a basis for the analysis of four[16] public, for-profit hospital providers, extracts from their 2006 Form 10-Ks follow below. From these extracts, the primary state locations and the extent of concentration can be observed as well as the rationale for locating there (see Tenet and Vanguard Health below). Two other hospital chains not discussed below are LifePoint and Community Health. LifePoint,[17] based in Brentwood, Tenn., has operations primarily in the rural South and border states including Alabama, Louisiana, Kentucky, and Virginia. Community Health,[18]

15 Repealed in the Tax Reform Act of 1986.

16 HCA has since been taken private in one of the largest leveraged buy outs ever.

17 LifePoint Hospitals operated 50 hospitals in 19 states as of May 2007.

18 As of Dec. 31, 2006, it owned, leased, or operated 77 hospitals, with an aggregate of 9,117 licensed beds in 22 states.

based in Franklin, Tenn., has many of its facilities in Texas, Alabama, Tennessee, northeastern Illinois, and southeastern Pennsylvania.

HCA (now privately held)

> We operated 173 hospitals at Dec. 31, 2006, and 73 of those hospitals are located in Florida and Texas. Our Florida and Texas facilities' combined revenues represented approximately 51% of our consolidated revenues for the year ended Dec. 31, 2006. This concentration makes us particularly sensitive to regulatory, economic, environmental, and competition changes in those states.

Tenet

> As of Dec. 31, 2006, the largest concentrations of licensed beds in our general hospitals were in California (23.6%), Florida (22.8%), and Texas (18.3%). Strong concentrations of hospital beds within market areas help us contract more successfully with managed care payors; reduce management, marketing and other expenses; and more efficiently utilize resources. However, such concentrations increase the risk that, should any adverse economic, regulatory, environmental, or other development occur in these areas, our business, financial condition, results of operations or cash flows could be materially adversely affected.

HMA Health Management Associates Inc.

> As of Dec. 31, 2006, we operated 60 hospitals, with a total of 8,589 licensed beds. During the year ended Dec. 31, 2006, we operated facilities in Alabama, Arkansas, Florida, Georgia, Kentucky, Mississippi, Missouri, North Carolina, Oklahoma, Pennsylvania, South Carolina, Tennessee, Texas, Virginia, Washington, and West Virginia.
>
> Our facilities are heavily concentrated in Florida and Mississippi, which makes us sensitive to regulatory, economic, and competitive changes in those states, as well as the harmful effects of hurricanes and other severe weather activity in such states. We operated 61 hospitals on Feb. 23, 2007, with 29 of those hospitals in Florida and Mississippi. Such geographic concentration of our hospitals makes us particularly sensitive to regulatory, economic, environmental, and competitive changes in those states. Any material changes therein in Florida or Mississippi could have a disproportionate effect on our business.

Vanguard Health

> Our ability to negotiate favorable contracts with health maintenance organizations, insurers offering preferred provider arrangements and other managed care plans significantly affects the revenues and operating results of our hospitals. Revenues derived from health maintenance organizations, insurers offering preferred provider arrangements and other managed care plans, including Medicare and Medicaid managed care plans, accounted for approximately 52% of our net patient revenues for the year ended June 30, 2007. Managed

> care organizations offering prepaid and discounted medical services packages represent an increasing portion of our admissions, a general trend in the industry which has limited hospital revenue growth nationwide and a trend that may continue if the Medicare Modernization Act increases enrollment in Medicare managed care plans. In addition, private payors are increasingly attempting to control healthcare costs through direct contracting with hospitals to provide services on a discounted basis, increased utilization review, including the use of hospitalists, and greater enrollment in managed care programs such as health maintenance organizations and preferred provider organizations. Additionally, the trend toward consolidation among private managed care payors tends to increase their bargaining prices over fee structures.
>
> Approximately 35% of our net patient revenues for the year ended June 30, 2007 came from Medicare and Medicaid programs, excluding Medicare and Medicaid managed plans. In recent years, federal and state governments have made significant changes in the Medicare and Medicaid programs. Some of those changes adversely affect the reimbursement we receive for certain services. In addition, due to budget deficits in many states, significant decreases in state funding for Medicaid programs have occurred or are being proposed.
>
> Historically, we have concentrated our operations in markets with high population growth and median income in excess of the national average.

At first glance, Vanguard may represent a partial anomaly in the public companies discussed herein. Seventeen percent of its hospital beds are located in Massachusetts, with approximately half of those in Framingham and Natick[19] and the other half in Worcester, 20 miles west. The Framingham and Natick facilities were acquired from Tenet after that entity's difficulties stemming from a federal government investigation of its Alvaredo facility in San Diego, Calif.; Tenet had acquired them in 1999 from the predecessor of Hospital Corporation of America (HCA) after that entity encountered regulatory problems leading to a fine of nearly $1 billion. Prior to that, Columbia and HCA acquired the facilities as a result of financial difficulties experienced by the local nonprofit institutions in competing with larger nonprofit entities.

Vanguard is a much smaller entity than either HCA or Tenet as can be seen from Exhibit 8 of the total number of beds each entity has and therefore, is less significant to the analysis. It is clear once again that Florida and Texas are primary locations for for-profit hospital providers.

19 The author lives in Framingham and formerly resided in Natick, a bordering community located in Middlesex county, which has the 19th highest total Medicare spending in the nation.

Exhibit 8. Number of Beds by State

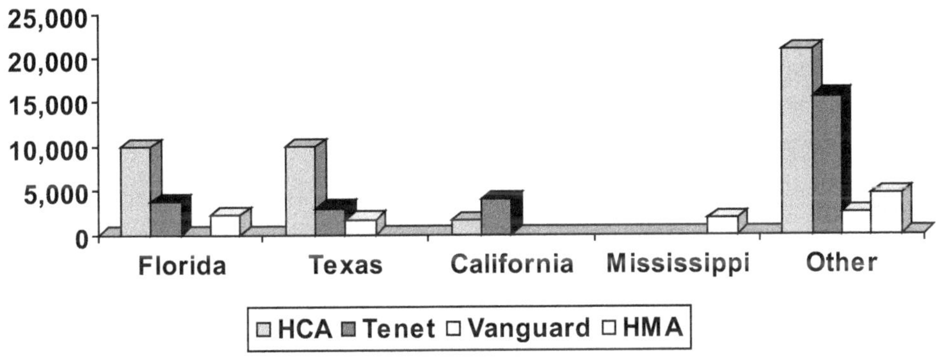

On a percentage basis, HCA and Tenet each have more than 40% of their hospital beds in Florida and Texas (see Exhibit 9).

Exhibit 9. Percentage of Beds by Company by State

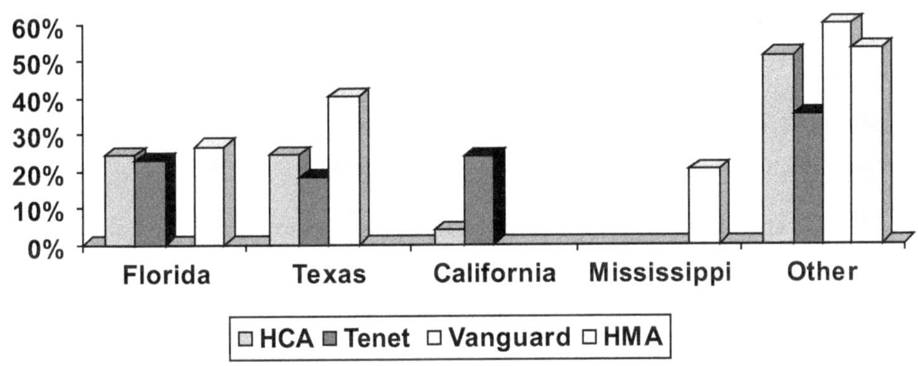

For the valuation of an individual hospital in a state other than Florida, Texas, or California, what is the relevance of transactions by one of these publicly traded entities? As the author and Reed Tinsley, CPA, CVA noted in a co-authored article in the December 2006 American Bar Association's *The Heath Lawyer*:

> What does [out of market] transaction data say or reveal about the value of a hospital with EBITDA of $1 million located in North Carolina? Does it tell a valuator that it could be worth the median [multiple] value of $5 million or the [average multiple] value of $7.5 million—the average being 50% greater than the median? Could it be worth [the highest multiple value of] $18.2 million? Given the Stark regulations requirement that comparable transactions be in a particular market at the time of acquisition, can any of these [out-of-market] multiples be used?

7.0 Medicare Part A Spending

Medicare divides providers into two general groupings: Part A hospital insurance, which is paid for by the combined employer-employee 2.9% Medicare tax, and Part B physician insurance, which is paid for out of general federal revenues, after a nominal premium contribution by beneficiaries withheld from Social Security checks. Medicare Advantage, the risk-based Medicare HMO program, publishes per-capita rates county by county across the country split into Part A and Part B components. There are more than 3,200 counties, including Puerto Rico and Guam, with published rates. Because these rates are one proxy for local county Medicare spending,[20] they provide useful insight into a public healthcare provider's location strategy.

Medicare spending is driven by two principal factors: utilization or volume of service, typically expressed in per-beneficiary measures, and price or rate per unit of service. Although beyond the scope of this chapter, utilization data are readily available from such sources as the Medicare Payment Advisory Commission's (MedPAC) 2007 report *Assessing Alternatives to SGR*.[21] While price or rate is a function of statutory formulas and local cost of service differences, utilization is a function of medical practice styles. The differences in utilization are dramatic and warrant study by an appraiser looking to use out-of-market valuation multiples.

The previous sections discussion on location of for-profit hospitals is consistent with high levels of Medicare spending. Of the top 50 counties, five are in Florida (which has nine of the top 100), four in Texas (which has 15 of the top 100 and another 22 in the next 200) and one in California (which also has nine of the top 100). Two of the top 10 counties (Dade and Okeechobee) are in Florida. The location of individual facilities in other states, such as Louisiana, is typically driven by high localized spending as reflected in Medicare Part A or B statistics.

For total Medicare spending, both Part A and Part B, the pattern is similar but more dramatic for Florida and California as shown in Exhibits 10 and 11.

Exhibit 10. Number of Top 200 Counties for Part A Per Capita Spending

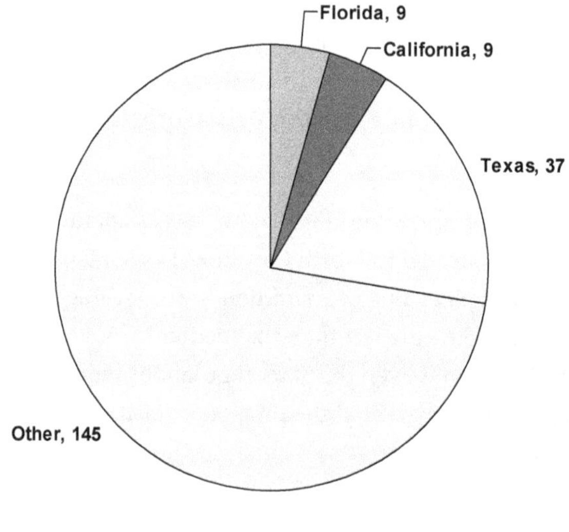

20 At least for the high-cost counties; low-cost counties have artificially higher rates than their fee-for-service equivalents as a means of inducing Medicare Advantage Plans to offer coverage.

21 Utilization and utilization growth is very high in Florida, for example, and low in mature managed care markets such as San Francisco and Portland, Ore.

Exhibit 11. Number of Top 200 Counties for Part A and B Total Spending

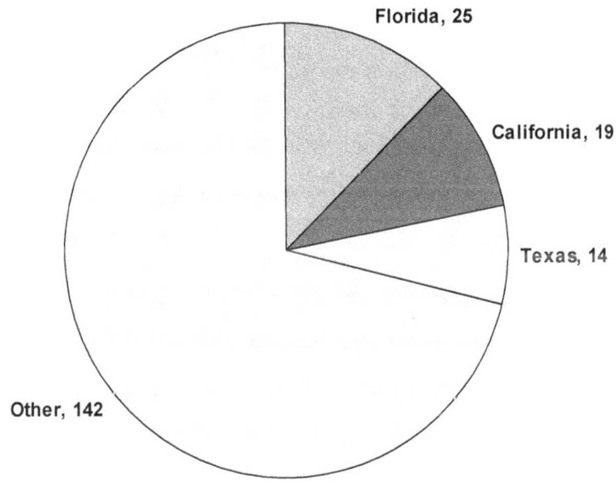

The counties shown in Exhibit 12 have the largest total dollar Medicare spending. Two counties—Maricopa County, Ariz. and Middlesex County, Mass.—which appear elsewhere in the article where the presence of public for-profit providers was not explained by other factors are clearly explained in this chart. Despite the high levels of Medicare spending, no significant for-profit hospitals are present in Cook County (Chicago) or the various boroughs of New York City,[22] for example. These are counties where unions have historically been very strong.

Exhibit 12. 20 Largest Counties for 2005 Medicare Spending ($Billions)

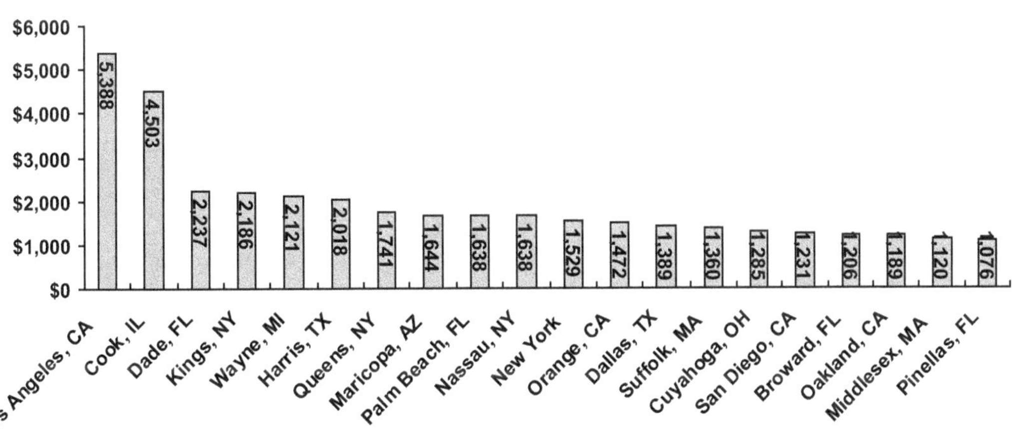

22 Less than 3.2% and 1% of hospital beds in Illinois and New York, respectively, are for-profit according to the Kaiser Family Foundation.

8.0 Other Hospital Market Factors

Perhaps the most difficult factor to quantify without local market knowledge or study is the presence of not-for-profit hospitals, particularly large, wealthy teaching hospitals. These institutions tend to be present in large urban markets. Examples include the Harvard-Affiliated Partners Health System in Boston, which includes the Massachusetts General and Brigham & Women's Hospitals; Baylor Health Care System in Dallas;[23] Yale-New Haven Hospital in New Haven, Conn.; any number of institutions in New York City, including Mount Sinai Hospital, Beth Israel Medical Center, and NYU Medical Center; The University of Chicago Health System and Northwestern Memorial Hospital and Health System in Chicago; and Johns Hopkins Hospital and Health System in Baltimore. These institutions frequently have market power not only in terms of hospital volume, but also in terms of physician affiliations, managed care contracts, and political influence.

Another example of nonprofit hospitals are the multistate religious health systems, such as Ascension Health. Many times these institutions are located in underserved areas where access to healthcare is limited by income considerations. They may also be small institutions located in rural areas where providing multidiscipline and emergency care is unprofitable and requires charitable support.

There is nothing that precludes the reporting of acquisitions by not-for-profit hospitals of other hospitals, physician practices, surgery centers, and the like. However, there is often no requirement of reporting, and it is certainly less common than reporting by the public for-profit companies described herein.[24] Some transactions may warrant reporting under generally accepted accounting principles (GAAP) and generally accepted auditing standards (GAAS) and many states require not-for-profits to file financial statements with the state Attorney General's office; fairness opinions may also be required. Analysts and appraisers need to keep in mind that single-state or single-locale not-for-profit transactions[25] likewise reflect only that local market's considerations and are equally suspect as value indicators in other markets.

9.0 Valuation Imperative

Appraisers and analysts should bear in mind that in addition to the Stark laws and anti-kickback statutes that apply to all healthcare providers, nonprofit and tax-exempt providers are subject to the requirements of the Internal Revenue Code, including anti-inurement and intermediate sanctions provisions.

23 A highly competitive market with both for-profit and nonprofit hospitals.

24 For competitive reasons and regulatory fear, among others.

25 For example, North and South Carolina not-for-profit integrated healthcare system Novant Health's acquisition of imaging provider MQ Associates.

10.0 Example

One common business strategy that hospitals utilize in acquiring physician-owned entities such as ambulatory surgery centers and imaging centers include converting them to hospital outpatient billing or so-called "provider-based billing."[26] This typically results in a higher revenue stream for the same services as both government and nongovernment insurers frequently have different payment levels for the same service based upon the type of provider submitting the bill, i.e., higher revenue for hospital entities than physician entities. Notwithstanding the business strategy, including the enhanced revenue in a valuation where the standard is fair market value raises serious if not fatal concerns. Since physicians cannot access this billing routine when they own the entity outright, including the enhanced revenue available to a hospital owner creates issues under both the Stark Law and anti-kickback statute as well as anti-inurement issues for tax-exempt entities.

11.0 Surgery Centers

After medical practice purchases, surgery center transactions are perhaps the most common form of healthcare transaction. As a result of private equity deals, AmSurg (AMSG) is one of the few remaining public companies in this business. Due to the importance of acquisitions to the value of this company and to the valuation of individual surgery centers, the chapter addresses AMSG in detail. Although the primary location of its facilities is Florida, followed by Tennessee and California, it does, in fact, have locations in many other states, which make it a particularly interesting subject for analysis. A number of these other locations are examined for consistency with the factors discussed elsewhere herein.

A review of AMSG's Dec. 31, 2006 10-K filing with the SEC revealed the following:

> Practice-based [ambulatory surgery centers] ASCs, such as those in which we own a majority interest, depend upon third-party reimbursement programs, including governmental and private insurance programs, to pay for services rendered to patients. We derived approximately 35%, 35%, and 37% of our revenues in the years ended Dec. 31, 2006, 2005, and 2004, respectively, from governmental healthcare programs, primarily Medicare. The Medicare program currently pays ASCs and physicians in accordance with predetermined fee schedules.
>
> At Dec. 31, 2006, 30 of the 156 surgery centers we operated were located in the state of Florida. This concentration makes us particularly sensitive to adverse weather conditions and other factors that affect the state of Florida.
>
> Ninety-two percent of our centers specialize in gastroenterology or ophthalmology procedures. These specialties have a higher concentration of older patients than other specialties,

26 Medicare requires eligible healthcare providers to bill services in two parts: one for the facility or technical fee to the hospital or facility for owning the building and equipment and employing nonphysician staff and one for physicians for interpreting and performing the test or procedure known as the professional fee; a hospital-owned facility may be able to bill under higher hospital rates.

> such as orthopedic or [gastro]enterology. We believe the aging demographics of the U.S. population will be a source of procedure growth for these specialties. We target these medical specialties because they generally involve a high volume of lower-risk procedures that can be performed in an outpatient setting on a safe and cost-effective basis.
>
> We begin our acquisition process with a due diligence review of the target center and its market. We use experienced teams of operations and financial personnel to conduct a thorough review of all aspects of the center's operations, including the following:
>
> - Market position of the center and the physicians affiliated with the center;
> - Payor and case mix;
> - Growth opportunities;
> - Staffing and supply review; and
> - Equipment assessment.
>
> In presenting the advantages to physicians of developing a new practice-based ASC in partnership with us, our development staff emphasizes the proximity of a practice-based surgery center to a physician's office, the simplified administrative procedures, the ability to schedule consecutive cases without preemption by inpatient or emergency procedures, the rapid turnaround time between cases, the high technical competency of the center's clinical staff that performs only a limited number of specialized procedures and the state-of-the-art surgical equipment. We also focus on our expertise in developing and operating centers. In addition, as part of our role as the manager of our surgery center limited partnerships and limited liability companies, we market the centers to third-party payors.

The 10-K also reveals that 105 of the 156 centers are gastroenterology, four multispecialty, 40 ophthalmic, and seven orthopedic. Appraisers and analysts should consider the prospects for these service lines versus other (*non*gastroenterology—also called endoscopy—or ophthalmology) medical service lines when contemplating using AMSG acquisition multiples. It is critical to understand precisely what types of procedures a facility is performing as part of the assessment of market data's relevance.

Exhibit 13 displays AMSG's historical cumulative acquisitions of surgery centers (103, or 66% of the total), and Exhibit 14 shows its cumulative total centers (156) to emphasize the importance of acquisition growth to the value of the company.

Exhibit 13. AMSG Cumulative Acquisitions

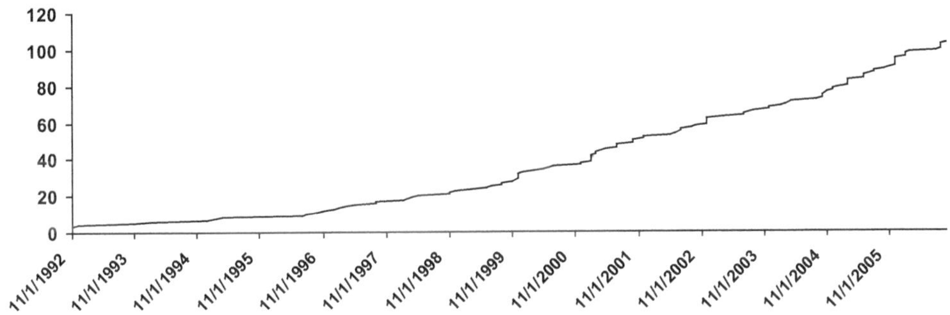

Exhibit 14. AMSG Cumulative Centers

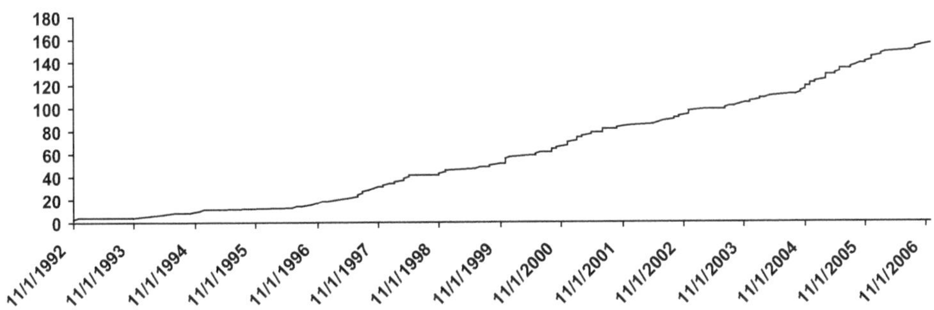

Exhibit 15 shows the location of AMSG's operating rooms (ORs) by state for purposes of the later analysis of the reason for locating in certain states and not others.

Exhibit 15. AMSG ORs by State

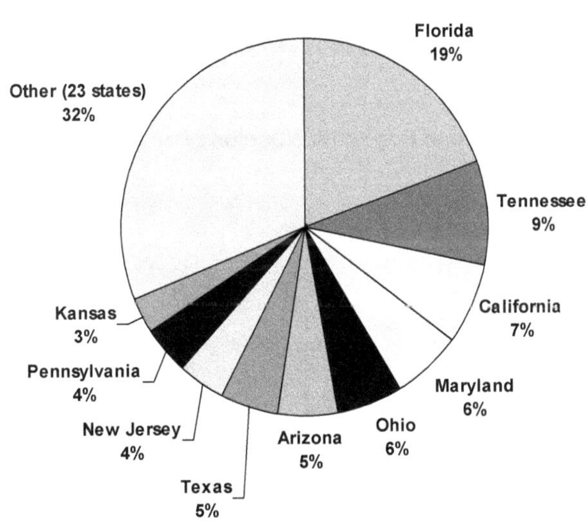

12.0 Medicare Part B Spending

The states in which AMSG is located consistently have the highest rates for Part B physician spending—and that is where such transactions are or may be relevant depending upon further analysis. Of the 200 counties with the highest Part B Medicare Advantage rates, half (101) are located in the 10 states in which AMSG has most of its facilities. Of the top 50 counties, five are in Florida, four in Texas (which has 15 of the top 100 and another 22 in the next 200) and six in New Jersey. Two of the top 10 counties (Dade and Okeechobee) are in Florida. Only Arizona does not appear in the top 200 (see Exhibit 16).

Exhibit 16. Number of Top 200 Counties for Part B Per Capita Spending

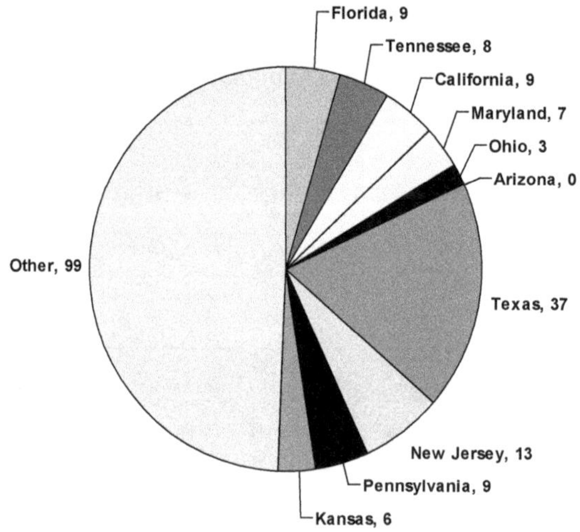

13.0 Prevalence of For-Profit Hospitals

Earlier, the presence of for-profit hospitals and health insurers was examined. Exhibit 17 shows the percentage of for-profit hospitals[27] for each of the 10 states where AMSG has the largest number of ORs, with the largest states at the left. Florida, Tennessee, and California have 35% of AMSG's capacity. Florida has the second highest percentage of for-profit hospitals in the country, with Tennessee seventh.

Exhibit 17. Prevalence of For-Profit Hospitals For AMSG's Major States

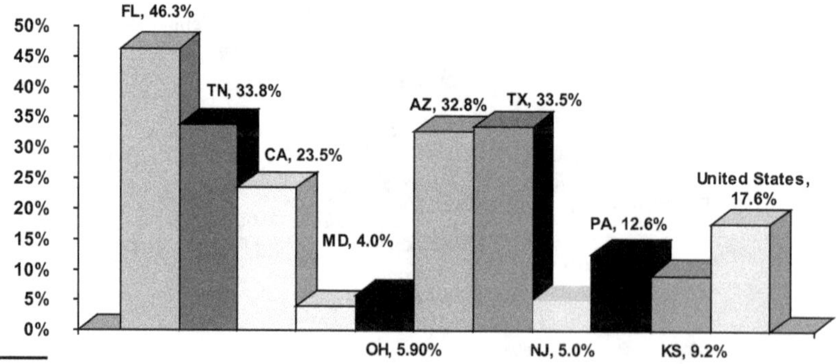

27 Kaiser Family Foundation State Health Facts, www.statehealthfacts.kff.org/.

Pennsylvania is below the national average, but the activity in this state could be explained in part by a strong state government commitment to rating outpatient surgery facilities, including going so far as to require extensive financial disclosure[28] on top of clinical quality.

Another manner to evaluate for-profit presence is by the number of hospital beds (see Exhibit 18) as opposed to the number of hospitals. Both data sets are relevant because a number of specialty hospitals, such as cardiac and orthopedic, may have relatively few beds but extremely high profitability. Cardiac and orthopedic care is at the core of most hospitals' profitability. Appraisers seeking to value a hospital should be certain to understand the underlying case mix of both the purported comparables and the subject. A specialty orthopedic hospital transaction is likely of little use in valuing a general hospital.

Exhibit 18. Prevalence of For-Profit Beds For AMSG's Major States

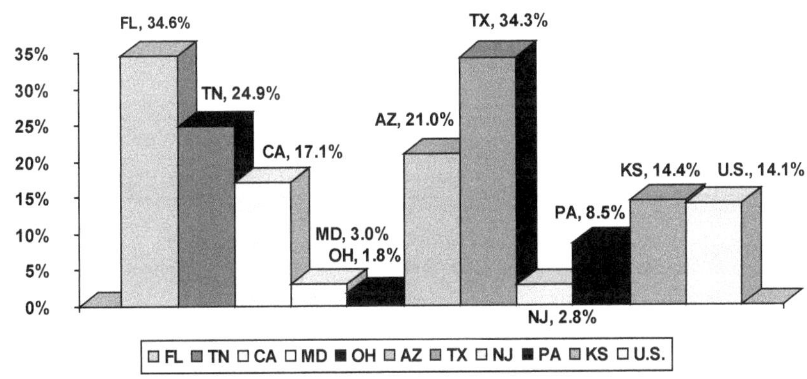

Exhibit 19 summarizes criteria that impact the desirability of locating a surgery center in a given state based upon the 10 states above. Bold items are those that appear partially determinative. For example, Florida has the third highest number of for-profit hospital beds in the country, is ranked 4th in overall healthcare spending, 6th in the concentration of population in metropolitan areas, 9th in spending on physician services, and 19th in per-capita healthcare spending. The percentage of overall spending in the state on physician services is more than 3% greater than the national average.

For certain of the principal states in which AMSG does business, the listed factors do not appear to readily explain the desirability. For example, Kansas is ranked 8th in overall physician spending as a percentage (31.5%) of healthcare expenses but otherwise does not appear attractive based on the criteria. This is where individual local market conditions become important.

28 Pennsylvania Health Care Cost Containment Council, www.phc4.org.

Exhibit 19. Criteria That Impact the Desirability of Locating a Surgery Center in a Given State

			RANKINGS				
Top 10 AMSG States	For-Profit Beds %	MD Spending%	For-Profit Beds	Total Healthcare Spending	Metropolitan Pop	MD Spending	Per Capita
Florida	**34.6%**	31.5%	**3**	**4**	**6**	**9**	19
Tennessee	**24.9%**	31.4%	**10**	15	26	**10**	21
California	**17.1%**	33.4%	18	**1**	**2**	**3**	44
Maryland	**3.0%**	28.7%	34	19	**7**	20	18
Ohio	1.8%	26.8%	39	7	25	35	15
Arizona	**21.0%**	33.0%	15	21	14	**5**	50
Texas	**34.3%**	30.8%	**4**	**3**	**11**	**11**	45
New Jersey	2.8%	28.2%	35	**9**	**1**	27	13
Pennsylvania	8.5%	26.6%	28	**5**	22	38	11
Kansas	14.4%	31.5%	22	31	35	**8**	24
United States	14.1%	28.2%	NA	NA	NA	NA	

Explanations
For-Profit Beds %: The percentage of all hospitals beds owned by for-profit hospitals.
MD Spending %: The portion of the state's healthcare spending that goes to physician services.
Rankings
For-Profit Beds: The rank based on total for-profit beds, with 1 being highest,
Total Healthcare Spending: The rank based upon total dollars spent.
Metropolitan Population: The rank based upon the percentage of the states' population located in metropolitan areas (as opposed to rural).
MD Spending: The rank based upon total dollars spent.
Per Capita: The rank based upon per capita income.

Kansas is a largely rural state with population centers in larger cities. The following is the location of the AMSG facilities:

- Hutchinson, Kan.
- Overland Park, Kan.
- Shawnee, Kan.
- Topeka, Kan.
- Wichita, Kan.

Overland Park and Shawnee are part of suburban Kansas City (the metropolitan area includes the larger Kansas City, Mo.), while Hutchinson is a suburb of Wichita. Thus, the ranking of Kansas as a rural state is misleading with respect to the location of the AMSG facilities.

Similarly, Arizona has only high total spending for health care as a positive criteria in the analysis. Arizona, however, has a very high percentage of Medicare-eligible retirees and as noted earlier, Medicare is a key source of revenue for AMSG. Below is a listing of AMSG's Arizona locations.

- Mesa, Ariz.
- Peoria, Ariz.
- Phoenix, Ariz.
- Sun City, Ariz.
- Yuma, Ariz.

Sun City, Mesa, and Peoria are part of greater Phoenix (Maricopa County, described earlier herein), one of the fastest growing metropolitan areas in the nation, with Sun City a prime locale for retirees. Maricopa County has the third highest total Medicare spending in the country at *$1.64 billion.* Yuma is near the Mexican border, and an even more localized market analysis would be in order.

New Jersey is a particularly interesting case in point where the criteria do not appear to explain the presence of AMSG. Fortunately, the Center for Studying Health System Change,[29] which tracks development in 12 markets nationally, includes Northern New Jersey, where three of the faculties are located. This is an area where specialist physicians—which would include gastroenterology and ophthalmology—have been terminating provider agreements with insurers to compel higher fees as out-of-network providers. Ambulatory surgery centers are being developed as part of this strategy to shift revenue from hospitals to physicians.

13.1 Characteristics of Areas With No AMSG Locations

AMSG has no facilities in Vermont, Massachusetts, Maine, New Hampshire, and Rhode Island and a single one in Connecticut. Thus, the New England area, for example, would not appear to be a target market. These states have comparatively few for-profit beds (Rhode Island and Vermont have none) and high market concentration of insurers (see Exhibit 20). Maine, New Hampshire, Connecticut, and Vermont have more than 94% market concentration as defined earlier herein, and the largest insurer in each market is a Blue Cross plan, with 67%, 38%, 33%, and 60% market share, respectively.

Exhibit 20. For-Profit Beds in AMSG's No Facility States

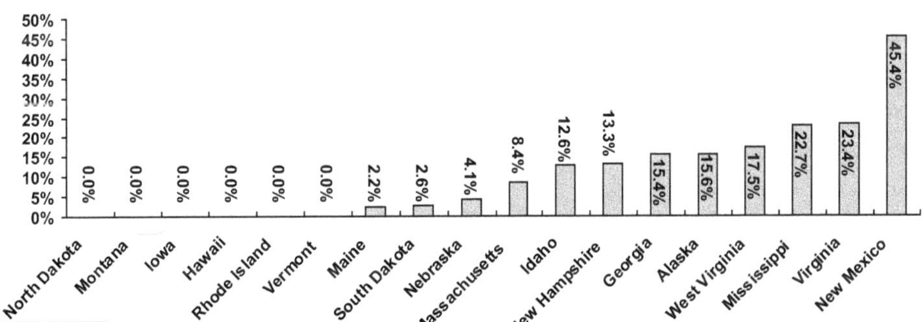

29 www.hschange.org.

14.0 Valuation Imperative

An appraiser or analyst should also consider the requirement or lack thereof for a certificate of need (CON) in each state[30] where a purported comparable operates and in the state where the valuation subject is located. Florida, Texas, Pennsylvania, and California do not require a CON for an ASC! Lack of a CON makes it easier to establish an ASC—although actually having a difficult-to-obtain CON in a state that requires them is generally a valuation positive, assuming the CON is transferable. Some states waive a CON for expenditures below a specified level, e.g., $1 million for an MRI in Missouri.

15.0 Radnet

The one large publicly traded[31] provider of fixed location imaging services, Radnet—which acquired its principal competitor Radiologix in the fall of 2006—has the majority of its facilities in three of the same states (California, Maryland, and Florida) listed above, with a concentration in California.

Exhibit 21 reflects total units of equipment (e.g., MRI, CT, and so on).

Exhibit 21. Radnet, Units by State

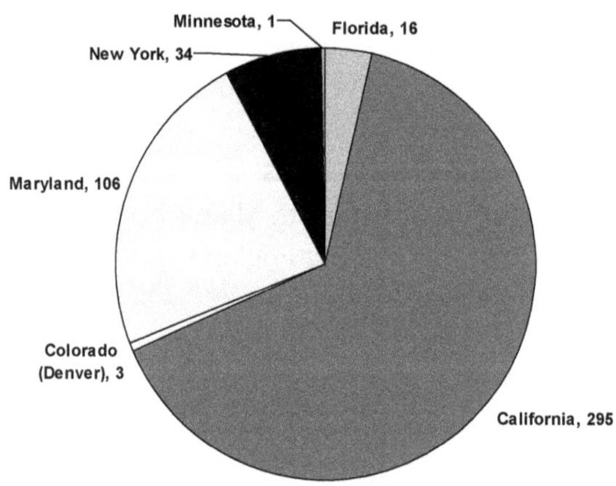

Certainly, a substantive argument could be made that the multiples paid by Radnet for imaging centers in California would be relevant to the valuation of an imaging center located in California (see Exhibit 22). It seems questionable, particularly in light of regulatory considerations, that those transactions would be relevant in New Mexico or Georgia, for example. At best, the multiples might provide some insight, especially if the effect of acquisition growth could be eliminated.

30 www.ncsl.org/research/health/con-certificate-of-need-state-laws.aspx, a CON is basically a form of state-issued license.

31 Alliance is the other with primarily mobile imaging and locations in many states. It has recently turned its attention to development of PET and CT. The revenue prospects for different types of imaging can vary dramatically.

Exhibit 22. Radnet, California Units

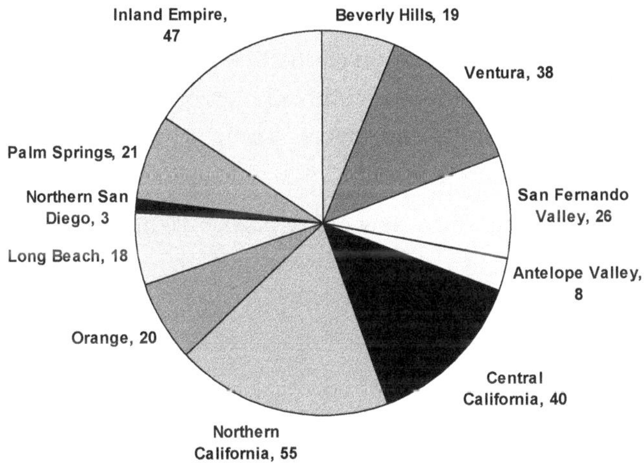

16.0 Acquisition Versus Same Store Growth

One of the most important and fundamental differences between a single location valuation subject and a large multilocation, multimarket alleged comparable is the availability of acquisition growth to enhance value through the earnings or cash flow capitalization rate[32] or to offset a decline in same-store revenue and profit growth. Consider the following statement from Lehman Brothers analyst Adam Feinstein about AMSG in anticipation of the announcement of the final rule by the CMS with respect to the adoption of a new revenue model for ASCs that would contain significant cutbacks for endoscopy:

> In regards to an LBO, AMSG has noted that it believes that the overhang created by the proposed changes in Medicare reimbursement (with a final rule expected sometime this summer [*2007*] and the changes expected to take effect on Jan. 1, 2008) reduces the likelihood that a financial sponsor would be interested in acquiring the company (due to the anticipated negative impact in 2008 and 2009). In addition, we get the sense that the company is not interested in going private since *the company has noted that it believes it needs to undertake 12 to 15 acquisitions per year in 2008 and 2009 in order to generate the same cash flow in those years as it will in 2007 (with the anticipated negative impact from the changes in Medicare reimbursement being offset by the cash flow the company acquires)*[33] (emphasis added).

17.0 Valuation Imperative

One observation about the valuation implication of AMSG's statement regarding new acquisitions is that for those acquisitions to be accretive to earnings—a necessity if the stock price is to be maintained—acquisition multiples are likely to drop! This is a key test that the appraiser or analyst should employ as part of the reality check for an ultimate valuation conclusion if

32 Defined as the discount rate less the long-term or perpetual growth rate.

33 Lehman Brothers Health Care Facilities: March Quarter Review: "Buyouts Rule the Day", May 18, 2007.

the merged and acquired company method is being used: Would the acquisition be accretive to earnings?

Another observation is that a single-location endoscopy center, for example, is unlikely to be in a position to respond to per-unit revenue cutbacks by acquiring other endoscopy centers; at best, it might hope to attract additional providers to its facility assuming it had excess capacity.

Exhibit 23. New Centers: 2005-2006

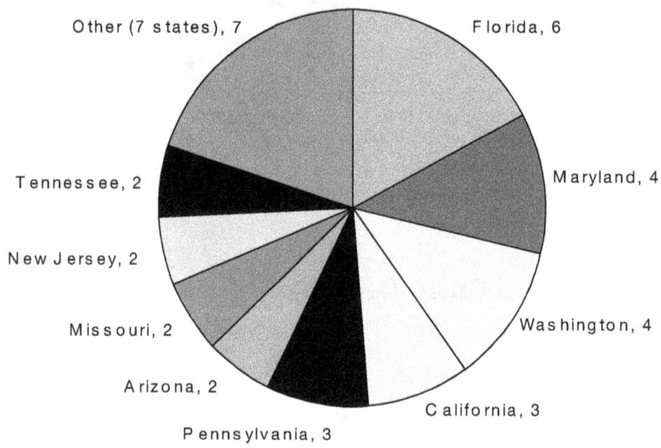

How would the plan by a public surgery center consolidator to offset per-unit revenue declines impact the transaction price for a single-location provider? Unless that provider is located in a state that the consolidator is active in or likely to become active in, there would be no impact. The universe of hypothetical buyers under the fair market value standard or even for strategic value does not include buyers who are not present in the market. Exhibit 23 presents AMSG's 35 most recent centers by state.

18.0 Implications for Valuation of Private Healthcare Providers

18.1 Follow the Money

The old adage "follow the money" is employed in many professions. As the analysis in this chapter demonstrates, to some extent you can find large for-profit providers by looking at high local rates of healthcare spending. Or perhaps it is more accurate to say you will *not* find those providers where there is low healthcare spending. Factors in addition to total and per-capita spending play a significant role in the desirability of a particular location for larger for-profit entities and highlight the importance of understanding local market conditions, including:

- Income levels of population;
- Health insurance coverage statistics, including coverage by Medicaid;
- Hospital spending per capita and in total;

- Physician spending per capita and in total;
- Competing nonprofit providers, including whether the entities have established integrated healthcare networks;
- Identity and market share of health insurers; in large states, regional market concentration should be considered along with statewide data; HMO penetration (reported by KFF) versus indemnity and other types of health insurance should also be considered; and
- Competing for-profit local providers, e.g., Shields MRI in Massachusetts.

18.2 All Healthcare Is Local

Healthcare markets are highly localized. When seeking to apply comparable transactions under the merged and acquired company method or the guideline publicly traded company method, it is incumbent on the analyst to establish that an acquirer or public company is likely to be active in the market of the valuation subject. Failure to establish that limits the usefulness of the market data and may, in fact, lead to an erroneous conclusion of value.

Other relevant local market factors:

- The concentration of the population in urban versus rural areas; urban areas provide easier access;
- In rural areas, the extent and quality of road systems enabling access to healthcare providers; barriers to access such as bridges or ferries from peninsula or island communities; and
- Age distribution of population.

Earlier, portions of public hospital company 10-Ks were cited that described the economies of scale and negotiating leverage with managed care insurers that were obtained through concentrating activities in a given state. It stands to reason that acquisition multiples in that state could properly reflect the inherent value from the economies of scale, but it is difficult to see how that acquisition multiple could be applied to a valuation subject in another state.

Another element to consider is localized supply and demand for a particular healthcare provider. Hospitals often compete to acquire physician practices, seeking to increase or defensively maintain inpatient admissions and referrals for tests. Nonetheless, there are regulatory prohibitions against considering such admissions and referrals in the purchase price and any demand-driven increase in value is limited to factors not precluded by law. Many times, it is difficult to appropriately include even factors such as reduced cost of capital or economies of scale due to the need to rely upon the fair market value standard.

19.0 Other Uses of Market Data

There is an arbitrage effect when private company cash flows are moved into the public markets via acquisition, as described earlier with respect to evaluating whether a particular acquisition would be accretive to earnings. If possible, an appraiser or analyst might attempt to extract acquisition growth from valuation multiples to obtain an indication of market value when acquisition-driven market data are used to value a subject in a market where no such buyer is present. This would require analyzing the out-of-market acquirer's stock and EBITDA valuation multiples and extracting that portion representing acquisition-driven growth. A fundamental analysis can also be performed on the subject to derive discounts from the public company's value for size and growth, for example.[34]

20.0 Valuation Imperative

Of course, not all transaction data represents activity of publicly traded companies. However, it is reasonable to believe that privately held or nonprofit buyers of healthcare entities in markets dominated by public for-profits find acquisition prices driven by what the public for-profit is willing to pay, *even if* the nonprofit cannot match the growth rate. There are many policy and economic implications beyond the scope of this chapter with respect to the availability of tax-exempt bonds to lower a nonprofit's cost of capital.

21.0 Regulatory Issues

At the outset of the chapter, it was stated "that the government agencies' views of 'fair market value' should be seriously considered by appraisers and analysts in their own opinions of fair market value." The core of the Stark regulations limitations on use of market data in establishing fair market value can be found in the following extract:

> Usually the fair market price is the price at which bona fide sales have been consummated for assets of like type, quality, and quantity in a particular market at the time of acquisition.[35]

The presence of this statement, drafted at the Department of Health and Human Services (DHHS), which operates the Medicare program, likely reflects that agency's intimate familiarity with differences in local healthcare spending and providers.

Appraisers conforming to uniform standards of professional appraisal practice (USPAP) and other standards frequently cite those standards as the basis for employing certain methods even in the face of apparent government rejection, typically in tax court or other tax-oriented proceedings. For example, USPAP Standards Rule 9-4 provides in part that

34 See, e.g., Goeldner, "Adjusting Market Multiples of Public Guideline Companies for the Closely Held Business," ASA 18th Annual BV Conference, October 1999.

35 420 CFR 411.351.

> An appraiser must, when necessary for credible assignment results, analyze the effect on value, if any, of: … sales of capital stock or other ownership interests in similar business enterprises.

However, the Jurisdictional Exception Rule provides

> If any part of USPAP is contrary to the law or public policy of any jurisdiction, only that part shall be void and of no force or effect in that jurisdiction.

Appraisers and analysts should not assume that government's views of fair market value are inconsistent with the usage of that term in the appraisal profession and do well to remember that the law always trumps professional standards. Improper use of market data in the face of the above regulation could result in unlawful conduct.

22.0 Conclusion

The results of this study are important to appraisers and analysts working in the healthcare industry. Healthcare markets are highly localized and use of out-of-market data for the valuation of a healthcare business requires a detailed analysis of conditions in the source market as well as the subject market (see Exhibit 24). Regulatory restrictions on the use market data in the Stark laws cannot be dismissed because there are fundamental economic reasons for those restrictions as well as professional standards that require they be respected.

Markets in which larger for-profit provider entities are present will have transactions that reflect not only the local market conditions, but also the revenue and earnings growth inherent in the motivation of public companies. Public healthcare providers, such as AMSG, are consolidators driven by acquisition growth. Even those nonprofit markets where healthcare spending and insurer concentration are *otherwise* similar to for-profit markets may have very different values for local entities than is indicated by consolidator-driven multiples. Thus, methods under the market approach have to be used with considerable skill and intensive analysis.

There are few absolutes in valuation in general and healthcare valuation in particular. However, terms such as "north," "south," "Rust Belt," and "Mason-Dixon Line" seem to have consequential importance. Finally, there is an abundance of readily available and often free data on local healthcare markets that enable the appraiser or analyst to accomplish the tasks necessary for the appropriate application and weighting of the market approach.

My thanks to Barry Sziklay, James Rigby, Michael Crain, Nancy Fannon, Don Barbo, Kevin Yeanoplos, and Carol Carden who contributed to the review of this chapter but may or may not agree with its conclusions.

Exhibit 24. Factors to Consider When Evaluating Out-of Market Transactions

Factor	Subject Market	Comparable Market	Data * Source(s)
Economic and demographic factors			
Medicare Part A spending total and per capita			1, 2
Medicare Part B spending total and per capita			1, 2
Medicare Geographic Practice Cost Indices (GPCI)			
Cost of Living for local market versus national			
Pending or anticipated per unit revenue changes			3, 4
Hospital spending per capita and in total			1
Physician spending per capita and in total			1
Per capita income levels of population			1
Age distribution of population			1
The concentration of the population in urban versus rural areas			1
In rural areas, the extent and quality of road systems enabling access to healthcare providers; barriers to access such as bridges or ferries from peninsula or island communities			
Health insurance coverage statistics, including coverage by Medicaid			1
Presence of Medicare Advantage plans			2
Medicaid spending and crisis status (Medicaid is typically the single largest line item in a state budget)			1
Health insurer factors			
Identity and market share of health insurers; in large states, regional market concentration should be considered along with statewide data; HMO penetration versus indemnity and other types of health insurance should also be considered			1, 5, 6, 7
Whether or not insurers use network fee schedules or individually negotiated fee schedules			
Utilization factors			
Hospital length of stay			1
Hospital days per 1,000			1
Hospital cost per day			1
Imaging per capita, rate of increase			3
Inpatient versus outpatient surgery			1
Market competition factors			
Presence of publicly held provider entities			6
Competing for-profit local providers			

Factor	Subject Market	Comparable Market	Data * Source(s)
Competing not-for-profit providers			
The percentage of all hospitals beds owned by for-profit hospitals			1
The rank by state based on total for-profit beds			1
Presence of integrated hospital systems			
Presence of integrated delivery systems with physician networks			
Potential economies of scale resulting from multiple locations in terms of costs, negotiating strength, marketing, etc.			
Whether or not insurers use network fee schedules or individually negotiated fee schedules (again)			
Intensity of market competition for acquisitions			6
Impact of acquisition growth on stock price			
Legal factors			
For physician practices, enforceability of noncompete laws including judicial precedent			
Certificate of need laws for various provider entities			8
Federal regulatory status			9
Anti-kickback Stark laws False Claims Act CMS administrative sanctions Enforcement trends, e.g., hospital systems suffering losses as the result of physician employment			
State regulatory status			
Political factors			
Lobby strength of state hospital association, medical society, imaging, ASC, chiropractic, etc.			
Board representation on provider entities, particularly exempt hospitals and teaching hospitals			

*Data Sources:
1. kff.org/statedata/.
2. www.cms.gov/Medicare/Health-Plans/MedicareAdvtgSpecRateStats/index.html/.
3. www.medpac.gov.
4. Centers for Medicare & Medicaid generally.
5, 6. SEC filings.
7. State Insurance Commissioners.
8. www.ncsl.org/research/health/con-certificate-of-need-state-laws.aspx.
9. www.cms.gov/Regulations-and-Guidance/Regulations-and-Guidance.html.

Chapter 2.
Factors in Estimating Cost of Capital and Forecasting Cash Flow in Healthcare

CONTENTS

Chapter 2.
Factors in Estimating Cost of Capital and Forecasting Cash Flow in Healthcare

By Carol W. Carden, CPA/ABV, ASA, CFE, and Mark O. Dietrich, CPA/ABV

It is critical when undertaking the valuation of any company to have a good understanding of the risks associated with its future cash flows. In today's healthcare industry environment, it has never been more important or more difficult to appropriately assess risk and correctly apply discount or capitalization rates. It is equally difficult with the uncertainty of this environment to develop revenue forecasting assumptions that are reasonable and reflective of likely trends in the various healthcare industry sectors. This chapter offers some guidance on the myriad of factors that impact the cost of capital, risk assessment, and cash flow forecasting for healthcare industry transactions.

1.0 What Comprises the 'Healthcare Industry'?

Before delving into a discussion about the risk and uncertainty associated with the healthcare industry, it is important to first establish the different types of organizations included under this broad umbrella. Comprising 17.7% of the U.S. economy, healthcare is the single largest segment. The treatment of healthcare as a single industry obscures the reality that it is really a complex set of separate subsections that are, to one extent or another, interrelated, and may have vastly different prospects at various points in time.

Primary components of the industry include physicians, patient care facilities, pharmaceutical and life sciences, medical equipment manufacturers and technology, provider networks and accountable care organizations (ACOs), and home healthcare. As a further division, facilities include acute care hospitals, long-term care hospitals, skilled nursing facilities, freestanding ambulatory surgery centers (ASCs), and senior housing. These are all dramatically different businesses. Acute care hospitals compete with ASCs for outpatient surgery, for example, but ASCs are paid only 60% of what a hospital outpatient department receives for the same case.

Therefore, even two businesses that essentially provide the same service have very different risk characteristics and future revenue prospects.

In the physician sector, hospital-based physicians, such as anesthesiologists or neonatal intensive care unit (NICU) physicians favored by private equity investors, are highly different from one another and from other types of practices, which typically have greater overhead than they do.

Each of these sectors is likely to have a different risk profile. That risk, to a large extent, is a function of the relative success or failure of industry lobbyists in winning government payors' support (e.g., Medicare and Medicaid) for their subsection payors. As such, identifying trends in future government program revenue is one key to the accurate assessment of risk, as well as the forecasting of future cash flow.

2.0 Deriving the Discount Rate

Some within the academic finance community recently have begun to rethink the manner in which the appropriate return on investment is calculated. This reconsideration is the result of new challenges to the capital asset pricing model (CAPM) that underlie equity cost of capital in business valuation (e.g., by Pablo Fernandez of the University of Navarra in Spain[1]). Perhaps more important to the broad business valuation community is the challenge to the continued existence of the historical small-stock risk premium, which is the basis for the belief that risk and size are inversely proportional, a critical element in valuing privately held businesses. Michael Crain, a thought leader in business valuation, has been at the forefront of the challenge. One hypothesis is that the introduction of small-cap stock funds in the early 1980s substantially increased those firms' liquidity as institutions and investors impacted supply and demand.[2] Crain further states:

> Practitioners seem to pay little or no attention to more recent research on the size effect showing its diminishment or disappearance. When they refer to empirical research, it is to earlier studies. First, investment advisers still tell investors that small firms have historically produced higher returns over the long run. But they do not acknowledge increasing underperformance of smaller stocks....
>
> Secondly, practitioners who value unlisted SMEs [small and midsized enterprises] have a perspective that is similar to investment advisers of not explicitly recognizing more recent research on the size effect. These practitioners seem to believe either the size effect is persistent over the long run or they are not aware the size effect has diminished or disappeared since the 1980s. According to business valuation handbooks, practitioners who value unlisted SMEs rely on long-term historical averages of the size effect in listed firms

1 *CAPM: An Absurd Model*, papers.ssrn.com/sol3/papers.cfm?abstract_id=2505597.

2 Michael A. Crain, *A Literature Review of the Size Effect*, Florida Atlantic University; University of Manchester—Manchester Business School, Oct. 29, 2011, citing research by Horowitz et al.; papers.ssrn.com/sol3/papers.cfm?abstract_id=1710076.

> when estimating costs of capital. These averages are usually based on data beginning either in the 1920s or 1960s. Practitioner texts generally do not acknowledge more recent size-effect studies.

In his conclusions, Crain observes:

> When the size effect is observed, theory suggests that superior returns in smaller firms arise from higher risk in these firms compared to larger firms. Researchers do not claim that size per se is a source of risk that drives superior returns of smaller firms. Instead, firm size may be a proxy for one or more underlying risk factors linked to smaller firms. Such factors could be endogenous or exogenous and explain variations in the size effect. Empirical research suggests one such embedded factor in smaller firms is liquidity risk. Logically, these findings on liquidity seem linked to the emergence of small-cap investment funds in the 1980s. Small-cap funds increase the liquidity of smaller firms and, thus, liquidity risk in these firms ought to be lower on average after these kinds of funds launch. It follows that superior returns of smaller firms should decline when liquidity risk decreases.
>
> In addition to the discoveries of the size effect and variations in the effect, two areas of research are related to these findings. First, research shows that when the size effect is observed, it is nonlinear and concentrated in smaller listed firms. One study finds the effect is five times larger in firms in the 20th percentile using NYSE breakpoints for size and only marginal across the remaining larger firms. Another study finds the size effect is significant only in listed firms under $5 million in market capitalization.

Since value and the discount rate are inversely proportional, e.g., the lower the discount rate, the higher the value, this current research likely has significance to the values ultimately determined for privately held healthcare businesses. Supply, demand, and illiquidity are all important to the discount rate in healthcare valuation. If, in fact, the small-stock premium for public companies has disappeared or shrunk significantly due to liquidity, that does not mean the illiquidity discount for nonpublic companies ceases to exist. However, as the discussion in the remainder of this chapter demonstrates, volatility in the payment for healthcare services trumps other factors in assessing the risk of future cash flow.

3.0 Weighted Average Cost of Capital (WACC)

Once equity discount rate is determined, the relevant discount rate for determining the market value of invested capital or operating asset value is the WACC, reflecting some measure of debt in the entity's capital structure. Of course, the more debt one assumes in the capital structure, the lower the discount rate. It is important to remember that the CAPM's beta suggests that the more leverage an entity employs, the higher its cost of equity will be. The appropriate percentage of debt will vary by the nature of the entity being valued, with capital-intensive segments such as facilities and imaging centers using more debt, and physician practices using less. As a general rule, the amount of debt in the typical nonintegrated primary care practice's capital structure would not exceed 15% or 20%. In contrast, an imaging center may have 30% to 40% debt. The amount of debt is also influenced by whether a control or noncontrol interest is being valued as well as expected future capital outlays.

4.0 Government Influence

The healthcare segment of the industry is closely tied to the action of federal and state governments. Government influence flows from the executive branch through regulatory authorities such as the Office of the Inspector General (OIG), Federal Trade Commission (FTC), Anti-Trust Division of the Department of Justice (DOJ), states' attorneys general, DOJ Civil and Criminal Division, Centers for Medicare & Medicaid Services (CMS), and numerous others. Each of these agencies plays a critical role in the prospects of the various components of the healthcare industry.

The legislative branch plays a less frequent, but often dramatic, role in subsector prospects as discussed in greater detail later in this chapter. At the federal level, passage of the Affordable Care Act (ACA) in 2010 (also referred to as healthcare reform) has caused fundamental shifts in how healthcare reimbursement works and has, therefore, introduced greater uncertainty into cash flow projections. At the state level, the Medicaid program for low-income and indigent individuals is a significant factor for many individual companies within each subsector but may not be significant to others who do not service that population. Owing to differences in state-defined covered benefits and policy design, healthcare reform has had a highly localized effect. It is critical in assessing the risk and cash flows associated with a healthcare company that you have a good understanding of the potential impact of government action or inaction on your particular healthcare subsector.

5.0 Identifying Factors That Contribute to Risk

One of the great challenges of business valuation is quantification of future changes in cash flow through the forecast or the discount rate. Due to the high level of regulation and government influence in healthcare, the forecasting of revenue growth assumptions is much more difficult than a similar undertaking for a less-regulated industry. On the other hand, there are a number of sources for near-term trend analysis for the healthcare industry as well as longer-term crystal ball gazing to assist in this undertaking.

One of the most important things for an appraiser to understand about forecasting healthcare industry cash flow is that there is a long history of radical changes in the rates that Medicare pays for services. There is virtual certainty that explosive growth in spending on a particular service will be met with equally explosive cuts in the payment for those services. The discussion below and the proceeding sections detail a series of examples of significant changes since 2003. These illustrations are by no means exhaustive but rather representative of the kinds of changes that happen routinely in the healthcare industry and lend themselves to either cash flow modification or enhanced risk in the discount rate.

6.0 Near-Term Forecasting and Risk Assessment: MedPAC, the MPFS Proposed and Final Rules, and the Market

Each March, the Medicare Payment Advisory Commission (MedPAC) issues its report to Congress regarding Medicare payment policy. While the MedPAC report is not authoritative, it serves as a good indicator of potential areas of Medicare payment action as well as which sectors are likely to be targeted for significant reimbursement changes or industry restructuring. Many times, recommendations from the MedPAC report will be included in the proposed physician fee schedule as discussed below.

Also annually, CMS publishes proposed and—after a comment period—final regulations announcing rates for the subsequent calendar year. For example, the proposed Medicare Physician Fee Schedule (MPFS) Rule is typically published in July or August and the final rule in early November, allowing approximately three months' notice for what is likely to occur in the next calendar year. While labeled "physician fee schedule," the MPFS also contains proposed fees for outpatient, physician-based healthcare entities, such as ASCs. There have also been instances, such as when the ASC fee schedule was completely revamped in 2005, when fee changes are so significant that they will be phased in over a number of years, providing a reliable revenue assumption forecasting tool for the short term. The MPFS assumptions and trends also can be applied to commercial insurance payors as commercial plans typically follow the lead of CMS in establishing reimbursement policy.

6.1 Example 1: The Sustainable Growth Rate

Notably, since 2003, massive cuts in the physician fee schedule have been announced in the proposed rule (in the order of magnitude of 25% or more) only to be overturned by Congress in late December before a January 1 effective date, and replaced with small increases in the range of 0.5% to 1.5% due to the sustainable growth rate (SGR) formula. It is beyond the scope of this chapter to discuss the SGR in detail, but, in summary, the premise of the SGR was that budget neutrality was related to changes in the MPFS and was not achieved. Therefore, to place the MPFS back in "balance" would have required a significant, single-year, across-the-board reduction in physician fees.

After more than a decade of consternation and confusion over the SGR, it was finally repealed in early 2015. To attain budget neutrality, future increases in the MPFS conversion factor are limited to 0.5% in June 2015 and in each year 2016 through 2019. An increase is not expected from 2019 through 2025. At least for the next several years, valuators have a reasonable basis for anticipating the *overall* increase in physician fees. However, in 2019, quality and cost-of-care indicators are scheduled to determine whether physicians will be entitled to conversion factor updates. It is important to note that changes in the "relative value" of individual physician specialties' services can impact whether a specific specialty receives an overall increase or decrease in fees from Medicare.

6.2 Example 2: Imaging

The proposed and final rules are closely watched by management and industry analysts, although seemingly less so by investors, given the lag in some stock's price response. For example, Alliance Imaging (AIQ) is a provider of magnetic resonance imaging (MRI), positron emission tomography and computed tomography (PET/CT) and radiation therapy, primarily on an outpatient basis. Approximately 80% of its revenue comes from contracts with hospitals, and much of that is subject to the Hospital Outpatient Prospective Payment System (HOPPS). Nonetheless, it has a significant exposure to the MPFS.

Exhibit 1 plots AIQ's stock price and volume for the period from June 2009 to November 2009. The graph indicates some market reaction to the July 1, 2009, MPFS-proposed rule that called for significant cuts in the payment rates for MRI and radiation therapy, particularly intensity-modulated radiation therapy (IMRT), an expensive form of radiation therapy. Thereafter, the stock recovered much of the loss in value following the announcement, only to plunge following the company's earnings conference call when management quantified the loss in net revenue (and effectively operating income) at more than $5.5 million. From an appraiser's standpoint in looking at a comparable company, one would have to believe that the impact of the proposed cuts (which were in large part adopted as part of the final rule on October 31) was subject to calculation and therefore reasonably known at the beginning of July.

Exhibit 1. AIQ Price and Volume

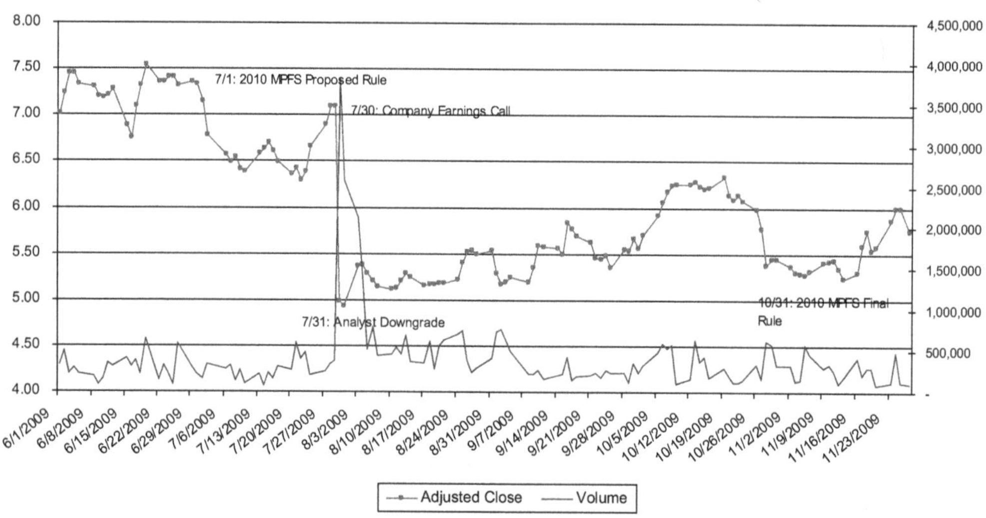

The drop of about 30% in the stock's price on July 31 is a function of three factors: (1) expected and known reduction in future cash flow; (2) increased risk of cash flows; and (3) selling pressure due to high trading volume. Note that despite the quantification of the loss in cash flow, the stock's price recovers after the downward price pressure of the sell-off is gone. When the proposed rule is finalized at the end of October, the stock's price declines again. Investor reaction appears more immediate, since the reductions under the proposed rule announced July 31 are confirmed on October 31, and "all hope is lost."

Point: The response of public market investors as reflected in stock prices often lags knowledge of likely or pending reimbursement changes. Aside from the tendency to view bad news about one's investment in the most favorable light, the lag may be pending the assessment of professional industry analysts, e.g., Joshua Raskin & Adam Feinstein of Barclays Capital.

7.0 Identifying Reimbursement Trends That Are Not Sustainable

Perhaps the single largest error made in forecasting cash flows for a medical practice or other entity that relies on the MPFS is failure to evaluate the likely direction that reimbursement for that particular sector is headed using the tools just discussed. Additionally, as a general rule, no single location, market, or service line healthcare entity will have reimbursement growth rate assumptions greater than 2% to 3% over the long term. Growth of this magnitude is possible in the discrete periods of the forecast, but given the complexity of the regulations just discussed, it is highly unlikely, and quite likely impossible, for any sector to grow at a rate greater than 2% to 3% over the long term. The key to identifying and addressing risk and future cash flows is understanding that frequently utilized, high-cost procedures and tests will be targeted for dramatic cutbacks. It is not a matter of if, but when, the cuts will be implemented, as demonstrated in the following examples.

7.1 Example 1: Dermatopathology in 2012

An example of these targeted cuts involves pathology. A rapid increase in the acquisition of dermatopathology laboratory equipment occurred during the 2000s as dermatologists merged their practices into larger entities. Fellowships in pathology were offered for boarded dermatologists, and fellowships for dermatopathology were offered for boarded pathologists. This sparked a significant increase in the utilization of skin biopsies and tests. A similar pattern occurred with urology practices that also are heavy users of tissue samples.

Dermatopathology involves both a professional component (PC) for interpreting the biopsy as well as a technical component (TC) for owning the equipment. In the MPFS Final Rule for 2013, CMS observed that: "In 2010, Medicare spent $1.3 billion on CPT® code 88305."[3] The total RVU value of current procedural terminology (CPT®) code 88305,[4] the primary pathology code, dropped from 3.04 in 2012 to 2.07 in 2013, a 33% reduction. The reduction in the TC RVU value of CPT® 88305 was actually 52%, and the impact on the global market was offset by a small increase of 2% in the PC. In 2014, the total RVU value declined to 1.97, but, owing to a change in the way the practice expense component was computed, the numbers are not entirely comparable.

3 Surgical Pathology, gross and microscopic examination.

4 Codes are copyright, American Medical Association. This code was "cross-walked," or changed, to 78452 in the period between the 2010 proposed and final rules—one more complication that emphasizes the importance of understanding CPT® codes.

7.2 Example 2: Cardiac Imaging in 2007

As further demonstration, CPT® code 78465, heart image (3rd) multiple, is a single photon emission computed tomography (SPECT) code for myocardial infusion that represented a staggering 10.3% ($2,072,176,147) of charges for cardiovascular physicians who billed Medicare in 2007. That single CPT® code trumped all other single codes both in terms of the frequency of billing and in the greatest amount of total charges.[5] CPT® code 78465 also represented 10.4% ($2,017,599,660) of charges in 2006 and 10.4% ($1,863,154,763) of charges in 2005.

Exhibit 2 depicts the growth in allowed charges (left axis)—those that Medicare actually approves for payment as opposed to those that are submitted—from 2003 to 2008, and billed charges (right axis)—those actually submitted by providers—from 2005 to 2007.

Exhibit 2. Growth in Allowed Charges and Billed Charges*

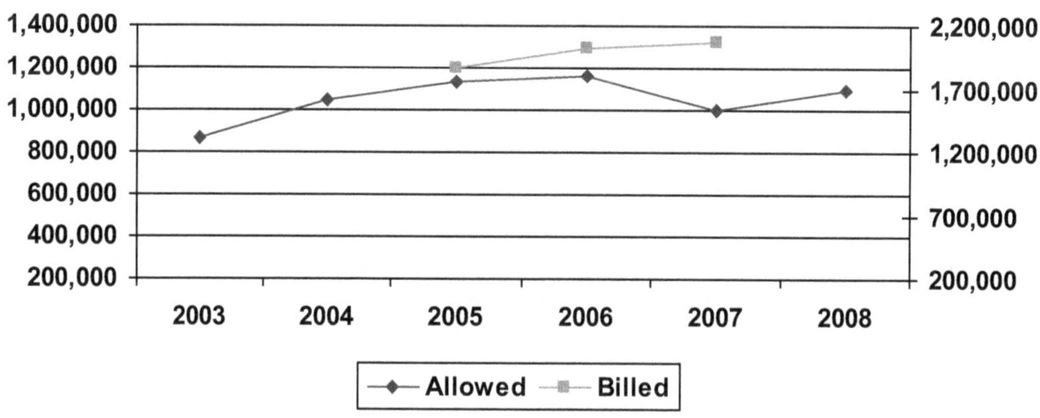

* Growth in allowed charges and billed charges for cardiac imaging

The TC paid in connection with ownership of the equipment, employment of a technician, and provision of supplies and other overhead, is approximately *85%* of the global fee for CPT® code 78465. The Medicare program sets fees by assigning to each code a value factor in terms of relative value units (RVU) and multiplying that by a dollar rate, called a conversion factor.[6] Thus, the fee paid for a code is proportional to the RVU value assigned to it.

RVU values are based upon three principal factors: the cost of providing the service, known as the practice expense component; the physician work associated with providing the service or interpreting the results of a test; and the cost of malpractice insurance. Therefore, the more

5 Current data can be downloaded at www.cmpasupport.com/download/files/Top10Procs_2008.zip, and historical data are available at www.cms.hhs.gov/MedicareFeeforSvcPartsAB/04_MedicareUtilizationforPartB.asp#TopOfPage.

6 The concept of RVUs is analogous to billable hours, while the conversion factor is analogous to a billing rate per hour. For example, if a code has an RVU value of 10 and the conversion factor is $50, it would have a fee of $500.

resources a particular service consumes in terms of physician time and effort, as well as operating costs, the higher the RVU assignment will be, and therefore, the higher the associated payment. The TC consists of a practice expense component and a small malpractice component.

In 2007, the TC had an RVU value of 11.51. That declined to 11.26 in 2008 and 10.73 in 2009. The final rule published in November 2009 set the RVUs for the TC at 8.32, a drop of 22%. This illustrates one of the critical insights that experienced healthcare industry appraisers possess: *expensive procedures eventually will be targeted for dramatic cutbacks. As previously stated, it is not a matter of if, but when, this will occur. The 78465 CPT® code was eliminated in 2010 and replaced with* 78452, which also encompassed two other eliminated codes, 78478 and 78480. This pattern highlights another means of cutting payments that is less obvious: combining and/or eliminating codes.

7.3 Example 3: High-Tech Imaging in 2005

Other notable examples of payment cutting measures include the Deficit Reduction Act of 2005—perhaps the most significant of the past decade, and part of a continuing trend highlighted by the earlier discussion of AIQ—which dramatically reduced the explosive growth in spending on high-tech imaging (e.g., MRI and CT).

The 2010 ACA is the most recent instance of a major revaluation of imaging services, raising the utilization assumption to 90% for purposes of establishing the practice expense RVU value of the TC. CMS has suggested further reductions in physician office-based imaging and even hospital outpatient department imaging.

7.4 Example 4: In-Office Infusible Drugs in 2003

The Medicare Modernization Act of 2003 (MMA) changed the methodology for paying for physician office chemotherapy drugs from one based on published list prices (average wholesale price) to one based on actual average selling price. The scale of the cuts was such that many physicians were unable to continue in-office chemotherapy, and the incomes of affected specialists, such as medical oncologists, dropped dramatically. The MMA also expanded the Medicare Advantage program in a manner that proved to be highly questionable from a cost-benefit standpoint, causing MedPAC, in its 2009 Report to Congress, to devote an entire chapter outlining related problems.

7.5 Example 5: G Codes

A comparatively subtle means of cutting reimbursement, similar to that of Example 2, involves combining codes that were once billable separately into a single "G" code. G codes are Medicare-specific and are used when CPT® code descriptions do not conform to CMS's desired description of a covered service. In 2010, for example, in response to the growth in knee arthroscopy, CMS combined CPT® 29877 (multiple procedures at the same time in the same knee) and another code into a single code: G0289. This action effectively eliminated the ability to bill for multiple procedures that were commonplace at the time. Many commercial insurers then followed suit.

This combination of codes is a form of "bundled" payment.[7]

The above examples span more than a decade.

Point: If a healthcare service or procedure reflects dramatic profits, it is likely to change, change soon, and change in a significant, negative fashion.

8.0 The MedPAC Crystal Ball

The appraiser can identify trends in the high-dollar-value services offered by a practice specialty by reviewing multiple years' worth of data for the practice as well as Medicare claims data for the same services by all similar specialists, or even for specialists located only within that state.[8] As suggested above, the annual MedPAC Reports to Congress offer additional resources for prospective change and risk. Exhibit 3—taken from the 2015 Report—generally appears every year. The average annual change in services per beneficiary, as well as volume[9] per beneficiary, is shown along with the year-over-year change for the most recent period, here 2013 over 2012.

Exhibit 3. Use of Services Provided by Physicians and Other Health Professionals, per FFS Beneficiary

	Change in units of service per beneficiary		Change in volume per beneficiary		
Type of service	**Average annual 2008–2012**	**2012–2013**	**Average annual 2008–2012**	**2012–2013**	**Percent of 2013 allowed charges**
All services	**0.6%**	**–0.2%**	**N/A**	**0.5%**	**100.0%**
Evaluation and management	**0.2**	**1.4**	**N/A**	**1.4**	**47.3**
Office visit—new and established	0.5	2.8	N/A	2.8	26.8
Inpatient visit—hospital and nursing facility	–0.6	–0.5	N/A	–0.6	15.6
Emergency room visit	2.2	–1.1	3.5%	–0.1	3.1
Hospital visit—critical care	4.7	0.6	4.8	0.5	1.4
Home visit	3.8	1.0	4.3	1.1	0.4
Imaging	**–0.5**	**–0.6**	**–1.4**	**–1.0**	**11.5**
Advanced—CT: other	1.8	2.2	0.6	0.9	1.6
Advanced—MRI: other	0.0	1.6	–2.3	0.4	1.1

7 For a more in-depth explanation, see www.hcpro.com/HOM-247616-8160/Auditing-for-coding-mistakes-on-outpatient-orthopedic-cases.html.

8 This data is available at www.frankcohengroup.com/, for example.

9 "Volume is measured as units of service multiplied by each service's relative value unit (RVU) from the physician fee schedule. To put service use in each year on a common scale, we used the RVUs for 2013. For billing codes not used in 2013, we imputed RVUs based on the average change in RVUs for each type of service." MedPAC 2015 Report to Congress.

Exhibit 3. Use of Services Provided by Physicians and Other Health Professionals, per FFS Beneficiary, Continued

	Change in units of service per beneficiary		Change in volume per beneficiary		
Type of service	Average annual 2008–2012	2012–2013	Average annual 2008–2012	2012–2013	Percent of 2013 allowed charges
Echography—other	4.5	4.1	6.7	6.8	1.1
Echography—heart	–0.8	–1.2	–2.1	–7.3	1.0
Standard—nuclear medicine	–6.8	–7.9	–10.1	–10.2	0.9
Standard—musculoskeletal	0.0	0.5	–0.6	0.3	0.9
Standard—breast	1.4	0.9	1.1	0.1	0.7
Imaging/procedure—other	–3.5	–2.0	0.4	5.3	0.7
Advanced—MRI: brain	–1.3	–0.3	–4.4	–1.8	0.5
Advanced—CT: head	1.2	–0.3	–0.6	–0.8	0.4
Standard—chest	–2.1	–3.5	–2.7	–3.6	0.4
Echography—abdomen and pelvis	1.5	0.0	1.8	0.4	0.4
Major procedures	**0.3**	**–1.1**	**1.2**	**1.2**	**7.4**
Cardiovascular—other	–1.4	–7.6	0.4	–2.9	1.7
Orthopedic—other	1.6	2.5	3.1	3.6	1.1
Knee replacement	0.9	3.2	1.3	4.4	0.6
Hip replacement	3.2	4.1	3.7	5.2	0.3
Explore, decompress, or excise disc	2.6	0.3	4.7	2.7	0.3
Hip fracture repair	–2.3	0.3	–2.2	0.8	0.3
Coronary angioplasty	–3.3	7.2	–3.2	6.8	0.2
Coronary artery bypass graft	–7.0	–2.8	–7.0	–2.0	0.2
Other procedures	**1.9**	**–0.9**	**1.9**	**0.1**	**22.2**
Skin—minor and ambulatory	0.7	1.4	2.3	1.0	4.8
Outpatient rehabilitation	3.9	–2.4	4.7	–1.9	3.3
Radiation therapy	–2.7	–2.5	–1.1	–2.4	1.9
Minor—other	0.6	–1.4	1.2	–0.8	2.0
Cataract removal/lens insertion	–0.4	1.2	–0.2	1.2	1.4
Minor—musculoskeletal	1.8	0.0	2.5	0.6	1.4
Eye—other	10.1	4.8	4.8	2.5	1.1
Colonoscopy	–2.0	0.4	–1.9	0.7	0.9
Upper gastrointestinal endoscopy	0.5	–1.1	1.0	–0.6	0.5
Cystoscopy	0.1	0.1	–0.3	0.2	0.4
Tests	**0.8**	**0.5**	**2.0**	**–2.1**	**4.6**
Other tests	1.2	4.9	1.1	0.5	1.7
Laboratory tests—other	3.7	0.7	5.0	0.0	1.6
Electrocardiograms	–0.4	–2.5	–0.2	–3.2	0.5

One thing that the appraiser should recognize is the subset of services on which MedPAC is focusing out of the many thousands of services offered by physicians. This focus gives the appraiser some insight into areas where MedPAC might potentially think reimbursement is too high. Generally speaking, when you see high growth rates in units of service per beneficiary or strong growth rates in overall utilization, MedPAC has a tendency to recommend fee reductions that have the effect of reducing utilization levels. As can be seen in Exhibit 3, imaging services totaled 11.5% of allowed charges for Medicare physician services. Those imaging areas previously singled out for reimbursement reductions include CT, MRI, and echography. There is an uptick in the utilization pattern in the current data for CT and MRI compared to the five-year average; this pattern would not bode well for future action to reduce utilization, likely through fee reductions. Recognition of patterns such as this directly impacts the appraiser's assessment of risk when appraising an imaging center focused in one of the modalities.

8.1 Example 1: Skin Lesion Removal in 2013

Dermatologists also saw an explosion in the growth of lesion removal (see Exhibit 4), included in Exhibit 3 in the category "Skin—minor and ambulatory." CMS moved to reduce costs here as well.

Exhibit 4. Growth of Lesion Removal

Description	CPT®	2013	2014	Change
Destruction premalg les	17000	91.81	82.61	10.02%
Destruction premalg les, 2-14	17003	7.37	11.23	52.37%
Destruction premalg les, 15+	17004	186.79	162.74	12.88%

8.2 Example 2: Home Health Payments

A final example, and one that garnered much attention due to the tax court case *Caracci,* involved home health agencies and the changeover from a cost-based payment system to a prospective payment system (PPS) in the late 1990s. The ACA made dramatic cuts to that HH PPS, commencing in 2014 and phasing in over four years. This followed years of MedPAC recommending that Congress cut payments. For example, in the 2009 Report, one year before the ACA, MedPAC stated: "The Congress should eliminate the market basket increase for 2010 and advance the planned reductions for coding adjustments in 2011 to 2010, so that payments in 2010 are reduced by 5.5% from 2009 levels."

9.0 Primary Care: The Baseline for Risk in Physician Practices

Pure primary care is generally regarded as the least risky of all physician practices. Key elements of this risk-analysis include:[10]

10 www.cms.gov/Medicare/Medicare-fee-for-Service-Payment/sharedsavingsprogram/faq.html, answer A6; generally, at least 60 percent of the allowed charges under Part B for the practitioner must be for specified codes. See also www.cms.gov/Regulations-and-Guidance/Guidance/Transmittals/downloads/R2161CP.pdf.

1. Severe shortage of internists and family practitioners to provide adult primary care;
2. Renewed focus on preventive care and management of patient illness;
3. General requirement for a health system to claim "covered lives" in an ACO, integrated delivery system, or capitation model; and
4. Consistently favorable reimbursement trends reflected in legislation such as the ACA and recommendations by MedPAC.

In the 2014 Report to Congress, MedPAC reported on the availability of primary care physicians and the increase in midlevel providers (advanced practice nurses and physician assistants):

> Our analysis of Medicare FFS claims data for 2010 to 2012 shows that the number of physicians and other health professionals providing services to Medicare beneficiaries kept pace with growth in the beneficiary population. For physicians in specialties eligible for the Primary Care Incentive Payment Program (PCIP), the ratio of these physicians per 1,000 beneficiaries remained constant at 3.8 per 1,000.
>
> Between 2011 and 2012, the ratio of physicians in other specialties fell slightly from 8.5 per 1,000 to 8.4 per 1,000. Meanwhile, the number of advanced practice nurses and physician assistants billing Medicare grew from 2.8 per 1,000 to 3.0 per 1,000.

The Report goes on to address compensation issues:

> The Commission remains concerned that the fee schedule and the nature of FFS payment lead to an undervaluing of primary care and overvaluing of specialty care. First, the Commission has concerns that the resource-based relative value scale, which forms the basis for the fee schedule, includes mispriced services and that these mispriced services can cause an income disparity between primary care and specialty physicians. Second, FFS payment allows some specialties to increase the volume of services they provide more easily (and therefore increase their revenue from Medicare), while other specialties, particularly those that spend most of their time providing E&M services, have limited ability to increase their volume. This difference in ability to increase volume can also lead to the compensation differences between primary care and specialty care.
>
> The physician fee schedule must be rebalanced to achieve greater equity of payments between primary care and other specialties. Given the important role primary care will play in delivery system reform, the Commission believes that the imbalance in payment between primary care and specialty care must be corrected to ensure adequate beneficiary access to these services and to support the role of primary care in delivery system reform.

In its March 2015 Report to Congress, MedPAC made the following recommendation:

> Therefore, the Commission recommends that the additional payments to primary care practitioners be in the form of a per-beneficiary payment as a step away from the service-oriented FFS payment approach and toward beneficiary-centered payments that encourage care coordination. The Commission recommends funding the per-beneficiary payment by reducing fees for all services in the fee schedule other than PCIP-defined primary care services provided by any practitioner, regardless of the practitioner's specialty designation or whether PCIP-defined primary care services accounted for at least 60% of the practitioner's allowed charges. Beneficiaries would not pay cost sharing, just as beneficiaries do not pay cost sharing to fund the PCIP. This method of funding would be budget neutral and would help rebalance the fee schedule to achieve greater equity of payments between primary care and other services.

Note that the source of the additional payment for primary care physicians (PCP) is the result of a reduction in the payment to non-PCP physicians! This is an important risk factor for the Medicare portion of a specialist's practice, as well as for any share represented by a payor who uses the CMS resource-based relative value scale (RBRVS) upon which physician fees in the MPFS are based.

10.0 Understanding the Impact of Payor Relationships

To this point in the chapter, we have focused much of our discussion on understanding the direction that governmental payors, such as Medicare and Medicaid, are headed. However, it is critical that the appraiser also understands the composition and reimbursement trends for the remaining payors, which means looking at several years' worth of data. Often, commercial payors tend to follow the direction of Medicare, albeit with a lag of one or more years. Therefore, the analyst should review and be familiar with the reimbursement terms for the most significant commercial contracts held by a healthcare organization to effectively forecast cash flows.

An often overlooked but important consideration is whether or not the company has a significant amount of out-of-network business. In this situation, the company does not hold a contract with the commercial payor, but treats patients of the payor nonetheless. In the early periods of this practice, it can be a lucrative arrangement for the healthcare company because it may receive fees that are higher than would be included in a contract. However, over the long term, this tactic will generally fail, resulting in a decrease in fees, if not in the complete elimination of a portion of the company's patient base. Therefore, when determining the level of revenues to forecast as well as the associated risk, it is critical to understand whether the company has exposure in this area and to factor such risks into the assessment of the discount/capitalization rate.

In the post-reform era, virtually everyone has some form of health insurance, and health insurance companies are arguably the "customer" for providers' services. As with any company being appraised, it is critical to assess concentration of customer risk when determining the appropriate discount rate/cost of capital. The tool used to assess concentration of risk for a healthcare company is the "payor mix." The payor mix is a reflection of the proportionate level of revenues attributable to the various payors, such as Medicare and Medicaid, as well as significant commercial health insurers, such as BlueCross/BlueShield or United Healthcare. If the appraiser determines that the healthcare company has a concentration with a particular payor, it would likely increase the assessment of risk related to the cash flows. Additionally, it would be imperative that the appraiser gain a very thorough understanding of the direction of reimbursement trends for that particular payor to ensure the revenue forecast is achievable.

Another important factor to analyze in terms of payor mix is the proportion of patients who are self-pay, or any significant changes in the proportion of self-pay patients. Many of the health insurance policies sold on state and federally operated exchanges established by the ACA contain very high deductibles, co-pays, and maximum out-of-pocket expenses for consumers. A significant increase in self-pay patients or in the patient's share of expense can trigger the appraiser to the fact that the company: has gained patients with poor insurance, lost an important commercial insurance contract, or geographically has been harder hit by economic changes than anticipated. Generally speaking, the collections rate on self-pay patients will be extremely low and most collections will happen very early in the process, if at all.

Point: You cannot assess the risk and discount rate or estimate future cash flow without knowledge of the underlying revenue sources. The risk of Medicare and Medicaid revenues is substantially different, and both of these may be very different from those of nongovernment payors; those individuals with insurance, co-pays, and deductibles; and uninsured individuals.

11.0 Using Guideline Company Data to Forecast Cash Flows and Assess Risk

To the extent that a public company's operations are representative of a given valuation subject's risk and prospects, it can provide insight into both the discount rate and forecast of cash flow. However, there are several often-overlooked, critical limitations on the use of the data in a healthcare industry context.

There have been two significant trends in the broader healthcare industry that affect the availability of guideline data and their usefulness. The first of these is consolidation within the payor industry. Consolidation of health insurers was possible due to their long-standing anti-trust waiver. This has, in turn, led to an ongoing and dramatic consolidation trend among providers, spurred by regulatory waivers for ACOs and a push to value-based payments for providers requiring closer coordination between hospitals, physicians, and other healthcare workers. The practical outcome of these interrelated and parallel trends has been to create a situation in many markets where providers pass increasing costs back to insurers that then pass those costs back to employers and insureds through their premiums. Consolidation among many healthcare sectors also has led to a declining number of guideline companies. The remaining companies are larger, more diverse in their revenue sources, and therefore, less exposed—or at-risk—to changes in a given market area.

Point: Future cash flow depends upon the relative market power of a company.[11] *Market risk is a function of many factors, and in the healthcare industry, size and diversity—particularly diversity as to revenue sources and number of distinct geographic market areas in which the company operates—are drivers of market or negotiating power.*[12]

Importantly, the detail regarding the guideline's payor contracts will likely not be known to the appraiser. Therefore, it is impossible for the appraiser to make the necessary adjustments to render the guideline truly "comparable." It is worth noting that one goal of the ACA is to increase the price transparency of healthcare services, so some data may be available in the future.

As discussed previously, commercial insurance contracts can have a dramatic impact on the risk assessment as well as the revenue forecast. Therefore, even if the guideline operates in only one industry segment that coincides with the subject company, the guideline can still have a much different revenue outlook and cost of capital due to interaction with commercial insurance payors across different geographic markets. To illustrate, if you are appraising a healthcare company that operates in the state of Alabama where BlueCross/BlueShield is by far the most dominant commercial payor, application of revenue trends from a guideline would have very little, if any, relevance to determining the revenue forecast or risk assessment of the company.

As an example, much of the consolidation of physician practices by hospital buyers was driven by the ability of a larger, integrated entity to obtain better contracts and rates from insurers, in addition to positioning the larger entity to better participate in population health initiatives. Many times, independent physician practices are unable to obtain the higher rates available to physicians who are part of a hospital-physician entity. Certain affiliation structures leave the physician practices as freestanding entities that obtain their insurer contracts through the affiliation structure, but otherwise are independent. These practices will earn better incomes and therefore, have higher values, all things equal. The relevance of market transactions of these practices to those without such payor contracts is limited or nonexistent.

Smaller, privately held companies with one or a few locations are typically less diverse and more exposed to local market conditions. Therefore, to extrapolate reimbursement trends from a guideline to a local healthcare company is a recipe for disaster! A guideline company may be able to achieve higher growth rates over a longer period of time related solely to the fact that it has a diversified revenue base that insulates it from the impact of significant changes to any one segment of its business. In contrast, the local healthcare company typically has "all its eggs in one basket" and can significantly benefit from or be harmed by changes to one industry segment. Additionally, using the cost of capital of a guideline for purposes of assessing the risk of

11 For a detailed analysis of health insurer and payor market strength, see *Competition in Health Insurance, Comprehensive Study of U.S. Markets,* updated annually by the American Medical Association.

12 For further healthcare industry risk factors, see "Healthcare Market Structure and Its Implication for Valuation of Privately Held Provider Entities: An Empirical Analysis;" *Business Valuation Review,* Summer 2008, Mark O. Dietrich, CPA/ABV.

a local healthcare company again ignores the impact of size and diversity on the assessment of risk, and would likely result in an overvaluation of the local healthcare company.

Point: You cannot assess the relevance of revenue-based market multiples to a valuation subject without knowing the underlying quality of the payor contracts of both comparable and subject.

Point: In healthcare, only pure-play comparable companies are typically appropriate. Even a pure play may have limits due to geographic diversity or difference in markets served, revenue sources, and localized trends.

Because public stock prices do not react as one might "expect" them to, or it might be better said "when" one expects them to, attempting to draw conclusions about cost of capital and trends using guideline companies becomes even more difficult in a healthcare industry context. This fact, combined with the limitations just discussed, makes determination of discount rates and cost of capital and revenue forecasting assumptions using a guideline company approach a virtual exercise in futility for a healthcare company. Therefore, the appraiser is better served to rely upon a buildup or capital asset pricing model for purposes of assessing risk for healthcare companies. Comparisons can be made to guideline companies' benchmarks, but this approach is better suited as a pressure test rather than a primary method.

A note on looking to guideline companies for weightings in the weighted average cost of capital: The availability of equity capital and conditions in the stock market at a given point for a specific comparable may limit the usefulness of this approach.

12.0 Conclusion

It is critical in any valuation assignment to develop a cash flow projection that is reasonable and achievable including the terminal growth rate, and to then estimate value based on a realistic assessment of risk related to those cash flows. In the healthcare industry in particular, these tasks are complicated by the myriad of regulations that govern healthcare companies and impact their ability to achieve projected results. When you add to this complication significant potential changes in how healthcare is delivered and reimbursed in the U.S., the result is an assignment that is extremely complex and requires a substantial amount of experience to accomplish successfully. This chapter examined various factors that contribute to the risk of a healthcare company as well as provided guidance regarding the means by which a business appraiser can go about doing the necessary research to appropriately forecast cash flows and assess cost of capital.

Part II.
Regulatory Considerations in Healthcare Valuation

Chapter 3.
The Anti-Kickback Statute and Stark Law: Avoiding Valuation of Referrals

CONTENTS

Chapter 3.
The Anti-Kickback Statute and Stark Law: Avoiding Valuation of Referrals

By James M. Pinna, Esq., and Matthew D. Jenkins, JD

The federal anti-kickback statute, 42 U.S.C. § 1320a-7b(b), sets forth the general principle that healthcare providers cannot exchange remuneration in return for referrals of federal healthcare program business. The federal physician self-referral law or Stark Law, 42 U.S.C. § 1395nn, incorporates a similar principle by prohibiting certain physician referrals to entities that physicians have compensation arrangements with unless the arrangement meets an applicable exception by, among other things, not providing compensation based on the volume or value of referrals by the physician. The fundamental prohibition on providing remuneration in return for referrals exemplified in these two statutes has important consequences in the valuation context and requires that healthcare providers and their advisors be careful to avoid ascribing value to prior or anticipated referrals when structuring transactions involving healthcare providers. This chapter explores the framework created by the anti-kickback statute and the Stark Law and some of the specific valuation contexts in which healthcare providers and their advisors should be attentive to avoiding the attribution of value to referrals.

1.0 The Anti-Kickback Statute

The anti-kickback statute prohibits the knowing and willful offer, payment, solicitation, or receipt of "any remuneration (including any kickback, bribe, or rebate) directly or indirectly, overtly or covertly, in cash or in kind," to induce or reward referrals of items or services reimbursable by a federal healthcare program.[1] In addition to criminal penalties, violations of the anti-kickback statute can lead to the imposition of civil sanctions and administrative exclusion from participation in federal healthcare programs (which carries a lower burden of proof than that which is

1 42 U.S.C. § 1320a-7b(b). A "federal healthcare program" includes any plan or program that provides health benefits, whether directly, through insurance, or otherwise, which are funded directly, in whole, or in part by the federal government. 42 U.S.C. § 1320a-7b(f).

required to sustain a criminal conviction). To prove a violation of the anti-kickback statute, the government must show that an entity: "(a) knowingly and willfully; and (b) with the intent to induce the referral of federal healthcare program business solicited, received, offered, or paid remuneration."[2]

Courts have interpreted the anti-kickback statute to prohibit arrangements if one purpose of the arrangement is the inducement of referrals of federal healthcare program patients, regardless of whether there are other appropriate purposes for the arrangement.[3]

Investment and compensation arrangements between healthcare providers should be structured in a manner that does not ascribe value to referrals of federal healthcare program business to avoid implicating the anti-kickback statute. Several courts, as well as the Office of Inspector General of the Department of Health and Human Services (OIG), have indicated that certain facts and circumstances in such arrangements, such as paying greater than fair market value for services or items, can support an inference that improper remuneration is being paid to induce referrals.[4] When structuring and valuing investment and compensation arrangements, healthcare providers and their advisors should look to guidance provided by the OIG and court decisions to identify what could be considered improper remuneration for referrals and how to structure their arrangements to avoid problematic remuneration.

1.1 Remuneration

Health care providers and their advisors should first understand what could be considered improper remuneration under the anti-kickback statute. In plain English, the term "remunerate"

2 *Hanlester Network v. Shalala*, 51 F.3d 1390, 1397-1400 (9th Cir. 1995).

3 *United States v. Greber*, 760 F.2d 68 (3d Cir. 1985), cert. denied, 474 U.S. 988 (1985).

4 See *United States v. Lipkis*, 770 F.2d 1447 (9th Cir. 1985) (Noting that the fair market value of services provided under an arrangement was substantially less than the compensation received, and there is no question that there was payment for the referrals as well as the described services); *United States ex rel. Constantino Perales v. St. Margaret's Hospital*, 243 F. Supp. 2d 843, 851 (C.D. Ill. 2003) (Indicating that payment in excess of fair market value for a physician practice may create an inference of improper remuneration); *United States ex rel. Obert-Hong v. Advocate Health Care*, 211 F. Supp. 2d 1045, 1049 (N.D. Ill. 2002) (Indicating that payment in excess of fair market value for a physician practice may create an inference of improper remuneration); *OIG Special Fraud Alert: "Arrangements for the Provision of Clinical Laboratory Services"* (Issued October 1994), republished at 59 Fed. Reg. 65372 (Dec. 19, 1994) (Whenever a laboratory offers or gives to a source of referrals anything of value not paid for at fair market value, the inference may be made that the thing of value is offered to induce the referral of business. The same is true whenever a referral source solicits or receives anything of value from the laboratory. By "fair market value," we mean value for general commercial purposes. However, fair market value must reflect an arms-length transaction that has not been adjusted to include the additional value that one or both of the parties has attributed to the referral of business between them); Letter from D. McCarty Thornton, Associate General Counsel, OIG to T.J. Sullivan, Technical Assistant, Office of the Associate Chief Counsel, Employee Benefits and Exempt Organizations dated December 22, 1992 (available at oig.hhs.gov/fraud/docs/safeharborregulations/acquisition122292.htm) (Indicating that payment in excess of fair market value may create an inference of improper remuneration); *OIG Supplemental Compliance Program Guidance for Hospitals*, 70 Fed. Reg. 4858, 4866 (Jan. 31, 2005) (Arrangements under which hospitals (a) provide physicians with items or services for free or less than fair market value; (2) relieve physicians of financial obligations they would otherwise incur; or (3) inflate compensation paid to physicians for items or services pose significant risk. In such circumstances, an inference arises that the remuneration may be in exchange for generating business).

is defined as "to pay an equivalent for."[5] Congress used the term "any remuneration" in the anti-kickback statute to more broadly capture various forms of value that may be traded in exchange for referrals to strengthen the capability of the government to detect, prosecute, and punish fraudulent activities under the Medicare and Medicaid programs.[6] The language "directly or indirectly, overtly or covertly, in cash or in kind" makes clear that the form or manner of remuneration can include indirect, covert, and in-kind transactions. Courts have held that remuneration encompasses both traditional kickback payments, where no actual service was performed, as well as payments for which some service was performed.[7] The fact that Congress included a specific exception for discounts under the anti-kickback statute demonstrates that it otherwise extends even to arrangements where there is no direct payment at all from the party receiving referrals.

Even the mere opportunity to earn profits can constitute improper remuneration to induce referrals. For instance, giving a person the opportunity to generate consulting or service fees, even if those fees are the result of actual services provided, could potentially constitute improper remuneration if coupled with an improper intent to induce referrals.[8] The ability to generate a fee could also potentially constitute improper remuneration when an existing supplier of a healthcare service (e.g., a lab company or radiation therapy center) contracts to supply those services to a provider in a position to refer business (e.g., a physician group) that can then bill and collect fees for business typically provided by the existing supplier.[9] Additionally, the OIG

5 Merriam-Webster Online Dictionary (2011).

6 See H.R. Rep. No. 95-393, Pt. II, 95th Cong., 1st Sess. 53 *reprinted in* 1977 U.S.C.C.A.N. 3039, 3056; *Medicare and State Health Care Programs: Fraud and Abuse; OIG Anti-Kickback Provisions*, 56 Fed. Reg. 35952, 35958 (July 29, 1991) (Congress' intent in placing the term "remuneration" in the statute in 1977 was to cover the transferring of anything of value in any form or manner whatsoever. The statute's language makes clear that illegal payments are prohibited beyond merely "bribes," "kickbacks," and "rebates," which were the three terms used in the original 1972 statute); Hanlester Network, 51 F.3d at 1398 (Noting that the phrase "any remuneration" was intended to broaden the reach of the law that previously referred only to kickbacks, bribes, and rebates); Greber, 760 F.2d at 71 (Indicating that Congress included "any remuneration" to make it clear that even if the transaction was not considered to be a "kickback" for which no service had been rendered, payment could nevertheless violate the statute).

7 *Greber*, 760 F.2d at 71; *United States v. Bay State Ambulance and Hospital Rental Service, Inc.*, 874 F.2d 20, 30 (1st Cir. 1989).

8 See *Bay State Ambulance*, 874 F.2d at 29 (Court acknowledged that opportunity to earn consulting fees could constitute improper remuneration, rejecting defendant's argument that consulting fees had to be of substantially more value than services performed to constitute illegal remuneration and upholding jury instruction indicating that payments could be illegal remuneration if they were made with improper purpose); *Medicare and State Health Care Programs: Fraud and Abuse; Clarification of the Initial OIG Safe Harbor Provisions and Establishment of Additional Safe Harbor Provisions Under the Anti-Kickback Statute*, 64 Fed. Reg. 63518, 63548 (Nov. 19, 1999) (Noting that the opportunity to split a global fee may constitute something of value to a referring party apart from any payment for the referral, such as where an optometrist and ophthalmologist network refers patients for cataract surgery only to ophthalmologists who agree to split the global surgical fee by referring patients back to the optometrist for post-operative care).

9 *OIG Special Advisory Bulletin on Contractual Joint Ventures*, 68 Fed. Reg. 23148 (April 30, 2003); see also OIG Advisory Opinion No. 04-17 (Dec. 10, 2004); OIG Advisory Opinion No. 08-10 (Aug. 19, 2008) (Noting that arrangement where intensity-modulated radiation therapy facility block leases time to urologists who then bill Medicare for the professional and technical components could potentially result in problematic remuneration to the urologists in the form of the difference between the fees collected and the fixed amounts to be paid to the facility under the block lease arrangement).

has taken the position that the mere opportunity to invest in a joint venture (and consequently receive profit distributions) may in certain circumstances constitute improper remuneration if offered in exchange for past or anticipated referrals.[10]

As indicated by the examples discussed above, healthcare providers should bear in mind that potentially problematic remuneration may take many forms, including: (a) payments or kickbacks for referrals where no services are performed in return; (b) payments for which some services or items was were provided in return; (c) discounts or rebates off the price of an item or service received; or (d) the opportunity to earn profits by generating fees for services or receiving distributions from an investment.

1.2 Fair Market Value

One of the primary means to ensure there is no remuneration for referrals in an arrangement is to make sure that the parties pay or receive fair market value in exchange for the items or services provided. Some of the most commonly cited instances of potentially improper remuneration are where a party provides items or services to another party for more or less than fair market value or provides an inappropriate discount or premium to the fair market value purchase price of an investment interest. For example, in the context of purchasing physician practices, courts have held that "to the extent that a payment exceeds the fair market value of the practice, or the value of the services, it can be inferred that the excess amount paid over fair market value is intended as payment for the referral of program-related business."[11]

Conversely, it can be argued that when the amount paid for services, items, or investment interests is fair market value, there is a presumption that there is no remuneration in exchange for referrals because the amount paid is solely attributable to the service, item, or investment interest provided.[12] Note, however, that the OIG has not chosen to provide safe harbor protection to all arrangements that are consistent with fair market value, but rather only a small subset of such arrangements, and the OIG has taken the position that fair market value alone will not insulate an arrangement from violating the anti-kickback statute.[13]

10 OIG Advisory Opinion No. 98-19 (Dec. 14, 1998); OIG Advisory Opinion No. 97-5 (Oct. 6, 1997).

11 *Perales*, 243 F. Supp. 2d at 849; Obert-Hong, 211 F. Supp. 2d at 1049.

12 See Letter from D. McCarty Thornton (Noting the importance of fair market value in the context of physician practice acquisitions and stating that "it is necessary to consider the amounts paid for the practice or as compensation to determine whether they reasonably reflect the fair market value of the practice or the services rendered, to determine whether such items in reality constitute remuneration for referrals"); *United States ex rel. Goodstein v. McLaren*, 202 F. Supp. 2d 671 (E.D. Mich. 2002) (Holding that a lease for medical office space was based on fair market value and not remuneration for referrals of Medicaid patients to the defendant based on applying the statutory allowances for lessee and lessor relationships); U.S. ex rel. Obert-Hong, 211 F. Supp.2d at 1049 (Holding that "the Anti-Kickback Act does not prohibit hospitals from acquiring medical practices, nor does it preclude the seller-doctor from making future referrals to the buyer-hospital, provided there are no economic inducements for those referrals. To comply with the statute, the hospital must simply pay fair market value for the practice's assets").

13 70 Fed. Reg. at 4864 (Neither a legitimate business purpose for the arrangement, nor a fair market value payment, will legitimize a payment if there is also an illegal purpose to induce federal healthcare program business).

When considering the question of fair market value in the context of healthcare transactions, traditional methods of economic valuation may not always comport with the proscriptions of the anti-kickback statute. For example, parties unfamiliar with the limitations imposed by the anti-kickback statute might normally expect the purchase price for a physician practice acquisition by a hospital to account for potential revenues from anticipated referrals by the selling physician to the hospital for nonphysician services. However, the anti-kickback statute dictates that anticipated referrals to the hospital must be excluded from the calculation of a fair market value purchase price.[14]

The safe harbor regulations under the anti-kickback statute also dictate that for purposes of determining the value of space or equipment rentals, "fair market value" is specifically defined to exclude the additional value one party would attribute to the property or equipment as a result of its proximity or convenience to sources of referrals (such as the added value a hospital places on having referring physicians located in a medical building the hospital owns on its property).[15] Additionally, parties should be careful in evaluating comparable market data in healthcare transactions. Merely because another buyer is willing to pay a particular price does not mean the price is fair market value especially if the price offered attributes value to referrals expected to result from the arrangement. Thus, in a market where physician practice acquisition activity is strong, those involved in structuring a transaction should be alert to the risks posed by relying on uninformed pronouncements of the "going rate" as a reliable indication of fair market value in the context of the anti-kickback statute.

1.3 Investment Arrangements

The OIG has provided guidance as to appropriate structures for investment arrangements by creating safe harbors that protect certain types of investment interests and provide that the distributions related to such investment interests will not constitute "remuneration" under the anti-kickback statute when all of the safe harbor requirements are satisfied.[16] These safe harbors contain two common requirements that are important to consider in the valuation context: (a) terms on which an investment interest is offered to an investor must not be related to previous or expected volume of referrals, and (b) payment to an investor in return for the investment interest must be directly proportional to the capital investment of that investor.[17]

The OIG has provided further guidance on investment arrangements in its Special Fraud Alerts identifying problematic features that could result in a business arrangement that violates the anti-kickback statute.[18] In the OIG's view, these improper investment arrangements are not intended "to raise investment capital legitimately to start a business, but to lock up a stream of

14 *Obert-Hong,* 211 F. Supp.2d at 1049.
15 42 C.F.R. § 1001.952(b) and (c); 56 Fed. Reg. at 35971-73.
16 42 C.F.R. § 1001.952(a) and (r).
17 Id.
18 OIG Special Fraud Alert: Joint Venture Arrangements (Issued August 1989), republished in 59 Fed. Reg. 65372 (Dec. 19, 1994).

referrals from the physician investors and to compensate them indirectly for these referrals."[19] Two of the "questionable features" identified by the OIG as potential indicators of a "suspect joint venture" are: (a) the amount of capital invested by the physician is "disproportionately small" and the returns on investment may be "disproportionately large" when compared to a typical investment in a new business enterprise; and (b) investors may be paid what the OIG terms "extraordinary returns" on the investment in comparison with the risk involved, often well over "50% to 100% per year."[20]

One of the key principles in the guidance on investment arrangements from the OIG is that the amount of payment to each investor must be directly proportional to capital invested. The OIG has issued two separate advisory opinions related to investment in surgery centers that have created some confusion as to what the OIG considers to be disproportionate returns to investors and whether valuation of intangible assets could be construed as attributing value to investor referrals.

In Advisory Opinion 07-05, the OIG took the surprising position that a hospital's purchase of ownership interests in an existing surgery center for fair market value from certain physician owners could potentially generate prohibited remuneration under the federal anti-kickback statute.[21] This result turned in part on the fact that the hospital and the physicians would not receive investment returns directly proportional to the dollar amount of their invested capital (although returns would be directly proportional to percentage ownership interests) because the price paid for investment interests by the hospital (as a later investor) would be higher (due to appreciation in value) than price originally paid for investment interests by the physicians.

The position taken by the OIG in Advisory Opinion 07-05 stands in stark contrast to its position in Advisory Opinion 01-21, which concluded that the distribution of profit and losses in direct proportion to each investor's percentage of equity ownership in a surgery center (as opposed to original capital investment) does not increase the risk of fraud and abuse, even though it does prevent the arrangement from meeting the anti-kickback statute safe harbor for surgery centers.[22] In fact, the OIG explained in Advisory Opinion 01-21 that there was a reasonable basis for different prices paid by later investors, namely, the appreciation in value of the surgery center over time. The sale of ownership interests in an existing surgery center must occur at fair market value to avoid an inference of improper remuneration to the purchaser or seller, and the OIG could not possibly condone a later investor paying the same price as an original investor when such price is below fair market value due to subsequent appreciation in the value of the underlying security. It should also be noted that when the OIG originally established the safe harbor for investment interests, it explained that "to receive protection, dividend payments can only be tied to the number of shares owned by an investor, and not to his or her referrals," an

19 Id.
20 Id.
21 OIG Advisory Opinion No. 07-05 (June 12, 2007).
22 OIG Advisory Opinion No. 01-21 (Nov. 16, 2001).

acknowledgment that dividends are tied to shares of ownership interest held rather than the amount of capital invested.[23] Advisory Opinion 07-05 may be distinguished, however, based on the unique concerns raised by the OIG that the investment by the hospital appeared to be intended to allow specific physician investors to realize a gain on their investment, raising the possibility that the hospital's investment was intended to influence the referrals of those selected physicians.

In Advisory Opinion 09-09, the OIG took the position that the independent development of two surgery centers by a hospital and a group of physicians and the merger of those surgery centers into a joint venture could potentially generate prohibited remuneration under the anti-kickback statute because the hospital and the physicians might receive investment returns that were not directly proportional to their invested capital, but that the risk of abuse was low in part because the valuation of the surgery centers contributed to the joint venture was based on a tangible asset valuation.[24] The OIG noted, however, that under certain circumstances it might be concerned if the valuations of the surgery centers included intangible assets by using a cash flow analysis that could potentially include the value of referrals by the parties to their respective surgery center prior to the merger.

Advisory Opinion 09-09 dealt with a unique, multistep transaction that appeared to be structured to avoid state certificate of need restrictions by developing separate single operating room surgery centers (that would not require certificate of need approval) and then merging them together to create a two operating room surgery center (which would have required certificate of need approval if developed on its own). The key distinguishing feature of this transaction was that the contribution of the surgery centers to the joint venture was agreed to ex ante ("before the event") by the parties. Absent certificate of need restrictions, one could reasonably expect that the parties would have taken the more simple approach of making initial capital contributions to the joint venture and having it develop a two operating room surgery center. As a result, it is reasonable for the OIG to view the contributions of the surgery centers as initial capital investments, rather than contributions of going concerns, and using a tangible asset valuation of the surgery centers serves to prevent either party from abusing the agreed-to arrangement by directing referrals to a particular surgery center to increase the value of their capital contribution. In contrast, if either of the surgery centers had been in operation for many years, and the proposed joint venture had not been agreed to ex ante by the parties, then the contribution of the surgery center, or the purchase of ownership interests therein, should not be viewed merely as an initial capital investment. Dictating a tangible asset valuation in such circumstances could actually lead to the very situation that the OIG wants the parties to avoid: improper remuneration that could be related to referrals. For example, if the physicians purchased ownership interests in an existing surgery center owned by the hospital based on a tangible asset valuation of $1 million when the fair market value of the surgery center was

23 *Medicare and State Health Care Programs: Fraud and Abuse; OIG Anti-Kickback Provisions;* Rule, 56 Fed. Reg. 35952, 35970 (July 29, 1991).

24 OIG Advisory Opinion No. 09-09 (July 22, 2009).

actually $5 million (based on the income approach), then the physicians could be viewed as receiving remuneration (in the form of a discounted purchase price) in exchange for referrals.

At first blush, the OIG's position in Advisory Opinion 09-09 appears to create an untenable conflict between the regulatory framework of the anti-kickback statute and business valuation standards that require a valuator to consider all appropriate valuation approaches and which indicate that the income approach may be the preferred approach for businesses with positive cash flow. However, upon further examination of the unique structure of the transaction at issue, the OIG's position proves to be a reasonable one in the specific scenario where the parties agree to contribute the surgery centers to a joint venture ex ante to their development, and these contributions are, in effect, treated as initial capital investments by parties to the joint venture rather than as contributions of going business concerns. Advisory Opinion 09-09 should not be read in any way to discredit valuations based on the income approach, and in many cases the income approach may be absolutely necessary to ensure that none of the parties to a transaction give or receive improper remuneration by transaction at other than fair market value.

1.4 Compensation Arrangements

The OIG has provided guidance regarding appropriate structures for compensation arrangements by creating safe harbors that protect certain types of compensation arrangements when all of the safe harbor requirements are satisfied. There is a safe harbor for employment arrangements that protects "any amount paid by an employer to an employee, who has a bona fide employment relationship with such employer, for employment in the furnishing of any item or service for which payment may be made in whole or in part under Medicare, Medicaid or other federal healthcare programs."[25] This safe harbor gives broad protection for compensation paid to employees, regardless of whether such compensation is fair market value or whether it takes into account the volume or value of referrals. However, as discussed below, the Stark Law does require that compensation to physician employees be consistent with fair market value and not take into account the volume or value of referrals.

With respect to other types of compensation arrangements, the safe harbors for space rentals, equipment rentals, and personal services and management contracts generally include the following characteristics: (a) the aggregate compensation paid over the term of the agreement is set in advance, is consistent with fair market value in arms-length transactions, and is not determined in a manner that takes into account the volume or value of any referrals or business otherwise generated between the parties for which payment may be made in whole or in part under a federal healthcare program,; and (b) the aggregate services contracted for do not exceed those that are reasonably necessary to accomplish the commercially reasonable business purpose of the services.[26] The OIG has noted that per patient, per order, per click, and percentage-based compensation arrangements are disfavored under the anti-kickback statute because they inherently vary based on the volume and value of business generated between the parties.[27]

25 42 U.S.C. § 1320a-7b(b)(3)(B); 42 C.F.R. § 1001.952(i).

26 42 C.F.R. § 1001.952(b), (c), and (d).

27 See 56 Fed. Reg. at 35973 (noting that percentage or per-unit agreements between healthcare providers in

2.0 The Stark Law

The Stark Law prohibits physicians having a financial relationship with an entity from referring patients to such entity for certain "designated health services" provided to Medicare beneficiaries, unless such financial relationship meets one of the exceptions enumerated under the statute or the regulations promulgated thereunder.[28] The Stark Law also prohibits entities from billing individuals or Medicare for designated health services furnished pursuant to a prohibited referral, and any payments (including co-payments) received in violation of this prohibition must be refunded. A financial relationship under the Stark Law can take the form of a direct or indirect ownership interest or compensation arrangement. The Stark Law and the regulations promulgated thereunder define a referral as the request by a physician for, or ordering of, or the certifying or recertifying of the need for, any designated health service for which payment may be made under Medicare, but not including any designated health service personally performed by the referring physician.[29]

2.1 Fair Market Value

For a compensation arrangement between an entity providing designated health services and a referring physician to avoid the prohibitions on physician referrals, the exceptions under the Stark Law generally require that remuneration under such compensation arrangement be: (a) set in advance; (b) consistent with fair market value; and (c) not determined in a manner that takes into account the volume or value of referrals or other business generated.[30] Note that, unlike the employment safe harbor to the anti-kickback statute, the employment exception to the Stark Law does require that compensation paid to physician employees be consistent with fair market value and not determined in a manner that takes into account the volume or value of referrals. The Centers for Medicare and Medicaid Services (CMS) has also noted that the definition of "fair market value" under the Stark Law is qualified in ways that do not necessarily comport with the usage of the term in standard valuation methodologies. In particular, the Stark Law requires that the methodology for analyzing fair market value exclude valuations where the parties to the transactions are at arm's length but in a position to refer to one another.[31]

---

a position to refer Medicare or Medicaid business threaten to violate the statute because the payments in these arrangements are directly tied to the volume of business or amount of revenue generated, providing an improper incentive to refer); OIG Advisory Opinion 03-8 (April 3, 2003) (noting that that "per patient", "per order", "per click" and similar payment arrangements with referral sources are disfavored); OIG Advisory Opinion 06-02 (March 21, 2006) (noting that percentage-based compensation was inherently problematic from a fair market value perspective because the compensation necessarily relates to the volume and value of business generated between the parties).

28 42 U.S.C. § 1395nn. Designated health services include clinical laboratory services; physical therapy, occupational therapy, and speech-language pathology services; radiology and certain other imaging services; radiation therapy services and supplies; durable medical equipment and supplies; parenteral and enteral nutrients, equipment, and supplies; prosthetics, orthotics, and prosthetic devices and supplies; home health services; outpatient prescription drugs; inpatient and outpatient hospital services. 42 U.S.C. § 1395nn(h)(6); 42 C.F.R. § 411.351.

29 42 U.S.C. § 1395nn(h)(5); 42 CFR § 411.351.

30 See 42 C.F.R. § 411.357(a) (rental of office space), (b) (rental of equipment), (c) (employment), (d) (personal services), (f) (isolated transactions), (i) (payments by physician) and (l) (fair market value).

31 *Medicare Program; Physicians' Referrals to Health Care Entities With Which They Have Financial Relationships (Phase II); Interim Final Rule*; 69 Fed. Reg. 16054, 16107 (March 26, 2004).

For purposes of the Stark Law, fair market value is defined as the value in arm's-length transactions, consistent with the "general market value," which means the price that an asset would bring as the result of bona fide bargaining between well-informed buyers and sellers who are not otherwise in a position to generate business for the other party, or the compensation that would be included in a service agreement as the result of bona fide bargaining between well-informed parties to the agreement who are not otherwise in a position to generate business for the other party, on the date of acquisition of the asset or at the time of the service agreement.[32] The Stark Law regulations also note that a "fair market price" is usually the price at which bona fide sales have been consummated for assets of like type, quality, and quantity in a particular market at the time of acquisition, or the compensation that has been included in bona fide service agreements with comparable terms at the time of the agreement, where the price or compensation has not been determined in any manner that takes into account the volume or value of anticipated or actual referrals.[33] Note that the foregoing language reflects that the particular market in which a transaction occurs is important in assessing the relevance of comparable transactions.

With respect to space and equipment rentals, the Stark Law regulations specifically define fair market value as the value of rental property for general commercial purposes (not taking into account its intended use, provided that costs incurred by the lessor in developing or upgrading the property or maintaining the property or its improvements may be considered), and in the case of a space rental, this value may not be adjusted to reflect the additional value the prospective lessee or lessor would attribute to the proximity or convenience to the lessor when the lessor is a potential source of patient referrals to the lessee.[34]

2.2 Per-Unit and Percentage-Based Compensation

The exceptions under the Stark Law permit per-unit and percentage-based compensation in certain limited circumstances. Unlike the safe harbors under the anti-kickback statute, per-unit or percentage-based compensation can meet the Stark Law requirement of being "set in advance" as long as the per-unit of service amount or specific formula for calculating the compensation is (a) set forth in the written agreement between the parties in sufficient detail so that it can be objectively verified; and (b) may not be changed or modified during the course of the agreement in any manner that takes into account the volume or value of referrals or other business generated by the referring physician.[35] Per-unit compensation (but not percentage-based compensation) is also deemed not to take into account "the volume or value of referrals" under the Stark Law if the compensation is fair market value for services or items actually provided and does not vary during the course of the compensation arrangement in any manner that takes into account referrals or other business generated by the referring physician.[36]

---

32 42 C.F.R. § 411.351.

33 Id.

34 Id.

35 42 C.F.R. § 411.354(d).

36 Id.; See also 69 Fed. Reg. at 16066-70 (Indicating that percentage compensation arrangements can meet the set in advance requirement, but must also meet the volume or value and other business generated requirement).

Per-unit or percentage-based compensation may not, however, be used in space or equipment rentals if the per-unit charge reflects services provided to patients referred by the lessor to the lessee or the compensation is based on a percentage of revenue raised, earned, billed, collected or otherwise attributable to the services performed or business generated in the rented space or using the leased equipment.[37] Although CMS has not prohibited percentage-based compensation in arrangements involving nonprofessional services (such as management or billing services), it has indicated that it intends to continue to monitor these types of compensation arrangements for potential abuse.[38]

CMS has also noted that it does not consider an agreement to be at fair market value if the lessee is paying a physician-owned lessor substantially more for equipment than it would have to pay a non-physician-owned lessor and has serious questions as to the commercial reasonableness of an agreement if the lessee is performing a sufficiently high volume of procedures such that it would be economically feasible to purchase the equipment rather than lease it.[39] In the view of CMS, these types of arrangements raise the question of whether the lessee is paying more than what it would have to pay another lessor (or if the lessee purchased the equipment) to avoid losing referrals from the lessor.[40] Potential issues that can arise when a lessee is paying a physician lessor more for equipment than it would have to pay a third-party lessor are illustrated in the *Bradford* case discussed below.

3.0 Valuation Scenarios to Consider

The following examples of valuation contexts are intended to identify particular scenarios in which healthcare providers and their advisors should be attentive to avoiding the attribution of value to referrals of federal healthcare program business when structuring and valuing business arrangements. These examples also draw on lessons that can be learned from OIG advisory opinions and court cases involving healthcare providers engaged in similar business arrangements.

3.1 Compensation Arrangements With Physicians

To avoid prohibited referrals under the Stark Law or an inference of improper remuneration for referrals under the anti-kickback statute, compensation arrangements between healthcare providers and referring physicians should be at fair market value for actual items or services furnished and should not take into account, directly or indirectly, the value or volume of any past or anticipated referrals or other business generated by the physician. When structuring

37 42 C.F.R. § 411.357(a), (b), (l) and (p).

38 See *Medicare Program; Changes to the Hospital Inpatient Prospective Payment Systems and Fiscal Year 2009 Rates*; 73 Fed. Reg. 48434, 48710 (Aug. 19, 2008). Note that in its 2009 Hospital Inpatient Prospective Payment System Proposed Rule, CMS originally proposed to limit percentage compensation arrangement only to personally performed services. *Medicare Program; Proposed Changes to the Hospital Inpatient Prospective Payment Systems and Fiscal Year 2009 Rates*, 73 Fed. Reg. 23528, 23694 (April 30, 2008).

39 See 73 Fed. Reg. at 48714.

40 Id.

compensation arrangements with physicians within the regulatory framework of the Stark Law and anti-kickback statute, it is important to consider both the amount and type of compensation provided.

Compensation that is fixed in advance may more easily fit within a Stark Law exception or safe harbor to the anti-kickback statute because there is no opportunity for compensation to vary during the term of the arrangement based upon referrals. However, healthcare providers must be attentive to make sure the fixed compensation amounts are fair market value for the actual services provided. For example, although compensation based on actual hours worked may not be considered fixed compensation, it may more accurately reflect the fair market value of services provided than a fixed monthly payment (particularly if physicians work less than the anticipated time per month). Health care providers should also be careful when resetting fixed compensation amounts under an arrangement to make sure that the compensation is not adjusted in a manner that provides incentives for increases in referrals.

An example of how fixed compensation arrangements can still pose potential problems is the case of *U.S. v. Campbell* (2011).[41] This case was based on part-time employment contracts between the University of Medicine and Dentistry of New Jersey and local cardiologists serving as clinical assistant professors with fixed salaries ranging from $50,000 to $180,000 that were alleged to have been entered into by the hospital to ensure a sufficient number of cardiac procedures to avoid losing Level 1 Trauma Center accreditation. The hospital entered into a settlement agreement with the government for alleged violations of the False Claims Act related to these contracts and the government then sought damages from an individual cardiologist related to his contract with the hospital. This case illustrates that healthcare providers and their advisors should carefully consider the specific facts and circumstances of compensation arrangements with referring physicians and keep in mind that even fixed salaries may still pose a problem if the salary is not tied to actual services provided by the physician.

Percentage and per-unit based compensation arrangements with physicians are more prone to being viewed as tied to the volume or value of referrals and should be carefully reviewed to ensure they meet all of the applicable requirements under a Stark Law exception and do not involve space or equipment rentals where the rental charge reflects services provided to patients referred by the lessor to the lessee. Even if a per-unit or percentage-based compensation arrangement meets a Stark Law exception, there is no safe harbor protection for such arrangements under the anti-kickback statute. Moreover, while percentage or per-unit based compensation methodologies may be common in certain business arrangements, such methodologies may be disfavored under the anti-kickback statute when they involve physicians. For instance, although management agreements often include fees based on a percentage of revenue, this type of management fee may raise concerns when the manager is owned by physicians in a position to make referrals to the business being managed.

41 *U.S. v. Campbell*, 2011 WL 43013, No. 08-1951 (D.N.J., Jan. 4, 2011).

The need for careful attention when structuring compensation arrangements with physicians is illustrated by the case of *U.S. ex rel Drakeford v. Tuomey Healthcare System, Inc.* (2010).[42] This was a qui tam case brought by an orthopedic surgeon contending that the hospital's part-time employment of surgeons violated the Stark Law because the compensation was based on the volume or value of referrals from the physicians to the hospital. The part-time employment agreements tied physician compensation to collections for personally performed professional services, which by itself is a fairly common structure and unlikely to raise concerns under the Stark Law because personally performed services are not considered referrals. However, the agreements also had several unusual features, including 10-year terms, only applying to outpatient surgeries (but not inpatient surgeries or work done in the office), imposing significant noncompete covenants requiring all outpatient surgeries to be performed in the hospital's outpatient surgery center and providing total compensation and benefits that were approximately 30% higher than actual collections for professional services. Taken as a whole, the government characterized these part-time employment agreements as an attempt to limit competition from physician-owned surgery centers by providing compensation and benefits that were significantly higher than what the physician could reasonably expect to collect for their professional services. Although the hospital contended it had legal opinions and third-party valuations supporting the appropriateness of the arrangements, the jury found that these part-time employment agreements violated the Stark Law and the hospital had improperly billed Medicare for approximately $45 million in services tied to referrals that were prohibited under the Stark Law. The *Tuomey* case serves as a reminder that even though employment arrangements with physicians may have safe harbor protection under the anti-kickback statute, they are still susceptible to violating the Stark Law and should be evaluated as a whole to ensure that compensation is fair market value, commercially reasonable, and not tied to volume or value of referrals.

3.2 Physician Practice Acquisitions

Hospital acquisitions of physician practices are transactions that commonly require the parties to determine the fair market value of the practice being acquired. As mentioned above, hospitals cannot attribute value to prior or anticipated referrals for hospital services by physician owners when calculating the purchase price for a physician practice. When a physician practice is valued on a going concern basis, revenues tied to referrals from physician owners to the hospital for nonphysician services must be excluded because they are unrelated to the going concern value of the business being acquired. This does not mean, however, that the hospital has to disregard revenues of the physician practice attributable to (a) professional services of the physician owners, because these services do not constitute a referral to another person or entity for reimbursable services or items; or (b) other revenue of the practice, to the extent this revenue is reflective of the going concern value of the practice's business. It is also important that the value of a physician practice on a going concern basis incorporate the post-transaction compensation paid to the physicians by the acquiring hospital. This issue was highlighted in

42 *U.S. ex rel. Drakeford v. Tuomey Healthcare System, Inc.*, No. 3:05-CV-02858-MJP (D.C.S.C., March 29, 2010).

the case of *Derby v. Commissioner* (2008), where the tax court denied a charitable deduction for the intangible value of a medical practice claimed by the physician owners in connection with the acquisition of a health system that included a purchase price tied solely to tangible assets.[43] This case illustrates that intangible value may not exist if post-transaction compensation to physicians eliminates any potential cash flow to the acquirer of the practice.

When substantially all of the cash flows from a physician practice are allocated to physician compensation, thereby eliminating any residual going concern value, it is common for the practice to be valued on a cost approach basis. This approach determines the liquidation value of the individual assets of the practice as opposed to the going concern value of the practice as a whole. While establishing the value of tangible assets such as equipment and furniture under the cost approach may be fairly straight forward, determining what value, if any, can be attributed to other intangible assets of the practice under the cost approach requires careful consideration. Certain types of intangible assets (like goodwill) may not have any value in the absence of any going concern value for the business (i.e., in the absence of positive post-transaction cash flow net of physician compensation).

For an asset to be attributed value in a liquidation scenario, the practice must have a bona fide right of ownership to the asset that it can legally transfer to the buyer.[44] This may require valuators to consider contractual rights and relevant laws governing the right to ownership of such assets (for example, the transferability of a noncompete under an employment contract). For an asset to have quantifiable value under the cost approach, it must also generate some measurable amount of economic benefit to the buyer, whether in the form of an income or cost avoidance.[45] In other words, the buyer must have a need to acquire the asset for its employment of the physicians such that it would otherwise have to go out and incur the cost of acquiring the asset independently. The value of the asset should take into consideration any functional or economic obsolescence as well as any obligations and costs associated with ownership of the asset. For example, costs of storage and retrieval should be considered in the context of placing value on medical records. Similarly, credit for prior years of service granted to nonphysician employees should be considered in analyzing the value of any trained workforce whose employment contracts are transferred to the buyer.

3.3 Acquisitions of Physician-Owned Ancillary Businesses

Another type of transaction that often requires careful consideration under the regulatory framework of the Stark Law and anti-kickback statute is the acquisition of physician-owned ancillary businesses. In-office ancillary businesses such as laboratory, imaging, and surgical suites that are operated as part of a physician practice will often derive substantially all of their business from referrals by the physician owners of the practice. As a result, healthcare providers

43 *Derby v. Commissioner*, T.C. Memo 2008-45 (2008).

44 See Shannon P. Pratt, Robert F. Reilly & Robert P. Schweihs, *Valuing a Business: The Analysis and Appraisal of Closely Held Companies*, 325 (4th Ed., 2000).

45 Id.

acquiring these in-office ancillary businesses need to be careful to structure the acquisition in a manner that does not improperly attribute value to anticipated referrals by the physician owners of the practice.

Some of the potential pitfalls to consider when structuring acquisitions of physician-owned ancillary business are highlighted in the case of *United States ex rel. Singh v. Bradford Regional Medical Center*, involving a qui tam action brought against a hospital and local physicians relating to a nuclear camera sublease arrangement.[46] The court in this case concluded that the sublease arrangement between the parties created financial relationships that violated the Stark Law and resulted in prohibited referrals by the physicians to the hospital. Central to this conclusion was the court's determination that payments under the sublease, which included substantial amounts attributable to a noncompete agreement, were greater than what would be paid in the absence of the ability of the physicians to generate referrals to the hospital and inflated to compensate the physicians for their ability to generate such referrals. Thus, the court was able to conclude that the noncompete payments were arrived at by taking into account the volume and value of anticipated referrals by the physicians and were therefore not fair market value for purposes of the Stark Law. Although the hospital had obtained a report from an accountant analyzing the noncompete payments under the sublease using the competitive business valuation method and concluding that they were fair market value, in reaching this conclusion, the accountant had improperly taken into account anticipated revenues to the hospital for not only nuclear imaging services but also CT/ MRI, inpatient, and outpatient services based on the assumption that the physicians would likely refer this business to the hospital in the absence of a financial interest in their own facilities (although not required to do so by the noncompete).[47]

The *Bradford* case underscores the need for careful attention when structuring acquisitions of physician-owned ancillary businesses and valuing intangible assets (such as noncompetes) in these arrangements. It also emphasizes the need to consider the element of commercial reasonableness in these types of arrangements. One of the problems in the *Bradford* case was that the parties structured what would typically be a business acquisition as an equipment lease. While it is common for value to be allocated to intangible assets as a component of the larger assemblage of assets in a business acquisition, this allocation of value is rarely applicable to leasing arrangements. Moreover, paying for intangible assets over time (through monthly lease payments) increases the risk that such payments may be linked to a continued expectation of referrals. When evaluating payments for intangible assets in acquisitions of physician-owned ancillary businesses, healthcare providers and their advisors should also keep in mind the general concept of commercial reasonableness that is embodied in the regulatory framework of the Stark Law and anti-kickback statute. In essence, the parties need to ask whether it is commercially reasonable for a purchaser to pay for intangible assets associated with a physician-owned ancillary business absent any expectation of referrals from the physician sellers. Facts to

46 *United States ex rel. Singh v. Bradford Regional Medical Center*, 752 F. Supp. 2d 602 (W.D. Pa., 2010). *Editor's Note: The* Bradford *case is also discussed in Chapter 9.*

47 Report of Charles T. Day (attached as Exhibit 7 to Relators' Appendix), 752 F. Supp. 2d 602.

consider in this analysis are (a) whether the location and services of the acquired business are well suited for integration with the purchaser; (b) whether the purchaser will have to relocate or restructure the business; and (c) whether acquiring the business is more cost-effective than the alternative of independently developing a facility, buying or leasing equipment, recruiting staff, incurring start-up losses, and competing with the physicians.

Another issue highlighted in the *Bradford* case is the importance of making sure that payments for intangible assets do not take into account the volume or value of referrals from physician sellers, particularly when the fair market value of intangible assets is determined using discounted cash flows reflecting revenues from referrals by physician sellers under the income approach. Generally accepted valuation standards require consideration of all appropriate valuation approaches, including the asset approach, income approach, and market approach, and for a business that generates positive cash flows, the income approach is in many cases the preferred methodology.[48] When applying the income approach, it is extremely important that fair market value be determined using projected cash flows that reflect the ability of the business to generate cash flows in the absence of any obligation of physician sellers to continue referring to the business. The risk that physician sellers will no longer refer to the business should be accounted for by using appropriate growth assumptions and discount rates. This risk will be higher and the fair market value will be lower if physician sellers are the primary or only source of referrals to the business (which is often the case with physician-owned ancillary businesses). Assuming the income approach appropriately accounts for the risk that physician sellers will no longer refer to the business, arguably there will be no consideration tied to anticipated referrals from physician sellers. Conversely, disregarding the income approach when projected cash flows reflect referrals from physician sellers could actually lead to a purchase price that is below fair market value and may raise concerns under the anti-kickback statute. For example, if a physician-owned ancillary business is sold at below fair market value to a physician-owned hospital or surgery center in which the physician sellers are investors, the discounted purchase price could be viewed as consideration for anticipated referrals by other physician owners of the acquiring entity (which could result in higher distributions to the physicians sellers from such acquiring entity). Those involved in structuring transactions where such discounting assumptions are invoked to eliminate value attributable to future referrals from physician sellers should be alert to communications between the parties where, in pursuit of a higher valuation, selling physicians or their representatives may inappropriately attempt to argue that future referrals should be anticipated. Such communications may have a tendency to taint an otherwise appropriately structured transaction with evidence of improper intent.

48 See National Association of Certified Valuation Analysts Professional Standards, Section 3.7; American Society of Appraisers Business Valuation Standards BSV-I, Section IV; American Institute of Certified Public Accountants Statement on Standards for Valuation Services No. 1, paragraph 31; Shannon P. Pratt, Robert F. Reilly and Robert P. Schweihs, *Valuing a Business: The Analysis and Appraisal of Closely Held Companies*, 40 (4th Ed., 2000).

3.4 Noncompete Agreements

Like other types of intangible assets, valuation of noncompete agreements with healthcare providers requires careful consideration. Noncompete agreements may be attributed value to the extent the noncompete is an enforceable mechanism to preserve the value of an acquired business by prohibiting the detrimental effect of a seller from competing with the acquired business. Assessing the enforceability of the noncompete requires consideration of applicable state laws. The value of a noncompete is related to the avoidance of the potential negative impact on cash flows from allowing the seller to establish a competing business and should not be based on the anticipated volume or value of referrals from the seller because the seller could refer business to another entity regardless of the presence of a noncompete. The value of a noncompete should also take into account the reasonable ability of the seller to engage in competitive activity. For example, a physician might be able to establish an inexpensive surgery or imaging suite in his or her office relatively easily, but establishing a separately licensed surgery or imaging center may not be a realistic scenario.

The competitive business valuation method is a commonly accepted methodology for analyzing the value of a noncompete in the context of a larger assemblage of assets. However, as illustrated by the *Bradford* case discussed above, this methodology must be appropriately applied by assessing the present value of anticipated economic damage to the buyer if the seller were allowed to compete.[49] This requires an analysis of the realistic potential loss in earnings from the specific business being acquired by allowing the seller to compete with the business (in contrast, the accountant's report in the *Bradford* case included revenues associated with CT/MRI, inpatient, and outpatient services that were unrelated to the nuclear camera business). Moreover, the result of the competitive business valuation method should conform with or fit into the context of the overall purchase price for the business. For example, if the total enterprise value of the business is $100, the logical fair market value of the noncompete would be significantly less than $100 after accounting for the value of other identifiable assets included within the enterprise value.

When the enterprise value of a business is determined on a going concern basis, the value of a noncompete would be encompassed within the overall purchase price for the business (unless the noncompete was not factored into the enterprise value). However, when a business is valued using the cost approach, the value of a noncompete, if any, would have to be determined separately from the value of other identifiable assets based on the impact to projected cash flows of the business by allowing the seller to compete with the business in the future. In such case, valuators should carefully consider the reasonable ability of the seller to compete with the business. If the business is being valued on a cost approach because the sellers are losing money, then the sellers may have little ability to successfully compete with the business and the value of a noncompete may be may be minimal or nonexistent. In the context of noncompetes from physician sellers, it is important to remember that physician sellers cannot be prohibited

49 See Robert F. Reilly and Robert P. Schweihs, *Valuing Intangible Assets*, 400-09 (1999); IRS Coordinated Issue All Industries Covenants Not to Compete (February 19, 1996); *Ansan Tool v. Commissioner*, T.C. Memo 1992-121.

from making referrals to competing businesses (i.e., they can only be prohibited from owning a competing business). Therefore, the value of a noncompete from a physician seller cannot be determined based on referrals made by the physician seller to the acquired business because they can make those referrals to a competing business regardless of the presence of a noncompete.

Noncompete agreements often arise in the context of physician practice acquisitions where the selling physicians agree not to compete with the purchaser under the terms of their employment agreements with the purchaser. In this case, the noncompete agreement is given in return for compensation provided under the employment agreement, rather than the purchase agreement. If the practice assets were valued using the cost approach, there would be no separate consideration for the noncompete as part of the purchase price.

Another situation that sometimes arises is when physicians desire to receive consideration for contributing a noncompete agreement in connection with their investment in a joint venture. If physicians are making a cash investment in a joint venture, then there is no associated business being acquired that they could adversely compete with and there would be no value to attribute to their noncompete agreement. In comparison, if physicians are contributing an existing business to a joint venture in return for investment interests in the joint venture, then the consideration for their noncompete would be encompassed within the fair market value purchase price paid for the business being contributed.

3.5 Investment in De Novo Joint Ventures

When valuing investment interests in de novo (new) joint ventures that include investors in a position to make referrals to the joint venture, the anti-kickback statute generally requires that anticipated referrals from such investors, which might otherwise be taken into account in a normal commercial setting, must be disregarded in determining the value of contributions to the joint venture or the value of the joint venture itself. In the context of a de novo joint venture, there is no existing business to be valued and the purchase price for investment interests should be based solely on the capital required to start up and operate the business. The purchase price for investment interests should not vary between individual investors, as such variance could give rise to an inference of improper remuneration in exchange for anticipated referrals and the OIG has indicated its concern when investors who are potential referral sources for the investment entity are permitted to obtain their investment interests at insider prices or at prices more favorable than those available to the general public.[50]

In contrast, if a party is contributing capital to a de novo joint venture in the form of assets related to an ongoing business, then it is important that such assets be fairly valued and that the contributing party receives fair market value investment interests in exchange. Additionally, investors may contribute capital in the form of pre-operational services or sweat equity, provided that the investment interests received in return are fair market value for actual services contributed.[51]

50 64 Fed. Reg. at 63522.
51 See 56 Fed. Reg. at 35970.

However, it is important that the valuation of any assets or sweat equity contributed does not assign any value to anticipated referrals by the contributing party to the de novo joint venture.

3.6 Investment in Existing Joint Ventures

Just as with de novo joint ventures, the value of investment interests in existing joint ventures that include investors in a position to make referrals to the joint venture also should not attribute value to anticipated referrals from such investors. In contrast to a de novo joint venture, an existing joint venture typically has going concern value that may be affected by revenues stemming from referrals made by investors. Additionally, the inflow and outflow of investors actively involved in providing services in connection with a joint venture (which may actually be required to meet the anti-kickback statute safe harbor for ambulatory surgery centers) could potentially impact future revenues of the joint venture. In these circumstances, it is important that the value of investment interests is determined using projected cash flows based on the historical operations of the joint venture, as opposed to the projected future referrals by investors. When a business is valued using projected cash flows based on historical operations, the value of the business is based on the projected ability of the business to continue to operate in a profitable manner. Potential outflows of investors and losses in revenue would be reflected in the discount premium applied to the cash flows of the joint venture (reflecting a higher risk with respect to future operations), however potential inflows of investors and additional revenues attributable to potential referrals from those investors should not be reflected in the purchase price because this could be construed as attributing value to anticipated referrals.

For example, if a physician owner of a surgery center is retiring and selling his or her ownership interests to a new physician and the new physician performs procedures that receive higher reimbursement than the retiring physician, the valuation of the ownership interests in the surgery center should not reflect any anticipated increase in reimbursement from the activity of the new physician at the surgery center because it would reflect the value of anticipated referrals. In contrast, if a surgery center invests in a new piece of high-technology equipment enabling it to perform certain cutting-edge procedures that receive higher reimbursement, the valuation of the surgery center should reflect the projected revenues from this new equipment. The important distinction here is that in the latter case, the valuation is appropriately based on the projected ability of the business to perform new procedures and is not based on projections of anticipated referrals from a new physician investor.

In valuing an existing joint venture, it is also important that an appropriate discount premium is applied so that the amount of capital invested by new investors is not disproportionately small compared to disproportionately large returns that an enforcement authority might assert to be "extraordinary returns" in comparison with the risk involved.[52] Assuming that a joint venture

52 Note that the OIG has stated that "a reasonable return can be appropriately measured only in light of the risk of the investment. An investor would surely expect a much higher return from an investment in an expensive piece of diagnostic equipment that might soon become obsolete than from an investment in a relatively inexpensive piece of equipment that can be expected to generate a steady profit stream for the foreseeable future." 56 Fed. Reg. at 35970.

has a significant operating history and a relatively stable risk profile that allows for the application of an appropriate discount premium, the mere purchase of an investment interest should avoid any inference of improper remuneration to the purchaser, the seller, or other investors as long as the purchase is not targeted toward certain investors in return for their referrals and the purchase price is fair market value. The logical argument that can be made here is that if the price paid for an investment interest is fair market value, then the value of the purchase price consideration is equivalent to the value of the investment interest received and there is no additional remuneration that could be attributed to referrals.

3.7 Investment in Existing Joint Ventures With Limited Operating History

Sometimes investors may purchase ownership interests in an existing joint venture that has a limited operating history and minimal or no cash flow. This scenario presents unique challenges for valuators. The valuation of investment interests in an existing joint venture with a limited operating history should be careful to avoid (a) underestimating the value that has been created by the formation of the business; or (b) overestimating the value that has been created by the formation of the business by ascribing value to anticipated referrals from physician investors.

To be sure, there is some value created by the syndication of ownership interests and the formation of a joint venture. This value is likely to increase as the business reaches additional milestones such as obtaining additional financing, constructing a facility, purchasing equipment, obtaining licenses and other regulatory approvals, and commencing operations because the related risk of future cash flows declines. Until those milestones are reached, the risk that they might not be met would warrant additional discounts to the value of the business. The attainment of certain milestones means that the purchase price for ownership units in the business likely is no longer based solely upon the equity capital required to start up the business. If, following syndication and formation of the joint venture, the fair market value of the business has increased, then it would no longer be appropriate to sell units to physician investors at the initial offering price if this price is less than the then-current fair market value of the business.

On the other hand, a joint venture with a limited operating history has significantly higher risks than an existing business with stable, continuing operations, and there is less certainty that a startup business will be able to meet projected cash flow levels. When there is no operating history upon which to base cash flow projections, valuators may be relying principally on their analysis of management's preliminary projections for future cash flows. Management's future cash flow projections, in an attempt to be more accurate, may incorporate an analysis of procedures expected to be performed by physician owners and other physicians in the community. This analysis might be particularly relevant in the context of surgery centers, where the anti-kickback statute safe harbor affirmatively requires that physician owners perform at least one-third of their procedures in the surgery center. To avoid attributing value to anticipated referrals from physician owners, the valuation of a business with a limited operating history should avoid ascribing certainty to any referrals from physician investors. Thus, a discounted cash flow analysis should include an appropriate discount rate to reflect, among the many other business risks, that physician owners are not required to make referrals to the facility (except to the extent to meet regulatory requirements under the anti-kickback statute safe harbor for surgery centers) and that there can be no assurance that the business will meet its cash flow projections.

Chapter 4.
The Volume or Value Standard: Navigating the Stark Law's Prohibition on 'Taking Into Account' Designated Health Service Referrals

CONTENTS

Chapter 4.
The Volume or Value Standard: Navigating the Stark Law's Prohibition on 'Taking Into Account' Designated Health Service Referrals

By Joseph N. Wolfe, Esq., and Alyssa C. James, Esq.

As evidenced by a wave of recent cases and settlements, the federal government continues to focus on pursuing perceived healthcare fraud and abuse. A combination of aggressive enforcement efforts and a hypertechnical regulatory framework make today's environment particularly challenging for healthcare organizations. Enforcement continues to focus on the federal physician self-referral law and its implementing regulations (collectively, the "Stark Law," or "Stark").[1]

As a central premise, remuneration paid by healthcare organizations to referring physicians must satisfy three key substantive tenets of defensibility: it must be consistent with *fair market value* (FMV); it must be paid under an arrangement that is *commercially reasonable* (CR); and it cannot be determined in a manner that *takes into account* the *volume or value* of the physician's referrals of designated health services (DHS). Accordingly, these three tenets are critical to structuring compensation arrangements that comply with the Stark Law.

Even though a number of recent cases and settlements have centered on alleged violations of the third tenet (also referred to as the "volume or value" standard), the prohibition on "taking into account" DHS referrals typically receives far less industry attention than the FMV or CR standards. This chapter focuses on the Stark Law's volume or value standard, including the underlying regulatory framework, relevant guidance from the Centers for Medicare & Medicaid Services (CMS), and the inherent tensions in the standard as illustrated in recent enforcement actions. This chapter seeks to provide context and direction to healthcare organizations, appraisers, and legal counsel as they navigate this confounding area of health law.

1 42 U.S.C. § 1395nn.

1.0 Stark Law Overview

The Stark Law was established to provide a bright-line test to determine whether impermissible conflicts of interest were present in financial arrangements with referring physicians. For a variety of reasons, this objectivity and certainty have proven to be elusive.[2]

Stark generally prohibits a physician from making referrals of DHS[3] to any entity with which the physician has a financial relationship, unless the arrangement qualifies for one of its specified exceptions.[4] No entity furnishing DHS may submit a claim for services performed pursuant to a physician's prohibited DHS referral.[5] This prohibition applies regardless of the underlying terms of the financial relationship or purposes of the DHS referral. Therefore, unlike other fraud and abuse laws such as the anti-kickback statute, Stark is a strict liability statute, and no finding of unlawful intent or knowledge is generally required to trigger a violation of the Stark Law.[6]

The Stark Law defines a "financial relationship" as an ownership or investment interest in an entity or a compensation arrangement between a physician and an entity.[7] Financial arrangements include any arrangement that involves the exchange of remuneration (directly or indirectly, covertly or overtly, in cash or in kind) between an entity and a physician.[8] The Stark Law and its corresponding regulations define a "referral" as the request by a physician for, the ordering of, or the certifying or recertifying of the need for, any DHS for which payment may be made under Medicare but not including any DHS that the referring physician personally performs or provides.[9] However, as described in more detail later in this chapter, a referral of DHS may still be present if the entity bills a corresponding "technical component" DHS in connection with a physician's personally performed service.[10]

While it is referred to in healthcare compliance circles as a fraud and abuse law, the Stark Law is fundamentally a billing and payment rule. In cases where an entity has billed and collected for a DHS in violation of the Stark Law, the entity is required to refund the inappropriately

2 The court in *United States ex. rel. Villafane v. Solinger*, 543 F. Supp. 2d 678; 2008 U.S. Dist. LEXIS 28766 (W.D. Ky., 2008), acknowledged the inordinate complexity of the Stark Law and regulations, which it noted "has resulted in a 'Homeric odyssey' for attorneys attempting to advise clients on the troublesome and elusive goal of compliance."

3 Designated health services (DHS) under Stark include: clinical laboratory services; physical therapy, occupational therapy, and outpatient speech-language pathology services; radiology and certain other imaging services; radiation therapy services and supplies; durable medical equipment and supplies; parenteral and enteral nutrients, equipment, and supplies; prosthetics, orthotics, and prosthetic devices and supplies; home health services; outpatient prescription drugs; inpatient and outpatient hospital services; and nuclear medicine services. See 42 C.F.R. § 411.351.

4 42 U.S.C. § 1395nn(a)(1)(B).

5 42 C.F.R. § 411.353(b).

6 See 42 U.S.C. § 1320a-7b. The relevant inquiry in an action brought under the anti-kickback statute focuses on the subjective intent of the parties to exchange remuneration for referrals.

7 42 U.S.C. § 1395nn(a)(2); 42 C.F.R. § 411.354.

8 Id.

9 42 U.S.C. § 1395nn(h)(5); 42 C.F.R. § 411.351.

10 66 Fed Reg. 856, 941 (Jan. 4, 2001).

collected amount in a timely manner. The government may impose a civil penalty of up to $15,000 for each DHS provided by a physician or entity who knew, or should have known, that the DHS was rendered in violation of the Stark Law. The violation also may cause the person or entity to be excluded from federal healthcare programs and may result in the imposition of a civil penalty of up to $100,000 against any parties that enter into a scheme to circumvent the Stark Law's prohibition.[11] Similar to the anti-kickback statute, a Stark Law violation may also serve as the basis for liability and trebled damages under the False Claims Act.[12]

From a compliance and process perspective, as a threshold matter all compensation arrangements with referring physicians must fit squarely within one of Stark's enumerated exceptions.[13] In addition to meeting strict technical elements that vary depending on the applicable Stark exception (e.g., in writing, signature, term requirements, etc.), compensation arrangements must also meet the more substantive tenets of defensibility introduced above, including the requirement that the compensation not take into account the volume or value of a physician's actual or anticipated referrals of DHS.[14] Because the standard is common to most Stark exceptions, healthcare organizations looking to manage their Stark Law risk should focus their attention on compliance with the volume or value standard, regardless of the exception that is ultimately relied upon.

2.0 Navigating the Volume or Value Standard—Documenting Compliance

As discussed throughout this chapter, healthcare organizations looking to manage risk should focus on developing governance and documentation processes that support compliance with Stark's volume or value standard.[15] There is no one-size-fits-all strategy for documenting compliance, and healthcare organizations will utilize different approaches due to their different delivery models, market dynamics, existing governance framework, tax-exempt status, organizational size and complexity, risk tolerance, and other factors unique to their particular circumstances.

Many healthcare organizations engage appraisal professionals to analyze and confirm that their compensation arrangements with referring physicians meet the applicable FMV and CR standards required for compliance. The appraiser's role may encompass performance of financial projections, compensation planning and design (e.g., examination of local, national, and specialty-specific trends, conceptual modeling, etc.), development of compensation structures and compliance parameters, and the issuance of objective third-party opinions supporting compliance with the FMV and CR standards.

11 Social Security Act § 1877(g); 42 U.S.C. § 1395nn(g); 42 C.F.R. §§ 411.351(b)-(d).
12 42 U.S.C. § 1320a-7b.
13 See 42 C.F.R. § 411.357.
14 The U.S. district court in *United States ex rel. Singh v. Bradford Reg'l Med. Ctr.*, 752 F. Supp. 2d 602 (W.D. Pa. 2010), interpreted the term "referral" as encompassing both *actual* and *anticipated* referrals.
15 This chapter focuses on the Stark Law's volume or value standard. A healthcare organization's governance processes should also support compliance with Stark's FMV and CR standards.

Professional appraisers in other industries typically consider all financial aspects of an arrangement as part of their analysis. In contrast, in the healthcare setting, any consideration of actual or anticipated DHS referrals by the appraiser may carry with it legal risk under the Stark Law. Thus, when a compensation arrangement with a referring physician is evaluated, appraisers should not analyze the physician's anticipated or actual downstream DHS referral data. Further, to manage potential risk, appraisers should not ascribe value to a physician's past, present, or future DHS referrals when performing their analysis and should state the same in their written opinion and work papers. These safeguards will reduce the risk that a whistleblower or the government will successfully allege that a physician's DHS referrals were taken into account when compensation was determined.

Given the inherent complexities, healthcare organizations should engage appraisers that appreciate the constraints of the volume or value standard and that have the requisite expertise to opine on the Stark Law's unique definitions of FMV and CR.[16] Consideration should also be given to engagement of an appraiser directly by legal counsel to increase the likelihood that communications related to the appraisal and any written opinions obtained under the engagement may be protected under the attorney-client privilege. Consistent with the terms of the privilege, the appraiser should work at the direction and under the control of legal counsel.

To the extent appropriate, the nonreferral purposes and reasoning supporting all compensation arrangements should be emphasized and contemporaneously documented in the underlying correspondence and in the appraiser's written opinion and work papers. Further, the proper and legally appropriate purposes of the compensation arrangement should be communicated in all planning and transaction documents (e.g., business plans, presentation materials, term sheets, letters of intent, services agreements, final contracts, etc.).

In addition, healthcare organizations should educate personnel involved in physician contracting and should periodically re-evaluate any processes, actions, or communications that may be at a higher risk for being misconstrued as inappropriate under the volume or value standard. To the extent possible, governance processes should ensure that physicians, employees, and members of the governing board and/or compensation committee are familiar with the appropriate nonreferral purposes supporting any financial arrangement with a referring physician.

3.0 Understanding the Volume or Value Standard—Guidance From CMS

Following enactment of the Stark Law, CMS issued implementing regulations and commentary in the form of the 1998 Proposed Rule, which was followed by three subsequent phases of regulations (Phases I, II, and III).[17] The phases of rule-making are intended to be read together

16 For example, CMS has noted that the definition of FMV in the statute and regulations is qualified in ways that do not necessarily comport with the usage of the term in standard valuation techniques and methodologies. See 69 Fed. Reg. at 16107 (March 26, 2004).

17 CMS issued the 1998 Proposed Rule on Jan. 9, 1998. 63 Fed. Reg. at 1659 (Jan. 9, 1998). CMS issued Phase I of its regulations on Jan. 4, 2001. These regulations became effective on Jan. 4, 2002, 66 Fed. Reg. at 855 (Phase I).

as a unified whole.[18] In particular, CMS has provided the following guidance and commentary on specific matters related to Stark's volume or value standard.

3.1 Personally Performed Services

As noted above, the Stark Law definition of "referral" expressly excludes DHS that the referring physician performs or provides.[19] According to CMS, "personally performed work—DHS or otherwise—is not considered a referral under [the Stark Law]."[20] Thus, compensating a physician based on his or her personally performed services traditionally has not been viewed as violating the volume or value standard.[21]

In many of the recent Stark Law enforcement actions, the government has focused its attention on whether the physician's work effort generated a corresponding technical component DHS. The basis for this position is the Phase I commentary where CMS clarified that, while a physician's personally performed services are not referrals, the corresponding technical component service the DHS entity billed would still constitute a referral of a DHS. Below is the applicable text from the Phase I CMS commentary:

> We have concluded that when a physician initiates a DHS and personally performs it him or herself, that action would not constitute a referral of the service to an entity under [the Stark Law]. However, in the context of inpatient or outpatient hospital services, there would still be a referral of any hospital service, technical component or facility fee billed by the hospital in connection with the personally performed service.[22]

However, historically, CMS did not interpret the mere fact that a healthcare organization received payment for a corresponding DHS as triggering the volume or value standard.[23] In fact, CMS made express statements to the contrary in the Phase II commentary. A commenter posed the following scenario to CMS:

> A hospital employs a physician at an outpatient clinic and pays the physician for each patient seen in the clinic. The physician reassigns his or her right to payment to the hospital and the hospital bills for the Part B physician service (with the site of service reduction). The hospital also bills for the hospital outpatient services. The commenter's concern is that the payment to the physician is inevitably linked to the facility fee, which is a DHS (that

---

CMS issued Phase II of the Stark regulations in the form of an interim final rule implementing the portions of Stark not addressed in the Phase I regulations, 69 Fed. Reg. at 16053 (March 6, 2004) (Phase II). This interim final rule became effective on July 26, 2004. CMS issued Phase III, its final set of regulations implementing Stark, three years later, 72 Fed. Reg. at 51011 (Sept. 5, 2007) (Phase III). These regulations became effective on Dec. 4, 2007.

18 72 Fed. Reg. at 51013 (Sept. 5, 2007).

19 69 Fed. Reg. at 16067 (March 6, 2004).

20 Id.

21 See 42 C.F.R. § 411.351 and 69 Fed. Reg. 16054, 16067 (March 26, 2004). In Phase II, CMS clarified that it defined "referral" under Stark to include only DHS referrals and to exclude a physician's personally performed DHS.

22 66 Fed. Reg. at 941 (Jan. 4, 2001).

23 66 Fed. Reg. at 871 (Jan. 4, 2001); 69 Fed. Reg. at 16067 (March 26, 2004).

> is, a hospital service). Accordingly, the commenter wondered whether the payment to the physician would be considered an improper productivity bonus based on a DHS referral (that is, the facility fee).[24]

CMS gave the following response:

> The fact that corresponding hospital services are billed would not invalidate an employed physician's personally performed services for which the physician may be paid a productivity bonus (subject to the FMV requirement).[25]

Thus, the commentary from CMS expressly states that a DHS entity may compensate a referring physician based on personal productivity and that the presence of corresponding DHS is not sufficient, on its own, to violate the volume or value standard.

That being said, in the recent enforcement actions, the government has alleged that a mere *one-to-one* relationship between a physician's compensation for personally performed services and the volume of their corresponding DHS referrals may implicate Stark's volume or value standard.[26] This position taken by the government has created uncertainty and industry confusion since the arguments advanced are seemingly inconsistent with the express statements by CMS above regarding the circumstances that would trigger a violation of Stark's volume or value standard.

3.2 The Fair Market Value Standard

FMV is defined in both the Stark statute and its implementing regulations.[27] CMS has provided some general explanatory guidance on FMV and its relationship with the volume or value standard in its interpretive commentary but has declined to set forth a specific methodology for determining whether the FMV standard has been satisfied.[28] As background, Section 411.351 of the Stark regulations defines FMV as:

> The value in arm's-length transactions, consistent with the general market value. "General market value" means the price that an asset would bring as the result of bona fide bargaining between well-informed buyers and sellers *who are not otherwise in a position to generate business for the other party*, or the compensation that would be included in a service agreement as the result of bona fide bargaining between well-informed parties to the agreement *who*

24 69 Fed. Reg. at 16088-89 (March 26, 2004).

25 Id.

26 Memorandum in Support of the United States' Motion for Partial Summary Judgement at 11, *United States ex rel. Drakeford v. Tuomey Healthcare Sys., Inc.*, No3:05-cv-02858-MBS (D.S.C. Aug. 24, 2012), citing 42 C.F.R. § 411.354(c)(2)(ii). Because the part-time employment arrangements in the *Tuomey* case were uniquely structured, even following the court's logic, it is unclear whether the existence of a one-to-one relationship would be sufficient for a similar finding under full-time employment or other circumstances.

27 42 U.S.C. § 1395nn(H)(3); 42 C.F.R. § 411.351.

28 See 69 Fed. Reg. at 16107 (March 26, 2004); see also 72 Fed. Reg. at 51015-16 (Sept. 5, 2007). In 2004, CMS created a "safe harbor" provision in the definition of FMV for hourly payments made to physicians for their personal services. Due in part to concerns regarding the availability of the surveys identified in the safe harbor, CMS eliminated the FMV safe harbor in 2007.

> *are not otherwise in a position to generate business for the other party,* on the date of acquisition of the asset or at the time of the service agreement. Usually, the fair market price is the price at which bona fide sales have been consummated for assets of like type, quality and quantity in a particular market at the time of the acquisition, or the compensation that has been included in bona fide service agreements with comparable terms at the time of the agreement, where the price or compensation *has not been determined in any manner that takes into account the volume or value of anticipated or actual referrals.*[29]

In the recent enforcement actions, the government has argued that the italicized text above means that a compensation arrangement will not satisfy the FMV standard if it varies with the volume or value of a physician's actual or anticipated DHS referrals.[30] CMS initially articulated this position in the following Phase I commentary:

> To establish the FMV of a transaction that involves compensation paid for assets or services, we intend to accept any method that is commercially reasonable and provides us with evidence that the compensation is comparable to what is ordinarily paid for an item or service in the location at issue, by parties in an arm's length transaction *who are not in a position to refer to one another.* As discussed in Section V of this preamble, *in most instances the FMV standard is further modified by language that precludes taking into account the "volume or value" of referrals,* and, in some cases other business generated by the referring physician. Depending on the circumstances, the "volume or value" restriction will preclude reliance on comparables that involve entities and physicians in a position to refer or generate business.[31]

As discussed later in this chapter, CMS has noted in the commentary that fixed compensation could take into account referrals if the compensation is *inflated* or *excessive* to reward referrals or appears to have been calculated based on the physician's referrals. This language suggests that determining whether compensation takes into account referrals may require a subjective inquiry. Specifically, in Phase II, CMS noted:

> Depending on the circumstances, fixed aggregate compensation can form the basis for a prohibited direct or indirect compensation arrangement. This will be the case if such fixed aggregate compensation takes into account the volume or value of referrals (for example, the fixed compensation exceeds FMV for the items or services provided or is inflated to reflect the volume or value of a physician's referrals or other business generated).[32]

Furthermore, CMS noted that arrangements may pose a risk of abuse even if the compensation does not explicitly reflect the volume or value of a physician's DHS referrals.

29 42 C.F.R. § 411.351 (emphasis added).

30 The federal district court in *United States ex rel. Sing v. Bradford Reg'l Med. Ctr.*, 752 F. Supp. 2d 602 (W.D. Pa. 2010), interpreted that the term "referral" encompasses both actual and anticipated referrals.

31 66 Fed. Reg. at 944 (Jan. 4, 2001).

32 See 60 Fed. Reg. 16054, 16059 (March 6, 2004).

Simply stated, Stark establishes a straightforward test that compensation arrangements should be at FMV for the work or service performed or the equipment or space leased—not inflated to compensate for the physician's ability to generate other revenues.[33]

Taken together, from an FMV standpoint, it seems that CMS's position in the commentary is that the compensation in arrangements where *anticipated* referrals were actually taken into account will necessarily be greater than what parties who are not in a position to refer would pay, regardless of the objective support obtained. And while the compensation agreed upon by such parties would be appropriate as negotiated at arm's length *between the parties*, under the narrower FMV and volume or value standards in the Stark regulations, the compensation would ultimately still fail because anticipated referrals were taken into account. Such a subjective approach to FMV seems inconsistent with the objective definition of FMV in the Stark regulations and the guidance from CMS regarding the appropriateness of supporting FMV by referencing multiple and objective third-party salary surveys.[34]

3.3 The 'Other Business Generated' Standard

As discussed above, nearly all of the Stark exceptions prohibit payments of compensation to physicians that take into account the "volume or value" of such physician's DHS referrals. Some of the Stark Law exceptions also include language prohibiting the taking into account of "other business generated" between the parties.[35] CMS has explained that other business generated refers solely to referrals of non-DHS activity.[36] As background, in the 1998 Proposed Rule, CMS initially took the position that the volume or value standard necessarily included the other business generated restriction in all instances, even when the exception did not expressly state as such.[37] However, CMS subsequently adopted its current position that the other business generated restriction would apply only to those exceptions where the language expressly appears.[38] For Stark exceptions without such a restriction (e.g., the employment exception, etc.), the taking into account of a physician's "other business generated" (referrals of non-DHS activity) would not conflict with the standard.

3.4 Compensation Conditioned on Referrals to a Particular Provider

Section 411.354(d)(4) of the Stark regulations expressly authorizes a DHS entity to condition a physician's employment or independent contractor arrangement on referrals to the entity's designated provider, practitioner, or supplier.[39] CMS's historic interpretation with respect to directed referrals has substantially evolved over time. In the 1998 Proposed Rule, CMS initially interpreted the Stark Law as prohibiting an entity from placing restrictions on a physician's

33 66 Fed. Reg. at 877 (Jan. 4, 2001).
34 72 Fed. Reg at 51015 (Sept. 5, 2007).
35 See 42 C.F.R. § 411.357.
36 66 Fed. Reg. at 877 (Jan. 4, 2001).
37 63 Fed. Reg. at 1699 (Jan. 9, 1998).
38 66 Fed. Reg. at 877 (Jan. 4, 2001).
39 See 42 C.F.R. § 411.354(d)(4).

referrals.[40] CMS was concerned that compensation predicated, either expressly or otherwise, on a physician's referrals of DHS necessarily violated the volume or value standard.[41]

After receiving a number of comments objecting to its initial interpretation, CMS reversed its position.[42] In the final Phase I Stark regulations, CMS added Section 411.354(d)(4), which explicitly authorizes a physician's compensation to be conditioned on directed referrals provided the restriction is appropriately structured and contains certain safeguards.[43] Notably, the arrangement must be set in advance, must be consistent with FMV, must be in writing, and must otherwise fit within an existing Stark Law exception.

As an additional safeguard, the referral restriction must be structured so it doesn't apply: (1) when the patient expresses a different choice; (2) when the patient's insurer determines the provider; or (3) when the referral is not in the best medical interest of the patient in the physician's judgment.[44] The referral restriction must "relate solely" to the physician services covered under the arrangement and must be "reasonably necessary to effectuate the legitimate business purposes" of the compensation relationship.[45] Healthcare organizations that utilize referral restrictions should ensure they are appropriately structured to meet these requirements.

3.5 Special Treatment for Stark Group Practices

The Stark Law provides additional compensation flexibility for independent, hospital, or system-affiliated physician practice entities that qualify as a Stark physician "group practice."[46] As a threshold matter, a Stark group practice must meet all nine structural and operational requirements identified in Section 411.352 of the Stark regulations to receive this favored treatment.[47]

Unlike other healthcare organizations, Stark group practices can distribute certain profits from DHS to physicians without violating the volume or value standard, as long as the distribution methodology does not *directly* take into account a physician's DHS referrals.[48] This favored treatment and additional latitude with respect to the volume or value standard is statutory.[49]

40 63 Fed. Reg. at 1699 (Jan. 9, 1998).
41 Id.
42 Commenters noted that directed referral requirements were necessary to develop integrated networks and quality controls and that a prohibition on directed referrals would interfere with exclusive hospital-physician relationships and managed care arrangements was inconsistent with the duty of loyalty, and would have far-reaching effects and unintended consequences. See 66 Fed. Reg. at 878 (Jan. 4, 2001).
43 66 Fed. Reg. at 877 (Jan. 4, 2001).
44 42 C.F.R. § 411.354(d)(4)(iv)(B).
45 69 Fed. Reg. at 16081 (March 26, 2004).
46 42 C.F.R. § 411.355.
47 42 C.F.R. § 411.352; see also 69 Fed. Reg. at 16077 (March 26, 2004).
48 42 C.F.R. § 411.352; see also 66 Fed. Reg. at 909 (Jan. 4, 2001). CMS has identified safe harbored methodologies for distributing productivity bonuses and profit shares that it deems to be indirect under the volume or value standard. Group practices may use other methodologies provided they are reasonable, objectively verifiable, and are only indirectly related to DHS referrals.
49 42 U.S.C. § 1395nn; see also 69 Fed. Reg. at 16077 (March 26, 2004).

CMS noted in Phase I that group practices should be prepared to demonstrate compliance with the group practice regulatory standards at all times.[50] Periodically confirming and documenting compliance with the hypertechnical structural and operational requirements is a prudent practice that will enhance defensibility in the event a group practice's status is ever challenged.

4.0 The Volume or Value Standard—Case Law Illustrations

In several recent enforcement actions, the government has expressly alleged Stark law violations based on the volume or value standard. As discussed below, the arguments the government advanced in these enforcement actions have resulted in confusion regarding what it means for compensation to "take into account" the volume or value of referrals. To some extent, the cases indicate that the determination of whether the standard has been violated should be left up to a jury's discretion.

The recent enforcement actions point to an ongoing battle between the government and healthcare organizations on a few key issues related to the standard. Perhaps the biggest issue arising from the enforcement actions is whether compliance with the volume or value standard should be an objective determination or a subjective one. Two other areas of uncertainty arising from the enforcement actions are whether compensation that exceeds professional collections and/or whether a healthcare organization's examination (or tracking/monitoring) of DHS referrals should be permissible under the volume or value standard. Regrettably, the government has advanced an expansive interpretation of the volume or value standard in these areas, even though many of its interpretations do not appear to be based in law, rule, or regulation and are seemingly inconsistent with the express statements and clarifications provided in the commentary from CMS as discussed in Section 3.0 above.

The discussion below is not intended to summarize all of the facts or issues in these cases or their extended procedural history, which have been recounted elsewhere. Rather, it illustrates the tensions inherent to the volume or value standard that are underscored in these cases.

4.1 *Villafane*—An Objective Test

In the *Villafane*[51] case, the court analyzed the volume or value standard in the context of Stark's academic medical center exception.[52] The court adopted an objective test that focused on whether a violation of the volume or value standard appeared on the face of the contracts.[53]

The court noted the objective approach was appropriate because of the Stark Law's desire to create a "bright-line rule" upon which physicians and hospitals could rely. The court applied the following reasoning:

50 66 Fed. Reg. at 909 (Jan. 4, 2001).

51 *Villafane,* 543 F. Supp.2d 678 (W.D. Ky.2008).

52 42 C.F.R. § 411.357(e).

53 *Villafane,* 543 F. Supp.2d 678 (W.D. Ky.2008).

> Thus, where no violation appears on the face of the arrangement, either in the form of above market-value compensation or of a provision allowing for increases or decreases in payment based on the number of referrals made, the text and history of the Stark Law's desire to create a "bright-line rule" would seem to argue against establishing a violation on the basis of intent alone. As such, the Court is convinced that when, as here, the faculty salary paid to the physician is initially set at fair market value and where the faculty salary does not vary once set, this requirement is easily met.[54]

Given the ongoing confusion related to the volume or value standard, a reasonable and practical solution could include clarifying the Stark regulations with an objective definition or safe harbor for "takes into account" that follows the *Villafane* interpretation. Such a change could more closely align the features of the standard with the "bright line" test that Congress intended.[55]

4.2 *Bradford*—A Subjective Test

In contrast to the *Villafane* case, in the *Bradford*[56] case, the court applied a subjective test and looked beyond the four corners of an equipment sublease with Bradford's referring physicians and concluded that the volume or value standard had not been satisfied.[57] Even though the equipment sublease had fixed payments and was supported by a third-party appraisal, the court still determined that the arrangement was not consistent with FMV and violated the volume or value standard.[58]

Notably, the court carefully scrutinized the underlying analysis and conclusions in an external appraisal Bradford obtained.[59] The revenue projections in the appraisal had assumed that certain referring physicians would refer DHS to the hospital.[60] The *Bradford* court concluded as a matter of law that that the sublease arrangement violated the Stark Law because the valuation of the noncompete took into account the volume or value of "anticipated referrals."[61]

The *Bradford* case illustrates an expansive and subjective interpretation of the volume or value standard. It acknowledges the fact that the compensation paid to physicians may include an amount for anticipated referrals that is not obvious from the contract itself. For that reason,

54 Id.

55 On Oct. 30, 2015, CMS issued its 2016 Physician Fee Schedule Final Rule. In its discussion of the volume or value standard, CMS stated that a commenter had asked CMS to include a proposed definition of the phrase "takes into account" in Section 411.351 of the Stark regulations. CMS decline to do so but noted it was considering the commenter's proposed definition and related discussion as part of its solicitation of comments on the perceived need for clarification regarding permissible physician compensation. If ultimately adopted, perhaps the definition CMS is referencing will alleviate some of the inherent tensions in the volume or value standard that are discussed in this chapter.

56 *U.S. ex rel. Singh v. Bradford Regional Medical Center,* 752 F. Supp. 2d 602 (W.D. Penn. 2010). In *Bradford,* the court determined that fixed compensation that does not vary with referrals, and is not contingent on referrals, may nevertheless be found to take into account if it was determined based on anticipated referrals.

57 Id.

58 Id.

59 Id. at 610.

60 Id.

61 Id. at 640.

under a subjective approach, the volume or value test will include an examination beyond the four corners of the contract to determine the true nature and design of the arrangement. A fact finder may scrutinize aspects of the arrangement that are not apparent on the face of the challenged agreements, and any conduct that may be misconstrued as "taking into account" referrals will result in heightened risk. Healthcare organization, appraisers, and legal counsel should consider the lessons of *Bradford* and should ensure that their valuation processes and written valuation opinions and work papers are prepared for the scrutiny of a subjective validation.

4.3 Compensation That Exceeds Professional Collections

In a number of recent cases, the government has alleged that payment of compensation that exceeds a physician's collections for professional services gives rise to an inference that the compensation must be related to the volume or value of referrals. For example, in the *Tuomey*[62] case, the court focused on the fact that the compensation paid to the physicians at issue far exceeded his or her collections.[63] The government's statements and arguments with respect to practice losses do not appear to be based in law, rule, or regulation. That being said, healthcare organizations, appraisers, and legal counsel should continue to monitor developments in this area of enforcement to see whether new guidance or risk management strategies emerge.

4.4 Examination of 'Downstream Data' and Tracking of Referrals

The government has also alleged that a healthcare organization's tracking of a physician's referrals of DHS demonstrates that the DHS entity determined the physician's compensation in a manner that took into account the physician's actual or anticipated referrals. For example, in the *Halifax*[64] case, the government alleged that a single email from the hospital's CFO to its director of finance requesting the referral volume of its neurosurgeons and a single document from the hospital's CFO questioning referral volumes for a medical oncologist were sufficient to violate the volume or value standard.[65]

The government's statements and arguments with respect to examination of DHS referral data do not appear to be based on law, rule, or regulation. The *Halifax* case illustrates that the government may misconstrue the review of a physician's referral information as evidence that actual or anticipated referrals were taken into account. While it makes business sense for an organization to consider all financial aspects of its arrangements, when entering into arrangements with physicians, it is important to remember that an examination of downstream referral data carries with it a heightened risk of being construed as violating the volume or value standard. How such downstream data are calculated, assessed, and utilized may affect the level of risk associated with the examination (or tracking/monitoring) of such data. For example, the associated risk would be reduced if the downstream referral data are not provided to individuals within the organization who have the authority to make or influence compensation decisions.

---

62 *U.S. ex rel. Drakeford v. Tuomey*, 792 F.3d 364 (4th Cir. 2015).

63 *Tuomey*, 792 F.3d at 377.

64 *U.S. ex rel. Baklid-Kunz v. Halifax Hosp. Med. Ctr.*, No. 6:09-cv-1002-Orl-31DAB (M.D. Fla. March 19, 2012).

65 Id. See United States' November 4, 2011 Complaint in Intervention at 8.

The ability to do so may be dependent upon the size of the organization; however, to the extent possible, downstream referral information should be insulated from those individuals who make or influence physician compensation decisions. Healthcare organizations, appraisers, and legal counsel should periodically evaluate their processes and continue to monitor developments with regard to tracking of a physician's referrals to see whether new guidance or risk management strategies emerge.

5.0 Conclusion

Healthcare organizations face significant potential liability in the current regulatory environment. Given the potential risks under the Stark Law generally, and its volume or value standard in particular, it is of the utmost importance that healthcare organizations, appraisers, and legal counsel focus on maintaining compliance as they navigate this confounding area of the law.

Chapter 5.
The Imperative to Meeting the Stark Group Practice Definition

CONTENTS

Chapter 5.
The Imperative to Meeting the Stark Group Practice Definition[1]

By Alice G. Gosfield

Almost 20 years after the Stark Law's effective date (1995), in August 2014, the Office of the Inspector General and the Department of Justice entered into the very first settlement with a physician group based on internal compensation practices that did not meet the definition of a group practice.[2] Paying more than $1.3 million for compensation practices in 2007 and 2008, the partners in New York Heart Center allegedly compensated themselves based on the volume of their internal referrals for designated health services (DHS), primarily CT scans and nuclear diagnostic studies. They were not obligated to enter into a Corporate Integrity Agreement.

Although no whistleblower is mentioned in the settlement, and it has gotten relatively little press, it is extraordinarily important for several reasons: (1) when the law was enacted, it was almost impossible to imagine how the government would ever be in a position to look at internal private practice operations unless they were investigating a group for something else; and (2) to take such a long time to enforce with regard to a basic and fundamental definition in the statute and regulations means that now every aspect of the law is fair game for the enforcers, even if they have never taken action before.

This is a warning shot over the bow. Every group practice should not only re-examine their compensation formulas involving DHS, but also look very closely at whether they are meeting the other indicia of a physician group set forth in regulation.

1 "The Imperative to Meeting the Stark Group Practice Definition," written by Alice Gosfield, first appeared in the February 2015 issue of *Compliance Today*, published by the Health Care Compliance Association, Copyright 2015. Reprinted here with permission.

2 www.justice.gov/usao-ndny/pr/new-york-heart-center-pay-more-133-million-settle-allegations-false-claims-act-and. Please note: The original footnote published in *Compliance Today* was changed by the editor of this book due to an error in the web link.

This chapter looks at each of the elements of the definition of a group practice and elucidates the complexities lurking there. The drafters of the legislation were protecting against ills they little understood themselves. Their language is replete with misused terms that have long had meaning in Medicare, such as "personal supervision," "direct supervision," and "incident-to." Fortunately, regulation fixed many of these confusions. In the only attempt to repeal parts of the statute in the Balanced Budget Act of 1995 (which President Clinton vetoed, thus shutting down the government), one of the major elements was removing the implications of the law for the internal operations of a group practice. Nothing like that has happened since.

1.0 Why the Definition Matters

Many people still think that there is a group practice exception in the Stark Law. There is no such thing. To avail oneself of some of the exceptions, you must be a group practice. The principal exceptions that require this precondition are: (1) the referral to a physician in the group practice; (2) in office ancillary services; and (3) certain group practice arrangements with hospitals, which no longer has much relevance since the arrangements had to have been in place before Dec. 19, 1989. The safe harbor regulations under the anti-kickback statute (AKS) have added a couple of protections that turn on meeting the group practice definition. These include investments in group practices as well as referral agreements among specialists within group practices.

The fundamental prohibitions under the Stark Law are against an improper referral by a physician where the referral does not meet an exception under the law, and then the real impact is the prohibition on submitting claims, which include violating transactions. From the original statutory provisions, the paid claim is an overpayment, which is also subject to a civil money penalty of $15,000 and potential exclusion from Medicare.[3] The same provision of the statute requires repayment to be made to the patient for any amounts paid in association with the overpayment. There had long been a debate as to whether Stark violations could be false claims. There is no longer any question about this. The Affordable Care Act provided that any claims submitted pursuant to a Stark or AKS violative transaction must be repaid within 60 days, or they convert to false claims.[4] This is now whistleblower country.

2.0 Single Legal Entity

To qualify as a group practice, the group must consist of a single legal entity operating primarily for the purpose of being a physician group.[5] The regulations are widely liberal with respect to what kind of legal structure may be used, permitting partnerships, professional corporations, limited liability companies, foundations, nonprofit corporations, faculty practice plans, or virtually anything else. There are no specifications with regard to who must or may own or organize the entity, which can include physicians as well as healthcare facilities or any other persons or entities.

3 42 USC §1395nn(g).
4 Section 6402(d) of the Affordable Care Act.
5 42 CFR §411.352(a).

To qualify as a single legal entity, the group practice may be owned by another group, but it may not be owned by a group that continues to practice as a group. As rigid as that qualification appears to be, it is somewhat undermined by a sentence further on in the same paragraph, which says, "A group practice that is otherwise a single legal entity may itself own subsidiary entities." One could well imagine a primary care physician group that continues to operate as a group practice owning and operating a separate professional corporation or limited liability company that consisted solely of specialists. Going all the way back to the first final regulations in 2001, the regulators rejected the concept of allowing separate entities under common control to qualify as a group practice. In response to fairly extensive comments on the proposed regulations, the regulators agreed that many group practices are formed out of merging prior practices. It was in that context that they took the position that the practice should consist of a single legal entity.

Even today, attorneys ask me whether a group of physicians employed by a hospital can constitute a group practice. While the old line fully integrated medical groups such as the Cleveland Clinic, the Billings Clinic, and Park Nicollet, these are in fact physician practices that own the hospitals and do meet the definition of a group practice. The traditional community hospital that now employs physicians likely cannot claim that it is a group. When it sets up a separate entity that employs the physicians, then that entity may well constitute a group practice, even though the sole member is the hospital with which it is affiliated.

3.0 Physicians

The group practice must have at least two physicians who are members of the group. Members are defined as those physicians who are a direct or indirect physician-owner of a group practice, a physician employee of the group practice, a locum tenens physician, or an on-call physician covering for a member of the group practice. A physician is a member of the group practice during the time he or she furnishes "patient care services" to the group as defined in the regulatory definition. An independent contractor is not a member of the group. This was a major controversy when proposed regulations were published. An independent contractor can be a physician "in the group" for purposes of supervising personnel and receiving referrals from other physicians in the group. Independent contractor physicians are only physicians "in the group" when they are using the group's offices. The regulation actually says the group's "facilities," which is nowhere defined.

4.0 Range of Care

Each physician who is a member of the group must furnish substantially the full range of patient care services that he or she routinely furnishes, including medical care, consultation, diagnosis, and treatment through the joint use of shared office space, facilities, equipment, and personnel. This means that, if a physician really only does one service, such as Mohs surgery, and if that is all he or she does with the group practice, there is no problem. However, this provision was intended to prevent groups consisting of members who served in that status only to deliver a limited range of services, such as cardiac catheterizations from which the referring physicians in the group would profit. But, because the provision only refers to the members of the practice, there can be independent contractor arrangements for limited services provided by other physicians, billed by the group practice.

5.0 Services Furnished by Group Practice Members

At least 75% of the total patient care services of the group practice members must be furnished through the group and billed under a billing number assigned to the group. Revenues received from that billing must be treated as receipts of the group. In calculating whether the members of the group meet the 75% standard, the regulations look at the total time each member spends on patient care services documented by any reasonable means (including, but not limited to, time cards, appointment schedules, or personal diaries). The regulations offer the example of a physician who practices 40 hours a week and spends 30 hours on patient care services for the group practice as meeting the 75% rule. If, however, a physician is only engaged in clinical practice 10 hours a week but spends all of those 10 hours with the group practice, he would meet the standard at 100%. The calculation has to take into account all of the members of the group practice so that the average is 75% among them. This provision is intended to limit loosely knit organizations of clinicians who do not practice together most of the time.

Any other alternative measure that is reasonable, fixed in advance of the performance of the services being measured, uniformly applied over time, verifiable, and documented is also permitted. These rules do not pertain to a group practice that is located solely in a health-professional shortage area. The regulations offer a grace period of 12 months for a new physician who joins a practice.

6.0 Distribution of Expenses and Income

The regulations say relatively little about how expenses must be allocated but require that the expenses and income must be distributed according to methods that are determined before the receipt of payment for the services that give rise to the overhead expense of producing the income. In the preface to the regulations, there is little discussion of this provision. The regulators did state explicitly that many types of cost center and location or specialty-specific allocations are permitted, as long as they are prospectively determined.[6]

7.0 Unified Business

The regulations require that the group practice must be a unified business. The government has taken the position that this would be manifested by having at least the following features: (1) centralized decision making by a body representative of the group practice that maintains

6 66 Fed Reg 907 (Jan. 4, 2001).

effective control of the group's assets and liabilities (including, but not limited to, budgets, compensation, and salaries); and (2) consolidated billing, accounting, and financial reporting. This is typically referred to as "one tax ID number, one checkbook." However, the extent of the required consolidation is not described.

8.0 Volume or Value of Referrals

As the touchstone for safety, the regulations set forth that no physician who is a member of the group practice may directly or indirectly receive compensation based on the volume or value of his or her referrals, except in compliance with the regulations pertaining to productivity bonuses and profit shares. However, the regulators have also made clear that as incident-to services often are reflective of a referral for a DHS, they are an exception to the rule because they are part of the definition of a group practice.

9.0 Physician-Patient Encounters

In yet a second 75% rule applied to group practices, the regulations require that members of the group must personally conduct no less than 75% of the physician-patient encounters of the group practice. Again, there is almost no explanation of what this provision means, other than it is based on a per-capita calculation rather than a time-based calculation. The term "encounters" is unclear. Generally speaking, under Part B, one would talk about visits rather than encounters. Is the interpretation of a diagnostic test an encounter? What happens if in an oncology practice, for example, there are infusions that are conducted with virtually no physician involvement on multiple patients during the day?

Are those encounters? In the absence of any real guidance, it would be hard to imagine a whistleblower making much of this, unless a group used mostly independent contractors to conduct the practice.

10.0 Productivity Bonuses

Here, the regulators address the issue of allocating to physicians revenues associated with services that they have personally performed. In addition, the revenues from services incident-to the physician's services to the patient may also be allocated to that physician, provided that the bonus is not determined in any manner that is directly related to the volume or value of referrals of DHS by the physician.

Many lawyers have continued to be confused about this. The regulation goes on directly to say "except that the bonus may directly relate to the volume or value of DHS referrals by the physician if their referrals are for services 'incident to' the physician's personally performed services."[7] The regulators made this point clearly in the discussion of incident-to services in

7 42 CFR §411.352(i)(1).

the preface to the 2001 regulations.[8] Although commenters were apparently still confused, in 2004 the regulators noted that "a number of commenters asked that we clarify that physicians in the group practice can be paid a productivity bonus or profit share based directly on services that are 'incident to' services personally performed by the physician,"[9] and they did so again. For example, independent contractors may be paid 60% of the revenues they generate through personally performed and incident- to services. Finally, in 2007, after some debate as to whether handing a continuous positive airway pressure (CPAP) machine to a patient would qualify as a personally performed service, the regulators made it clear that such a transaction would not qualify as an incident-to or personally performed service. They did clarify, again, that revenues from services and supplies such as drugs were allocable under the incident-to provision, which, by that time, they had said three times—in 2001, 2004, and 2007.[10]

What qualifies as incident-to under Medicare's general reimbursement rules applies to what is permissible under Stark. In 2007, turning their back on the entire 40-year history of the Medicare program, the regulators announced that diagnostic testing could no longer be considered incident-to a physician's services.[11] This may well be where the New York Heart Group went wrong. Note that the dates at issue in the "allocation formulas" were 2007-2008, when rules that had been in place for years were trashed in these little-known regulatory publications. Revenues from diagnostic tests that are DHS must be allocated in a profit-sharing formula. The regulators took this position because, they say, diagnostic testing has its own benefit category in the Medicare statute, but so do physical therapists, occupational therapists, nurse practitioners, physician assistants, and others, and their services all can be billed incident-to a physician.

The basic requirements for incident-to Medicare services must be met. There has to be a physician service to which the ancillary services are incidental in a course of treatment established by the treating physician. A physician in the group—meaning a member or an independent contractor who reassigns payment to the group—must be on the premises, in the office suite, and immediately available to assist the ancillary personnel. The supervising physician need not be the treating physician. Incident-to services can be billed on a day when no physician sees the patient at all. Incident-to services are paid at 100% of the Medicare physician fee schedule, and they are billed as if the physician performed them himself. The Stark regulators have repeatedly stated that the level of supervision that is required (despite the statute's misguided reference to "direct supervision" in some instances and "personal supervision" in others) is the level of supervision that otherwise pertains under Medicare policy: (1) general—no physician on premises required; (2) direct—a physician in the office suite required; or (3) personal—physician and patient in the same room while the service is rendered.

8 66 Fed Reg 909 (Jan. 4, 2001).
9 69 Fed Reg 16080 (March 26, 2004).
10 72 Fed Reg 51016-51020 (Sept. 5, 2007).
11 72 Fed Reg 51016 (Sept. 5, 2007).

A related concept for the allocation of productivity bonuses is the shared visit, which pertains only to hospital services—inpatient, outpatient, and in the Emergency Department. Here, a nonphysician practitioner in the same group as the treating physician can perform and document most of an evaluation and management (E&M) service. The physician can later perform any portion of the visit in a face-to-face encounter with the patient, and both of their services can be "grossed up" and billed in the physician's name.[12] These count as personally performed services for Stark, but they are actually not DHS at all, so Stark has little to say about them. The same is true of visits billed by nurse practitioners (NPs), physician assistants (PAs), and clinical nurse specialists (CNSs) on their own provider numbers and paid at 85% of the physician fee schedule. Unless they are performing Stark diagnostic tests, most of their interactions with patients are not DHS and their revenues can be directly attributed to the treating physician. That is not the case for physical therapists or occupational therapists billing on their own provider numbers and paid at 100% of the physician fee schedule because physical therapy and occupational therapy are DHS. This brings us to profit sharing, which is often not well understood. There is much more liberality to be found there than many practices and even attorneys realize.

11.0 Profit Sharing

Although the statute says that a physician in a group practice may be paid a share of overall profits of the group, in fact, Stark has little to say about profits from services that are not DHS. Profit sharing is sharing in the revenues from the fruits of others' labors from DHS, such as sharing diagnostic testing revenues or physical therapy revenues from services that were not provided incident-to.

The rules allow subgroups within a group as long as each pod consists of at least five physicians.[13] A single group of fewer than five means that all must be paid in accordance with the same formula, which need not produce the same amount of compensation to each. Profit sharing cannot include current DHS ordering patterns, but there is nothing to prohibit a historical look at ordering projected forward for the coming year. This does not directly reward current referrals.

Some groups allocate on the basis of the volume of E&M services or the work relative value units (RVUs) associated with nondesignated health services. Some use number of patients. Some share equally. Nothing is mandated nor, in a larger group, is there a requirement that everybody participate in profit sharing. In very large groups, we have seen profits shared by historical referral patterns by differing ancillary services (e.g., the physical therapy pod, the infusion pod, the CT and MRI pod, the imaging pod, etc.). As long as each subgroup is at least five physicians and the formula does not directly reflect the volume of referrals, it will be compliant with the statute and regulations.

12 First published in Transmittal 1776 in 2002, the provisions have now been manualized at Medicare Claims Processing Manual Chapter 12 §30.6.1B.

13 42 CFR §411.352(i)(1) and 66 Fed Reg 908 (Jan. 4, 2001), 69 Fed Reg 1680-1 (March 26, 2004).

12.0 Conclusion

The definition of a group practice is a fundamental predicate to being able to refer in accordance with any of the exceptions under the Stark Law that make reference to group practices. With the New York Heart Center settlement, it is abundantly clear that this will be fertile ground for enforcers and whistleblowers. All group practices should review each of the relevant criteria to make sure they comply.

Chapter 6. Valuation Issues Affecting Tax-Exempt Healthcare Entities

CONTENTS

Chapter 6. Valuation Issues Affecting Tax-Exempt Healthcare Entities

By Robert F. Reilly, MBA, CPA/ABV/CFF

1.0 Introduction

This discussion describes many of the regulatory reasons why a tax-exempt healthcare entity may retain a valuation analyst (analyst) to perform a transaction-related property valuation, a reasonableness of compensation valuation analysis, or a similar type of fair market value analysis. This discussion does not explain the generally accepted valuation approaches, methods, and procedures with regard to the transfer of healthcare business entities ("property") or professional/other services ("services"). Such explanations of valuation and transfer pricing methodologies are presented elsewhere in this text. In addition, the generally accepted business and intangible asset valuation approaches and methods are described in numerous valuation textbooks. And the arm's-length price methods for the analysis of transferred professional and other services are described in numerous transfer pricing and economics textbooks.

Instead, this discussion summarizes the regulatory considerations that the analyst (and the parties to a proposed transaction) should be aware of with respect to the valuation of a healthcare business entity or a contract to provide employment, leased real estate, or other services.

With regard to a healthcare transaction including at least one tax-exempt entity, the principal parties (and the analyst) should be concerned with a series of laws and regulations including (but not limited to): (1) the Medicare fraud and abuse statutes; (2) Internal Revenue Service (IRS) private inurement issues; and (3) the various Stark laws and regulations. This discussion introduces the analyst's transaction-related considerations with regard to the Medicare fraud and abuse statutes and the various Stark statutes and regulations. However, this discussion primarily focuses on the analyst's considerations with regard to federal income tax issues related to tax-exempt healthcare entities. These transaction-related issues relate primarily to private inurement considerations and the related intermediate sanctions excise tax penalties.

In particular, this discussion focuses on the following income-tax-related valuation issues involving tax-exempt healthcare entity property and services transfers: what type of transaction price or structure may result in a private inurement, what parties are subject to the private inurement considerations, what types of transactions are encompassed in the spectrum of private inurement considerations, what the IRS looks for in its consideration of private inurement issues, and how the intermediate sanctions penalties work in instances of alleged private inurement.

This discussion is not a primer with regard to all of the regulatory requirements facing healthcare providers. Ignoring the associated professional regulations, the business practices-related regulations facing healthcare providers are voluminous. While some of these regulations may be mentioned in passing, they are not the focus of this discussion. The focus of this discussion is very specific: requirements related to the determination of the fair market value standard in the transfer of: (1) a professional practice or other healthcare entity ownership interest; and (2) services (e.g., employee, professional, property lease, and other services) related to a healthcare provider.

The first section of this discussion summarizes the tax-related regulatory issues related to a healthcare property or services transfer transaction including a tax-exempt organization as one of the transaction participants. The analyst should be generally aware of these issues in the fair market value analysis of any healthcare transaction involving either: (1) a tax-exempt entity and a for-profit entity; or (2) a tax-exempt entity and any "disqualified person."

The second section of this discussion considers non-tax-related regulatory issues involving the valuation of healthcare property or services transfer transactions.

Finally, the last section of this discussion provides a list of common analyst misconceptions with regard to the fair market value valuation of a healthcare property or services transfer transaction.

2.0 Valuation Issues

The private inurement and excess benefit issues related to tax-exempt healthcare entities encompass two types of transfer transactions: (1) the transfer of property and (2) the transfer of services. Both of these types of transfer transactions involve valuation issues and fair market value valuations. Both of these types of transactions are assessed by an analyst who concludes a fair market value opinion related to a proposed or completed transfer transaction.

"Fair market value" is defined the same way for both types (i.e., property and services) of transfer transactions. According to Treasury Regulation Section 53.4958-(b)(1)(i):

> Fair market value is defined as the price at which property or the right to use property would change hands between a willing buyer and a willing seller, neither being under any

compulsion to buy, sell, or transfer property or the right to use property and both having reasonable knowledge of relevant facts.

Many analysts may be more familiar with valuations related to property transfer transactions. This type of transaction occurs when the tax-exempt entity buys or sells a business entity, a business ownership interest, or business operating assets. Some common examples of such a property transfer include a tax-exempt healthcare entity buying or selling the equity of—or the assets of—a hospital, clinic, physician practice, outpatient surgical center, dialysis center, MRI center, urgent care center, HMO, home healthcare agency, medical equipment provider, or any other healthcare delivery organization. And, these property transfer transactions encompass the purchase or sale of either the assets or the equity of the healthcare provider entity. Such property transfer transactions also include the tax-exempt entity either buying or selling a medical office building, specialty medical equipment, or other type of real estate or tangible personal property. As part of the analysis of such property transfer transactions, the analyst is asked to opine on the fair market value of the property transfer.

Many analysts may be less familiar with valuations related to the services transfer transactions. This type of transaction occurs when a tax-exempt entity hires employees or contracts for professional services. Some common examples include when the tax-exempt healthcare entity compensates a chief executive officer (CEO) or other executives, pays a medical director (or other physician professionals), hires a physician group to manage emergency room or operating room operations, rents office or professional space to (or from) physicians, leases equipment to (or from) physicians, provides billing or other administrative services to physicians (or from other for-profit service providers), or generally enters into any joint venture or related contractual agreement with physicians or other healthcare providers. As part of the analysis of such service transactions, the analyst is asked to opine on the fair market value of the services transfer.

The taxation and other federal (and many state) regulations use the term fair market value as the benchmark for the transfer of services to or from the healthcare provider entity. From the analyst's perspective, much of the professional guidance with regard to the price analysis of services uses the term "arm's-length price." This statement is particularly true with regard to income-tax-related guidance related to the pricing of transferred services. One example of this is the body of literature (and the voluminous Treasury regulations) related to the arm's-length price measurement of the intercompany transfer of services pursuant to Internal Revenue Code Section 482. For purposes of this discussion, the analyst can think of the terms "fair market value" and "arm's-length price" as synonymous. However, to comply with the appropriate regulatory requirements, the analyst is cautioned to use the term fair market value in the analysis of a services transfer transaction related to healthcare providers.

The private inurement prohibition requires that a public charity that has been granted tax-exempt status under Internal Revenue Code Section 501(c)(3) operate so that none of its income or assets unreasonably benefits any of its board members, trustees, officers, or key employees. These types of individuals are commonly referred to as "insiders." Therefore, the private inurement prohibition precludes any of the income or assets of a tax-exempt healthcare entity from unfairly or unreasonably benefiting (either directly or indirectly) individuals who have: (1) close relationships with the tax-exempt entity; and (2) the ability to exercise control over the tax-exempt entity.

The most common type of private inurement is excessive compensation paid to the tax-exempt entity insiders (discussed below). There are, however, many other forms of private inurement that can also result in the revocation of the healthcare entity's tax-exempt status and/or in the imposition of significant "intermediate sanctions" (discussed below). These other forms of possible private inurement include, but are not limited to, transactions such as:

- The sale of the tax-exempt entity's asset to an insider;
- The entity's purchase of an asset from an insider;
- The entity's rental of real estate or tangible personal property from, or to, an insider;
- The entity's lending of money to an insider; and
- The use of the tax-exempt entity facilities and/or any other assets by an insider.

Just as when the analyst assesses the appropriateness of an insider's compensation, the important factor in determining whether any tax-exempt entity transaction with an insider violates the private inurement prohibition is whether the transaction is fair and reasonable under the circumstances. For example, it would not be improper for a tax-exempt hospital to buy a medical office building from a physician group at, or below, its fair market value. However, it would be improper for the tax-exempt hospital to lease the medical office building to a physician group for less than its fair market value rent.

The courts and the IRS have consistently concluded that any unreasonable benefit or inurement, however small, is impermissible and can result in the revocation of the healthcare entity's tax-exempt status. Even, however, if private inurement is clearly present in a particular fact situation, it can be argued that the ultimate sanction of revoking the healthcare entity's tax-exempt status should not be imposed if the unreasonable benefit an insider receives was only incidental or insignificant. In these instances, an argument can be made to only have "intermediate sanctions" (discussed below) imposed instead.

As noted above, the most common type of private inurement is the payment of excessive compensation to insiders. Recently, the IRS has significantly increased its enforcement efforts in this area. And the IRS has assessed millions of dollars in penalties for these compensation-related violations. In addition, the IRS has indicated that it will include excess compensation analyses in every tax-exempt entity audit it conducts.

Editor's note: Readers should be aware that reasonable compensation under Section 4958[1] *is determined under the general principles of Section 162's ordinary and necessary test.*

Of course, individuals working for a tax-exempt healthcare entity are not expected to donate their services, and they are allowed to be reasonably compensated. Such employees are not expected to work for free or accept reduced compensation simply because they provide their services to a tax-exempt entity rather than to a taxable healthcare organization. The private inurement prohibition simply requires that the total compensation a tax-exempt entity pays to an insider be fair and reasonable.

Whether an insider's total compensation is fair and reasonable is determined on a case-by-case basis. Such a fair market value analysis of compensation involves a process similar to that used to value any other type of transfer. This valuation process requires the analyst to gather comparable data regarding what similarly situated individuals employed by similar organizations are paid. There are numerous publicly available data sources for obtaining this type of empirical compensation information. For example, Economic Research Institute (ERI—www.erieri.com) and GuideStar (www.guidestar.org) are two executive compensation data sources that analysts use in healthcare entity reasonableness of compensation valuation analyses.

For an insider's compensation to be considered fair and reasonable, there should be an approximately equal exchange of benefits between the tax-exempt entity and the insider. In that case, the insider does not receive an unreasonable or unwarranted benefit from the tax-exempt entity. The analyst typically considers several factors in the evaluation of the reasonableness of insider compensation valuation, including:

- The compensation paid by a similar entity, both tax-exempt and taxable, for equivalent positions in the same community or geographic area;
- The tax-exempt entity's need for the particular services of the subject individual;
- The uniqueness of the subject person's background, education, training, experience, and responsibilities;
- Whether an independent board of directors approved the compensation;
- The size and complexity of the tax-exempt entity's income and assets and the number of employees that the entity employs;
- The subject individual's prior compensation arrangements. the subject individual's job performance. the relationship of the individual's compensation to the compensation paid to the tax-exempt entity's other employees; and
- The number of hours the subject individual spends performing his or her job.

1 Treas. Reg. § 53.4958-4(b)(1)(ii)(A).

Total compensation a tax-exempt healthcare entity pays to an insider includes more than just the insider's salary or wages. It also includes all other forms of compensation that the insider receives. These other forms of compensation may include bonuses, commissions, royalties, fringe benefits, deferred compensation, severance payments, retirement and pension benefits, expense allowance, and insurance benefits.

The analyst should be aware that an unreasonably large or excessive salary paid by a tax-exempt entity to an insider can be considered private inurement. This conclusion is especially true when the insider also receives other forms of compensation from the tax-exempt entity. The analyst should note, however, that very large salaries and noncash benefits paid to certain key employees can often be reasonable when one considers the employee's experience and expertise. For example, highly skilled and experienced physicians at a tax-exempt hospital are sometimes paid significantly more than the hospital's CEO and its other executive-level staff.

The analyst should be aware that a tax-exempt healthcare entity can avoid violating the private inurement prohibition for the compensation it pays to an insider as long as it is able to:

- Describe fully and accurately all aspects of the insider's total compensation package;
- Explain exactly how the tax-exempt entity determined the insider's total compensation package;
- Describe adequately and accurately the insider's duties and responsibilities;
- Provide adequate documentation, such as comparable salaries paid by similar entities, that demonstrate the reasonableness of the insider's compensation;
- Demonstrate through appropriate documentation that the entity's governing body approved the amount of the insider's compensation and that the insider (or someone related to the insider) did not participate in the approval process;
- Demonstrate that the amount of the insider's total reportable compensation agrees with the amount reported on the insider's Form W-2 or Form 1099—in order to avoid an automatic excess benefit transaction; and
- Demonstrate through appropriate documentation that the insider's use of any of the tax-exempt entity assets (such as cars, real estate, credit cards, laptops, or cell phones) for any reason other than fulfilling the entity's tax-exempt purpose were properly included in his or her compensation and properly included in the insider's Form W-2 or Form 1099—in order to avoid penalties for automatic excess benefit transactions.

As described more completely below, not all findings of private inurement will result in the revocation of the healthcare entity's tax-exempt status. Internal Revenue Code Section 4958 provides for "intermediate sanctions." Intermediate sanctions allow the IRS to impose significant taxes on tax-exempt entity insiders, whom the applicable regulations refer to as "disqualified person," when they engage in excess benefit transactions with a tax-exempt healthcare entity.

Therefore, Section 4958 provides the IRS with the authority to impose a sanction short of revocation when tax-exempt status revocation would be inappropriate and/or unnecessarily harsh.

In an excessive compensation case, the "excess benefit" is the amount by which: (1) the total compensation the tax-exempt entity paid to an insider exceeds (2) the reasonable value of the services provided by the insider to the entity. So, for example, if a comparison of comparable executive salaries indicates that the tax-exempt hospital CEO is being paid $100,000 more than comparable individuals performing similar functions at similar hospitals and that there is no legitimate reason for such excess compensation, then the amount of the "excess benefit" the insider receives would be $100,000.

Internal Revenue Code Section 4958(a)(1) imposes an initial tax equal to 25% of the excess benefit. In this example, the hospital CEO insider (i.e., not the tax-exempt hospital itself) would have to pay a $25,000 penalty to the IRS. In addition, the CEO insider would have to make the hospital whole by repaying the $100,000 excess benefit, plus interest.

In this example, if the CEO insider does not make the tax-exempt hospital whole within the time frame set by the IRS, Section 4958(b) imposes an additional tax equal to 200% of the excess benefit of the CEO insider—i.e., an additional $200,000 tax penalty in this example.

Section 4958(a)(2) also imposes a tax equal to 10% of the excess benefit on any tax-exempt healthcare entity executive, typically a board member who knowingly approved the excess benefit transaction, unless his or her participation was not willful. Again, in the above example, the tax on any hospital board member who knowingly approved the unreasonable or excessive CEO salary would be $10,000.

It is important to note that the term "participation" includes a board member's silence or inaction where he or she is under a duty to speak or act—as well as any affirmative action by the board member. The healthcare entity's tax-exempt board member is not considered to have participated in an excess benefit transaction, however, if he or she opposed the transaction. For example, the entity's board member could have his or her objection to the compensation transaction noted in the entity's board meeting minutes.

In addition, a board member's participation is normally not considered to be "knowing" within the meaning of Section 4958(a)(2) if there was full disclosure of all relevant facts to an appropriately qualified analyst and the entity's board member relied on a reasoned written opinion by that analyst that the subject transaction payment was reasonable.

To help tax-exempt healthcare entities comply with these regulations, the IRS established a "rebuttable presumption" that payments to insiders are presumed to be reasonable and not excessive if the following procedures were taken:

- The tax-exempt entity's board obtained and relied on appropriate comparability data prior to making its determination;
- The tax-exempt entity's board approved the total compensation package in advance, and no individuals who had an actual or potential conflict of interest with respect to the compensation arrangement participated in the deliberations; and
- The tax-exempt entity's board adequately and contemporaneously documented the basis for its determination.

If the above three procedures are performed, then the IRS may only rebut the presumption of reasonableness if it can demonstrate that the comparability data the tax-exempt entity board relied on was inappropriate. For a tax-exempt healthcare entity with annual gross receipts of less than $1 million, a board is considered to have appropriate comparability data if it has data on compensation paid for similar services by three comparable organizations in the same or similar communities.

3.0 Other Regulatory Considerations

In addition to these IRS and taxation considerations, tax-exempt healthcare entities should comply with numerous other federal and state regulations regarding the transfer of property or services. This section provides a brief overview of some of the regulatory considerations that the analyst should be aware of. Again, this overview only considers property or services transfer transactions. This section does not consider all of the business practices regulations that healthcare providers must comply with.

Numerous federal laws govern Medicare fraud and abuse. Most of the provisions of these laws do not encompass the property or services transfer transactions considered in this discussion. Therefore, the analyst does not have to be familiar with most of these laws. Healthcare providers, of course, have to be familiar with—and comply with—all of these laws. For this discussion, these laws are referred to collectively as the Medicare fraud and abuse statutes (or, simply, the statutes). These statutes include the following:

1. The False Claims Act;
1. The anti-kickback statute;
2. The Physician Self-Referral Law;
3. The Social Security Act; and
4. The United States Criminal Code.

These statutes specify the criminal and/or civil remedies that the government can impose on individuals or provider entities that commit fraud and abuse in the Medicare program, including Medicare Parts C and D, as well as the Medicaid program. Violations of any of these statutes may result in the nonpayment of claims, civil monetary penalties, exclusion from participation in federal health care programs, and criminal and civil liabilities. A healthcare provider's liability can exist without proof of actual knowledge or a specific intent to violate the law.

Each of these statutes is briefly introduced below.

3.1 The False Claims Act

The False Claims Act protects the government from being overcharged or sold substandard goods or services. The False Claims Act imposes civil liability on any "person" who knowingly submits, or causes the submission of, a false or fraudulent claim to the federal government. The "knowing" standard includes acting in deliberate ignorance of—or reckless disregard of—the truth related to the claim.

There is also a criminal False Claims Act statute through which an individual or entity healthcare provider that submits false claims can face criminal penalties.

3.2 The Anti-Kickback Statute

The anti-kickback statute makes it a criminal offense to knowingly and willfully offer, pay, solicit, or receive any remuneration directly or indirectly to induce or reward referrals of items or services reimbursable by a federal healthcare program. An example of an anti-kickback statute violation would be a healthcare provider who benefits from a below fair market value rent on a hospital-owned medical office building in exchange for patient referrals.

Civil penalties for violating the anti-kickback statute can include fines up to three times the amount of the kickback. Criminal penalties for violating the anti-kickback statute can include fines, imprisonment, or both.

If certain types of healthcare provider arrangements satisfy regulatory safe harbors, then the anti-kickback statute will not treat these arrangements as offenses.

3.3 Physician Self-Referral Law (Stark Law)

The Physician Self-Referral Law, often called the Stark Law, prohibits a physician from making a referral for certain designated health services to a healthcare provider entity in which the physician (or member of his or her immediate family) has an ownership/investment interest or with which he or she has a compensation arrangement, unless an exception applies. The Stark Law is further discussed below.

3.4 Criminal Health Care Fraud Statute

The Criminal Health Care Fraud Statute prohibits knowingly and willfully executing, or attempting to execute, a scheme or artifice in connection with the delivery of or payment for healthcare benefits, items, or services to:

1. Defraud any healthcare benefit program; or

2. Obtain (by means of false or fraudulent pretenses, representations, or promises) any of the money or property owned by, or under the custody or control of, any healthcare benefit program.

4.0 Other Medicare Fraud and Abuse Penalties

Aside from the civil and criminal actions brought by law enforcement agencies, the Medicare program itself has additional administrative remedies applicable for certain healthcare fraud and abuse violations.

Under the Exclusion Statute, the Office of Inspector General must exclude from participation in all federal healthcare programs any healthcare providers and suppliers that are convicted of:

1. Medicare fraud;
2. Patient abuse or neglect;
3. Felony convictions related to fraud, theft, embezzlement, breach of fiduciary responsibility, or other financial misconduct in connection with the delivery of a healthcare item or service; or
4. Felony convictions for unlawful manufacture, distribution, prescription, or dispensing of controlled substances.

The Department of Health and Human Services Office of Inspector General also has the discretion to impose exclusions on a number of other grounds. Excluded providers cannot participate in federal healthcare programs for a designated period. An excluded healthcare provider may not bill federal healthcare programs (including, but not limited to, Medicare, Medicaid, and State Children's Health Insurance Program) for services he or she orders or performs. At the end of an exclusion period, an excluded healthcare provider must affirmatively seek reinstatement; reinstatement is not automatic.

Under the Civil Monetary Penalties Law, civil monetary penalties apply for a variety of misconduct. The Civil Monetary Penalties Law authorizes penalties of up to $50,000 per violation and assessments of up to three times the amount claimed for each item or service or up to three times the amount of remuneration offered, paid, solicited, or received. Healthcare provider violations that may give rise to a civil monetary penalty include:

1. Presenting a claim that the healthcare provider knows or should know is for an item or service not provided as claimed or that is false and fraudulent;
2. Presenting a claim that the healthcare provider knows or should know is for an item or service for which Medicare will not pay; and
3. Violating the anti-kickback statute.

In general, the Medicare fraud and abuse statutes make it illegal to pay, offer, or induce any remuneration in exchange for patient referrals. For example, a hospital cannot pay a physician in exchange for patient referrals to that hospital. Accordingly, in a physician practice acquisition transaction, a hospital cannot pay any portion of the purchase price in exchange for the physician's current or expected patient referrals to that hospital. Therefore, both tax-exempt acquirers and taxable acquirers in the healthcare industry should not structure a transaction that appears to involve either; (1) a "kickback" payment for physician patient referrals; or (2) a "lockup" of physician patient referrals.

The various Stark laws prohibit physicians with a financial relationship with a healthcare entity from referring patients to the entity for "designated health services" covered by either Medicare or Medicaid programs. The Stark laws are named for United States Congressman Peter Stark, who sponsored the initial bill.

The Stark laws provide a limitation on certain physician referrals. The law prohibits physician referrals of designated health services for Medicare and Medicaid patients if the physician (or an immediate family member) has a financial relationship with that healthcare entity. A financial relationship is defined to include ownership, investment interest, and compensation arrangements.

Under the Stark laws, the term "referral" is defined more broadly than merely recommending a vendor of designated health services to a patient. Instead, the Stark laws definition of the term "referral" means, for Medicare Part B services, "the request by a physician for the item or service" and, for all other services, "the request or establishment of a plan of care by a physician which includes the provision of the designated health service."

The term "DHS" is defined to include clinical laboratory services as well as the following: physical-therapy services; occupation-therapy services, radiology, including magnetic resonance imaging, computerized axial tomography scans, and ultrasound services; radiation-therapy services and supplies; durable medical equipment and supplies; parenteral and enteral nutrients, equipment, and supplies; prosthetics, orthotics, and prosthetic devices; home health services and supplies; outpatient prescription drugs; and inpatient and outpatient hospital services.

As described below, the Stark laws contain several exceptions. The statutory exceptions include physician services, in-office ancillary services, ownership in publicly traded securities and mutual funds, rental of office space and equipment, bona fide employment relationships, and the like.

The Stark laws penalties include denial of payments for the designated health services provided; refund of any monies received by physicians and facilities for amounts collected; payment of civil penalties of up to $15,000 for each healthcare service that a person "knows or should know" was provided in violation of the Stark laws, and three times the amount of improper payment the healthcare entity received from the Medicare program; exclusion from the Medicare program and/or state healthcare programs including Medicaid; and payment of civil penalties for attempting to circumvent the Stark laws of up to $100,000 for each circumvention scheme.

The Medicare anti-kickback laws prohibit both the giving and the receipt of anything of value to induce the referral of medical business reimbursed under the Medicare or Medicaid programs. Unlike the Stark laws (summarized below), the Medicare anti-kickback law is an "intent-based" statute. In addition, the Medicare anti-kickback law statutes make it clear that the healthcare entity payments for any property or services should be based on a fair market value price (and should not be priced based on a variable formula, such as a patient volume or patient referrals formula).

The Stark II statute became effective on Jan. 1, 1995. Like the Stark I statute (which became effective on Jan. 1, 1992), the Stark II law was intended to curb abuses inherent in physician self-referral arrangements. Like Stark I, the Stark II statute prohibits physicians who have a financial relationship with a healthcare entity (whether tax-exempt or taxable) from referring patients to the entity for "designated health services" covered by either Medicare or Medicaid programs.

A financial relationship consists of: (1) an ownership or investment interest in the healthcare entity; or (2) a compensation arrangement with the healthcare entity. If the physician: (1) does not own any portion of the healthcare entity; and (2) does not pay the healthcare entity or receive any kind of payment from the entity for the referral or for anything else, then there is no financial relationship. Under the various Stark laws, a financial relationship can exist between a physician and a healthcare entity even if that relationship does not involve designated health services or the Medicare or Medicaid programs.

For example, a compensation arrangement is defined in the Stark II statute as any arrangement involving any remuneration between (1) a physician (or family member) and (2) a healthcare entity. This remuneration can involve payments for anything, such as payments for rent, payments for nonmedical services, or payments for housing or travel expenses. Accordingly, the Stark statutes would interpret the purchase of a physician's practice by a hospital (and the related payment to the selling physicians) as a financial arrangement.

Section 18779(e)(6) of the Stark II regulations provides that an isolated transaction, such as a one-time sale of property (such as a professional practice), is not considered to be a compensation arrangement for purposes of the prohibition on patient referrals. This statement is true if the following conditions are met:

- The amount of remuneration for the one-time transaction sale is consistent with fair market value and is not determined, directly or indirectly, in a manner that takes into account the volume or the value of physician patient referrals;
- The remuneration is provided under an agreement that would be commercially reasonable even if no patient referrals are made to the acquirer healthcare entity; and

- The arrangements meet any other requirements the Secretary (of Health and Human Services) may impose by regulation as needed to protect against Medicare program or patient abuse.

It is noteworthy that the term "isolated transaction" is defined as a transaction involving a single payment between two or more persons. A transaction that involves long-term or installment payments is not considered to be an isolated transaction.

To comply with the various Stark laws, a healthcare entity's property or practice purchase transaction (1) should be priced at fair market value and (2) should be structured with a purchase price that is not paid in patient referral-related installments.

To comply with the various Stark laws related to the payment for services, the healthcare entity services transaction should be structured as follows:

1. There should be a written agreement signed by parties that specified the services to be covered under the arrangement;
2. The term of the agreement should be specified;
3. The aggregate services contracted for should not exceed those that are reasonable and necessary for the legitimate business purpose of the subject arrangement;
4. The compensation to be paid by the healthcare entity over the term of the agreement should be:
    a. Defined in advance,
    b. Not in excess of fair market value, and
    c. Not determined in a manner that takes into account patient volume or the value of any patient referrals or other business generated by the parties.

The Phase III final rule of the Stark II law became effective on Dec. 4, 2007 (except for certain "stand in the shoes" provisions described below, which became effective on Dec. 4, 2008). And the Centers for Medicare & Medicaid Services (CMS) self-referral disclosure protocol rules (described below) were published on Sept. 23, 2010.

The Phase III final rules are sometimes referred to as the Stark III regulations. These Stark III regulations (and particularly the transaction—and valuation-related—provisions) are summarized below:

1. *The "stand in the shoes" provision.* A physician's relationship with an entity providing designated health services (such as a hospital) through a direct single intervening physician organization (such as a group practice) may no longer take advantage of

the favorable provisions of the Stark laws' indirect compensation exception. Under Stark III, a physician is considered to "stand in the shoes" of his or her physician organization. Therefore, the relationship between the physician organization itself and the entity providing designated health services must meet a Stark law exception.

In making this rule change, the Stark III regulations tighten the indirect compensation exception. The indirect compensation exception is still available for compensation relationships where there is more than one entity between: (a) the provider of designated health services; and (b) the physician. But this is only the case as long as the physician is paid in a manner that does not reflect the volume or value of patient referrals to the healthcare entity providing the designated health services.

2. *Shared space.* To the extent that a physician or practice relies on the Stark Law "in office" ancillary services exception to provide designated health services to patients (such as imaging or clinical lab services), such services: (a) must truly be provided in office; or (b) must be leased on a block-time basis, rather than a per-click basis.

3. *Independent contractors.* A group practice that obtains the services of an independent contractor physician (such as a pathologist or radiologist) in connection with the provision of designated health services must contract with that physician directly. Contracting with the physician's practice or with a staffing service will not allow the group practice to bill for the independent contractor's services as a "physician in the group practice."

4. *Recruited physicians.* A group practice that accepts economic assistance for the recruitment of a physician: (a) must abide by certain new accounting rules that are tightened; and (b) must abide by certain restrictions that have been loosened as to noncompetition items.

5. *Academic medical centers.* The Stark III regulations make some clarifications to the academic medical center exception. The academic medical center exception as a whole provides greater latitude as to specific compensation payments as long as the aggregate compensation paid is at fair market value. Some of the clarifications include: (a) the requirement to aggregate physician faculty member compensation relationships to determine fair market value; and (b) the method for counting faculty member physicians.

6. *Productivity bonuses.* The Stark III regulations permit payment of a productivity bonus to a physician for income directly derived from designated health service referrals that are "incident to" the physician's performance of services. This expansion is of limited practical effect because: (a) this benefit is limited to productivity bonuses but not profit sharing; and (b) referrals truly "incident to" the physician's referrals are generally few.

7. *Fair market value.* The Stark laws fair market value exception is expanded to include arrangements whereby a physician makes payments to an entity providing designated health services (such as a payment for health services), and not just to situations where an entity makes payments to a physician (such as a medical director agreement).

8. *Amendments.* The Stark III regulations clarify that amendments to agreements implicated by the Stark laws are acceptable as long as the economic elements of the agreement (such as the rate of physician compensation or the square footage of a lease) remain materially unchanged by the amendment.

9. *Holdovers.* The Stark III regulations specifically allow for month-to-month holdover payments after the expiration of a rental agreement or a personal services arrangement (such as an agreement with a pathologist or radiologist): (a) for up to six months; and (b) as long as the terms and conditions of the expired agreement do not change during the holdover period.

10. *Other issues.* The Stark III regulations provide additional clarifications and minor revisions that provide some practical guidance regarding nonmonetary compensation, compliance training, and professional courtesy.

The Stark laws Phase II created a "safe harbor" in the definition of fair market value for hourly payments to physicians for their personal services. Although acknowledging that several methods of measuring fair market value exist, pursuant to this provision, the CMS would automatically consider the following compensation measurement methods to result in fair market value: (1) an hourly payment less than or equal to the average hourly rate for emergency room physician services in the relevant physician market; and (2) the 50th percentile national compensation level based on one of several specified compensation data surveys.

In response to healthcare industry comments, the CMS made two statements regarding the fair market value hourly rate compensation.

First, while a fair market value rate may be used to compensate a physician for both clinical and administrative work, the CMS stated that there may be a distinction between the rate paid to a physician for administrative work and the rate paid to a physician for clinical work.

Second, the CMS stated that a fair market value hourly rate could be used to determine an annual salary, provided that the hourly multiplier used to calculate such salary accurately reflected the number of hours a physician actually worked.

Prior to the issuance of the Stark III regulations, the fair market value exception protected arrangements whereby an entity providing designated health services paid compensation to a physician, family member of a physician, or group of physicians for the provisions of items or services if the arrangement met five specific requirements.

The Stark III regulations expand the fair market value exception to also include compensation made from a physician to an entity providing designated health services. Under the Stark III regulations, the fair market value exception covers payment made from the entity to a physician, as well as from the physician to a healthcare provider entity, provided:

1. The arrangement is set out in a writing signed by the parties describing the items or services;
2. The writing sets out a time frame for the arrangement;
3. The writing specifies the compensation, which must be set in advance, consistent with fair market value, and not determined in a manner that takes into account the volume or value of the physician's referrals;
4. The arrangement is commercially reasonable and furthers the legitimate business purpose of the parties; and
5. The arrangement does not: (a) violate the anti-kickback statute; or (b) involve the promotion of any business arrangement that violates state or federal law.

In addition, the Stark III regulations clarify that the fair market value exception does not apply to the leases of office space but that such arrangements must fit the stricter lease of office space exception.

On Aug. 19, 2008, the CMS finalized the Stark IV regulations. The Stark IV regulations became effective on two different dates: Some provisions became effective on Oct. 1, 2008, and other provisions became effective on Oct. 1, 2009.

Prior to the Stark IV regulations, the CMS proposed to revise the Stark space and equipment lease exceptions to prohibit per-use or per-click charges under a lease with: (1) the healthcare provider entity as the lessee; and (2) the physician as the lessor. In the Stark IV regulations, the space, equipment, fair market value, and indirect compensation exceptions prohibit rental charges that use a formula that is based on:

1. A percentage of the revenue attributable to the services performed or generated in the office space or with the equipment; or
2. Per unit of service, to the extent the charges reflect services provided to a patient referred between the parties.

That Stark IV regulations revision became effective on Oct. 1, 2009.

As mentioned above, the Stark III regulations had included a "stand in the shoes" provision under which referring physicians are treated as "standing in the shoes" of their physician organizations for purposes of applying the rules for direct and indirect compensation arrangements. A "physician organization" was defined as a physician, a physician practice, or a group practice.

In the more recent Stark IV regulations, the "stand in the shoes" provisions were revised to clarify when a physician must, and when a physician may, "stand in the shoes" of his or her physician organization. Physicians who have an ownership or investment interest in a physician organization must be treated as standing in the shoes of that physician organization. In contrast, a physician with a titular ownership interest is not required to stand in the shoes of his or her physician organization, although such a physician is permitted to do so.

The CMS defined a "titular" ownership or investment interest as an interest that does not include the ability or right to receive financial benefits or ownership or investment, including distribution or profits, dividends, proceeds of sale, or similar returns on investment. The Stark IV regulations "stand in the shoes" revisions were effective on Oct. 1, 2008.

5.0 Tax-Exempt Entity Definitions

This section summarizes the definitions of certain terminology in the Internal Revenue Code and the Treasury Regulations. This terminology is associated with the valuation of property and/or services transfer transactions involving a tax-exempt healthcare entity.

5.1 Tax-Exempt Organization

First, a not-for-profit entity is not the same as a tax-exempt entity; and, a tax-exempt entity is not the same as a charitable institution. As described below, there are several types of tax-exempt entities:

- Section 501(c)(4)—civic leagues and social welfare organizations;
- Section 501(c)(5)—labor, agricultural, and horticultural organizations;
- Section 501(c)(6)—business leagues; and
- Section 501(c)(7)—social and recreational clubs.

This discussion focuses on the regulations with regard to a property transfer and/or a services transfer involving Section 501(c)(3) "charitable organizations." The requirements to be a Section 501(c)(3) organization include:

- The organization is organized and operated exclusively for tax-exempt purposes;
- The net earnings of the organization do not inure to the benefit of individuals;
- The organization is without substantial lobbying activity;
- The organization is without any political activity; and
- Examples of Section 501(c)(3) organizations include schools, churches, and hospitals.

Again, this discussion focuses on Section 501(c)(3) public charity healthcare organizations.

There are numerous advantages of the Section 501(c)(3) statutes, including:

- Exemption from most federal and state income taxes;
- Exemption from most state sales taxes;
- Exemption from certain payroll taxes;
- State and local property tax benefits;
- Preferred U.S. postal service mailing rates;
- Charitable contribution deductions allowed for its donors; and
- Eligibility for tax-exempt bond financing.

To maintain its Section 501(c)(3) status, the healthcare entity is required to operate "exclusively" for exempt purposes. However, the term "exclusively" does not actually mean exclusively. As explained below, the term "exclusively" is actually defined in the Internal Revenue Code as "primarily."

The private benefit standards do not relate to "the net earnings of the organization" mentioned above. Rather, the Treasury Regulations consider the private benefit standards based on that portion of Section 501(c)(3) that requires an organization to be "operated exclusively" for exempt purposes. However, the term "operated exclusively" has two meanings. Both meanings are contained in Regulation 1.501(c)(3)-1(c)(1):

> (c) Operational test. (1) Primary Activities. An organization will be regarded as "operated exclusively" for one or more exempt purposes only if it engages primarily in activities which accomplish one or more of such exempt purposes specified in section 501(c)(3). An organization will not be so regarded if more than an insubstantial part of its activities is not in furtherance of an exempt purpose.

The "primary activities" portion of the regulation helps to harmonize the regulation with the unrelated business income tax provisions set forth in Regulation 1.501(c)(3)-1(e)(1). This provision allows an exempt organization to engage in unrelated trade or business activity as long as engaging in such trade or business is not the organization's primary purpose.

5.2 Disqualified Person

This term (which is also used in the private foundation tax statutes) refers to the person or persons who have a close relationship with a tax-exempt entity.

5.3 Excess Benefit Transaction

This is the type of property transfer or services transfer transaction that is at the heart of the intermediate sanctions rules. It is an impermissible transaction between (1) a tax-exempt entity and (2) a disqualified person.

5.4 Excess Benefit

An excess benefit is the impermissible aspect of a tax-exempt entity transaction that constitutes an excess benefit transaction. It is the amount that is used to compute one or more of the intermediate sanctions excise tax penalties.

5.5 Revenue-Sharing Transaction

This is a transaction between a tax-exempt entity and a disqualified person, where the benefit flowing to the disqualified person is based, in whole or in part, on the revenue flow of the tax-exempt entity.

5.6 Initial Contract Exception

This is one broad exception to the concept of the excess benefit transaction. Based on the initial contract exception, the transaction created by the initial relationship between the tax-exempt entity and the disqualified person is exempted from the intermediate sanctions excise tax penalties.

5.7 Initial Tax

This is the tax that is initially levied on an excess benefit amount. This tax is also referred to as a first-tier tax.

5.8 Additional Tax

This is the tax that can be imposed on an excess benefit amount, if the initial tax is not timely paid.

5.9 Correction

A correction is the process that is required to undo an excess benefit transaction and return the parties to the economic position they were in before the excess benefit transaction was entered into.

6.0 Tax-Exempt Organization Transactions—Private Inurement and Excess Benefits

Tax-exempt entities are exempt from federal income tax as organizations described in Section 501(c)(3) only if they are organized and operated exclusively for charitable purposes within the meaning of the statute. However, such tax-exempt entities are subject to certain restrictions with regard to acquisition, professional services, employee compensation, and other types of transactions.

The IRS and many state attorneys general view tax-exempt entities as charitable trusts for the benefit of the public. The regulatory scheme of Section 501(c)(3) is designed to:

1. Ensure the furtherance of public purposes; and

2. Prevent the diversion of charitable assets into private hands.

6.1 Private Inurement

The first type of restriction relates to private inurement. For Section 501(c)(3) tax-exempt entities, no part of the net earnings may inure to other benefit of any private shareholder or individual. This means that an individual can't receive the tax-exempt entity's funds, except as reasonable payment for goods or services. There is no minimum threshold related to the private inurement restriction, and there is no de minimis exception.

The private inurement restriction applies only to "private shareholders or individuals," commonly referred to as "insiders" (i.e., those having a personal and private interest in or opportunity to influence the activities of the entity from the inside). It is noteworthy that the term "insider" does not appear in either the Internal Revenue Code or the Treasury Regulations. However, it is widely used in the related legal, accounting, and valuation literature.

The intermediate sanctions provisions of Section 4958 were added to the Internal Revenue Code in 1996 and (as discussed below) used the terms "excess benefits transaction" and "disqualified person." The legislative history of Section 4958 states that "[t]he Committee intends that physicians will be considered disqualified persons only if they are in a position to exercise substantial influence over the affairs of an organization." The tax-exempt entity's payment of excessive or greater-than-reasonable compensation to an insider, such as a tax-exempt healthcare entity's officer or director, is a prime example of prohibited private inurement.

6.2 Private Benefit

The second type of restriction relates to private benefit. Section 501(c)(3) tax-exempt entities should be organized and operated to serve public rather than private interests. Unlike the private inurement transaction restrictions, the private benefit transaction restrictions are not absolute. To be a permissible transaction, a private benefit transaction should be incidental to (or a necessary concomitant of) accomplishment of the public benefits involved. Private benefit should be balanced against the public benefit. And, the Treasury (through the IRS) has issued regulations that provide examples illustrating the test for serving a public rather than a private interest.

The private benefit prohibition is not limited to insiders. For example, some incidental private benefit is always present in hospital-physician relationships (e.g., when a private practice physician uses a tax-exempt hospital facilities to treat his or her paying patients).

Any private inurement or too much (i.e., other than incidental) private benefit could cause a tax-exempt hospital to lose its tax exemption. Until 1995, the revocation of the organization's tax exemption was the only sanction available to the IRS. However, with regard to both private inurement and excess private benefit, the IRS currently relies principally on the imposition of Section 4958 intermediate sanctions excise tax penalties.

6.3 Excess Benefit

Section 4958, enacted as part of the 1996 Taxpayer Bill of Rights, allows the IRS to impose penalty excise taxes on certain excess benefits transactions between "disqualified persons" and tax-exempt entities described in Section 501(c)(3) or 501(c)(4).

Excess benefit transactions include:

1. A transaction priced at other than fair market value in which a disqualified person: (a) pays less than fair market value to the tax-exempt entity; or (b) charges the tax-exempt entity more than fair market value for a property or service;

2. An unreasonable compensation transaction, in which a disqualified person receives greater than a fair market value level of compensation from the tax-exempt entity; and

3. A prohibited revenue-sharing transaction, in which a disqualified person receives payment based on the revenue of the tax-exempt entity in an arrangement specified in the Section 4958 regulations that violates the inurement prohibition under current law.

6.3.1 Disqualified Persons

Section 4958 defines certain individuals to be "disqualified persons" with respect to a tax-exempt entity, including:

1. Voting members of the tax-exempt entity's governing board;

2. Individuals who have or share ultimate responsibility for implementing the decisions of the governing body or for supervising management, administration, or operation of the tax-exempt entity (such as president, chief executive officer, chief operating officer, treasurer, and chief financial officer unless demonstrated otherwise); and

3. Individuals with a material financial interest in a provider-sponsored organization.

The regulations related to Section 4958 clarify that this category of disqualified persons can include entities such as management companies.

Section 4958 identifies other parties as not being a disqualified person:

1. All organizations described in Section 501(c)(3) (although the Pension Protection Act of 2006 created an exception for supporting organizations);

2. With respect to Section 501(c)(4) organizations, other Section 501(c)(4) organizations; and

3. Full-time or part-time employees receiving total direct and indirect economic benefits in an amount less than the amount of compensation necessary to be highly compensated, as defined in Section 414(q)(1)(B)(i) (i.e., $100,000 in 2007), who are not substantial contributors within the meaning of Section 507(d)(2) (taking into account certain adjustments) or otherwise within the definition of "disqualified person."

In all other cases, the Section 4958 regulations indicate that a "disqualified person" is (1) any individual who was, at any time during the previous five years, in a position to exercise substantial influence over the affairs of the organization, (2) certain family members (lineal descendants, brothers and sisters, whether by whole or half-blood, and spouses of any of them), or (3) an entity 35% or more of which is controlled by such individuals.

The legislative history of Section 4958 recognizes that a nonemployee, such as a management company or the employee of a subsidiary (even a taxable subsidiary), could be in a position to exercise substantial influence. The Section 4958 regulations provide that, in the case of multiple entities affiliated by common control or governing documents, the determination of whether a person does or does not have substantial influence is made separately for each applicable tax-exempt entity.

The Pension Protection Act of 2006 added several classifications of disqualified persons. Any disqualified person with respect to a Section 509(a)(3) supporting organization is a disqualified person with respect to the supported organization. Any substantial contributor to a donor-advised fund is a disqualified person with respect to the donor-advised fund. Any investment advisor to an organization sponsoring a donor-advised fund is a disqualified person with respect to the sponsoring organization.

7.0 The Initial Contract Rule

The Section 4958 regulations establish an "initial contract rule" to protect from intermediate sanctions liability certain "fixed" payments for the provision of services or the sale of property made under a binding written contract. The initial contract only applies to persons who were not disqualified persons immediately before entering into the initial contract. Fixed payments are defined to include an amount of cash or other property that is either (1) specified in the contract or (2) determined using a fixed formula specified in the initial contract. And payments that include a variable component (such as achieving certain levels of revenue or business activity) may qualify as a fixed payment—as long as the components are calculated pursuant to a pre-established, objective formula.

8.0 Section 4958 Penalty Excise Taxes

Under Section 4958, a disqualified person is liable for (1) an initial 25% penalty excise tax on the amount of the excess benefit and (2) an additional penalty tax of 200% on the amount of the excess benefit if the transaction is not timely corrected. A tax-exempt entity manager who knowingly, willfully, and without reasonable cause participates in an excess benefit transaction is personally liable for a 10% penalty tax (up to a maximum of $20,000) on the amount of the excess benefit.

It is noteworthy that no Section 4958 penalties are assessed on the tax-exempt entity itself. Of course, a tax exemption revocation remains an option available to the IRS in extreme cases.

9.0 Intermediate Sanctions

The purpose of the intermediate sanctions provisions of the tax law is to prevent wrongdoing by persons who have a special relationship with tax-exempt entities, particularly charitable entities. Before the enactment of the intermediate sanctions laws, the IRS, when faced with an inappropriate transaction, essentially had two choices:

1. Apply the private inurement doctrine or the private benefit doctrine and revoke the tax-exempt status of the subject entity; and

2. Ignore the matter (and perhaps informally attempt to influence the behavior of the parties involved on a going-forward basis).

From the perspective of the IRS, these two options were not sufficient. Accordingly, the Treasury and the IRS urged Congress to enact the intermediate sanctions legislation.

Revocation of an entity's tax-exempt status is a particularly harsh consequence. Moreover, the loss of the subject entity's tax-exempt status does not necessarily resolve the underlying problem—the party that obtained the inappropriate benefit still has it. Often, the only individuals truly punished in these situations are the beneficiaries of the tax-exempt entity's programs.

Intermediate sanctions are penalties imposed on the person or persons who engage in the inappropriate transaction with the tax-exempt entity. These sanctions are called "intermediate" because they fall between (1) the revocation of tax-exempt status and (2) inaction on the part of the IRS. Also, the sanctions are not applied to the tax-exempt entity that was abused. Rather, they are imposed on the person or persons who improperly benefited from the subject property or services transfer transaction.

It is noteworthy that the intermediate sanctions law does not replace either (1) the private inurement doctrine or (2) the private benefit doctrine. Rather, the IRS has a range of taxpayer penalty options. The IRS can impose the sanctions alone. The IRS can impose both the sanctions and the private inurement doctrine, or the IRS can find the sanctions do not apply and nonetheless invoke the private benefit doctrine.

9.1 Intermediate Sanction Taxes

The intermediate sanctions are, in fact, federal excise taxes. These federal excise taxes are applied to the amount involved in the impermissible transaction—i.e., the excess benefit. The person who pays for intermediate sanctions tax (again, not the tax-exempt entity itself) is referred to as a disqualified person.

The first intermediate sanctions tax is an "initial tax." The initial tax is 25% of the amount of the excess benefit. Also, the excess benefit property or services transaction must be reversed. This reversal or refund of the excess benefit transaction is intended to put the parties in the same economic position they were in before the excess benefit transaction was entered into. This process is referred to as correction of the transaction.

If (1) the initial tax is not timely paid and (2) the offending transaction is not timely and properly corrected, then an "additional tax" may be imposed. This intermediate sanctions tax is 200% of the amount of the excess benefit. In some instances, the trustees, directors, or officers with the tax-exempt entity may also be required to pay a tax of 10% of the amount of the excess benefit.

Under certain circumstances, the intermediate sanctions tax may be abated. Generically, the Section 4958 intermediate sanctions excise taxes are referred to as "penalties."

9.2 Intermediate Sanctions and Applicable Tax-Exempt Organizations

The Section 4958 intermediate sanctions statute and the associated regulations apply with respect to public charities and tax-exempt social welfare organizations. These entities are called "applicable tax-exempt organizations" for this Section 4958 purpose.

Applicable tax-exempt organizations include any organization described in either of these two categories of tax-exempt entities at any time during the five-year period ending on the date of the property sale or services transfer transactions. Accordingly, public charities can be:

1. Churches, integrated auxiliaries of churches, and associations and conventions of churches;
2. Colleges, universities, and schools;
3. Hospitals, other providers of healthcare, and medical research organizations;
4. Foundations supportive of governmentally operated colleges and universities;
5. Units of government;
6. Publicly supported charitable, educational, religious, scientific, and similar organizations; and
7. Organizations that are supportive of other types of public charities.

Tax-exempt social welfare organizations include entities that are (1) civic in nature, (2) assist a community in various ways, and (3) engage in more advocacy (usually lobbying) than is allowed for charitable organizations. Therefore, an entity qualifies as an applicable tax-exempt organization if it operated as either type of tax-exempt entity at any time in the five-year period before the excess benefit transaction occurred. This five-year period rule is referred to as the "lookback rule," and this five-year period is referred to as the "lookback period."

Section 4958 provides for no exemptions from these rules (e.g., for small organizations or religious entities). That is, all domestic public charities and all social welfare organizations are applicable tax-exempt organizations. However, a foreign organization that is tax-exempt, by determination of the IRS or by treaty, as a charitable or social welfare entity is not an applicable tax-exempt organization if it receives substantially all of its support from sources outside the United States.

The Section 4958 definition of the term "applicable tax-exempt organization" encompasses the concept of recognition of the entity's tax-exempt status. Most categories of tax-exempt entities are tax exempt because they satisfy one or more federal tax law definitions of the term. However, to be recognized as tax exempt, some entities (1) must file notice with the IRS to that effect and (2) have their exempt status recognized by the IRS. This recognition is accomplished by using the IRS determination letter or private ruling.

For an organization to be a tax-exempt charitable organization, it typically files notice with, and has its tax-exempt status recognized by, the IRS. Some charitable organizations, such as churches and certain other religious organizations and small organizations, are exempt from this requirement of recognition. For a charitable organization to be recognized as an applicable tax-exempt organization, it should be in compliance with the recognition requirements.

To be tax exempt, social welfare organizations do not need to have their exempt status recognized by the IRS. An organization can qualify as an applicable tax-exempt organization by reason of being an exempt social welfare organization in these four ways:

1. The organization has applied for and received recognition from the IRS as an exempt social welfare organization;

2. The organization has filed an application for recognition with the IRS seeking exempt social welfare status;

3. The organization has filed an annual information return as an exempt social welfare organization; and

4. The organization has otherwise held itself out as an exempt social welfare organization.

A governmental unit or an affiliate of a governmental unit will not be recognized as an applicable tax-exempt organization if the governmental unit is (1) exempt from or not subject to taxation without regard to the general statutory basis for exemption or (2) relieved from the requirement of filing an annual information return. A governmental entity may be recognized as tax-exempt as an integral part of the state (1) by reason of the doctrine of intergovernmental immunity or (2) because its income is excluded from federal taxation.

An entity qualifies as a governmental unit if it is:

1. A state or local governmental unit as defined in the rules providing an exclusion from gross income for interest earned on bonds issued by these units;

2. Entitled to receive deductible charitable contributions as a unit of government; or

3. An Indian tribal government or a political subdivision of this type of government.

9.3 Intermediate Sanctions and Individual Executives and Professionals

Under the Section 4958 intermediate sanctions law, excise taxes are imposed on excess benefit transactions that occur on or after Sept. 14, 1995. The Section 4958 excise taxes do not apply to any transaction made pursuant to a written contract that was binding on Sept. 13, 1995, and continued in force through the time of the subject transaction.

An excess benefit transaction is any transaction in which a Section 501(c)(3) or 501(c)(4) organization provides an economic benefit to a disqualified person that has a greater value than what it receives from that person. An excess benefit transaction would include: (1) providing compensation to a person in excess of the value of the services rendered; or (2) selling or renting property to a person for less than the property's sale or rental value. The excess benefit is measured as the difference between: (1) the fair market value of the benefit provided to the person; and (2) the fair market value of the consideration received by the tax-exempt entity.

As summarized above, there are two types of Section 4958 excise taxes. The first type of excise tax is imposed on the disqualified person who receives an excess benefit. That tax is equal to 25% of the amount of the excess benefit if it is not corrected before (1) the date that the IRS deficiency notice is mailed for the 25% tax or (2) the date that the 25% tax is assessed, whichever comes first. The second type of excise tax is imposed on "organizational managers" who knowingly, willfully, and without reasonable cause or participate in the excess benefit transaction. This Section 4958 tax is equal to 10% of the amount of the excess benefit, but no more than $20,000.

A disqualified person is defined in Section 4958 as someone who, at any time during the five years preceding an excess benefit transaction, was in a position to exercise "substantial influence" over the affairs of the tax-exempt entity. If an individual is considered to be a disqualified person, then certain related parties are also considered disqualified persons. These related parties include spouses; brothers or sisters; spouses of brothers or sisters; direct ancestors; direct descendants and their spouses; and corporations, partnerships, and trusts in which the disqualified person has more than a 35% interest.

Certain individuals within tax-exempt entities are automatically identified as disqualified persons. These individuals include (1) any individual who serves as a voting member of the governing body of the tax-exempt entity; (2) any individual who has the power or responsibilities of the president, chief executive officer, or chief operating officer of the tax-exempt entity; and (3) any individual who has the power or responsibilities of treasurer or chief financial officer of the tax-exempt entity.

An employee of a tax-exempt entity is not considered a disqualified person if he or she (1) receives less than $100,000 of direct or indirect benefits from the tax-exempt entity for the year (adjusted for inflation), (2) is not a member of a specifically included category above, and (3) is not a substantial contributor of the entity.

The IRS looks at specified facts and circumstances to indicate whether a person has "substantial influence" over the subject tax-exempt entity. In particular, the IRS often considers the following factors in deciding whether an individual has "substantial influence" over the tax-exempt entity:

1. The person founded the tax-exempt entity;
2. The person is a substantial contributor;
3. The person's compensation is based on the revenue derived from the activities of the tax-exempt entity;
4. The person has authority to control or determine a significant portion of the entity's capital expenditures, operating budget, or compensation for employees; and
5. The person has managerial authority or serves as a key adviser to a person with managerial authority.

The following types of facts and circumstances would indicate to the IRS that a person does not have "substantial influence" over the tax-exempt entity:

1. The person has taken a bona fide vow of poverty;
2. The person is an independent contractor (e.g., an attorney) who would not benefit from a transaction aside from the receipt of professional fees; and
3. The person is a donor who receives no more preferential treatment than other donors making comparable contributions as part of a solicitation intended to attract a substantial number of contributions.

An individual can be liable for the 10% excise tax penalty on organization managers if he or she is an officer, director, or trustee of the tax-exempt entity or is a person with powers or responsibilities similar to those of officers, directors, or trustees. Attorneys, accountants, and investment advisers acting as independent contractors are typically not considered to be organizational managers. Any person who has authority merely to recommend particular administrative or policy decisions, but not to implement them without approval of a superior, is also excluded.

A tax-exempt entity's manager is considered to have "participated" in an excess benefit transaction not only by affirmative steps, but also by silence or inaction. That would be the case when the entity's manager does not exercise a duty to speak or take action. However, the tax-exempt entity manager will not be considered to have participated in a transaction when he or she opposed it in a manner consistent with that manager's responsibilities to the tax-exempt entity.

Tax-exempt entity managers can avoid the 10% penalty if they can show that they did not act willfully or knowingly. Tax-exempt entity managers can meet this requirement if, after disclosing all facts to an attorney, they receive a reasoned written legal opinion that a transaction does not provide an excess benefit. This procedure will protect the manager even if a transaction is later determined to be an excess benefit transaction.

Compensation to the entity's management for services rendered will not be considered an excess benefit if it is an amount that would ordinarily be paid for similar services in a similar situation. For purposes of this Section 4958 excise tax, compensation includes, but is not limited to, salary, fees, bonuses, severance payments, and all forms of deferred compensation that are earned and vested, whether paid under a tax-qualified plan or not. If deferred compensation is paid to a manager in one year for services performed by the manager in two years or more, then that compensation will be allocated to the years in which the services are performed.

Compensation also includes all benefits, whether included in incomes for federal tax purposes. For example, such benefits include medical, dental, life insurance, disability, and both taxable and nontaxable fringe benefits (other than job-related fringe benefits and fringe benefits of inconsequential value).

An economic benefit will not be treated as reasonable compensation unless the tax-exempt entity clearly indicates its intention to treat it as compensation at the time it is provided. For example, if the tax-exempt entity fails to include compensation or other payments to disqualified persons on a Form W-2 (for employees) or Form 1099 (for board members and other nonemployees) and does not treat the payments as compensation on its Form 990, then the payments will be considered an excess benefit.

A special rule applies to arrangements that compensate a disqualified person in proportion to the revenue generated by the tax-exempt entity. Such compensation may be considered an excess benefit even if it does not exceed the fair market value of the services provided. This result can occur if, at any point, the arrangement permits a person to receive additional compensation without providing proportional benefits to the tax-exempt entity.

Whether such compensation is an excess benefit depends on the facts of the individual case. The IRS considers such factors as: (1) the relationship between the size of the benefit provided and the quality and quantity of the services provided; and (2) the ability of the party receiving the compensation to control the activities that generate the revenue.

To avoid the above-mentioned 200% excise tax, the excess benefit must be undone to the extent possible. In addition, other procedures may be necessary to place the tax-exempt entity in the same position that it would have been in if the excess benefits transaction was made under the highest fiduciary standards. An excess benefit can be corrected if the disqualified person repays the tax-exempt entity an amount equal to the excess benefit plus an interest element for the period the excess benefit was outstanding. A correction may also be accomplished, in some situations, by (1) returning the transferred property to the tax-exempt entity and (2) making any additional procedures necessary to make the tax-exempt entity whole.

10.0 Excess Benefit Transaction Presumption of Reasonableness

There is an important "presumption of reasonableness" that every tax-exempt entity subject to the intermediate sanctions law may endeavor to take advantage of. That presumption is in favor of the tax-exempt entity that a compensation arrangement or property sale or rental is not an excess benefit. To qualify for this presumption of reasonableness, the tax-exempt entity must meet the following three requirements:

1. The compensation arrangement or property sale or rental must be approved by the tax-exempt entity's governing body or a committee of the governing body composed entirely of individuals who do not have a conflict of interest with respect to the subject transaction;

2. The governing body or its committee must have obtained and relied on "appropriate data" as to comparability prior to making its decision; and

3. The governing body or its committee must have "adequately documented" the basis for its decision at the time that it was made.

These three presumptions of reasonableness requirements are further described below.

11.0 Conflict of Interest

A member of a tax-exempt entity governing body or its committee will be treated as not having a conflict of interest if he or she:

1. Is not: (a) the disqualified person benefiting from the subject transaction; or (b) a person related to the disqualified person;

2. Is not an employee subject to the control or direction of the disqualified person;

3. Does not receive compensation or other payments subject to approval of the disqualified person;

4. Has no financial interest affected by the subject transactions; and

5. Will not receive any economic benefit from another transaction in which the disqualified person must grant approval.

12.0 Appropriate Data

The category of "appropriate data" includes such information and documents as (1) the compensation levels actually paid by similarly situated entities, both for-profit and tax-exempt, for similar positions; (2) independent compensation surveys compiled by independent consulting firms; (3) actual written offers from similar entities competing for the services of the disqualified person; and (4) independent appraisals of the fair market value of the to-be-transferred property.

There is a special "appropriate data" relief provision for tax-exempt entities with annual gross receipts of less than $1 million. Such a tax-exempt entity will be automatically treated as satisfying the appropriate data requirement if it has data on the level of compensation actually paid for similar services by five comparable entities in similar communities.

13.0 Adequate Documentation

To meet the "adequate documentation" requirement, the tax-exempt entity governing body or its committee must have written or electronic records showing (1) the terms of the transaction and the date it was approved, (2) the members of the tax-exempt entity governing body or committee who were present during debate on the transaction and the names of those who voted on it, (3) the comparability data obtained, and (4) what actions were taken about the members who had a conflict of interest.

For a decision to be documented concurrently, the records must be prepared by the next meeting of the governing body or committee occurring after the final action is taken. Also, the records must be reviewed and approved by the governing body or committee as reasonable, accurate, and complete within a reasonable time period thereafter.

For purposes of this presumption of reasonableness exclusion, a tax-exempt entity governing body is (1) a board of directors, (2) a board of trustees, or (3) an equivalent controlling body of the tax-exempt entity. A committee of the tax-exempt entity governing body (1) may be composed of any individuals permitted under state law to serve on such a committee and (2) may act on behalf of the governing body to the extent permitted by state law.

The tax-exempt entity should note that if a committee member is not on the governing board and the presumption of reasonableness is relied on, then the committee member comes an "organization manager" for purposes of the 10% excise tax penalty. In other words, the committee member is treated like a member of the tax-exempt entity governing body if the presumption of reasonableness relied upon is rebutted by the IRS.

Also, a person will not be treated as a member of the entity's governing body or its committee if he or she (1) meets with other members only to answer questions and (2) is not present during debate and voting on the transaction.

In addition, a tax-exempt entity subject to the intermediate sanctions law should note that this presumption of reasonableness is only a presumption. The IRS can rebut the presumption of reasonableness if there is information indicating that (1) the amount of the compensation was not reasonable or (2) the property transfer was not at a fair market value price. However, these three requirements should go a long way toward helping a tax-exempt healthcare entity avoid the Section 4958 intermediate sanctions penalties.

14.0 Analyst Considerations Regarding Private Inurement

This section presents a list of analyst considerations with regard to valuations performed for tax-exempt healthcare entities. These valuations include both (1) fair market value valuations of property (such as business equity interests or business operating assets) bought and sold by the healthcare entity and (2) fair market value valuations of the services paid for (or provided) by the healthcare entity (such as employee compensation or vendor fees or rents).

These analyst considerations may not affect the valuation approaches, methods, and procedures that the analyst selects and performs. And, these considerations may not affect the analyst's conclusions regarding the fair market value of the property or services transfer transactions. However, these analyst considerations relate to the intermediate sanctions law and regulations that the analyst should be aware of during the conduct of the tax-exempt healthcare entity valuation.

14.1 Tax-Exempt Healthcare Organizations

The Internal Revenue Code grants a tax exemption for not-for-profit hospitals and other healthcare organizations provided that their net earnings do not inure (1) to the benefit of private shareholders or (2) to individuals with a "personal and private" interest in the healthcare entity's activities.

14.1.1 Criteria to Be Recognized as a Tax-Exempt Organization

To meet the statutory criteria to be recognized as a tax-exempt healthcare entity, the entity must comply with the following rules:

- Physicians cannot be "in a position to exercise substantial influence over the affairs of (the hospital);
- The total compensation must be "reasonable" and the incentive arrangement may not be a disguised distribution of profits;
- The compensation arrangements must be negotiated or established in the context of an arm's-length relationship; and
- There is a ceiling or reasonable maximum compensation level.

14.2 No Inurement

No portion of a tax-exempt healthcare entity's income or assets may inure to the benefit of "insiders." For purposes of this consideration, the term "insiders" may be defined as someone with decision power (e.g., board members, officers, founders, selected physicians, and so on). Examples of such private inurement may include:

- Excessive employee or subcontractor compensation;
- Compensation based on the "net earnings" of the tax-exemption entity; and
- Any transfer of property or services at less than a fair market value price.

14.2.1 Penalty for Private Inurement

There are taxation-related penalties for any violation of this no-inurement rule. The IRS may apply a broad spectrum of remedies, including:

- Revocation of the subject healthcare entity's tax-exempt status;
- Settlement of the amount of the inurement; and
- The Section 4958 intermediate sanctions excise taxes.

15.0 Purpose of Intermediate Sanctions

The objective of the Section 4958 intermediate sanctions law is to curb potential abuses by penalizing participating parties (both those that benefit from the abuse and those that knowingly authorize it). The intermediate sanctions law applies if there is an "excess benefit" transaction with a "disqualified person."

An excess benefit transaction occurs when the economic benefit given in a transaction is greater than the consideration received by the healthcare tax-exempt entity. A disqualified person is any person having the ability to exercise influence over the affairs of the tax-exempt entity.

16.0 Imposition of Penalty Excise Taxes

Section 4958 imposes excise tax penalties on:

1. The disqualified person who has to correct the excess amount (i.e., pay it back to the tax-exemption healthcare entity) plus pay a penalty tax of 25%; and
2. The entity manager who has to pay a tax equal to 10% of the excess benefit amount (not to exceed $20,000 per transaction).

17.0 Rebuttal Presumption of Reasonableness

There is a rebuttable presumption of a reasonableness with regard to the tax-exempt healthcare entity entering into a property or services transfer transaction when:

1. The transaction is approved in advance by an independent, authorized body of the tax-exempt entity;
2. The decision was based on the appropriate comparability data; and
3. The decision is adequately and timely documented (i.e., written down by the later of the next meeting or 60 days).

18.0 Excess Benefit Transaction

An excess benefit transaction is any transaction in which an economic benefit is provided by the tax-exempt healthcare entity directly or indirectly to or for the use of any "disqualified person" if the fair market value of the benefit exceeds the fair market value of the consideration.

18.1 Disqualified Persons

For purposes of the Section 4958 intermediate sanctions rules, a "disqualified person" includes:

1. A voting member of a board of the tax-exempt healthcare entity;
2. The chief executive officer, chief operating officer, treasurer, or chief financial officer;
3. Any person, at any time during the previous five years, in a position to exercise substantial influence over the affairs of the healthcare entity;
4. Identified family members of the above; and
5. A 35% controlled entity.

18.2 Not Disqualified Person

For purposes of the Section 4958 intermediate sanctions rules, the following "persons" are not disqualified persons:

1. Entities described in Section 591(c)(3); this exception was created by the Pension Protection Act of 2006;
2. Other Section 501(c)(4) organizations (applicable for Section 501(c)(4) entities only); and
3. Employees receiving less than $100,000 a year in compensation.

19.0 Reasonableness of Tax-Exempt Entity Compensation

One of the current controversy areas related to the intermediate sanctions requirements relates to the reasonableness of employee or contractor compensation. This is particularly true with regard to tax-exempt healthcare entities. This reasonableness of compensation issue appears to be the current focus of IRS scrutiny with regard to tax-exempt healthcare entities. To alleviate concerns regarding intermediate sanctions, the tax-exempt healthcare entity should establish that its executive and physician employees are not paid more than a fair market value-level of compensation.

Related to this reasonableness of compensation issue, many tax-exempt healthcare entities benefit from reliance on a dedicated compensation committee. Such a board-level compensation committee would:

1. Adopt a written charter;
2. Be comprised of independent directors; and
3. Be authorized to approve the healthcare entity's executive compensation.

And such a board-level compensation committee would likely adopt a written compensation policy.

When considering the reasonableness of tax-exempt healthcare entity compensation, the IRS looks at how the entity determined and documented the comparability of its executive compensation to other similarly situated entities. In particular, the analyst can assist the tax-exempt healthcare entity with the following:

1. Compensation levels paid by similarly situated healthcare entities, both taxable and tax-exempt;
2. Independent compensation surveys compiled by independent consulting firms;
3. Actual written offers from similar healthcare entities; and
4. Independent valuations of the fair market value of the subject executive compensation.

The analyst can assemble compensation data and prepare a compensation fair market value valuation that considers the following:

1. Make sure that any compensation consultant relied on is independent and has no incentive to support higher pay and benefits;
2. Use data for the same or the closest functional position, and support these data in the board minutes; and
3. Use data for entities with a similar level of annual revenue, or show that the compensation data was "normalized" to fit entities of a similar size.

In the preparation of a compensation fair market value valuation (also called a reasonableness of compensation study), the analyst should note the following caveats:

1. For-profit entity compensation data are permitted, but the analyst should avoid relying exclusively on for-profit entity compensation data;
2. Include compensation data related to the value of any significant or unusual employee benefits; and
3. Make sure that every element is considered and the total compensation is assessed for reasonableness (and approved by an authorized body of the tax-exempt healthcare entity).

The approving body of the tax-exempt healthcare entity is protected in its reliance on the analyst's written reasoned analysis, if the analyst certified that he or she:

1. Holds themselves out to the public as a compensation consultant;
2. Performs this type of compensation valuation regularly; and
3. Is qualified to perform such a compensation valuation.

Such a written certification should be included in every type of compensation valuation performed by the analyst.

20.0 Revocation of Tax-Exempt Status

As indicated in the regulations related to Section 501(c)(3), the IRS still possesses its ultimate weapon with regard to the tax-exempt healthcare entity—i.e., the revocation of the entity's tax-exempt status. With regard to healthcare entities and other tax-exempt entities, the analyst should be aware that the IRS may seek revocation—in addition to the provision of the Section 4958 intermediate sanctions excise taxes.

The IRS has indicated that it will consider a list of facts and circumstances in determining when the level of excess benefit transactions will jeopardize a healthcare entity's tax exemption. These factors include, but are not limited to, the following:

1. The size and scope of the tax-exempt healthcare entity's regular and ongoing activities that further exempt purposes before and after the excess benefit transaction or transactions occurred;
2. The size and scope of the excess benefit transaction(s) (collectively, if there are more than one) in relation to the size and scope of the tax-exempt healthcare entity's regular and ongoing activities that further exempt purposes;
3. Whether the tax-exempt healthcare entity has been involved in repeated excess benefit transactions;
4. Whether the tax-exempt healthcare entity has implemented safeguards that are reasonably calculated to prevent future violations; and
5. Whether the excess benefit transaction has been corrected or the tax-exempt healthcare entity has made good-faith efforts to seek correction from the disqualified persons who benefited from it.

In other words, both the analyst and the tax-exempt healthcare entity board should be aware that the imposition of the Section 4958 excise taxes are the "intermediate" weapon of the IRS. Revocation of the tax-exempt entity's exemption status is still the ultimate weapon of the IRS.

21.0 Analyst Common Misconceptions Regarding Healthcare Property and Services Valuations

This section describes and responds to 10 analyst common misconceptions when performing valuations of healthcare entity property and/or services transfer transactions. These misconceptions are considered in this discussion because they generally relate to a misunderstanding of one or more of the relevant regulatory provisions. That is, these misconceptions typically relate to an erroneous understanding that "the IRS only accepts this" or "the Office of Inspector General doesn't accept that." Therefore, these analyst common misconceptions are addressed from the perspective of the regulatory compliance of the valuation analysis.

21.1 There Is a Preferred Valuation Approach or Method

Some analysts believe that certain healthcare transaction audit or regulatory authorities have a preferred valuation approach or method. This belief is simply not correct. None of the healthcare transfer statutes or regulations mandate a property or services valuation preferred approach. Any of the generally accepted property or services valuation approaches and methods may be used in a healthcare transaction analysis—as long as the analysis conclusion is fair market value.

21.2 There Is a Prohibited Valuation Approach or Method

Some analysts believe that there is a prohibition against using certain valuation approaches and methods. For example, some believe that the income approach, and particularly the discounted cash flow method, is inappropriate to healthcare property or services valuations. The basis for this erroneous belief is that such a methodology has to include the income from prohibited patient referrals. Of course, no healthcare entity can pay a transaction price that includes patient referrals. However, that statement does not invalidate the use of the income approach. The analyst simply has to be careful to exclude any income from post-transaction prohibited patient referrals in the income approach analysis.

Likewise, some analysts believe that an adjusted net asset value method is inappropriate if it incorporates some type of a capitalized excess earnings procedure. The basis for this erroneous belief is that no healthcare entity is allowed to earn excess earnings. In fact, there is no prohibition on using this valuation method. And there is no prohibition on any particular healthcare entity earning a high profit margin (as long as there is no fraud and abuse contributing to that income, of course). Let's assume that, for purposes of the subject valuation, excess earnings are defined as excess above the median profit margin level for that healthcare industry segment. Based on that excess earnings definition, half of all of the entities in the industry segment may earn excess earnings (i.e., half of the healthcare entities will earn income above the median level, and half of the healthcare entities will earn income below the median level).

21.3 All Healthcare Valuations Should Be Performed on a Before-Tax Basis

To adjust for the fact that some healthcare industry acquirers are tax-exempt and some healthcare industry acquirers are for-profit entities, some analysts ignore income taxes altogether—and perform all valuations on a pretax basis. Some analysts erroneously believe that this procedure prevents the tax-exempt entity from paying more than fair market value for a target healthcare entity. This objective is certainly appropriate. However, there is no regulatory requirement that all healthcare property (or services) valuations be performed on a pretax basis—or on an after-tax basis, for that matter.

Typically, if the property (or services) valuation variables are derived in a consistent basis, then the subject healthcare property (or services) should have one fair market value—whether the variables are measured on a pretax basis or an after-tax basis. That is, the valuation can be performed with all valuation variables (discount rates, capitalization rates, pricing multiples, income metrics) derived on a pretax basis, or the valuation can be performed with all valuation variables derived on an after-tax basis. The fair market value conclusion should be about the same. So there is no regulatory (or theoretical) preference—or prohibition—for performing healthcare property (or services) valuations on a pretax basis compared to an after-tax basis.

21.4 There Should Be No Goodwill Included in the Healthcare Valuation

Some analysts erroneously believe that audit and regulatory authorities do not allow the inclusion of either an individual practitioner's goodwill or an entity's institutional goodwill in a healthcare property transfer valuation. These analysts may conclude that any goodwill value includes the value of prohibited patient referrals or the value of excess (and suspicious) earnings.

However, there is no legislative or regulatory prohibition on the healthcare entity (tax-exempt or otherwise) paying for the goodwill of a target healthcare entity. And there is no prohibition on including the value of goodwill in the healthcare property valuation. Goodwill can be measured many different ways. But goodwill is basically the value of the healthcare entity's ongoing business operations in excess of the value of the entity's tangible assets. For a successful going-concern business operation, the analyst would expect the healthcare entity to have some amount of goodwill. Of course, the goodwill value should not include future prohibited transactions or expected post-acquisition synergies or economies of scale. But, if the target entity's historical results of operations indicate a positive goodwill value, then that goodwill value should be included in the healthcare property transfer valuation.

Typically, the goodwill value is included in the asset-based approach valuation analysis of the target entity value. And that goodwill value may be measured in either the asset accumulation method or the adjusted net asset value method of the asset-based approach to business enterprise valuation.

21.5 There Should Be No Patient Relationships Value Included in the Healthcare Valuation

Often the same analysts who exclude goodwill value will also exclude the value of any patient relationships-related intangible asset from the healthcare valuation. This procedure (or lack of performing a procedure) is particularly important when the analyst uses the asset-based business valuation approach (and, specifically, the asset accumulation method) to value the healthcare property transfer.

First, the statutory and regulatory prohibition relates to any healthcare provider (tax-exempt or otherwise) paying for patient referrals to the acquirer entity. Second, there is no prohibition of a healthcare acquirer paying for the current patient relationships of the target healthcare entity.

In virtually any industry or profession, a good part of the value of a target business relates to the income earned from the entity's current customer (in this case, patient) relationships. The value of these current patient relationships is often measured based on the expected future income from the current patients returning to the current healthcare services provider. That value does not (and should not) include the expected future income from the future referrals of current patients to the acquirer healthcare entity.

21.6 No Healthcare Entity Can Pay Reasonable Compensation Over $1 Million Per Individual

Some analysts erroneously believe that there is an arbitrary dollar amount (say, $1 million per year) of reasonable compensation above which healthcare regulatory authorities will not accept. These analysts may also erroneously believe that there are arbitrary "ceilings" on fair market value compensation for different professional positions—for example, a chief executive officer, chief medical officer, chief research officer, operating room director, emergency room director, etc. The fact is, there are no such arbitrary limits on the fair market value level of compensation—either in the relevant statutes or in the relevant regulations.

An analyst should consider numerous factors in assessing the fair market value of a healthcare entity executive or professional compensation. Likewise, an analyst should consider numerous factors in assessing the fair market value compensation-related contract terms for healthcare entity contractors. All of these factors are consistent with the overarching consideration with regard to the fair market value of either employee or contractor compensation: The compensation should be commensurate with the compensation levels paid to similarly qualified individuals performing similar functions at similar organizations.

21.7 The Analyst Should Not Use For-Profit Organizations as Comparables in a Fair Market Value Compensation Analysis

Some analysts believe that for-profit business entities do not provide meaningful guidance with regard to the fair market value compensation assessment of a tax-exempt entity employee or contractor. As mentioned above, the general regulatory guidance with regard to fair market value compensation is that the analyst should consider comparable individuals in comparable situations at comparable organizations.

First, with respect to providing empirical evidence regarding market-derived compensation levels, tax-exempt healthcare entities and for-profit healthcare entities are comparable in at least one important respect. Both types of healthcare entities are subject to the Medicare fraud and abuse statutes and regulations. Therefore, ignoring income tax status considerations, neither type of healthcare entity may seek reimbursement for employee or contractor compensation expense in excess of fair market value compensation levels.

Second, healthcare entities and many related industry entities are comparable in at least one other important respect. That is, they all compete for the same pool of executive and professional talent. Healthcare providers, insurance companies, pharmaceutical companies, research institutes, universities, and other organizations all are competing to recruit the same pool of executive, technical, and professional talent. In addition, when a healthcare entity employee or contractor decides to change jobs, he or she can interview with all of these related-industry entities.

The employers will recruit—and compensate—the most talented employees (even if that means recruiting an employee from a related industry). Likewise, the employees will interview with—and work for—the highest-paying employers (even if that means working for an employer in a related industry).

Therefore, in a fair market value compensation analysis, the analyst should consider the "big picture" with regard to compensation paid by competing employers and compensation received by competing employees. With regard to the supply and demand for executive, technical, and professional talent, comparable organizations can be: (1) either for-profit or not-for-profit; and (2) in related industries.

21.8 A Services Supplier Cannot Earn Excess Profits on a Fair Market Value Compensation Services Contract

Like the fair market value of employee and contractor compensation, the general rule for the fair market value of supplier contract price is that it should be supported by empirical market data. That is, the subject healthcare entity contract price should be comparable to prices paid by comparable entities for comparable contract services.

Like employees offering employment services, service providers are free to offer their services to both for-profit entities and tax-exempt entities. Likewise, service providers are free to offer their services to entities in related industries. Accordingly, for-profit entities and related industry entities may provide a source of empirical data for assessing the fair market value of market-derived contract services prices.

Further, there is no statutory or regulatory prohibition that an efficient services provider cannot earn a profit margin (even a high profit margin) providing services to a healthcare entity. Rather, the services providers must charge fair market value prices for the services they provide to the healthcare entity. Excess earnings methods and profit split methods may have certain applications in healthcare property valuation circumstances. However, neither of these methods is used to measure the fair market value price for professional, administrative, technical, or other contract services provided to a healthcare entity.

21.9 Analysts Should Only Consider Data From For-Profit Acquirers in Healthcare Property Valuations

Some analysts believe that they should only consider valuation variables extracted from empirical data with regard to for-profit buyer transactions. Such valuation variables may include discount rates, capitalization rates, pricing multiples, etc. These analysts erroneously believe that this procedure will prevent the subject healthcare entity (particularly a tax-exempt entity) from paying more than fair market value for property or services. Presumably, this belief is based on the erroneous premise that tax-exempt buyer transactions (related to property or services) include some amount of price premium associated with the buyer's tax-exempt status. In other words, this belief is based on the misconception that tax-exempt entities generally pay more than a fair market value price for purchased property or services.

It is possible that any buyer (healthcare or otherwise, tax-exempt or otherwise) could occasionally pay more than fair market value for property or services. Likewise, it is possible that any buyer could occasionally pay less than fair market value for property or services.

However, there is no empirical evidence to indicate that any class of buyer (and particularly healthcare buyers or tax-exempt buyers) consistently pay more than (or less than) fair market value for property or services. Therefore, there is no empirical or theoretical reason to exclude a tax-exempt healthcare property or services transfer from the analyst's data gathering or valuation analysis.

21.10 Paying a Fair Market Value Price Is the Same as Having a Commercially Reasonable Purpose

To comply with federal statutes and regulations, healthcare entities (and their legal counsel) often ask the analyst to opine both that a pending transfer: (1) is priced at fair market value; and (2) is commercially reasonable. Some analysts erroneously believe that proving one of these propositions (i.e., that the transfer is priced at fair market value) also provides the second of these propositions (i.e., that the property or services transfer is commercially reasonable has a valid business purpose). That analyst belief is a misconception.

A proposed property or services transfer could be priced at fair market value—and still there is no valid business purpose for the proposed transfer. In other words, that transfer would not be commercially reasonable. Likewise, there could be a perfectly valid business purpose for the healthcare entity to enter into the proposed property or services transfer—yet the transfer could be priced at above fair market value. In other words, that transfer could still be commercially reasonable (even though it was not priced at a fair market value price).

Each of these two opinions (i.e., fair market value price and commercially reasonable purpose) deserves its own individual consideration and analysis. And each of these two transfer transaction opinions can be reached by the analyst independently of the other opinion.

In summary, this discussion section considered 10 common analyst misconceptions with regard to healthcare transfer fair market value analyses. Each of the above-listed analyst beliefs is considered a misconception when it is compared to the professional guidance provided by the relevant statutory authority and regulations.

There are, of course, valid analyst beliefs with regard to healthcare entity fair market value valuations. First, in the valuation of any healthcare property transfer, the analyst should understand the subject transfer transaction. For example, the analyst should understand if a pending healthcare entity transaction will be the purchase of the entity assets or the purchase of the entity equity.

Second, in the healthcare property transfer valuation, the analyst should consider both the payment price and the payment terms. For example, the analyst should investigate if there is any seller financing. And the analyst should investigate whether the property purchase price will be paid in cash at the closing—or whether there will be a series of payments over a time period. If there are payment terms, then the analyst should assess whether those terms are at fair market value.

Third, the analyst should consider if there are several contracts being entered into as part of the healthcare property transfer. For example, the analyst should consider whether there are earn-out provisions to the healthcare property transfer transaction. And the analyst should consider whether there are employment agreements, noncompete agreements, intellectual property licensees, lease transfers, or other agreements that are part of the overall transaction. If so, the analyst should assess the fair market value of the total (multicontract) transaction.

Editor's note: This third consideration is perhaps the most important in all healthcare valuation, i.e., the transaction must be viewed in its entirety.

Fourth, the analyst should consider whether the healthcare transaction includes both a property transfer and a services transfer. And the analyst should consider the direction (i.e., from whom to whom) of both the property transfer component and the services transfer component. Both components of the healthcare transfer have to be at fair market value if the total transaction is considered to be a fair market value transaction.

Finally, this section considered both analyst misconceptions and analyst correct understandings with regard to the fair market value analysis of a healthcare entity property transfer or services transfer.

22.0 Summary and Conclusion

This discussion focused on the role of fair market value valuations with regard to the transfer of property and services when one transaction participant is a tax-exempt healthcare entity. Therefore, this discussion focused principally on tax-related transaction guidance. All healthcare services providers (tax-exempt or otherwise) have to comply with a variety of federal laws governing Medicare fraud and abuse. This discussion does not consider most of the business practices-related regulations that healthcare providers must comply with. However, with regard to the healthcare entity transfer of property or services, this discussion touched on the relevant provisions of the following statutes: the False Claims Act, the anti-kickback Statute, the Physician Self-Referral Law (the various Stark statutes and regulations), the Social Security Act, and the Internal Revenue Code.

In the consideration of healthcare entity transactions, the valuation analyst should be aware of the relationship of Internal Revenue Code Section 4958 with other federal tax laws[2] and with other federal and state healthcare profession regulations. Numerous federal laws are intended to achieve the same objective: prevent persons who have a close relationship with a tax-exempt healthcare entity from manipulating the flow of income or assets to them for their private benefit. These federal laws include the Stark legislation (including up to the Stark IV regulations), the Medicare fraud and abuse statutes (including but not limited to the False Claims Act and the anti-kickback Statute), and the tax-exempt organization provisions of the Internal Revenue Code.

Of course, this list of statutes does not include all of the laws and regulations that healthcare providers have to comply with. Rather, this list is deliberately limited to the regulatory environment with regard to the transfer of property and/or services between a for-profit entity and a tax-exempt healthcare entity. This is the transactional (and regulatory) environment that the analyst typically works in with regard to the preparation of property or services transfer fair market value valuations.

Nonetheless, even in this limited portion of the regulatory environment, the analyst's fair market value valuations of property and/or services transfers are often subject to a contrarian review by numerous agencies, including the IRS, the DHHS Office of Inspector General, the Department of Justice Criminal Division, the various state attorneys general, and other regulatory authorities.

All of the above-mentioned federal laws (and corresponding state laws)—and the regulatory authorities that enforce them—are directly influenced by these legal concepts:

1. The private inurement doctrine;
2. The private benefit doctrine; and
3. The self-dealing rules.

The analyst should be aware that the private inurement doctrine directly influences the Internal Revenue Code Section 4958 intermediate sanctions rules. In many ways, the Section 4958 rules are a codification of the private inurement legal doctrine. With regard to tax-exempt healthcare entities, the legal concepts of private inurement and excess benefit transactions are essentially the same. The same is true with respect to the legal concepts of the insider and the disqualified

2 *Editor's note: Notably, Section 162.*

person. In the case of the private inurement doctrine, the ultimate sanction is the IRS revocation of the entity's tax-exempt status. The IRS can apply the private inurement doctrine either (1) in lieu of the intermediate sanctions excise tax penalties or (2) in addition to the Section 4958 excise tax penalties.

The analyst should be aware that the private benefit doctrine is applicable only to charitable entities. That is, this legal doctrine is not applicable to other types of tax-exempt organizations, including social welfare organizations. The private inurement doctrine is applicable to both public charities and private foundations. In many ways, the legal concepts of private benefit and private inurement are very similar. That is, every transaction that is a private inurement is also a private benefit. The ultimate sanction, too, is the same: the IRS revocation of that entity's tax-exempt status.

The two principal differences between these legal doctrines are (1) a private benefit transaction does not require an insider and (2) the tax law recognizes the idea of incidental private benefit. Therefore, the private benefit doctrine can apply even where the private inurement doctrine and the Section 4958 intermediate sanctions tax penalties cannot apply.

The analyst should be aware that the rules concerning self-dealing and the Section 4958 intermediate sanctions rules do not overlap. This is because the legal rules concerning self-dealing apply to charitable organizations only with respect to private foundations. In contrast, the Section 4958 intermediate sanctions tax rules apply only with respect to public charities. Nonetheless, the self-dealing rules are still significant within the intermediate sanctions context. This is because the Section 4958 intermediate sanctions rules are patterned largely on the private foundation rules.

The analyst should be aware that most healthcare industry professional advisers consider the Section 4958 intermediate sanctions rule to be a good idea. The Section 4958 provisions place the sanction—i.e., the excise tax penalties—where it should be: on the persons who inappropriately extracted a benefit from charitable and social welfare organizations and not on the tax-exempt healthcare entity itself. The intermediate sanctions rules—based on a standard of reasonableness—are an improvement over the unnecessarily stringent private foundation rules. Those rules effectively prohibit transactions with foundations and any disqualified persons related to them.

The analyst who performs valuations of healthcare entity property or services transfer transactions should be aware of the various regulatory requirements with regard to such fair market value valuations. The analyst should be familiar with the regulatory environment with regard to private inurement, excess benefit transactions, intermediate sanctions excise tax penalties, and other tax-exempt entity regulatory issues. The analyst should be aware of these issues in order to provide property and services transfer valuations to tax-exempt healthcare entities that will address these regulatory concerns.

Chapter 7.
Patient Medical Records, HIPAA, and State Medical Records Law in Valuation and Litigation

CONTENTS

Chapter 7.
Patient Medical Records, HIPAA, and State Medical Records Law in Valuation and Litigation

By Mark O. Dietrich, CPA/ABV, MBA, MST

Editor's note: The author gratefully acknowledges the substantial contributions made by Lara B. Winn, Esq., to the regulatory descriptions and analyses that appear throughout this chapter.

1.0 Introduction

The Health Insurance Portability and Accountability Act of 1996, or HIPAA, is an every-engagement element of healthcare industry practice. This chapter is based upon the cited research along with the author's 38 years doing auditing, consulting, valuation, and litigation support in the healthcare industry. Appraisers and valuators are encouraged to consult with HIPAA-qualified legal counsel about establishing safeguards for information that is subject to HIPAA and especially about what business associate agreements (BAA) should and should not be signed. Due to the draconian penalties for violating HIPAA, some healthcare entities attempt to have BAAs signed that shift liability to, or eliminate defenses for, business associates. These latter two factors impact the liability for storage and retrieval the purchaser or transferee of PHI assumes.

In general, HIPAA will trump individual state law where it is contrary to HIPAA, unless an exception applies—for example, where state law relating to the privacy of individually identifiable information provides greater privacy protections or privacy rights with respect to such information.[1] Accordingly, it is important to be familiar with state laws when taking possession of any medical information or, more commonly, attempting to value patient charts. Relevant laws constrain the value of any asset—a cocaine dealership may have large profits but no fair

1 Other exceptions include the following: (i) state law providing for the reporting of disease or injury, child abuse birth, or death, or for public health surveillance, investigation, or intervention; and (ii) state law requiring certain health plan reporting, such as for management or financial audits.

market value for obvious reasons—and thus HIPAA and state law, which impose restrictions on charges for copies of medical records, often act to limit or eliminate any value to patients' medical records on a stand-alone basis. HIPAA and many states regulate not only the cost a patient can be charged for a copy of his or her medical record, but also the length of time a physician or hospital must maintain that record and the period of time for response to a request for a copy of a record.

2.0 The Health Insurance Portability and Accountability Act of 1996[2]

HIPAA is a far-reaching statutory framework that originated in 1996, when it was known as the Kennedy-Kassebaum Act, after the two U.S. senators who sponsored it. HIPAA contained important sections on fraud and abuse enforcement, income taxation (including expansion of the repatriation tax), and, notably, health insurance and limitations on pre-existing-condition exclusions and other antidiscrimination rules. Thus, it is integral to an understanding of the context of the Patient Protection and Affordable Care Act, P.L. 111-148 (PPACA), as well. As part of a comprehensive overhaul of electronic data storage and transmission requirements, the Health Information Technology for Economic and Clinical Health Act (the HITECH Act, adopted as part of the American Recovery and Reinvestment Act of 2009) significantly expanded the reach of HIPAA's privacy rules beyond "covered entities," which are defined as health plans, healthcare clearinghouses, and healthcare providers that electronically transmit health information. Regulations under the HITECH Act's revisions to HIPAA were published in January 2013, and certain requirements became effective in September 2013.

The notable changes the HITECH Act wrought include expansion of the patient protection provisions and, more importantly for appraisers, the expansion of the data security compliance requirements beyond healthcare providers and to their "business associates," such that business associates now are directly liable for compliance with HIPAA security requirements and certain HIPAA privacy requirements. Understanding HIPAA is thus more important than ever for appraisers with clients in the healthcare industry.

2.1 Key Terminology

HIPAA coined a number of defined terms that appraisers need to be familiar with to implement appropriate practices in their firms.

2.1.1 Protected Health Information (PHI)

PHI is *individually identifiable health information* that a covered entity maintains or transmits by electronic media or in any other form or medium. Individually identifiable health information is defined as information, including demographic data, that identifies the individual (or which could reasonably be used to identify the individual), relating to at least one of the following:

2 Portions of this chapter originally appeared in "How Health Care Data Security Rules May Affect You," Mark O. Dietrich, CPA/ABV, *Journal of Accountancy*, January 2015.

- The individual's past, present, or future physical or mental health or condition;
- The provision of healthcare to the individual; or
- The past, present, or future payment for the provision of healthcare to the individual.

Merely knowing of the provision of healthcare to an individual through an engagement—that is, a patient's name, in combination with the name of a healthcare provider—is considered PHI, and, for purposes of HIPAA, conversations about a patient constitute disclosures of PHI. HIPAA covers dentists, physical therapists, home health aides, and many social workers, in addition to physicians, hospitals, nursing facilities, imaging centers, and all forms of healthcare providers (to the extent that they transmit health information in electronic form in connection with a transaction covered by HIPAA).

The definition of PHI is quite expansive and could include the following identifiers of a patient (or of a patient's relatives, employers, or household members): name, address, e-mail address, fax number, telephone number, birth date, and other elements of dates (e.g., service date), biometric identifiers (e.g., finger and voice prints), photographic images/x-rays, Social Security number, Internet protocol address numbers, and Web Universal Resource Locators, vehicle/device identifiers and serial number, medical record number, health plan number, account number, certificate/license number, and any other unique identifying number, characteristic, or code.

2.1.2 Privacy Rule

The Privacy Rule applies to all PHI, while the Security Rule discussed in the next paragraph applies only to electronic PHI. "A major purpose of the Privacy Rule is to define and limit the circumstances in which an individual's protected heath information may be used or disclosed by covered entities. A covered entity may not use or disclose protected health information, except either: (1) as the Privacy Rule permits or requires; or (2) as the individual who is the subject of the information (or the individual's personal representative) authorizes in writing."[3] The Privacy Rule permits use and disclosure of PHI without an individual's authorization for the following 12 "national priority purposes":

1. Required by law;
2. Public health activities;
3. Victims of abuse, neglect, or domestic violence;
4. Health oversight activities;
5. Judicial and administrative proceedings;
6. Law enforcement purposes;

3 HHS Office for Civil Right, *Summary of the HIPAA Privacy Rule* and 45 C.F.R. § 164.502(a).

7. Decedents;
8. Cadaveric organ, eye, or tissue donation;
9. Research;
10. Serious threat to health or safety;
11. Essential government functions; and
12. Workers' compensation.

Note, however, that certain conditions must be met under HIPAA in order for the use or disclosure to be considered as one of these national priority purposes. Furthermore, note that some states impose additional requirements prior to certain disclosures relating to these national priority purposes.

In litigation practice, a court order or a patient's HIPAA-compliant authorization typically is required for disclosure of any PHI under many circumstances, but, outside the practice of healthcare law, many lawyers and judges seem unaware of this requirement.

2.1.3 Security Rule

The Security Rule is arguably the most important of HIPAA's provisions. Under the Security Rule, *electronic PHI* must be protected with reasonable administrative, technical, and physical safeguards to ensure its confidentiality, integrity, and availability and to prevent unauthorized or inappropriate access, use, or disclosure. The regulations contain five general requirements for conforming to the security rule, including: (1) administrative safeguards, including risk analysis and risk management; (2) physical safeguards; (3) technical safeguards; (4) organizational requirements; and (5) policies, procedures, and documentation requirements. The key thing for an appraiser to recognize here is that, in the event that a covered entity client discloses electronic PHI to you so that you can provide services to or on behalf of the client, you are a business associate of the covered entity client, and as such you are required to comply with the Security Rule.

The Security Rule does not expressly prohibit the use of e-mail for sending electronic PHI. However, a business associate[4] (see below) is required to implement policies and procedures to restrict access to, protect the integrity of, and guard against unauthorized access to electronic PHI. This may involve, for example, confirming that the sender's e-mail is *secure* and that *the recipient's e-mail is secure*, and, in some instances, may require encryption. Confirming that a recipient's e-mail address is, in fact, secure is beyond the capacity of most e-mail users.[5]

4 You are also a business associate of a covered entity client under the Privacy Rule if you receive PHI in paper format so that you can provide services to or on behalf of the client.

5 The Security Rule does not expressly prohibit the use of email for sending e-PHI. However, the standards for access control (45 CFR § 164.312(a)(1)), integrity (45 CFR § 164.312(c)(1)), and transmission security (45 CFR § 164.312(e)(1)) require covered entities to implement policies and procedures to restrict access to, protect

Encryption is not mandatory under HIPAA, but it is the best way to prevent data breaches and any communication of large amounts of PHI should always be encrypted whenever possible.

The Security Rule requires not only a plan for securing PHI, but also regular security evaluations and training of employees and consultants who will have access to PHI. Technically, the Security Rule does not apply to PHI on paper, unless it was previously in electronic format. As a practical matter, because the Privacy Rule applies to both electronic and paper PHI, appraisers will find it necessary to physically secure paper documents to prevent unauthorized or inappropriate access, use, and disclosure of PHI in violation of the HIPAA Privacy Rule and Security Rule.

2.1.4 Disclosure of PHI for Judicial and Administrative Proceedings

45 C.F.R. §164.512 deals with those circumstances in which disclosure of PHI can be made without authorization of, or an opportunity to agree or object by, the individual. The regulations distinguish between court and administrative tribunal orders and subpoenas or other discovery requests. PHI can be disclosed in response to a court order without a patient's authorization, but such disclosure must be limited to only that PHI the court order expressly authorized. This is particularly important with respect to highly confidential information (e.g., HIV/AIDS status) that is subject to extra protection in some states and therefore cannot be disclosed in response to a court order unless it specifically lists that type of highly confidential information.[6]

Pursuant to the HIPAA Privacy Rule, in the case of a subpoena, the entity receiving the request must receive satisfactory assurance in the form of a written notice from the party seeking the information that such party has made reasonable efforts to ensure that the individual whose PHI is sought has been given written notice of the request or receive satisfactory assurance that reasonable efforts have been made to secure a qualified protective order. In the alternative, the covered entity may disclose the requested PHI in response to the subpoena without receiving the satisfactory assurances described above if the covered entity makes reasonable efforts to notify the individual about the request in the manner described above or to seek a qualified protective order for the information from the court.

The written notice described above must: (1) contain sufficient information about the litigation or proceeding to permit the individual to raise an objection to the court or administrative tribunal; (2) specify that the time to raise objections has lapsed; and (3) state that the individual filed no objections or the court has resolved all objections filed and the disclosures being sought are consistent with such resolution. The qualified protective order described above must prohibit

the integrity of, and guard against unauthorized access to e-PHI. The standard for transmission security (§ 164.312(e)) also includes addressable specifications for integrity controls and encryption. This means that the covered entity must assess its use of open networks, identify the available and appropriate means to protect e-PHI as it is transmitted, select a solution, and document the decision. The Security Rule allows for e-PHI to be sent over an electronic open network as long as it is adequately protected.

6 For example, in Massachusetts, information about HIV/AIDS status should not be disclosed in response to a court order unless it expressly orders the disclosure of information about the individual's HIV/AIDS status.

the parties from using or disclosing the protected health information for any purpose other than the litigation or proceeding for which such information was requested and require the return to the covered entity or destruction of the protected health information (including all copies made) at the end of the litigation or proceeding.

Note that state law always should be reviewed before disclosing PHI in response to a subpoena as certain states impose requirements that are more restrictive than the HIPAA requirements described above and do not authorize disclosure in response to a subpoena, even if the covered entity has received satisfactory assurances.[7]

2.1.5 Minimum Necessary

The minimum necessary rule provides that, when protected health information is requested, used, or disclosed, the information must be limited to only that which is needed for the intended purpose. Of all the terms defined in the statute, minimum necessary is among the most important because you need a reason to have PHI as a condition precedent to receiving it. As suggested by the definition, it is incumbent upon the covered entity (client) not to provide an appraiser with PHI unless necessary, and it is incumbent upon the appraiser not to request PHI unless necessary, but many unnecessary disclosures occur.

2.2 Business Associate

Knowing when an appraiser becomes a business associate of a covered entity (or of a covered entity's existing business associate) is critical to understanding your HIPAA responsibilities. HIPAA defines a "business associate" as an individual (or entity) who, on behalf of a covered entity, creates, receives, maintains, or transmits PHI. Appraisers can come into contact with PHI in the conduct of a forensic investigation through testing of internal controls, while reviewing a healthcare provider's revenue cycle activities, or even in utilizing bookkeeping and accounting data. Something as simple as a client's patient refunds account in the general ledger can constitute PHI. To the extent that an appraiser needs such PHI to provide a service to or on behalf of the covered entity client, the appraiser becomes a business associate of the covered entity client and becomes subject to HIPAA privacy and/or security obligations.[8] Examples of

7 For example, under Massachusetts law, the HIPAA provision allowing disclosure in response to a subpoena applies only to hospitals and clinics and only if the patient is a named party in the caption and the information is not otherwise additionally privileged or protected under federal or state law. Otherwise, a court order or patient authorization is required. Furthermore, with respect to physicians and other licensed practitioners, Massachusetts law provides no statutory authority to release medical information in response to a subpoena alone, even with the satisfactory assurances described above. Accordingly, even if a physician or other healthcare practitioner receives the satisfactory assurances described above, he or she should not release information in response to a subpoena unless it is accompanied by a court order or the patient has executed a HIPAA-compliant authorization. In addition, as noted earlier, certain types of highly confidential information should not be disclosed unless expressly required.

8 If the appraiser's functions, activities, or services do not involve the use or disclosure of protected health information, and where any access to protected health information by the appraiser would be incidental, if at all, it may be possible to conclude that the appraiser is not a business associate of the covered entity client. This determination will depend on the specific facts and circumstances, including, but not limited to, the extent to which the appraiser's access to PHI is limited in nature.

other business associates (or business associate functions) of a covered entity client that an appraiser may encounter include:

- Claims processing;
- Data analysis;
- Medical consultants—e.g., in child custody/support proceeding;
- Billing;
- Legal (including litigation counsel);
- Actuarial—retirement plan data you might receive;
- Accounting firms;
- Consulting;
- E-discovery vendors;
- Copier technicians (if your copier has memory);
- Records subpoenas/duplication services;
- Shredding services—likely a problem-source area as well; and
- Storage vendors of paper PHI who are not subject to the standards of the Security Rule but are subject to the requirements of the Privacy Rule.

When an appraiser is the business associate of a covered entity, the appraiser and the covered entity must enter into a business associate agreement. The definition of business associate also applies to subcontractors of the business associate. Thus, if an appraiser utilizes the services of independent contractors who have access to PHI to provide a service to or on behalf of the covered entity client and/or its business associate, the appraiser must enter into a "downstream" business associate agreement (BAA) with that subcontractor (where the subcontractor is the "downstream" business associate) (the appraiser also must enter into a BAA with the covered entity). Similarly, if the appraiser firm becomes a business associate of a healthcare provider's existing business associate, the appraiser firm and the existing business associate will need to enter into a "downstream" BAA (where the appraiser is the "downstream" business associate).

2.2.1 Obligations of a Business Associate

HIPAA's privacy and security rules are at the heart of protecting PHI from unauthorized access, use, and disclosure. Business associates must limit the uses and disclosures of PHI to what is permitted under the Privacy Rule, subject to what is allowed under the business associate agreement. This includes complying with the minimum necessary standards, providing breach notification to the covered entity, and providing an accounting of certain disclosures. Business associates also must prepare and implement HIPAA security policies and procedures and complete risk assessments concerning electronic PHI.

2.2.2 Business Associate Agreement (BAA)

Appraisers who provide services to covered entities or other users of PHI are likely to encounter a need to sign a BAA; in fact, covered entities that share PHI with appraisers (including patient payment and demographic data) are required to obtain a BAA. Although the Department of Health and Human Services has a sample basic BAA on its website, in practice, BAAs vary considerably and can impose legal and indemnity obligations on an appraiser that are beyond the minimum requirements. Further, such obligations can implicate the coverage provisions of an appraiser's professional liability insurance and other forms of liability insurance coverage. Thus, a BAA should never be signed without a thorough review and understanding of its terms. Appraisers may wish to seek legal advice in this regard and consider having their own standard BAA prepared if their client base warrants it.

Most healthcare providers will have their own version of a BAA as part of their mandatory HIPAA compliance plan, but, as noted above, not all BAAs are alike. For example, the sample business associate agreement from the HHS website does not contain an indemnity provision. On the other hand, the sample agreement from the American Medical Association states in part:

> Contractor shall defend, indemnify and hold harmless the Physician Practice from and against any or all cost (including but not limited to any and all costs incurred by Covered Entity in complying with the breach notification requirements of 45 C.F.R. Part 164, Subpart D), loss, interest, damage, liability, claim, legal action or demand by third parties (including costs, expenses and reasonable attorney fees on account thereof) arising out of Contractor's activities under the Agreement.

It should be readily clear that signing this type of a document could seriously restrict the ability of an appraisal firm to defend itself and limit any liability.

Another common clause with variations on the writing is the disposition of any PHI after the termination of the engagement. The sample BAA from HHS provides the following optional language:

> Return to covered entity [or, if agreed to by covered entity, destroy] the protected health information retained by business associate when it is no longer needed by business associate for its proper management and administration or to carry out its legal responsibilities.

In a valuation or litigation engagement, the appraisal firm may have a policy of retaining all file documentation for a period of time; CPA firms may need to retain file documentation for professional standards compliance; many firms may need to retain PHI pursuant to their professional liability policies. By the same token, if the PHI is retained and not returned or destroyed, HIPAA's privacy, security, and other requirements will continue to apply to the firm.

Note: Lawyers should determine whether their obligations to protect data arise under the attorney-client privilege and/or a BAA pursuant to HIPAA.[9] For example, where the lawyer is representing a patient in a malpractice or personal injury case and has possession of his or her client's medical records, the lawyer must protect such information under the attorney-client privilege. If, however, the lawyer is representing the healthcare provider in a malpractice case, the lawyer is a business associate of the healthcare provider and is obligated to protect the patient's medical records under both the attorney-client privilege and the BAA the lawyer should have entered into with the healthcare provider pursuant to HIPAA.

2.3 The HIPAA Security Compliance Plan

HHS has an entire series of brochures in PDF format summarizing the various provisions of the HIPAA Security Rule.[10] These include:

1. Security 101 for Covered Entities;
2. Security Standards—Administrative Safeguards;
3. Security Standards—Physical Safeguards;
4. Security Standards—Technical Safeguards;
5. Security Standards—Organizational, Policies and Procedures and Documentation Requirements;
6. Basics of Risk Analysis and Risk Management; and
7. Security Standards: Implementation for the Small Provider.

Earlier, it was stated that the Security Rule only applies to electronic PHI but that other PHI is subject to privacy protection as well. Security 101 for Covered Entities describes the difference as follows:

> The Privacy Rule sets the standards for, among other things, who may have access to PHI, while the Security Rule sets the standards for ensuring that only those who should have access to EPHI will actually have access. With the passing of both the privacy and the electronic transactions and code set standards compliance deadlines, many covered entities are focusing on the security requirements. In developing the Security Rule, HHS chose to closely reflect the requirements of the final Privacy Rule. The Privacy Rule requires covered entities to have in place appropriate administrative, physical, and technical safeguards and to implement those safeguards reasonably. As a result, covered entities that

9 See, e.g., www.hhs.gov/ocr/privacy/hipaa/faq/business_associates/709.html describing lawyers as business associates and www.americanbar.org/publications/gp_solo/2011/september/navigating_hipaa_claims_litigation.html.

10 www.hhs.gov/ocr/privacy/hipaa/administrative/securityrule/securityruleguidance.html.

have implemented the Privacy Rule requirements in their organizations may find that they have already taken some of the measures necessary to comply with the Security Rule. The primary distinctions between the two rules follow:

> Electronic vs. oral and paper: It is important to note that the Privacy Rule applies to all forms of patients' protected health information, whether electronic, written, or oral. In contrast, the Security Rule covers only protected health information that is in electronic form. This includes EPHI that is created, received, maintained or transmitted. For example, EPHI may be transmitted over the Internet, stored on a computer, a CD, a disk, magnetic tape, or other related means. The Security Rule does not cover PHI that is transmitted or stored on paper or provided orally.
>
> "Safeguard" requirement in Privacy Rule: The Privacy Rule contains provisions at 45 CFR § 164.530(c) that currently require covered entities to adopt certain safeguards for PHI. While compliance with the Security Rule is not required until 2005 for most entities (2006 for small health plans), the actions covered entities took to implement the Privacy Rule may already address some Security requirements.

Item No. 7 above, Security Standards: Implementation for the Small Provider, is a particularly useful read for a firm considering receiving, storing, and/or transmitting PHI in electronic form. One strategy worth considering is viewing electronic PHI only in the client's office on the client's computers or equipment, thus minimizing the firm's obligations under the HIPAA Security Rule. HIPAA's standards for electronic security are well in excess of those that are the norm for nonhealthcare entities.

2.4 HIPAA's Restrictions on Charges for Copies of Medical Records

Under the HIPAA Privacy Rule, covered entities may impose only "reasonable, cost-based fees" for copies of medical records, which include supplies and labor for copying the record along with postage when applicable. It is important to note that no charge can be made for search and retrieval of the record or any other arguably incurred cost.[11] This legal requirement is a significant restriction on any cost-based valuation of patient records, which is described in more detail later in the chapter. Some states define what reasonable costs for obtaining a medical record are while some states or provider agreements with insurers also impose limitations on charges for copies of medical records based on continuity of care—the latter something appraisers using the cost approach generally overlook. The HIPAA Privacy Rule provides the following in 45 CFR 164.524(c)(4):

> (4) Fees. If the individual requests a copy of the protected health information or agrees to a summary or explanation of such information, the covered entity may impose a reasonable, cost-based fee, provided that the fee includes only the cost of:

11 45 CFR 164.524(c)(4).

i. Labor for copying the protected health information requested by the individual, whether in paper or electronic form;

ii. Supplies for creating the paper copy or electronic media if the individual requests that the electronic copy be provided on portable media;

iii. Postage, when the individual has requested the copy, or the summary or explanation, be mailed; and

iv. Preparing an explanation or summary of the protected health information, if agreed to by the individual as required by paragraph (c)(2)(ii) of this section.

It is important to note that covered entities also must comply with state law when setting copy fees and that such state laws may be more restrictive than the copy fees permitted by HIPAA.

2.5 Civil Penalties for Violating HIPAA

The HITECH Act provides four categories or tiers of violations that reflect increasing levels of culpability for the violation of HIPAA. The four corresponding tiers of penalty significantly increase the minimum penalty amount for each violation, and the maximum annual penalty is $1.5 million for all violations of an identical provision.

The four tiers of violations are: (1) the offender did not know (and by exercising reasonable diligence would not have known) that it violated the provision; (2) the violation was due to reasonable cause and not willful neglect; (3) the violation was due to willful neglect but was corrected within the required time period; and (4) the violation was due to willful neglect and was not corrected.

HIPAA Violation	Minimum Penalty	Maximum Penalty
Individual did not know (and by exercising reasonable diligence would not have known) that he or she violated HIPAA	$100 per violation, with an annual maximum of $25,000 for repeat violations (Note: maximum that can be imposed by State Attorneys General regardless of the type of violation)	$50,000 per violation, with an annual maximum of $1.5 million
HIPAA violation due to reasonable cause and not due to willful neglect	$1,000 per violation, with an annual maximum of $100,000 for repeat violations	$50,000 per violation, with an annual maximum of $1.5 million
HIPAA violation due to willful neglect but violation is corrected within the required time period	$10,000 per violation, with an annual maximum of $250,000 for repeat violations	$50,000 per violation, with an annual maximum of $1.5 million
HIPAA violation is due to willful neglect and is not corrected	$50,000 per violation, with an annual maximum of $1.5 million	$50,000 per violation, with an annual maximum of $1.5 million

2.6 Criminal Penalties for Violating HIPAA

Covered entities and business associates that knowingly violate the HIPAA rules also may be subject to criminal penalties. Penalties range from a fine of not more than $50,000 and/or imprisonment for not more than one year. Moreover, if the offense is committed under false pretenses, the offender can be fined up to $100,000 and/or imprisoned for up to five years. More severe penalties exist if the offense is committed with the intent to sell, transfer, or use the health information for commercial advantage, personal gain, or malicious harm. In these cases, monetary penalties may be as high as $250,000 and/or imprisonment for as long as 10 years. Individuals such as directors, employees, or officers of the covered entity or business associate, where the covered entity or business associate is not an individual, also may be directly criminally liable under HIPAA in accordance with principles of "corporate criminal liability." Where such an individual is not directly liable under HIPAA, he or she still can be charged with conspiracy or aiding and abetting.

2.7 Engagement Letters

One colleague observed that HIPAA PHI is toxic, in the same manner as hazardous waste subject to the Environmental Protection Act: If you have it, you are responsible for it. Thus, appraisers should consider adding a provision to their engagement letter specifically dealing with the improper provision of PHI by a client and the related costs of unauthorized transmission. Here is sample language that might form the basis for such a provision. You should consult your own legal advisor, of course.

> Practice agrees not to provide me, directly or indirectly, any Protected Health Information ("PHI") without advance written notification including an explanation of the need to do so and a fully executed Business Associate Agreement which is acceptable to and has been signed by [Representative of Firm]. Any such data must be the minimum necessary for the purposes of this engagement. For this purpose, PHI and minimum necessary have the meaning set forth in the Health Insurance Portability and Accountability Act of 1996 ("HIPAA"), the American Recovery and Reinvestment Act of 2009 ("ARRA"), and their implementing regulations set forth at 45 C.F.R. Parts 160 and 164 (the "Privacy and Security Rules"). Additionally, if Practice provides me with PHI in violation of the Privacy and Security Rules, the Business Associate Agreement, and/or the terms specified above, then Practice agrees to indemnify and hold me harmless for any related damages or costs incurred by me or any other third party as a result of such unauthorized transmission.

2.8 Engagement Examples

2.8.1 PHI in Valuation

In valuation of healthcare provider entities, it is necessary to obtain reports from the revenue cycle system that show the units, charges, payments, and adjustments by service and by insurer, as well as an aged accounts receivable. It is not necessary, however, for any of the data to contain patient identifying information in the ordinary course.

When no PHI is necessary in the engagement, appraisers should carefully structure their data requests and be certain that the client understands that no PHI should be provided. If the appraiser needs direct access to the client's revenue cycle system containing PHI during the engagement, a BAA will be required, but the appraiser should consider whether maintaining any written or electronic patient identifying information in workpapers is necessary. Although the appraiser is responsible for maintaining the confidentiality of all PHI encountered in accordance with the HIPAA Privacy Rule, leaving all physical and electronic PHI in the client's office may result in the appraiser avoiding having to implement a costly physical and electronic security plan.

The key to being subject to HIPAA's privacy and security standards is that the expert must be a business associate of a covered entity or a downstream business associate of a business associate of a covered entity. If the information is not created or received by a healthcare provider, health plan, or healthcare clearinghouse, it is not protected under HIPAA and can be gathered under applicable discovery rules.[12]

Example: PHI in Shareholder Buyouts

A concierge medical practice retains a well-known expert to value the practice for purposes of a buyout of a retiring shareholder. The concierge practice offers primary care to wealthy and well-known individuals at an annual cost of $10,000. Pursuant to a data request from the expert, the practice provides a list of accounts receivable and patient encounter data. Both reports contain patient names, and the encounter data includes diagnosis and treatment information, even though de-identified data would have been sufficient for the engagement. The expert had signed a BAA at the request of the practice administrator, without recognizing the implications.

The data are provided on paper reports and arrive in the office of the expert. Pursuant to established practice, the office secretary opens the mail and scans all valuation material for storage in PDF format. While engaged in scanning, the secretary notices a number of "famous" individuals. After work, she goes out for drinks with a friend and discusses the medical issues of several of the "famous" patients. The friend later posts some of these issues to social media, citing "rumors."

This example highlights the import of staff training on HIPAA privacy. The employee's impermissible disclosure has caused the expert employer, as a business associate of a covered entity client, to violate HIPAA and its BAA. It also emphasizes that a BAA should not be signed if the expert can provide the services using only data that have been de-identified in accordance with the HIPAA Privacy Rule. In the fact pattern, the concierge practice may also have violated HIPAA by providing data that exceed the "minimum necessary" for the valuation service being provided to the covered entity.

12 Note, however, that the information still may be subject to state statutes and/or regulations that protect the privacy of certain information.

2.8.2 PHI in Litigation Support

The number of possible litigation engagements where PHI might be involved is perhaps limitless, but common examples include divorce matters and claims for damages by or against healthcare providers. Experts should realize that lawyers who specialize in marital dissolution matters or damages litigation may be completely unaware of HIPAA. Due to the broad reach of legal discovery, it may be relatively easy for legal counsel to obtain PHI, even when it is not necessary for the expert's engagement; opposing counsel may be unaware of HIPAA as well. HIPAA and state privacy requirements provide specific rules for the use of court orders and subpoenas to obtain PHI, but many judges are also unfamiliar with the rules. Many attorneys provide experts with a "data dump" so that the expert needs to sort through the material and determine what is relevant. Experts attending depositions or obtaining deposition transcripts will often see PHI. Clearly, where PHI is concerned, the expert should see only that data, if any, constituting the minimum necessary for the task. Thus, it is incumbent upon both attorney and expert to comply with the minimum necessary requirement throughout the engagement.

Forensic experts should be extremely cautious with any healthcare engagement. Searching for unreported income is more than likely to require access to significant levels of PHI, requiring a BAA and implementation of a security plan to protect electronic PHI, training, and ongoing evaluation of compliance with the privacy and security rules—or a court order to obtain access to same if the expert is not a business associate of the covered entity.

It is advisable for the expert to discuss the expectation of PHI at the outset of the engagement and before any data changes hands to be certain that the expert receives no PHI unless absolutely necessary and that the necessary HIPAA privacy and security compliance plan(s), as applicable, is in place before the expert receives the PHI.

Example: PHI in Marital Dissolution

As noted above, to be subject to HIPAA, an expert must be a business associate of a covered entity or a downstream business associate of a business associate of a covered entity; the expert must be involved in providing services to the covered entity—as opposed to providing services to the marital litigant/physician or the estranged spouse of a physician-owner of a covered entity. In a marital dissolution proceeding, it is unlikely that opposing counsel representing the nonphysician spouse will be a business associate or that the opposing expert will be a downstream business associate, unless they are providing services to a covered entity. If they are not a business associate or downstream business associate of a covered entity, they will not be subject to HIPAA's privacy and security rules. However, in the event that either party from the covered entity—here the practice of the physician—seeks PHI, the practice can only provide the data pursuant to federal and state law, generally with patient authorization unless another exception to HIPAA is satisfied.

> Where the covered entity is not a party to the proceeding, the covered entity may disclose protected health information for the litigation in response to a court order,

subpoena, discovery request, or other lawful process, provided the applicable requirements of 45 CFR 164.512(e) (GPO) for disclosures for judicial and administrative proceedings are met.[13]

Individual states may also have rules on the disclosure of PHI that are stricter than the federal requirements. In this case, *the state law takes precedence* over HIPAA.[14]

2.8.3 PHI in the Appraiser's Office

HIPAA imposes obligations on a firm beyond those that seem readily apparent. For example, modern photocopiers and fax machines utilize computer hard drives. If a photocopier maintenance person has access to a hard drive that has been used to copy PHI for inclusion in workpapers, the firm is likely required to obtain a downstream BAA from the maintenance person. Of course, selling or trading in a photocopier with a hard drive requires removal of all PHI in accordance with HIPAA's Security Rule, which means that any PHI is unrecoverable using modern forensic data reconstruction techniques.[15]

Another example arises when document shredding companies are hired to destroy workpapers that are outside the firm's retention period. If these workpapers contain PHI, the firm is likely required to obtain a downstream BAA from the shredding company.

Example: Document Destruction

A valuation firm hires a shredding company to destroy workpapers that are beyond the firm's and state law retention policy/rules, some of which contain PHI, including general ledger refund accounts of mental health providers. On a windy day, the shredding company employee heaves a box into the back of his truck and a couple papers fly away. He is behind schedule and figures no one will know anyway if he does not chase after them. These papers contain PHI that is subsequently found on the street. The finder returns it to the individual whose PHI is in the papers.

In this case, the valuation firm may be liable for disclosure of PHI even though the error occurred as a result of an action by the shredding company. The valuation firm should consider having one of its own employees physically supervise each phase of the document destruction to be certain there is no break in security. The valuation firm also should consider adding an indemnification clause to the downstream BAA between it and the shredding company, such that the shredding company will be required to reimburse the valuation firm for any damages

13 www.hhs.gov/ocr/privacy/hipaa/faq/judicial_and_administrative_proceedings/704.html.

14 For example, in Massachusetts, a physician practice may disclose the requested information only pursuant to the patient's authorization or a court order.

15 Note that CMS guidance provides the following: "When covered entities dispose of any electronic media that contains EPHI they should make sure it is unusable and/or inaccessible." HIPAA Security Series 3, Security Standards: Physical Safeguards (revised 3.2007) at www.hhs.gov/ocr/privacy/hipaa/administrative/securityrule/physsafeguards.pdf (viewed July 21, 2015).

or other costs relating to impermissible uses and disclosures of PHI by the shredding company and its employees.[16]

2.9 State Laws on Maintenance and Disposition of Medical Records

States regulate several fundamental issues for patient medical records. These include the period of time such records must be retained, the time period in which a healthcare provider must respond to a patient's request for a copy of his or her record, the cost the patient may incur for that copy, and rights of action for violations of state requirements. Curiously, HIPAA does not provide a federal right of action to a patient, though a patient can file a complaint against a healthcare provider with the Office for Civil Rights. Within those areas governed by state law, the states impose a range of requirements, all of which are subject to pre-emption by HIPAA if they are contrary to HIPAA (unless the state law is more protective than HIPAA or another exception applies).

2.9.1 Time Period for Medical Record Retention

HealthIT.gov maintains a file of record retention rules by state.[17] Generally speaking, there are different retention periods for different types of healthcare providers (e.g., physicians and hospitals) and different periods depending on whether the patient is an adult or child, with a child's record required to be retained for a certain number of years following discharge/last date of contact or until the child reaches a certain age, whichever period is longer. For example, Alaska requires a hospital to maintain a record for seven years following "discharge of the patient" or until age 21 for a patient under the age of 19, whichever is longer.[18]

As previously noted, some states impose different retention periods for physicians and hospitals. Connecticut requires physicians to maintain the record for seven years from the last date of treatment or, upon the death of the patient, for three years, whereas hospitals must maintain the record for a minimum of 10 years after the patient has been discharged.[19] In Florida, it is a period of at least five years from the last patient contact for physicians and seven years after the last record entry for hospitals.[20]

Many states, including Alaska, Arkansas, California, Colorado, Idaho, Illinois, Kentucky, Maine, Minnesota, Mississippi, Montana, Nebraska, North Carolina, North Dakota, Ohio, Oklahoma, Oregon, Utah, Vermont, Washington, West Virginia, and Wyoming, do not have *specific* retention

16 www.beckershospitalreview.com/healthcare-information-technology/confetti-used-for-us-women-s-soccer-victory-parade-found-to-be-shredded-medical-records.html.

17 www.healthit.gov/sites/default/files/appa7-1.pdf, from Privacy and Security Solutions for Interoperable Health Information Exchange: Report on State Medical Record Access Laws (August 2009), viewed June 21, 2015—an invaluable resource, however, individual state laws should be checked for changes since 2009.

18 Alaska Stat. § 18.20.085(a).

19 Conn. Agencies Regs. § 19a-14-42 and Conn. Agencies Regs. §§ 19-13-D3(d)(6).

20 Fla. Admin. Code Ann. 64B8-10.002(3) and State of Florida General Records Schedule GS4 for Public Hospitals, Health Care Facilities and Medical Providers (Effective: Feb. 19, 2015), viewed July 8, 2015 at dos.myflorida.com/media/693585/gs04.pdf.

periods for physicians in their statutes.[21] In some of these states, state medical boards or state medical societies may set the standard or provide guidance. General statute of limitations provisions may also impact the holding period and should be considered by all healthcare providers, even those licensed in a state that sets a minimum retention period by statute.

2.9.2 Time Period for Response to Request for Medical Record

George Washington University's Hirsh Health Law and Policy Program and the Robert Wood Johnson Foundation maintain a site called Health Information and the Law.[22] HIPAA provides a 30-day period for a response to a patient's request for a copy of a medical record.[23] If an existing state law provides for a longer period, HIPAA will trump that and mandate a period that is no more than 30 days.

Based on the Health Information and the Law website referenced above, the following states have response time laws that are pre-empted by HIPAA: North and South Dakota, Minnesota, Wisconsin, Iowa, Missouri, Arkansas, Oklahoma, Mississippi, Alabama, Florida, South Carolina, West Virginia, Pennsylvania, Delaware, Maine, New Hampshire, Massachusetts, Arizona, New Mexico, and Alaska.

Also based on the Health Information and the Law website referenced above, the following states have response time laws that are more favorable to patients than HIPAA (and therefore are not pre-empted by HIPAA): Hawaii ("upon request" to patient and within 10 days from the authorization to provide a copy to the patient's attorney), Washington state (15 days generally), California (15 days for copy, five working days for inspection), Nevada (examination within five working days and copies upon request), Wyoming (10 days for hospitals, 30 for physicians), Colorado (10 days for hospitals, 30 for physicians), Texas (15 days generally), Nebraska (10 days to examine, 30 days for copy), Louisiana (15 days in general), Tennessee (10 working days for practitioners, without unreasonable delay for hospitals), Virginia (15 days generally), Maryland (21 days), and New York (10 days to inspect, reasonable time for copy). (Response days are summarized in parenthesis, but additional factors may apply.)

The balance of the states impose requirements that are the same as HIPAA's 30-day requirement or do not impose any time-specific requirement, which again leaves providers subject to HIPAA's 30-day requirement.

21 www.healthit.gov/sites/default/files/appa7-1.pdf, from Privacy and Security Solutions for Interoperable Health Information Exchange: Report on State Medical Record Access Laws (August 2009); an invaluable resource; individual state laws should be checked for changes since 2009.

22 www.healthinfolaw.org/comparative-analysis/individual-access-medical-records-50-state-comparison The site was last updated in 2013, so individual state laws should be checked for changes.

23 Note, however, that if the covered entity is unable to provide a copy of the medical record no later than 30 days after receipt of the request, the covered entity may extend the time by no more than 30 days, provided that the covered entity, within the initial 30-day period, provides the individual with a written statement of the reasons for the delay and the date by which the covered entity will complete its action on the request and provided further that the covered entity may have only one such extension of time for action on the request. 45 C.F.R. §164.524(b).

A record request can be denied in limited circumstances.[24]

2.9.3 Cost to Obtain Copy of Medical Record

There are several sources[25] for obtaining this information, which is critical to any attempt to value medical records. There is a separate question as to whether those medical records have any stand-alone value in excess of the cost of/liability for storage and retrieval, which must offset the calculation of medical record/chart value. Many times, appraisers will value records on the basis of the cost to reproduce in terms of photocopy labor and supplies, a standard not dissimilar to the HIPAA Privacy Rule. However, individual states can interpret what labor and supply costs are reasonable.

Another nuance of this cost issue that was earlier pointed out as commonly ignored by appraisers is the impact of continuity of care rules based on state law or provider agreements with payors. For example, in Arizona, a healthcare provider or contractor shall not charge for the pertinent information contained in medical records provided to: (1) another healthcare provider for the purpose of providing continuing care to the patient; (2) the patient the medical record pertains to for the demonstrated purpose of obtaining health care; or (3) the healthcare decision-maker for a patient for the demonstrated purpose of obtaining healthcare for that patient.[26]

Another important element of medical record requests is the requirement under the HITECH Act that patients may receive their records in electronic format, if the provider has electronic records. The covered entity may impose a reasonable, cost-based fee for an electronic copy, including labor for copying the PHI requested, supplies for creating the electronic media, and postage when the individual has requested the copy be mailed.

2.10 Review of Valuation Issues

The asset value of patient charts or medical records involves two basic issues: allocating a portion of any intangible value derived from a method under the income approach and valuing the charts directly as a stand-alone asset using the cost approach. The directly related issue of measuring the liability assumed when taking possession of charts is described separately.

As previously described, one typical application of the cost approach to paper record value under either scenario is the cost of labor and supplies associated with photocopying, something that is consistent with HIPAA. However, given the HITECH Act's requirement that a patient be able to obtain a copy of his or her record electronically if an EHR is in place, this approach may be different for electronic health records where the cost is likely different. The difference between the cost of electronic copies and paper copies should be built into any valuation model. Of course, given the requirement to adopt electronic health records to avoid Medicare and other

24 www.hhs.gov/ocr/privacy/hipaa/understanding/special/healthit/eaccess.pdf.

25 medicopy.net/who-we-are/blog/guide-of-state-statutes-for-copies-of-medical-records, www.lamblawoffice.com/medical-records-copying-charges.html.

26 A.R.S. §12-2295.

payor penalties, paper medical records will soon be functionally obsolete and that obsolescence would have to be computed under accepted use of the cost approach.

Another question that needs to be asked is how state law impacts the value of medical records, i.e., all things equal, does a record's value differ from state to state based upon the limitations on charges in that state for records? The answer will depend in part on whether the state limitations are consistent with the HIPAA Privacy Rule.

More important, perhaps, is the threshold question of whether the chart has any value if the provider agreement with a payor requires a chart to be provided free of charge to another provider for continuity of care purposes or if state law has the same provision.

2.10.1 Storage and Retrieval Costs

HIPAA and the HITECH Act have, or should have, a dramatic impact on the stand-alone value of medical charts or records. As previously described, no charge can be made for search and retrieval of the record or any other arguably incurred cost.[27] For a prospective purchaser of a medical practice still using paper charts, storing those paper charts securely in accordance with HIPAA's Privacy Rule and providing access to patients within the period mandated by state law and HIPAA can be expensive indeed.

The oft-cited IRS 1996 Exempt Organization CPE text *Valuation of Medical Practices* by Charles F. Kaiser and Amy Henchey contains insights that are still useful today:

> The cost method is commonly used to value medical records, based on the concept that the value of each medical record incorporates the cost of creating and maintaining it. For a large practice, cost is calculated based on annual medical records department expenditures for creating/maintaining records, minus the portion of those departmental expenditures for withdrawal of records, divided by the number of records created/maintained in that year. (For smaller practices a similar methodology, using the salary of records retention personnel or a portion thereof, is used.) Applying this approach typically results in a new per record value ranging from $12-$20. Rough validation of the per record value can, where appropriate, be secured by comparing the amount determined under the cost method to what it would cost to secure copies of the records at rates imposed by state and federal social service agencies, insurance companies, and law firms.
>
> Medical records diminish in value once a patient is no longer a regular patron of the practice. Thus, a reasonable allowance for depreciation is made when valuing medical records under the cost approach. Two bases sometimes used to establish a depreciation period (useful life) are the average term of residence in the community where the practice is located and the legally required retention period for medical records. Thus, if a seven-year depreciation

27 45 CFR 164.524(c)(4).

> period is used, one-year-old records lose 14% of their cost value while six-year-old records lose 86% of their cost value.

The discussion above with respect to the useful lives of medical records is of special importance as it reinforces the earlier discussion herein that inactive charts have no value, only a liability associated with storage and retrieval.

Example: Urgent Care Practice

A family practice physician operates an urgent care center for 30 years using paper medical records. As he nears retirement, he has accumulated more than 40,000 medical records, the older of which are stored in boxes in the attic of his office building. Many of the patients seen were children, and relevant state law requires that a child's records be maintained until three years after the patient reaches age 18. Thus, a prospective buyer faces a storage and retrieval obligation that could last 21 years for a newborn—and has no idea how many records in the attic may be for children.

In attempting to sell this otherwise profitable practice, the physician is unable to obtain a buyer because of the state of the medical records.

Example: Internal Medicine Practice

A Missouri hospital is considering the purchase of an IM practice with 1,800 active patients, in this case those seen within the last three years, and a total of 5,000 charts. Post-transaction compensation for the selling physician is such that the practice will not generate a profit and may generate a loss. The terms of the transaction require the hospital system to assume responsibility for all 5,000 charts. The hospital identifies an appraiser who is willing to opine on the stand-alone value of the paper charts based on state law. Missouri law provides as follows:

> Effective February 1, 2015, the maximum fees for paper copies of medical records is $23.94 plus 55¢ per page for the cost of labor and supplies for copies provided in paper form. An additional $22.41 may be charged if records are maintained offsite. If copies are provided electronically, the maximum fee is $23.94 plus 55¢ per page or $104.91 total, whichever is less. Mo. Rev. Stat. Section 191.227.

Reiterating the HIPAA Privacy Rule limitations described above, as set forth in 45 CFR 164.524(c)(4):

> (4) Fees. If the individual requests a copy of the protected health information or agrees to a summary or explanation of such information, the covered entity may impose a reasonable, cost-based fee, provided that the fee includes only the cost of:
>
> i. Labor for copying the protected health information requested by the individual, whether in paper or electronic form;

ii. Supplies for creating the paper copy or electronic media if the individual requests that the electronic copy be provided on portable media;

iii. Postage, when the individual has requested the copy, or the summary or explanation, be mailed; and

iv. Preparing an explanation or summary of the protected health information, if agreed to by the individual as required by paragraph (c)(2)(ii) of this section.

Earlier herein, it was stated that HIPAA pre-empts Missouri law in part. Here, the $23.94 (apparently a handling fee) and $22.41 (a retrieval fee for off-site records) charges appear to be inconsistent with HIPAA's prohibition on a search and retrieval fee. The 55¢ per page would be allowed if it is a reasonable, cost-based fee. Assume there are 20 pages per active record, resulting in 36,000 pages and an *asset* value of $19,800.

It is incorrect for the analysis to stop here. Missouri law (Mo. Rev. Stat. § 334.097(2) (2008)) requires that physicians maintain records for seven years from the date the last professional service was provided; the rule for hospitals is longer. Ignoring for the moment the 1,800 active charts, what is the assumed liability of storage and retrieval of the 3,200 inactive charts? Notwithstanding the HIPAA pre-emption,[28] and assuming Missouri law has some factual basis as to the cost of storage, it would be $23.94 per record if stored on-site and an additional $22.41 if stored off-site. Three thousand two hundred records at $23.94 is $73,408, nearly four times the alleged recoverable value of the active charts of $19,800, resulting in a net liability for the hospital system. In point of fact, an appraiser would want to obtain estimates of storage and retrieval fees from companies engaged in this line of business along with the aforementioned continuity of care rules. Nonetheless, it seems reasonably certain that the liability associated with the inactive charts would exceed the value of the active charts.[29]

2.10.2 Electronic Health Records (EHR)

Earlier, HIPAA's requirement that patients are entitled to an electronic copy of their medical record if an EHR (or EMR, for electronic medical record) system is in place was described. One of the complexities that arise in the valuation of EHR is the vast number of such software programs that are on the market. The value of EHR, if any, is likely highest to a buyer who is on the same software program as the seller. Where fair market value is the standard—*any* willing buyer/seller—there is a substantive question as to the value since the hypothetical buyer and seller cannot necessarily be presumed to have the same software program.

Where the buyer is not using the same software as the seller, the buyer will have to purchase software licenses and train staff in how to use it. This is a cost/liability assumed in connection with the purchase that needs to be measured as part of any valuation. Fair market value

28 Again, the $23.94 (apparently a handling fee) and $22.41 (a retrieval fee for off-site records) charges appear to be inconsistent with HIPAA's prohibition on a search and retrieval fee.

29 See, e.g., www.hhs.gov/news/press/2014pres/06/20140623a.html.

is transaction-specific; it is the value of a specific transaction with a bundle of assets and liabilities to a hypothetical buyer and seller—not a hypothetical transaction's value. In addition, measuring liabilities assumed in connection with the purchase of assets seems necessary for commercial reasonableness purposes.

Appraisers should also consider the life expectancy of an EHR system. There is an ongoing consolidation[30] in the EHR industry with the number of vendors declining, resulting in significant costs to convert existing records to a new system, including training for providers and staff and the resultant loss of income from decreased productivity.

2.10.3 Value Under the Income Approach

Generally speaking, finance and valuation would derive the value of an asset by discounting to present value the cash flow that asset generates at an appropriate discount rate. In the case of medical records, it is generally deemed impractical to allocate income from a going concern's aggregate intangible assets to medical records. Among the many reasons for the impracticality is that generating income from the medical record usually requires a provider to deliver a medical service.

An appraiser may gain some insight into the difference in payment for an established patient versus a new patient. CMS defines a "new patient" for billing evaluation and management services "to mean a patient who has not received any professional services, i.e., evaluation and management service or other face-to-face service (e.g., surgical procedure) from the physician or physician group practice (same physician specialty) within the previous three years."[31] This suggests that, if a different practice than the selling physician buys the medical records, it will be eligible to bill for a new patient visit rather than an established patient visit, even though it has the benefit of the patient's medical history in the purchased record. For example, a Level 3 new patient visit CPT® 99203 has a 2015 national RVU value of 3.05, 50% more than the 2.04 RVUs for a Level 3 established patient visit CPT® 99213. The description[32] of a 99203 visit can be found on the CMS website as can the description[33] of 99213. Although not controlling for billing purposes, the description indicates that in a 99203 visit "typically, 30 minutes are spent face-to-face with the patient and/or family" and in a 99213 visit "typically, 15 minutes are spent face-to-face with the patient and/or family."

One area where medical records may have a unique value beyond their use in the provision of medical care is as part of a database where individually identifiable health information has

30 See, e.g., www.healthtechzone.com/topics/healthcare/articles/2014/10/16/391527-whats-next-ehr-market-consolidation.htm, www.cio.com/article/2378865/healthcare/why-the-ehr-market-is-poised-for-disruption.html, and www.bostonglobe.com/business/2015/05/31/partners-launches-billion-electronic-health-records-system/oo4nJJW2rQyfWUWQlvydkK/story.html#.

31 questions.cms.gov/faq.php?id=5005&faqId=1969.

32 www.cms.gov/medicare-coverage-database/staticpages/cpt-hcpcs-code-range.aspx?DocType=LCD&DocID=32007&Group=1&RangeStart=99201&RangeEnd=99205.

33 www.cms.gov/medicare-coverage-database/staticpages/cpt-hcpcs-code-range.aspx?DocType=LCD&DocID=32007&Group=1&RangeStart=99211&RangeEnd=99215.

been de-identified. There is a growing demand by researchers, pharmaceutical companies, and medical device developers among others for data on the success of various treatment regimens. This creates a circumstance where the transaction-specific character of fair market value is critical: the value of a specific transaction to a hypothetical buyer and seller. Medical record data in this circumstance will likely have considerably more value than in the provider-use context.

3.0 Conclusion

The legal and contractual rights associated with any asset govern the value of that asset. As is the case with many assets, such as FCC licenses, franchise agreements, trademarks, copyrights, certificates of need, noncompete agreements, and, in the instant case, medical records, the appraiser must take into account the law and any contract of transfer. HIPAA and individual state laws play an unavoidable role in determining medical record asset value and the related liability assumed via the cost of maintaining those records. In generic business transactions, the hypothetical *and* actual buyer do not ignore the liabilities attached to the assets of a business they are acquiring—e.g., warranty costs of the seller's products previously sold—and there is no rational basis for ignoring those liabilities in healthcare transactions.

The author gratefully acknowledges the review of this chapter and contributions of examples by Ken Miller, CPA, CIA, CRMA, CHC, CISA. Miller is a senior manager in healthcare at Horne LLP in Ridgeland, Miss.

Chapter 8.
By the Numbers: A Case-Based Understanding of Healthcare Valuation Fraud

CONTENTS

Chapter 8.
By the Numbers: A Case-Based Understanding of Healthcare Valuation Fraud

By Mark O. Dietrich, CPA/ABV

Author's note: This chapter analyzes allegations and related issues and expert testimony that involve matters of finance and valuation as they affect the determination of fair market value. It is not intended to evaluate whether a given party to an action did or did not engage in the alleged activities and what, if any, liability they incurred. The settlement agreements in each case speak for themselves.

1.0 Introduction

Healthcare industry consolidation, driven in part by the historical business cycle and enhanced by the Affordable Care Act's (ACA) accountable care organizations (ACO) and related provisions, has heralded an unprecedented number of business and compensation valuations—and opportunities for qui tam or whistleblower complaints. In this chapter, recent cases and case law highlighting new areas of inquiry and risk are explored along with some thoughts about how that risk might be minimized. Notable issues in these cases include the difference between the values of control and noncontrol interests, the assumptions utilized in discounted cash flow models and multiple of EBITDA models, losses incurred from the employment of physicians, and the requirement for industry knowledge on the part of valuation experts.

2.0 Principal Statutes Related to Valuation Fraud

Discussed in more depth elsewhere in this guide, the anti-kickback statute, Stark Law, and False Claims Act along with exclusions and administrative sanctions by the United States Department of Health and Human Services (HHS) Office of Inspector General (OIG) are the principal areas of criminal and civil penalties.

3.0 Import of Qui Tam Relators

As noted by the Department of Justice in a 2014 press release:[1]

> Whistleblower lawsuits were in the range of three to four hundred per year from 2000 to 2009, when they began their climb from 433 lawsuits in fiscal year 2009 to 752 lawsuits in fiscal year 2013. Due to the complexity of fraud investigations generally, the outcomes of many of the qui tam cases filed this past fiscal year are not yet known, but the growing number of lawsuits filed since 2009 have led to increased recoveries. Qui tam recoveries exceeded $2 billion for the first time in fiscal year 2010 and have continued to exceed that amount every year since. Qui tam recoveries this past fiscal year bring the department's totals since January 2009 to $13.4 billion. During the same period, the department paid out $1.98 billion in whistleblower awards.

3.1 *United States of America et al. ex rel. David Barbetta v. DaVita, Inc.*

The first of several high-profile, large-dollar cases against dialysis giant DaVita raised significant business valuation issues. The complaint,[2] which was filed under seal and subsequently joined by the federal government, was released after a $389 million settlement was reached.

In the settlement agreement with the government, DaVita denied any wrongdoing:

> DaVita expressly denies the allegations of the United States and Relator as set forth herein and in the Civil Action and the Complaint in Intervention and denies that it engaged in any wrongful conduct in connection with the Covered Conduct.

Counsel for the relator is well-known amongst the *qui tam* bar and has a history of successful large settlement cases. As such, the complaint is both well written and well documented, displaying an unusual understanding of valuation issues as applied to healthcare. Paragraph numbers below and on the following pages are taken directly from the unsealed complaint.

> 39. Accordingly, HHS OIG has cautioned that valuing a physician practice or other physician investment using a formula based on the practice's revenue stream raises concerns under the AKS.[3] *Cash flow based valuation is not per se a violation of the AKS, but it presents a significant concern because such a valuation would potentially lead to a payment based on the value of Medicare, Medicaid or other federal program referrals the selling physician made to the practice and/or might make to the practice in the future.* Cf. Ex. 3 (HHS OIG Advisory Opinion 09-09, at 7 n.5 (July 29, 2009)) ("a cash flow-based valuation of that business potentially would include the value of the [physicians'] referrals over the time that their [practice] was in existence prior to the [sale]")). Accordingly, it is appropriate to apply heightened scrutiny to such transactions (emphasis added).

1 www.justice.gov/opa/pr/justice-department-recovers-38-billion-false-claims-act-cases-fiscal-year-2013.
2 First Amended Complaint, Case No. 09 cv 02175 WJM-KMT.
3 Anti-kickback statute.

Recognizing this is a complaint targeting cash flow valuation, the concession that it "is not per se a violation of the AKS" is significant, given that many appraisers relying solely on the cost approach use the rationale that cash flow valuation automatically implicates referrals. That rationale is, of course, a red herring[4] or canard. A skilled appraiser can use one or both of the cash flow forecast and the discount rate (risk-based future cash flow and valuation multiple) to eliminate the volume or value of future referrals by substituting a hypothetical seller and buyer for the actual seller and buyer. Adjustment of the discount rate (rate of return) as a means to account for the hypothetical buyer/seller is borne out by OIG Special Fraud Alert, 59 Fed. Reg. 65372 at 67374 (Dec. 19, 1994), and other rulings that express concern where referral sources receive extraordinary returns on an investment—something, again, also known as the discount rate.

The complaint contains a number of illustrative discounted cash flow valuation models.

3.1.1 Purchasing Control and Selling Noncontrol Interests

One of the most significant issues raised in the complaint is the difference between the value of a control interest and a pro rata share (noncontrol or minority value) of that interest. (This was also a critical issue in the *Meridian* case discussed infra.) A minority interest is generally accepted as being worth less than a pro rata share of a control interest, while the extent of the discount between the two is subject to intense debate, dispute, and disagreement. It appears that the differences in the DaVita valuations were based upon assumptions used in the discounted cash flow models, rather than on discounts for lack of control pegged to market studies.

> A. DaVita's "Buy High/Sell Low" Strategy
>
> 57. The AKS allows physicians to engage in certain business transactions with entities to which they refer patients. As discussed above, however, an essential limitation on such relationships is that any payments made to the physicians must be at fair market value. This rule is designed to prevent dialysis centers (and other referral-receiving companies) from disguising illegal kickbacks as inflated payments to physicians for other assets or services.[5]
>
> 58. The prices DaVita pays for dialysis centers it buys, and similarly its charges for centers it sells, violate this restriction. An elementary feature of the marketplace is that participants try to sell their goods and services for as much as possible, and buy goods and services as cheaply as possible (i.e., Buy Low/Sell High). DaVita's approach to dialysis center joint ventures turns this dynamic on its head. DaVita deliberately pays more than fair market value for dialysis centers and joint-venture shares it buys from physicians in a position to refer business to the centers, and regularly charges cut-rate, below market prices when it sells shares of dialysis centers to physicians.

4 A red herring is something that misleads or distracts from a relevant or important issue. It may be either a logical fallacy or a literary device that leads readers or audiences toward a false conclusion. en.wikipedia.org/wiki/Red_herring.

5 Observation: Even a compensation arrangement meeting a fair market value test would violate the AKS if any party to the arrangement had the "bad" intent that the AKS prohibits.

> 59. This "Buy High/Sell Low" strategy is the cover DaVita uses to mask the illegal kickbacks it gives these physicians to secure a steady flow of referrals from them.
>
> 60. DaVita masks and supports its "Buy High/Sell Low" strategy primarily through manipulation of the financial models its analysts and its outside appraisers use to calculate the value of dialysis centers. DaVita personnel in its "Deal Depot" Mergers and Acquisitions department, under direct orders from the Vice Presidents and other managers in charge of the department, manipulate the valuation process with both ad hoc adjustments to various financial models, and through the application of non-standard—even illogical—(from an accounting point of view) formulas and algorithms.

This latter allegation, "ad hoc adjustments to various financial models," is especially significant in that it demonstrates the critical import of industry subsector knowledge. This edition and earlier editions of this guide contain an entire chapter[6] devoted to dialysis valuation. The following is a relevant extract:

> Before undertaking a valuation of a dialysis clinic, it is important to understand the mechanics and any potential changes in the reimbursement methodology. Patients having end stage renal disease (ESRD) become eligible for Medicare four months after they begin dialysis treatments even if they have not reached the age of 65. Eligibility can begin sooner if the patient elects to train for home-based dialysis. As a result, a significant portion of a dialysis clinic's patient base is covered by Medicare. Commercial insurance companies will cover dialysis services until the patient becomes eligible. Additionally, patients are not required to accept Medicare benefits and can elect to retain their commercial insurance benefits. Even though commercially insured patients do not typically comprise a significant portion of the patient base, they can have a tremendous impact on the profitability of the clinic because the reimbursement from commercial insurance companies is generally significantly greater than Medicare.

Thus, the status of non-Medicare patients that "have a tremendous impact on the profitability of the clinic" is critical in dialysis center valuation. The advent of the ACA has increased the complexity of this analysis as more individuals may have the opportunity to remain covered by private health insurance. Given that one is eligible for Medicare four months after commencing dialysis, why would there be many non-Medicare patients? "If you are eligible for Medicare because of a disability, your employer insurance is primary to Medicare if you, your spouse, or other family member are currently working and there are 100 or more employees at the company where you, your spouse or other family member work."[7] There are other examples as well that warrant understanding. For example, patients may desire to keep their commercial insurance plan if the overall out-of-pocket cost of their treatment will be less.

6 *Valuing Dialysis Clinics*, Carol W. Carden, CPA/ABV, ASA, CFE.

7 www.medicareinteractive.org/page2.php?topic=counselor&page=script&script_id=1715.

In the complaint, dialysis patients with commercial insurance payors were labeled "HIPPERS," a DaVita-specific acronym for high-paying patients. HIPPER is the algorithm referred to in the following paragraphs:

> 61. Some of the non-standard algorithms DaVita uses to "game" its projections tend to decrease the projected value of a dialysis center. Others generally have the opposite effect, increasing the projected value of a center. When DaVita sells centers to physicians, it uses the algorithms that decrease the value of the centers, thus decreasing the purchase price to the physicians. Conversely, when it buys centers from physicians, DaVita tends to use only the algorithms that increase the values of centers, thus increasing the price paid to the physicians. The manipulative application of these algorithms, as standard practice, leads to the occasional over-valuing of the centers DaVita buys, and the systematic undervaluing of the centers it sells.
>
> 62. The primary mechanism DaVita uses to depress the value of centers DaVita sells is the application of a financial algorithm known as HIPPER compression. In addition to this structural machination, DaVita routinely manipulates its financial models by using artificial and unreasonable values for expected costs or other key financial indicators.

The following allegation seems very odd, at least as far as its use as an assumption in a valuation model prepared by the third-party appraiser. Historical insurer data for multiple years are a usual and required part of any data request, and one would think the validity of the HIPPER assumption would be ascertainable.

> 66. One way that DaVita hides these machinations is through the selective use of third-party valuations. DaVita generally uses an outside firm, [redacted], to provide a "fair market value" opinion whenever DaVita sells ("divests" in DaVita's parlance) all or part of a dialysis center. DaVita manipulates these opinions to ensure they support the proposed sale price by "gaming" the revenue and cost assumptions given to [redacted]. Because [redacted] relies on these assumptions without independent confirmation, DaVita is able to ensure that these opinions say whatever DaVita wants them to say (i.e., they are not "independent" third-party valuations, but rather are valuations of projections which DaVita has manipulated).
>
> 69. HIPPER compression is an algorithm developed by DaVita and utilized as a policy from at least 2006. It is based on the presumption that insurance companies that pay the most for dialysis treatments will, within three years, be able to negotiate lower reimbursement rates to more closely mirror average rates. In DaVita's parlance, a HIPPER is a "High Paying Patient" (i.e. a patient with an insurance plan that reimburses at a high rate).
>
> 70. The HIPPER compression algorithm assumes that no insurer will pay more than $750 per dialysis treatment, beginning in year 3 of a financial model. Therefore, for patients whose insurance company would likely pay $1,200 per treatment, DaVita assumes that the insurance company will, in fact, lower its payment by nearly 40% per treatment from year

3 onward. DaVita CEO Kent Thiry pushed the use of the HIPPER Compression algorithm on company departments, over objections.

71. The predictable and expected result of applying HIPPER compression to a financial analysis is that the dialysis center will be expected to have substantially lower future revenue, and thus will be less valuable. HIPPER compression, however, is an overly conservative and unrealistic assumption, acknowledged even by DaVita's CFO, Richard Whitney, in a May 19, 2009 email. In the email, Mr. Whitney (and other recipients) are asked about aspects of the acquisition revenue build up model, including specifically that it "compresses revenue to $750 all in for years 3 and beyond." Mr. Whitney responds: "If all of our private pay compresses to 750 without increases in the lower rate biz or mcare [Medicare] ... we are out of business. In other words this is not a realistic assumption." Ex. 10 (May 19, 2009, email "RE: Acquisition Revenue Build Up Assumptions").

The complaint alleges other manipulations of valuation assumptions, the impact of which should be familiar to any user of discounted cash flow models. As described below, per-unit costs of treatment, per-unit revenue, volume of epogen (an IV drug used to treat anemia associated with ESRD), and terminal value calculations were targeted. Notably, terminal value calculations were based on EBITDA[8] multiples rather than the Gordon growth model.

73. DaVita routinely manipulates the estimate of how much it will cost to provide each treatment. For example, in most of its internal financial modeling and reporting, DaVita's accountants estimate that it costs the company $25-$35 in general and administrative ("G&A") expenses to provide each dialysis treatment. However, when projecting the value of dialysis centers DaVita intends to purchase, the analysts in Deal Depot are instructed to use an estimate of $13.50 per treatment for G&A expenses. In addition, they estimate that these expenses will remain constant from year to year regardless of inflation. By artificially underestimating the dialysis center's costs, this manipulation unrealistically inflates the profit the center is expected to generate and increases the projected "value" of the center.

83. DaVita also increased the expected revenue per transaction by artificially increasing the amount of epogen each patient was projected to receive. Epogen is a drug given to patients during dialysis treatment. A substantial portion of the revenue DaVita receives for each treatment is attributable to the profit it makes on epogen. Id. Artificial increases in epogen are not factored into divestiture valuations.

84. In other situations, DaVita's method was far more direct—it simply increased the expected revenue per treatment. For example, in a transaction in Kansas in June 2008, DaVita "gamed" the revenue by simply bumping the expected revenue per treatment up from $310 to $350. Ex. 15 (Kansas—Post DD Model 06-05-08 $18.75M with Budgets//Summary

8 Earnings before interest, taxes, depreciation, and amortization.

worksheet). This tactic, known within DaVita as "plugging revenue," is not used in divestiture financial models.

85. Of late, DaVita has relied more on artificially increasing the "terminal value" of a center to boost its projected value. DaVita's financial models (as is standard) estimate projected revenue year-by-year for a certain number of years going forward, and then account for all expected revenue beyond that point through use of a lump-sum amount. That lump sum is the "terminal value." This terminal value is usually calculated as a certain multiple of the center's expected annual earnings. A higher terminal value produces a higher overall projected value for the center.

86. In recent years, DaVita has used progressively higher EBITDA multipliers, without justification, to produce higher terminal values and thus further arbitrarily inflate the projected value of centers it intends to buy. In 2007 the average terminal value was 5.3 times expected EBITDA. Ex. 7 (DaVita M&A Transactions). In 2008, the multiple increased to 5.8 and in 2009 it is close to 7.0. Id. On one deal that was active at the time Relator left the company, the multiple was 7.8. Ex. 16 (KantTucker Model 2009-06-16//Assumptions Summary worksheet). No such efforts to increase terminal values are used in DaVita's divestiture models. In order to artificially depress the value of centers DaVita sells to physicians, its managers and analysts reverse the ad hoc "gaming" method, artificially inflating the expected amounts to be paid for labor and other expenses and using HIPPER compression to artificially decrease the expected revenue. Thus, to the extent ad hoc adjustments are made to financial models for divestitures, the manipulations are employed to effect a decrease in the valuations (rather than an increase as in the case of acquisitions).

3.1.2 Specific Valuation Example

The following is an example from the complaint that contained a spreadsheet example of the assumptions used in an acquisition of a dialysis center:

82. On the revenue side of the transaction, DaVita uses multiple methods to inflate the valuation and hence the purchase price. For some transactions, DaVita increased the expected revenue by inflating the projected number of high paying (HIPPER) patients the center was expected to treat. This method, which effectively turns the usual HIPPER assumption on its head, is known colloquially within DaVita as using the "HIPPER bus"—i.e., assuming a mythic bus full of HIPPERs will routinely drop patients off at the center. For example, in the "Fayetteville" transaction in Arkansas in February 2008—a transaction involving centers treating 110 patients—the initial projected revenue was $243 [$253 in Exhibit 1] per treatment. DaVita increased this to $320 [$300 in Exhibit 1] per treatment, by assuming the HIPPER bus would drop off 10 patients whose insurance policies each paid $1050 per treatment. Ex. 1 (Fayetteville RKC Model Post DD ROD Review Final $3.79MM 080114// Summary worksheet). The "HIPPER bus" never appears in divestitures.

Exhibit 1 was replicated from the exhibit in the complaint.

Exhibit 1. Fayetteville Transaction

Extracted from Complaint	2004	2005	Base Year	Year 1	Year 2	Year 3	Year 4	Year 5
Average Patients			110	118	137	153	170	188
Treatments			15,840	17,032	19,693	21,987	24,421	27,036
Tx Growth				7.5%	15.6%	11.6%	11.1%	10.7%
Net Revenue	4,457,575	3,725,963	4,012,963	4,314,820	5,912,172	6,576,565	7,304,537	8,086,556
Per Tx			253.34	253.34	300.22	299.11	299.11	299.11
EBITDA	(558,818)	(595,634)	(425,218)	(423,233)	807,796	1,082,260	1,381,531	1,501,631
Per Tx			(26.84)	(24.85)	41.02	49.22	56.57	55.54
% of Revenue			-10.6%	-9.8%	13.7%	16.5%	18.9%	18.6%
Pre-Tax Income				(697,379)	525,793	790,218	1,081,631	1,193,874
Taxes				(281,741)	212,420	319,248	436,979	482,325
Book Net Income				(415,638)	313,373	470,970	644,652	711,549

The second part is an analysis of the assumptions, based in part on Paragraph 82 of the complaint above, along with customary analysis that would be done in a valuation model, such as year-over-year percentage and dollar change of line items, per treatment (Tx) analysis. Items not provided in the original exhibit were calculated, such as interest, depreciation, and amortization (IDA), which was calculated by subtracting pretax income from EBITDA. Expenses net of IDA were calculated by: (1) subtracting pretax income from revenue; and then (2) subtracting IDA.

Notable below is that the number of treatments per patient did not change from year to year—as well it should not have since dialysis patients are dialyzed approximately three days per week, or 12 times per month. Year-over-year patient growth is significant and would warrant inquiry if an independent appraisal were being done. Reasons for such growth would have to be substantiated by population increases, changing demographics, and similar items; it is unlikely an area served by an existing center would be "underserved" resulting in an influx of new patients. Total expense per patient is likely declining in this circumstance due to fixed overhead per patient declining.

3.1.3 Summary

In the government's complaint in intervention[9] filed in this *DaVita* case, a separate issue affecting valuation firms was raised. In the first amended complaint filed by the relator and discussed above, it was stated: "One way that DaVita hides these machinations is through the selective use of third-party valuations. DaVita generally uses an outside firm, [redacted], to provide a 'fair market value' opinion whenever DaVita sells ('divests' in DaVita's parlance) all or part of a dialysis center."[10] In the instance described below, a new firm was retained to value an acquisition.

9 Complaint in Intervention, Case 1:09-cv-02175-WJM Document 68 Filed Oct. 22, 2014 USDC Colorado.

10 Paragraph 66; Observation: The 4th Circuit in the *Tuomey* case faulted the hospital for legal opinion shopping; courts or enforcement authorities could use the same logic to question a hospital's or other buyer's reliance on

> 129. Near the time the transaction was set to close, Deal Depot's management sought a third-party opinion to reflect that the approximate $39 million price for these three centers was fair market value. This was unusual because *typically Deal Depot only sought fair-market-value opinions on the value of centers it was selling. Rather than use Deal Depot's usual valuation firm, they gave the task to a new firm.* The new firm's analysis did not support DaVita's desired $39 million price. Instead, even using the doctored financial data provided by DaVita, this new firm reported that fair market value for the three centers was no more than $30 million. When the valuation firm orally reported its findings, DaVita ordered the company not to produce a written report of its findings. DaVita then consummated the deal based on its inflated $39 million price. DaVita managers told Relator that DaVita paid the new valuation firm thousands of dollars for its unwritten services that DaVita ended up not using in the deal[11] (emphasis added).

It is likely that many if not most valuation firms make an effort to assess the history of a significant client—especially one that engages in many transactions—as part of the risk assessment

Exhibit 2. Analysis of the Assumptions

Analysis						
Patient Growth		6.8%	13.9%	10.5%	10.0%	9.6%
Tx per Patient	144.00	144.34	143.74	143.71	143.65	143.81
Net Revenue Growth	7.7%	7.5%	37.0%	11.2%	11.1%	10.7%
$ Revenue Growth	287,000	301,857	1,597,352	664,393	727,972	782,019
Per Tx Growth			18.5%	-0.4%	0.0%	0.0%
EBITDA Growth		0.5%	290.9%	34.0%	27.7%	8.7%
Pre-Tax Income Growth			175.4%	50.3%	36.9%	10.4%
Total Expense		5,012,199	5,386,379	5,786,347	6,222,906	6,892,682
IDA		274,146	282,003	292,042	299,900	307,757
Expense net of IDA		4,738,053	5,104,376	5,494,305	5,923,006	6,584,925
Expense net of IDA per Tx		278.19	259.20	249.89	242.54	243.56
Total Expense per Tx		294.28	273.52	263.17	254.82	254.94

in any new engagement. Skepticism of projections presented by management is de rigueur in healthcare appraisal practice as is detailed industry subsector knowledge and a data request that is highly detailed. This case lends credence to the practice often used in healthcare valuation engagements of having outside legal counsel retain and interact with the valuation firm to maintain attorney-client privilege.

3.2 *United States of America et al. ex rel. Parikh v. Citizens Medical Center*

The case involves issues associated with the fair market value of physician compensation along with the commercial reasonableness of hospitals losing substantial amounts of money when employing physicians in a position to refer. The lack of a fair market value opinion at the outset

more than one valuation expert on a particular matter.

11 Complaint in Intervention, Paragraph 129.

supporting the compensation paid may also be seen as significant. The physicians in the matter are cardiologists, and cardiovascular services are generally one of the most valuable in terms of revenue and profit to the typical acute care hospital. The paragraphs below from the complaint[12] are very self-explanatory as to the allegations and contain issues analogous to those in the University of Medicine and Dentistry of New Jersey (UMDNJ) case *U.S. v. Campbell*[13] as well as *Tuomey*[14] and *Halifax*.[15]

3.2.1 Summary of Allegations

76. CMC [Community Medical Center] and Brown's [CMC's administrator] illegal self-referral practices. CMC and Brown have violated the Anti-Kickback Act by illegally paying the CMC Cardiologists salaries many times more than what they earned in private practice and other benefits in return for their agreement to refer cardiology Patients requiring hospital services to CMC and, in many instances, to Dr. Yahagi for surgery at CMC. CMC pays the CMC Cardiologists a salary well above their salaries in private practice, bills and collects for all services they provide, provides malpractice coverage for the CMC Cardiologists, provides dictation services, and offers the cardiologists health and dental insurance. See Exhibits "I"-"M." For example, in the year prior to CMC's employment of Drs. Campbell, Krueger, and Oakley, they earned a combined salary of $630,000.00. Upon employment, CMC paid Dr. Campbell a guaranteed salary of $400,000 per year. His partners, Drs. Krueger and Oakley, received guaranteed salaries of $500,000 from CMC. *Thus, in the span of a single year, that group went from making $630,000.00 in 2006 to making $1,400,000.00 in 2007, an increase of $770,000.00 in one year. There were no market conditions that justified a two-fold salary increase; in fact, since reimbursement rates were declining at that time (as CMC and Brown have contended), the salaries should have decreased. Tellingly, neither CMC nor Brown conducted a fair-market salary study or analysis before offering the cardiologists the staggering salaries.* And their employment contracts certainly provide no justification or basis for their enormous salaries. Instead, the only justification offered by CMC and Brown for hiring the CMC Cardiologists is reflected in CMC's Board Meeting Minutes from March 6, 2007, which states that the cardiologists were hired to "improve their income level" and "help with their working situation." See Exhibit "N." Simply put, CMC and Brown knew and intended that by paying the CMC Cardiologists nearly double the amount they earned in practice, the CMC Cardiologists would refer nearly all of their patients to CMC, which is exactly what has happened.

77. In January 2007, CMC and Brown agreed to hire Dr. Chelif Junor, a new cardiologist, for a guaranteed salary of $400,000.00 for two years, a $50,000.00 "sign-on" bonus, and a $25,000.00 "show-up" bonus. Neither CMC nor Brown conducted any community need study prior to hiring the cardiologists and agreeing to pay them substantial, guaranteed salaries and bonuses. In return for the enormous salaries and increases, the CMC Cardiologists perform their services at CMC

12 Third Amended Qui Tam Complaint.

13 *United States v. Campbell,* 2011 U.S. Dist. LEXIS 1207 (D.N.J. Jan. 4, 2011).

14 *United States ex rel. Drakeford v. Tuomey Healthcare System, Inc.,* No. 10-1819.

15 *U.S. ex rel. Baklid-Kunz v. Halifax Hospital Medical Center et al,* No. 6:09-CV-1002-ORL-31 DAB, M.D. Fla.

and refer surgical Patients to Dr. Yahagi, CMC's exclusive cardiac surgeon. Dr. Campbell has admitted that his group is financially beneficial to CMC because of their referrals to the hospital. CMC's inducement or reward to the CMC Cardiologists for referring, recommending, or arranging for federally funded medical services violates the Anti-Kickback Act. Where a hospital "provides physicians with services for free or less than fair market value, or relieves physicians of financial obligations they would otherwise incur," evidence of inducement and a violation of the Anti-Kickback Act exists. 70 Federal Register 4858, 4866 (Jan. 31, 2005); see also 70 Federal Register 59015, 59018 (Oct. 11, 2005) (indicating that a computer has independent value to a physician and providing a free computer to a physician may constitute an illegal inducement). Campbell violated the Anti-Kickback Act, Stark Act, and the FCA [False Claims Act] by agreeing to accept illegal remuneration in exchange for patient referrals to CMC.

81. CMC's compensation to the CMC Cardiologists is not based on their actual work. Instead, the CMC Cardiologists are paid many times more by the county hospital than what they earned in private practice, as compensation for their patient referrals to CMC. *In fact, as referenced herein, the CMC Cardiologists' office practices have systematically lost money, but CMC continues to employ them because of the volume and value of their patient referrals to CMC.* CMC's illegal employment of the ER Physicians and hospitalists also violates the Anti-Kickback Act for the same reasons set forth above.

105. Similarly, CMC and Brown's employment agreements with the CMC Cardiologists fail to satisfy the bona fide employment safe harbor under Stark. Specifically, the amount of remuneration under the employment contracts is not consistent with fair market value. Indeed, as set forth above, Drs. Campbell, Kruger, and Oakley were paid nearly double the amount they earned in private practice in a declining cardiology market with declining reimbursement rates. Thus, the Stark safe harbor does not apply. See 42 C.F.R. § 411.357(c)(2)(i). Further, Drs. Tillman and Junor were offered guaranteed salaries of $625,000.00 in addition to significant signing bonuses. *According to CMC and Brown's expert, [redacted], the median salary for invasive cardiologists in 2009 was $481,878, which is substantially below what Drs. Junor and Tillman were paid in their first years of practice (2008 and 2007, respectively). For these same reasons, the employment contracts fail to satisfy the Stark employment safe harbor because the remuneration provided is not commercially reasonable even if no referrals were made to CMC. Indeed, as set forth above, CMC loses significant money on the CMC Cardiologists' office practices; it more than makes up for the losses on the CMC Cardiologists' patient referrals.* This is fatal to any claim that the agreements meet the safe harbor requirements. For these reasons, CMC's employment contracts with the CMC Cardiologists fail to satisfy the employment safe harbor of the Stark Act. As such, the referrals from the CMC Cardiologists to CMC in exchange for above-market salaries, discounted office rent, CME allowance, health and insurance allowance are subject to Stark liability.

3.2.2 Analyzing the Allegations

This case is significant in many ways. It occurs during the period when a rapid consolidation of cardiology practices was underway, culminating in the dramatic cuts in physician office-based nuclear medicine in 2010. More than half the cardiologists in the country are now employed or otherwise integrated with a hospital. Given that there is a long delay in the government reviewing such cases for a decision to join, many more are likely in the wings.

3.2.2.1 Dramatic Increase in Physician Compensation

"Thus, in the span of a single year, that group went from making $630,000.00 in 2006 to making $1,400,000.00 in 2007, an increase of $770,000.00 in one year."

From a valuation standpoint, this would be the required inclusion of historical compensation in the analysis to determine fair market value. Historical compensation reflects existing arm's-length payment rates between insurers and physicians, something also identified in the complaint: "There were no market conditions that justified a two-fold salary increase; in fact, since reimbursement rates were declining at that time (as CMC and Brown have contended), the salaries should have decreased."

3.2.2.2 Lack of Fair Market Value Opinion for Compensation

"Tellingly, neither CMC nor Brown conducted a fair-market salary study or analysis before offering the cardiologists the staggering salaries."

Obtaining an appraisal before entering into a compensation arrangement is not conclusive but is seen as supporting a party's contention that the compensation payments were not for referrals. "As we explained in Phase II, although a good faith reliance on an independent valuation (such as an appraisal) may be relevant to a party's intent, it does not establish the ultimate issue of the accuracy of the valuation figure itself (69 FR 16107)."

"In January 2007, CMC and Brown agreed to hire Dr. Chelif Junor, a new cardiologist, for a guaranteed salary of $400,000.00 for two years, a $50,000.00 "sign-on" bonus, and a $25,000.00 "show-up" bonus."

Here, it is important to recognize that the overall compensation being paid must meet the fair market value standard, and that includes any "sign-on" or other bonuses. (Note: The author has never heard of a "show-up" bonus.") When such large bonuses are utilized, it may be necessary to have employment contract terms that require repayment if the individual leaves employment within a specified period of time in order to allocate the bonus to more than one year.

3.2.2.3 Failure to Establish Community Need

"Neither CMC nor Brown conducted any community need study prior to hiring the cardiologists and agreeing to pay them substantial, guaranteed salaries and bonuses."

This is an area of increasing risk and particularly in those circumstances where physicians already working in a given local market area are recruited to a hospital also in that market area at much higher rates of pay.

3.2.2.4 'Recruiting' Physicians Already on Hospital Medical Staff

The payments to Drs. Campbell, Krueger, and Oakley were alleged to be in conflict with the Stark regulations because the bona fide employment exception as well as the recruitment exception requires that:

> "[T]he amount of the remuneration under the arrangement is not determined in a manner that takes into account (directly or indirectly) the volume or value of any referrals by the referring physician."[16]
>
> This language makes clear that the recruited physician cannot already be a member of the hospital's medical staff. We believe that the relocation requirement is insufficient to establish that a physician who is already a member of the hospital's active staff needs an incentive to move his or her practice. We are not persuaded that permitting recruitment of physicians who are not on a hospital's "active" medical staff, but who hold some type of medical staff privileges (for example, courtesy privileges), poses no risk of program or patient abuse. Moreover, defining "active" privileges is difficult, as many hospitals use different terminology to refer to different types of medical staff privileges."[17]

3.3.2.5 Physician Practice Losses and Commercial Reasonableness

"In fact, as referenced herein, the CMC Cardiologists' office practices have systematically lost money, but CMC continues to employ them because of the volume and value of their patient referrals to CMC." "For these same reasons, the employment contracts fail to satisfy the Stark employment safe harbor because the remuneration provided is not commercially reasonable even if no referrals were made to CMC. Indeed, as set forth above, CMC loses significant money on the CMC Cardiologists' office practices; it more than makes up for the losses on the CMC Cardiologists' patient referrals."

These two quotes contain the thrust of the argument that the employment contracts failed the commercial reasonableness test. The following is taken from the government expert's testimony in *Tuomey*, highlighting both the aforementioned community needs analysis as well as the commercial reasonableness requirement, suggesting the two are closely related:

> Over time, if a physician's production does not support even median compensation in an employed situation, the cause is usually one of two things. One, the physician does not want to work hard enough. Over time, the employer needs to determine if it is commercially reasonable to support an under-performing physician. Or two, there is not enough business in the community to support the physician or specialty. Over time, the employer

16 42 U.S.C. § 1395nn(e)(5); similarly in §411.357(c)(2).

17 72 F.R. 171, Sept. 5, 2007.

needs to determine if it is necessary and commercially reasonable to support a physician or specialty for the benefit of the community.[18]

3.2.2.6 Expert Use of Surveys to Establish FMV Compensation

"According to CMC and Brown's expert, [redacted], the median salary for invasive cardiologists in 2009 was $481,878, which is substantially below what Drs. Junor and Tillman were paid in their first years of practice (2008 and 2007, respectively)."

Subsequent to the claim being unsealed, Citizens sought expert appraisal services. The expert report is not available in the public record of the case, but, based upon the following quotes from the Defendant Citizens Medical Center's Motion to Dismiss Relators' Third Amended Qui Tam Complaint and Defendant CMC's Reply in Support of Motion to Dismiss, there appears to be an alternate interpretation of what that report said:

> As reflected in the expert report of [redacted] ("[redacted]Report"), which Relators rely upon and incorporate in their Complaint, these salaries at the time were near or below the median of the nationwide average compensation for invasive cardiologists of $481,878. ¶ 105; [redacted]Report at 5. Accordingly, the fact that these CMC Cardiologists were paid salaries very close to or below the national median for cardiologists negates the plausibility of Relators' allegations of above-market compensation.
>
> Moreover, the allegation that the CMC Cardiologists earned more money working for CMC than in private practice does not lead to the inference that these cardiologists were paid above fair market value. There are many legitimate reasons why compensation might vary between hospital employment and private practice, but that variance does not automatically equate to a Stark Law or AKS violation as Relators suggest. For example, the CMC Cardiologists might have provided significant amounts of uncompensated or undercompensated care while in private practice; or these physicians might have capitalized on strong market conditions to secure positions with CMC. Indeed, Exhibit N to the Complaint shows that Dr. Krueger received several competitive offers of employment from Scott & White Memorial Hospital in Temple and other hospitals. Exhibit N also reflects that employment was offered to the CMC Cardiologists in an effort to keep them practicing in Victoria, Texas—not for referrals. Relators do not attempt to negate these other reasonable, lawful explanations in their Complaint—nor could they.
>
> Next, Relators rely on the [redacted] Report to fallaciously claim that Drs. Tillman's and Junor's initial, start-up salaries of $625,000 (in 2007 and 2009, respectively) were above market because they were above the median salary of $481,878 for invasive cardiologists in 2009. ¶ 105; [Meridian Expert] Report at 5. The [redacted] Report, however, demonstrates that the CMC Cardiologists were not paid above fair market value. The Victoria market consists of

18 Kathleen A. McNamara, Myers and Stauffer Fair Market Value, Commercial Reasonable Assessment, *U.S. ex rel Michael K. Drakeford, M.D., v. Tuomey Healthcare System, Inc.*, March 13, 2009, at 12 ("Tuomey Report"), 6.

> only two cardiology groups—the CMC Cardiologists and the Relators. [redacted] Report at 10. Between 2007 and 2009, the [redacted] Report demonstrates that Relators' income far exceeded that of the CMC Cardiologists. [redacted] Report at 14, 32 (showing the compensation of the three Relators). *If anything, Drs. Tillman and Junor's compensation of $625,000 was vastly below market value when compared to the "market" in Victoria, as set by Relators—the chief competitors of the CMC Cardiologists*[19] (emphasis added).

The above is a significant argument and one that is underexplored at that: Local market conditions are an appropriate measure of fair market value. The argument was not sufficiently compelling in light of the hospital's losses on the arrangement, however, as noted infra in the court's ruling on the Motion to Dismiss. It would have required exploring the relative productivity of the physicians in the two practices, ownership and utilization of ancillaries such as a nuclear medicine camera, and whether both practices had the same rates from payors. Basically the same argument was made in the Motion to Dismiss:

> Relators, however, attempt to rely upon national median salaries in the [redacted] Report and the fact that the CMC Cardiologists made less in private practice to argue that it is "quite plausible" that the CMC Cardiologists were paid above-market salaries. Resp. at 25-26. This argument is contradicted by the [redacted] Report, which demonstrates that the CMC Cardiologists were paid significantly less than Relators in the relevant market at issue—Victoria, Texas. See *United States ex rel. Dennis v. Health Mgmt. Assocs., Inc.*, No. 3:09-cv-00484, 2013 WL 146048, at *13 (M.D. Tenn. Jan. 14, 2013).[20]

3.2.2.7 Court's Ruling on Motion to Dismiss

The court's ruling on the order on motion to dismiss is extracted in relevant part below as to the compensation valuation issues:

> Citizens also argues that Relators' allegations are insufficient because they do not allege that the cardiologists actually made above-market income and, instead, that an expert report they rely on shows that the cardiologists' salaries are below the national median.
>
> Given the Rule 12 posture in which Relators allegations must be taken as true, the Court disagrees. Relators have made several allegations that, if true, provide a strong inference of the existence of a kickback scheme. Particularly, the Court notes Relators' allegations that the cardiologists' income more than doubled after they joined Citizens, even while their own practices were costing Citizens between $400,000 and $1,000,000 per year in net losses. *Even if the cardiologists were making less than the national median salary for their profession, the allegations that they began making substantially more money once they were employed by Citizens is sufficient to allow an inference that they were receiving improper remuneration. This inference is*

19 Case 6:10-cv-00064 Document 53 Filed in TXSD on June 28, 2013.

20 Defendant CMC's Reply in Support of Motion to Dismiss; Case 6:10-cv-00064 Document 72 Filed in TXSD on Aug. 9, 2013.

> *particularly strong given that it would make little apparent economic sense for Citizens to employ the cardiologists at a loss unless it were doing so for some ulterior motive—a motive Relators identify as a desire to induce referrals.* Relators' allegations are more than sufficient to satisfy Rule 9(b) as interpreted by Grubbs. The AKS- and Stark-predicated FCA allegations concerning the cardiologist group survive the motion to dismiss.

The case was settled by Citizens agreeing to pay the United States $21.75 million.[21]

3.2.3 Concluding Thoughts

Losses are the crux of the issue in many compensation valuation engagements and many business valuation engagements, which are part and parcel of compensation arrangements. One can imagine that, if the hospital in this case had purchased the cardiology practice as well as paying salaries that generated dramatic losses, the result would have been the same. Hundreds of such transactions took place with large payments for cardiology practices based on the cost approach and then salaries higher than that earned by the physicians historically.[22] Whether for tax purposes or financial reporting, buyers have to amortize or impairment test most intangible assets, which in turn would increase the operating losses. The court might have said in this scenario: "This inference is particularly strong given that it would make little apparent economic sense for Hospital to purchase the cardiologists' practice and then employ the cardiologists at a loss unless it were doing so for some ulterior motive." Or, perhaps more straightforward: "This inference is particularly strong given that it would make little apparent economic sense for Hospital to purchase the cardiologists' practice then lose money operating it."

3.3 *United States of America et al. ex rel. Thomas Reed Simmons v. Meridian Surgical Partners, LLC, et al.*

This is arguably a peculiar case in which the government failed to join, but the defendant chose to settle. The government only joins something in the vicinity of 25% of such actions, and more than 90% of these result in the defendant making a settlement.[23] In contrast, relators fail in all but perhaps 5% of cases that the government does not join, making this case somewhat unique and the reason for its selection here. Notably, the relator's expert was the same individual the government retained in *Tuomey, Halifax,* and *Campbell,* among others, which may be instructive.

As described in the introduction to the *DaVita* case, the most significant issue raised in this complaint is the difference between the value of a control interest and a pro rata share (non-control or minority value) of that interest. However, the complaint reflects a fundamental lack of understanding of valuation terms, such as "asset purchase" versus "tangible assets," the allegation being made that payments in excess of tangible assets based on a multiple of earnings were for referrals, in violation of the anti-kickback statute. It apparently ignores as well

21 www.justice.gov/opa/pr/texas-based-citizens-medical-center-agrees-pay-united-states-2175-million-settle-alleged.

22 See, e.g., "MedAxiom Spring 2010 Integration Survey" or "2013 MedAxiom Annual Integration Report."

23 See, e.g., "DOJ's New 'No Decision' Tactic In 'Qui Tam' Cases Leaves Counsel Guessing," www.bna.com/dojs-new-no-n17179893168/. Gibson Dunn, "2014 Year-End False Claims Act Update," January, 2015.

the diminution in value in the post-transaction entity caused by Meridian charging that new entity a 6% management fee.[24]

The first complaint contained a number of significant errors as to the prices the various physician investors paid for interests subsequent to Meridian's involvement.

3.3.1 First Complaint, Valuation Multiple[25]

Meridian bought 60% of Treasure Coast Surgery ASC using an eight times multiple of earnings,[26] which the relator argued therefore included the value of referrals, in part because it exceeded the value of the tangible assets: "74. The purchase documents characterize the transaction as a purchase of 60% of an undivided portion of the company's assets" and "75. However, rather than the claimed asset purchase, Meridian's valuation was based on an eight times multiple of Treasure Coast Surgery, Inc.'s 2006 earnings." "80. Treasure Coast Surgery, Inc.'s entire tangible assets at the time were worth less than $550,000."[27]

3.3.2 First Complaint, Control and Minority Values

The transaction valued the entire entity at $9.6 million, and therefore 1% would be valued at $96,000. Nine months after the transaction, a 3% interest was sold to a physician for $25,183 and several 1% interests for $8,583: "85. On its face, these sales place a value of 1% of Treasure Coast at approximately $8,500 (average between $8,394 to $8,598) and the entire entity (100%) at $850,000, a more than a 90% reduction from the $9.6 million value calculated from what Meridian paid fewer than nine months earlier."

3.3.3 Amended Complaint, Minority Values

Six months after the transaction, a 3% interest was sold to a physician for *$69,786* and several 1% interests, one for *$26,000* and one for approximately *$27,000*. These values are around 275% of the original values.

3.3.4 First Complaint, Distributions

The complaint goes on to allege that distributions in the subsequent three years were more than double the amount invested in the above transactions. One of the physicians who purchased a 1% interest for $8,538 subsequently purchased a second 1% interest for $8,969. He then purchased an additional 1.07% interest for $7,408.[28] Similar allegations are made with respect to other transactions, namely that the discounted interests were compensation for referrals.

24 Meridian Answer to Amended Complaint, May 23, 2015, paragraph 53.
25 Complaint, May 10, 2011, Case 3:11-cv-00439.
26 Plaintiff's expert report on page 5 says, "Meridian used a multiple of least 8.9x up to 11.1x."
27 Complaint, May 10, 2011, Case 3:11-cv-00439
28 Paragraph 114.

3.3.5 Amended Complaint, Minority Interests[29]

The prices this physician paid for the additional interests are not provided in the Amended Complaint, although they appear in plaintiff's expert report.

3.3.6 First Complaint, Operating Agreement

Another interesting if not altogether absurd accusation is that the operating agreement for the LLC served "as a de facto mandate for patient referrals since, as explained below, the investment opportunities are limited to local surgeons, it allows for limited competition, and it mandates that if any of a specified number of 'triggering events' stops patient referrals, the shares will be purchased back and the physicians will be removed from the investment (i.e., no longer eligible for distributions)."[30] Such provisions are standard to one extent or another in ASC agreements, in part due to the desire to qualify for the AKS safe harbor for ASC ownership by surgeons performing at least 33.33% of their case volume and/or earning 33.33% of their income from procedures in the facility.[31]

3.3.7 Amended Complaint, Operating Agreement

The plaintiff seemingly recognized the issue above because the amended complaint alleged "contrary to the applicable safe-harbor regulation, Meridian offers physicians 'investments' in Treasure Coast LLC on terms that are 'related to the [physicians'] previous or expected volume of referrals' to the ASC 42 C.F.R. § 1001.952(r)(3)(i)."[32] Nonetheless, the complaint continues to emphasize that "Meridian offers these lucrative terms only to physicians who refer Medicare patients to the ASC."

3.3.8 The Meridian Valuation Models

There is a significant amount of information in the public record concerning the opposing experts' approaches to the valuation issues; at the same time, significant gaps exist with pages of Meridian's expert deposition not available or, notably, the actual report. The reader should bear that in mind.

The issues involved in the case, as suggested by the discussion of the complaint above, involve both the control value as well as the noncontrol or minority interest value.

Plaintiff's expert has served as the government's expert in a number of high-profile cases involving physician compensation including *Tuomey* and *Halifax* but has no experience in business valuation. Defendant's expert has extensive business valuation experience.

29 Case 3:11-cv-00439 Document 31 Filed Dec. 10, 2012.

30 Paragraph 145.

31 www.gpo.gov/fdsys/pkg/CFR-2009-title42-vol5/xml/CFR-2009-title42-vol5-sec1001-952.xml.

32 Paragraph 104.

3.3.9 Definition of Fair Market Value

Defendant's expert used the definition from Revenue Ruling 59-60. His deposition testimony stated, "Revenue Ruling 59-60 discusses the need for discounts, for lack of marketability, and discounts for lack of control. And it goes on to say that the valuation is based on a cash price paid in today's terms."[33] When questioned further about the definition and why he did not "use the definitions as recognized in the OIG opinions," he responded[34] that "my understanding is that the anti-kickback statute doesn't supply the definition of fair market value."

Plaintiff's expert report, which is part of the public record, had an extensive discussion of regulatory statements on fair market value in OIG fraud alerts, the 1992 Thornton letter, and then the Stark Law definitions.[35]

3.3.10 Valuations of Plaintiff Expert

According to the plaintiff's expert, Meridian used one approach at the control level and another at the minority level:

> To arrive at its internal FMV analyses for Meridian's 60% buy-in to TCSC, Meridian used the market approach by: (1) calculating earnings before interest, taxes, depreciation and amortization ("EBITDA"), and then (2) multiplying EBITDA by a valuation multiple. To determine the price for new minority physician owners, Meridian prepared a separate valuation as opposed to applying a DLOC and DLOM to its majority interest valuation. To value the minority investment interests, Meridian used the income approach by projecting future cash flows and applying a discount factor to arrive at the present value of the minority physician buy-in price.[36]

Multiples of EBITDA are fairly common means of acquiring control interests since EBITDA and EBITDA growth are two equally common means of measuring the success of a company; acquisitions of new entities must not dilute the company's existing EBITDA or earnings and will hopefully be accretive (increase).

3.3.10.1 Control Value

As is also seen in the use of surveys in establishing reasonable compensation for physicians, plaintiff's expert placed *exclusive* reliance on the Healthcare Appraisers (HAI) "2008 ASC Valuation Survey" (based on 2007 results). According to the federal government's Health Indicators Warehouse, there were just under 5,000 ASCs in 2007.[37] According to the HAI survey, "Thirteen respondents representing well over 300 surgery centers throughout the country responded to the survey this year." That is only 6% of the total of all ASCs. Further, since the sample is

33 Case 3:11-cv-00439 Document 142-2 Filed 05/12/14

34 Accurately

35 ASC's are not covered by Stark.

36 Case 3:11-cv-00439 Document 116-1 Filed 04/21/14, page 16

37 www.healthindicators.gov/Indicators/Ambulatory-Surgical-Centers-number_10033/Profile/ClassicData; 4,962 was the actual number, these being Medicare-licensed.

not random but rather a self-selected sample of 13 operators of ASCs, it would have little or no statistical significance for the other 4,700 ASCs and their operators absent a showing that those 4,700 operators were relying on this survey as well. "Becker's ASC Review," a well-known industry information source, published a list of 56 (as compared to 13) *ASC Management and Development Companies to Watch in 2011.*[38] Obviously, many of these entities did not participate since only 13 did participate in HAI's survey.

The HAI survey *is* used as a source of market data on what industry consolidators[39] are paying for ASCs but not on a stand-alone basis without considering other market-based evidence, such as earnings calls from publicly traded operators, as well as income approach-based methods. There were more publicly traded surgery center operators in 2007 than exist today, so more market data would have been available than simply the HAI survey.

All that said, the multiple of EBITDA was the only valuation "method" plaintiff's expert relied on.

> As shown in Exhibit 1, I adjusted Mr. Uden [a Meridian employee] risk score downwards from his overall rating of "4" to a neutral "zero." This is conservative and gives Meridian the benefit of the doubt, particularly in light of the fact case volume has declined since 2006, volume risk was concentrated with Dr. Fier, there was risk of declining Medicare reimbursement, the center was operating at capacity and some of the key physician owners had mature practices. A neutral risk score does not warrant a higher multiple to be applied in the valuation process. Rather, it proves that the multiple should be no higher than the multiplier used by the majority of the ASC management companies at the time, which is a multiple ranging from 6.0x-7.0x.[40]

3.3.10.2 Management Fee Impact

As noted above, as part of the purchase, Meridian was entitled to a 6% management fee that did not exist prior to the transaction. One analysis that should be done in evaluating EBITDA multiples is to compute them with and without the management fee. Exhibit 3 re-creates one[41] that appears in the plaintiff's expert report used to compare that expert's valuation based on EBITDA multiples to the price Meridian actually paid for its 60% interest.

38 www.beckersasc.com/lists/56-asc-management-and-development-companies-to-watch-in-2011.html noting the 2011 date; see also www.beckersasc.com/news-analysis/sixty-three-people-to-know-in-the-ambulatory-surgical-center-industry.html from June 30, 2007.

39 For a broader discussion of consolidators, see "Understanding the Difference Between Strategic Value and Fair Market Value in Consolidating Industries," *Business Valuation Review,* June 2002, by this author, reproduced elsewhere in this guide.

40 Plaintiff's expert report page 20; despite the fact that the Great Recession occurred during the period starting in December 2007 and was worst in 2008 and 2009 with recovery thereafter weak, plaintiff's expert report never addresses that Recession in its repeated discussion of case volume decline and the inaccuracy of Meridian's projections. In fact, only in its rebuttal of Meridian's expert report does plaintiff's expert claim the recession did not begin until 2008.

41 Expert Report, Feb. 10, 2014, Case 3:11-cv-00439 Document 116-1 Filed April 21, 2014, page 25.

Exhibit 3. Plaintiff's Calculation of Fair Market Value

		5/31/2007	3/31/2007	3/31/2007
TTM revenue		4,329,014	4,400,211	4,400,211
Operating expenses		3,462,932	3,462,250	3,462,250
EBITDA		866,082	937,961	937,961
FMV multiple		6.0	6.0	7.0
Enterprise value		5,196,492	5,627,766	6,565,727
Meridian ownership %		60%	60%	60%
Meridian's FMV price as calculated by Plaintiff's expert		3,117,895	3,376,660	3,939,436
Pro rata control value of 1%	1.0%	51,965	56,278	65,657

Note: Plaintiff's expert report seems to imply that a management fee is a synergistic adjustment: "To determine FMV, the valuator cannot consider the 'strategic' benefits the ASC management company could achieve from its investment. For example, ASC management companies may: Benefit from margins earned on management fees." This is a very peculiar position inconsistent with both standard industry operating practice as well as basic finance. There is nothing strategic about charging a profitable fee to run an ASC or paying fair market value for a share of a future revenue stream expressed as a percentage.

We do not know from the facts available if the management fee represented: (1) pure profit to Meridian; (2) partial profit—i.e., some expense was to be incurred against the management fee by Meridian (the most likely scenario); or (3) if Meridian expected to incur a like amount of cost. However, the management fee commonly contains a profit element and is part of the value that the purchaser pays for. Perhaps more important, not all surgery center operators charge management fees in the same fashion and the multiples relied upon in the report from Healthcare Appraisers 2008 ASC valuation survey (based on 2007 results) contain a mix and match of EBITDA and adjusted EBITDA calculations that influence the range of reported multiples. Thus, it is necessary to compute an adjusted EBITDA and a true multiple of the purchase price.

Exhibit 4 reflects the adjusted EBITDA substituted in the plaintiff's expert calculation and the resultant multiple, considerably less than the apparent multiple in the plaintiff's actual exhibit.

Exhibit 4. Calculation of Multiple Using Adjusted EBITDA in Plaintiff's Model

		5/31/2007	3/31/2007	3/31/2007
EBITDA		866,082	937,961	937,961
Meridian ownership %		60%	60%	60%
Meridian EBITDA share		519,649	562,777	562,777
Management fee	6%	259,741	264,013	264,013
Meridian adjusted EBITDA		779,390	826,789	826,789
Meridian's FMV price as calculated		3,117,895	3,376,660	3,939,436
Calculated multiple		4.0	4.1	4.8

Exhibit 5 calculates the valuation multiple based on adjusted EBITDA (that includes the management fee) from the actual purchase price Meridian paid. Note that it is exactly 7.0.

Exhibit 5. Calculation of Multiple Using Adjusted EBITDA in Meridian's Model

		5/31/2007	3/31/2007	3/31/2007
EBITDA		866,082	937,961	937,961
Meridian ownership %		60%	60%	60%
Meridian EBITDA share		519,649	562,777	562,777
Management fee	6%	259,741	264,013	264,013
Meridian adjusted EBITDA		779,390	826,789	826,789
Meridian's FMV price as calculated		5,748,446	5,748,446	5,748,446
Calculated multiple		7.4	7.0	**7.0**

Finally, Exhibit 6 revises the plaintiff calculation shown in Exhibit 3 using the adjusted EBITDA that Meridian actually purchased and the valuation multiple of 7.0 that plaintiff's expert concluded was appropriate. The value is the same as that paid by Meridian, adjusted for rounding. This would seem to be the way that Meridian viewed the transaction.

Exhibit 6. Recalculation of Plaintiff's Valuation Using Adjusted EBITDA

	5/31/2007	3/31/2007	3/31/2007	
TTM revenue	4,329,014	4,400,211	4,400,211	
Operating expenses	3,462,932	3,462,250	3,462,250	
EBITDA	866,082	937,961	937,961	
FMV multiple	6.0	6.0	7.0	
Enterprise value	5,196,492	5,627,766	6,565,727	
Meridian ownership %	60%	60%	60%	
Meridian's FMV price as calculated	3,117,895	3,376,660	**3,939,436**	**a +**
Management fee	259,741	264,013	264,013	
FMV multiple	6.0	6.0	7.0	
Additional enterprise value	1,558,445	1,584,076	**1,848,089**	**b =**
Meridian's FMV price as adjusted	4,676,340	4,960,736	**5,787,525**	**c**
Difference (rounding)	-1,072,106	-787,710	**39,079**	

Reiterating the earlier statements about gaps in the public record and the management fee itself, Exhibit 7 reduces the historic EBITDA by the management fee—which is what would happen prospectively—and calculates new valuation multiples. The revised multiples are still within the expect range based on the HAI survey the plaintiff's expert used, as the survey showed 33% of transactions at a multiple greater than 7.0.

Exhibit 7. Recalculation of Multiple Using Alternative Adjusted EBITDA in Meridian's Model

		5/31/2007	3/31/2007	3/31/2007
EBITDA		866,082	937,961	937,961
Management fee	6%	259,741	264,013	264,013
Alternative adjusted EBITDA		606,341	673,948	673,948
Meridian ownership %		60%	60%	60%
Meridian EBITDA share		363,805	404,369	404,369
Management fee	6%	259,741	264,013	264,013
Meridian adjusted EBITDA		623,546	668,382	668,382
Meridian's FMV price as calculated		5,748,446	5,748,446	5,748,446
Calculated multiple		9.2	8.6	8.6

For sake of illustration, Exhibit 8 recalculates the plaintiff's valuation based upon the alternative adjusted EBITDA above, i.e., reducing historical EBITDA for the prospective management fee. Here, using the assumption of plaintiff's expert that 7.0 was the appropriate valuation multiple, Meridian's FMV price as adjusted is approximately 4.7 million, still ~$1.1 million more than the actual purchase price.

Exhibit 8. Recalculation of Plaintiff's Valuation Using Alternative Adjusted EBITDA

	5/31/2007	3/31/2007	3/31/2007
TTM revenue	4,329,014	4,400,211	4,400,211
Operating expenses	3,462,932	3,462,250	3,462,250
Management fee	259,741	264,013	264,013
Alternative adjusted EBITDA	606,341	673,948	673,948
FMV multiple	6.0	6.0	7.0
Enterprise value	3,638,047	4,043,690	4,717,638
Meridian ownership %	60%	60%	60%
Meridian's FMV price as calculated	2,182,828	2,426,214	**2,830,583**
Management fee	259,741	264,013	264,013
FMV multiple	6	6	7
Additional enterprise value	1,558,445	1,584,076	**1,848,089**
Meridian's FMV price as adjusted	3,741,273	4,010,290	**4,678,672**
Difference	-2,007,173	-1,738,156	**-1,069,774**

Finally, Exhibit 9 recalculates the plaintiff's valuation based upon the alternative adjusted EBITDA above assuming that the acquirer (Meridian) would earn only 50% of the management fee as a profit.

Exhibit 9. Recalculation of Plaintiff's Valuation Using Second Alternative Adjusted EBITDA

		5/31/2007	3/31/2007	3/31/2007
TTM revenue		4,329,014	4,400,211	4,400,211
Operating expenses		3,462,932	3,462,250	3,462,250
Management fee	50%	129,870	132,006	132,006
2nd alternative adjusted EBITDA		736,212	805,955	805,955
FMV multiple		6.0	6.0	7.0
Enterprise value		4,417,269	4,835,728	5,641,683
Meridian ownership %		60%	60%	60%
Meridian's FMV price as calculated		2,650,362	2,901,437	**3,385,010**
Management fee profit	50%	129,870	132,006	132,006
FMV multiple*		6.0	6.0	7.0
Additional enterprise value		779,223	792,038	**924,044**
Meridian's FMV price as adjusted		3,429,584	3,693,475	**4,309,054**
Difference with actual		-2,318,862	-2,054,971	**-1,439,392**

* Note: Given that the management fee comes "off the top" as a percentage of revenue and is not subject to the risk of bottom-line performance such as EBITDA, a higher valuation multiple would likely be warranted.

3.3.10.3 Minority/Noncontrol Values From Control Value

After the purchase of the 60% interest, Meridian sold portions of that interest in 1% units to physicians.[42] In light of the above analysis, plaintiff's expert makes what should be considered an error, comparing the control value of $5,748,446 that *includes* the value of the 6% management fee to the post-transaction minority or noncontrol interest sales, which were not entitled to any of that management fee. The report states that the control value implies a value of $9,597,410, computed by dividing $5,748,446 by 60%, implying a value for a 1% interest of $95,974.[43] This is clearly incorrect. Assuming *only* for the sake of illustration that plaintiff's expert used an appropriate valuation multiple of 7.0 times EBITDA, the correct comparison would be as shown in Exhibit 10, *before* considering the reduction in value of a pro rata control interest for lack of control and lack of marketability discounts.

42 Amended Complaint, Case 3:11-cv-00439 Document 31 Filed Dec. 10, 2012, page 13.
43 Expert Report, Feb. 10, 2014, Case 3:11-cv-00439 Document 116-1 Filed April 21, 2014, Exhibit 6.

Exhibit 10. Calculation of Post-Transaction Noncontrol Value Using Alternative Adjusted EBITDA

TTM revenue	4,329,014	4,400,211	4,400,211
Operating expenses	3,462,932	3,462,250	3,462,250
Management fee	259,741	264,013	264,013
Adjusted EBITDA	606,341	673,948	673,948
FMV multiple	6.0	6.0	7.0
Enterprise control value	3,638,047	4,043,690	4,717,638
Meridian ownership %	60%	60%	60%
Meridian ownership	2,182,828	2,426,214	**2,830,583**
Pro rata control value of 1%	36,380	40,437	**47,176**

After Meridian assessed the 6% management fee that it purchased for a portion of the ~$5.75 million it paid, the EBITDA of the ASC declined by the amount of that management fee! Of course, the value of the remaining shares would have to decline—the physicians just sold that value to Meridian. If the value had not declined, one would have failed to meet fair market value at the same valuation date. In Exhibit 6 of plaintiff's expert report, the first sale after Meridian's involvement was on Nov. 14, 2007, for $23,262 for a 1% interest, at the low end of the range of values posited by plaintiff's expert, who concluded a value of $31,328 was appropriate.

Plaintiff's expert report does not mention the new operating agreement that would have been a standard part of any transaction involving Meridian or another ASC manager-owner. The operating agreement would have a significant impact on the right of the minority or noncontrolling owner group and therefore the value of its interests.

3.3.10.4 Noncontrol or Minority Interest Valuation

Plaintiff's expert effectively withdrew the original report's minority interest valuation using the income approach that claimed, "based on my analysis, TCSC undercharged new minority in all instances, in amounts ranging from $3,077 to $24,197." In the supplemental and rebuttal report *after* Meridian's expert had issued a report, plaintiff's expert stated, "Given the inherent access to information limitations in this matter, we were not in a position to question or validate Meridian's cash flow projections it developed for the minority buy-ins" and, "because of the reasons noted above, we now believe that we do not have enough information to opine on the fair market value of the minority interest transactions."

3.3.10.5 Return on Investment

In apparent homage to Advisory Opinion No. 07-05, plaintiff's expert report[44] states the following:

> As discussed above, to comply with the ASC safe harbor under the AKS, one of the eight

44 Page 26.

> requirements that must be met to comply with the safe harbor is that, "the amount of payment to an investor in return for the investment must be directly proportional to the amount of the capital investment of that investor."[45] In other words, distributions must be directly proportional to the amount of the capital investment.

In a statement that defies reconciliation with the opinions of the value of the minority interests ($31,328 for a 1% share or $1,253,120 for a 40% noncontrol share), plaintiff's expert claims:

> At the same time Meridian purchased its 60% share in TCSC, it started a new company TCSC, LLC. Meridian's contributed capital for its 60% investment in TCSC, totaled $5,833,127. In exchange for their 40% interest, the physician owners contributed just *$291,184.* As a result, TCSC's distributions made to Meridian and the original physician owners were not in direct proportion to the amount of contributed capital.

The physicians owning the remaining 40% after the sale of 60% to Meridian contributed those interests to a new LLC in exchange for 40% ownership. One cannot simultaneously value something at both $1,253,120 and $291,184.

3.3.10.6 Did Plaintiff's Expert Conform to AICPA Valuation Standards?

Defendants filed a motion[46] to have the plaintiff's expert testimony excluded, for among other reasons, failure to adhere to professional standards by using a rule of thumb as a sole valuation method and lack of any business valuation experience. The motion was denied.

The American Institute of Certified Public Accountants Statements on Standards for Valuation Services (SSVS) requires all certified public accountants[47] who are AIPCA members to adhere to its criteria for valuation. Although there is a specific exception for reports (see below) offered in a litigation context, there is no exception from the standards of developmental work done in connection with expressing an opinion of value. Plaintiff's expert expressed the following opinions of value:

1. It is my opinion that Meridian overpaid TCSC's referring physician owners for its purchase of its 60% ownership interest in TCSC. The amount paid in excess of fair market value ranges from $1,819,010 to $2,640,552. [*Editor's note: A CPA cannot express an opinion of amounts in excess of fair market value without first coming to their own opinion of fair market value.*]

45 42 C.F.R. § 1001.952(r)(4)(iii).

46 Case 3:11-cv-00439 Document 116 Filed April 21, 2014.

47 According to the CV attached to the supplemental expert report, the primary/testifying expert is not an AICPA member although other members of the engagement team cited as playing significant roles are. No senior member of the engagement team holds the Accredited in Business Valuation designation from the AICPA according to the CVs. One junior member holds that designation. Some states require adherence to SSVS if the firm is registered as a CPA firm.

2. Meridian's internal valuation of TCSC was inflated because it used higher than FMV multiples to determine TCSC's value. *It's my opinion that the FMV multiple that should have been used in this instance ranges from 6.0x to 7.0x.* Meridian used a multiple of least 8.9x up to 11.1x. [*Editor's note: The emphasized portion expresses an opinion as to a valuation multiple and was used in the report to reach the alleged amount in excess of fair market value paid by Meridian.*]

The following two sections are extracted from the AICPA standards. The development standards listed are some, but likely not all, of the ones relevant in this particular matter that the reader should evaluate. Given the reporting exemption, it is often difficult to determine precisely what development standards were and were not applied in a litigation engagement.

3.3.10.7 AICPA Valuation Standards Reporting Exemption

Reporting Exemption for Certain Controversy Proceedings .50 A valuation performed for a matter before a court, an arbitrator, a mediator or other facilitator, or a matter in a governmental or administrative proceeding, is exempt from the reporting provisions of this statement. The reporting exemption applies whether the matter proceeds to trial or settles. The exemption applies only to the reporting provisions of this statement (see paragraphs .47-.49 and .51-.78). The developmental provisions of the statement (see paragraphs .21-.46) still apply whenever the valuation analyst expresses a conclusion of value or a calculated value (Interpretation No. 1 [VS sec. 9100 par. .01-.89]).

3.3.10.8 Select AICPA Valuation Development Provisions[48]

i. Applicable premise of value;

ii. Assumptions and limiting conditions;

iii. Classes of equity ownership interests and rights attached thereto:

  a. Determine the type of ownership interest being valued and ascertain whether that interest exhibits control characteristics;

  b. Analyze the different ownership interests of other owners and assess the potential effect on the value of the subject interest;

  c. Understand the classes of equity ownership interests and rights attached thereto; and

  d. For a business, business ownership interest, or security: Shareholder agreements, partnership agreements, operating agreements, voting trust agreements, buy-sell agreements, loan covenants, restrictions, and other contractual obligations or restrictions affecting the owners and the subject interest.

48 Statement on Standards for Valuation Services No. 1, June 2007.

iv. In developing the valuation, the valuation analyst should consider the three most common valuation approaches:

a. Income (income-based) approach;[49]

b. Asset (asset-based) approach (used for businesses, business ownership interests, and securities) or cost approach (used for intangible assets); and

c. Market (market-based) approach.

v. For an intangible asset, the valuation analyst should also consider, when relevant, the following:

a. Whether any tax amortization benefit would be included in the analysis.[50]

3.3.10.9 Deposition Rebuttal of Plaintiff's Report by Meridian Expert

Meridian's expert correctly identified that plaintiff's expert in the original report revised Meridian's internal valuation multiples using an *after-tax* discount rate, despite the fact that the internal models were clearly based on *pretax* cash flows and therefore required a pretax discount rate. As shown in Exhibit 11 from documents contained on the federal PACER website for the case, the free cash flows are derived directly from EBITDA,[51] definitionally a pretax measure.

3.3.10.10 Rebuttal of Meridian's Expert report by Plaintiff Expert

> In reality, the application of a TAB [tax amortization benefit] in this context is virtually unheard of in the healthcare valuation community. Nowhere in credible valuation guidance or literature is it recommended, or even suggested, to add a TAB to an equity value,[52] and it is misleading for [Meridian's Expert] to suggest otherwise. The literature that does exist relates to fair value accounting, which has significant differences in theory and application from fair market value (defined previously), the standard of value required by the OIG and relevant to this case.[53]

First off, SSVS as cited in Item v.a. above specifically requires the consideration of an amortization benefit for an intangible asset, of which goodwill in a business valuation would be one. Further, as readers of each edition of this guide—and numerous other places in the literature—would

49 In the rebuttal to Meridian's expert rebuttal of their report, plaintiff's expert states: "We believe that: (1) we were unable to perform a credible DCF analysis due to the inherent limitations in this litigation matter, (2) we were in no position to validate Meridian's assumptions used to determine TCSC's TTM EBITDA24 used in its valuation, and (3) we were not provided Meridian's projected cash flows as of the June 29, 2007 transaction."

50 See Rebuttal of Meridian's Expert below.

51 Earnings before interest, taxes, depreciation, and amortization.

52 This statement is also wrong. Meridian's expert valued invested capital, the correct approach as the transaction was an asset purchase.

53 Plaintiff's Expert Rebuttal Report, page 23; the 2009 edition of this guide was cited elsewhere by plaintiff's expert and it contained discussion of the tax amortization benefit. *The Medical Practice Valuation Guidebook 2001/2002*, page 137, contains a comprehensive example of how to compute the TAB.

Exhibit 11. Free Cash Flows Derived From EBITDA

Treasure Coast Surgery Center, LLC
Valuation - 9/30/07

Discount Factor						
Discount Rate:	27.0%					
Years	0.5	1.5	2.5	3.5	4.5	5.0
Factor	0.8874	0.6987	0.5502	0.4332	0.3411	0.3027
Assumes mid-year convention, where cash flows occur evenly throughout the year						

Free Cash Flow	Year 1	Year 2	Year 3	Year 4	Year 5	
EBITDA	695,414	750,347	778,113	806,341	835,023	
Changes in Working Capital	(95,193)	(11,162)	(11,499)	(11,846)	(12,204)	
Capital Expenditures	(50,000)	(50,000)	(50,000)	(50,000)	(50,000)	
Debt Service	-	-	-	-	-	
Free Cash Flow	550,220	689,185	716,614	744,495	772,820	
Discount Factor	0.8874	0.6987	0.5502	0.4332	0.3411	
Present Value of FCF	488,242	481,538	394,254	322,514	263,610	1,950,157

Terminal Value			
Year 5 EBITDA	835,023		
Exit Multiple	3.00x	*- Multiple from Operating Agreement*	
Terminal Value	2,505,070		
Discount Factor	0.3027	*- Assumes that exit occurs at the end of year 5*	
Present Value	758,231		758,231

Discounted Cash Flow Analysis	
Total Present Value of FCF	1,950,157
Present Value of Terminal Value	758,231
Enterprise Value	2,708,387
Add: Cash	-
Less: Debt	-
Equity Value	2,708,387
Number of Shares	100
Per Share	27,084
Old	23,262.00

be aware, this statement is simply false. In fact, Chapter 16 of the *BVR/AHLA Guide to Healthcare Industry Finance and Valuation* contains the following quotations:

> "Bear in mind that healthcare transactions are usually of assets, not equity, and therefore the basis step-up in the hands of the acquirer is relevant. The same rationale applies to amortizing any intangible value under IRC Section 197."[54]

> "If the goal of the valuation is to value assets, the valuator should consider adding the present value of the tax benefit of amortizing the intangible value under Internal Revenue Code 197."[55]

> "For example the AICPA White Paper Intangible Asset Valuation Cost Approach Methods and Procedures states:
>
>> The tax amortization benefit adjustment is applicable to the application of the income approach to value intangible assets. The tax amortization benefit adjustment (1) decreases income tax expense and (2) increases after tax income in the application of the income approach to asset valuation. However, neither income tax expense nor after tax income is a component of a cost approach valuation.[56]

54 *BVR/AHLA Guide to Healthcare Industry Finance and Valuation*, 4th edition, Chapter 16, page 388.
55 Footnote on page 412.
56 American Institute of Certified Public Accountants white paper "Intangible Asset Valuation, Cost Approach

A Google search of the term "tax amortization benefit" returned many thousands of hits including numerous PowerPoint presentations and articles[57] on precisely this issue. Plaintiff's original expert report was dated Feb. 10, 2014, shortly before the white paper was published in March 2014, and the supplemental expert report was dated April 21, 2014, long after the white paper was published. Of course, SSVS was published in 2007.

Treasure Coast Surgery Center LLC was structured as an LLC taxed as a partnership, therefore the purchase of the interest and contribution to this new LLC by Meridian would have been treated as an asset purchase (*not* an equity purchase as plaintiff's expert alleges; further, Meridian's expert first correctly valued invested capital before subtracting debt to arrive at equity) and a basis step-up in the intangible assets eligible for amortization would exist. Similarly, an evaluation of the contribution to the capital of the LLC would be required for the physicians owning the 40% minority interest pursuant to IRC sections 704 and 737 and perhaps 751. Once the new LLC was established and then minority shares sold to physicians, an IRC section 754 election could—and in all likelihood should—have been made to adjust the basis of the purchased assets with respect to the new owner in order not to leave substantial tax and cash flow benefits "on the table."

3.3.11 Valuation of Meridian Expert

It does not appear that Meridian's expert report is available as part of the public record and as such information can be gleaned only from the limited extracts of deposition testimony that are in the record as well as the rebuttal of the report by plaintiff's expert.

3.3.11.1 Market Approach

Meridian's expert used both a guideline public companies method and a guideline transaction method[58] with a valuation date of June 29, 2007.[59] Both value indications were less than the transaction price, by ~$700,000 and $1.0 million, respectively. Plaintiff's expert, who employed only the EBITDA multiple described above in concluding the value of the control interest, criticized the selection of the guidelines and the failure to somehow weight the market approach with the income approach—this despite the fact that standard healthcare industry valuation practice is to base one's conclusion on a discounted cash flow model.

Methods and Procedures," page 52, March 2014; principal author Robert Reilly, CPA/ABV, ASA.

57 E.g., *Tax Amortization Benefit: Usage in Healthcare Transactions* from VMG Health, a valuation firm with extensive experience in ASC valuations; *Practical Application of Intangible Asset Valuation Approaches and Methods,* Robert F. Reilly, CPA of Willamette Management Associates, who also is principal author of the AICPA white paper and a member of the AICPA Business Valuation Committee that drafted SSVS; *Tax Considerations in M&A Transactions,* David Burton (Akin Gump Strauss Hauer & Feld LLP) and Anne Levin-Nussbaum (Attorney), Thomsen Reuters Business Law Currents; *Understanding Book Versus Tax Valuation Differences Improves M&A Planning and Reporting,* PricewaterhouseCoopers Transaction Services (August 2011).

58 The plaintiff's rebuttal incorrectly refers to these methods as approaches.

59 Prior to the record reached in the post-Recession period, the Dow Jones hit a record of 14,198 in October 2007, declining 6%, to 13,364, by Dec. 31, 2007. It hit a post-record low in February 2009.

3.3.11.2 Income Approach

Meridian's expert used a 4% terminal growth rate in the valuation. Certainly, this would be deemed high by recent historical standards, and, absent the report, there is no way to gauge the underlying rationale. However, the Survey of Professional Forecasters by the Philadelphia Federal Reserve for the second quarter of 2007 was reporting expected real economic growth for 2007 and 2008 of between 2.4% and 3.0% coupled with core inflation of 2.3%, suggesting that nominal near-term growth would be in the 5% range. In today's weak economy, that is unheard of, making a 4% terminal growth assumption seem inappropriate without some hindsight into the pre-Recession period. The rebuttal also maintained that there was no capital expense outlay to support a 4% growth rate.

Furthermore, it was also known at the valuation date that, as of Jan. 1, 2008, there would be a large expansion in the number of procedures eligible for Medicare reimbursement in an ASC setting that could have driven the terminal growth rate. "This proposed rule, in part, would revise the current list of procedures that are approved when furnished in a Medicare-approved ambulatory surgical center (ASC), which would be applicable to services furnished on or after January 1, 2008."[60]

> In CY 2008, we also are adding hundreds of surgical procedures to the already extensive list of procedures for which Medicare allows payment to ASCs, creating new opportunities for ASCs to expand their range of covered surgical procedures. For the first time, ASCs will be paid separately for covered ancillary services that are integral to covered surgical procedures, including certain radiology procedures, costly drugs and biologicals, devices with pass-through status under the OPPS, and brachytherapy sources.[61]

Again, plaintiff's expert inexplicably maintained that the management fee included in the Meridian expert's cash flow forecast was somehow a strategic value adjustment, despite a footnote in the rebuttal that stated: "It has been our experience that ASC managers generally charge a management fee of 5%- 6%. Meridian applies a 6% management fee." By logical extension, then, all ASC transactions including a management fee component would not be commercially reasonable, as plaintiff's expert concluded: "It is my opinion that the financial arrangements between Meridian and TCSC were not commercially reasonable because the amounts paid were not FMV."[62]

A weighted average cost of capital (WACC) based on 25% debt and 75% equity was used. As with a 4% growth rate, such a WACC weighting for an entity characterized by high intangible value relative to total value might be considered at the high end of the debt range *today*, although certainly not unheard of. The plaintiff's rebuttal suggests that Meridian's expert based this on

60 www.cms.gov/Medicare/Medicare-Fee-for-Service-Payment/ASCPayment/ASC-Regulations-and-Notices-Items/CMS1205832.html

61 72 Fed. Reg. 42542-43 (Aug. 2, 2007).

62 Plaintiff expert report, page 5.

an optimal mix of debt and equity. Whatever the capital structure or weightings assumed, the cost of debt and equity subject to the weightings has to reflect the dynamic relation between the two. As debt goes up relative to equity, the cost of equity will increase[63] and the cost of debt may well increase because a firm with more debt is more risky, all things equal, than one with less debt. The plaintiff's rebuttal displayed various combinations of debt and equity and recalculated WACCs without making the necessary adjustments to the cost of equity and debt. In fact, the cost of equity used by Meridian's expert based on the plaintiff rebuttal report was 20.3%. Given an equity risk premium of 7% and a small stock premium of 5.82%[64] and a 20-year Treasury bond rate of 5.21% on June 29, 2007, this yields a base equity rate of 18.03% and implies an additional risk premium for Meridian of ~2.3%. For reasons not clear in the plaintiff's expert report,[65] all the discount rate computations were done as of December 31 rather than on the actual valuation dates, but the one closest to the June 29, 2007, was 16.63%.[66] Thus, Meridian's expert could have accounted for the increased equity risk associated with more debt in an optimal capital structure.

3.3.12 Conclusions

This is a very peculiar case, as are many cases when seen from the outside without the benefit of all the facts, valuation and otherwise, known to the parties, their legal counsel, and experts. Whether the 60% interest was overvalued or not is less important, however, than the stated position of the plaintiff and its experts with respect to accepted ASC industry operations—e.g., management fees[67]—and required valuation industry practice—e.g., consideration of a tax amortization benefit, reliance on one's own work when expressing a conclusion of value, as opposed to manipulating someone else's work to generate a different result, and having a depth of expertise in healthcare industry business valuation as well as the regulatory environment. At the same time, it highlights the practical import of getting a contemporaneous independent third-party valuation for transactions at risk of attack under the AKS or Stark Law. In addition, it demonstrates the inherent difficulty and risk of preparing a valuation after the fact that purports to agree with a transaction that took place years earlier.

3.4 *United States of America ex rel. Michael Reilly, M.D. v. North Broward Hospital District, et al.*

Author's note: This case was settled shortly before the deadline for submission of chapters for this guide, so the analysis is abbreviated. The settlement of $69.5 million was announced Sept. 15, 2015, and North Broward denied the allegations.

63 Reflected by unlevering and relevering beta in the capital asset pricing model.

64 *Ibbotson SBBI Valuation Yearbook, 2008.*

65 Exhibit 7.

66 Notably, this included the use of an industry risk premium, something that in this author's view was debunked by my paper for *Business Valuation Review* "A Healthcare Appraiser Reviews a Judge-Appraiser's 'Report,'" Summer 2007, reproduced elsewhere in this guide; *Business Valuation Review* papers are generally considered to be peer-reviewed.

67 For a broader discussion of what constitutes strategic value and when, see "Understanding the Difference Between Strategic Value and Fair Market Value in Consolidating Industries," *Business Valuation Review,* June 2002, by this author, reproduced elsewhere in this guide.

3.4.1 Introduction

The Relator in this case clearly had extensive access to inside information, particularly for a physician who was practicing in the community, as opposed to, for example, a member of the hospital finance department or executive team.

> 67. The financial data cited in this Second Amended Complaint are derived from Broward Health's internal financial reports which are kept in secret by Broward Health financial strategists. Such internal reports are not publicly available. The contribution margin reports discussed below for each employed physician are kept in secret by Broward Health's financial strategists who have recruited physicians and determined their compensation terms. With respect to the employed physicians discussed below, Dr. Reilly has provided the identity of each physician and documentation of the detailed evidence discussed to the Department of Justice.[68]

According to the complaint, the hospital offered him employment on terms that he believed to violate the Stark laws, which he declined. The complaint also alleges "excessive compensation of employed physicians has caused estimated net operating losses in excess of 150 million dollars if referral profits are not considered."

3.4.2 Allegations

The Second Amended Complaint[69] in this matter stated the key allegations in connection with physician compensation:

> 2. Defendants North Broward Hospital District d/b/a Broward Health and Broward General Medical Center (collectively referred to as "Broward Health" or "the Broward Health Defendants") have compensated employed physicians (1) at levels which exceeded the fair market value of their personal services, (2) at levels which have caused major net operating losses and were not commercially reasonable if the physicians were not in a position to generate referral business for Broward Health, and (3) at levels which were determined based in part on the volume and value of inpatient and outpatient referrals by such physicians to Broward Health hospitals and clinics.

3.4.2.1 Operating Losses and How Funded

There is extreme detail throughout the complaint about operating losses, including analysis of overhead rates, operating expenses, and physician compensation. The allegations included physician practices in orthopedics, cardiology, hematology/oncology, and cardiology.

> 63. Practice overhead (which primarily represents physician compensation) for all practice groups totaled $25,047,758 as of December midway through Fiscal Year 2011, yet total collections for all practice groups totaled only $14,546,385. The overall percent of practice

68 Case 0:10-cv-60590-JEM, Document 19 Entered on FLSD Docket Sept. 29, 2011.

69 Id.

> overhead/collections was 172 percent. Such percentage would be economically unviable if the parties were not in a position to generate and receive referral profits.
>
> 73. For Year 3, Broward Health listed the "ancillary revenue" associated with these 3 [orthopedic surgeon] physicians as $820,706 and the "rehab revenue" associated with these 3 physicians as $520,200. For Year 4, Broward Health listed the "ancillary revenue" associated with these 3 physicians as $837,120 and the "rehab revenue" associated with these 3 physicians as $530,604. For Year 5, Broward Health listed the "ancillary revenue" associated with these 3 physicians as $853,863 and the "rehab revenue" associated with these 3 physicians as $541,216.
>
> 112. Broward Health's secretive internal financial reports demonstrate that for every employed physician and every group of employed physicians, Broward Health has tracked the volume and value of referrals from its physicians to Broward Health hospitals and clinics.
>
> 113. The analyses privately performed by Broward Health's internal financial strategists confirm that the employed physicians are being compensated at levels which produce major operating losses if profits from referrals by such physicians to Broward Health hospitals and clinics are not considered. Midway through Fiscal Year 2011, Broward Health calculated the year-to-date "net losses from operations" for its employed physicians to be $10,501,373.
>
> 116. Broward Health has systematically and secretly monitored and evaluated the inpatient and outpatient "contribution margins" from its employed physicians which changed the net operating losses of $10,501,373 caused by Broward Health's overcompensation of employed physicians into a profit of $5,929,288 for Broward Health plus $1,878,166 for indigent care compensation under the PPUC Program midway through Fiscal Year 2011.
>
> 122. The "inpatient contribution margin" or profits from inpatient referrals by employed primary care physicians were $3,279,365, which is the highest inpatient profits associated with referrals from any practice specialty at Broward Health. That fact further explains Broward Health's current focus on recruiting primary care physicians who have brought the highest inpatient referral revenues to Broward Health hospitals as discussed below.

3.4.2.2 Rationale for Recruitment

The complaint alleges that referrals rather than community need were the basis for the employment of the physicians.

> 70. The Proforma confirms that Broward Health did not recruit and hire these orthopedic surgeons based on the need for more orthopedic surgeons in Broward County. Rather, Broward Health targeted these orthopedic surgeons who were employed by a competitor hospital in the same region, Holy Cross Hospital in Fort Lauderdale. Broward Health's goal was to capture more of the lucrative market of outpatient visits and inpatient admissions for orthopedic surgeries and services.

> 102. In recent years, Broward Health has aggressively recruited, hired, and compensated cardiologists using a similar business model of valuing the referral revenue stream from such physicians. Broward Health has focused on recruiting and employing cardiologists due to its fear of losing the referral revenue stream from inpatient admissions and outpatient procedures to competing hospitals and its desire to profit from the lucrative ancillary revenues associated with inpatient cardiac admissions and outpatient cardiac procedures.
>
> 103. For example, in Fiscal Year 2011 as of December, the overall percent of the practice overhead/collections for Broward Health's employed orthopedic surgeons was 176 percent. The overall percent of practice overhead/collections for Broward Health's employed cardiologists was 188 percent.

3.4.2.3 'Survey Says'

In yet another over-reliance on the relevance of surveys in fair market value physician compensation analysis—whether by qui tam relators and their experts or by hospital experts—the complaint notes, "The compensation to collections ratio for orthopedic surgeons has been double the 90th percentile ratio for orthopedic surgeons in the southern United States."

> 92. Broward Health paid Dr. [redacted] at least $1,391,184.23 in 2008 and $1,557,984.40 in 2009, despite the fact that the 90th percentile (the highest percentile category) salary for orthopedic surgery-sports medicine in the Southern U.S. was $1,209,569 in 2008 and $1,236,276 in 2009. Broward Health paid Dr. [redacted] $1,557,984.40 in 2009 despite the fact that expenses from his practice exceeded 2 million dollars.
>
> 93. Dr. [redacted] compensation to collections ratio for 2009 was 1.20 which was approximately double the 90th percentile compensation to collections ratio (.615) for sports medicine orthopedic surgeons in the southern United States as reported in the *MGMA 2009 Physician Compensation and Production Survey.* The ratio of practice overhead to collections for Dr. [redacted] was 1.61 in Fiscal Year 2009.
>
> 178. For example, the Broward Health Operating Statement dated September 10, 2009 indicates that Dr. [redacted] aka Dr. [redacted] produced 3,672 RVUs for the two month period of July-August 2009. Her "planned budget" RVUs are even higher at 4,027. Such numbers are implausible for an invasive cardiologist like Dr. [redacted]. The *2009 MGMA Survey* indicates that the highest percentile (90th percentile) of invasive cardiologists in the southern United States produce 13,458 RVUs per year. Broward Health budgeted her RVU numbers at a pace to nearly double the RVU levels of the highest percentile (90th percentile) of invasive cardiologists in the southern United States.

3.4.2.4 Physician Compensation and Productivity

Aside from the survey-based allegation in the preceding paragraphs, the complaint alleges that compensation was not linked to high productivity or to the provision of uncompensated charity care.

> 174. With employed physicians producing major net operating losses if the value and volume of referrals are not considered, such physicians' compensation cannot be justified legitimately by the personal production or personal services of such physicians or physician RVUs.
>
> 175. The relatively modest net operating revenues produced by employed physicians' services do not reflect overall high personal productivity or collections based on high RVUs.
>
> 176. The modest operating revenues produced by employed physicians are not explained by charity care. Among all physician practice groups for Fiscal Year 2009 as of June, physician charity care totaled only $15,314 or .0008 of net revenue from physician services. According to the July 2011 Internal Operating Statement Report for Physician Groups, charity care for physician services is only 11 percent of net revenues for audited Fiscal Year 2010 and that percentage is inflated because charity care is internally calculated at gross charges. Midway through Fiscal Year 2011 as of December, the total indigent care write-offs were only 4.18 percent across all physician practice groups.
>
> 177. Employed physicians at Broward Health are not being compensated at levels which only contemplate their net revenues from personal production or RVUs. There is also evidence that some physicians' RVUs are implausible or abnormally disconnected from physician revenues and Dr. Reilly has provided that evidence to the Department of Justice for investigation.

3.4.2.5 Alleged 'Unbundling' of Multiple Surgical Procedures to Increase RVUs

> Dr. Reilly has also received information that the orthopedic surgeons' RVU codes have been unbundled in the past, allowing such physicians to receive excessive compensation. The RVU codes for surgical procedures commonly include multiple related procedures in a single RVU. If those RVU codes are "unbundled" which means each related procedure is listed as a separate RVU, the numbers of RVUs can be inflated.

3.4.2.6 Nonemployee Physicians

This is one of the more novel aspects of this complaint in that it involves allegations of excessive compensation to nonemployees, who could not be covered by the employment exception to the Stark law,[70] for example.

> 190. Under the same scheme discussed above, Broward Health's financial strategists also regularly run secretive "contribution margin reports" for every non-employed physician who refers patients to Broward Health hospitals and clinics. In such reports, Broward Health calculates the volumes and profits from inpatient and outpatient referrals by such physicians to Broward Health hospitals and clinics.

70 42 C.F.R. § 411.357(c).

191. One of these non-employed physicians tracked by Broward Health is Dr. [redacted] and his AIDS Healthcare Foundation, Inc. Dr. [redacted] has been and is a significant source of referrals of patients to Broward Health hospitals and clinics.

192. In approximately December of 2008, Broward Health gave nine months of free rent to Dr. [redacted] and his AIDS Healthcare Foundation under a lease which required monthly rent of $10,360.61 plus applicable taxes for office space at the Imperial Point Medical Office Complex located at 6405 North Federal Highway Suite 205, Fort Lauderdale, Florida 33308. There was no commercial justification for such free rent other than the value of profits from referrals by Dr. [redacted] to Broward Health hospitals and clinics.

193. The lease term began on July 1, 2000 for five years, was renewed for five years, and was set to expire in 2010.

194. In December of 2008, Broward Health executed an Assignment of the Medical Office Lease from Dr. [redacted] to his AIDS Healthcare Foundation, Inc. with Dr. [redacted] still serving as a guarantor. The parties ostensibly affirmed all of the obligations under the original Lease. In reality Broward Health agreed to give Dr. [redacted] and his AIDS Healthcare Foundation free rent for nine months in part based on the value of profits from referrals to Broward Health hospitals and clinics.

3.4.3 Conclusions

This case highlights the risk of "recruiting" into hospital employment settings physicians already on the staff of the recruiting institution or already working in the institution's service or catchment area at a competitor. Yet again, it emphasizes that the commercial reasonableness standard requires that hospitals and health systems employing physicians at significant losses be prepared to offer a community needs or other analysis for those losses that do not invoke the volume or value of referrals.

Physician compensation survey usage is a double-edged sword, as seen in *Community Medical* and this case as well as *Tuomey* and *Halifax* discussed elsewhere in this guide. Qui tam plaintiff experts, and defendant and regular appraisal experts, make unwarranted reliance on the surveys in attacking or justifying physician compensation under the fair market value standard.

Chapter 9.
Bradford Regional Medical Center: Lessons for the Inexperienced

CONTENTS

Chapter 9.
Bradford Regional Medical Center: Lessons for the Inexperienced

By Mark O. Dietrich, CPA/ABV

Author's note: This is one of the first in a line of qui tam cases involving valuation issues. The previous chapter in this guide describes three more recent cases in detail. The federal government reached a $2.75 million settlement with Bradford Regional in August of 2012. In June of 2014, the federal government reached a separate settlement of $500,000 with the two physicians who originally owned the nuclear medicine camera at issue. The relators objected to that settlement in August of 2014, but that objection was later withdrawn in the face of court rulings.

1.0 Introduction

The federal whistleblower or qui tam law allows a private citizen (plaintiff) to bring a civil action[1] on behalf of the government against an alleged violator seeking damages, of which the qui tam plaintiff (or relator) may claim 15% to 35% of the total damages ultimately paid. The government may choose to join in the action against the alleged violator, bringing the enormous prosecutorial clout of the federal government to bear against the defendant. Thus, there are significant financial incentives to bring a qui tam action. This November 2010 case involved a whistleblower on whose behalf the government had intervened.

The facts of the case include the sublease of a nuclear medicine camera[2] by two physicians on the Bradford Regional Medical Center (BRMC) staff who were threatened with loss of hospital admitting privileges for competing with BRMC in the provision of nuclear medicine scans. Nuclear

1 There is a segment of the litigation bar that specializes in these cases.

2 SPECT, or single photon emission computed tomography, is the technical term. The fixed units look like a small CT or MRI unit, while the mobile units have a chair in which the patient sits and the camera rotates around that chair, generating an image of the heart.

medicine scans represent the highest dollar cost to the Medicare Part B program performed by cardiologists. More importantly in the context of this guide, a valuation of a "noncompete" prepared by a CPA (referred to as CPA or [name] Redacted) is at the center of the case.

2.0 Court's Findings in *Bradford Regional Medical Center (BMRC)* Case

The background as summarized by the court is as follows:

> Before entering into a final sublease, BRMC had a fair market value assessment prepared by an accountant, Redacted. (Leonhardt[3] Dep. at 54; BRMC 30(b)(6) Dep. at 146-148.) BRMC sought this report to determine whether BRMC was paying fair market value under the proposed sublease arrangement. (Leonhardt Dep. at 54-55; BRMC 30(b)(6) Dep. at 148-149.) In September 2003, the board of BRMC received Mr. Redacted's report. The report concluded that the amounts to be paid pursuant to the proposed sublease were reasonable. (BRMC 30(b)(6) Dep. Appx., at 146-149.)
>
> In performing his fair market value analysis, Mr. Redacted compared the revenues BRMC expected to generate with the sublease in place to the revenues BRMC expected to receive without the sublease in place. (Report of Redacted, C.P.A.; Leonhardt Dep. at 55-56.) The projections were based on the expectation that V&S would refer such business to the hospital if the sublease arrangement was approved. (Id.) According to defendants, the basis of Mr. Redacted's report was what benefits BRMC would have lost had it terminated the medical staff appointment and clinical privileges of Drs. Vaccaro and Saleh pursuant to BRMC's policy. BRMC advised Drs. Vaccaro and Saleh that its valuation expert indicated that he could support the fair market value of the sublease, however neither Vaccaro nor Saleh received or reviewed a copy of Mr. Redacted's written valuation.

In denying, in part, both parties' cross-motions for summary judgment, the court concluded:

> Again, the record evidence is not strongly in favor of defendants [BRMC, et al.] as it tends to show that defendants entered into the equipment sublease fully aware that the arrangement, which had at its core a noncompete payment roughly equal to the referral business BRMC would gain from the doctors and the business V&S would lose from abandoning its own camera, may not be permitted under the Stark Act and Anti-Kickback Act. However, we are unable to conclude as a matter of law that defendants acted "knowingly" for purposes of the False Claims Act.
>
> For the foregoing reasons, we will deny defendants' motions for summary judgment and grant in part and deny in part relator's motion for summary judgment.[4]

3 The hospital's CEO.

4 docs.justia.com/cases/federal/district-courts/pennsylvania/pawdce/1:2004cv00186/3406/145/.

3.0 Key Valuation Issues in *BRMC* Case

As those of us trained in tax law[5] learn, court decisions are case-fact specific. The valuation report in this case was obtained through the federal court system's PACER service[6] since it was part of the public record. A review of that report indicates that it is not the typical valuation one would expect to see in a circumstance such as this; for example, the report states that the fair market value was tested against Section 482 of the Internal Revenue Code. As such, fewer risks might have been perceived from an initial reading of the court's decision in those circumstances where the parties are relying upon the fair market value exception based upon an appropriately prepared report. At the same time, even a good report is never an absolute defense against an allegation under the Stark Law or anti-kickback statute. Further, it is clear that in the court's view, factors cited in the valuation report were consistent with the purchase of referrals, e.g., "these statements, however, do not counter the record evidence that the analysis in the [CPA valuation] report was based on the assumption that the physicians would likely refer this business to the hospital" and that Mr. Leonhardt's summary presentation showed an expected profit for BRMC from entering into the lease agreement that was based on receiving business from V&S."

This suggests the court believed that the valuation had as an underlying assumption that all the nuclear scans done in the physicians' office would be referred post-transaction to the acquiring hospital. This, in turn, might indicate strategic value rather than fair market value, depending on how the valuation was performed. Given the requirement of the Stark regulations defining the modifications to fair market value, a compliant fair market value analysis would have considered the risk of the hospital (and other potential competitors) *not* receiving all of the referrals, to wit:

420 CFR 411.351 states: "Fair market value means the value in arm's-length transactions consistent with general market value. 'General market value' means the price that an asset would bring as the result of bona fide bargaining between well-informed buyers and sellers *who are not otherwise in a position to generate business for the other party*" (emphasis added).

And from Stark II-Phase 2: "Moreover, the definition of 'fair market value' in the statute and regulation is qualified in ways that do not necessarily comport with the usage of the term in standard valuation techniques and methodologies. For example, the methodology must exclude valuations where the parties to the transactions are at arm's length but in a position to refer to one another. In addition, the definition itself differs depending on the type of transaction: Leases or rentals of space and equipment cannot take into account the intended use of the rented item, and *in cases where the lessor is in a position to refer to the lessee, the valuation cannot be adjusted or reflect the value of proximity or convenience to the lessor*" (emphasis added).

Thus the cash flow analysis and the discount rate developed in connection with such a valuation would have to reflect something other than the actual relationship between purchaser

5 The author has a Masters in Taxation degree.
6 Thank you to Kathie Wilson, CPA/CVA one of the guide's contributing authors.

and seller. The court clearly believed that the actual relationship was the basis for the valuation. And, it is clear from the court's opinion that the modifications to fair market value spelled out in the above two quotes from the Stark regulations were not taken into account.

The OIG's office has long expressed concern with the sale of ancillary designated health services ancillaries (DHS) owned by physicians to a hospital or other buyer when the DHS will remain in the selling physician's office and continue to be used by the physicians. Although it involved a surgery center, similar issues in the OIG's perspective can be seen in Advisory Opinion No. 07-05.[7]

The following section illuminates key issues in the case and then what fair market value in a regulatory context (should) mean to an appraiser and how the fundamental measure of an appropriate discount rate and measure of cash flows *should* avoid much of the inherent issue of "valuing referrals."[8]

The quotation below is one of the most damning elements of the fact pattern. Although the court does not mention it, fair market value includes a criterion that neither party is under duress.

> Drs. Vaccaro and Saleh had a history of referring patients to BRMC for nuclear imaging until they invested in their own General Electric nuclear camera. With their own camera, they no longer needed to refer patients to BRMC for imaging. BRMC threatened to revoke the doctors' hospital privileges, which led to lengthy negotiations.

Equally as problematic are the contents of the valuation report:

> Mr. [CPA] explained that his table is "based on the assumption that the physicians would likely refer this business to the hospital in the absence of a financial interest in their own facilities or services, although they are not required to do so by virtue of any of the covenants contained in the agreements or otherwise."
>
> Therefore, the report itself indicates that the analysis of whether the noncompetition agreement represents a fair market value is based, in part, on anticipated referrals from the doctors. BRMC affirmed that the report evaluated expected revenues based on the assumption that defendants would likely refer the business to BRMC.

Here is additional material along the same lines taken from the deposition of the hospital CEO and the portion of the court's opinion that followed the excerpt:

7 As I and other observers noted at the time, this advisory seemed to misconstrue fair market value, while emphasizing the focus on referrals. oig.hhs.gov/fraud/docs/advisoryopinions/2007/AdvOpn07-05C.pdf.

8 Note: Chapter 3 of the this guide, "The Anti-Kickback Statute and Stark Law," looks at many of the issues discussed in this case, including noncompete agreements, and Chapters 26 and 27 in the *BVR/AHLA Guide to Healthcare Industry Finance and Valuation*, 4th edition, look at the mechanics of actually valuing a noncompete.

> Q. It's fair to say that the purpose of the noncompete agreement was to protect that revenue stream [referrals from Dr. Saleh and Dr. Vaccaro].
>
> A. The purpose of the noncompete, from my point of view, was to make sure that Drs. Vaccaro and Saleh didn't have a financial incentive to refer away from the hospital.
>
> Q. Because if they didn't have a financial incentive to refer away, they would refer it to you?
>
> A. We could hope that they would, yes.
>
> Q. You did more than hope. You expected they would refer to you?
>
> A. Expected they would refer a good bit of it to us, yeah.
>
> A compensation arrangement does not take into account the volume or value of referrals or other business generated between the parties if the compensation is fixed in advance and will result in fair market value compensation, and the compensation does not vary over the term of the arrangement in any manner that takes into account referrals or other business generated.
>
> While the value agreed upon by parties who are in a position to refer business to each other and who take into account anticipated referrals will be a fair value as between the parties, such an arrangement is not fair market value under the Stark Act. Here, the compensation arrangement between the parties is greater than what would be paid in the absence of the ability of Dr. Saleh and Dr. Vaccaro to provide referrals for BRMC's nuclear camera business.

As indicated above, the court concluded that the defendant hospital, et al., by their plain statements, considered the volume or value of referrals. Notwithstanding that, the court went on to say that even if that had not been the case, the defendants could not rely upon the fair market value exception because the *valuation itself* expressly considered referrals. Apparently key to this conclusion was the fact that the lease of the nuclear camera approximated $30,000 per month, of which nearly 80% was for a noncompete agreement. Further, a net present value analysis of the cost of the noncompete was compared to the revenues from inpatient and outpatient services the hospital expected to derive from the acquisition of the nuclear medicine camera.

Now, it would be foolhardy to suggest that a different valuation model might have caused the court to rule differently. However, assume for the sake of argument that none of the defendants or the valuation report was on record as stating that they considered referrals when negotiating or valuing the arrangements. What type of assumptions might an appraiser have put into a valuation model that would not take into account the volume of value of referrals from the seller to the buyer to conform to the requirement that "'general market value' means the price that an asset would bring as the result of bona fide bargaining between well-informed buyers and sellers *who are not otherwise in a position to generate business for the other party*" and "the definition itself differs depending on the type of transaction: Leases or rentals of space and equipment cannot take into account the intended use of the rented item, and *in cases where the lessor is in a position to refer to the lessee, the valuation cannot be adjusted or reflect the value of proximity or convenience to the lessor"* (emphasis added).

Before going to the Stark modifications of fair market value, it is important to note that the use of an appropriate equity discount rate and weighted average cost of capital are designed to account for the investment risk inherent in owning a business. One of the many differences between fair market value and strategic, investment value, or value to the [existing] owner is the use of a market-based rate of return to discount future cash flows to present value. There is no discussion in the case about this at all. A value to the owner standard in the instant case might have resulted from the use of a risk-free rate, which in turn would have resulted in a much higher value than if a market-based rate of return[9] were utilized. At least from the standpoint of an appraiser undertaking an exercise of determining fair market value, the very use of a market-based rate of return will eliminate a significant portion of the value of referrals from the existing owners, because a hypothetical seller or buyer is substituted through the discount rate for the actual seller or buyer. The next part of the discussion focuses on the adjustment to the cash flows subject to discounting necessary to move from a value to the owner standard to a fair market standard that from an appraisal standpoint, does not consider referrals.

The subject nuclear medicine camera had been and remained post-transaction in the offices of the selling physicians for several years (through December 2006, about three years). During time, of course, most of the cases would come from the two selling physicians. It is not clear whether before or after the transaction, any patients came from other physicians on the hospital staff, though that would clearly be relevant to the determination of fair market value as well as to the hindsight required in the prosecution of the litigation. To meet the requirement that "the valuation cannot be adjusted or reflect the value of proximity or convenience to the lessor," an appraisal of a nuclear medicine camera lease would merely look to what the rent on the piece of equipment might be—and that would already have been clear from the GE lease, which the hospital assumed.

An appraiser valuing a nuclear medicine business—which is where a noncompete would become relevant—as opposed to simply a lease would have to base volume assumptions and resultant cash flows on what a freestanding nuclear camera owned, say, by an independent nonphysician vendor would expect to receive in referrals from the medical community assuming that the referring physicians had no financial interest in the business. In a rural market such as that of BRMC, it is likely that before the physicians in the case acquired their nuclear camera, all of those cases had gone to the hospital and there was no competing provider. This would make the task challenging, indeed, but one would think the assumption would be two market competitors, the hospital and the independent vendor, and how that independent vendor might fare against the hospital— and not giving effect to the hospital's threat to revoke the staff privileges of physicians who did not refer to it.

9 The report in this case actually used an 18% discount rate.

A noncompete is part of the overall value of a business and represents the business that would be lost if the seller competed post-transaction, adjusted for the possibility that if allowed to compete, the seller would, in fact, do so, with the resultant cash flows discounted to present value at the discount rate used to determine the value of the business. This is referred to as the "with [the value with the noncompete in place] and without [the value without the noncompete in place] method." A noncompete is not in addition to the value of the business. In the instant case, there appears from the record to be confusion between the value of a lease, the value of a noncompete, and the value of a nuclear medicine business, among other things. Where that confusion originated is not clear.

One possible interpretation of the impact of the decision is that in circumstances such as this, the price paid for an operating business should be allocated to various component assets including the value of a noncompete to identify that portion of the value that is attributable to the sellers—assuming that noncompete value is based solely upon the sellers' DHS referrals. Such an approach would require some thinking about the traditional model of noncompete valuation. The two steps discussed above— an appropriate return to a hypothetical; buyer or seller and identifying cash flows available to a market participant not in a position to refer— need first to be considered in the noncompete analysis. Then, the appraiser also has to ask himself or herself how much business the buyer would lose if the sellers competed and what the likelihood of that competition is.

4.0 Conclusion

The larger question for the valuation community would seem to be whether an entire practice that owns DHS can be purchased *with* the valuation including the cash flows from DHS *and* the physicians being employed post-transaction by the purchaser. As suggested earlier, it has been clear to many for some time that purchasing DHS separately from a purchase of an entire practice and leaving the DHS physically present in the still independent practice is problematic from the government's standpoint.

It seems as well that a hospital buyer should be first guided not only by qualified legal counsel, but also by an opinion of fair market value from an appraiser with the requisite expertise to apply the regulatory standard to a valuation engagement *before* the hospital embarks on discussing price with a physician-seller in a position to refer DHS. This is a little different from retaining a neutral, subject to a confidentiality agreement, to evaluate financial terms in provider integration transactions subject to antitrust review before determining whether a memorandum of understanding is appropriate to move forward. Separately, the lack of statutory authority for the OIG to opine on fair market value is problematic and warrants extreme caution. Finally, threatening physicians in a position to refer DHS with loss of staff privileges if they compete is not a good idea.

Chapter 10.
Converting Physician Practices to Tax-Exempt Status

CONTENTS

Chapter 10. Converting Physician Practices to Tax-Exempt Status

By Mark O. Dietrich, CPA/ABV

Historically, hospitals and physician practices have integrated for a variety of non-tax-related reasons. Integrated delivery systems provide hospitals with immediate direct revenues from an expanded patient base and offer the potential for substantial indirect revenues flowing from inpatient referrals. Physicians who sell their practice may benefit from having access to an established hospital and its attendant perks, such as superior managed care contracts and the ability to offer patients a wider range of services. Another significant consideration, given the long-standing opposition of the Federal Trade Commission (FTC) and Department of Justice (DOJ) to physician joint-contracting efforts, includes qualification under the *Copperweld* doctrine,[1] where common legal control permits the negotiation of nonrisk contracts in addition to risk-based and quality-based contracts.

Tax benefits play a role, however. When the acquiring hospital is tax-exempt, another benefit is the ability to operate the acquired physician practice on a tax-exempt basis. The obvious incentive is the ability to retain the practice's profits free of income tax, but this strategy presents a variety of issues.

This chapter is concerned with the tax aspects of a physician practice's acquisition and conversion to tax-exempt status. Basic tax principles of the transaction are discussed first. The article then explains how to reduce the tax cost of the transaction through proper valuation techniques.

1.0 Basic Tax Consequences

A Section 501(c)(3)[2] hospital seeking to acquire a for-profit physician practice to operate on a tax-exempt basis typically structures the acquisition through a newly formed nonprofit

1 *See Copperweld v. Independence Tube*, 467 U.S. 752 (1984).

2 Unless otherwise specified, all section references are to the Internal Revenue Code of 1986, as amended (Code).

corporation, of which the hospital is the sole member and ultimate governing authority. The newly formed entity purchases the practice's assets or stock if the practice is in corporate form. When the physician practice is organized as a Subchapter C corporation, the selling physicians face an unavoidable "double tax" if they sell the corporation's assets to the hospital. First, the corporation pays tax on any gain realized from the sale of its assets,[3] leaving only the after-tax proceeds available for distribution to the physician shareholders. The shareholders are then individually taxed on any distributions received from the corporation.[4] Reversing the two steps does not change the result; double taxation similarly applies if the corporation first distributes its assets to its shareholders, who then sell them to the hospital. The Internal Revenue Service (IRS) illustrated these principles in the following example in its 2000 Exempt Organizations Continuing Professional Education Text (EO CPE Text):

> In 1990, 10 physicians invested $50,000 each ($500,000 in total) in a C corporation to purchase land and construct a freestanding ambulatory surgery center. The ambulatory surgery center was constructed and has thrived. In 1999, the physician-owners decided to sell the center to a local hospital. The hospital wanted to purchase the corporate assets instead of the stock because of liability concerns and to operate as a tax-exempt organization. Assume for this example that the C corporation's basis in its assets is $1 million and it has no liabilities. If it sells its assets to the hospital for $6 million, it will be taxed on its gain (35% × $5 million = $1.75 million), leaving $4.25 million for the physician-shareholders in liquidation. They will net about $2.57 million on the sale after paying individual tax (39.6% × $4.25 million = $1.68 million).[5]

The physician-shareholders can avoid double taxation, however, by instead selling their stock in the C corporation. In a taxable stock purchase, the selling shareholders are still subject to one level of tax on the gain realized from the sale of their stock, but there is no corporate-level tax on the sale. The above example continues:

> In contrast, if the hospital buys the C corporation stock from the physicians, the physicians will be taxed $1.68 million on their gain on the stock, but the corporate tax, $1.75 million, will be deferred.[6]

The preceding example illustrates that the selling shareholders are theoretically able to increase their after-tax proceeds by $1.75 million by selling their stock in the C corporation rather than selling the corporation's assets. But the 2000 EO CPE Text importantly points out that corporate-level tax is not eliminated; it merely shifts to the purchaser. Although the hospital could continue to defer the corporate-level tax as long as it operates the C corporation as a for-profit subsidiary, this is not an effective use of its tax-exempt status. If the hospital wishes to

3 Code Section 1001.

4 Code Sections 301 and 311.

5 Charles F. Kaiser III and Thomas Miller, *IRS Exempt Organizations Continuing Professional Education Text for FY 2000*, Topic U, Treas. Reg. Section 1.337(d)-4 and Exempt Organizations (2000 EO CPE Text), at p. 3 of the PDF, available at www.irs.gov/pub/irs-tege/eotopicu00.pdf.

6 *Id.* at p. 3 of the PDF.

operate the physician practice on a tax-exempt basis, it must either convert the subsidiary to a tax-exempt organization or distribute the subsidiary's assets to itself—both options trigger taxable gain to the hospital.[7]

IRC 337(b)(2) provides an exception to the above example. The purchasing exempt organization is not subject to corporate tax if, immediately after the distribution, it uses the property in an unrelated trade or business. However, this exception is usually moot because a hospital will use the corporate assets in an exempt function.

A hospital engaging in an arm's-length stock purchase should adjust the purchase price to account for the corporate-level tax it would eventually incur on the built-in gain.[8] The failure to consider the tax could constitute a private benefit to the selling shareholders and implicate the anti-inurement or intermediate sanctions provisions of the code, as well as violate the Stark Law or anti-kickback statute by failure to have the transaction meet the fair market value standard and commercial reasonableness standard. Thus, the shareholders in the preceding example have not necessarily increased their after-tax proceeds by $1.75 million by selling stock rather than assets. An appraisal prepared in connection with such a stock transaction must consider this tax, as described in detail below from the 2000 EO CPE text:

> When an IRC 501(c)(3) hospital or controlled entity within the tax-exempt system acquires a physician practice or related assets, it usually operates the business or assets on a tax-exempt basis. If the hospital acquired all the assets of a physician practice from the physicians' C corporation, the C corporation would be taxed under IRC 1001 on any gain from the sale of those assets. Only the after-tax proceeds would be available for distribution to the physician/shareholders, who would also pay individual tax (generally under IRC 331 or 301, depending on whether the corporation liquidates). Thus, in this example the physician/shareholders' proceeds are reduced twice.
>
> The results are similar if the C corporation first distributes the practice or assets to the shareholders, who then sell them to the hospital. The C corporation still recognizes gain on the distribution of assets under IRC 311 or 336 (depending on whether it liquidates) as if sold for fair market value and, the shareholders are taxed on the distribution, generally under IRC 301 or 331.
>
> If instead the hospital purchased the stock of the C corporation, the physician-shareholders still bear the individual level of tax on their gain, but the corporate level of tax on the C corporation would remain deferred. In this situation, the physician-shareholders' proceeds would be greater because only the individual level of tax would reduce the profits, as corporate tax is deferred. However, the hospital would be operating the C corporation as a for-profit subsidiary, which would not make effective use of the hospital's tax exemption.

7 Code Sections 311 and 337(b)(2); see Treas. Reg. Section 1.337(d)-4.

8 See 2000 EO CPE text, supra note 5, at page 2 of the PDF.

Therefore, to operate the corporate assets as an IRC 501(c)(3) function, the hospital would need to have the assets distributed to it. That distribution generally triggers the corporate level tax (which had been deferred), either under IRC 311 (if the physicians' C corporation, the C corporation would be taxed under IRC 1001 on any gain from the sale of those assets. Only the after-tax proceeds would be available for distribution to the physician/shareholders, who would also pay individual tax (generally under IRC 331 or 301, depending on whether the corporation liquidates). Thus, in this example the physician/shareholders' proceeds are reduced twice.

The results are similar if the C corporation first distributes the practice or assets to the shareholders, who then sell them to the hospital. The C corporation still recognizes gain on the distribution of assets under IRC 311 or 336 (depending on whether it liquidates) as if sold for fair market value and, the shareholders are taxed on the distribution, generally under IRC 301 or 331 (if the corporation is not liquidated) or under section 337(b)(2) (if the corporation is liquidated).

If instead the hospital purchased the stock of the C corporation, the physician shareholders still bear the individual level of tax on their gain, but the corporate level of tax on the C corporation would remain deferred. In this situation, the physician-shareholders' proceeds would be greater because only the individual level of tax would reduce the profits, as corporate tax is deferred. However, the hospital would be operating the C corporation as a for-profit subsidiary, which would not make effective use of the hospital's tax exemption.

Therefore, to operate the corporate assets as an IRC 501(c)(3) function, the hospital would need to have the assets distributed to it. That distribution generally triggers the corporate level tax (which had been deferred), either under IRC 311 (if the corporation is not liquidated) or under section 337(b)(2) (if the corporation is liquidated).

B. Adverse Effect on Charity

Both methods described above for the hospital to obtain the C corporation's assets result in two levels of taxation. They differ, however, in who is responsible for the tax. If the hospital purchases the C corporation's stock, the corporate level tax is borne while the corporation is owned by the exempt hospital, and does not reduce the proceeds available to the selling physician-shareholders.

However, in an arm's length purchase, the buyer would pay less for the stock than it would for the net assets because the buyer assumes the burden of the corporate level tax on the assets built-in appreciation. Thus, the hospital's failure to make a downward adjustment to the fair market value of the stock, as determined by an independent appraisal, to reflect the corporate level tax might be viewed as a private benefit to the selling physicians[9] (emphasis added).

9 www.irs.gov/pub/irs-tege/eotopicu00.pdf.

2.0 Valuing Intangible Assets

An arm's-length acquisition of a physician practice requires an independent appraisal, and thus a 1996 EO CPE Text discussing the valuation of medical practices has become a staple in the healthcare appraisal community.[10] Although instructional on the use of the discounted cash flow method under the income approach, the document importantly establishes criteria for the allocation of intangible asset value that while basic to valuation theory, are often overlooked in valuing medical practices.

For example, the 1996 EO CPE Text explains that although the value of goodwill can be allocated to specific intangible assets, "the value of the latter is limited to the value of the former, as calculated under the income approach."[11] In other words, the total value of the individual intangible assets cannot exceed the total value of the medical practice net of the aggregate fair market value of the tangible assets.

The authors of the 1996 EO CPE Text also point out that intangible value is not always present in a medical practice, a fact appraisers all too frequently overlook. Rather, they mistakenly attribute value to certain intangible assets even when the discounted cash flow method shows that the medical practice has no overall intangible value. This error often occurs with intangible assets that are typically valued using the cost method, such as medical records, assembled workforce, and trade name. Appraisers forget that using the cost method to value such intangible assets is only appropriate if the income approach first finds the presence of intangible value.

3.0 Personal Versus Enterprise Goodwill

Well-defined tax principles, originally enunciated by the U.S. Tax Court in *Martin Ice Cream,*[12] *Norwalk,*[13] and *Derby*[14] and re-emphasized in *Howard,*[15] establish a framework for potentially reducing the value of corporate-level intangible assets, thus reducing the tax cost of converting a physician practice to tax-exempt status.[16] These cases illustrate how to distinguish between personal goodwill, i.e., goodwill owned personally by the business' owners or employees, and goodwill owned by the corporation.

In *Derby,* a group of independent physicians decided to affiliate with a larger healthcare organization and sold the tangible assets of their practices to a tax-exempt medical foundation that

10 Charles F. Kaiser and Amy Henchey, *IRS Exempt Organizations Continuing Professional Education Text for FY 1996,* Topic Q, "Valuation of Medical Practices" (1996 EO CPE Text), *available at* www.irs.gov/pub/irs-tege/eotopicq96.pdf.

11 *Id.* at p. 22 of the PDF.

12 *Martin Ice Cream v. Commissioner,* 110 T.C. 189 (1998).

13 *Norwalk v. Commissioner,* T.C. Memo. 1998-279; *see "Goodwill Requires Enforceable Covenant Not to Compete," CPA Expert* (Spring 1999).

14 *Derby v. Commissioner,* T.C. Memo. 2008-45.

15 *Howard v. US,* 108 AFTR.2d 2011-5993 (Ninth Cir., August 29, 2011), affg 106 AFTR.2d 2010-5533 (DC Wash., July 30, 2010)

16 See also *Bross Trucking, Inc. v. Commissioner,* T.C., No. 7710-11, T.C. Memo. 2014-10.

was affiliated with multiple hospitals in an integrated delivery system. The acquiring organization, however, refused to purchase the goodwill or similar intangible assets associated with the physicians' practices, citing, in part, potential violation of the Medicare and Medicaid anti-kickback statute. Instead, the physicians donated their intangibles to the tax-exempt foundation and claimed charitable contribution deductions. The tax court, however, denied the physicians' deductions, finding that the physicians received consideration for their intangible assets in the form of future employment with the medical foundation.

The *Derby* court observed that the terms of employment contracts—and particularly noncompetition provisions—are a crucial factor in determining whether enterprise goodwill is present and whether a physician has assigned his or her professional goodwill to the practice, thereby making it a practice asset. However, many appraisers incorrectly believe that fair market value contemplates or requires the sellers agreeing to provide the buyers with a noncompete agreement. This assumption is often blindly included in the valuation without confirmation, as was the case in *Derby*.

Appraisers must keep in mind that noncompete agreements can be independently valued, and that such agreements do not contain standard provisions. The nature of the included (or excluded) provisions drives the value of noncompete agreements. Moreover, different states have different statutory and judicial precedents on what is and what is not enforceable in such an agreement, and these also may have a consequential effect on value. It is more accurate to state that fair market value contemplates understanding the terms of the transaction and the laws that govern it before attempting to assign value to the whole or its component parts.

Derby also emphasized the necessity of using negotiated post-transaction compensation in the valuation model. Reasonable compensation is a critical aspect of determining whether and to what extent any enterprise goodwill (as distinct from personal goodwill) is present and how much of that enterprise goodwill would be allocable to a noncompete agreement. A November 2005 article in the *Journal of Accountancy* articulated why an accurate valuation must incorporate compensation:

> If the selling physician(s) still will be employed by the practice after the sale, the cash flow the buyer is purchasing—the subject of the valuation—can't be known without including a realistic amount of post-sale compensation in the valuation model.[17]

The threshold question in such a valuation is relatively easy to state, if difficult to appraise or value: How much of the practice's value would be lost if the physicians competed or were able to compete with the practice following conversion. Importantly, this question applies *whether or not* the physicians have a pre-existing noncompete agreement, because it is the basis for the methodology used to value that noncompete agreements.

17 *"Medical Practices: A BV Rx," Journal of Accountancy* (Nov. 2005).

The valuation method's mechanics are beyond the scope of this chapter but can be summarized as follows:

1. Determine reasonable compensation under the fair market value standard for the physicians post-conversion;
2. Determine the value of the entity assuming that noncompete agreements are in place based on historical and forecasted entity cash flows using the discounted cash flow method;
3. Allocate that value first to working capital assets (cash, receivables, inventory), then to property and equipment, and finally any remainder to intangible assets in the manner contemplated by the residual method of allocation described in the regulations under Section 338;
4. Allocate that intangible value first to any readily identifiable intangible assets, such as a below-market lease on real property assumable by a purchaser, trade name, trained workforce, patient charts, or others that the buyer could retain if the sellers competed. (Trained workforce contemplates an enforceable nonsolicitation provision; patient chart valuation requires an understanding of the extent to which a patient requesting transfer of his or her personal health information to a new practice entity could be charged);
5. Any remaining value is attributable to the sellers' noncompete agreement (an ordinary income component) and personal goodwill (a capital asset component);
6. Assess and quantify the entity cash flows that would be lost if the sellers competed post-transaction;
7. Revisit any allocation in Step 3 above to identifiable intangible assets;
8. Assess and quantify the probability that the sellers would, in fact, compete post-transaction;[18]
9. The quantified probability is applied to the forecasted cash flow expected to be lost as a result of competition then discounted to present value to determine the noncompete's value. This step must consider the enforceability of a noncompete in the applicable jurisdiction; and
10. The balance is a capital asset in the nature of personal goodwill of the sellers.

18 For litigation, alternative damage causation theories may be relevant such as violation of fiduciary obligations or intent to defraud via the sale, among others.

4.0 Hypothetical Sale

Appraisers are often confused by the concept of the hypothetical buyer and seller in the fair market value standard. They mistakenly believe that it requires the use of hypothetical assumptions such as an enforceable noncompete agreement, even when the interest being valued has no such agreements in place.

Appraisers must understand that a valuation in an actual transaction is significantly different than a valuation based upon a hypothetical sale. Valuations accompanying an estate and gift tax reporting, litigation, or a property division for marital dissolution, unlike a business acquisition, lack transactional documents and do require the appraiser to make a variety of assumptions.

An interest in the assets or equity of a private company is a specific basket of legal and contractual rights and obligations and economic risks and rewards. Each of that basket's characteristics must be evaluated to determine at what price a member of the universe of hypothetical buyers and sellers would transact. The "hypothetical" aspect of the valuation in a real transaction is what buyer and seller would pay for the specific business or business interest being transacted *as reflected in the transaction documents.*

Understanding this difference is critical in a healthcare transaction because failure to do so may implicate the anti-kickback statute, Stark Law, or other civil and criminal penalty provisions. It is perhaps easier to understand within the concept of post-closing adjustments in an actual transaction. A typical post-closing adjustment in the purchase of the stock or equity of a business would be an increase or decrease in the sales price based upon the actual measure of the liabilities assumed and paid; in an asset transaction, those liabilities would typically not be assumed. Another adjustment would be for any difference in the value of accounts receivable purchased versus ultimately collected, if they are purchased at all. Certainly, a hospital purchasing a physician practice for a value that includes the accounts receivable when they are not transferred would be placed in significant jeopardy. Paying an amount that assumes a noncompete is in place without obtaining one as part of the transaction should be viewed no differently.

5.0 Current Economy Considerations

The current economic times feature low interest rates due to action by the Federal Reserve and resultant low discount rates in comparison to historical times, which translates to higher values, all other things equal, because risk and value are inversely related and an appraiser typically captures these factors in the valuation multiple through development of the discount rate or cost of capital. The Great Recession had offered an arguably counterintuitive benefit in terms of enhanced risk and reduced valuations to hospitals and physicians seeking to integrate via a conversion to tax-exempt status.

6.0 Conclusion

The contractual agreements a physician practice entity has in place with its owner- and nonowner-physicians determine how much of the goodwill or intangible value is owned by the practice and how much is owned personally by the physicians. To the extent that the enforceability of a noncompete, nonsolicitation, trade secrets, or other provision is limited or barred by state law, that portion of the agreement will have less or conceivably no value. A practice owned by physicians that has no post-termination noncompete agreements does not contractually own the personal goodwill of those physicians and therefore, should not recognize a taxable gain on that personal goodwill in a conversion to tax-exempt status.

Chapter 11.
What Goes Around Comes Around: *Derby v. Commissioner*

CONTENTS

Chapter 11.
What Goes Around Comes Around: *Derby v. Commissioner*

By Mark O. Dietrich, CPA/ABV

Author's note: Derby *remains one of the most significant tax cases for nonprofit hospitals and for-profit physician practices. The nine-factor checklist below should be a standard part of any valuation checklist.*

Established healthcare valuation principles from the 1990s remain in full force and effect.

The tax court case *Derby, et al. v. Commissioner*[1] is important for a variety of reasons, not the least of which is its instructive value as today's consolidation in the healthcare industry mirrors that in the early and mid-1990s when the *Derby* case originated. Key factors in the case include those which this author has repeatedly cited in numerous articles over the last 10 years in *CPA Expert* and the *Journal of Accountancy,* among others. Those factors are as follows:

1. The use of expected post-transaction physician compensation in the discounted cash flow model based on the transaction documents *rather than* use of some arbitrary compensation figure, such as the median, for a given physician specialty;
2. Allocating enterprise or invested capital value among working capital, fixed assets, and intangible assets;
3. Carefully studying transaction documents to discern the character and extent of any intangibles being transferred or not being transferred;
4. The critical import of allocating between personal and professional goodwill and enterprise goodwill when valuing a medical practice for acquisition by a hospital;
5. The importance of any noncompete agreement in determining the value of the medical practice and the import of *Norwalk v. Commissioner;*

1 *Charles A. and Marian L. Derby, et al.,1 Petitioners v. Commissioner,* Respondent, T.C. Memo. 2008-45, Gale, Judge.

6. The need for "donative intent" when claiming a deduction for the value of a medical practice or other enterprise allegedly donated to a tax-exempt entity;
7. The relevance of the Friendly Hills private letter ruling and the 1994 Exempt Organizations Continuing Professional Education Technical Instruction Program manuals;
8. The citation of the anti-kickback statute (AKS); and
9. The issue of the timeliness of the valuation versus the date of the transaction.

This is a well-written decision that highlights the typical issues in the valuation of a physician practice for sale or other transfer to a hospital or integrated delivery system. As such, Judge Gale's words are frequently quoted.

1.0 Case Summary

The case arose out of a claimed charitable deduction for the intangible value of the medical practices of more than a dozen physicians who sold their medical practices to Sutter Medical Foundation (Sutter) in 1994. The purchase agreements contained payments for fixed assets, while the selling physicians retained their accounts receivable.

The transaction took place during the period of consolidation of the healthcare industry associated with the rise of managed care and capitation on the West Coast in the early 1990s, which later spread across the country. Although restrictive managed care and capitation have fallen into disfavor and lost market share over the last six or seven years, consolidation is once again the rage in healthcare. Although some markets, such as Boston, are reconsidering the use of capitation, much of the present consolidation is driven by the more typical revenue concerns associated with fee for service medicine. Major hospital and ancillary testing revenue sources, such as cardiology, orthopedics, and high-tech imaging, are driving many of today's transactions.

The key decisions for the court were whether there had, in fact, been a *donative* transfer of intangible value, what the value was, and *if* the claimed value of the donation was overstated, whether the donor-physicians were subject to understatement of overvaluation penalties. As such, the valuations submitted by the taxpayers in connection with the donation received careful scrutiny from the court.

Critical in the ultimate resolution of the donation issue was a review of the history of the transaction with Sutter, which had declined to *pay* anything for intangible value, citing the AKS and the "famous" Thornton Letter in which the then Deputy Counsel of the Office of the Inspector General stated that a sale of goodwill by a physician to a hospital was problematic. Peter Grant, legal counsel in the seminal integrated delivery system transaction of the 1990s, represented the *Derby* physicians known as the Davis Medical Group (DMG).

> Unlike Foundation, Sutter Health was unwilling to pay anything for the intangible assets, or goodwill, that might be associated with petitioners' medical practices ... first, and principally, because Sutter Health's management believed that doing so might constitute a crime under the Medicare and Medicaid antikickback statute, 42 U.S.C. Sec. 1320a-7b(b), prohibiting payments for referrals of patients eligible for Medicare or Medicaid; and second, because Sutter Health's management believed, on the basis of their projections of the financial performance of the UHMG physicians' group after acquisition, that any additional payment for intangibles would have rendered the deal financially nonviable for Sutter Health.
>
> Mr. Grant recommended that petitioners structure the transfers of the intangibles as donations because that technique had been used in connection with an acquisition of a group medical practice by a nonprofit medical foundation (*Friendly Hills Healthcare Foundation*), for which Mr. Grant had served as an adviser. Mr. Grant was familiar with the annual *Exempt Organizations Continuing Professional Education Technical Instruction Program manuals*, including the manual for 1994 (emphasis added).

2.0 Transaction Overview

The parties retained Houlihan Lokey (Houlihan), the valuation firm in the Friendly Hills transaction, and arranged for an appraisal of the "business enterprise value" defined below. Note the emphasized items.

> The fair market value of the aggregate assets of [the Davis Medical Group] *exclusive of any benefit or element of value conferred upon Sutter* [Health] as a consequence of its current or proposed relationship with.... [Davis Medical Group], and *with consideration of proposed post-transaction compensation and benefits to the physician group.*

Houlihan also agreed to "allocate the appraised value ... to each of its physician/shareholders" using a method to be agreed upon in consultation [physician] steering committee, but the agreed-upon method "[had to] be acceptable to Houlihan" (emphasis added).

SWMG (Davis Medical Group later changed its name to Sutter West Medical Group, or SWMG) entered into a professional services agreement (PSA) or employment contract with Sutter as part of the transaction.[2] The court spelled out the key economic terms of the PSA, which included a very limited noncompete—the terms of which are critical in this valuation and, for that matter, any such valuation—and a complex revenue sharing formula that included a minimum compensation guaranty. The PSA also contained what amounted to a signing bonus that the court would see as in part a payment for goodwill.

> The PSA contained a noncompete provision, under which SWMG and its physician shareholder/employees were prohibited from participating in the ownership, management,

2 This is a standard feature of purchase transactions.

> operation, or control of any business or person providing healthcare services within the service area covered by the agreement. However, specifically exempted from this prohibition was any SWMG physician who left the employment of SWMG.... Departing physician may give written notice to the departing physician's patients named in the departing physician's patient list furnished to SMF on or before the ... effective date ... announcing the departing physician's separation from ... SWMG and his or her new practice location, and offering the patient an opportunity to choose whether his or her patient records should remain with SMF or be transferred to the departing physician.
>
> To provide an incentive to SWMG to form and sustain a group, SMF will pay SWMG a physician access bonus.... The "physician access bonus" was $35,000 for each of SWMG's full-time physicians.

The transaction documents stated that the seller and buyer believed the purchase price was less than the fair market value and that the difference was being donated. Significantly, the document contained a provision requiring the appraisal be completed within 60 days—designed to avoid a "stale" valuation. Finally, a discounted cash flow model was used. All of the factors outlined in the case closely track the Friendly Hills private letter ruling and the *1994 Exempt Organizations Continuing Professional Education Technical Instruction Program* manual.

As discussed above, the donation was to be allocated among 29 physicians who formed the group practice based on the valuation. In actuality, the donation was allocated using a formula designed by one of the physicians that attributed "(i) 50% of the aggregate value on the basis of each physician's share of gross revenues generated in the year preceding the transfer to SMF; (ii) 25% on the basis of each physician's 'years in the community,' with up to a maximum of five years being counted; and (iii) 25% on the basis of each physician's share of the aggregate fixed assets transferred to SMF by the SWMG physicians." Although the physicians attached a Form 8283 to their tax returns, Sutter never reflected the donation in its tax return—despite the transaction documents obligating it to do so.

3.0 Taxpayers' Valuation for Trial

For healthcare industry appraisers and valuation analysts, the issues surrounding the appraisal submitted for trial are the most important. Perhaps the most significant feature of the appraisal prepared for the trial was the use of median compensation for the physician-sellers rather than the actual compensation negotiated in the transaction! This remains an item of ill-considered debate and frequently results in mistaken assumptions in physician practice and other professional practice valuation, despite being long-settled and in direct conflict with fair market value.[3] The question can be stated as follows: Would the hypothetical buyer pay a price for the practice based on a *lower* compensation than he or she intended to pay post-transaction, thereby paying twice to the extent of the extra compensation.[4]

3 See, e.g., "Medical Practices: A BV RX," *Journal of Accountancy*, November 2005.

4 Besides the inurement risk under the Internal Revenue Code, this error creates risk under the AKS and Stark

> The national median for the "Western Region" for a weighted average of the medical specialties comprising SWMG, or 45.18%" in determining the physician compensation expense for the discounted cash flow model.[5] *However, the actual negotiated compensation negotiated in the transaction "provided for compensation to SWMG equal to 57.75% of fee-for-service revenue, 47% to 53% of capitation revenue, and at least 55% of risk pool revenue* (emphasis added).

The Dutcher Appraisal contained other significant weaknesses in the view of the court. There was no allocation of any intangible value to the professional goodwill of the physicians[6] as opposed to enterprise goodwill, which the court differentiated as follows:

> No allocation of any value to the professional goodwill of the SWMG physicians despite the fact that Mr. Dutcher distinguishes, in the case of the goodwill of a professional practice, between "practice" goodwill and "professional" goodwill, the former attributable to characteristics of the practice entity such as patient records, provider contracts, and workforce in place; and the latter attributable to the personal attributes of the individual practitioner, such as charisma, skill, and reputation and he acknowledge[d] that professional goodwill is not transferable.

Dutcher's testimony that professional goodwill is not transferable would have been one of many fatal blows to the taxpayers' position. The court went on to discuss the lack of noncompete agreements and importantly emphasized the continuing viability of *Norwalk v. Commissioner*,[7] perhaps the seminal case on the ownership and valuation of personal goodwill and noncompetes. A noncompete is the contractual basis for transferring personal or professional goodwill to an employer. The court also observed that the willing buyer would have insisted on "a significant discount" due to the lack of a noncompete!

> There is no adjustment for the fact that the SWMG physicians were not required to execute noncompete agreements. Mr. Dutcher treated each SWMG physician as transferring an allocable share of SWMG's intangibles, including goodwill, which was not treated as diminished in any way by the physicians' not having executed noncompete agreements with respect to SWMG or SMF. However, in *Norwalk v. Commissioner*, T.C. Memo. 1998-279, we found that there is no transferable or salable goodwill where a company's business depends on its employees' personal relationships with clients and the employees have not provided covenants not to compete.... We also believe that, under the willing buyer/willing seller standard of fair market value ... a willing buyer of SWMG on the transaction date would have insisted on a significant discount with respect to the value of the entity's

laws.

5 The phrase "national median for the 'Western Region'" appears to be a misnomer. The data were taken from the MGMA *Physician Compensation Survey* 1994 report based on 1993 data.

6 "Identifying and Measuring Personal Goodwill in a Professional Practice," *CPA Expert*, Spring 2005 and Summer 2005.

7 T.C. Memo. 1998-279; See "Goodwill Requires Enforceable Covenant Not to Compete," *CPA Expert*, Spring 1999.

> intangible assets, precisely on account of the absence of noncompete agreements from the SWMG physicians.

Other problems cited by the court included the taxpayers' use of an intangible value allocation model developed by one of the taxpayers rather than one based upon sound appraisal techniques and failure to include in the valuation any consideration of the $35,000 signing bonus described above.

4.0 The Donation

There is a fundamental requirement in a charitable transfer that the contributor have "donative intent" to receive a tax deduction. Donative intent contemplates a disinterested gift to a charitable organization without the donor receiving any corresponding benefit. It remains commonplace to attempt to structure physician practice transfers as part-sale, part-donation in the current environment.

> In its analysis of the transaction, the court found that the taxpayers received significant benefits from the transaction that belied any intent to make a disinterested donation with no consideration in return. The court cited the advantages of patient retention, negotiating leverage as part of a larger system, compensation based upon a percentage of net revenue, all of which was embodied in an employment contract with "carefully delineated terms."

5.0 Conclusion

Consolidation trends are cyclical and the wave that collapsed 10 years ago in the healthcare industry is back yet again. *Derby* reminds us that the old adage "those who fail to learn from history are doomed to repeat it" remains in full force and effect. From the standpoint of the hypothetical buyer, the court reiterated old guidance with respect to the common sense requirement that the value of the practice be based on expected post-transaction compensation. Equally important, the court restated the principles espoused in the *Norwalk* case that contracts—in this case the purchase and sale and professional services agreement—be part of the analysis of intangible value due to the impact of (any) noncompete agreements. Thus, when valuing a medical practice for purposes of an actual transaction, the appraiser must be familiar with the terms of that transaction if the buyer and seller are to rely upon it for regulatory purposes. As the court seemed to suggest of the appraisal submitted by the taxpayers in this case, something other than that which the parties transacted was valued. Transactional valuation *requires* understanding the terms of the transaction to opine on fair market value.

Chapter 12.
What Is to Be Learned From *Caracci*?

CONTENTS

Chapter 12. What Is to Be Learned From *Caracci*?

By Mark O. Dietrich, CPA/ABV, and Kenneth W. Patton, ASA

The appropriate use of the market approach in healthcare industry valuation is one of the most critical issues confronting the appraisal industry today. Many healthcare industry appraisers believe that market data are often unreliable or even misleading and must be used with abundant caution. Therefore, they focus primarily on the income approach. These appraisers cite such factors as local Medicaid coverage differences, the monopsonistic market power of local health insurers, the lack of sufficient data to determine comparability, and regulatory restrictions on the use of market data contained in the Stark regulations.

Appraisers who believe that the market approach, along with the income approach, should be given significant weight focus on the importance of actual transactions and not substituting one's judgment for that of the market. Where both groups agree is that use of market data in the healthcare industry requires significant skill and in-depth analysis. In this chapter, two leading experts, who have contrasting views on the topic, explore those issues in depth.

To illustrate our viewpoints, we discuss these issues in the context of the 5th Circuit's reversal of the tax court's opinion in *Caracci*,[1] which poses a number of questions to business valuation professionals. With respect to the valuation issues only, Mark Dietrich believes that the 5th Circuit's decision was more correct than the tax court's decision, while Ken Patton believes that the tax court's decision was more correct.[2] Ken Patton brings years of healthcare industry valuation expertise (although fewer years than Mark Dietrich) and more to the point, his knowledge of this specific market through his experience valuing other healthcare companies in the region during this time.[3]

1 118 TC 379 (2002), rev'd.: 456 F.3d 444, 98 AFTR2d 2006-5264: (CA-5, 2006).

2 The authors offer no opinion as to any of the legal aspects of this case.

3 Neither of the authors (or their firms) was involved in the case; therefore, they are relying solely on publicly available information.

1.0 The Key Valuation Issue and Valuation Experts

In *Caracci,* the key valuation issue was the value of the assets transferred from a not-for-profit entity to a for-profit entity.

The valuation expert for the taxpayers, Sta-Home entities and the Caraccis, was Allen D. Hahn, a director in PricewaterhouseCoopers Northeast Region Corporation Valuation Consulting Group. The valuation expert for the Internal Revenue Service (IRS) was Charles A. Wilhoite, a managing director of Willamette Management Associates and the national director of its healthcare industry services. In its opinion, the tax court recognized the experience and qualifications of the experts.

2.0 History of Sta-Home

Sta-Home was a collection of entities that provided home healthcare services primarily paid for by Medicaid to residents of Mississippi. Reimbursements were limited to the cost of providing the service, which apparently precluded the possibility of profitability. Sta-Home completed a corporate reorganization in 1995, which ultimately led to the litigation with the IRS.

Sta-Home was approximately 20 years old at the time of the reorganization. According to the courts' decisions, it:

- Had a well-established brand name;
- Had well-documented intellectual capital (manuals, procedures);
- Had a "generally good reputation";
- Had a certificate of need and accreditation by the Joint Commission on the Accreditation of Healthcare Organizations (JCAHO); and
- Was the largest provider of home healthcare services in Mississippi.

For perspective, as shown in Exhibit 1, Sta-Home's scale of operations had increased dramatically from 1991 to 1995. A question immediately comes to mind: Why would the owners grow the business to this extent if there was no chance of economic success?

Exhibit 1. Sta-Home's Revenues and Expenses (1991-1995)

Year	Revenue	Expenses	Net Income
1991	$11,736,061	$11,799,721	($63,660)
1992	$18,442,072	$18,414,315	$27,757
1993	$25,162,701	$25,208,255	($45,554)
1994	$36,882,957	$37,141,686	($258,729)
1995	$44,101,849	$44,535,239	($433,390)

3.0 Position of the Parties

This case involved the conversion of Mississippi's largest home health agency chain, Sta-Home, from tax-exempt to for-profit status in 1995.[4] The entity had more than $44 million in revenues and a loss of $433,390 in that year, as well as a large share of the Mississippi market. Such conversions were common at this time. They took place against the expectation[5] of a prospective payment system (PPS)[6] replacing Medicare's cost-based system for paying for home healthcare. The PPS was ultimately adopted in the Balanced Budget Act of 1997. It paid agencies in 60-day episodes of care, rather than on the basis of costs incurred. The cost-based system had led to the spending of excessive amounts on delivering care. Prior to the adoption of the PPS, home health agencies were often acquired by hospitals (and there was an active market in Mississippi). The hospitals, which were already paid by Medicare under a PPS, could therefore shift costs to the home health agency and obtain higher reimbursement for the same services.

The conversion was audited by the IRS, which found that the tax-exempt entities had approximately $18.5 million in net equity value that had been improperly transferred to the subsequent owners. The new owners maintained that the liabilities assumed exceeded the value of the assets received. The IRS asserted that the net excess benefit of $18.5 million triggered excise taxes and penalties of more than $250 million. The tax court subsequently reduced this to $46 million.

4.0 Tax Court Opinion

According to Judge Laro's opinion, a valuation prepared contemporaneously with the transaction at the insistence of special tax counsel for Sta-Home was initially rejected by that counsel for failure to conform to Revenue Ruling 59-60[7] and to address the existence of intangible assets. A second appraisal found that the equity value of the entities was negative, although the tax court record indicates that special tax counsel remained concerned about the quality of the appraisal.

5.0 The Standard of Value

A key issue in the case was the conflict between the normalization of earnings adjustments available to a hypothetical willing buyer and those available only to a specific buyer or specific class of buyers and whether the latter constituted fair market value. The following is quoted from the tax court's opinion:

> During 1995, the primary buyers of home health agencies were hospitals, nursing homes, and other home health agencies. They were able to take advantage of a mechanism known as "cost shifting."

4 The entities operated under state certificates of need.

5 A virtual certainty in the view of co-author Mark Dietrich. The tax court stated in its opinion that "national expenditures for home nursing care grew from $3.8 billion in 1990 to $20.5 billion in 1997," a circumstance that guaranteed congressional action and always has.

6 A PPS pays for services on the basis of a fee set in advance.

7 1959-1 CB 237.

Cost shifting was commonly used at that time by hospitals that were paid under a PPS. The PPS generated a fixed payment so that if costs could be transferred to the home health agency, additional revenue could be generated with no additional cost. The inclusion of this attribute by the tax court was critical in the determination of fair market value.

The taxpayer's expert, Hahn, valued the cost gap at $667,000 based upon his view that a buyer would have a one-year benefit from that strategy. The tax court disagreed:

> This value is too low. The cost gaps were available under the then-current reimbursement program. They would cease to exist under a PPS. Although there had been discussions of a PPS for several years, Congress had passed no such legislation at the time of the transfer, and there is no evidence that the prospect of such legislation had a negative effect upon the value of home health care agencies.

6.0 Hahn's Valuation Approaches

The tax court reviewed and critiqued each expert's use of the market approach. Hahn also relied primarily on an adjusted balance sheet methodology (a version of the cost approach), in which he valued the trained workforce and certificate of need. Hahn placed considerably less reliance on market comparables because purported comparables were "idiosyncratic" and lacked sufficient detail.

The tax court also noted Hahn's testimony that guideline public companies were not appropriate comparables because home health care was part of a broader service mix. In effect, there were no "pure-play" public companies.

7.0 Wilhoite's Valuation Approaches

Wilhoite relied primarily on the market approach utilizing both guideline public companies and guideline acquisitions. The tax court appeared to indicate a clear preference for this approach. Wilhoite derived revenue pricing multiples for market value of invested capital (MVIC), the use of which was a key issue in the 5th Circuit's decision.[8]

The tax court discussed the two comparable acquired companies deemed most like Sta-Home, according to Wilhoite. The court then went on to develop its own view of the proper multiple.

There was no discussion by the tax court of differences in payor mix between the purported comparables and Sta-Home, which was 95% Medicare-based. The court did observe that Mississippi had the largest per-capita spending on home health in the country under the Medicare program, but that speaks more to volume of services than rate per unit of service—and the latter

8 Of particular note is the IRS expert's reliance on revenue multiples from *out-of-market* transactions and public companies. This is a notoriously bad multiple in the view of many healthcare valuation experts and one specifically banned by the later-issued Stark II regulations discussed below.

drives profits. The court did allude to Hahn's testimony that successful home health agencies had nongovernment patients and more profitable lines of business, such as infusion therapy. These are all critical, and likely conclusive, differences as to comparability. Regardless of these concerns about the comparables, the tax court held that the taxpayers owed a crushing amount of excise taxes and penalties.

8.0 Appellate Court Opinion

The 5th Circuit severely criticized the IRS for its numerous errors in the assessment process, Judge Laro for engaging in valuation, and Wilhoite for his failure to understand the Mississippi marketplace. The 5th Circuit first observed that Sta-Home had looked for a hospital buyer unsuccessfully. Where Judge Laro had been dismissive of the taxpayer's expert, Hahn, the 5th Circuit embraced him, observing that the IRS had also attempted to retain him and that he spent eight weeks in Mississippi working on the case[9] compared to Wilhoite's two days. Wilhoite's lack of experience in the home healthcare industry in particular, as opposed to his general valuation experience, was also cited. Significantly, the 5th Circuit noted that: "Wilhoite used market-based and income-based approaches to assign values to all Sta-Home's assets in general, *without valuing any of Sta-Home's assets in particular*" (emphasis added).

9.0 Synonymous Standard of Value?

Caracci implicitly raises an issue regarding the standard of value. Without question, all of the parties believed that fair market value was applicable. The potential for sale of Sta-Home was discussed by the tax court and even more by the 5th Circuit. Although fair market value is generally considered to refer to hypothetical willing buyers and sellers, it is evident that the very specific circumstances of potential buyers were considered.

Wilhoite used a method known as cost shifting in his analysis. Economic profits are created by charging a portion of the expense base to another business unit. Cost shifting was in frequent use in the region as a means of creating value for Medicare home health agencies. Because cost shifting incorporates business synergies, it raises the specter that the standard of value had really morphed into investment value, which is defined in the *International Glossary of Business Valuation Terms* as "the value to a particular investor based on individual requirements and expectations."[10] If virtually every market participant has the potential to use the cost-shifting benefits, investment value might effectively become synonymous with fair market value.

The third standard of value, intrinsic value, is defined in the *International Glossary* as "the value that an investor considers, on the basis of an evaluation of available facts, to be the 'true' or 'real' value that will become the market value when other investors reach the same conclusion."

9 These facts do not appear in the tax court decision.
10 American Society of Appraisers Business Valuation Standards, Glossary, last revised June 2005. www.appraisers.org.

Why is intrinsic value important in this case? First, there was great debate about the future of home health care as a business due to the implementation of PPS. Market participants in the geographical area had widely different views. Market transactions occurring contemporaneously and after the valuation date indicated that Medicare-dependent home health agencies had value. Taking the opposite position with respect to Sta-Home clearly reflected a different view of the company's intrinsic prospects.

Second, the valuation of health care entities can be very volatile based on potential change in reimbursement rates. Note carefully the use of the word "potential." Medicare changes are often first rumored, followed by proposals that may not be implemented for a year or more, and then the actual implementation. The analyst is left to make key decisions about prospective economic conditions of a business in the face of both great and unique uncertainties. Without question, actual market transactions can differ from an individual analyst's belief about the future. The circumstances of Sta-Home reflect this conundrum. While hindsight may give comfort to an analyst's position, appraisers must look at the broader market and attempt to reconcile actual market activity with their expectations and the expectations of others.

10.0 Key Regulatory Issues in Health Care

Certain regulatory structures discussed here were not in place or well-understood at the time of the Sta-Home conversion. However, they are critical to assessing the relevance of the *Caracci* decision to appraisals in today's marketplace.

The following are excerpts from a synopsis of the anti-kickback statute extracted from an advisory opinion of the Office of the Inspector General:

> The anti-kickback statute makes it a criminal offense knowingly and willfully to offer, pay, solicit, or receive any remuneration to induce or reward referrals of items or services payable by a federal health care program. See Section 1128B(b) of the act. Where remuneration is paid purposefully to induce or reward referrals of items or services paid for by a federal health care program, the anti-kickback statute is violated. By its terms, the statute ascribes criminal liability to parties on both sides of an impermissible "kickback" transaction. For purposes of the anti-kickback statute, "remuneration" includes the transfer of anything of value, directly or indirectly, overtly or covertly, in cash or in kind.[11]

A buyer paying a seller for the profits associated with the buyer's subsequent provision of new services to the seller's patients may well be seen as paying a prohibited kickback for future referrals, particularly when the sellers remain employed by or active in the business.[12]

11 See Office of the Inspector General Advisory Opinion No. 03-12.

12 See *McLeod Regional Medical Center to Pay U.S. Over $15 Million to Resolve False Claims Act Allegations*, U.S. Department of Justice Press Release, Nov. 1, 2002.

11.0 Valuation Questions Raised by the Case

At this point, the authors engage in some point-counterpoint by addressing valuation questions raised by the tax court and 5th Circuit's decisions.

Q: *What is required for market comparability?*

Dietrich: Payment mechanisms are one of the most fascinating things about health care. Most health care is covered by private insurance or government programs such as Medicare (as in Sta-Home) or Medicaid. What is not widely understood is that the level of payment for those services varies radically from state to state and even market to market. Most urban markets are dominated by a few health insurers that hold significant influence over the fees paid to providers. Very few insurers have national market coverage, and those that do have significant market share in only a few states.[13] To use a guideline public company method or a guideline acquisition, the analyst would need to look at the payor mix for both the guideline and the subject and see whether they were similar. In a poor state such as Mississippi, the insurance market is unlikely to have been attractive because most patients would have had Medicaid, which pays the least. This would have made the out-of-market guideline transactions and public companies worthless.

Patton: The payment mechanism is clearly one of the most important factors in healthcare valuation. Reimbursement rates and sources vary by region and by state or even locality. Mississippi is a poor state that was experiencing a surge in home health visits, as compared with national activity. At the time, it shared these characteristics with the nearby states of Alabama, Louisiana, Arkansas, and portions of Tennessee and Kentucky. A market comparison to publicly traded companies or individual transactions outside the geographic region would likely be problematic. Nevertheless, there was acquisition activity in the aforementioned states in Medicare-based agencies, and demand for them was evident. Mercer Capital had observed market pricing in the range of $10 to $15 per visit for Medicare-based companies in the region.

Q: *Can appraisers differ reasonably about the implications of a foreseeable change?*

Dietrich: Perhaps the most important issue raised in *Caracci* is the tax court's specific rejection of the impending change to a PPS, which was the basis of Hahn's position. Medicare had been converting various healthcare industry sectors from cost-based and other reimbursement systems to PPS to control rapidly expanding costs. There was no doubt PPS was coming and, therefore, the change was reasonably foreseeable on the valuation date.

Patton: Although there was little doubt that the change to PPS was coming, there was apparently considerable doubt as to the precise timing and the implications of its implementation. The prevailing temporary payment system (PIP) had placed considerable strain on the financial resources of Sta-Home and other home healthcare agencies. Yet, the company continued to

13 See Government Accounting Office *Private Health Insurance: Number and Market Share of Carriers in the Small Group Health Insurance Market.*

grow the base of visits. Does this speak to a different view on the implication of the ultimate shift to PPS? Other companies were amassing size under a general theory that a well-operated company could prosper under PPS. Notwithstanding the ultimate wisdom of that position (based on a subsequent event), companies in the region were increasing their size in the belief that customer accumulation created value.

Q: *Does "market data" necessarily apply to the subject interest being valued?*

Dietrich: Another problem is the conflict between the 5th Circuit's view that Sta-Home had pursued buyers unsuccessfully and the tax court's apparent dismissal of this. It is important to understand that strategic buyers in a market do not need to buy every player in that market. Generally, they will buy only a sufficient mass to service the market area. There are antitrust implications to owning too much market share. If the hospitals in Sta-Home's service area had already acquired home health agencies, they would be unlikely to acquire another.

Patton: A market for Medicare-dependent home health agencies clearly existed in the region. Yet, was there a market for this specific company based on conditions in Mississippi? As the geographical market shrinks, the analysis moves away from hypothetical buyers and sellers to a very specific list of each. In this case, Sta-Home would be the seller, and the list of buyers was thought to be very limited. At the same time, why was it appropriate to limit the list of likely buyers to Mississippi-based entities? An analyst should not substitute his or her judgment for that of the marketplace and assume his or her analysis considers every reasonable type of buyer. In many respects, courts in these types of cases began to move toward an investment value standard that might well be reasonable in an industry highly influenced by regulations and dominated by a narrow payment structure.

Q: *When does data become "irrelevant history"?*

Dietrich: Historical transactions would have been increasingly irrelevant measures as the PPS loomed ever closer, at least to the extent they were based on the cost gap. Comparability can be a function of time. If a major change in the reimbursement program occurs, comparability is lost. Therefore, one must be able to relate the reimbursement systems to the timing of the transaction.

Patton: My co-author should be given great credit for emphasizing this crucial point. The viability of any healthcare business is extremely exposed to the payment system. To the extent that payments are made by a government entity (Medicare, Medicaid, or local tax support), the prospects for that business can (and do) change greatly as reimbursement changes. Home health care literally exploded in the early 1990s. It was obvious that some reaction from the U.S. government would occur. Transactions that occurred during the time frame of growth may not be relevant to a specific valuation. The underlying conditions are just not comparable. Nevertheless, transactions for Medicare-based agencies continued to occur within the region for several years after 1995 at pre-1995 levels. This was apparently due to the differences in outlook for the industry and the impact of PPS. The important point is, however, that allegedly comparable transactions can become dated literally overnight as the reimbursement rules change.

Q: *What does it mean to be reasonably informed of the relevant facts?*

Dietrich: Knowledge of impending legislative changes in health care, even if several years in the future, is critical to developing a realistic cash flow forecast. Many of these changes are driven by the recommendation of the Medicare Payment Advisory Commission, established by Congress as part of the Balanced Budget Act of 1997 to advise it about needed changes. Equally important, extremely rapid growth in revenues in a particular industry subsector is compelling evidence that future growth is likely to be curtailed. For example, this happened in the summer of 2005 with respect to high-tech imaging after four years of rapid growth, when payments for diagnostic exams, such as magnetic residence imaging (MRI) and computed tomography (CT), were curtailed and positron emission tomography (PET) was brought within the purview of the Stark laws, which govern physician self-referral for Medicare and Medicaid patients.

As the present author noted in an article,[14] discussing the then-just-released tax court's decision in *Caracci*:

> Moreover, these cost-shifting strategies have been the subject of numerous civil and criminal proceedings under the Medicare fraud and abuse statute. In fact, MedPAC's current [2002] report[15] notes that:
>
> > The new payment system's [The payment system was changed from a cost-based system to an interim system with stricter payment limits in 1997, then changed again to the prospective payment system in October 2000.] adjustments to eligibility and fraud and abuse reduction efforts were intended to reduce spending and redirect the benefit toward briefer, more intense care. Changes in spending and use between 1997 and 1999 demonstrate that these changes had some dramatic effects (*McCall, et al.* 2001): Total Medicare spending on home health fell 52%.

Allowing for the inherent distortions in reporting caused by the cost-shifting strategy used by hospitals with respect to home health agencies, Exhibit 2 presents a graph that illustrates the four-year margin, from 1996–1999, on Medicare home health business for hospitals (the arguably strategic class of acquirer that was the basis for the tax court decision). This shows the decreased spending in those years, which occurred even though the PPS was not finally implemented due to delays until 2000. The bottom dropped out two years before the implementation.

14 "Valuation, Tax Exemption, 'Fair Market Value,' and the Tax Court (*Caracci, et al. v. Commissioner*)", Medical Management Advisor, May, 2002.

15 *Report to the Congress: Medicare Payment Policy,* March 2002; see page 93 forward.

Exhibit 2. Four-Year Margin (1996-1999)

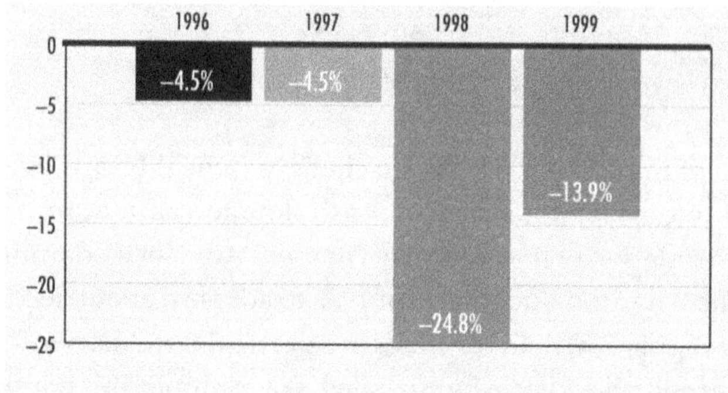

What is astounding about the tax court decision is that this information was known at the time of the trial; the court either was unaware of it or ignored it. The information very clearly demonstrates that Hahn was correct. The court's rationale seemingly cannot be that the information came after the valuation date as can be seen clearly from the following statement by the court concerning post-valuation date data.[16]

Home health agencies remained under a cost-reimbursement system until Sept. 30, 1999, when legislation passed by Congress in 1997 providing a PPS for home health agencies took full effect. The Health Care Financial Administration (HCFA) encountered problems implementing the system, and it was not finally implemented until Oct. 1, 2000. The requirement for regional market value evidence is now spelled out in the Stark laws. Although implemented well after the Sta-Home transaction, abuses in valuing such transactions are a principal reason for the rule:

> Fair market value means the value in arm's-length transactions consistent with general market value. "General market value" means the price that an asset would bring as the result of bona fide bargaining between well-informed buyers and sellers who are not otherwise in a position to generate business for the other party or the compensation that would be included in a service agreement as a result of bona fide bargaining between well-informed parties to the agreement who are not otherwise in a position to generate business for the other party, on the date of acquisition or at the time of the service agreement. Usually the fair market price is the price at which bona fide sales have been consummated for assets of like type, quality, and quantity in a particular market at the time of acquisition.[17]
>
> Moreover, the definition of "fair market value" in the statute and regulation is qualified in ways that do not necessarily comport with the usage of the term in standard valuation

16 Later in the opinion, the court stated that Hahn's inclusion of a one-year "cost gap" should have been a two-year "cost gap," apparently because the PPS was, in fact, passed in 1997, two years after the Sta-Home transaction.

17 420 CFR 411.351.

> techniques and methodologies. For example, the methodology must exclude valuations where the parties to the transactions are at arm's length but in a position to refer to one another.[18]

The following clarifying statement should be included immediately following the standard definition of fair market value: *Reasonable knowledge of the relevant facts contemplates an understanding of the regulatory environment for healthcare entities.*

Patton: It is surely essential to understand the legal and regulatory structure. Once again, however, market data from relevant transactions appear to offer a different interpretation of the specific implications of the prospective changes in the home healthcare industry. Nevertheless, the comments above are extremely important in understanding the rules of valuation in a highly regulated industry such as health care.

Q: *How does the valuation analyst balance historical results with changes in the strategic position of the industry and varying views of the industry?*

Dietrich: The single most powerful tool for differentiating "strategic" value inherent in acquisition prices from fair market value is a disciplined application of the income approach on a stand-alone basis. If the value indications under the market approach cannot be sustained on a stand-alone basis,[19] the analyst needs to perform an analysis to justify a crossover from strategic value to fair market value in the marketplace.[20] In other sectors of the economy, such as banking, most, if not all, buyers have "strategic" opportunities from things such as economies of scale. Because the definition of fair market value in health care is qualified by the regulatory environment, only certain types of otherwise strategic adjustments can be considered. Each category of "strategic" opportunity must be identified, evaluated for appropriateness under the statutes and regulations, and then, if appropriate, included in the valuation model (typically a discounted cash flow) to justify the value conclusion under the income approach. The value indications of the different approaches cannot be said to have been reconciled absent such an undertaking.

For example, it might be appropriate to value a subject in a sector that is being consolidated on the basis of consolidator transactions if the consolidators are active in the subject's service area. In that case, otherwise strategic adjustments such as a lower cost of capital, higher growth rates, and lower operating costs might be appropriate normalization adjustments in an income approach.[21]

---

18 "Medicare Program; Physicians' Referrals to Health Care Entities With Which They Have Financial Relationships (Phase II)"; Interim Final Rule; 69 Fed. Reg. 16053.

19 Damodaran describes stand-alone value in his writings on evaluating acquisitions. www.stern.nyu.edu/~adamodar/.

20 See Dietrich, "Understanding the Difference Between Strategic and Fair Market Value in Consolidating Industries," 21 *Business Valuation Review* 77 (June 2002).

21 *Id.*

At the same time, and more important, it is incumbent on the analyst to eliminate the possibility that market data may have included strategic considerations that violate the Stark laws, anti-kickback statute, or IRS regulations and rulings for exempt entities; *Caracci*, after all, was about excise taxes for an excess benefit transaction. In the two opinions, it is not clear whether there was testimony about the appropriateness from a regulatory standpoint of considering acquisition multiples based on agencies that included infusion or respiratory therapy. The tax court made it clear that Hahn, who was a leading expert in this area, eliminated them (appropriately):

> From these privately held transactions, Hahn excluded sales of privately held home health agencies that provided sophisticated "infusion or respiratory therapy" because those could attract reimbursement at a higher rate than those available to the more traditional home health care agencies such as Sta-Home.

Patton: An analyst must consider the regulatory structure. Once again, this is a situation in which many of the prospective buyers are likely to view acquisition targets from the perspective of investment value. Hence, fair market value and investment value begin to merge.

Q: *Can a business that appears to be losing money in perpetuity have goodwill or is there the potential for creating value even when there is no direct way to create profits?*

Dietrich: This question is certainly one that often confronts appraisers. I believe the prevailing view among appraisers who limit themselves to the healthcare industry is that if one cannot generate a cash return, one generally cannot have intangible value. Because the definition of fair market value is constrained by what is legally permissible (for example, a cocaine dealership has no fair market value because it is illegal), one cannot ascribe fair market value to potential exit strategies from a losing business that are inconsistent with the law.

Outside this regulatory constraint, a business that always loses money may have value to a larger entity due to economies of scale or other arguably strategic opportunities as discussed in the preceding section. A simple proscribed example would be a physician practice that earns the physician less than a reasonable salary, but generates significant revenues to a hospital through admissions and tests. The practice has a large value to the hospital, but the hospital cannot pay for that value since it violates both the Stark laws and the anti-kickback statute.

Value may exist on other than a stand-alone basis in such a circumstance as Sta-Home, but demonstrating that value to be consistent with fair market value is a required and significant burden on the appraiser and the parties to any transaction.

Patton: The 5th Circuit places great reliance on a strain of thought that Sta-Home's operations could not have goodwill because the court could not identify a stream of profitability. Consider the following comment by the court:

> For Sta-Home, the overwhelming dependence on Medicare reimbursement meant that added revenue meant added reimbursement costs, which in turn, generated greater losses.

Given the growth in revenue of 276% evident in Exhibit 1 and the strategies of similar companies, why didn't Sta-Home just stop growing if the owners really believed that there was no hope of an economic return?

The tax court explained that it believed that this apparently illogical conclusion made sense: It found that Sta-Home had the potential to make a profit, which demonstrated that its assets had substantial fair market value.

There is a disconnect between the court's theory and the behavior of the owners of Sta-Home and the owners of other companies in the marketplace.

> To operate despite their perennial cash flow problems, their lack of profitability, their increasing operating losses, and their increasing deficits....
>
> [I]ts patients—would only enable the agencies to lose money for the indefinite future.

Can a business that appears to be losing money in perpetuity have goodwill? Here again, the growth of the size of the business could indicate an alternative theory about the creation of value not linked to reported profitability. Again, there is a disconnect between the business strategy of Sta-Home (and other similar companies in the region) and the observations of the 5th Circuit. Rational people stop amassing assets when it continually increases their losses unless they believe that there is an economic return on some basis in the future.

The 5th Circuit posits the following argument that goodwill is derived from excess earnings; therefore, in this case, there can be no goodwill. It states:

> The tax court's mistaken belief that Sta-Home's intangible assets had substantial fair market value led it to ignore its own long-recognized position that unprofitable intangible assets do not contribute to fair market value unless those assets produce net income or earnings. Revenue Ruling 59-60 requires the IRS to assign zero value to unprofitable intangible assets. See Rev. Rule 59-60, 1959-1 C.B. 237 ("The presence of goodwill and its value, therefore, rests upon the excess of net earnings over and above a fair return on the net tangible assets.")

Putting aside the 5th Circuit's legal position, the court's implicit economic position requires discussion. First and foremost, all value is a function of future benefits. The past may be instructive but is not determinative of value. The core question for any asset or business value is: "What benefits will it produce in the future?"

Most assets and businesses have the prospect of a visible positive return in the hands of its current owners. Value is most visible when net income is present. However, every valuation analyst has to be open to an alternative view of value creation that is not apparent until the ultimate sale of the assets. Appraisers often place virtually all of the value in a discounted cash flow analysis in the terminal value; therefore, interim profitability is not essential.

What happens, however, when profitability is never likely or even expected to occur in the hands of the current owner? Can goodwill exist? Of course it can, and it does. How could this be true? In one simple scenario, value in excess of cost can be created by accumulating a customer base. By selling the amassed base in bulk, there is value to the buyer, which is often a typical market participant. The seller realizes the value of its efforts to accumulate the customers.

Q: *Did the tax court and Wilhoite err by basing the valuation of the assets on the market value of invested capital?*

Patton: The tax court and Wilhoite based the value of the assets, including the intangible assets, on the market value of invested capital. The 5th Circuit said this was in error, and the value of the assets, including the intangible assets, should be based on a valuation of the direct value of the assets themselves. Was the tax court in error? From a valuation perspective, the answer is an emphatic "no."

The 5th Circuit favors an approach to valuing goodwill by valuing the asset directly. Further, it seems not to accept the notion that the value of the assets must equal the value of the liabilities by referring to it as an accounting concept. This is incorrect. The value of the assets will, by definition, from a valuation perspective, be the value of the total invested capital plus other liabilities and nonoperating assets. Additionally, the concept of direct valuation of goodwill will require the use of income methods that ultimately require the determination of total invested capital.

Dietrich: Perhaps both courts got ahead of their knowledge in writing their opinions. The left-hand or asset side of the accounting equation must, of necessity, equal the right-hand or invested capital side. The 5th Circuit thought a more meaningful result could be obtained from the left-hand side, while the tax court believed in the invested capital approach inherent in use of the guideline methods in which individual assets are not valued. It is a useful exercise to allocate value to the assets after making a preliminary determination of invested capital, and the present author often does so both analytically and in reports. Identifying the amount of intangible value is important in healthcare appraisal because this is where the regulatory risk is greatest.

12.0 Looking Ahead

The opinions of the tax court and the 5th Circuit in *Caracci* raise very interesting questions for business valuation professionals. The authors have attempted to address several of them. While they may not agree on every point, hopefully readers will find their insights helpful and that this chapter furthers the discussion.

Part III.
Valuing Healthcare Enterprises

Chapter 13.
Understanding and Using the Technical and Professional Components of Ancillary Revenue When Valuing Medical Practices

CONTENTS

Chapter 13. Understanding and Using the Technical and Professional Components of Ancillary Revenue When Valuing Medical Practices

By Mark O. Dietrich, CPA/ABV, and Kathie L. Wilson, CPA/ABV

Valuing any business requires an understanding of how revenue is generated: what products or services are sold, how much revenue comes from each, competing products or services, and competing sellers. Valuing a medical practice is no different in that regard. It is important to understand that services sold by medical practices are commonly specified by current procedural terminology (CPT) codes and healthcare common coding procedure system (HCPCS or "Hickpicks") codes. For example, CPT code 99213 is a Level 3 office visit for an established patient. HCPCS codes can denote "products" such as certain injectable drugs or chemotherapy that are specified by J codes or services and procedures that are specified by G codes. The HCPCS codes are alphanumeric and start with a letter. For example, J0133 is the code for an acyclovir injection; G0202 is the code for screening mammography. Thus, considerable background is required by an appraiser to understand the revenue lines in the variety of medical practice specialties.

Many of the more common specialties require more expertise than simply being familiar with the codes for seeing patients in the office. Of particular note is the differentiation between the technical component and professional component of ancillary services for practices such as radiology, cardiology, neurology, and others. The technical component is paid in connection with ownership of equipment, provision of a technologist to operate the equipment, supplies, and general overhead. The professional component is paid to the physician specifically for interpreting the results of the test or study, e.g., an imaging study such as an X-ray or MRI. Revenue from the technical component, therefore, is related to the equipment investment of the practice, not the efforts of the physician.

This can be seen in the following quotes from the Centers for Medicare and Medicaid Services' Medicare Physician Fee Schedule 2010 Final Rule:[1]

> Services with technical components (TCs) and professional components (PCs). Diagnostic services are generally comprised of two components: a professional component (PC) and a technical component (TC), both of which may be performed independently or by different providers. When services have TCs, PCs, and global components that can be billed separately, the payment for the global component equals the sum of the payment for the TC and PC. This is a result of using a weighted average of the ratio of indirect to direct costs across all the specialties that furnish the global components, TCs, and PCs; that is, we apply the same weighted average indirect percentage factor to allocate indirect expenses to the global components, PCs, and TCs for a service. (The direct PE RVUs for the TC and PC sum to the global under the bottom-up methodology.)
>
> Modifier. A modifier is shown if there is a technical component (modifier TC) and a professional component (PC) (modifier -26) for the service. If there is a PC and a TC for the service, Addendum B contains three entries for the code. A code for: the global values (both professional and technical); modifier -26 (PC); and, modifier TC. The global service is not designated by a modifier, and physicians must bill using the code without a modifier if the physician furnishes both the PC and the TC of the service.

Within the relative value unit (RVU) allocations are components for physician work, practice expense, and malpractice insurance. As you might expect, the largest element in the TC is for practice expense, whereas the largest element in the PC is typically for physician work, known as wRVUs. In some circumstances, these can be important in measuring the productivity for reasonable compensation purposes as defined later herein.[2]

1.0 Some Common Mistakes

Most appraisers determine reasonable compensation when valuing a medical practice by reference to the physician's (or physicians' aggregate) productivity benchmarked against "norms" such as those from the Medical Group Management Association (MGMA). The definition of collected revenue in the MGMA data is with the technical component of ancillary services excluded! MGMA does have some data that include the technical component and nonphysician providers at two levels, greater than 10% or less than 10%, but that differentiation is generally not specific enough to be useful for reasonable compensation purposes.[3] Thus, to use the data appropriately, it is necessary for the appraiser to separate the revenues associated with the professional component (related to the efforts of the physician) from those of the ancillary or technical component (related to the equipment investment).

1 CMS-1413-FC.

2 Not all, or even many, practices track wRVUs. However, it is easy to obtain an RVU calculator, drop the CPT frequency distribution data into it, and compute RVUs for work, practice expense, malpractice for both professional and technical component.

3 See the Rhode Island example later herein for an important exception.

1.1 Example

While valuing a four-physician neurology practice with a single owner, the appraiser notes that the owner has collected revenue credited to him of more than twice the 90th percentile of MGMA. Upon investigation of the practice's reports of productivity by CPT (including HCPCS) code and the list of fixed assets, he determines that the practice owns an MRI unit in addition to other ancillary equipment. The technical component of the MRI services representing approximately 80%[4] of the global (or total) collected revenue has been credited to the owner-physician as well as the professional component. To determine the owner's productivity consistent with the MGMA definition, the technical component of the MRI and other ancillaries will have to be backed out. This has a dramatic effect on the reasonable compensation determination: After the appropriate modifications are made, the owner-physician's collections are only at the 75th percentile of MGMA. Failure to identify and appropriately adjust for the technical component collected revenue would have resulted in a dramatic understatement of the practice's value due to an overstatement of reasonable compensation for the services of the owner-physician.

2.0 Jurisdictional Issues

Aside from the obvious effect on the reasonable compensation determination, the source of profit in a practice can be quite significant from a jurisdictional standpoint. For example, in marital dissolution valuation, many jurisdictions distinguish between personal goodwill and enterprise goodwill. In many circumstances, the revenue, profit, and value resulting from the technical component of ancillary services may be included in enterprise goodwill and therefore, considered marital property subject to division, again, because it is not related to the personal efforts of the physician, but to the investment in the equipment of the practice. In other circumstances, even the technical component element may be considered nondivisible if a noncompete agreement is required from the seller to maintain the related revenue and profit in the hands of a buyer. Absent a jurisdictional rule, that portion of the practice value connected to technical component revenue that would be present absent the seller is perhaps the clearest element of enterprise goodwill.

3.0 Transactions

In the current transaction market, differentiating reasonable compensation along with enterprise and personal goodwill can be equally important. After a physician practice is acquired by a hospital, a number of employment settings are possible, including employment by the hospital, a hospital-controlled group practice, or the physician practice itself, if the hospital purchases the stock or uses a management company structure similar to that of Sheridan or Pediatrix. The Stark laws have different permitted compensation rules depending on the nature of the employment setting, which can impact how profits from the technical component of ancillaries are handled. This should, in turn, influence precisely what is being valued and how reasonable compensation is determined.

4 At the time of the engagement; today it is more like 74% on average, with a range of 64% to 81% depending on modality.

One of the most important practice types from a valuation and transaction standpoint in the recent past was cardiology. Cardiologists employ a variety of ancillary testing equipment including single photon emission computed tomography (SPECT),[5] used for myocardial perfusion, ultrasound (echocardiogram as distinct from an electrocardiogram, or EKG), coronary computed tomography angiogram, and cardiac MRI. Due to fairly dramatic cuts for SPECT and other nuclear medicine in the 2010 Medicare Physician Fee Schedule, these practices were attractive to hospital acquirers for the technical component of tests as well as for the highly profitable admissions they generate because the hospitals were able to switch the technical component billing to "provider-based" using the hospital outpatient department rates. It is important to note that this has caught MedPAC's attention and it has recommended CMS adopt a site-neutral payment policy for Medicare with respect to such testing.

3.1 Example

CPT code 78465,[6] heart image (3D) multiple, is a SPECT code for myocardial infusion and represented a staggering 10.3% ($2,072,176,147) of charges for cardiovascular physicians billing Medicare in 2007, the highest single code in terms of charges as well as frequency of billing. CPT code 78465 also represented 10.4% ($2,017,599,660) of charges in 2006 and 10.4% ($1,863,154,763) of charges in 2005. Exhibits 1 and 2 are taken from the indicated proposed and final rules and show the global, technical, and professional component breakdown by RVU. Both exhibits reflect the 2010 code change to 78452.

Exhibit 1. 2010 Final Rule

CPT[1]/ HCPCS	Mod	Status	Description	Physician Work RVUs[2,3,4]	Fully Implemented Non-Facility PE RVUs[2,4]	Year 2010 Transitional Non-Facility PE RVUs[2,4]	Fully Implemented Facility PE RVUs[2,4]	Year 2010 Transitional Facility PE RVUs[2,4]	Mal-Practice RVUs[2,4]	CPT[1]/ HCPCS
78452		A	Ht muscle image spect, mult	1.62	8.84	8.84	NA	NA	0.06	XXX
78452	TC	A	Ht muscle image spect, mult	0.00	8.32	8.32	NA	NA	0.01	XXX
78452	26	A	Ht muscle image spect, mult	1.62	0.52	0.52	0.52	0.52	0.05	XXX

In 2011, CPT 78452 represented $790 million of allowed charges. In 2013, it had dropped to $507 million.[7]

5 Due to its ability to generate true three-dimensional images, it is gradually replacing traditional gamma (ray) cameras.

6 Codes are Copyright, American Medical Association. This code was "cross-walked," or changed to 78452 in the period between the 2010 proposed and final rules. This illustrates one more complication that emphasizes the import of understanding CPT codes.

7 www.cms.gov/apps/ama/license.asp?file=/Research-Statistics-Data-and-Systems/Downloadable-Public-Use-Files/Part-B-National-Summary-Data-File/Downloads/PartBNational2013.zip.

Exhibit 2. 2009 Final Rule

CPT[1]/ HCPCS	Mod	Status	Description	Physician Work RVUs[2]	Fully Implemented Non-Facility PE RVUs[2]	Year 2009 Transitional Non-Facility PE RVUs[2]	Fully Implemented Facility PE RVUs[2]	Year 2009 Transitional Facility PE RVUs[2]	Mal-Practice RVUs[2]	Global
78465		A	Heart image (3d), multiple	1.46	10.96	11.32	NA	NA	0.67	XXX
78465	TC	A	Heart image (3d), multiple	0.00	10.23	10.64	NA	NA	0.62	XXX
78465	26	A	Heart image (3d), multiple	1.46	0.73	0.68	0.73	0.68	0.05	XXX

In some practices the professional component and technical component may be billed separately either because of payor rules or because the practice, in fact, only provides one or the other. In this case, a modifier is used for billing and should appear in the billing system reports: "26" is the modifier used for the professional component only and "TC" is the modifier used for the technical component only. If the billing is global (has no modifier), it is necessary to separate the professional component and technical component. The accompanying checklist provides detail on how to accomplish this.

Professional and Technical Component Analysis Checklist

1. What is the practice's specialty?

   Note: Certain specialties may include technical component revenue (neurology, cardiology), while other specialties (family practice, pediatrics) would probably not include technical component revenue.

2. Does the practice own ancillary equipment that has a technical component?

   Note: Look through the depreciation schedule for expensive pieces of equipment. Technical equipment purchases typically stand out from the routine office equipment and furnishings.

3. Identify expected technical component CPT codes for equipment identified in Step 2.

   Discuss with provider and billing staff. Inquire as to whether ancillary revenues are billed globally separately for professional and technical component, or both; this may be payor-specific.

   Some practices may bill globally for in-office ancillary services and professional only for hospital-based services when the hospital owns the equipment. This is common for cardiology practices where the physician may interpret the result of hospital-based stress tests, for example.

4. Request production data by provider and CPT code for your period of analysis. If available, request both charges and receipts by CPT code.

   Review services by CPT code; professional component only income is denoted with a "26"; technical component income is typically denoted with "TC," but other acronyms may be used. Global is typically not specified, but assumed by default if no modifier is present.

5. Calculate production, by provider, preferably using receipts, excluding technical component receipts

Receipts are used because best MGMA data is based upon collections. Because payment rates are set by insurers, the amount a practice charges has little significance except to an uninsured patient or noncontracted insurer.

For globally billed ancillary tests, it is necessary to separate out the professional component. Download the Medicare Physician Fee Schedule for the years the data related to, state, and region in which the practice is located.

www.cms.gov/Medicare/Medicare-Fee-For-Service-Payment/PhysicianFeeSched/Index.html

For example, Exhibit A lists codes for certain imaging procedures from the Massachusetts Medicare fee schedule,[1] with the modifier:

Exhibit A. Codes for Select Imaging Procedures From Massachusetts 2015 Medicare Fee Schedule

CPT Code	Modifier	Fee Nonfacility	Fee Facility	Percent
70490		$217.58	$217.58	100.0%
70490	26	68.17	68.17	31.3
70490	TC	149.41	149.41	68.7
70491		267.011	267.01	100.0
70491	26	73.71	73.71	27.6
70491	TC	193.29	193.29	72.4

Exhibit B lists the same codes from the **2010** fee schedule—note the dramatic reduction in the TC.

Exhibit B. Codes for Select Imaging Procedures From Massachusetts 2010 Medicare Fee Schedule

CPT Code	Modifier	Fee Nonfacility	Fee Facility	Percent
70490		$309.59	$309.59	100.0%
70490	26	70.80	70.80	22.9
70490	TC	238.79	238.79	77.1
70491		373.21	373.21	100.0
70491	26	76.19	76.19	20.4
70491	TC	297.02	297.02	79.6

Not all payors use the same split between professional and technical component, so make inquiries of the practice.

1 www.cms.gov/Medicare/Medicare-Fee-for-Service-Payment/PhysicianFeeSched/PFS-Carrier-Specific-Files-Items/CY2015-CarrierFiles.html?DLPage=1&DLEntries=10&DLSort=1&DLSortDir=descending

Consider alternative measures of productivity including wRVUs depending upon data available from client.

For forecasting purposes, the values of CPT codes may change dramatically from year to year, particularly when ancillary testing is involved. You may want to look at the subsequent year's fee schedule, for example, if using 2015 data as a basis for forecasting 2016 results.

6. Compare calculated production to applicable statistical data to determine reasonable compensation.

Subtract reasonable compensation from the practice's pre-compensation profit to determine cash flow to capital and equity.

(Alternatively, add difference between actual compensation and reasonable compensation to the practice profit and loss.)

7. Isolate the cash flow attributable to the technical component production. Be sure to identify expenses associated with technical equipment.

Note: Examples include billing and collection, technician wages and benefits, insurance, maintenance contracts, certifications, and so on.

8. Compare the cash flow profit in Step 7 to the practice's profit in Step 6.

Consider Jurisdictional rules as to determination of personal and enterprise goodwill.

E.g., if a noncompete agreement is nondivisible in a marital dissolution, calculate the impact on TC profit due to a noncompete.

4.0 Individual Market Idiosyncrasies

In some poorly reimbursed markets, it may, in fact, be necessary for the technical component income to supplement reasonable compensation for the physicians. For example, Rhode Island is notorious for the low levels of fees paid to physicians. This is due in large part to the fact that two insurers control nearly all of the health insurance market in that state and rates are artificially low as a result. Houston is another example, where insurers typically pay physicians less than Medicare; in contrast, Dallas has much better physician fee schedules. As such, to attract and retain physicians, many practices have profitable ancillaries in place. In such a circumstance, it may be necessary to test the reasonable compensation analysis against an alternative measure of production, such as compensation per RVU, wRVUs, or annual encounters. This is an example where the productivity data *including* technical component revenue may need to be evaluated as well.

5.0 Conclusion

Valuing medical practices requires an in-depth understanding of the individual practice and the healthcare industry. This article highlights just one aspect of a myriad of issues unique to medical practice valuation and the determination of reasonable compensation (see sidebar,

What Is 'Incident to' Billing?

Many medical practices increase revenue through the use of nonphysician providers (NPPs), also called midlevel providers. These are employees who provide separately billable services to patients, but are not physicians. Physician assistants (PAs), nurse practitioners (NPs) and midwives are examples of NPPs.

Although they provide separately billable services, there are options for how to bill these services. The services can be billed directly and, because they are not physicians, the reimbursement for these services is a portion of the physician's fee schedule (Medicare sets the rate for many services at 85% of the rate for a physician; non-Medicare payors may have different rules). Another option is to bill the services as "incident to" the services of a physician. If the requirements for incident to billing are met,[1] the services are billed under the physician's provider number and reimbursement is at the full physician's fee schedule. The physician is required to participate in the services provided by the NPP (e.g., supervision, chart review, physical presence in the office suite when the services are provided, among others), but the bulk of the effort is provided by the NPP. Other requirements include that the physician must initiate the plan of care for a patient; if the midlevel changes the plan of care during a visit—e.g., by changing a prescription—the service cannot be billed incident to; if a midlevel sees an existing patient for a new condition, the visit cannot be billed incident to. Appraisers should note that, while nurse practitioners (NP) can bill Medicare directly for those services when working in a state where the scope of practice laws permit them to practice without physician supervision, a physician assistant's (PA) services can only be billed by the PA's employer or contractor.[2]

The expansion of the use of midlevels has caught the attention of the Office of the Inspector General.[3] The final Medicare Physician Fee Schedule for 2014 providers can only bill Medicare for "incident to" services that are furnished in accordance with applicable state laws, as a result of the OIG's finding in the 2009 report that personnel not licensed to perform the service had performed 21% of the services billed incident to.

This becomes an issue in valuation because, like the technical component billing, the productivity related to the nonphysician providers' services could be included in the physician's productivity. Without identifying and segregating the production unrelated to the efforts of the physician from the productivity related to the efforts of the physician, the valuation analyst can end up with an inconsistent reasonable compensation calculation. This is complicated by the fact that CMS does not presently require a modifier in incident to billing to reflect the fact that the service was not provided by the supervising/billing physician, although most practices track midlevel productivity and the related billing physician in their billing systems. A further complication is that practices often incorrectly bill for the services of midlevels under the national provider identifier (NPI) of the physician who originated the plan of care, rather than under the NPI of the supervising physician, as required by CMS. Additional effort in terms of data request and interview questions is required in these circumstances for an appropriate result.

In addition to understanding technical component revenue, understanding the use of nonphysician providers and the methodology for billing their services is important to developing reasoned valuation conclusions.

1 A number of examples can be found here: www.ismanet.org/pdf/membership/incident%20to.pdf.

2 www.cms.gov/Outreach-and-Education/Medicare-Learning-Network-MLN/MLNProducts/Downloads/Medicare-Information-for-APRNs-AAs-PAs-Booklet-ICN-901623.pdf.

3 *Prevalence and Qualifications of Nonphysicians Who Performed Medicare Physician Services,* August 2009

What Is "Incident to" Billing?). The environment that physicians work in, dominated by the Medicare system, changes frequently. Some of these changes can be anticipated, such as the annual Medicare fee schedule modifications. Other changes are less predictable but can have a far greater impact, such as legislation. As any other highly regulated industry, it is critical that valuators remain current. The goal is always to have your valuation upheld, be it in court or in a settlement conference. Failure to understand the industry and its related terminology can undermine your authority as a valuation analyst and reduce the value of your opinion.

Thanks to Jackie Coult, CHBC for her review of this chapter.

Chapter 14. Valuation Considerations Specific to Diagnostic Imaging Entities

CONTENTS

Chapter 14.
Valuation Considerations Specific to Diagnostic Imaging Entities

By Douglas G. Smith, FRBMA

Editor's introduction: Appraisers and valuation analysts are often confronted with complex businesses or industries that require detailed study to understand or the retention of an industry expert for assistance. The healthcare industry is a broad example of such an area, and the subset involving imaging and particularly high-tech imaging is more complex still. This chapter includes a contribution by a leading industry consultant who "talks" to the valuation community about how to approach the development of revenue and expense forecasts, which form the underlying basis for a conclusion of value under the income approach.

There have been a number of significant regulatory, rule-making, and healthcare landscape changes with material significance over the past several years. This is especially true in 2014, 2015, and as proposed by the Center for Medicare & Medicaid Services (CMS) for 2016 through 2018.

Additionally, the healthcare landscape is undergoing significant change as hospitals and health systems consolidate, integrate, and, in some cases, radically change healthcare delivery from hospital-centric services to a broader market penetration strategy including providing more services in stand-alone facilities more directly accessible by patient populations in the communities they serve. Healthcare is a transaction-rich environment.

Simultaneously, federal, state, and commercial health insurance products are evolving. Risk-based products and other alternate payment mechanisms are increasingly replacing traditional fee-for-service payment mechanisms.

These changes in landscape and payment mechanisms continue to highlight the unique considerations related to diagnostic imaging facilities, which may not be understood with sufficient specificity by many highly skilled valuation specialists who have not had the opportunity to routinely participate in the diagnostic imaging business space. Diagnostic imaging is a business sector in which the old adage of if you "see one," or "perform one," valuation, you can be relatively sure the other valuations following will be the same is definitely far from reality. The differences between one facility and another, or one market and another, today, can be quite substantial due to a number of variables in imaging center content and local-area competitive influences on the business.

In this section, we will provide a detailed understanding of the many unique considerations specific to diagnostic imaging entities. Although many of the core elements of a medical practice valuation for other medical specialties can be directly applicable to diagnostic imaging entities, a number of unique elements of revenue and expense requires specific knowledge and experience to assure a valuation of these entities is an accurate representation of its value.

To set the stage and to make sure we are all using the same language and references, I will list a rather universal set of diagnostic imaging entities you may be engaged to value. The list is not necessarily in any order of interest or importance. Nuances within the construct of each entity type need to be taken into consideration when valuing these entities. You should become familiar with each. However, in the interest of time and space available, we will not go into the nuances and subtleties of each entity type with any depth or specificity at this time. The core considerations for all imaging entities we will discuss will apply to all entity types mentioned here:

- Provider entity—hospital-owned freestanding imaging center;
- Radiology group-owned "office" imaging center;
- Radiology group-/hospital-owned clinic imaging center;
- Radiology group/hospital independent diagnostic testing facility (IDTF);
- Radiology group/physician group/hospital freestanding imaging center;
- Physician office imaging entity;
- Corporate imaging center;
- Mobile diagnostic imaging services;
- Specialty hospital imaging center; and
- OWA (other weird arrangements).

1.0 The Unique Structure of Diagnostic Imaging Services Requiring Analysis

Diagnostic imaging services, unlike medicine services, are billed to third-party payors as:

1. Global services (technical component and professional component together);

2. Technical component only services;

3. Professional component only services; or

4. For certain payors, a mix of global, technical, and professional services.

Generally, a diagnostic imaging entity will bill global services and receive a global payment from third-party payors. The revenue line in the financial statement will include, by definition, payment for the professional interpretation of the studies performed at the facility as part of the global fee. The entity will then pay a radiologist, radiology group, or other professional services entity for the professional interpretation in accordance with a professional services agreement, and such costs should appear as a line item of expense in the financial statement. *The technical component revenue is the principal source of net revenue.* The exception to this rule is in the private practice radiology clinic setting where the professional component may not be expressed as a separate expense to the group. A purchaser is typically only buying the technical component revenue.

The importance of understanding the nuances of diagnostic imaging revenue elements is well known to those who have valued diagnostic imaging facilities. For those who have not had the experience of doing so, you are in for a real treat when performing an analysis of historical revenue streams, then trying to develop a base year with certain adjustments, and finally springboarding off of this analysis to forecast revenue streams into the future to determine value.

Exhibit 1 illustrates how the Medicare Physician Fee Schedule is structured utilizing 2014 MPFS as an example.

Exhibit 1. Medicare Physician Fee Schedule

MPFS CALCULATION

(Medicare Physician Fee Schedule)

Non-Facility Pricing Amount =
Work GPCI* Work RVU
+
(Transitioned Non-Facility PE RVU * PE GPCI)
+
(Malpractice RVU * Malpractice GPCI)
X
Conversion Factor (with Budget Neutrality Factor Applied)

2011- $33.9764 2012 = $34.0376 2013 = $34.0230 2014 = $35.8228

% PC to Global has Changed

You Need to Know the Facts

PC ACTUAL 2014 GPCI ADJ RBRVS VS 2012 = -3% to -4%

TC ACTUAL 2014 GPCI ADJ RBRVS VS 2012 = -8% to - 16%

THIS IS A FORMULA YOUR OTHER PAYORS ARE USING AS WELL
AN UNINTENDED CONSEQUENCE BY CMS

1.1 Why Is All This Important?

If the facility bills "globally" instead of "split billing" separately for the technical component and professional component, one must examine how the payments were made for the professional interpretations. Some entities owned by the physicians may intentionally pay for the professional interpretations either at a higher or lower value than a true TC/PC split may dictate. If that is the case, then the technical revenues may be either overstated or understated and will need to be "normalized" in order to accurately forecast future streams of revenue for the contemplated entity post transaction.

In our experience, more often than not, radiology group-owned imaging centers do not split bill but rather bill globally. Accordingly all revenues are stated as global receipts, which will need to be recalculated into technical revenue only, and expense will require restatement to eliminate any expense related to professional services. And all of this must reflect "fair market value" restatement.

2.0 Diagnostic Imaging: Influences on Revenue, Historical Performance Analysis, and Revenue Forecasting

A watershed event in the diagnostic imaging space occurred in 2005 with the introduction of the Deficit Reduction Act of 2005, which was effective Jan. 1, 2006 (DRA 2005). Since then, there have been continuous annual changes to payments for diagnostic imaging services about which you must know the details and the effects to historical revenues as well as the effects of policy changes to future streams of revenue, by modality.

The aftershock of DRA 2005, 2008 MPFS, 2009 MPFS, 2010 MPFS, 2011 MPFS, 2012 MPFS, 2013 MPFS, 2014 MPFS, and 2015 MPFS has been continuous year-to-year adjustments in payment by certain third-party payor contractual arrangements with diagnostic imaging centers. Certain national payors released new policies on payment for *"advanced imaging"* (CT, CTA, MRI, MRA, PET, PET/CT) services before the ink dries each year as posted in the *Federal Register* and have followed suit on every CMS payment policy change and rule-making change ever since. Most national payors have been quick to say "me, too" in their fee schedules, ratcheting down reimbursement for MRI, CT, and PET progressively over the past two to three years.

(Editor's note: This "me, too" or "piling on" phenomenon is common to healthcare fees.)

Exhibit 2 illustrates the historical policy and legislative changes to the Medicare Physician Fee Schedule.

Exhibit 2. MPFS Regulatory History

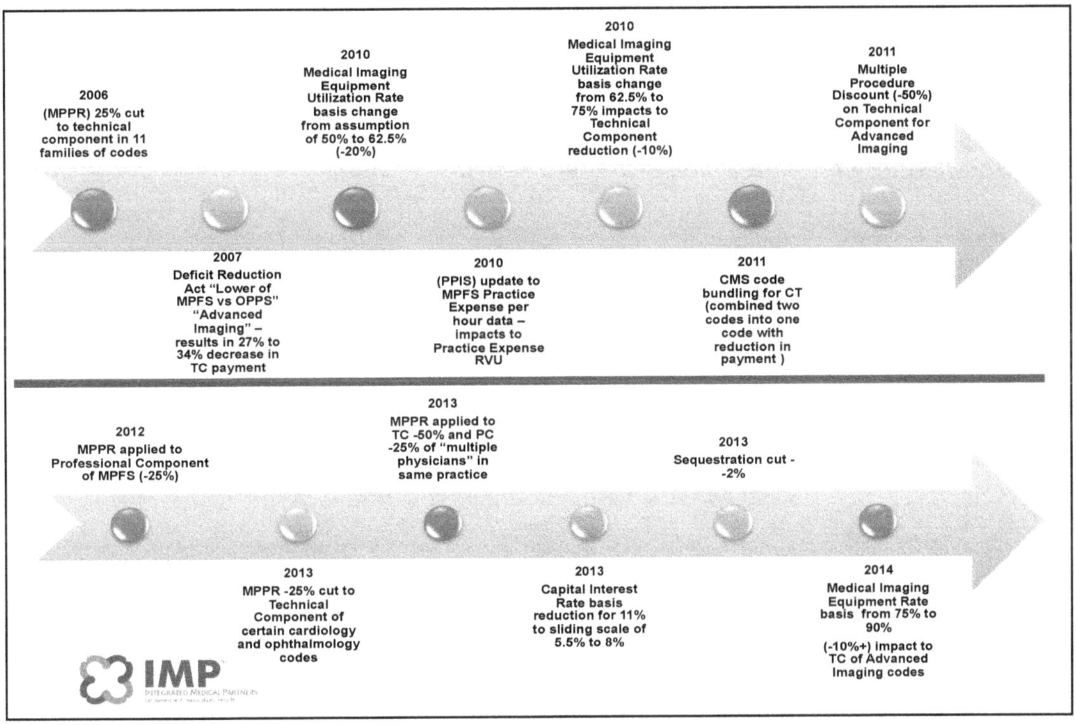

In addition to the above listed impacts to payments for services, there are also a whole host of other regulatory influences and "market forces" influences on imaging entities about which the valuator must be aware and take into consideration. (See Exhibit 3 and Exhibit 4.)

Analysis needs to be performed definitively and with specificity on content performed for Medicare, Champus, Medicaid, and other federal program secondary payors as well as commercial payors with whom the entity contracts and their payor fee schedules if tied to RBRVS (the Medicare Physician Fee Schedule).

Depending on the payor mix and modality mix in the facility, the outcome of these payment policies may be either material to your forecasts or minimal. You need to find out with specificity. The only way to gain specificity is to obtain a report providing count, charges, payments, adjustments by CPT® code, by modality, by payor, for the past two years and the current year (what we call a CPT Frequency Report by Payor). In the absence of such data, you are likely going to face a challenge on certain assumptions in your forecast that will quickly become a personality fight instead of a discussion on the merits.

A recent example is a valuation being performed on a radiology group-owned imaging center by a hospital and imaging center operator newly formed joint venture. Historical performance of the imaging center revealed, after the valuation was complete and a sale price determined, a rather material reduction in volume for MRI and CT volume beginning late 2014 into early 2015,

Exhibit 3. Government Policy

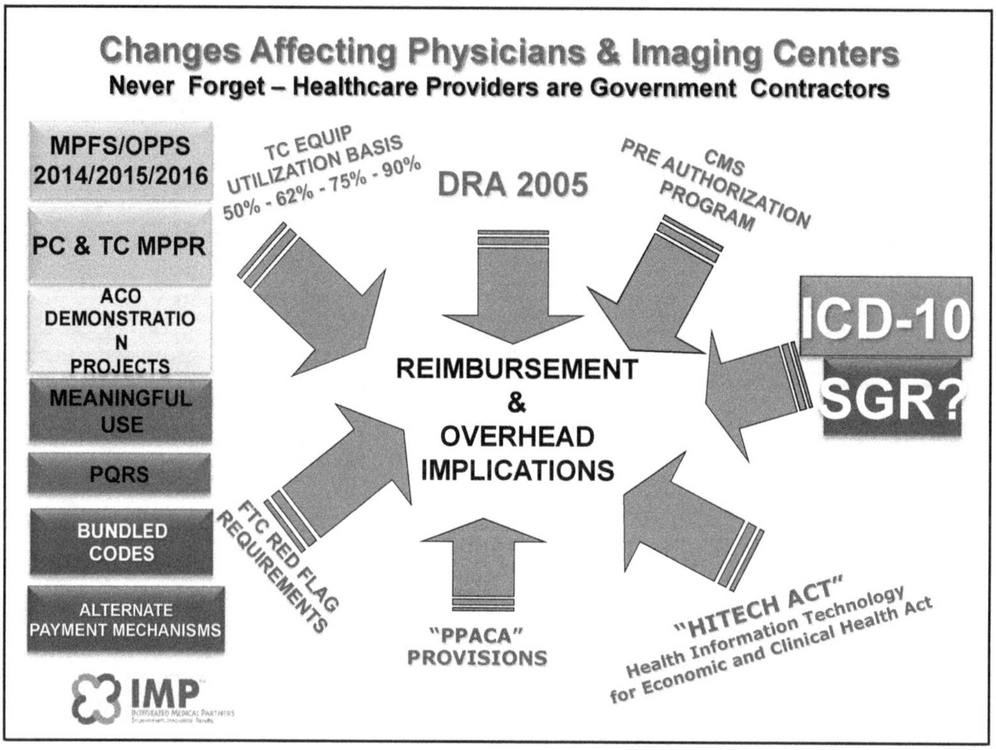

Exhibit 4. Primary Influences on Future Revenue Streams at Diagnostic Imaging Entities

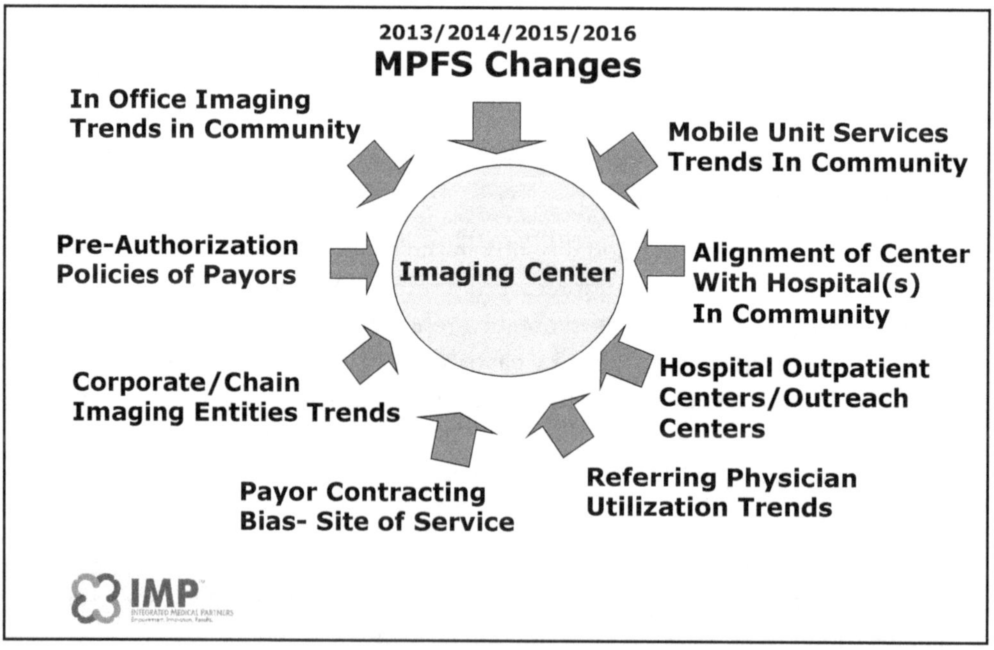

which made the potential buyer quite nervous. Diving deeply into the root cause of the reduction in volume and thus reduction in revenue for the seller revealed that the imaging center had decided to not participate in certain state exchange insurance products in late 2014 since a sale of the imaging center appeared eminent and the pricing offered for exchange insurance plans was well below an "acceptable level" determined by the owners. Further investigation found that historically loyal referring physicians contracted with the exchanges, with many seeing up to 40% of their patient populations shifting from better paying health plans to exchanges. Since the imaging center was not enrolled as a provider of services in the exchanges, the populations of patients typically referred to the imaging center instead had competitor imaging sites of service perform their imaging.

You can imagine the potential impact to the original conclusion of value with those facts present. At the end of the day, the imaging center enrolled in the exchange products, and within 30 days substantially all the volume previously lost returned.

2.1 Lesson Learned

Get into the details. Examine what has changed, and gain insight from management on the ground before leaping off with assumptions that may materially impact the results of your work and thus implications to both the buyer and seller. In this case, the Patient Protection and Affordable Care Act (PPACA) triggered the establishment of state insurance exchanges, which, when offered in the community, resulted in a material shift of patient populations and referral patterns.

Of equal consideration with respect to healthcare landscape effects upon the valuation of diagnostic imaging centers as illustrated in Exhibit 4 are "events" in the marketplace as a result of consolidation and integration, which may well affect referral patterns.

For example, if upon review of historical referring physician metrics the valuator learns that material numbers of referrals to the entity being valued have come from private practice physicians who have recently become employees of a hospital with its own imaging centers, one would have to assess to what degree, if any, historical referrals to the imaging center will continue in the future.

More on "market forces" influences later.

2.2 Medicare Physician Fee Schedule (MPFS)

For illustration purposes, we will use the 2014 Medicare Physician Fee Schedule as an example of the importance of understanding changes in regulatory and rule making by the CMS on forecasting imaging entity performance once a historical trend has been established on past performance. For those of us valuing entities in 2013, it was imperative we understood, with specificity, the impact of changes in the MPFS on each modality. Once the 2014 MPFS was finalized, we had to make many adjustments to payment rates for services the changes impacted in the final bill signed into law for Year 1 performance forecasts.

Although the "conversion factor" (payment per relative value unit) went up, technical component RVU values were significantly reduced for advanced imaging (CT, CTA, CCTA, MRI, and MRA as well as PET/CT). Additional changes were also made to ultrasound and plain film but to a lesser degree.

There were also changes made to the Hospital Outpatient Prospective Payment System (HOPPS) we needed to understand since the technical component for advanced imaging, by law, is paid at the "lower of" the Medicare Physician Fee Schedule (MPFS) or the HOPPS.

It is also important to understand and take into consideration other "regulatory" changes implemented in the fiscal year with respect to the multiple procedure discount applied to both the technical component and professional component as well as any changes to the Geographic Practice Cost Index (GPCI) in the locality of the imaging entity. Exhibit 5 shows the changes made to the Medicare Physician Fee Schedule in 2014.

Exhibit 5. Final 2014 Medicare Physician Fee Schedule

- ❑ **Medical Imaging Equipment Utilization Factor** Increase from 50% TO 62.5% to 75% IN 2013 to **90% in 2014 – results in 10% to 15% reduction in TC for Advanced Imaging**
- ❑ **Multiple Procedure Discount** Increase 11 Families from 25% to 50% reduction – NOW MOVING TO PC AS WELL as TC.
- ❑**Breast Interventional Codes Changes** – Bundles Two Codes, Eliminates 4 Codes
- ❑ **RVU Changes, PE RVU Changes, Malpractice RVU Changes (PC/TC/Global)**
- ❑ **Budget Neutrality Adjustment Application to CF**
- ❑ **Commercial Insurance are "following" CMS Changes**
  - ❑ **Humana, Anthem BC, United – and more**
- ❑ **OPPS Payment Changes effecting the "Lower of" MPFS/ OPPS Determination for TC Payments**
  - ❑ **OPPS Changes:**
    - ❑ **CT -24% to -38%**
    - ❑ **MRI – 18.9% to -19.4%**

IMP Integrated Medical Partners

Cautionary note: When "forecasting" revenue per unit of service and "adjusting" payment per unit of service for each modality, it is necessary to perform a "weighted average" by modality by CPT® code analysis for the specific entity being valued. Individual CPT® codes within a modality are based upon individual relative value units. In our experience, one cannot simply review "aggregate reductions" in the technical component per modality for a given year. Doing so will result in either significant undervalue or significant overvalue of the changes in RVU and payment depending upon the actual CPT® codes used at the facility being valued. For example, CMS and ACR "estimated" the effect of the 2014 Medicare Physician Fee Schedule for CT at a decrease of 24% or so and MRI at 37% or so. We have not seen any outpatient imaging center with more than a 7% decrease in CT or more than a 24% to 28% decrease to

MRI as a result of the changes in the technical component in FY 2014. You must do your homework and obtain a CPT® frequency report from the entity and perform a side-by-side comparison of the "base year" to the "prior year" same period by CPT®, by modality, to understand, with specificity, the actual impact on the facility for which you are performing a "forecast."

Likewise, the 2015 Medicare Physician Fee Schedule (see Exhibit 6) contained additional impacts to diagnostic imaging, which required analysis to determine the implications to future streams of revenue versus historical streams of revenue—by modality, by payor.

Exhibit 7. 2016 to 2018 MPFS Draft

- **Transition from Film to Digital Imaging** (page 44) – CMS intends to update the price for the PACS workstation from $2,501 currently to $5,557 based on new information; public input is sought on clinical labor tasks associated with digital imaging (Table 5, page 47)
- **Review of High Expenditure Services across Specialties with Medicare Allowed Charges of $10,000,000 or More** (page 74) – Table 8 (page 75) lists 118 codes that account for high Medicare expenditures and may be potentially misvalued. **Several radiology and interventional radiology codes are so identified.**
- **XR-29 Reporting** (page 112) – Pursuant to the Protecting Access to Medicare Act (PAMA), the proposal would reduce payment for the technical component (TC) (and the TC of the global fee) of the MPFS service and the HOPPS payment for specified computed tomography (CT) services furnished using equipment that does not meet the National Electrical Manufacturers Association's (NEMA) XR-29 standards by 5 percent in CY 2016 (15 percent in CY 2017).
- **Proposed Relative Values for New or Revised Codes for CY 2016** (page 115) – For CY 2016, CMS is proposing new values in the proposed rule for new or revised codes for which the agency received complete RUC recommendations by February 10, 2015. Final values will be published in the CY 2016 MPFS final rule. CMS denotes new or revised services with an alternative 5-character alphanumeric placeholder code for this proposed rule. New or revised codes for CY 2016 of interest include:
  - New bundled codes for intravascular ultrasound (noncoronary vessel) (3725A-B)
  - New bundled codes for genitourinary interventions (5039A-5039M; 5069G-5069I)
  - New spine x-ray codes (7208A-7208D)
- **Phase-In of Significant RVU Reductions** (page 106) – CMS proposes that, pursuant to a PAMA requirement to phase-in RVU reductions of 20 percent or more, it will adopt a 19 percent cut in year 1, followed by the remaining percentage in year 2. The agency says it believes "this approach avoids differential treatment due to an arbitrary cutoff (e.g., 19 percent reduction vs. 20 percent reduction)."

IMP
INTEGRATED MEDICAL PARTNERS

It is important to understand the influences of changes to each and every payor contract reimbursement over the retrospective two to three years and fully understand the contracting environment specific to the entity you are valuing.

In many cases, we have seen imaging centers maintain a level of "clout" resulting in attractive reimbursement for advanced imaging, while in other markets we have seen reimbursement follow Medicare in a proportional adjustment to prior contracts—all downward. There are certain states in which some payors refuse to contract with IDTFs, or contract with single modality clinic model imaging entities, or in-office imaging entities serving certain medical group practices.

Exhibit 6. 2015 CMS Provisions and Rule-Making Implications to Radiology

- **Good News:**
  - MPFS Conversion Factor only reduced by .001% - Jan-March 2015 $37.7547 as of 1/20/2015 Update (original 2015 CF was $35.8013)from prior $35.8228
  - Screening Colonoscopy Approved Service
  - Digital Breast Tomosynthesis Codes Added
  - Screening and Diagnostic Mammography G Codes Remain in place – for now
- **Bad News:**
  - Technical Component Practice Expense RVU's for Advanced Imaging Seriously Reduced – recent additional changes have been made
    - MRI, MRA – up to 6% to 10% reduction
    - CT, CTA – up to 4% to 21% reduction
  - Digital Breast Tomosynthesis Codes - Not being paid by Many Insurance Companies – Depends upon area of country – some do, some don't.
  - "Imaging Cap" Additions – Breast Ultrasound, Dexa, Stereotactic Guided X-Ray

IMP INTEGRATED MEDICAL PARTNERS

HCPCS	Modifier	Description	Jan 2015 Non-Facility Total RVU	Oct 2014 Non-Facility Total RVU	Variance Total Non-Facility
72146	TC	Mri chest spine w/o dye	4.16	4.74	-12.24%
73721	TC	Mri jnt of lwr extre w/o dye	4.67	5.23	-10.71%
73221	TC	Mri joint upr extrem w/o dye	4.67	5.22	-10.54%
72148	TC	Mri lumbar spine w/o dye	4.12	4.74	-13.08%
72141	TC	Mri neck spine w/o dye	4.16	4.74	-12.24%
72270	TC	Myelogphy 2/> spine regions	1.66	3.69	-55.01%
72265	TC	Myelography l-s spine	1.38	2.41	-42.74%
72240	TC	Myelography neck spine	1.44	2.39	-39.75%
72255	TC	Myelography thoracic spine	1.42	2.20	-35.45%
77002	TC	Needle localization by xray	1.80	2.09	-13.88%
76770	TC	Us exam abdo back wall comp	2.15	2.71	-20.66%
76775	TC	Us exam abdo back wall lim	0.81	1.03	-21.36%
76700	TC	Us exam abdom complete	2.48	2.84	-12.68%
76856	TC	Us exam pelvic complete	2.12	2.54	-16.54%
76857	TC	Us exam pelvic limited	0.64	0.98	-34.69%
76870	TC	Us exam scrotum	0.99	1.18	-16.10%

We *strongly suggest* you analyze reimbursement in six-month increments rather than 12-month periods for the preceding years and current year to pick up any changes in contractual reimbursement and trends emerging in the specific market in which the entity operates.

Anecdotally, we recently were retained to analyze certain assumptions a valuator made with respect to forecast payment for technical component services over the period of the valuation. We discovered a rather material variance between the valuator's payment per procedure assumptions for MRI and CT services forecast in Year 1 and the actual current payment per procedure for MRI and CT services by an amount close to 35% understated—a material difference.

The difference was due to a lack of investigation into actual reimbursement in a defined recent six-month period versus "average reimbursement" for a rolling historical 12-month period resulting in an understatement of reimbursement. The valuator's analysis did not recognize a major recent shift in reimbursement from all principal payors with whom the facility was contracted for MRI, CT, and ultrasound procedures.

In contrast, we also reviewed a set of assumptions for another party in which the valuator overstated current payments per procedure by close to 28% due to a lack of consideration and analysis of changes in modality mix, payor mix, and contract reimbursement following an intense period of contract renegotiations with certain payors in the area.

Another important note: As alluded to earlier, if the entity being valued is radiologist owned, and the purchasing entity will not benefit from the professional component revenue (PC), the valuator will need to restate any global revenue as technical component revenue only, or make accurate assumptions in the expense lines of the forecast to account for payment of the professional component at "fair market value." With respect to the determination of professional component, one needs to consider the change in the ratio of PC to global for DRA 2005 technical component impacts for all federal and state program content. The ratio of PC to global is material when the TC is reduced due policy and rule making. Using the traditional professional component RVU as a percentage of global RVU may not be a valid analysis since the advent of DRA 2005. The MPFS reimburses advanced imaging services at the lower of the HOPPS or MPFS. The only appropriate way to segregate the PC and TC is to express the PC dollars as a percentage of global dollars to be sure all changes in the conversion factor as well as RVU changes are captured.

Other considerations to be applied to revenue streams, on a prospective basis, include an understanding of a number of "environmental" or market-specific forces that may impact future streams of revenue, in addition to the regulatory implications discussed previously.

All or some of the factors illustrated above can have a significant influence on determining and forecasting the value of future streams of revenue. These influences can be accounted for in "risk factors" applied to the determined value or can be reflected through more conservative or aggressive assumptions of volume per modality, reimbursement per modality, or a combination of both in the forecast. Whichever methodology is employed, the valuator should clearly state the assumptions, bases, and rationales used to create the values used in the forecast.

Exhibit 8. Revenue History Analysis Considerations

- ❑ **Retrospective** (3 years – 6 month intervals to assess seasonality impacts, if any)
  - ❑ **Volume**
    - ❑ By Modality (Total and Per Day)
    - ❑ By Payor, By Modality
    - ❑ By Referring Physician, By Modality (top 25)
  - ❑ **Charges and Receipts Trends**
    - ❑ By Modality
    - ❑ By Payor, By Modality
    - ❑ By Referring Physician, By Modality (top 25)
  - ❑ **Charges & Payments per Procedure Trend**
    - ❑ By Modality
    - ❑ By Payor
  - ❑ **Accounts Receivable Aging** (2012, 2013, 2014 YTD)
    - ❑ Special attention to "Self Pay" Patient Responsible

You NEED a CPT Frequency Report

Technical Component Only

Watch For:
Payor Mix Shift, Modality Shift, Referring Volume Shift

IMP

Often, the buyer or seller may attempt, either intentionally or unintentionally, to influence the valuator with respect to the potential effects of each of these factors of influence related to diagnostic imaging entities listed above.

2.3 Emerging Landscape Changes Influence on Valuation Considerations

Over the past two to three years, a new consideration hit the imaging center universe we typically did not need to take into consideration: hospital and physician group alignment. Today, this matter is of material concern with respect to the future stream of revenues to be expected at the entity being valued.

Consolidation is *not* "coming" to healthcare—*consolidation is happening with increasing velocity and vector.* Hospitals are purchasing physician group practice entities at an increasing rate. Groups are merging or finding other "affiliation and integration" models at an increasing pace.

It is important to understand, with as much specificity as is available at the time of the valuation, existing or emerging trends with respect to competition, regulatory changes effecting revenue and operations, referring physician pattern changes, center alignment in the community, and the other factors listed above. These factors of influence can make a material difference in the forecasts and ultimate value determination. For example, if consolidation is occurring in the community, certain providers may be implementing an "employment model" for their medical staff. If the entity being valued historically received referrals to the facility from certain physicians now employed by a hospital not aligned with the entity, it is highly probable the historical referrals to the facility from these physicians will go to another facility aligned with the hospital that has now become their employer.

Exhibit 9. Phase 1 Reaction: Integration and Market Expansion

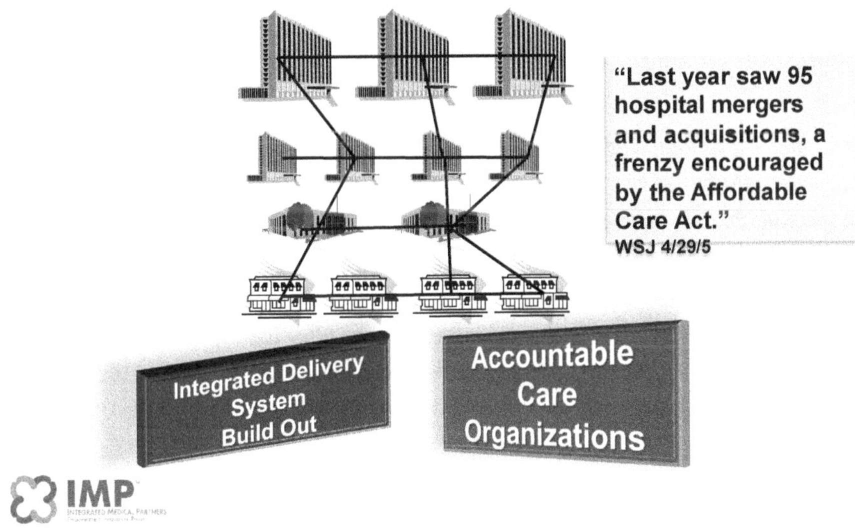

These are matters requiring "homework" to allow you to arrive at your own conclusions with respect to the degree to which the future will follow the documented history of the entity. For example, if the entity being valued is owned by a radiology group or physician group with a historical alignment relationship with a hospital and its medical staff in the community, and the relationship with the hospital has changed, then one needs to consider to what extent the change in relationship will affect future streams of revenue—positively or negatively.

Likewise, one needs to examine the historical sources of patients presented to the facility and competitive trends in the service area:

- Are there recent new entrants into the market?
- Is there evidence the new entrant is "stealing patients" from the entity?
- Is the new entrant a compliment to the entity or a competitor?
- Are the community's referring physicians taking imaging into their practices instead of referring to the entity?
- Are long-standing referring physicians being purchased by the hospital resulting in a shift in referral patterns away from the entity to the hospital-owned facilities?
- Are there emerging regulatory changes to the in-office ancillary services self-referral prohibition exceptions on the horizon that may change the market dynamics?
- Have certain in-office imagers found it financially unattractive to be in the imaging business and plan to return to the market as referring physicians?

- Have certain tightly managed third-party payors entered the area or increased their subscriber populations at the expense of more liberal paying companies?
- Have any major employers in the area changed insurance carriers or covered services benefits for their employees?

You get the idea. *Do the homework.* Do not rely totally upon input from either the buyer or seller. *However, the seller and buyer can provide valuable local knowledge as to trends and influences on the business you should listen to carefully.*

In diagnostic imaging, due to the high fixed costs associated with the business, a change in volume of as little as two to three procedures per day (260 to 286 days per year) can make a material difference in net revenue. Once breakeven is reached (a certain volume at a certain payment per procedure covers all fixed and variable costs), the lion's share of revenue per unit of service will drop straight to the bottom line. Conversely, the loss of two to three procedures per day (260 to 286 days per year) can turn the financial picture upside down in a hurry if the facility is dominated, as most are, by MRI and CT revenue.

3.0 Regulatory Impacts Specific to Diagnostic Imaging Entities and Their Influence on Forecasting Revenue Streams

We need to closely examine certain documents regarding the structure of the entity to determine what, if any, existing or pending regulatory or policy changes may impact future performance of the entity or exact additional expense on the entity for which we must provision in the forecast of either revenue or expense if not already experienced by the entity.

Closely examine any existing operating agreements, contracts with outside providers of services, especially management services and professional services. We also urgently need to examine any contracts with third parties related to leasing of the entity infrastructure (slot leases, per unit of service leases, under arrangement agreements with hospitals to provide technical component services to inpatients) that may need to be eliminated from revenue streams due to the nature of the transaction for which the valuation is being performed on behalf of the seller or buyer. New federal or state policies on these matters may eliminate these streams of revenue. Currently IDTF sites of service are walking around with targets on their backs due to contracting bias in the payor universe.

Valuators should monitor announcements from CMS during the course of the valuation engagement, notably the MPFS Proposed Rule that is released in July of each year about planned changes for the subsequent calendar year. Monitoring is necessary to see which of the proposed changes in the MPFS, if any, actually find their way into the regulations when the final rule is released in late October or early November, find their way into law if Congressional action is required, and then find their way into commercial payor policies affecting future reimbursement.

Exhibit 10. Additional Regulatory and Industry Actions to Consider When Valuing Diagnostic Imaging Entities

- ❑ Utilization Management Policies (Commercial Payors)
  - ❑ Pre-Authorization Policies
    - ❑ Advanced Imaging Modalities
      - ❑ CT
        - ❑ CTA, CCTA
      - ❑ MRI
        - ❑ MRA
      - ❑ PET & PET/CT
- ❑ IDTF Classification
  - ❑ Compliance with IDTF Rules
- ❑ Slot Lease and Per Unit Lease Arrangement Legislation and recent actions
- ❑ Under Arrangement Legislation
- ❑ Anti-Mark-up Legislation
  - ❑ Accreditation of Diagnostic Imaging Entities
- ❑ OIG and CMS Utilization Audits and Investigations
- ❑ CON Laws (State by State)

IMP Integrated Medical Partners

You are not done with the revenue side yet.

3.1 Revenue Forecast Considerations

After collecting all of the historical material provided by the client, analyze it by modality, by site of service, by payor, by modality, by top 20 to 25 referring physicians, and by year. Then step back and see whether any metric stands out as unreasonable or pops out as a red flag to future performance. (See Exhibits 11 and 12.)

Items that should scream out at you also demand you return to the client or source of data and ask probing questions as to potential root causes for results you did not expect. Search for possible errors in data and explanations for variances from expectations not available to you in your interviews with management—both buyer and seller. It is important you gain a full picture that meets the test of reason before you proceed on with a forecast of the future with all of the considerations mentioned herein.

Of special interest today is the trend related to capture of patient-responsible portions of payment such as copays, deductibles, health savings accounts, and other patient-responsible portions of payments. If the entity has "forecast" capture of these accounts at full value, the entity is either totally out of touch with reality or misrepresenting the facts. Take a hard look at what payments, if any, are received on these categories of revenue in the 90-day-or-longer AR. Our experience suggests nothing more than 3% of the charge value will be realized. How

Exhibit 11. List of Revenue Forecasting Considerations

- **Volume Assumptions**
  - **By Modality (total and Per Day)**
    - **Calculate Total Market Demand**
      (Utilization Per Thousand Population in Service Area)
      - Per Year - over Forecast Period
    - **Calculate Total Market Supply**
    - **Calculate Current Market Share**
    - **Calculate Available Market**
    - **Determine Assumptions for Market Share Growth/Decline**
      - Competitive Landscape
      - Entity Leverage in Market – Specific Contributors

At what point does the entity require new or replacement equipment to accommodate forecast volume?

IMP

Exhibit 12. Revenue Forecasting Considerations

- ❑ **Revenue Per Procedure Assumptions**
  - ❑ By Modality
  - ❑ By Payor Category
  - ❑ Throughout Period of Forecast (reimbursement does not go up unless there is a significant rationale for Payor Mix Shift based upon evidence available at the time of the forecast)
- ❑ Test Forecast against History for Consistency does the forecast make sense given the history and facts?
- ❑ **Test Volume assumptions against throughput capacity of imaging equipment and staffing to determine:**
  - ❑ **What, if any, additional provisions in the forecast need to be made for additional medical imaging equipment, maintenance and repair contracts and additional technician and administrative staff to accommodate additional volume forecast.**

You NEED a CPT Frequency Report

IF AN ACQUISITION – WILL BUYER PAYOR PORTFOLIO MATCH SELLER PAYOR PORTFOLIO????

IMP

does the actual experience of the entity then play into your forecast of revenue over the period of the valuation?

Author's note: Recently we have seen and been party to valuations of certain disparate entities in contemplation of combining outpatient imaging entities, owned by the respective parties, into a joint venture entity. Often, the two parties are a hospital and a radiology group. Most frequently, the hospital entity is a "provider model" entity, or one that is an extension of the outpatient department of the hospital, and the radiology group entity is enrolled either as an "office" or as an independent diagnostic imaging facility (IDTF).

The hospital entity, operating as an extension of the outpatient department of the hospital, bills Medicare for its diagnostic imaging services under the Hospital Outpatient Prospective Payment System (HOPPS) and uses the hospital contracts with third-party payors to bill for services to the nonfederal and state patient populations.

If the contemplated joint venture created as a result of the two parties "contributing" their "businesses" to the new entity, the valuator must take special precaution with respect to valuing both the revenue and expense of the hospital department contributed revenue streams if the contemplated entity is intended to be enrolled in Medicare as either a "clinic" or as an IDTF under the MPFS.

Two issues must be engaged:

1. *Revenue*—Historical Medicare and Medicaid revenue at the hospital setting must be converted from the OPPS basis to the MPFS basis. Additionally, the hospital-contracted rate reimbursement should also be converted to the physician entity-contracted rates so that there is parity in assessing the future contribution of the existing stream of revenues. Reiterating, the contributed volume will, on a prospective basis, be realized using the MPFS for Medicare and Medicaid, and the new entity-contracted rates of payment from other third-party payors will likely not benefit from hospital-contracted payor rates. The hospital outpatient rates are typically 15 points to 28 points higher than is available in other settings, so this adjustment is significant.

2. *Expense*—In our experience, it is difficult (if not nearly impossible) to obtain accurate hospital imaging department expense data upon which one can rely for purposes of "forecasting." Many hospitals are not able to segregate shared diagnostic imaging expenses between the outpatient department use of the facilities, inpatient use of the facilities, and ER use of the facilities. Nor do many hospitals have at their disposal a uniform "allocation" of common resources to support their contentions regarding the allocations.

In such cases, the valuator may have to abandon a discounted cash flow or earnings methodology of calculations of value in favor of alternate approaches in order to arrive at conclusions of the value of the contributed "business" to the contemplated venture. In the alternative, the valuator could model the hospital expense structure based on operation as a freestanding entity.

4.0 The Primary Influences and Considerations Required When Analyzing and Forecasting Infrastructure Expense Unique to Diagnostic Imaging Entities

Now let's turn our attention to the expense side of valuation considerations. As with all medical practice settings, there are a number of unique matters to consider when forecasting entity expense. Diagnostic imaging entities have especially unique elements of cost one needs to examine closely. The list provided here may not be totally exhaustive but points to many material matters that need to be understood. (See Exhibits 13 and 14.)

We sometimes find the owners have "prepped" a certain facility for sale.[1] This means certain normal expenses related to equipment maintenance and repair contracts have been deferred or eliminated in favor of "at risk" expense as required or that certain critical technician and/or administrative staff have been recently eliminated. It will be important to examine staffing ratios and credentials of certain technicians to determine what, if any, additional adjustments need to be made to the base year and subsequent years.

Another often missing analysis, when creating a forecast of expense, over the period of the valuation, is an analysis of assumptions of volume cross-referenced to each modality of medical imaging equipment's throughput capacity and cross-referenced to staffing requirements to support the volume forecast—technical staff and administrative support staff.

Exhibit 13. Diagram of Primary Influences on Expense at Diagnostic Imaging Entities

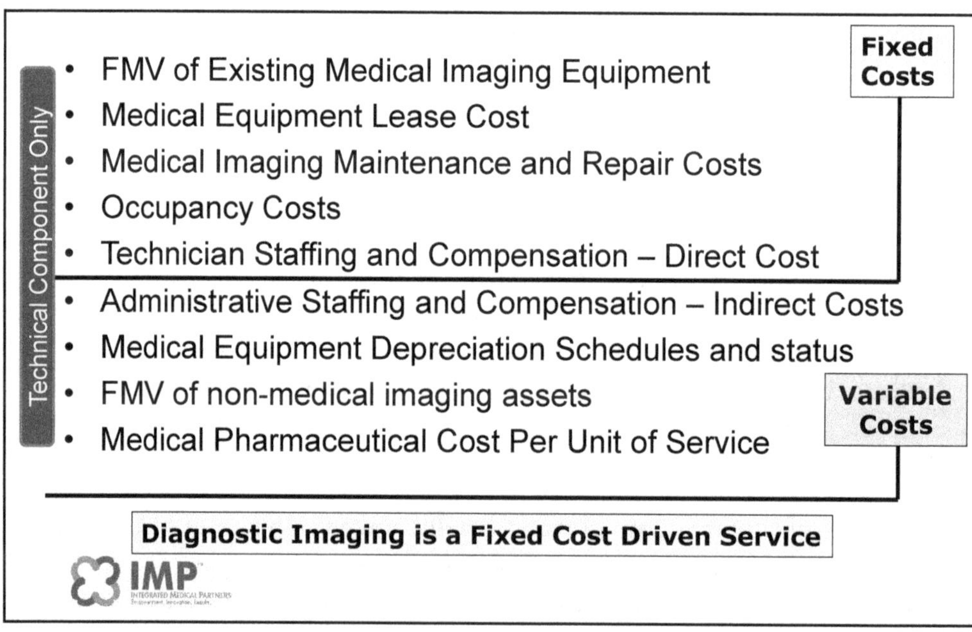

1 *Note: CPAs will recall from their audit training that this was termed "window dressing."*

Exhibit 14. Primary Influences on Expense at Diagnostic Imaging Entities

- ❑ Medical Imaging Equipment Technology
    - ❑ Relevance to Competitive Community Standard
- ❑ Additional Capacity Forecasts – Medical Imaging Equipment, Space, Personnel, Supply Costs – **Useful Life is not the same as Depreciation Life**
- ❑ Technician Licensing Status/Requirements
- ❑ PACS Status and Links to outside images
- ❑ RIS Status
- ❑ Management Fees
- ❑ Medical Director Fees
- ❑ Accounts Receivable Management (Billing) Fees
- ❑ Marketing Expense Status and Forecast
- ❑ Accreditation Status and investments required
- ❑ Compliance Program Implementation
- ❑ HIPAA Program Implementation
- ❑ OSHA Compliance Implementation

It is very easy, and not unusual, to witness forecasts of volume that exceed the throughput capacity of the existing medical imaging equipment at some point in the out years of the forecast.[2] One must look at the viability of expanding operating hours to absorb the increase in volume in the specific market. But expanding hours of operation may not completely absorb the forecast volume. If throughput capacity is breached, then one must make a provision for the addition of additional equipment, maintenance and repair of the equipment, and additional radiologic technicians, with their associated cost of employment to staff the facility.

Exhibit 15. Recommended Additional Investigations

Technical Component Only

- ☐ **Number of Studies per day – by Modality**
    - ☐ **Machine loading capacity by modality per day**
- ☐ **ALL UP COST PER UNIT OF SERVICE PER FTE** (SALARY, BENEFITS, OT)
    - ■ TECHNICIANS
    - ■ NURSING & OTHER CLINICAL
    - ■ ADMINISTRATIVE
        - ☐ DIRECT
        - ☐ INDIRECT
- ☐ **UTILIZATION TRENDS BY ORDERING PHYSICIAN**
    - ■ BY MODALITY
    - ■ BY SITE OF SERVICE
    - ■ BY MAJOR PAYOR
- ☐ **REVENUE CYCLE MANAGEMENT COSTS** (BILLING AND COLLECTION)
- ☐ **Days in AR Trends (three years)**
- ☐ **Content in AR Trends (Payor Mix Shift)**
    - ☐ **Self Pay Category**

2 *Note: This is particularly critical not only for revenue, but also for terminal Capex and depreciation.*

If the entity has a multislice CT unit (32 slice or 64 slice), slot times may be shorter due to the increased scan speed of these devices thus increasing throughput capacity. Other modifications may need to be made to the times listed above based upon the unique characteristics of the medical imaging device in place. Likewise, a 3.0 Tesla[3] MRI may be faster than a "vintage" 1.5 Tesla MRI or a 0.7 Tesla Open MRI.

In our consulting practice, we always request a document from the client describing its patient scheduling times for each modality. The "slot times" will include prescan preparation time, actual scan time, and post-scan time escorting the patient from the scanner room. In the case of procedures for which a contrast agent was administered, the total patient time will include the prescan injection time and post-procedure "recovery" time. The actual "scan time" (time the patient is on the table) is not the true throughput determination—it is the total episode of care time.

If the valuation results in the need for a net asset determination due to lack of excess net profit available to the owners, then the author recommends you retain the services of a qualified and experienced independent medical imaging equipment appraiser to perform a fair market appraisal of the equipment, furniture, and fixtures. To perform such an appraisal, the appraiser will require a comprehensive listing of all assets noting their purchase date and model number.

Other elements of expense that require examination include general medical supply cost per unit of service (linens, gowns, and general medical supplies) as well as pharmaceutical costs per unit of service including contrast agents for CT and MRI services performed with and without contrast, as well as radiopharmaceutical costs per dose for PET and PET CT services.

As you forecast volume for these services, you also need to forecast the associated costs for these items on a per-unit-of-service basis.[4] It is substantially more accurate.

5.0 Potential Land Mines and Valuation Considerations That Can Come Back to Haunt You

As you enter the forecast stage of the engagement, it is important to do a good deal of homework with respect to very specific conditions on the ground in the specific location of the entity being valued. Although the thought of going back to the basic supply and demand calculations, which should have preceded the development of the imaging entity forecast, could make you lose sleep at night in anticipation, it is almost inevitable that the "fight" over the results of the valuation will rest primarily in the revenue forecast side and less so on the expense forecast side.

As discussed earlier, diagnostic imaging services are capital-intensive services. Reimbursement for the technical component, on a per-unit-of-service basis, can indicate either substantial value

3 Tesla is the measure of the field strength or magnetic flux density of the magnet in the machine and is named for Thomas Edison's principal competitor, Nikola Tesla, who promoted AC (alternating current) in contrast to Edison's DC (direct current).

4 Note that per-unit expense is not the same as using a percentage of collected revenue.

or certain impending financial death for the entity being valued. A diagnostic imaging entity has several key moving parts impacting revenue streams, which, examined individually, may not indicate the true trajectory of the business. But taken altogether several factors will definitely paint a brightly colored picture of the entity and its future capacity to generate excess revenue for the owner.

A more recent matter that must be addressed in the valuation is potential medical imaging equipment replacement costs over the period of the forecast and incorporated into the CapEx determinations. Unlike many prior years, we are finding more imaging centers have delayed either replacement of aged equipment or are investing in upgrades to extend the useful life of the equipment. Be sure to examine the entity depreciation schedule to identify equipment at, beyond, or near the benchmark 10-year life expectancy.

Volume projections will, by definition, be based upon the facts of recent history. If the entity has experienced an erosion of volume in key reimbursing modalities, one will need an impressive and quantitative rationale for a step function increase in volume in the forecast. Likewise, if recent history results in erosion per-unit-payment dollar amount, then any forecasts of improvement must be directly linked to quantitative explanations for any forecast increases in per-unit-of-service per modality.

An anxious buyer or seller often asks us to consider or ignore, in forecasts, past trends in reimbursement and/or known events. The dilemma for us all is the representation we make as to the fair market value determination. Can we ignore current facts in the forecast? Should we accommodate the probability of such an occurrence in the risk factors instead? That is a question for the valuator.

A simple supply and demand analysis for the specific area may be required to test the assumptions of growth. If we know the population demographics of the primary and secondary service area of the entity, then we can, using current, available utilization-per-thousand population by modality data, estimate the total demand for diagnostic imaging services in the area. (See Exhibit 16.) If we then know the current market share of the entity, we can forecast with some degree of certainty the "available" population we should reasonably expect to capture. However, we also need to closely examine the age and sex mix to be more precise and take into consideration known shifts, if any, in the construct of the medical staff in the area.

Are more specialist physicians who are high users of imaging services coming into the area? Are certain known high medical specialty users of imaging services fleeing the area? Are high referring specialist physicians being purchased by a hospital? Do the population metrics support or deny the growth assumptions in the forecast?

If a particular geographic area population is flat or declining, does the natural increase in a certain imaging modality per population fit the forecast? One also needs to test the service area declared by the entity. A quick look at a historical patient population by ZIP code can either

Exhibit 16. Modality Forecast Tool Population Utilization Per Thousand

		ACTUAL			FORECAST						
IMAGING UTILIZATION		**2010**	**2011**	**VAR**	**2012**	**2013**	**2014**	**2015**	**2016**	**2017**	**2018**
CT UTILIZATION PER 1000		130.9	132.0	0.79%	133.0	134.1	135.1	136.2	137.3	138.3	139.4
MRI UTILIZATION PER 1000		90.0	90.3	0.37%	90.7	91.0	91.3	91.7	92.0	92.3	92.7
US UTILIZATION PER 1000		522.0	503.7	-3.50%	486.1	469.1	452.7	436.8	421.5	406.8	392.5
X-RAY UTILIZATION PER 1000		1091.0	1074.6	-1.50%	1058.5	1042.6	1027.0	1011.6	996.4	981.5	966.8
PET/CT UTILIZATION PER 1000		7.7	8.0	4.00%	8.1	8.2	8.3	8.4	8.5	8.6	8.6
IMAGINGBIZ.COM REPORT 2012											

	Actual 2010 CENSUS		Calculated	Actual	Actual	Actual	Forecast	Forecast	Forecast	Forecast
US Census Bureau	**ACTUAL 2010 CENSUS**	**Estimated Population Growth**	**2011**	**2012**	**2013**	**2014**	**2015**	**2016**	**2017**	**2018**
TOTAL POPULATION	124,442	**1.1%**	125,266	127,677	130,997	134,403	137,898	141,483	145,161	148,936
LOCALITY PER THOUSAND	124.4		125.3	127.7	131.0	134.4	137.9	141.5	145.2	148.9

confirm or question the assertion of the reach of the entity. It is generally a good idea to at least perform a "back of the envelope" head check on these metrics.

It is important to recognize the source date of the data. Typically, utilization by modality data lag the real world by at least three years. The 2010 data, for example, do not contain effects of utilization management controls certain national payors put in place including preauthorization policies and other utilization management policies for advanced imaging. As evidence, a recent (April 2013) MedPAC Report to Congress noted a decrease in utilization per thousand population for certain modalities due to, in its opinion, DRA 2005, and other CMS policies related to in-office imaging services and utilization controls put in place by commercial insurance companies and radiology benefits management companies. There are no "point numbers" upon which we can rely with confidence. Rather we suggest using a range of utilization per thousand as a metric for the purposes described here. If we were performing a feasibility study to examine the viability of establishing an imaging center in a certain locality, then we would need to be significantly more precise.

Both consultant and appraiser are often challenged on the forecast revenue per unit of service per modality—especially for entities with heavy CT and MRI content. The only way revenue per unit of service ever goes up over time is either:

1. A major payor mix shift to more highly paying third-party payors versus historical payor mix data; or

2. If the managed care portfolio has been recently renegotiated to higher-than-historical aggregate rates.

In today's universe, neither is probable, but the author has experienced situations in which it happens. If evidence can be provided in support of the contention, then we should, by all means, include the evidence and adjust the forecast accordingly.

5.1 Summary and Parting Comments

Diagnostic imaging entities, regardless of structure or setting, are in a state of change. Some recent transactions indicate material changes in historical multiples of EBITDA (a metric that drives this author crazy). Some recent transactions have been strategic purchases and sales.

Others have been made on the merits. Some diagnostic imaging entities will prosper despite regulatory changes, rule-making changes, local landscape changes, and other negative impacts to diagnostic imaging entities. In spite of downward pricing pressures and utilization management directives to reduce access to imaging services, some entities find a way to thrive. Each transaction needs to be assessed at the local level. Valuing these unique entities requires a detailed understanding of the business unit in question.

To obtain such an understanding, take the following steps and ask the following questions:

1. *Get into the details. Make a detailed examination of past performance:*
   - By modality;
   - By payor; and
   - By site of service.
2. *Examine referral patterns* just as you examine them for other medical practices:
   - Who is coming?
   - Who is going?
   - Why?
3. *Understand the specifics* of certain modalities such as CT and MRI as well as other unique modalities.
   - How many studies with contrast are performed?
   - How many studies without contrast are performed?
   - What effects have code bundling made on the entity?
   - How many screening versus diagnostic mammograms are performed—not how many total mammograms are performed?
   - How many mammography CAD (computer-assisted detection) studies are performed?
4. *Do the data make sense* given the patient population demographics and referring physician demographics?
5. *Do reimbursement and payor mix* suggest the entity is capturing its fair share of better paying health plans, or has it been relegated to the low-pay and "self-pay-no-pay" population?
6. *What events on the horizon do we need to accommodate* in the forecast buildup as known facts, and how many events on the horizon do we accommodate as risk factors?

Once you have the details and are comfortable that you understand the past with specificity, then employ the same diligence in forecasting the future, based upon past trajectory and known or reasonable assumptions of local conditions and their likelihood of continuation, expansion, or contraction. The answers will not come from financial statements and balance sheets alone. The answers will come through the tough drilling down into the details of each modality, payor trends, accounts receivable analysis, payor analysis, denied services analysis, bad debt trends, operational efficiency, and expense by line item.

The diagnostic imaging sector is subject to quite rapid changes. Look for them, understand them, and assess their impact to the entity you are valuing. The devil is clearly in the details.

Do not get caught up in discussions of comparable EBITDA transactions. First, there are not many published sources upon which we can rely that provide us with any of the material facts we would need to know to assure ourselves the transactions are indeed "comparable." Many of the most noted transactions in the press have been strategic acquisitions having little to do with "fair market value." The prices paid, and the multiple of earnings paid, had little to do with the future stream of revenues any particular unit was expected to spin off to the owners and more to do with the effects of the addition of the business to a larger picture. Many of these transactions have been structured with strings attached to the ultimate payout price based upon certain metrics being achieved in the future.

A final note: For those of you advising imaging center owner clients as a "business advisor," we offer the following: Any owner of a diagnostic imaging entity considering a sale of the entity at a future date should understand, with specificity, the "factors of influence" to determine value discussed here and take all actions necessary to enhance the value of the entity today. *Any new volume coupled with reductions in cost per unit of service will add to net profit—the most influential metric of future value by a buyer. Added efforts to "brand" the facility and differentiate the facility with referring physicians and, today more than ever, the consumer, for a potential buyer to leverage will also add to value.*

Advise your clients to take actions today to enhance future value. Actions taken at the time of the valuation will not result in a positive outcome—it will be too late.

Chapter 15.
Ambulatory Surgery Centers

CONTENTS

Chapter 15. Ambulatory Surgery Centers

By Todd J. Sorensen, MBA, CVA

1.0 Introduction

During the first decade of the new millennium, surgery-center transactions became one of the most popular joint-venture relationships involving both for-profit and not-for-profit healthcare providers and surgeons who perform outpatient surgery. Due to the economic slowdown and the hospital-physician employment phenomenon, the volume of new joint-venture relationships has slowed substantially in the second decade. However, outside of engagements associated with physician practice transactions, valuation engagements associated with ambulatory surgery center (ASC) transactions continue to represent the highest-volume healthcare segment for business valuation engagements in our firm. As with most healthcare segments, ensuring that transactions between potential referral source physician owners and healthcare systems occur within the range of fair market value is critical to compliance with the Stark regulations, federal fraud and abuse statutes, and, in some cases, state law.

Types of private ASC equity transactions include: (1) controlling interests in stand-alone licensed freestanding surgery centers; (2) minority or noncontrolling equity transactions in freestanding ASCs; and (3) controlling and noncontrolling equity transactions in hospital outpatient departments relicensed as freestanding ambulatory surgery centers. Each of these transactions typically has a different value.

Minority equity interests in private ASCs tend to trade at much lower levels than controlling interests in those same ASCs. In general, valuations of any equity interest are based not only on external market factors, but also on the facts and circumstances of the particular ASC being valued. As an example, surgery centers with little or no physician ownership tend to be valued lower than those with significant ownership.

The ASC industry is highly fragmented, composed of several large publicly or privately owned companies and many small, independent operators. Of the 5,476 freestanding Medicare-certified ASCs operating in the United States, multifacility chains own or manage only 1,456 facilities, or approximately 26.7%. AmSurg, United Surgical Partners International (USPI), Surgical Care Affiliates (SCA), SurgCenter Development, and HCA Inc. (HCA) are the largest owners and operators (see Exhibit 1).

Exhibit 1. Overview of ASC Industry

Surgery Center Operators	# of Centers	Multifacility Surgery Center Chain	# of Centers	Multifacility Surgery Center Chain	# of Centers
AmSurg	247	Nueterra [4]	30	Surgem	13
USPI [1]	202	Covenant Surgical Health	29	Physicians Surgery Centers	11
Surgical Care Affiliates [2]	186	ASD Management	25	Community Visionary Enterprises	14
SurgCenter Development	130	Regent Surgical Health	23	Meridian Surgical Partners	10
HCA	115	Ambulatory Surgical Centers of America	22	Foundation Healthcare	10
Surgery Partners [3]	96	Practice Partners in Healthcare	21	Ortmann Healthcare Consultants	9
Medical Consulting Group	47	Surgical Management Professionals [5]	18	Merritt Healthcare	9
Tenet Healthcare Corporation [1]	44	Blue Chip Surgical Center Partners	17	Surgery One	4
Community Health Systems (est.)	41	Interventional Management Services	17	Murphy Healthcare	8
Physicians Endoscopy	36	Constitution Surgery Partners	15	Laser Spine Institute	7
				Total	1,456
				% of Total Medicare Certified ASCs	26.7%

Footnotes:

(1) In March of 2015 Tenet acquired USPI. At the time of the transaction, UPSI and Tenet owned and operated 202 and 44 surgery centers,

(2) SCA does not have an ownership interest in 26 of the total 186 facilities it manages

(3) Surgery partners acquired Symbion in November 2014. At the time of the transaction Symbion owned approximately 44 centers

(4) Based on 2010 data

(5) Includes surgery centers under development

Sources: Company websites, press releases, and SEC filings as of June 2015.

This chapter provides an overview of the ASC segment, typical ASC legal structures, ASC financial performance and primary value drivers, and the most common ASC valuation applications.

2.0 Segment Overview

Ambulatory surgery refers to relatively lower-acuity surgical procedures performed on an outpatient basis that do not require an overnight stay. These surgeries can occur in either a hospital outpatient (surgical) department (HOPD) or in a freestanding ASC.

ASCs offer a more productive and comfortable environment for both physicians and patients. A surgeon using an ASC may practice more efficiently while maintaining a schedule with more consistent weekly time blocked to schedule surgeries ("block time") and quicker, more reliable turnaround times. Patients who receive treatment at an ASC may recognize benefits from a convenient, less-institutionalized environment, streamlined care, specialized services and proven lower infection rates.

ASCs provide the surgical equipment and supplies, specialized personnel and other support services that enable their surgeon-users to perform surgeries. Physicians typically do not pay for these services. Instead, the ASC bills a technical fee, or facility fee, to the patient or payor. The physician bills the patient or payor a professional fee separately. The ASC neither employs nor pays compensation to the surgeon-users. Consequently, an ASC's success or failure relates directly to its ability to provide the necessary technical services to enable its surgeon-users to perform their surgical cases.

3.0 History of ASCs

The idea of performing outpatient surgery first materialized in 1966, in an article in the *Journal of the American Medical Association* (*JAMA*). Shortly thereafter, the health insurance industry began exploring alternatives to the high costs associated with procedures in hospitals, and the U.S. National Advisory Commission on Health Facilities began experimenting with ways to lower them. In 1970, the first ASC opened. In 1971, the American Medical Association (AMA) endorsed ASCs performing surgery under general and local anesthesia for selected procedures and patients. By 1976, 67 ASCs existed around the country.

Although the government, through Medicare, began collaborating with six ASCs in 1974, it wasn't until 1982 that the program approved payment for 200 selected procedures performed in ASCs. Today Medicare, Medicaid, and private insurers allow and pay for more than 3,600 procedures performed in ASCs, and these numbers are expected to grow. Approved procedures generally are those offered in a hospital inpatient setting that also can be performed safely in outpatient facilities. ASC-approved procedures generally require less than 90 minutes of operating-room time, less than four hours of recovery-room time, and no overnight stay.

Expanded acceptance by Medicare and other payors led to large growth in the number of ASCs and total Medicare payments to ASCs for services performed. For example, data show that Medicare payments to ASCs more than quadrupled between 1992 and 2005.

The 2000-to-2008 period was characterized by particularly strong growth in both the number of Medicare-certified ASCs and Medicare payments to ASCs. The number of Medicare-certified ASCs grew at an average annual rate of 7%, or 240 new ASCs, from 3,028 in 2000 to 4,941 in 2008. Medicare payments over this period increased approximately 10.4% compounded annually from approximately $1.4 billion in 2000 to $3.1 billion in 2008.

While both the number of Medicare-certified ASCs and Medicare payments have continued to grow since 2008, the rate of growth has slowed. The number of Medicare-certified ASCs and Medicare payments to ASCs has slowed to 1.6% and 3.9%, respectively. As of 2014, there were 5,476 Medicare-certified facilities nationwide and total Medicare payments to ASCs were $3.9 million. In addition to the Medicare-certified facilities, there are an additional 600 ASCs that are not Medicare-certified.

4.0 Certificate of Need Requirements

Some states require a certificate of need (CON) to operate an ASC. A CON is a regulatory review process that evaluates whether a proposed service or facility is actually needed in a specific market. Those subject to CON regulations include hospitals, nursing homes, outpatient surgery centers, and anyone purchasing medical equipment valued above certain state-determined thresholds.

The CON mandate began in response to overwhelming requests for federal funding spurred by the 1946 Hill-Burton Program, which matched grants for the construction of hospitals in medically underserved areas. Congress needed to infuse effective measures to appropriately manage the billions of dollars in federal assistance being requested in response to the program.

In 1974, Congress passed the National Health Planning and Resources Development Act, offering states powerful incentives to enact laws implementing CON programs. By 1980, all states except Louisiana had one. Congress repealed the federal law in 1986, and many states have since relaxed or eliminated CON laws.

Exhibit 2 illustrates the states that require a CON, those that do not, and the number of Medicare-certified ASCs in the United States in 2014.

Exhibit 2. States That Require a CON

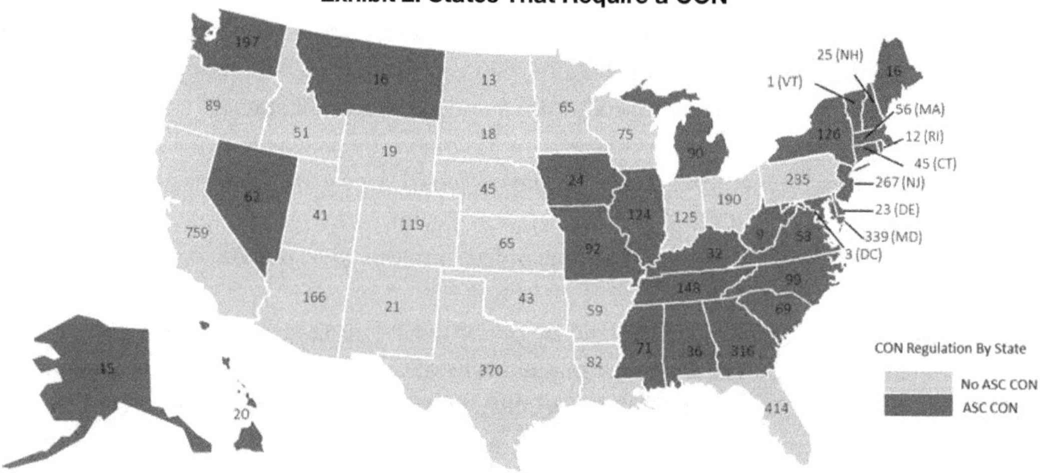

5.0 ASC Growth

That healthcare costs have increased at rates in excess of inflation is considered the primary factor in the development and increased use of surgery centers. Procedures performed in an outpatient setting generally cost between 30% and 60% less than the same procedures performed in a hospital. As a result, Medicare, managed care, and other payors have encouraged moving procedures to ASCs.

While cost containment may have been the initial driver in the growth of ASCs, the historical growth in the industry was also driven by advantages to both patients and physicians. In a survey completed by the Office of the Inspector General (OIG), part of the U.S. Department of Health and Human Services (HHS), Medicare beneficiaries who underwent procedures in ASCs strongly preferred the facilities to hospitals.[1] Reasons included less paperwork, lower costs, more convenient locations, better parking, less wait time, better organization and friendlier staff. The study also determined that ASCs provided safety and post-operative care comparable to a hospital.

For physicians, the benefits of performing surgeries in ASCs go beyond increased patient satisfaction. Not only are their patients happier, but they can also achieve larger volumes and more efficiency. Unlike doctors at a hospital that provides a variety of surgical procedures and uses an array of supplies and equipment, doctors at freestanding surgery centers typically focus on a few select procedures. This increases patient volume and decreases turnaround time between surgeries because the operating room needs minimal preparation for the next patient.

Physicians who act as partial owners or investors in the venture (by partnering with a multicenter ASC owner/operator chain such as AmSurg, SCA, or USPI, for example), have an additional incentive to prefer the ASC environment: They earn income for the procedures they perform. In other words, physicians capture a portion of a technical fee not accessible to them at a hospital.

Technological developments also have contributed to substantial growth in the ASC segment. Advances in laser, endoscopic, and arthroscopic minimally invasive procedures have allowed for more variance in the array of procedures conducted at ASCs.

Demand for outpatient surgery will continue to increase during the next decade, driven by growth in the 55-plus population, as baby boomers shift into the senior-citizen bracket. This is largely because utilization rates for many outpatient surgical procedures appear to correlate directly with age.

Of all the surgery cases performed in the United States in 2013, approximately 65.6% were performed in the outpatient setting. Outpatient surgery as a percentage of total surgery has increased significantly from 1980 to 2013. The increase in surgical procedures performed in outpatient settings is primarily linked to both the rise of ASCs as well as innovations in technological and surgical procedures that have expanded the types of procedures suitable for an outpatient setting. Beginning in the early to mid-1990s, the shift in surgical volume from inpatient to outpatient began to flatten. While the number of ASCs and Medicare payments to ASCs has grown substantially, the percentage of surgeries performed in the outpatient setting since 2000 has only grown slightly, from 62.7% to 65.6% of total surgeries. This lack of growth in outpatient surgery versus inpatient surgery suggests a maturing of the ASC industry.[2]

1 Richard P. Kusserow, inspector general, *Patient Satisfaction With Outpatient Surgery, A National Survey of Medicare Beneficiaries*, December 1989.

2 Avalere Health for American Hospital Association, *Trendwatch Chartbook 2011*.

Exhibit 3. Medicare ASC Trends: MedPAC June 2015 Data Book

Medicare ASC Trends: MedPac June 2015 Data Book															
	2000	2001	2002	2003	2004	2005	2006	2007	2008	2009	2010	2011	2012	2013	2014
Medicare ASC Payments (Billions)	$1.4	$1.6	$1.9	$2.2	$2.5	$2.7	$2.8	$2.9	$3.1	$3.2	$3.3	$3.4	$3.6	$3.7	$3.9
Growth	n/a	14.3%	18.8%	15.8%	13.6%	8.0%	3.7%	3.6%	6.9%	3.2%	3.1%	3.0%	5.9%	2.8%	5.4%
Number of Medicare Certified ASCs	3,028	3,302	3,545	3,848	4,140	4,298	4,530	4,740	4,941	5,049	5,135	5,217	5,287	5,363	5,437
Growth	n/a	9.0%	7.4%	8.5%	7.6%	3.8%	5.4%	4.6%	4.2%	2.2%	1.7%	1.6%	1.3%	1.4%	1.4%
Medicare Payments per Facility (in thousands)	$462	$485	$536	$572	$604	$628	$618	$612	$627	$634	$643	$652	$681	$690	$717
Growth	n/a	4.8%	10.6%	6.7%	5.6%	4.0%	-1.6%	-1.0%	2.5%	1.0%	1.4%	1.4%	4.5%	1.3%	4.0%

This is further supported by the reduction in growth of both the number of Medicare-certified ASCs and Medicare payments to ASCs previously discussed. As Exhibit 3 illustrates, total Medicare payments for ASC services more than doubled between 2000 and 2008 but only grew about 25% between 2008 and 2014. Compounded annual growth in Medicare payments to ASCs slowed from 10.4% between 2000 and 2008, to 3.9% between 2008 and 2014. As Exhibit 3 illustrates, total Medicare payments for ASC services more than doubled between 2000 and 2008 but only grew about 25% between 2008 and 2014. Compounded annual growth in Medicare payments to ASCs slowed from 10.4% between 2000 and 2008, to 3.9% between 2008 and 2014. This slower growth in Medicare payments appears to be a function of slower growth in both the number of ASCs and reduced reimbursement. Compounded annual growth in the number of Medicare ASCs slowed from 6.3% between 2000 and 2008, 1.6% between 2008 and 2014. The growth in Medicare payments to ASCs far outpaced the growth in Medicare certified ASCs during the period prior to 2005. Since 2005, this trend slowed significantly, coinciding with the freeze in Medicare grouper payments to ASCs which became effective in 2005. Growth in Medicare payments to ASCs has fallen from a high of 18.8% in 2002 to 2.8% in 2013.

6.0 Changes in Medicare Payment System for ASCs

The Medicare Prescription Drug, Improvement, and Modernization Act of 2003 (MMA) set in motion some much-anticipated changes to the ASC payment system. Through the MMA, CMS eliminated the update for ambulatory surgical center services for fiscal year 2005, changed the update cycle to a calendar year, and eliminated updates for calendar years 2006 through 2009. The MMA also removed the requirement that CMS survey ASCs' costs and charges every five years. It also asked the General Accounting Office (GAO) to study the relative cost of services in ASCs and HOPDs and determine whether the outpatient prospective payment system's (OPPS) procedure groups reflected ASC procedures. The results of this study formed the basis for the 2007 Proposed ASC Rule.

On Aug. 8, 2006, CMS unveiled its proposal for a new ASC payment system. On Jan. 1, 2008, CMS implemented the new system for payments to ASCs for the provision of medical services to Medicare beneficiaries. Exhibit 4 gives a brief description of the major events leading up to the implementation of the new system.

Exhibit 4. Major Events Leading Up to the Implementation of the New System for Payments to ASCs

NEW ASC PAYMENT SYSTEM TIMELINE	
1998	CMS proposes a new ASC payment system and a new hospital outpatient department ("HOPD") payment system.
2000	CMS Begins paying HOPD using prospectively determined rates for bundles of services, called APCs. Congress prohibits CMS from implementing a new system for ASCs without a new cost survey.
2003	Congress requires CMS to implement a new ASC payment system by January 1, 2008, and freezes ASC payment rates through 2009.
2005	Introduction of Ambulatory Surgical Center Medicare Payment Modernization Act of 2005 (legislation) by Congressman Herger (R-CA) and Senator Crapo (R-ID).
2006	CMS issues proposed rule detailing its recommendations for a new payment system.
2007	On August 2, 2007, CMS issues a final rule establishing a new payment system for ASCs, including the methodology to be used in determining rates, and proposes rates for 2008. On November 27, 2007, CMS issues final rates for 2008.

The new payment system is similar to the old Medicare payment system in that CMS pays ASCs a facility fee intended to cover the nonprofessional costs associated with providing a surgical procedure. But instead of categorizing payments into one of nine groupers, the new payment is based on one of 201 ambulatory payment classifications (APCs). Medicare uses the same APCs for ASCs and HOPDs. Each procedure performed is assigned a common procedural terminology (CPT) code, which in turn cross-walks to an APC, and each APC has a specific payment rate. But, because CMS continues to report payment rates by CPT code, ASCs continue to bill and collect from Medicare using CPT codes.

Though ASCs and HOPDs both use APCs, payment rates vary between the two. The rate paid to an HOPD for each APC is based on relative weight, a measurement that ranks the costs to perform the procedures in one APC compared to the costs of those in another. CMS determines the relative weight for each APC using hospital cost reports. The relative weight is then multiplied by a uniform dollar conversion factor to get the national HOPD payment rate. ASCs payment is a percentage of the national HOPD rate. For 2008, ASCs received, on average, 65% of HOPD payments. Since 2008, this gap has increased. The gap between ASC and HOPD reimbursement widened to 56% by 2011 and has remained at similar levels since then.

Medicare added a significant number of reimbursable procedures in 2008. Medicare reimbursed ASCs for providing 3,390 surgical procedures in 2008, 819 more than were reimbursable in 2007. Some of the new procedures realized reimbursement significantly higher than 65% of HOPD rates. For example, procedures that required the use of a device estimated to cost more than 50% of the procedure's total APC reimbursement, the ASC payment rate included the same dollar value that an HOPD received for the device, without any discount. In 2015, the threshold for the device-intensive policy was lowered to 40%, resulting in the addition of 47 more procedures to the program.

For procedures performed in physician offices more than 50% of the time, the ASC payment is the lesser of either the payment rate determined using the HOPD conversion factor or the amount Medicare typically pays the physician for performing the procedures in the office. This payment methodology only applies to new procedures introduced under the new payment system, not to procedures on the list prior to 2007.

When it comes to multiple procedures, the policy in effect prior to the implementation of the new payment system remained. ASCs earn 100% for the primary procedure (defined as the one with the highest reimbursement rate), and 50% for each additional procedure. Certain procedures are not subject to the multiple-procedure discount; the classification of these procedures did not change.

CMS established a four-year transition period for procedures already on the ASC list, to give individual ASCs more time to adjust to the new payment system. In 2008, Medicare ASC payment rates for these procedures were based on a blended rate of 75% of the 2007 ASC payment rates and 25% of the amount Medicare would have paid in 2008 under the new system. In 2009, the ASC rate was based 50% on the 2007 rate and 50% on the 2009 rate. In 2010, the payment was made based on 25% and 75% of those respective payment rates, and in 2011, the transition was complete.

The new payment methodology affected surgical specialties differently. Using the 2008 rates, the Federated Ambulatory Surgery Association (FASA), which has since been merged with the American Association of Ambulatory Surgery Center (AAASC) to form the Ambulatory Surgery Center Association (ASCA), estimated a 5% decline for GI rates and a 23% increase for orthopedics. FASA estimated that, once fully implemented, the new payment system would cause an overall decline of 19% for GI and an overall increase of 92% for orthopedics. FASA's analysis, detailed in the November/December *Update Magazine,* is summarized in Exhibit 5.

Exhibit 5. FASA's Analysis of New Payment System

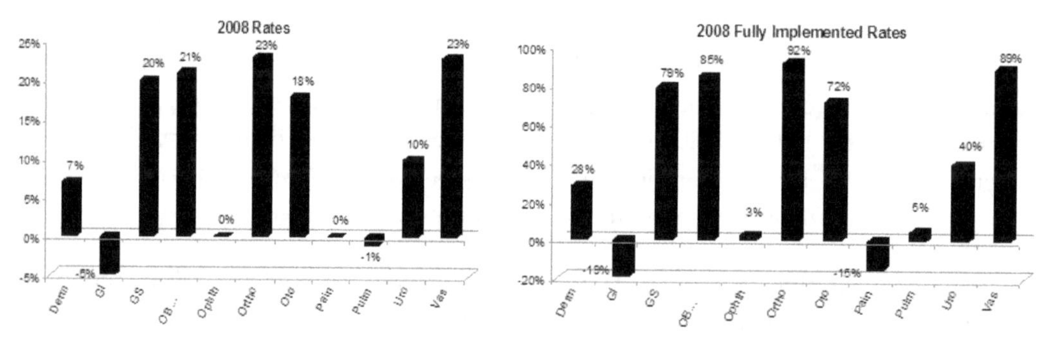

Under the new payment system, Medicare reimbursed nine of the 10 highest-volume procedures performed in ASCs at a lower rate. According to CMS, the overall lower payment rates, taking into consideration the 819 newly covered procedures, resulted in the same total 2008 Medicare spending on ASCs than if a new payment system had not been adopted.

CMS continued to use the prefloor, prereclassified wage index to adjust ASC payments for geographic differences in the relative cost of labor. The differences in some markets starting in 2011 were particularly pronounced because of a policy in the health reform law that sets the hospital wage index for inpatient and outpatient services in so-called "frontier states" at 1.0. The states affected by the frontier wage index policy include Montana, Wyoming, North Dakota, South Dakota, and Nevada.

CMS updated their estimate of productivity and applied a reduction of 1.3% in 2011, instead of the 1.6% reduction that had been proposed. This is inconsistent with MedPAC's recommended productivity update of 0.6%. In this time frame, CMS received criticism from the ASC industry and the hospital industry for an overly aggressive assumption of productivity gains between 2008 and 2010. In the final rule, CMS did respond to the concerns about the productivity calculation and reduced the productivity adjustment by 0.3%.

CMS applied a secondary budget neutrality calculation to the ASC relative weights to ensure that changes to the APC relative weights used to determine HOPD rates did not result in an aggregate increase or decrease in ASC payments. The final rule established a scaling factor more favorable to ASC rates of 0.9238 (CMS had originally proposed the factor to be 0.9090 for 2011). Although the final rule was better than the proposed rule, the 2011 factor was lower than the 2010 factor of 0.9567, partly due to the fact that these are the fully transitioned weights and due to increases in the OPPS relative weights for ASC procedures.

The final rule did not require ASCs to report quality data for CY 2011 but did express CMS's intention to implement ASC quality reporting in future rulemaking. In the 2011 final ruling, CMS also added four new quality measures for ASC quality reporting to a total of 23 measures. CMS suggested that 2012 would be the first year of required quality reporting.[3]

In the CY 2012 final rule, CMS adopted seven quality measures to be reported by ASCs that were expanded by subsequent rulings. Beginning in CY 2014, ASCs that did not meet the reporting requirements under the Ambulatory Surgical Center Quality Reporting (ASCQR) program are subject to a 2.0% payment reductions. Exhibit 6 outlines the measures finalized for purposes of the CY 2014-2017 payment determinations.

3 CMS, Final Ruling for ASC's 2011.

Exhibit 6. ASC Quality Reporting Program Measurement Set for Payment Determination

Measure	CY 2014	CY 2015	CY 2016	CY 2017
ASC-1: Patient Burn	X	X	X	X
ASC-2: Patient Fall	X	X	X	X
ASC-3: Wrong Site	X	X	X	X
ASC-4: Hospital Transfer/Admission	X	X	X	X
ASC-5: Prophylactic Intravenous (IV) Antibiotic Timing	X	X	X	X
ASC-6: Safe Surgery Checklist Use		X	X	X
ASC-7: ASC Facility Volume Data on Selected ASC Surgical Procedures		X	X	X
ASC-8: Influenza Vaccination Coverage among Healthcare Personnel			X	X
ASC-9: Endoscopy/Polyp Surveillance: Appropriate Follow-Up Interval for Normal Colonoscopy in Avg. Risk Patients			X	X
ASC-10: Endoscopy/Polyp Surveillance: Colonoscopy Interval Patients w/ a History of Adenomatous Polyps			X	X
ASC-11: Cataracts: Improvements in Patient's Visual Function within 90 Days Following Cataract Surgery*			X	X
ASC-12: Facility Seven-Day Risk-Standardized Hospital Visit Rate after Outpatient Colonoscopy**				X

Exhibit 7. ASC Reimbursement as a Percentage of HOPD Reimbursement

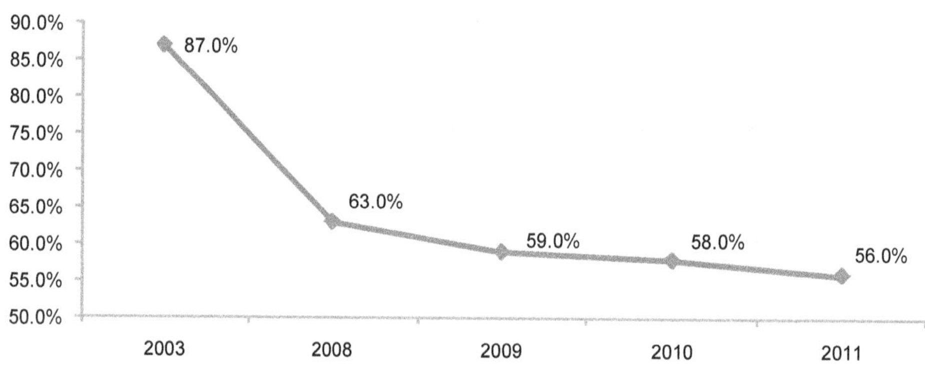

7.0 Discrepancy in Payments

The discrepancy between ASC payments and hospital outpatient departments has grown substantially since 2003. As illustrated in Exhibit 7, ASC reimbursement rates when compared to HOPD reimbursement rates for the same services decreased significantly from 87.0% in 2003 to 63.0% in 2008. As Medicare reimbursement transitioned to the new payment methodology, this declined to 56.0% by 2011 and remains near this rate for 2015. The discrepancy between ASC reimbursement rates and HOPD reimbursement rates exists because CMS uses different factors to annually update ASC rates and HOPD rates and a process called "secondary rescaling," which ensures that changes to the APC relative weights used to determine HOPD rates do not result in an aggregate increase or decrease in ASC payments. The ASC industry has lobbied to close the discrepancy, and, while recently CMS has expressed some interest in closing the gap for certain lower acuity procedures, there has not been any indication that this would result in any significant increase in ASC rates for these procedures.[4]

4 CMS, ASC Association.

8.0 CY 2015 Final Ruling

On Oct. 31, 2014, CMS released the calendar year (CY) 2015 Hospital Outpatient Prospective Payment System (OPPS) and Ambulatory Surgical Center (ASC) payment system policy changes and payment rates final rule. Based on the final ruling, ASC payment rates will increase by 1.4% in CY 2015. The increase is determined based on a 1.9% inflation adjustment per the Consumer Price Index for All Urban Consumers (CPI-U) less the multifactor productivity (MFP) reduction of 0.5% mandated by the Affordable Care Act (ACA). In addition, CMS calculated a wage index budget neutrality adjustment of 0.9998 for 2015. Therefore, the final FY 2015 ASC conversion factor for ASCs that meet quality reporting requirements is set at $44.071, which is calculated as the product of the CY14 conversion factor of $43.471 multiplied by the wage index budget neutrality adjustment of 0.9998 and the MFP-adjusted CPI-U update of 1.4%.

CMS also finalized a significant change to its device-intensive policy, which will benefit ASC providers. ASC device-intensive procedures are now defined as procedures that are assigned to any APC group with a device cost greater than 40% of the total cost of the procedure in the HOPD setting (previously the threshold was 50%). Device-intensive procedures are eligible for a carve-out payment for the device portion of the procedure, which is equal to the cost of the actual device minus the generic device cost included in the APC payment. According to the ASCA, approximately 47 additional codes will now meet the definition of "device-intensive" and be subject to carve-out payments. Finally, the FY 2015 ruling added nine spine codes to the list of procedures eligible to be performed in an ASC.

Based on the 2015 reimbursement update along with estimated changes in enrollment, utilization, and case mix, CMS estimates that total payments to ASCs for CY 2015 will be approximately $4.147 billion, an increase of approximately $236 million compared to estimated CY 2014 Medicare payments.

Exhibit 8. Estimated Impact of the CY 2015 Update to the ASC Payment System on Aggregate CY 2015 Payments by Surgical Specialty

Surgical Specialty Group	Estimated CY 2015 ASC Payments (in Millions)*	Estimated CY 2015 Percent Change
Total	$3819	1.0%
Eye and ocular adnexa	$1,560	(1.0%)
Digestive system	$781	6.0%
Nervous system	$568	1.0%
Musculoskeletal system	$472	2.0%
Genitourinary system	$165	3.0%
Integumentary system (skin, hair, and nails)	$137	5.0%
Respiratory system	$53	3.0%
Cardiovascular system	$36	(1.0%)
Ancillary items and services	$24	(4.0%)
Auditory system	$14	1.0%
Hematologic and lymphatic systems	$6	14.0%

Exhibit 9. Estimated Impact of the Final CY 2015 Update to ASC Payment System on Aggregate Payments for Selected Procedures

CPT/HCPCS Code	Short Descriptor	Estimated CY 2014 ASC Payments (in Millions)*	Estimated CY 2015 Percent Change
66984	Cataract surg w/iol, 1 stage	$1,131	-1.0%
43239	Upper GI endoscopy, biopsy	$170	10.0%
45380	Colonoscopy and biopsy	$167	7.0%
45385	Lesion removal colonoscopy	$107	6.0%
66982	Cataract surgery, complex	$93	-1.0%
64483	Inj foramen epidural l/s	$90	0%
62311	Inject spine l/s (cd)	$79	0%
45378	Diagnostic colonoscopy	$72	6.0%
66821	After cataract laser surgery	$63	3.0%
64493	Inj paravert f jnt l/s 1 lev	$47	0%

* The values above do not reflect reductions in Medicare payments caused by the sequester.

9.0 2015 Sequestration

The payment updates discussed above do not include the sequestration cuts that went into effect on April 1, 2013, as a result of the Budget Control Act of 2011. On Dec. 26, 2013, President Obama signed into law the Bipartisan Budget Act of 2013 (partisan), which set the federal budget targets for 2014 and 2015. The Act provided limited relief from sequestration cuts in FY 2014 and 2015 to certain defense and nondefense programs. However, it did not provide Medicare relief from sequestration cuts and actually extended the current sequestration cuts for an additional two years until 2023 to provide budget savings to help offset the cost of the temporary SGR patch included within the bill. Therefore, barring additional congressional action, the 2.0% reduction to ASC payments will continue in 2015, resulting in a net payment decrease to ASCs in 2015 of -0.6%.

10.0 Typical ASC Legal Structures

Typically, ASC entities are either structured as limited liability corporations (LLCs) or limited partnerships (LPs). In name and in legal form, these entities may differ, but they are similarly governed by the applicable agreement governing operations associated with ASCs, the operating agreement for LLCs, and the partnership agreement for LPs.

The most critical elements that may affect the valuation of assets or an ownership interest in an ASC include:

- Cash distributions;
- Ownership restrictions; and
- Buy/sell provisions.

In particular, these elements in turn have a direct or indirect impact on minority and marketability issues flowing from the valuation of an interest in an ASC.

10.1 Cash Distributions

Most ASC operating or partnership agreements include detailed provisions that provide for the distribution of virtually all of the discretionary cash on at least a quarterly, and sometimes monthly, basis. Since the cash distributions are normally defined in this manner, this may reduce the impact of any applicable discounts for both lack of control and lack of marketability.

10.2 Ownership Restrictions

As previously discussed, federal regulations allow physicians who perform surgery in and refer patients to ASCs, to maintain ownership in an ASC. To fit in a safe harbor from the federal fraud and abuse statutes, physicians who maintain an ownership interest in a multispecialty ASC must:

1. Derive one-third of their professional income from outpatient surgery; and
2. Perform one-third of their eligible cases in the ASC in which they invest.

For physicians who have an interest in a single-specialty ASC, only the first one-third test applies. Through the relevant operating or partnership agreement, some ASCs require that all physician-owners meet these one-third tests to maintain ownership in the ASC, while other ASCs are more flexible and the terms for maintaining ownership are less defined. Not all, but most ASCs require that physician owners be approved for admission to ownership and that they be redeemed upon their disability, retirement or move from their service area.

10.3 Buy/Sell

In either case (purchase or redemption), many ASC operating or partnership agreements require that physicians are redeemed or purchase shares at either fair market value or an amount based on a formula—often three to four times EBITDA less interest-bearing debt—that is meant to simulate fair market value. While on occasion ASC operating or partnership agreements may in effect penalize owners selling an interest, more often than not the buy/sell provisions ensure that the amount received for a redemption is either at or similar to fair market value.

To summarize, the provisions for cash distributions, ownership, and buy/sell arrangements typically included in ASC operating or partnership agreements reduce the impact of lack of control and marketability for noncontrolling equity interests.

11.0 Typical ASC Financial Structure and Performance

All facilities are different. However, VMG Health annually completes benchmarking studies, which are free to download at the company's website (www.vmghealth.com). The *Multi-Specialty Intellimarker Study* is based on analyses of actual detailed financial and operating performance information from more than 200 multispecialty surgery centers across the United States. Exhibits 10, 11, and 12 summarize the aggregate statistical analysis of the income statements from the *Multi-Specialty ASC Intellimarker 2013*. Our observations on the data then follow.

Exhibit 10. Income Statement

$ in thousands	Mean	Standard Dev.	25%	Median 50%	75%	90%
Patient Revenues						
Gross Charges	$ 34,987	$ 20,451	$ 20,580	$ 31,136	$ 45,354	$ 62,274
Adjustments	(25,958)	(18,206)	(14,302)	(22,036)	35,455	(47,122)
Other Revenue	17	33	2	4	12	46
Net Revenue	8,252	4,602	5,079	7,218	10,614	14,552
Operating Expenses						
Employee Salary & Wages	1,743	883	1,178	1,575	2,137	2,850
Employee Taxes & Benefits	396	230	243	355	509	640
Occupancy Costs	515	321	275	474	650	911
Medical & Surgical Supplies	1,796	1,229	1,048	1,528	2,292	3,028
Other Medical Costs	100	182	23	46	78	195
Insurance	62	43	33	49	75	125
Depreciation & Amortization	328	257	159	277	421	669
General & Administrative						
Bad Debt	166	139	58	120	245	384
Management Fees	418	287	229	350	510	676
Other G & A	733	376	480	687	905	1,211
Total G & A	1,177	666	713	1,062	1,548	1,994
Total Operating Expenses	5,995	3,102	4,041	5,680	7,203	9,964
Operating Income	2,074	2,668	513	1,533	2,959	6,158
Other Expense (Income)	92	267	2	6	22	55
Net Interest Expense	85	113	12	45	110	213
Earnings Before Taxes	1,996	2,664	473	1,427	2,957	6,001
EBITDA	$ 2,387	$ 2,731	$ 801	$ 1,871	$ 3,356	$ 6,602

VMG HEALTH Multi-Specialty ASC Intellimarker 2013

Exhibit 11. Common Size Income Statement

	Mean	Standard Dev.	25%	Median 50%	75%	90%
Patient Revenues						
Gross Charges	445.6%	180.7%	335.7%	430.0%	515.6%	642.7%
Adjustments	-335.2%	191.0%	227.2%	-327.6%	-415.4%	-541.5%
Other Revenue	0.2%	0.5%	0.0%	0.0%	2.0%	0.6%
Net Revenue	100.0%	0.0%	100.0%	100.0%	100.0%	100.0%
Operating Expenses						
Employee Salary & Wages	23.1%	6.1%	18.2%	23.2%	27.8%	31.4%
Employee Taxes & Benefits	5.2%	2.0%	3.9%	5.0%	6.1%	7.7%
Occupancy Costs	7.2%	4.0%	4.2%	6.8%	9.3%	12.3%
Medical & Surgical Supplies	22.1%	7.1%	16.7%	22.1%	27.4%	31.1%
Other Medical Costs	1.3%	2.4%	0.3%	0.6%	1.0%	2.1%
Insurance	0.9%	0.7%	0.5%	0.8%	1.0%	1.5%
Depreciation & Amortization	4.3%	3.1%	2.5%	3.4%	5.2%	8.4%
General & Administrative						
Bad Debt	1.9%	1.3%	0.9%	1.6%	2.6%	3.6%
Management Fees	5.0%	1.7%	3.8%	5.0%	6.0%	6.9%
Other G & A	10.1%	4.2%	7.2%	9.6%	12.2%	16.0%
Total G & A	15.3%	5.3%	1.3%	15.3%	18.6%	21.6%
Total Operating Expenses	77.9%	17.4%	66.1%	79.1%	88.4%	97.5%
Operating Income	23.2%	19.6%	11.7%	21.5%	34.4%	47.0%
Other Expense (Income)	1.0%	2.9%	0.0%	0.1%	0.2%	1.1%
Net Interest Expense	1.1%	1.8%	0.2%	0.5%	1.5%	2.8%
Earnings Before Taxes	22.2%	19.9%	10.8%	20.1%	33.8%	46.0%
EBITDA	27.3%	18.5%	16.4%	25.1%	38.6%	48.1%

VMG HEALTH Multi-Specialty ASC Intellimarker 2013

Exhibit 12. Operating Expense Analysis

	Mean	Standard Dev.	25%	Median 50%	75%	90%
as a % of Net Revenue						
Employee Salary & Wages	23.1%	6.1%	18.2%	23.2%	27.8%	31.4%
Employee Taxes & Benefits	5.2%	2.0%	3.9%	5.0%	6.1%	7.7%
Occupancy Costs	7.2%	4.0%	4.2%	6.8%	9.3%	12.3%
Medical & Surgical Supplies	22.1%	7.1%	16.7%	22.1%	27.4%	31.1%
Other Medical Costs	1.3%	2.4%	0.3%	0.6%	1.0%	2.1%
Insurance	0.9%	0.7%	0.5%	0.8%	1.0%	1.5%
General & Administrative	15.3%	5.3%	1.3%	15.3%	18.6%	21.6%
Total Operating Expenses	77.9%	17.4%	66.1%	79.1%	88.4%	97.5%
per Square Foot						
Employee Salary & Wages	$ 117.66	$ 52.74	$ 88.29	$ 110.75	$ 138.80	$ 186.67
Employee Taxes & Benefits	25.26	15.00	15.89	23.80	33.97	46.52
Occupancy Costs	33.45	15.28	24.40	34.22	41.73	48.03
Medical & Surgical Supplies	114.66	56.15	77.61	106.50	152.04	193.27
Other Medical Costs	3.51	6.83	-	1.36	3.79	8.39
Insurance	4.28	3.45	2.04	3.60	5.46	8.10
General & Administrative	80.34	43.74	51.97	76.65	98.85	133.21
Total Operating Expenses	$ 399.33	$ 157.86	$ 298.81	$ 398.98	$ 476.56	$ 602.12
per OR ($ in thousands)						
Employee Salary & Wages	$ 419.9	$ 194.7	$ 303.4	$ 407.7	$ 501.2	$ 634.0
Employee Taxes & Benefits	89.5	57.6	52.8	86.6	118.7	172.7
Occupancy Costs	121.9	68.3	76.8	117.0	161.4	203.3
Medical & Surgical Supplies	408.3	203.4	268.1	404.0	539.7	688.2
Other Medical Costs	12.6	25.8	-	5.0	13.2	26.4
Insurance	15.2	11.5	6.9	13.0	20.2	28.4
General & Administrative	292.1	170.4	172.9	269.2	394.4	503.9
Total Operating Expenses	$ 1,435.1	$ 611.0	$1,058.0	$ 1,437.2	$ 1,792.5	$ 2,166.6
per Case						
Employee Salary & Wages	$ 358.70	$ 133.96	$ 287.95	$ 351.44	$ 433.07	$ 522.28
Employee Taxes & Benefits	77.89	48.02	53.37	74.47	98.25	124.25
Occupancy Costs	113.39	71.46	60.98	112.72	146.48	212.28
Medical & Surgical Supplies	368.72	212.13	266.17	341.57	452.01	586.96
Other Medical Costs	4.29	12.60	-	-	5.38	10.81
Insurance	12.88	10.72	7.35	11.07	15.79	21.90
General & Administrative	253.29	142.96	158.75	235.43	313.52	438.35
Total Operating Expenses	$1,265.54	$ 559.66	#######	$1,201.84	$1,534.83	$1,931.23

VMG HEALTH Multi-Specialty ASC Intellimarker 2013

12.0 Income Statement Observations

Median net revenue, or reimbursement for ASCs participating in the *Multi-Specialty ASC Intellimarker 2013* is $7.2 million and median earnings before interest taxes depreciation and amortization (EBITDA) is $1.9 million. The single largest expense component is employee cost, including salaries, wages, taxes and benefits, representing 28% of net revenue. Median medical and surgical supplies costs represent 22% of net revenue. Median EBITDA is 25% of net revenue.

Net revenue for ASCs is driven by volume and specialty mix and varies widely across the spectrum of specialties. Exhibit 13 summarizes the median net revenue per case by specialty from the *Multi-Specialty ASC Intellimarker 2013*.

Exhibit 13. Revenue Per Case

	Specialty	Gross Charges
ENT	ENT	$8,092
GI	GI/Endoscopy	$4,132
GEN	General Surgery	$6,733
GYN	OB/GYN	$8,023
OPH	Ophthalmology	$6,015
ORA	Oral Surgery	$5,446
ORT	Orthopedics	$10,324
PM	Pain Management	$4,814
PS	Plastic Surgery	$9,292
POD	Podiatry	$9,545
URO	Urology	$6,266

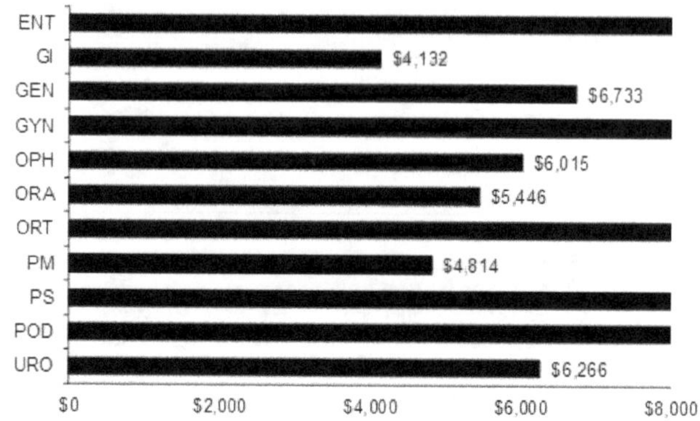

	Specialty	Net Revenue
ENT	ENT	$1,919
GI	GI/Endoscopy	$840
GEN	General Surgery	$1,877
GYN	OB/GYN	$2,302
OPH	Ophthalmology	$1,286
ORA	Oral Surgery	$1,028
ORT	Orthopedics	$2,816
PM	Pain Management	$938
PS	Plastic Surgery	$1,707
POD	Podiatry	$2,340
URO	Urology	$1,627

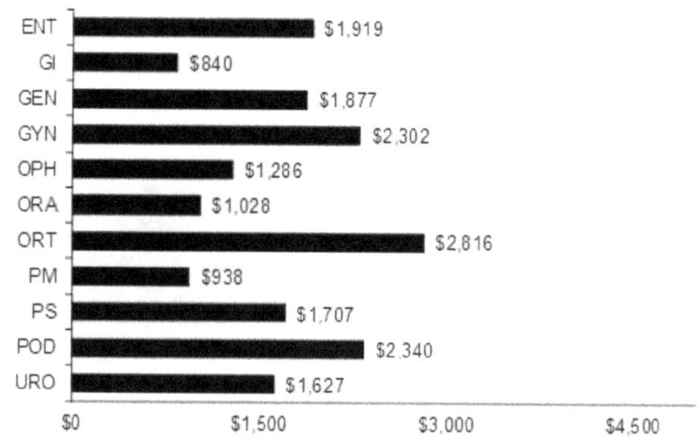

VMG HEALTH Multi-Specialty ASC Intellimarker 2013

From the *Multi-Specialty ASC Intellimarker 2013*, net revenue per case ranges from $840 for GI/endoscopy and $938 for pain management on the low end to $2,816 for orthopedics on the high end.

While there is some variability in operating expenses from center to center, the largest components—employee costs and medical and surgical supplies—are both driven primarily by the case specialty mix in an ASC. Generally speaking, less complex cases such as those procedures for GI/endoscopy and pain require fewer staffing hours and supplies than more complex cases such as those in orthopedics. Exhibit 14 contrasts costs per case for all multispecialty ASCs and ASCs with greater than 50% orthopedics.

Unlike employee costs and medical and surgical supplies per case, median employee costs and medical and surgical supplies as a percentage of net revenue are fairly consistent across the spectrum of case complexity.

Exhibit 14. Operating Expense Analysis Comparison

	Median		
as a % of Net Revenue	GI	All MS	MS > 50% Ortho
Employee Salary & Wages	22.3%	23.3%	17.5%
Employee Taxes & Benefits	5.2%	5.0%	3.7%
Occupancy Costs	4.3%	6.8%	7.9%
Medical & Surgical Supplies	7.6%	22.1%	23.3%
Other Medical Costs	1.8%	0.6%	0.8%
Insurance	1.2%	0.8%	0.3%
General & Administrative	13.8%	15.3%	8.5%
Total Operating Expenses	60.0%	79.1%	67.3%
per Case			
Employee Salary & Wages	$ 135.92	$ 351.44	$ 545.48
Employee Taxes & Benefits	36.86	74.47	99.37
Occupancy Costs	27.14	112.72	172.32
Medical & Surgical Supplies	44.63	341.57	610.67
Other Medical Costs	10.44	-	-
Insurance	5.94	11.07	9.73
General & Administrative	99.37	235.43	266.49
Total Operating Expenses	$ 368.60	$1,201.84	$1,934.96

VMG HEALTH Endoscopy Intellimarker 2007 and Multi-Specialty ASC Intellimarker 2013

Since the most significant operating expense categories tend to vary somewhat consistently with revenue, the primary driver of surgery-center profitability is relative reimbursement levels. Relative reimbursement levels are, in turn, determined by both the payor mix and an individual center's commercial reimbursement. Government payors such as Medicare and Medicaid tend to reimburse ASCs less than commercial or managed care payors. Local market conditions and/or the strength of the ASC's commercial and managed-care contracts may affect that ASC's relative commercial reimbursement.

13.0 Balance Sheet Observations

Median total assets for ASCs participating in the *Multi-Specialty ASC Intellimarker 2013* is $2.9 million and median long-term debt is $0.8 million. Median total current assets and net property, plant and equipment represent 51% and 40% of total assets, respectively. Median long-term debt is 35% of total assets. In comparison to the income-statement categories, the standard deviation for balance-sheet categories, and in particular, net property, plant, and equipment and long-term debt, are much higher.

Exhibits 15 and 16 demonstrate the aggregate statistical analysis of the balance sheets from the *Multi-Specialty ASC Intellimarker 2013.*

Exhibit 15. Balance Sheet

$ in thousands	Mean	Standard Dev.	25%	Median 50%	75%	90%
ASSETS						
Cash & Equivalents	$ 693	$ 676	$ 239	$ 486	$ 946	$ 1,445
Net Accounts Receivable	848	788	457	620	1,018	1,546
Other Current Assets	275	258	125	223	339	555
Total Current Assets	1,658	1,312	839	1,361	1,994	3,202
Gross PP&E	4,015	2,428	2,324	3,473	5,564	7,236
Accumulated Depreciation	(2,710)	1,695	(3,701)	(2,376)	1,482	(804)
Net PP&E	1,397	1,233	509	1,055	1,787	3,327
Other Assets	1,051	1,907	18	129	1,446	3,610
Total Assets	$ 3,592	$ 2,568	$ 1,782	$ 2,850	$ 4,750	$ 7,012
LIABILITIES						
Current Liabilities	$ 569	$ 512	$ 267	$ 434	$ 700	$ 1,148
Current Portion of LTD	302	374	57	218	418	646
Total Current Liabilites	698	651	312	499	845	1,504
Total Long-Term Debt	1,134	1,270	154	626	1,749	3,058
Other LT Liabilities	288	522	11	48	252	1,128
Total Liabilities	1,586	1,555	444	992	2,227	3,814
EQUITY						
Total Shareholders' Equity	2,175	2,200	776	1,495	2,513	5,337
Total Liabilities & Equity	$ 3,592	$ 2,568	$ 1,782	$ 2,850	$ 4,750	$ 7,012

VMG HEALTH Multi-Specialty ASC Intellimarker 2013

Exhibit 16. Common Size Balance Sheet

	Mean	Standard Dev.	25%	Median 50%	75%	90%
ASSETS						
Cash & Equivalents	21.3%	16.4%	10.7%	17.4%	27.4%	41.8%
Net Accounts Receivable	24.4%	12.6%	16.5%	22.7%	29.8%	39.2%
Other Current Assets	8.7%	6.9%	3.8%	6.8%	11.6%	18.1%
Total Current Assets	49.7%	21.9%	34.8%	50.8%	64.6%	79.0%
Gross PP&E	144.7%	85.9%	83.2%	136.2%	180.6%	256.8%
Accumulated Depreciation	-107.9%	-83.5%	-142.5%	-88.4%	-51.1%	-25.1%
Net PP&E	40.4%	22.4%	21.4%	40.0%	56.7%	71.2%
Other Assets	19.7%	25.3%	0.8%	7.0%	32.0%	64.6%
Total Assets	100.0%	100.0%	100.0%	100.0%	100.0%	100.0%
LIABILITIES						
Current Liabilities	17.9%	17.7%	10.2%	15.3%	20.8%	29.8%
Current Portion of LTD	9.6%	16.0%	1.9%	5.7%	10.1%	18.0%
Total Current Liabilites	22.0%	20.5%	11.6%	17.8%	24.8%	41.0%
Total Long-Term Debt	32.7%	31.6%	4.4%	28.8%	55.2%	72.1%
Other LT Liabilities	8.3%	14.8%	0.4%	1.8%	7.9%	25.3%
Total Liabilities	47.5%	41.4%	18.9%	35.0%	69.0%	94.9%
EQUITY						
Shareholders' Equity	59.7%	27.8%	36.5%	67.6%	81.8%	89.7%
Total Liabilities & Equity	100.0%	100.0%	100.0%	100.0%	100.0%	100.0%

VMG HEALTH Multi-Specialty ASC Intellimarker 2013

14.0 Does the Past Tell Us Anything About the Future?

Yes. No. Maybe. Maybe not. It depends. These all could be appropriate answers in a given situation. Whether an appraiser attempts to attach an appropriate market multiple to historical earnings or to develop "most likely case" projections, the future is much more important than the past. For ASCs with a substantial portion of out-of-network revenue (and all other things equal), the sustainability of maintaining relatively high out-of-network reimbursements is in question. In other words, there is a substantial "risk" in relying on the past to project future performance.

15.0 ASC Risk-Assessment Matrix

In addition to a thorough analysis of the historical performance of the ASC, the following represents a listing of the risk factors that should be considered when evaluating the historical performance of the center and expectations for future performance:

- Contracting;
- Service-area growth;
- Competition;
- Physician ownership;
- Nonowner utilization;
- Concentration by specialty;
- Out-of-network concentration;
- Staff and supplies efficiency;
- Location; and
- Condition of the facility and equipment.

15.1 Primary ASC Value Drivers

An ASC is an accumulation of the practices of the individual surgeons using the facility. Physician practices may be generally characterized as growing, mature or declining. To assess where an ASC falls on this continuum and the potential for its volume growth, it is critical to analyze the historical case volume by physician and by specialty. If, for example, the largest physician utilizers of an ASC are, for the most part, approaching the end of the mature stage of their respective practices, the current volumes and earnings may be relatively strong. However, this may not translate into expectations for growth or a strong future.

As we saw with the 2008 transition from a payment system based on ASC groupers to one based on a percentage of HOPD APCs, the specialty mix and the disparate impact of reimbursement changes are also important to consider. While the 2008 transition was designed to be neutral overall to Medicare payments, it resulted in significant financial losses for GI/endoscopy and pain cases and significant gains for orthopedics and general surgery. For multispecialty ASCs with a balanced case mix, this change may not have affected overall revenues and earnings. However, the future performance of ASCs with a concentration in one or more of the specialties was significantly affected. Based on the 2015 Final Ruling by CMS, GI/endoscopy is expected to experience a fairly positive increase in Medicare reimbursement compared to 2014 while ophthalmology is expected to experience a slightly negative impact.

In addition, projected reimbursement should take into account out-of-network payments. In many states, large commercial/managed care payors such as Blue Cross have developed statewide fee schedules that apply to all contracted (in-network) ASCs. Rather than simply accepting the relatively low rates, which may range between 110% and 130% of Medicare, ASCs using an out-of-network strategy may collect significantly more based on the usual and customary rates. Because reimbursement may be higher out of network, some ASCs contract with few or no commercial or managed care payors.

To address this strategy, many commercial and managed care payors have taken steps to eliminate or reduce the level of out-of-network payments. In many markets, commercial and managed care payors have instituted measures in response to the increased costs of out-of-network payments. Examples of these include the following:

- Increased patient responsibility for payment for procedures performed in out-of-network facilities;
- Payment to patients rather than to facilities, requiring ASCs to seek payment for out-of-network services from the patient; and
- Requirement that physicians conduct procedures in contracted facilities to receive professional fees.

Though the efforts of the commercial and managed care payors to curb out-of-network payments have either not been attempted or have not been entirely successful, the industry appears to agree that high out-of-network payments are not likely sustainable over the long term. In some cases, the conversion from out-of-network to in-network rates could be immediate; in others, it could take several years.

Regardless of how long the transition takes, it's crucial to consider not only the impact on projected reimbursement, but also the impact an ASC's out-of-network or in-network status on future volumes. If assuming that an ASC is going to maintain an out-of-network strategy, and managed care payors can effectively require physicians to do procedures in contracted facilities to receive professional fees, this combination may result in movement of those surgeries to hospitals or in-network surgery centers. If assuming that an ASC is transitioning from out of network to in network, the increase in volume that often comes with converting an ASC from out of network to in network may partially or entirely offset the reduction in rates.

15.2 ASC Valuation Purpose

As is the case with most valuations in the healthcare industry, the predominant purpose for most ASC valuations is compliance with the fair market value requirements established by the Stark regulations and the federal fraud and abuse and anti-kickback statutes.

While the federal anti-kickback statutes include a safe harbor for surgeons who wish to own an equity interest in an ASC to which they refer patients, pricing for any transaction involving a potential referral source physician must be consistent with fair market value. Whether they are buyers or sellers, hospital systems that have some level of ownership in an ASC are most concerned with ensuring that the purchase of an ownership interest from a physician does not exceed fair market value or the sale of an interest is not less than fair market value. Hence, most ASC valuation engagements happen at the request of a hospital or nonphysician ASC owner/operator for either the hospital system or the ASC owner/operator. The most common specific applications involve:

1. Purchase or sale of controlling equity interest;
2. Purchase or sale of noncontrolling equity interests; and
3. Conversion of a center operated as an HOPD to a freestanding joint venture and simultaneous offering of noncontrolling equity interests in the freestanding joint venture.

16.0 Purchase or Sale of Controlling Equity Interest

The most common buyers of a controlling equity interest in an ASC are the national developers and operators of ASCs/hospital systems. Our experience and surveys have consistently found that the ASC owner/operators most commonly analyze and price controlling equity interest transactions using a multiple of EBITDA less interest-bearing debt.[5] In light of their talent for recruiting additional physician-owners and improving or maintaining efficient operations, ASC owner/operators are typically less concerned than noncontrolling equity interest holders or hospital systems about the risks associated with potential volume loss.

ASC owner/operators often prefer to own a controlling equity interest to gain control over decisions typically associated with ASC entities such as:

- Deciding which physicians retain or receive equity in the ASC; and
- Maintaining the contractual relationship for management of the ASC.

5 VMG Health, "2011 Value Driver ASC Survey," and HealthCare Appraisers Inc.: "2008 ASC Valuation Survey" and "2007 ASC Valuation Survey."

Unlike ASC owner/operators who typically price controlling equity interest transactions using a multiple of EBITDA, most hospital systems rely on the fair market value opinion provided by an independent appraiser to ensure that they meet Stark and fraud and abuse statute requirements and private inurement concerns. Various professional standards require that business appraisers consider all relevant approaches and methods in developing an opinion of value. These other approaches and in particular, the income approach or discounted cash flow method, may provide a superior framework for measuring the impact of the individual facts and circumstances surrounding a subject ASC.

16.1 Cost Approach

Some ASCs are either not profitable or are not expected to provide a return greater than the required return on the working capital and fixed assets employed in the operation of the ASC. The key is not historical earnings or cash flows, but instead projected earnings and cash flows under the control of a typical owner/operator.

In a transaction for a controlling interest, an ASC owner/operator is not likely to pay for all, or maybe even any, of the intangible value that may result specifically from their ownership and management of an ASC. However, in the context of a "make or buy" decision typical of this type of transaction, the buyer may pay for the assembly of all tangible and some intangible assets (e.g., CON, an ASC license, and payor contracts) under the premises of value in continued use, as part of a mass assemblage of assets, or even in exchange.

This application of the cost approach may provide a "floor," or lowest minimum value related to a controlling or noncontrolling interest in an ASC and may be appropriate when the market and income approaches (which are discussed later) produce lower values. However, please note that, when applying the cost approach utilizing the premise of value in continued use as part of a mass assemblage of assets, the concept of economic obsolescence should be considered.

Surgery centers are an asset-intensive business. The median gross property and equipment plus working capital per operating room from VMG Health's *Multi-Specialty ASC Intellimarker 2013* is approximately $1.2 million. Depending on the age and condition of the furniture and equipment, the costs associated with these assets for an ASC may be substantial. Often, the application of the cost approach is important in situations in which an ASC has been overbuilt in terms of the space (e.g., number of operating and procedure rooms) and equipment required to accommodate the book of business.

16.2 Intangible Assets

Even for an ASC that has historically generated operating losses, the appraiser must consider the potential for the existence of intangible assets. The intangible assets in this case would be those that almost always have some legal title and are often separately marketable, including:

1. Certificate of need (CON);

2. ASC license; and
3. Payor contracts.

16.2.1 Certificate of Need

Some states require a CON for an ASC to be licensed by the state and receive reimbursement from public payors such as Medicare and Medicaid. Again, in the context of the "make or buy" decision, a potential buyer will evaluate the probability of obtaining a CON. In states such as New York, North Carolina, and Tennessee, for example, many markets are saturated, making it extremely unlikely that a CON for a new surgery center could be obtained.

The valuation methodology for a CON may take the form of a cash flow comparison under two scenarios: (1) the first assumes the CON is in place; and (2) the second assumes it is not. Using this "with and without" methodology, the value of the CON is quantified as the differential in the present value of the cash flows. In cases where it is likely that a CON might be obtained after legal and consulting costs are incurred and the passage of time, the incremental cash flows simply represent the present value of these incremental costs and cash flows foregone during the time required to obtain a CON. In extreme cases where the perceived probability of getting a CON seems remote, the present value of the incremental cash flows resulting from this analysis may make up a significant portion of the unidentified intangible value of the ASC. Since in this case the cash flows without a CON simply reflect the liquidation of the ASC's assets, the present value in the first scenario should be reduced by the value of the working capital, tangible assets, and identified intangible assets. While the probability of getting a CON today may currently be near zero in many markets, the probability likely increases over time. As a result, some discount to the incremental cash flows may also be considered. In addition, this analysis may need to consider the potential impact of other intangible assets, such as covenants not to compete typically included in ASC operating agreements, that are implied in the projected "with CON" cash flow stream.

Another consideration in the application of the "with and without" methodology is the use of actual/expected versus typical financial performance in the cash flow projections for the two scenarios. The volumes, reimbursement, and operating expenses assumed in the model should consider whether the buyers' or sellers' expectations reflect their specific circumstances or those of a typical buyer. This assumption is of particular import when either historical operations or future reimbursement expectations reflect the operation of the ASC as a department of a hospital. In particular, if either the historical or projected financial statements provided reflect reimbursement at hospital rates rather than normalized freestanding rates, the rates utilized in the projections for this analysis should reflect normalized freestanding ASC rates.

16.2.2 ASC License

An ASC is normally licensed by both the particular state in which it operates and by Medicare. It may take two or three months before an ASC receives licensure from both entities. This delay causes a delay in commencing the ramp-up period for operations, and in turn, a delay in reimbursement.

An ASC with a license in place can avoid this period of reduced cash flows. Like with a CON, the valuation methodology normally takes the form of a "with and without" analysis. The value of a CON exceeds that of a license because licenses are much easier to obtain. However, there is still uncertainty surrounding the licensing process. In California, for example, it's unclear how long it could take to obtain an ASC license. Some developers believe that it could take more than a year. In states requiring a CON, the value of an ASC license is generally not separated from the value of the CON.

16.2.3 Payor Contracts

Recent experiences in California also point to the need to consider payor contracts as a potential source of significant value, particularly in cases in which the ASC has contracts with reimbursement in excess of market levels or in which large payors are threatening not to extend contracts to new ASCs. ASC payor contracts that cannot be terminated without cause and multiyear terms are uncommon, but there may be circumstances in which ASCs expect current reimbursement levels to extend beyond the legal term of the contract. Once again, the valuation methodology for payor contracts normally takes the form of a "with and without" analysis.

16.3 Market Approach

ASC developers and operators generally rely on the market approach in pricing transactions. More specifically, they rely on the individual transactions method and use a multiple of EBITDA less interest-bearing debt in pricing a controlling equity interest in an ASC. Surveys have found that most respondents typically observed valuation multiples for controlling equity interests of six to eight or more times EBITDA less interest-bearing debt.[6] While ASC developers and operators nearly always reference and utilize these general market guideline multiples, many factors may lead to an adjustment of the historical EBITDA or an ultimate transaction price that resides outside of this range.

In the discussion of the primary ASC value drivers, we detailed the need to consider changes in Medicare and out-of-network reimbursement when analyzing historical information and developing future projections. Based on our experience, the six to eight or more times multiple used to price the purchase of a controlling interest is often applied to prospective or adjusted, rather than raw historical EBITDA. Accordingly, ASC developers and operators often adjust for changes in reimbursement to estimate the EBITDA to which that multiple is applied. Due to expected changes in the practices of physician utilizers or competitive factors that historical performance might not reflect, prospective or adjusted EBITDA may also reflect case-volume changes.

In addition to adjusting for potential reimbursement and volume changes, historical EBITDA may not reflect the payment of a management fee.

6 HealthCare Appraisers Inc., "2014 ASC Valuation Survey."

16.3.1 Valuation Impact of Management Fees

Nearly all multicenter owner/operators of ASCs charge the centers a fee of between 4% and 7% of net revenues to provide management services. For this fee, the manager typically does the following:

- Manages the ASCs finances and annual operating budgets;
- Administers all accounting, accounts payable, and purchasing functions;
- Manages human resources;
- Oversees information technology;
- Handles public relations;
- Develops plans for facilities and services;
- Maintain all necessary licenses and regulatory compliance;
- Designs, institutes, and supervises the physical and administrative operations of the ASC;
- Prepares and submits all tax returns and cost reports; and
- Negotiates and consummates agreements and third-party contracts.

Incremental costs associated with providing these services are generally fairly minimal. As a result, the contribution margin is very high. In addition, because the owner/operator receives the management fee off the revenue line before operating expenses, the risk associated with the fee is significantly less than the earnings generated by the owner/operator's equity investment in the ASC. Accordingly, when evaluating multiples from guideline transactions, it is particularly critical to understand whether the buyer received a management fee contract pursuant to the transaction.

To illustrate, suppose that an ASC owner/operator pays an amount equal to seven times EBITDA less debt for a 60% interest in the ASC, and enters into a long-term management contract at 5% of net revenues. Assuming the subject ASC's revenues are $4 million, its EBITDA is $1 million and the contribution margin on the management fee is 50%, this seven multiple becomes a six multiple after consideration of the additional $100,000 margin associated with the management contract. If the management fee is greater than 5% or if the assumed contribution margin is greater than 50%, the management contract could play an even greater role. There is a direct relationship between the level of the management fee and the assumed contribution (i.e., the higher the management fee, the higher the assumed contribution margin). We have not discovered any definitive data in the public domain on the exact level of the contribution margins associated with management fees. While this question should certainly be posed to management for the subject ASC owner/operator, a definitive answer supported with any type of analysis would be the exception rather than the norm. Perhaps this is a function of the fact that many ASC owner/operators do not appear to make an attempt to isolate the costs or perhaps the ASC owner/operators do not simply wish to share this information. In any event, our experience with ASC owner/operators and review of transaction pricing would indicate that the contribution margin is likely in excess of 50% for management fees equal to 5% or higher of net revenues. Exhibit 17 demonstrates this analysis.

Exhibit 17. Management Fee Valuation Impact

Subject ASC			
Revenues			$ 4,000,000
Operating Expenses (Excluding Depreciation)			3,000,000
EBITDA			$ 1,000,000
	Management Fee	5.0%	$ 200,000
	Contribution Margin	50.0%	**$ 100,000**

Valuation of 60% Interest (assumes no Long-Term Debt)			
EBITDA (60% Interest)	$ 600,000	**$100,000**	$ 700,000
X	X		X
Invested Capital / EBITDA Multiple	**7.0**	------------------>	**6.0**
Value Indication - 60% Interest	$ 4,200,000		$ 4,200,000

Another method utilized to address the management fee impact is to separately value the management fee. Based on our experience with many of the multifacility ASC owner/operators previously cited, many have transitioned over the last five years to this alternative method in the process of pricing transactions. As a result, we have transitioned to favor this method as well. If executed properly, however, the same result can be achieved utilizing either method.

It should be noted as well that, though the existence of the management contract effectively lowers the multiple of EBITDA paid by the beneficiary of the management contract in the previous example, hospitals and health systems purchasing a controlling interest in an ASC do not necessarily benefit from the management contract. This factor should be considered in utilizing guideline transactions and their application in a valuation of the hospital or health system's interest in the ASC in comparison to the valuation of the ASC owner/operator.

16.3.2 Guideline Public Company Method

The pricing of the ASC owner/operator companies in the public sector, in terms of multiples of revenues or earnings, provides little in the way of guidance regarding the pricing of either a controlling or noncontrolling interest in an individual ASC.

The universe of ASC owner/operators in the public sector is limited. Through sales to private equity and other healthcare providers, several of the largest ASC owner/operators have moved in and out of the public sector over the past 10 years. In addition, though HCA and now Tenet, through their acquisition of USPI in 2015, have significant ASC operations, their primary operations fall outside of the ASC segment, in acute care hospitals. Arguably, even AmSurg, the ASC owner/operator with the most tenured, uninterrupted stay in the public sector as a pure-play ASC company, may no longer be categorized as a pure-play ASC company as a result of its acquisition of Sheridan Healthcare in 2014.

AmSurg operates over 240 centers, with a majority of these being single-specialty GI/endoscopy and ophthalmology centers and remains the largest owner/operator of ASCs in the public sector. Besides AmSurg, SCA is the only other ASC owner/operator in the public sector with ASCs being their primary business. SCA operates nearly 180 centers and is arguably the better pure-play ASC owner/operator. Exhibit 18 summarizes the key valuation multiples for AmSurg and Surgical Care Affiliates. Trailing 12-month EBITDA multiples are approximately 11.4x for AmSurg and 9.4x for Surgical Care Affiliates.

Exhibit 18. Public Company Multiples

$ in Millions — *As of August 7, 2015*

	Market Cap	LTD	Minority Interest	Preferred Equity	MVIC		TTM Revenue	TTM EBITDA		MVIC / LTM Rev	MVIC / LTM EBITDA
AmSurg Corp (AMSG)	$ 3,993.6	$ 2,249.5	$ 1,189.6	$ 1,189.6	$ 7,077.8		$2,249.5	$ 1,189.6		3.1x	11.4x
Surgical Care Affiliates, Inc. (SCA)	$ 1,492.3	$ 803.5	$ 382.3	$ -	$ 2,678.1		$ 934.7	$ 286.2		2.9x	9.4x

Source: Capital IQ

Companies such as AmSurg and Surgical Care Affiliates, and others before they went private or sold, appear to trade at higher multiples than individual ASCs due to growth achieved through acquisition, access to and lower cost of capital, geographic diversification, and size. There is a fairly substantial spread between acquisition prices and the public company multiples, thereby making it fairly easy for public companies to add substantial value from acquisitions.[7]

Accordingly, while it's necessary to consider the guideline company method, it rarely has a direct application to the valuation of either a controlling or noncontrolling equity interest in an individual ASC, other than, perhaps, as a point of reference in relation to the amounts these companies pay for acquisitions.

7 This is an example of arbitrage; see this guide's chapter, "Healthcare Market Structure and Its Implication for Valuation of Privately Held Provider Entities—An Empirical Analysis," and "Understanding the Difference Between Strategic Value and Fair Market Value In Consolidating Industries," *Business Valuation Review*, June 2002.

16.4 Income Approach/Discounted Cash Flow Method

In this method, the total equity value is calculated using equity cash flows. Whether the appraiser projects a number of scenarios with a range of applicable discount rates or develops a single most-likely case scenario with a single appropriate discount rate, the mechanics of the projections should be similar.

Volume is the first primary determinant of financial performance. Volume is typically analyzed and projected in terms of number of surgical cases. However, each case may consist of a number of individual procedures. As such, it is important to understand whether the information that has been provided is measured in cases or procedures. As previously discussed, reimbursement varies widely by specialty. In addition, volumes are driven by the sum of individual physician practice expectations. The combination of these factors makes it absolutely essential to analyze and develop volume projections by specialty, by physician.

Reimbursement levels are the second primary determinant of financial performance. Like most healthcare services, ASCs maintain a fee schedule consisting of gross charges, by procedure, for services performed and supplies utilized during surgery. Gross charges, though somewhat arbitrary, are often set as a percentage of the Medicare reimbursement for a procedure, say 300% to 400%.

Most governmental (including Medicare and Medicaid), commercial and managed care payors reimburse according to a set fee schedule (either their own or one negotiated during the contracting process). A large share of commercial and managed care payors either directly or indirectly base their fee schedules on Medicare rates, making Medicare reimbursement and reimbursement trends particularly important to future projections.

Except in the fairly rare event that an ASC has a substantial number of payors that reimburse based on a percentage of gross charges, gross charges are somewhat irrelevant.

In addition, employee costs and medical and surgical supplies vary significantly by specialty. To properly accommodate the largely variable component of employee costs, base projections on staffing hours per case and/or costs per case. Other expenses that typically vary based on volume, specialty mix or revenues may include contract services, insurance, office supplies and postage and management fees.

Capital expenditures (CapEx) are also significant to the discounted cash flow method for ASCs. A surgery center is typically an asset-intensive business. While the dangers of following rules of thumb have been subject to lively debate throughout the history of the valuation profession, we typically look at annual amounts ranging from $50,000 to $100,000 per operating room and slightly less per procedure room as a starting point for maintenance CapEx. In addition to considering the age and condition of the existing furniture and equipment and the potential maintenance required, CapEx assumptions should also consider and be matched with projected growth in volume.

Consistent with the tendencies of ASC owner/operators, we typically execute the indirect convention of the discounted cash flow method whereby the market value of invested capital (MVIC) is calculated using debt-free cash flows and book value of debt is deducted from MVIC to arrive at a total equity value. Use of debt in the capital structure of ASCs varies widely based on the range of long-term debt to total assets from the *Multi-Specialty ASC Intellimarker 2012*. Based on our experience, use of substantial amounts of long-term debt is more prevalent for newer surgery centers and is almost entirely asset-based. While most ASCs typically use long-term debt to fund initial operations, many ASCs fund subsequent furniture and equipment purchases out of cash flows.

ASCs are generally located in either a medical office building or a separate freestanding facility. While it is certainly not uncommon for an ASC to own the land and building, particularly if the ASC is a separate facility, most lease their facilities. This comes into play in the ASC's valuation. If the ASC owns the real estate as well, the business appraiser should consider the potential difference in required returns on the real estate and ASC operations. The preferred solution is to engage a real estate appraiser to value the land and/or building and to then combine the values of the real estate and the ASC operations. This convention requires coordination with the real estate appraisal through the use of the fair market rental rate from the real estate appraisal.

If a separate real estate appraisal cannot be obtained, the discount rate utilized in the discount cash flows should be adjusted to reflect the generally lower expected returns associated with the real estate. An adjustment to account for real estate may be considered when using the market approach (discussed earlier) and is applicable in the valuation of either a controlling interest or noncontrolling interest.

The valuation of a controlling equity interest approaching 100% requires an additional consideration. Under the income and market approaches, the pricing of most controlling interest transactions is for 51% to 60% interest. The same market multiples and rates of return may not apply to the incremental 40% to 49% interest of a 100% equity purchase. Generally the market multiples and implied rates of return reflect the buyer's assumption that the physician utilizers will maintain meaningful ownership. Buyers may not be willing to pay the same premium for ownership in excess of 60%.

17.0 Purchase or Sale of Noncontrolling Equity Interests

Generally speaking, ASC owner/operators and healthcare systems are the typical buyers of controlling equity interests. Whether an ASC is a joint venture between a healthcare system and physicians; a three-way joint venture between ASC owner/operators, a healthcare system and physician utilizers; or wholly owned by physicians, individual physician utilizers are generally the noncontrolling equity interest buyers.

Noncontrolling equity interests in ASCs typically transact at relatively lower values compared to controlling equity interests. The same survey in which a large majority of respondents typically observed valuation multiples for controlling equity interests of 6.0 to 8.0 or more times EBITDA less interest-bearing debt found that a large majority of respondents typically observed valuation multiples for noncontrolling equity interests of 3.0 to 5.0 times EBITDA less interest-bearing debt.[8]

While the lower values associated with a noncontrolling interest are consistent with the levels of value framework from general valuation theory, in which there may be discounts from the value associated with a controlling interest for both lack of marketability and lack of control, we generally prefer to view the differential outside of this framework. Because the continued success of an ASC depends so much on the continued support of its physician owners, most ASC operating or partnership agreements include provisions that:

1. Provide liquidity to noncontrolling equity interest holders through formulas or requirements for the completion of an independent fair market value opinion; and

2. Clearly define discretionary cash flows, but require periodic distributions. ASC operating agreements or partnership agreements typically require monthly or quarterly cash distributions.

Within the levels of value framework from general valuation theory, a premium for control implies an inverse discount for lack of control. However, the difference in values for a controlling equity interest and a noncontrolling equity interest may be more appropriately, and perhaps more specifically, attributed to ASC owner/operators, or the typical buyers of a controlling equity interest:

- Obtaining a management fee;
- Having better access to, and a lower cost of, capital; and
- Having the ability to successfully manage and expand ownership.

Based on these factors and because ASC operating and partnership agreements provide some level of built-in liquidity, we prefer to simply view the valuation of a noncontrolling equity interest as entirely separate rather than starting with a controlling equity interest valuation and applying marketability and lack-of-control discounts typically utilized in valuations.

17.1 Cost Approach

Like for a controlling equity interest, the application of the cost approach for a noncontrolling equity interest provides a "floor," or lowest minimum value. However, for a noncontrolling equity interest, specific facts and circumstances may ultimately impair the value of any intangible assets.

8 HealthCare Appraisers Inc., "2014 ASC Valuation Survey."

17.2 Market Approach

ASC owner/operators observed that transactions for noncontrolling equity interests in ASCs occur at 3.0 to 5.0 times EBITDA less interest-bearing debt. Interestingly, for noncontrolling interest buy-ins and buy-outs, 50% of the respondents rely on a formula to determine pricing, while 25% rely on independent fair market value opinions.[9] This is not surprising considering that a large share of ASC operating or partnership agreements typically include formulas in the buy/sell provisions.

Based on our experience, a slightly smaller, but nonetheless large percentage of comprehensive valuations fall above or below the 3.0-to-5.0-times EBITDA range. In addition, the appropriate multiple to apply may vary widely within the range. Because the range is broad, and because of the lack of detailed information from both public and private sources, we typically use the market approach secondarily when valuing a noncontrolling equity interest.

17.3 Discounted Cash Flow

The overriding distinguishing feature in the valuation of a noncontrolling interest is that the projected volumes and revenues do not anticipate the change in ownership associated with the potential transaction. For example, if a noncontrolling equity interest is being valued for the purposes of allowing a new physician buy-in, the projections would not include any consideration of the case volumes that the physician would likely perform following the purchase of an interest in the ASC.

Further, while an ASC owner/operator with a controlling equity interest may be in a position to effect changes to respond to the potential loss of volumes to either existing or potential competitors, a noncontrolling equity owner, on the other hand, is not in as favorable a position to do so. In addition, the typical buyer or seller of a noncontrolling equity interest may have a higher cost of equity in comparison to the typical buyer or seller of a controlling equity interest.[10]

18.0 Conversion of an HOPD

The purpose of the valuation of an ASC being converted from an HOPD to a freestanding center is generally to estimate the fair market value of a noncontrolling equity interest. Though the application of the three approaches to value is generally the same as the application of the approaches to value for a noncontrolling equity interest, modeling the expected financial performance of an ASC that has historically operated as a HOPD can be particularly challenging.

With this in mind, rather than explore the valuation of an ASC converting from a HOPD to a freestanding entity based on the application of the approaches to value, it seems appropriate

9 HealthCare Appraisers Inc., "2008 ASC Valuation Survey" and "2007 ASC Valuation Survey."

10 This is an example of arbitrage; see this Guide's chapter, "Healthcare Market Structure and Its Implication for Valuation of Privately Held Provider Entities—An Empirical Analysis," and "Understanding the Difference Between Strategic Value and Fair Market Value In Consolidating Industries," *Business Valuation Review*, June 2002.

to expand on the challenges an appraiser faces in modeling this type of center's expected financial performance.

There are three primary challenges, driven by the fact that the financial performance of a HOPD, as presented in the historical accounting for a department of a hospital, bears little resemblance to the financial performance of the operation of the unit as a freestanding entity:

1. Proper volume assumptions;
2. Proper reimbursement assumptions; and
3. Proper operating-expense assumptions.

While the cost accounting may be very complex, the historical accounting for a department of a hospital requires a maze of assumptions and allocations that are rarely useful in estimating the performance of the business unit as a freestanding entity.

18.1 Volume Assumptions

The level of difficulty in projecting volumes for this type of ASC depends on whether the volumes expected to transition come from the main operating rooms in the hospital or from a separate outpatient unit. As a result, the first consideration in estimating proper volume assumptions involves carving out the outpatient volumes expected to transition to the freestanding entity.

Historical financial and operating data provided by the hospital may include not only cases expected to transition, but also the commingling of outpatient volumes not expected to transition to the freestanding ASC and inpatient volumes that have historically been performed in the hospital's main operating rooms or the separate facility. Estimating volumes expected to transition will require analyzing the case volumes by specialty and by physician and interviewing the hospital staff, any outside parties assisting the hospital with the development of the freestanding ASC joint venture, and the physicians currently performing surgery in the HOPD.

A second consideration in estimating proper volume assumptions involves evaluating the risk to the hospital of maintaining these volumes. Particularly in states that don't require a CON, a hospital may base its desire to transition from an ASC to a freestanding entity entirely on the perception that the physicians currently performing cases in the HOPD have an opportunity to either develop a competitive ASC venture or join an existing one. The volumes assumed in the valuation should consider the probability that these cases will remain with the HOPD being converted to a freestanding entity, absent the anticipated change in ownership and any non-competition provisions in the post-transaction operating agreement. In many cases, hospitals are converting the HOPD to a freestanding ASC joint venture in response to the competitive threat that the physicians currently performing surgeries in the HOPD are entertaining the potential to invest in and move all or a portion of their cases to a competitive ASC. Considering this potential risk may result in a much lower value for the HOPD than the current earnings levels might indicate.

Editor's note: It is not possible to value any ASC—or, for that matter, any entity—for purposes of a purchase or sell without knowledge of the actual transaction documents and how they impact post-transaction cash flows to the buyer and any seller who retains a minority interest. Fair market value is not a hypothetical transaction but rather an actual transaction where the fair market price is what a hypothetical buyer and seller acting at arm's length and not taking into account the volume or value of referrals would agree to. Referrals in an ASC context have to be considered in light of the previously described AKS safe harbors for surgeon-investors as to their case volume and share of revenue derived from the ASC.

18.2 Reimbursement Assumptions

Generally speaking, hospital reimbursement is significantly higher than ASC reimbursement for the same outpatient procedures. As previously discussed, Medicare reimbursement for ASCs is less than 60% of the amount received by hospitals for the same procedure. In addition, while ASCs usually contract with commercial and managed care payors at rates from a negotiated fee schedule, hospitals often receive a percentage of charges for outpatient surgery.

Due to this differential in reimbursement, net revenues from the historical data set provided by the hospital for an HOPD must shift to reflect the conversion of the HOPD to a freestanding ASC. Depending on the specialty mix and commercial and managed care reimbursement in the specific market, this could be a significant downward adjustment.

18.3 Operating-Expense Assumptions

Typically, expenses such as supplies and staffing are the only direct expenses that a hospital can identify in its departmental financial information. The remaining operating-expense information is not extremely useful in projecting the performance of an HOPD as a freestanding entity.

Fortunately, hospitals often include a developer or an ASC owner/operator in the joint-venture process who will work with the hospital to make financial projections to be included in the offering documents. Because the projections usually anticipate the change in ownership, they may include case volumes from physicians not currently doing cases in the HOPD and/or case volumes not adjusted for the potential risk of maintaining the case volumes if there is not a joint-venture opportunity. Operating-expense assumptions should be analyzed and/or developed specifically based on volume and specialty mix.

19.0 Data Request

As we have discussed throughout this chapter, the analysis of volumes and revenue by specialty and by physician are critical to the valuation of any interest in an ASC. Since all ASCs bill for services on a per-procedure basis using CPT codes, all volumes and revenues should be readily available, though the ease with which the data can be prepared depends on the sophistication of the information system.

In any event, the nature of billing for ASC services puts all ASCs on a common framework for analysis of both revenues and expenses. Exhibit 19 is an example data request for the valuation of either a controlling or noncontrolling equity interest.

Exhibit 19. Freestanding ASC Data Request

1. Income statements and balance sheets for Fiscal Year (FY) 2011, FY 2012, FY 2013, FY 2014 and year-to-date (YTD) 2015 (including the same period YTD 2014).

2. Copies of any current budgets or projections for the ASC.

3. Data for FY 2011, FY 2012, FY 2013, FY 2014 and year-to-date (YTD) 2015 (including the same period YTD 2014) ***by physician***, ***by specialty*** detailing the following:

    - Case Volume
    - Gross Charges
    - Contractual Adjustments
    - Net Revenues
    - Collections
    - Medical Supplies Costs (if available)

4. Top ten procedures (based on charges) ***by specialty***.

5. For the ASC, Total FY 2011, FY 2012, FY 2013, FY 2014 and YTD 2015 data ***by payor type*** detailing the following:

    - Case Volume
    - Gross Charges
    - Contractual Adjustments
    - Net Revenues
    - Collections

6. Summary of managed care contracts for outpatient surgery. Please provide info regarding the average insurance reimbursement as a percentage of Medicare.

7. Copy of most recent Accounts Receivable Aging summary.

8. A listing of employees for the ASC: (a) name (may be omitted for confidentiality); (b) compensation; (c) average hours worked per week; (d) benefits; (e) responsibility/position description; and (f) tenure / date-of-hire.

9. Copies of facility leases and/or detailed information concerning square footage for the ASC.

10. Summary and/or copies of any furniture or equipment leases for the ASC.

11. A detailed listing of fixed assets for the ASC including the following: original acquisition cost, date of acquisition, and depreciation.

12. A copy of any market research or demographic data for the ASC's service area.

13. A copy of any organizational documents relating to the ASC, including the following:

    - Articles of Incorporation
    - Partnership Agreement
    - Operating Agreement
    - Management Agreement
    - Detailed Ownership Roster
    - Most recent Offering

14. For completed transactions or any offers to buy assets or equity in the ASC during the last 2 years, details regarding any completed transactions or offers to buy assets or equity in the ASC. If no transactions or offers in the last 2 years, please provide details regarding the most recent transaction(s) or offer(s).

Because hospital-based facilities often perform outpatient and inpatient procedures, the data request varies slightly. Exhibit 20 is an example data request for the valuation of either a controlling or noncontrolling equity interest in an ASC being converted from an HOPD to a freestanding entity.

Exhibit 20. HOPD Data Request

1. Departmental income statements and balance sheets for Surgery for Fiscal Year (FY) 2011, FY 2012, FY 2013, FY 2014 and year-to-date (YTD) 2015 (including the same period YTD 2014).

2. Copies of any current budgets or projections for the subject Surgical Department.

3. For ***inpatient*** and ***outpatient*** cases currently being performed in the Hospital, FY 2011, FY 2012, FY 2013, FY 2014 and YTD 2015 (including the same period YTD 2014) data ***by physician***, ***by specialty*** detailing the following:

    - Case Volume
    - Gross Charges
    - Contractual Adjustments
    - Net Revenues
    - Collections
    - Medical Supplies Costs
    - Any additional Operating Expense Information Available

    Note: Please provide separate inpatient and outpatient data sets

4. Top ten ***outpatient*** procedures (based on charges) ***by specialty***.

5. For ***outpatient*** cases in the Hospital, FY 2011, FY 2012, FY 2013, FY 2014 and YTD 2015 data ***by payor type*** detailing the following:

    - Case Volume
    - Gross Charges
    - Contractual Adjustments
    - Net Revenues
    - Collections

6. Summary of managed care contracts for outpatient surgery. Please provide info regarding the average insurance reimbursement as a percentage of Medicare.

7. A listing of employees for the Hospital's ORs: (a) name (may be omitted for confidentiality); (b) compensation; (c) average hours worked per week; (d) benefits; (e) responsibility/position description; and (f) tenure / date-of-hire.

8. Copies of facility leases and/or detailed information concerning the space plan (square footage and estimated FMV rental rates) for the ASC JV.

9. Copies of any furniture or equipment leases for OP Surgery and/or the ASC JV.

10. A detailed listing of fixed assets for OP Surgery and/or the ASC JV including the following: original acquisition cost, date of acquisition, and depreciation (if available).

11. A copy of any market research or demographic data for the ASC JV's service area.

12. A copy of any organizational documents relating to the ASC JV, including the following:

    - Offering Documents
    - Partnership Agreement
    - Operating Agreement
    - Management Agreement
    - Detailed Ownership Roster

20.0 Conclusion

In this chapter, we provided an overview of the ASC segment, typical ASC legal structures, ASC financial performance and primary value drivers and the most common ASC valuation applications. The operations of an ASC and the framework for the valuation of an ASC are not complex. However, the myriad of legal, competitive, reimbursement, out-of-network, and other market and industry considerations complicate the analysis of historical data, the projection of future earnings and cash flows, and the application of the approaches to value.

21.0 Bibliography

AmSurg Corp., 10-Q, 2015.

ASC Association, Changes to Conditions for Medicare Coverage, June 2008.

Avalere Health for American Hospital Association, *Trendwatch Chartbook 2014,* "Inpatient vs Outpatient Surgery 1980-2013."

Avalere Health for American Hospital Association, *Trendwatch Chartbook 2014,* "Number of Freestanding Ambulatory Care Surgery Centers, 1996, 1998, and 2000-2013."

Avalere Health for American Hospital Association, *Trendwatch Chartbook 2014,* "Percent of Outpatient Surgery by Facility Type, 1980-2013."

2015 *Federal Register* CY 2015 Hospital Outpatient Prospective Payment System (PPS) Policy Changes and Payment Rates, and CY 2015 Ambulatory Surgical Center Payment System Policy Changes and Payment Rates (CMS-1613-P).

Federated Ambulatory Surgery Association, "Outpatient Prospective Payment System," *FASA Update Magazine,* November/December 2007.

HCA, 10-Q, 2015.

MedPAC, Healthcare Spending and the Medicare Program, June 2015.

SCA, 10-Q, 2015.

USPI, 10-Q, 2015.

Verispan, *2007 Guide to Healthcare Market Segments.*

VMG Health, *Multi-Specialty Intellimarker,* 2012.

Chapter 16.
Valuing Dialysis Clinics: Reasons for Valuation

CONTENTS

Chapter 16.
Valuing Dialysis Clinics: Reasons for Valuation

By Carol Carden, CPA, ASA, ABV, CFE

The primary reasons for dialysis clinic valuations: (1) ownership buy-in/buy-out transactions; (2) joint-venture transactions between a physician and an operating partner; and (3) asset distribution in divorces. In recent years, we have seen a fair amount of consolidation in the industry in the form of joint-venture transactions with large, national dialysis companies. Although unique considerations apply for each of the above reasons, the underlying valuation approach is generally consistent.

When valuing a clinic for ownership buy-in/buyout purposes, it is critical to understand the control elements associated with the particular interest being transferred, as well as any restrictions on transferring the subject interest that could limit the pool of potential future investors.

Noncompetition agreements are often used to help protect the business from departing physicians who try to take part of the business with them. In some cases, noncompetition agreements can have significant value; this value is part of the overall value of the business and represents that portion of the value that would be lost if the departing physician were to compete. However, to have value, the agreement must be enforceable,[1] and the departing physician must actually be in a position to compete. For example, a noncompetition agreement may not have much value in connection with physicians who are retiring or relocating to other geographic regions since they are less likely to compete with the clinic in the future. Even if the noncompetition agreement does not have much value itself, the clinic as a whole may be just as valuable due to the reduced risk of competition. However, if there is an opportunity for the departing physician

1 When determining the value of a noncompete agreement, it is necessary to be familiar with local law—both statute and court precedent—to determine the extent of enforceability. For example, Massachusetts General Law 112.12x precludes enforcement of geographic covenants not to compete among physicians.

to compete and no such agreement exists, the potential impact should be considered when estimating the clinic's future cash flows.

The absence of a noncompetition agreement can be particularly harmful to the value of a dialysis clinic as the lifeblood of the clinic revolves around its relationship with area nephrologists. Additionally, since dialysis clinics are not particularly capital intensive, it is fairly easy for a departing physician to start or join a competing clinic and attract patients away from other dialysis clinics.

Generally speaking, noncompetition agreements will prohibit the departing physician from having a financial interest (defined as ownership or, more importantly, a compensation agreement such as a medical directorship) in a competing dialysis clinic within a specified geographic range for a specified time period following his or her departure from the clinic. Given the nature of dialysis services (patients generally arrive three times per week for a three- to four-hour block of time), the geographic limitation tends to be more narrow for dialysis than it might be for other services. Generally speaking, the physician will be prohibited from competing within a 25-mile radius of the current center, a smaller radius for large, metropolitan areas. The rationale for this distance is that it becomes too inconvenient for current patients to follow the physician.

In addition to being prohibited from having a financial relationship, the physician is also generally prohibited from soliciting existing clinic employees for the same time period as the financial interest prohibition. Because patients spend such a significant amount of time at the clinic, they develop relationships with the staff. If a departing physician recruits experienced staff from that clinic, it could be detrimental to the clinic's patient satisfaction. Patients spend more time with support staff than they do with the physician, so this prohibitive measure may actually serve as better protection for the clinic than the feature prohibiting financial relationships.

A valuation for joint-venture purposes can be a much more complicated undertaking. It is critical to understand the nature of the joint venture to ensure that it does not contain unnecessary regulatory risks. In particular, it is important to ensure that the operating agreement does not reward incentives for referrals to the clinic. Also, it is important to understand any medical directorships that are attached to the operating agreement.

A medical directorship is typically awarded to a physician for clinical oversight of the center. If there are other physicians in the medical director's group, they will typically be included in any noncompetition and nonsolicitation provisions of the medical director agreement through a joinder. Under the medical director agreement, the physician agrees to head the governing body, provide supervision of the clinic's staff, oversee the safety of the clinic with regard to medical-grade purified water, and give input into staffing and capital replenishment. In return, the physician generally receives a fixed amount per year paid monthly. Medical directorship fees can range from \$25,000 to \$50,000 annually, or more, depending on the size of the center. Payment of the medical directorship must be at fair market value to avoid the perception that the payment is being made in exchange for referrals to the clinic (anti-kickback statute—AKS—concern); or, if the clinic is not-for-profit, the payment must not appear excessive in nature (private inurement/excess benefit concern to the Internal Revenue Service [IRS]). If a medical directorship exposes the clinic to undue regulatory risks, this factor must be considered when determining its value. This consideration is generally incorporated into the development of the discount rate. A higher discount rate would be attributed to the center, resulting in a lower value than the center would otherwise have absent the risky medical director agreement.

1.0 Regulatory Considerations

The following section briefly covers the three main areas of regulatory compliance considerations when appraising a dialysis clinic. A detailed discussion of the myriad of regulatory complications that can arise with healthcare transactions is beyond the scope of this chapter, but interested readers may want to explore additional reading from the referenced materials.

1.1 Stark

In general, the Stark regulations govern referrals from a provider of designated health services (DHS) to an entity in which the provider has a financial interest, unless the arrangement falls into one of several safe harbor classifications. Dialysis services are not among the 11 categories of DHS subject to Stark requirements.[2] Therefore, Stark restrictions generally do not significantly impact dialysis clinic valuations.

1.2 Anti-Kickback Regulations

The AKS prohibits the receipt or payment of anything of value to induce referrals of healthcare services.[3] There are 25 established safe harbors; however, even if the arrangement does not fit squarely into a safe harbor, that does not necessarily mean it will be illegal per se. In addition to treating patients at the dialysis clinic, any physicians involved in ownership of the clinic also admit patients for a variety of other kidney-related ailments. If a hospital is involved in the transaction, the parties must ensure that the remuneration paid is not impacted by past or future anticipated referral patterns to avoid AKS issues. Therefore, any analysis of the proposed dialysis transaction requires careful scrutiny to ensure the value of the interest is not negatively impacted by exposure to criminal, or alternatively, civil monetary penalties.

1.3 Private Inurement/Excess Benefit

The third regulatory area to consider is private inurement and excess benefit transactions as defined by the IRS. In general, the IRS is concerned about financial or other arrangements that result in a benefit to private individuals in excess of the benefit supported by arms-length market transactions.[4] These concerns come into play most heavily when valuing joint-venture transactions involving a not-for-profit clinic or venture partner. In particular, the IRS is concerned that

2 *Federal Register*/Vol. 69 No. 59/Friday, March 26, 2004/Rules & Regulations, XI. Definitions (Section 1877(h) of the Act; Phase I-66 FR 922-49; §411.351)..

3 *Federal Register*/Vol. 79, No. 192/Friday, Oct. 3, 2014, 42 CFR 1001.952 (a) through (y)

4 *Intermediate Sanctions – Excess Benefit Transactions*, IRS Revenue Manual, Section 7.27.30 and *Inurement*—Section 501 (c)(4), Internal Revenue Service.

not-for-profit assets will be transferred in excess amounts to private individuals. If a transaction is determined to contain private inurement or excess benefits, excise taxes may apply to both the organization making the payment as well as the individual receiving the benefit, if that individual is a "disqualified person" under the excess benefit regulations.

2.0 Reimbursement Models

Before undertaking a valuation of a dialysis clinic, it is important to understand the mechanics and any potential changes in the reimbursement methodology. Patients having end-stage renal disease (ESRD) become eligible for Medicare four months after they begin dialysis treatments even if they have not reached the age of 65. Medicare is administered by the Centers for Medicare and Medicaid Services (CMS). Eligibility can begin sooner if the patient elects to train for home-based dialysis. As a result, a significant portion of a dialysis clinic's patient base is covered by Medicare. Commercial insurance companies will cover dialysis services until the patient becomes eligible. Additionally, patients are not required to accept Medicare benefits and can elect to retain their commercial insurance benefits. Even though commercially insured patients do not typically comprise a significant portion of the patient base, they can have a tremendous impact on the profitability of the clinic as the reimbursement from commercial insurance companies is generally significantly greater than Medicare.

Since dialysis services are largely paid for by Medicare, the focus of our reimbursement discussion will include Medicare's payment methodology and any forecasted changes. In past years, outpatient maintenance dialysis treatments (typically done in the free-standing dialysis clinic setting), were paid on a per-treatment basis using what was referred to as the composite payment rate. The composite payment rate was a partially bundled rate that covered dialysis treatments except for some drug and laboratory costs, which were billed and paid for separately on a fee-for-service basis.

Section 153(b) of the Medicare Improvements for Patients and Providers Act of 2008 (MIPPA) replaced the composite rate system with a bundled ESRD payment prospective payment system (PPS) effective Jan. 1, 2011. Following a four-year transition period, the PPS was fully implemented in 2014. The PPS provides a case-mix adjusted single payment to clinics for dialysis services delivered in the clinic setting or in the patient's home. The case-mix adjustments take into consideration factors such as age, body mass index, and co-morbidities. For calendar year 2015, CMS elected to provide no increase to the PPS base rate.[5] In its March 2015 *Report to the Congress*, the Medicare Payment Advisory Commission (MedPAC) recommended elimination of the update to the PPS base rate for calendar year 2016 as well.[6] Acceptance of MedPAC's recommendations is not required, but many times these recommendations are implemented either in the suggested year or soon thereafter.

5 www.cms.gov/Medicare/Medicare-Fee-for-Service-Payment/ESRDpayment/Spotlight.html.
6 www.medpac.gov.

3.0 Valuation Approaches

There are three basic approaches utilized for determining the value of any asset or business enterprise. Depending upon the facts and circumstances of the particular clinic being valued, some of the approaches may be more applicable than others.

3.1 Asset Approach

This approach is generally not used for operating companies, such as dialysis clinics, unless the business is not generating sufficient cash flows to make its operations more valuable than the underlying net assets, less any outstanding debt obligations. Because dialysis clinics are not capital-intensive in nature, the net asset value is generally not a good indicator of value for a clinic that is anticipated to produce future cash flows. The exception to this can be with regard to a new center under construction (commonly referred to as a de novo center), where the asset approach can be commonly used to value the clinic.

3.2 Market Approach

The market approach values a business based upon publicly traded guideline companies or sale transactions of other similar privately held businesses. The challenges of applying this approach are twofold. Due to merger and acquisition activity of recent years, there are only two remaining publicly traded dialysis companies, Fresenius and DaVita. When utilizing the publicly traded guideline method, it is critical to make the necessary adjustments to the public company information so that it is comparable to the private company being valued. These adjustments involve an analysis of the balance sheet differences, such as levels of debt as well as differences in growth rates. This type of analysis can be quite time consuming and difficult to accomplish.

When utilizing merger and acquisition transaction data to develop valuation estimates for the subject company, it is important to gather and consider as much information about the sale transactions as possible. You should ascertain items about the sale such as:

1. Was there a noncompete included in the transaction;
2. Was the buyer a large, national player or smaller local or regional company;
3. What are the demographics of the market for the sold clinic;
4. What is the term of the medical director agreement and renewal options;
5. Are other physicians in the group bound to the noncompete agreement by a joinder; and
6. Are there any significant changes expected in the market demographics or competition in the short term.

Unfortunately, these details can be difficult, if not impossible, to obtain. Additionally, sometimes the published transactions include assets (such as real estate) that may or may not be included in your transaction.

Market differences[7] also must be taken into consideration. However, dialysis clinics are typically dominated by Medicare patients (many times as high as 85% of patients); therefore, individual payor differences between markets do not have the same impact on the use of private transaction multiples for dialysis clinic valuations as they do for other segments of healthcare. Unfortunately, many times the transaction data is limited, making application of the approach difficult.

3.3 Income Approach

The income approach values a clinic based upon its ability to generate future cash flows and the anticipated risk associated with those cash flows. Depending upon the circumstances, the income approach can be a single period capitalization of earnings or a discounted cash flow analysis. Many times, an income approach will be stated as a multiple of earnings before interest, taxes, depreciation, and amortization (EBITDA). Publicly traded companies will generally state their acquisition prices as a multiple of EBITDA. The income approach is the most commonly used valuation approach for privately held businesses such as dialysis clinics.

In applying the income approach, you will need to evaluate potential volume growth and capacity. Clinic volume is stated on a per-patient basis. Dialysis clinics typically run two shifts per day, although a third can be added. Shifts will run three days a week, and the clinic will operate either three days per week or six days per week as demand dictates. Generally speaking, for a two-shift clinic, there will be a morning shift that runs from approximately 6 a.m. to 10 a.m., and an afternoon shift that runs from 10 a.m. to 2 p.m. If the clinic runs a third shift, it will run from 2 p.m. to 6 p.m. To calculate capacity, determine the number of stations (each treatment is performed at a station comprised of a recliner and dialyzer machine) multiplied by the number of shifts being run. For volume and future growth to exceed capacity, additional stations or shifts must be added. If there is space in the physical location, and the plumbing was planned in advance, adding additional stations is a relatively easy thing to do as the capital requirements are not extensive. However, if the current space is utilized, expansion will require a significant amount of leasehold improvements or build-out costs as the dialyzer machines require medical-grade purified water and a substantial amount of plumbing.

In terms of projecting revenue, the valuation must consider changes in the reimbursement. As previously discussed, Medicare eliminated the increase to the base PPS rate for calendar year 2015 and will likely do so for 2016 as well.

4.0 Value Drivers

There are five primary drivers of value for any dialysis clinic. The following section explores each of these drivers and their potential impact on value.

7 For an extensive discussion of market differences, see Chapter 1, "Healthcare Market Structure and Its Implication for Valuation of Privately Held Provider Entities—An Empirical Analysis."

4.1 Demographics of the Community

Senior adults, African-Americans, and Native American adults use dialysis services more heavily than other ethnic groups.[8] Therefore, it is critical to understand the current demographics of the community where the clinic is located as well as the projections for future population growth in the area. Medicare patients often make up as much as 85% of the patient load for many dialysis clinics, although 50% or more (depending on the type of dialysis modality) of dialysis patients are under the age of 65.[9] As stated previously, patients can become eligible for Medicare without being seniors. On average, however, elderly patients comprise approximately one-third to one-half of the total population. Therefore, the composition of senior adults in the community as well as the projections for growth of this segment can have a tremendous impact on a clinic's ability to grow. It is also important to consider the geographic placement of the clinic. A location too far from the dominant patient base is vulnerable to competition from another clinic that is more conveniently located.

4.2 Relationship With Area Nephrologists

For any dialysis clinic to survive long term, relationships with area nephrologists are a key success factor. It is important to establish relationships with nephrology groups that have a good reputation in the community and that have a good mix of experienced physicians, preferably some of whom are still early in their career. Many times, the dialysis clinic will formalize its relationship with a key nephrologist or group by negotiating a medical directorship contract. Medical directorships generally help build the physician's loyalty to the clinic, thereby reducing the risk of losing revenues to a competing center. However, as stated previously, the terms and compensation of the medical directorship should be carefully evaluated to ensure the agreement does not unduly expose the clinic to regulatory risks.

4.3 Competition

The existence and aggressiveness of competitors can have a significant impact on the value of a dialysis clinic, just as with any other business. When considering investing in a dialysis clinic, it is important to understand the competitive landscape in the community and any expansion plans that dominant groups may be considering. A community with one or two dominant nephrology groups will be a more difficult competitive environment than a community primarily comprised of many independent practices. The value of a clinic can be substantially eroded if the dominant group in a community is planning a competing center in close proximity. Typically, certificate of need (CON) regulations do not govern the establishment of new dialysis clinics as the capital investment is not as significant as with some other healthcare ventures. However, the existence and extent of CON regulations are state-specific so it is important to understand any limitations specific to your community.

8 *2014 USRDS Annual Data Report*, United States Renal Data System.

9 Id.

4.4 Merger and Acquisition Activity

The dialysis industry has undergone extensive consolidation over the past several years. There are currently only a handful of companies that dominate the industry on a national basis, with Fresenius and DaVita being the largest players with a combined 65% market share.[10] When considering the value of a clinic for merger and acquisition purposes, it is critical to understand the status of current consolidation activity taking place, especially in the clinic's geographic area. These acquisition transactions could have a substantial impact on what a clinic could be worth in the marketplace.

4.5 Recent Payor Initiatives

A clinic's payor mix can have a substantial impact on its value. However, because dialysis clinics are typically dominated by governmental payors, specifically Medicare, it is very important to stay abreast of any upcoming changes in Medicare reimbursement rates. As previously mentioned, in March of each year, MedPAC issues its recommendations for changes in Medicare reimbursement rates for the upcoming year.

5.0 Government Enforcement Environment

In recent years, there has been an increase in qui tam (i.e., whistleblower) lawsuits related to the dialysis industry. In some of the larger cases, the fines have been in the hundreds of millions of dollars. It is important as an appraiser to stay abreast of enforcement actions in the particular industry segment you are appraising, as these types of actions can be future predictors of changes in processes for the industry and can be indicators of heightened scrutiny and risk associated with achieving financial projections.

6.0 Conclusion

Determining the value of a dialysis clinic is a complex undertaking. Therefore, it is important to ensure the valuation professional not only understands valuation techniques and methodologies, but also the regulatory issues of the healthcare industry. Additionally, a thorough analysis must be performed of the current and projected demographics of the community, the relationship with area nephrology groups, and the state of merger and acquisition activity going on in the industry.

10 www.wikinvest.com/stock/DaVita_(DVA).

Chapter 17.
The Valuation of Pathology Services

CONTENTS

Chapter 17.
The Valuation of Pathology Services

By Darcy Devine, CVA

The need to value pathology services arises when a hospital, physician group, or another provider contracts to buy or sell pathology-related services. Since the parties to these contracts often refer business to one another, compensation needs to be at fair market value for compliance purposes. The technical nature and confusing reimbursement structure of pathology services can often make these assessments more complex than those for most traditional physician service arrangements, creating a challenging engagement. The goals of this chapter are to describe the two major types of pathology services, identify the different reasons they are purchased, and provide a basis for determining their fair market value.

1.0 Clinical and Anatomic Pathology Background

To value pathology services, the appraiser first needs to recognize the two major disciplines in pathology: clinical pathology and anatomic pathology. Anatomic and clinical pathology services are dissimilar in many ways: They involve a different type of work effort on the physician's part, and insurance reimburses them differently. For these and other reasons, it is important to be able to unlink and separately analyze these services when they are both included in a pathology services agreement.

2.0 Clinical Pathology Services

Clinical laboratory (or clinical pathology) tests are medical procedures that involve testing samples of blood, urine, tissue homogenates, or substances in the body. They are generally performed using high-tech computerized and automated equipment. The results help physicians and other healthcare providers detect, diagnose, and treat disease. More than 4,000 clinical tests have been developed, with larger clinical laboratories offering test menus of 1,000 or more.

The federal government regulates laboratory testing on humans through the Clinical Laboratory Improvement Amendments (CLIA). Although the Centers for Medicare & Medicaid Services (CMS) administers the CLIA standards, the standards apply nationally and are not exclusive to laboratories serving Medicare and Medicaid patients. In place since 1988, the primary purpose of CLIA's laboratory testing standards is to ensure the accuracy, reliability, and timeliness of results regardless of where a test is performed.

Clinical laboratory tests (see Exhibit 1) are categorized as waived (simple), moderate complexity, or high complexity. CLIA requires that laboratories have properly trained and qualified staff, and the higher levels of testing complexity require more qualified staff. A board certified pathologist will meet the minimum criteria at all levels of testing including moderate and high complexity procedures.[1,2]

Exhibit 1. Common Clinical Laboratory Tests

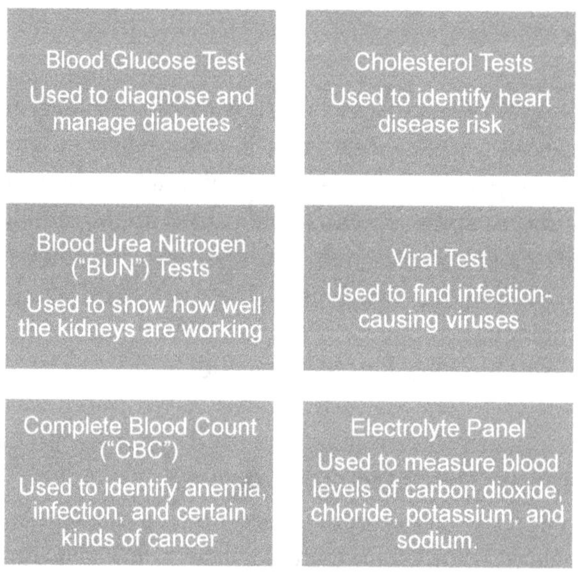

2.1 Clinical Laboratory Providers

The resources necessary to provide a clinical laboratory test are divided into two categories: technical component (TC) resources and professional component (PC) resources. The TC resources include the laboratory space, staff, equipment, and supplies. Hospitals, physician practices, and reference laboratories are common providers of these resources. PC resources are the physician-required services under CLIA, including medical directorship and supervision of the laboratory. These services are not patient-specific, meaning they benefit the laboratory's entire population of patients and are not provided to patients individually. Clinical pathologists provide laboratory oversight and other PC services.

1 clients.cola.org/files/pdf/LabGuide4.pdf.
2 www.mass.gov/eohhs/docs/dph/clinical-lab/clia-lab-qualifications.pdf.

It is common for different healthcare providers to provide the technical and professional components of a clinical laboratory test. For example, a hospital laboratory may perform the TC of a diagnostic test while a private practice pathologist who the hospital has contracted provides the PC. For certain services, Medicare will only reimburse the TC provider who is performing the test, with the assumption being that the provider is responsible for the cost of all the resources including pathologist time spent evaluating equipment, supervising laboratory staff, and other PC services. In these cases, the clinical pathologist is actually prohibited from billing Medicare for the PC because Medicare has already paid the TC provider all it will pay for the test.[3]

How Medicare pays for the TC varies based on patient setting. If a clinical test is performed on a hospital inpatient, Medicare Part A funds the payment using the Inpatient Prospective Payment System (IPPS). For a hospital outpatient, Medicare Part B funds the payment using the Outpatient Prospective Payment System (OPPS). If the clinical test is performed on a patient in a physician office setting, payment will generally be through Medicare Part B using the Clinical Laboratory Fee Schedule (CLFS).[4] Exhibit 2 summarizes the Medicare Fee Schedules, and Exhibit 3 provides an overview of Medicare's payment methodologies, by setting, for clinical laboratory testing.

Exhibit 2. Overview of Medicare's Fee Schedules

PART A (HOSPITAL INSURANCE)

Medicare program covering inpatient hospital services for aged and disabled individuals who meet the eligibility requirements.

- **Inpatient Prospective Payment System ("IPPS")** A payment system for hospital inpatient stays. Services and resources provided to inpatients are bundled into diagnosis-related groups ("DRGs"). DRGs are paid a set rate based on the resources expected to be consumed during the patient's stay.

PART B (MEDICAL INSURANCE)

Medicare program covering physician services, outpatient hospital care, durable medical equipment, and some medical services that are not covered by Part A.

- **Outpatient Prospective Payment System ("OPPS")** Resources and services provided to an outpatient are bundled together into Ambulatory Payment Classifications (APCs). Each APC is paid a set rate based on the resources expected to be consumed during the service.
- **Physician Fee Schedule ("PFS")** Individual services are identified by the Current Procedural Terminology (CPT®) code system. Each CPT is assigned a certain number of relative value units in consideration of the physician work, practice expense, and malpractice liability insurance expenses associated with the service. Medicare publishes a conversion rate each year that converts relative value units into reimbursement dollars.
- **Clinical Laboratory Fee Schedule ("CLFS")** Laboratory services identified by the CPT and Healthcare Common Procedure Coding ("HCPC") systems are paid on the basis of the lesser of the amount billed, the local fee for a geographic area, or a national limit identified by the CLFS.

3 When the requirements for a clinical consultation service are met, Medicare allows for a PC payment under the Physician Fee Schedule (PFS).

4 Outpatient services provided by hospital laboratories were previously reimbursed under the CLFS. Effective Jan. 1, 2014, CMS began packaging laboratory services related to the applicable primary outpatient service and reimbursing them using the OPPS.

Exhibit 3. How Medicare Pays for Clinical Laboratory Testing

<table>
<tr><th></th><th>Provider</th><th>Hospital Inpatient</th><th>Hospital Outpatient</th><th>Physician Office Patient</th></tr>
<tr><td>Technical Component</td><td>Clinical Laboratory</td><td rowspan="2">PART A
IPPS</td><td rowspan="2">PART B
OPPS</td><td>PART B
CLFS</td></tr>
<tr><td>Professional Component</td><td>Clinical Pathologist</td><td>PART B
CLFS</td></tr>
</table>

Like Medicare, some private or commercial insurance carriers also bundle the PC and TC of each clinical laboratory test into a combined facility fee. However, others split the reimbursement and allow clinical pathologists to bill the patient or insurer directly for the PC services. When this is allowed, patients who have a laboratory test may receive a bill from the pathology group for oversight and supervision of the laboratory even though they never saw or received individual service from the group.

3.0 Anatomic Pathology Services

Anatomic pathology services include the processing and microscopic examination of specimens of human tissues or fluids. Examples of anatomic laboratory services include the biopsy and examination of a mole for skin cancer or the collection and screening of cervical cells for abnormalities. Compared to clinical pathology, which is largely automated, anatomic pathology services involve more patient-identifiable, hands-on work. The technical and professional components are also more distinct.

3.1 Anatomic Pathology Providers

TC resources for anatomic pathology services include the laboratory space, staff, equipment, and supplies to provide the test. This includes the work of histology and cytology technicians who prepare the specimens prior to examination.[5] The PC of anatomic services is provided by anatomic pathologists who examine the prepared slides through a microscope and write diagnostic reports. (See Exhibit 4.) Pathologist oversight of an anatomic laboratory is also necessary, as anatomic pathology services are categorized as high complexity testing under CLIA.

Medicare pays for the TC of anatomic services provided to hospital inpatients and outpatients using the IPPS and OPPS systems. However, unlike clinical laboratory testing, the anatomic pathologist is not precluded from billing the PC of the anatomic service. The PC provided by an anatomic pathologist will generally be paid separately under the Part B PFS (see Exhibit 5) and will not be bundled into a facility fee paid to the TC provider. If the physician provides

5 Medicine.net defines histology as the anatomical study of the structure and composition of plant or animal tissues seen under the microscope, as opposed to gross anatomy, which involves structures that can be observed with the naked eye. Cytology is the study of the microscopic appearance of cells, especially for the diagnosis of abnormalities and malignancies. Cytological examinations may be performed on body fluids or cells that are aspirated, scraped, or washed from a part of the body.

Exhibit 4. The Anatomic Pathology Process

Technical Component (Histology Processing)	• Accessioning	Labeling and identifying specimen for tracking purposes
	• Sectioning	Sectioning specimen into small slices
	• Fixation	Hardening sliced specimen with a fixative to stop degradation
	• Processing	Dehydrating specimen in alcohols
	• Embedding	Embedding processed specimen into hot wax
	• Staining	Staining the mounted sections to improve visibility for the anatomic pathologist
Professional Component	• Examination	Specimen is examined microscopically by anatomic pathologist
	• Report	Pathologist documents examination findings in a written report

both the technical and the professional component, a global fee is paid for both components under the PFS. This is also true for commercial and nongovernment insurers.[6]

A complicating factor is, although every hospital in the U.S. provides its patients with some measure of anatomic laboratory services, not all hospitals have in-house histology or cytology labs. In those cases, the hospital generally purchases these services from a pathology group. Because pathology groups can only bill Medicare for the TC if the patient was not seen in a hospital setting, when a group provides the TC to a hospital patient, it has to seek payment from the hospital, which is responsible for billing Medicare.[7]

Exhibit 5. How Medicare Pays for Anatomic Pathology Testing

	Provider	Hospital Inpatient	Hospital Outpatient	Physician Office Patient
Technical Component	Anatomic Pathology Lab	PART A IPPS	PART B OPPS	Part B PFS
Professional Component	Anatomic Pathologist	Part B PFS	Part B PFS	Part B PFS

6 www.cms.gov/Regulations-and-Guidance/Guidance/Transmittals/downloads/R2714CP.pdf.

7 CMS implemented a policy in 1999 to pay only the hospital for the technical component of an anatomic pathology service provided to a hospital inpatient or outpatient. Congress responded by passing a grandfather clause that allowed independent laboratories and pathology groups providing these services at that time to be grandfathered in and continue to bill Medicare directly for these services. The final extension of the grandfather clause ended on July 1, 2012, and now only hospitals can be paid for these services.

4.0 Market for Professional Pathology Services

Clinical pathologists oversee the clinical laboratories, staff, and automated equipment that perform tests on various bodily fluid or tissue samples. Anatomical pathologists actually examine the tissue and cells obtained from biopsy samples through a microscope in an effort to aid in the diagnosis and prognosis of disease. Pathologists may specialize in one or both disciplines.

Becoming a pathologist requires approximately eight to 10 years of postgraduate education and training, including four years of medical school and four years of residency. The large majority of pathology residents also complete at least one fellowship (see Exhibit 6) that provides one to two years of more narrowly focused training.[8]

Exhibit 6. Pathology Fellowships in the U.S.

Anatomic/Clinical Pathology Fellowships Approved by the Accreditation Council for Graduate Medical Education (ACGME)
•Blood Banking / Transfusion Medicine •Clinical Informatics •Chemical Pathology •Cytopathology •Forensic Pathology •Hematopathology •Medical Microbiology •Neuropathology •Pediatric Pathology •Selective Pathology

There are 19,237 pathologists in the country, according to the most recent American Medical Association (AMA) study of physicians in the United States.[9] Out of the entire population of pathologists, approximately 13,420 are physicians providing patient care in a physician practice or hospital setting. Therefore, there are four patient care pathologists per 100,000 people[10,11] and one pathologist for every 68 hospital beds in the United States.[12,13] Interestingly, about 68% of the patient care pathologists recognized by the AMA study identify their area of practice as anatomic/clinical pathology, showing significant overlap between the two disciplines in the market.[14]

8 American Society of Clinical Pathology (ASCP), "ASCP Fellowship & Job Market Surveys, A Report on the 2014 RISE, FISE, FISHE, NPISE, PISE and TMISE Surveys." www.ascp.org/PDF/Fellowship-Reports/2014-Job-Market-Surveys.pdf.

9 American Medical Association, *Physician Characteristics & Distribution in the US,* 2015 edition.

10 According to the U.S. Census, the United States population is approximately 321 million.

11 www.census.gov/

12 According to the AMA, there are 914,513 staffed hospital beds in the United States.

13 www.aha.org/research/rc/stat-studies/fast-facts.shtml.

14 Many different pathology subspecialties were identified in the AMA report, including separate designations for those who practice anatomic pathology and clinical pathology exclusively.

Exhibit 7. Percentage of Respondents to CAP Survey by Practice Size

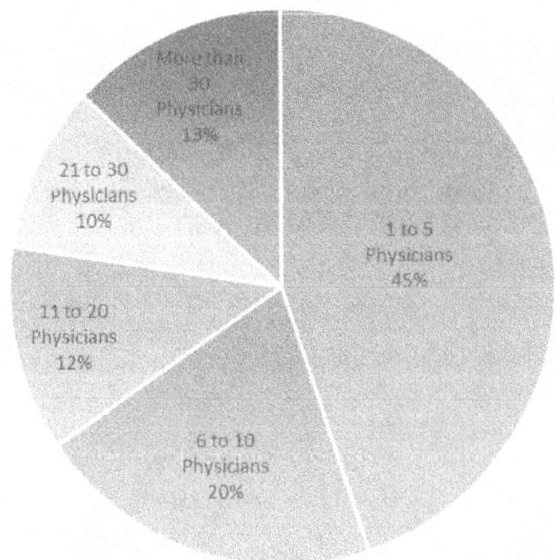

An in-depth study of members of the College of American Pathologists (CAP) shows that the majority of pathologists work in small group practices of one to 10 physicians in academic medical centers or community-based hospital settings (see Exhibit 7).[15] In terms of their professional time allocation, pathologists responding to the study indicated that they spend 67.4% of their professional time providing services related to individual patients, including reading slides, making diagnoses, interpreting tests, and consulting with other providers about individual patients. These services are likely to fall under Part B services and be reimbursed under the PFS.

Survey respondents also indicated that they spend another 17.5% of their professional time providing other types of services to general patient populations, such as laboratory direction and management. Given this description, these efforts are not likely to be billable to patients or insurers and are more likely to be reimbursed by payors to a hospital as part of a facility fee payment. These services are often labeled as the "PC of clinical pathology services" or, more generally, "Part A services."

Responses to the CAP survey also indicate that pathologists spend, on average, the remaining 15.1% of their professional time on other professional responsibilities (see Exhibit 8), including participation on hospital committees and professional societies, research and teaching efforts, life-long learning, and management of their practice. These services are generally not patient-identifiable services and are not billed to patients or insurers. As discussed later in the chapter, these additional services will sometimes be included in the basket of "Part A services" for which pathologists seek to be compensated under pathology services agreements with hospitals.

15 CAP 2014 *Practice Characteristics Survey Report* www.cap.org/ShowProperty?nodePath=/UCMCon/Contribution%20Folders/WebContent/pdf/practice-characteristics-survey-report.pdf.

Exhibit 8. Professional Time Allocation of Respondents to CAP Study

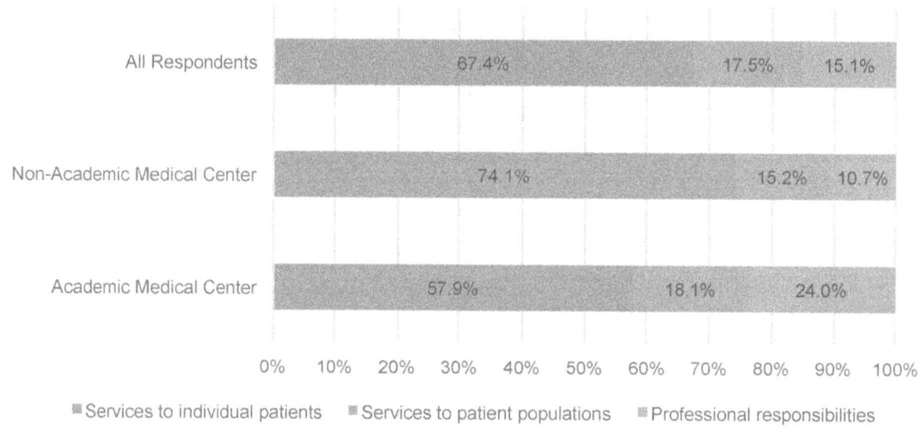

5.0 Pathology Services Agreements

Two common transactions for pathology services include the purchase of the PC of clinical pathology "Part A services" (as defined by the parties) or the purchase of the TC of anatomic services. These two transaction types include very different sets of services and resources. The following details possible approaches for the valuation of each type.

5.1 Clinical Laboratory Agreements—Purchase of Part A Services

Hospitals purchase Part A services from clinical pathologists because of CLIA requirements as well as standards and best practices in the industry. Years ago, it was more common for clinical pathologists to go uncompensated for Part A services. However, in addition to reductions in reimbursement, regulatory concerns have caused a significant increase in the number of clinical pathologists successfully seeking payment from hospitals for these responsibilities. More specifically, a 1991 Office of the Inspector General (OIG) Management Advisory Report, *Financial Arrangements Between Hospitals and Hospital-Based Physicians,*[16] identified arrangements that required pathologists to provide Part A services to hospitals for less than fair market value as being suspect. The implication is that if the hospital is not paying for the services at fair market value, the pathologists are providing the PC of clinical pathology services in order to illicit referrals from other physicians for anatomic services that are compensable under Part B. If true, this would be a violation of the anti-kickback statute. For this reason, appraisers are sometimes asked to determine the fair market value of the Part A services private practice pathology groups are providing to hospitals.

5.1.1 Identify Compensable Services

A good first step when valuing Part A services is to identify which services are included. Terminology varies in the industry, and sometimes the terms "medical director services," "PC

16 Office of Inspector General, "Financial Arrangements Between Hospitals and Hospital-Based Physicians," OEI-09-89-0330 oig.hhs.gov/oei/reports/oei-09-89-00330.pdf.

of clinical pathology services," and "Part A services" are used interchangeably. Technically, these terms can mean different things. For example, the PC of clinical pathology services can be a subset of a larger basket of "Part A" services that a pathology group may be providing. These broader services include activities such as hospital committee work, participation in strategic growth opportunities, in-services for hospital staff, conference attendance, leadership of technology initiatives, community activities, and continuing professional education. These contributions benefit more than just the clinical lab, often extending to anatomic pathology services and beyond, and sometimes to the entire hospital.

Given the varied nature of pathologists' activities from organization to organization, it is important that the parties to an agreement to purchase "Part A services" understand and agree on the basket of services being purchased. A good practice is to require a detailed breakdown of services provided. Ideally, this breakdown will detail whether the service is provided to individual patients, a patient population, or falls into another professional service category. It is also helpful to determine whether a clinical or anatomic pathologist provides the services. The hours may be further categorized as billable or nonbillable to patients. An example of such a breakdown is shown in Exhibit 9.

Exhibit 9. Example of Hourly Breakdown of Pathology Services Being Provided

	Total Hours			"Part A" Hours		
Activity Description	Anatomic Pathology	Clinical Pathology	Combined	Anatomic Pathology	Clinical Pathology[1]	Combined
Patient Specific Activities	**6,760**	**0**	**6,760**	**0**	**0**	**0**
Patient Population Activities	**330**	**2,792**	**3,122**	**330**	**1,257**	**1,587**
Accreditation Activities	4	80	84	4	36	40
Evaluating Equipment	6	108	114	6	49	55
Committee Work	80	208	288	80	94	174
Informatics	0	0	0	0	0	0
Lab Administration Activities	30	300	330	30	135	165
Laboratory Staff Management	20	200	220	20	90	110
Medical Direction	36	360	396	36	162	198
Medical Staff Inquiries	30	208	238	30	94	124
New Testing Protocols	8	80	88	8	36	44
Outcomes Assessments	40	520	560	40	234	274
Reviewing Policies & Procedures	36	208	244	36	94	130
Utilization Management	40	520	560	40	234	274
Other Professional Activities	**188**	**330**	**518**	**188**	**149**	**337**
Community Education & Outreach	4	40	44	4	18	22
Conference Attendance	40	82	122	40	37	77
Managing the Physician Practice	36	48	84	36	22	58
Continuing Professional Education	60	80	140	60	36	96
Society Activities	48	80	128	48	36	84
Total	**7,278**	**3,122**	**10,400**	**518**	**1,405**	**1,923**
Percentage of Hours	***70.0%***	***30.0%***	***100.0%***	***5.0%***	***13.5%***	***18.5%***
Full-time Equivalency (FTE)	**3.5**	**1.5**	**5.0**	**0.2**	**0.7**	**0.925**

[1] *Total clinical pathology hours were adjusted by the government payer mix of 45% based on the assumption that clinical pathologists can bill non-government insurers and patients for the professional component of Part A services.*

5.1.2 Determine the Amount of Compensable Time

Once the services have been defined, the amount of time necessary to provide them must be determined. In certain situations, time documentation does not exist or needs to be evaluated. How much Part A time a group provides is highly dependent on the setting, the needs of the hospital, mutual understanding between the parties, etc. Drawing from the CAP data, it is reasonable to anticipate 15% to 40% of pathologists' time will be spent providing services that are not patient specific and could potentially be classified as Part A services for the purpose of the appraiser's assessment. However, this is just a guide and only an indication of overall professional time spent in Part A activities. When estimating the amount of time needed for Part A services, there may be situations when fewer pathologists serve the needs of a hospital and therefore a larger percentage of those pathologists' time is needed for Part A work. Also, specific pathologists in a group may provide the majority of the Part A services while others provide little or no Part A services.

In any situation, it is best to have the pathologists' historical hours documented (see Exhibit 9) and have the hospital or buyer of the Part A services represent that the time is needed and reasonable given the relevant facts and circumstances.

5.2 The Value of Professional Pathology Services

Once the hours or physician FTEs necessary to provide Part A services are determined, numerous resources can be used to determine their value. Both the Medical Group Management Association (MGMA) and the American Medical Group Association (AMGA), for example, publish statistics on pathology compensation annually. Respondents to the most recent MGMA survey included 311pathologists, a small share of the estimated 13,420 practicing pathologists in the U.S. Respondents to the most recent AMGA survey included 574. Pathology-focused organizations such as CAP also provide data on pathology salaries. There were 1,691 respondents to the "CAP 2014 Practice Characteristics Survey." Total compensation in these surveys generally includes base salaries and incentive pay but does not include the value of fringe benefits or employment-related expenses such as cell phones, society dues, continuing medical education, or malpractice premiums.

Another source for valuing physician services is CMS, which has established reasonable compensation equivalents (RCEs) for physicians providing services to critical access hospitals and other providers paid by Medicare on a reasonable cost basis. These entities are limited to the lower of either the actual cost of services furnished by the physician or the RCE. The RCE includes all monetary benefits, fringe benefits, deferred compensation, and other items of value (excluding office space and billing and collection services). The calendar year 2015 RCE limit for pathology is $260,300.[17] (See Exhibit 10.)

17 www.gpo.gov/fdsys/pkg/FR-2014-08-22/pdf/2014-18545.pdf.

Exhibit 10. Comparison of Pathology Compensation Benchmarks

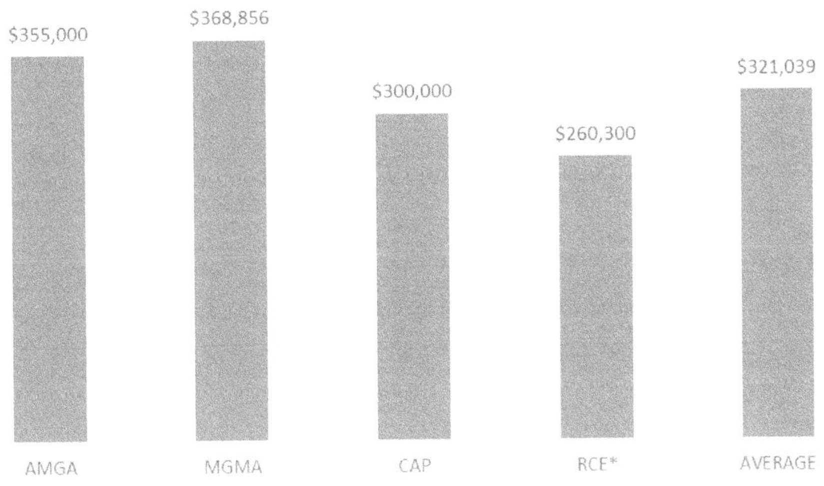

*Inclusive of benefits
Sources:
AMGA 2015 Medical Group Compensation and Financial Study
MGMA Physician Compensation and Production Survey: 2015 Report Based on 2014 Data
CAP 2014 Practice Characteristics Survey Report
CMS calendar year 2015 RCE for pathology

An example of how to assign value to Part A services is shown in Exhibit 11. In the example, the number of pathologists needed is estimated using pathologist-to-hospital-bed and pathologist-to-population ratios. These ratios reflect the current distribution of pathologists across the country. The ratios indicate that 5.0 FTE pathologists are needed to meet the needs of a 340-bed hospital serving a 150,000-person service area (adjusted to reflect market share). These FTEs reflect what is needed to provide all pathology services, including billable Part B services. Therefore, adjustments are necessary to find the number of FTEs needed to provide the nonbillable Part A services. Based on the professional time allocation and payor mix, the sample hospital needs a 0.925 pathology FTE for these services. Applying a compensation rate of $321,039 per FTE pathologist (the average of the median benchmarks), the analysis indicates the fair market value of the Part A services at the sample hospital to be $296,961 per year.

This example provides a way to either help establish or to provide a sanity check for physicians' Part A hours or the Part A stipend. Additional support for determining the right amount of hours or Part A stipend can be found by reviewing compensation for comparable services in comparable institutions. Pathology agreements can be very diverse from one facility to another, so the obvious difficulty is finding comparable agreements.

5.3 Anatomic Pathology Agreements—Purchase of TC Resources

The purchase of the TC of anatomic pathology services is also a common transaction. These services include histology and cytology preparations. As previously discussed, these agreements can be configured in two ways: a hospital can buy the TC of anatomic services from

Exhibit 11. Estimating Part A FTE Demand and Part A Stipend

Pathologist Demand	
Pathologist: Bed Ratio Method	
Hospital Bed Size	340
Pathologist to Bed Ratio	1:68
Pathology FTEs Needed to Serve Beds	**5.0**
Pathologist: Population Ratio Method	
Hospital Service Area Population	150,000
Pathologist to 100k Population	1:4
Hospital Market Share	82.5%
Pathology FTEs Needed to Serve Hospital Patient Base	**5.0**

Pathologists' Professional Time Allocation at Hospital	
Billable Anatomic Services	65.0%
Billable Clinical Pathology Services	16.5%
Non-Billable Anatomic Services	5.0%
Non-Billable Clinical Services[1]	13.5%

Hospital's Payer Mix	
Government Insurance	45%
Commercial Insurance	40%
Other Insurance	15%

Calculation of Part A Stipend	
Total Pathologist Demand	5.0 FTEs
Percentage of Time Spent on Part A / Non-Billable Activities	18.5%
Part A FTEs	**0.925**
Median Benchmark Compensation	$321,039
Part A Stipend	**$296,961**

[1] *Assumes a 45% government payer mix and the ability of the physician group to bill commercial and other non-government payers and patients for the professional component of clinical laboratory services*

physician groups that own a histology lab or physician groups can buy the TC of anatomic services from a hospital.

Market data for histology and cytology laboratory services is a helpful resource for the appraiser for determining the fair market value of these resources. The Medicare PFS is one such resource that provides values for such services. However, there are concerns with relying on the PFS for valuation purposes. Of principal concern is the wide fluctuation in values assigned to anatomic pathology TC services over the last few years. The most common anatomic procedure code, accounting for 54% of Medicare Part B spending on anatomic procedures and described by CPT® 88305, saw its TC reimbursement grow by over 250% from 1999 to 2012 and lopped off by over 52% in 2013.[18] There have also been other significant changes to Medicare funding

18 G2 Intelligence, "U.S. Clinical Laboratory and Pathology Testing 2013-2015: Market Analysis, Trends, and Forecasts."

and to the CPT® code set for pathology procedures that make it difficult to use the PFS as a constant when valuing pathology services.

Other market data include the prices independent histology/cytology laboratories charge for slide preparation. The challenge becomes creating a crosswalk between the services histology labs offer and the CPT® system. This is important because compensation included in agreements between hospitals and physicians for these services is often on a fee-for-service basis using the CPT® code set. The disconnect between histology lab pricing and the CPT® system is that the primary unit of service in the CPT® coding system is the "specimen." The number of blocks and slides needed, as well as the different staining and other work steps involved in the preparation of a specimen, vary significantly for different types of specimens. Meanwhile, histology labs generally price services on a per-block or per-slide basis, with additional charges for special staining and other extra services requested.

Although translating histology services into CPT® codes is challenging, there are resources that make it possible. For example, appraisers can find histology labs serving researchers and medical professionals online that publish their fee-for-service rates for paraffin block processing and embedding and slide preparation including hematoxylin and eosin (H&E) staining (the standard stain used in histology). The services offered will generally include comprehensive histologic services for diagnostic and research specimens, including tissue processing and preparation. The laboratories advertising these services are affiliated with medical schools, independent histology labs serving biotech and pharmaceutical companies, clinical research organizations, independent pathologists, medical examiners' offices, research companies, and others. Exhibit 12 provides a few examples of histology laboratories that publish their fee schedules on their websites.

Exhibit 12. Examples of Histology Laboratory Websites With Published Histology Fee Schedules

Mass Histology Service masshistology.com	North Bay Histology Lab, Inc. northbayhistologylab.com	Cureline BioPathology Laboratory curelinebiopathology.com
UConn Health Center researchhistology.uchc.edu/services_fees/	NYU School of Medicine med.nyu.edu/ocs/histopathology/fees	University of VA School of Medicine medicine.virginia.edu/research/cores/histology/rates-page

Using these published fee schedules, an appraiser can estimate what these facilities would charge, on average, for the services defined by an 88305 CPT® code, for example. A study published in the *American Journal of Clinical Pathology* on anatomical pathology workloads indicates that the average number of blocks and slides per 88305 is 1.8 blocks and 3.1 slides.[19] (This is roughly equivalent to saying that, per specimen, 1.8 paraffin blocks are processed and embedded and 3.1 slides are prepared and stained.) Again, this can vary substantially based on the source of the tissue and the purpose of the examination. However, it is a helpful guide for the purposes of this chapter. Using online fee schedule data, and estimating approximately 1.8 blocks and 3.1 slides per specimen, it appears that histology labs would charge in the neighborhood of $30 to $31 for the TC of an 88305 comparable service (or approximately 90% of the Medicare fee schedule).[20] These rates do not reflect discounts advertised for medical school employees or insiders or any high volume discounts.

There are other ways to value the TC of an anatomic pathology service. For example, using a cost plus approach, which assumes the cost to re-create the service plus a reasonable rate of return, to price TC services is possible if costs are known. Estimating these costs may also be possible given the numerous cost and output studies associated with histology and cytology staff.

6.0 Summary

Valuing pathology services is complicated by the very technical nature of the services involved as well as the complicated reimbursement systems associated with these services. It is likely that a large percentage of the professional component of clinical pathology services provided to a hospital's patients cannot be billed directly to the patient or the insurer. A hospital contracting with a pathology group for these services will need to understand the effort and resources the group is providing to fairly compensate the group for these and other "Part A" services it provides the hospital. Since pathologists experienced a tremendous decrease in reimbursement for anatomic services a few years ago, they seem to have turned up the pressure on hospitals related to Part A compensation. The government has also shown concern over arrangements involving hospital-based physicians, such as pathologists, who do not receive fair market value compensation for their Part A services. All of these pressures have driven, and will continue to drive, the demand for the valuation of pathology services to ensure fair market value is paid under these arrangements. As described in this chapter, although determining the value of pathology services provided under a pathology services agreement may present a challenge, many resources are available to an appraiser when providing a fair market value opinion.

19 Raymond T.A. Maung, "What Is the Best Indicator to Determine Anatomic Pathology Workload?" *American Journal of Clinical Pathology*. 2005.

20 This estimate was developed with approximately 25 fee schedules including, but not limited to, those shown in Exhibit 12.

Chapter 18.
The Valuation of Hospitals

CONTENTS

Chapter 18.
The Valuation of Hospitals

By G. Don Barbo, CPA/ABV, and Robert M. Mundy, CPA/ABV, CVA

Valuing hospitals may involve unique circumstances and nuances relative to other types of healthcare and non-healthcare entities. Therefore, it is imperative that an appraiser undertaking these complex assignments is both mindful and understanding of these nuances in order to generate a sound opinion of value. This chapter will examine the various distinctions that separate hospital valuations from nonhealthcare valuations.

While this chapter will focus solely on performing fair market valuations for general acute care hospitals (within the context of transactions), the appraiser should recognize that other "types" of hospitals are present in the market, such as:

1. Specialty surgical hospitals, such as heart or spine hospitals;

2. Critical access hospitals (CAHs);

3. Rehabilitation hospitals; and

4. Long-term acute care hospitals (LTACs).

Valuation of these types of hospitals is somewhat similar in nature to general acute care hospitals, but each has unique characteristics and trends that must be considered. The appraiser must be aware of the hospital industry, the challenges hospitals face, and trends that could impact the hospital's value.

1.0 Overview of the Hospital Industry

The hospital industry in the United States is highly fragmented. According to the American Hospital Association, there were 5,686 registered hospitals in the United States in 2013, with the overwhelming majority being community hospitals, numbered at 4,974. Of these community hospitals, over 58% were not-for-profit, and 20% were state and local government hospitals.[1]

The industry is highly regulated by both state and local governments and at the federal level through the Centers for Medicare & Medicaid Services (CMS). Federal laws, such as the Stark Law, False Claims Act and the Internal Revenue Service code sections 501(c)(3) anti-inurement rules and 4958 Intermediate Sanctions, commonly apply to healthcare valuations. As such, the appraiser needs to be aware of not only the federal regulations affecting hospitals, but also the state and local regulations, which can vary by locality.

2.0 Hospital Value Drivers

Many factors can influence the value of a hospital. Accordingly, an appraiser must gain a thorough understanding of such factors through research and management interviews before rendering an opinion of value. Several examples of value drivers for hospitals are discussed below.

2.1 Location and Demographics of the Community

Similar to the real estate market, a hospital's location can have a significant impact on its value. Numerous aspects of a hospital's operations will be impacted by its location, such as its admission patterns, payor mix, and workforce. A hospital located near a major highway or in a highly populated area will tend to have high patient volumes. Rural hospitals may face difficulty in attracting and retaining physicians, particularly specialized physicians and surgeons.

Local community demographics can also significantly impact a hospital's value. Hospitals operating in an area with a large percentage of the population over 65 years of age may have a greater demand for its services than a similar hospital located in a college town with a younger population. A hospital operating in a lower socio-economic area will tend to have higher levels of Medicaid or uninsured patients.

2.2 Age and Appearance of the Facility

A hospital's age and appearance can significantly impact patient volumes, as patients and physicians prefer newer, modernized facilities. Hospitals are moving away from the older institutionalized construction toward a warmer and inviting "home-like" experience. Additionally, hospitals are focusing on providing convenient patient care by investing in ambulatory care settings and delivering services into the community rather than adding new inpatient beds. The shifting of patient volumes from inpatient to outpatient settings has been a developing trend for a number of years, and the Affordable Care Act's emphasis on population health management and the medical home concept has escalated this outpatient shift. As such, hospitals have focused new construction efforts on urgent care and primary care clinics to improve patient convenience and strengthen physician alliances.

1 American Hospital Association website, www.aha.org/research/rc/stat-studies/fast-facts.shtml.

2.3 Medical Staff Composition

Coordinated relationships with physicians in the community are integral to the success of a hospital. In past years, hospitals have concentrated their physician alignment strategies on direct employment of physicians. Recently, however, alignment strategies have become especially nuanced, including a variety of models such as co-management agreements, professional service agreements, clinically integrated networks, and Accountable Care Organizations (ACOs). With the shift from fee-for-service models to value-based healthcare, a hospital's physician alignment strategy needs to be consistent with its overall mission and strategic plans.

2.4 Competition

As with any other business, the level of competition in the market area will generally have a material impact on a hospital's value. In recent years, hospitals have faced competition from not only hospitals, but also other facilities such as ambulatory surgery centers (ASCs). ASCs, also known as day surgery centers, are used by doctors to perform a variety of surgical procedures that do not require patients to stay overnight, including eye surgery; orthopedic and hand surgery; plastic surgery; pain management (spinal injections); podiatry; ear, nose, and throat surgery; endoscopy; laparoscopy; and various other surgical specialties.

Since ASCs only provide day surgery services, they are much smaller than general hospitals, which offer a much broader range of medical services. Because of their smaller size and considerably narrower medical service focus, ASCs are able to operate with smaller staffs and lower overhead levels. This leads to lower operating costs than larger, full-size hospitals.

Additionally, since ASCs do not provide emergency room services, but instead schedule surgery cases in advance, physician-users may prefer them over hospital operating rooms. Due to their focus on select types of surgeries, ASCs typically offer the following benefits over hospitals:

- Patients are less at risk of being bumped or losing their scheduled surgery to more critical cases, as may often occur in a hospital setting. Also, because of the lack of critical trauma cases being treated, the waiting room experience is typically less hectic and more pleasant than in full-service hospitals.
- Because of their lower operating cost structure and efficient operating environment, managed care companies and insurance companies look favorably on ASCs and can often negotiate lower payments with ASCs for these medical services.
- Physicians are able to schedule their surgery cases in advance with less risk of being bumped. Also, the nursing staff is familiar and well-trained in supporting the surgeries performed in the ASC. Physicians also may have a greater voice in the type of equipment and medical supplies offered at ASCs.

Because of their focus on day surgeries, ASCs can draw less urgent cases from the hospitals, allowing hospitals to treat the more serious and traumatic cases. However, this migration of outpatient cases from the hospital setting and into ASCs can have a significant negative impact on hospital profitability. Additionally, healthcare regulations allow physicians to have an ownership interest in the ASC, where they perform surgical cases as long as certain safe harbors are met.

2.5 Contracting Strength

A hospital's ability to negotiate and secure favorable reimbursement contracts with third-party commercial payors will generally have a positive impact on its profitability and value. Many small community hospitals have partnered or affiliated with larger healthcare systems in an attempt to garner more lucrative payor contracts. Typically, hospitals or health systems with a large presence in a market area can negotiate better commercial insurance rates than smaller hospitals. An appraiser attempting to value a hospital needs to understand the local commercial insurance market, the major commercial insurers within the community, and the hospital's leverage with these payors.

These are only some of the key value drivers for a hospital. All hospitals and the communities in which they operate have unique characteristics that must to be examined and properly considered in connection with the valuation.

3.0 Healthcare Reform Law

The Patient Protection and Affordable Care Act (ACA), signed into law on March 23, 2010, is bringing widespread changes to the U.S. healthcare system and is having a profound impact on the hospital industry. The many legal challenges against the ACA have left it fundamentally unscathed, aside from the failure of mandatory expansion of Medicaid. As such, hospitals are confronted with the sweeping changes brought about by the ACA.

The three primary goals of the ACA are as follows: (1) increase access to healthcare services; (2) improve the quality of healthcare services; and (3) reduce the overall costs of providing healthcare services. The following are some of the major healthcare reform law initiatives that are impacting hospitals.

3.1 Increase Access to Healthcare Services

Two of the major healthcare reform provisions that are intended to increase access to healthcare services are the individual insurance mandate and the expansion of the Medicaid program.

3.1.1 Individual Insurance Mandate

A major challenge to the constitutionality of the ACA involved the individual insurance mandate; however, the Supreme Court ultimately ruled in favor of the ACA. Under the ACA, Americans are required to purchase healthcare insurance or face a tax penalty. The primary goal of this initiative is to reduce the number of uninsured in the U.S., thereby reducing hospitals' bad debt and uncompensated care costs.

To assist Americans in obtaining health insurance, the ACA prescribed a federal health insurance exchange where individuals can shop for healthcare insurance. States were given the option of either setting up their own state exchanges or partnering with the federal exchanges. To date, only 17 states have set up their own exchanges, with the remaining states either partnering in some fashion with the federal exchanges or relying solely on the federal exchanges.[2]

3.1.2 Expansion of Medicaid

Under the original form of the ACA, states were required to expand Medicaid eligibility to cover individuals up to 133% of the poverty level. However, the Supreme Court ruling on the ACA gave states the option to opt out of this Medicaid expansion. Currently, only 28 states and the District of Columbia have elected to expand coverage with either Medicaid or a similar alternative plan.[3] This provision also intends to decrease the number of uninsured Americans and thereby decrease uncompensated care levels for hospitals.

A recent study by the Department of Health and Human Services (HHS) estimated that hospital uncompensated care costs were reduced by $7.4 billion in 2014, with $5 billion of this reduction attributable to states that elected to expand Medicaid coverage.[4] This study demonstrates that hospitals located in the states electing to expand Medicaid coverage experienced the largest decline in uncompensated care costs.

3.2 Improve the Quality of Patient Care

3.2.1 Value-Based Purchasing

The ACA established the Medicare hospital value-based purchasing (HVBP) program, which is designed to incentivize hospitals to improve quality of patient care. Under the HVBP program, a percentage of Medicare payments to hospitals is withheld in order to fund incentive payments to hospitals that provide high-quality patient care. By law, the HVBP program must be budget-neutral, such that the total incentive payments paid to hospitals equal the amounts withheld from the Medicare hospital base payments. In 2015, Medicare base payments to hospitals are reduced by 1.5%, and this reduction increases to 2% by 2017. Hospitals that achieve certain quality benchmarks are rewarded with these incentive payments. In this manner, CMS is reallocating a portion of Medicare hospital payments to the higher-performing hospitals, which incentivizes hospitals to improve patient quality.

3.2.2 Hospital-Acquired Conditions and Hospital Preventable Readmissions

Provisions included in the ACA related to hospital-acquired conditions (HACs)—conditions acquired by patients during a hospital stay—and preventable readmissions also aim to improve quality of care at hospitals. For 2015, Medicare payments related to HACs are reduced by 1%, with the goal of improving infection control programs at hospitals. According to CMS, 724

2 The Henry J. Kaiser Family Foundation. "State Health Insurance Marketplace Types, 2015." kff.org/health-reform/state-indicator/state-health-insurance-marketplace-types. Accessed July 18, 2015.

3 The Advisory Board Co., "Where the States Stand on Medicaid Expansion." www.advisory.com/daily-briefing/resources/primers/medicaidmap. Accessed July 18, 2015.

4 Department of Health and Human Services Office of the Assistant Secretary for Planning and Evaluation, "Insurance Expansion, Hospital Uncompensated Care, and the Affordable Care Act," March 25, 2015. www.aspe.hhs.gov/health/reports/2015/MedicaidExpansion/ib_UncompensatedCare.pdf. Accessed July 18, 2015.

hospitals fell within the worst-performing quartile and face a 1% reduction in their reimbursement for all Medicare discharges in 2015.[5]

The ACA also penalizes hospitals that have a higher-than-expected readmission rate for certain diagnoses. For purposes of this calculation, a readmission is defined as a patient admitted to a hospital within 30 days after being discharged from a previous inpatient stay. The intent of this provision is to incentivize hospitals to improve patient discharge instructions and the coordination of post-acute care services. For 2015 and beyond, the largest potential reduction for Medicare readmissions is 3%. According to a study conducted by the Kaiser Family Foundation, a projected 83% of 2015 Medicare admissions will be to hospitals receiving either no readmission penalty or penalties less than 1%.[6]

3.3 Reduce Costs to the Healthcare System

3.3.1 Hospital Market Basket Reductions

Similar to the Consumer Price Index (CPI), the hospital market basket is a fixed-weight index of the costs of hospital goods and services that is utilized by CMS to determine hospital fee schedule changes. Under the ACA, the hospital market basket is automatically reduced by 0.2% in 2015 and 2016, and 0.75% for 2017 through 2019.

3.3.2 Disproportionate Share Hospital Payment Reductions

The Disproportionate Share Hospital (DSH) program provides additional payments to hospitals that serve a high percentage of low-income or indigent patients. The ACA included cuts to the Medicare DSH payments by $22.1 billion from 2014 through 2019.[7] DSH cuts were included in the ACA under the theory that the uninsured population would decline due to individual insurance mandates and Medicaid expansion initiatives. However, with many states not electing to expand Medicaid coverage, the actual declines in the uninsured population have been less than initially estimated.

4.0 Current Challenges Facing Hospitals

In the midst of the sweeping changes brought about by the ACA, hospitals also are facing numerous operational challenges. These challenges are changing the way hospitals conduct business and the delivery models for patient care. Accordingly, hospital management needs to have proactive strategies to address these issues.

5 Maureen McKinney, "Hospital-Acquired Conditions Mean Medicare Penalties for 700-Plus Hospitals," *Modern Healthcare*, Dec. 18, 2014. www.modernhealthcare.com/article/20141218/NEWS/312189995. Accessed July 18, 2015.

6 Cristina Boccuti and Giselle Casillas, "Aiming for Fewer Hospital U-Turns: The Medicare Hospital Readmission Reduction Program," The Henry J. Kaiser Family Foundation, Jan. 29, 2015. Accessed July 19, 2015.

7 American Hospital Association, "Medicare DSH Fact Sheet," March 11, 2015. www.aha.org/content/13/fs-dsh.pdf. Accessed July 19, 2015.

4.1 Transition to Value-Based Reimbursement

No other issue presents as many challenges to the U.S. healthcare system as the shift to value-based reimbursement; however, every challenge presents an opportunity for success. Traditionally, hospitals (and most other health service providers) have been paid under a fee-for-service model in which payment was made for procedures performed regardless of the efficacy of the procedure or the quality of patient care. However, the trend of paying for quality care was kicked into high gear with the passage of the ACA. Many commercial insurers are following the government's lead and have now begun reimbursing hospitals for the quality of care provided.

This transformation in reimbursement is generating changes in the way healthcare services are provided. Hospitals are affiliating with other health service providers in various initiatives to better coordinate patient care, reduce costs, and provide more efficient healthcare services. Some of these initiatives include accountable care organizations, clinical co-management arrangements, clinically integrated networks, patient-centered medical homes, and retail health clinics. Gone are the days when a hospital only concerned itself with caring for the patients within its four walls. In this new era of healthcare, successful hospitals will proactively seek out partnerships and affiliations with other service providers in the community to provide higher quality and better coordinated patient care.

4.2 Increased Reporting Requirements

The shift to value-based reimbursement brings about increased administrative and reporting requirements for hospitals. Hospitals now must monitor and record patient outcomes and quality metrics in order to appropriately report the results to third-party payors. To appropriately address these new reporting requirements, hospitals need to train and educate physicians and providers to document the quality data in a manner that can be efficiently reported to outside parties.

Another administrative burden to hospitals is the impending conversion from ICD-9 to ICD-10. International Classification of Diseases (ICD) is the coding system used to submit patient claims to payors. ICD-10 is a total redesign of the diagnosis codes of ICD-9, requiring hospitals to make significant capital investments in information technology. The ICD-10 implementation deadline has been postponed several times; however, the current implementation deadline is set for Oct. 1, 2015.

4.3 Increased Governmental Scrutiny

Hospitals are facing unprecedented governmental scrutiny and regulatory enforcement actions. CMS created the Health Care Fraud Prevention and Enforcement Action Team (HEAT) in 2009 to prevent and prosecute fraud and abuse in the Medicare and Medicaid programs. Additionally, the Medicare Recovery Audit Contractor (RAC) program was instituted in 2006 to identify Medicare overpayments and underpayments to healthcare providers. The ACA increased the funding levels for these and other fraud prevention programs and expanded the reach of the RAC program. As a result, the Health Care Fraud and Abuse Control (HCFAC) program reported that the government recovered over $2.3 billion in healthcare fraud judgments and settlements in 2014.[8]

Several whistleblower cases also have been successfully brought against hospitals that were alleged to be in violation of the Stark Law. The penalties imposed were severe, reaching into the multi-million-dollar range and beyond. In several such instances, these hospitals had relied upon a third-party fair market value opinion. It is therefore imperative for healthcare appraisers to understand the potential risks associated with such transactions.

4.4 Physician Shortages

A growing problem facing hospitals is a shortage of medical service providers. According to a March 2015 study conducted by IHS Inc. at the request of The Association of American Medical Colleges (AAMC), demand for physician services will outpace the supply of physicians, leading to a projected shortfall of approximately 46,000 to 90,000 physicians by 2025.[9] The majority of the projected shortfall is anticipated for specialty surgeons. Rural hospitals will most likely feel the brunt of these shortages, as many already experience difficulty in attracting physician specialists.

5.0 Hospital Reimbursement

5.1 Inpatient Admissions and Inpatient Reimbursement

An inpatient is admitted to the hospital when the patient's medical procedure requires an overnight stay. Inpatient admissions drive the amount of inpatient revenue the hospital receives. The total number of days that a patient remains in the hospital after being admitted is referred to as patient days. Patient days also drive another important performance measure for hospitals known as average length of stay (ALOS). ALOS is generally computed as total patient days divided by patient admissions (or patient discharges).

Inpatient services are reimbursed for Medicare patients under the Medicare inpatient prospective payment system (IPPS). Under the IPPS, patients are grouped into Medicare severity diagnosis-related groups (MS-DRGs) based upon the patient's diagnosis and the severity of the diagnosis assigned at the time of discharge. Reimbursement for an MS-DRG is based on the estimated hospital cost for a specific diagnosis. Medicare inpatient payment rates are updated annually based upon market basket updates. The market basket is designed to reflect price inflation by indexing the prices of a mix of goods and services for a certain time period to a base time period.[10]

8 The Department of Health and Human Services and The Department of Justice, "Health Care Fraud and Abuse Control Program Annual Report for Fiscal Year 2014." March 19, 2015. oig.hhs.gov/publications/docs/hcfac/FY2014-hcfac.pdf. Accessed July 19, 2015.

9 Association of American Medical Colleges, "New Physician Workforce Projections Show the Doctor Shortage Remains Significant." March 3, 2015. www.aamc.org/newsroom/newsreleases/426166/20150303.html. Accessed July 19, 2015.

10 The Centers for Medicare & Medicaid Services website, cms.hhs.gov/MedicareProgramRatesStats/downloads/info.pdf.

It is important to note that the MS-DRG is a flat rate, meaning that a hospital is reimbursed the same amount regardless of a particular patient's cost. In other words, a hospital receives the same reimbursement for a diagnosis whether the patient stays one day or three days. Accordingly, under the Medicare MS-DRG system, a hospital has the economic incentive to reduce its ALOS.

A hospital's Medicare base reimbursement rate for inpatient services is divided into a labor and nonlabor portion. The labor portion is adjusted by the hospital's local wage index, and the nonlabor portion is adjusted by a cost-of-living adjustment factor.[11] However, a hospital can receive various supplemental payments—for instance, if its costs for treating a patient exceed the usual Medicare reimbursement for that patient's treatment by a certain threshold (referred to as "outlier payments")[12] or if it serves a disproportionately high percentage of low-income patients (referred to as "disproportionate share hospital payments").[13]

Some commercial insurance payors reimburse inpatient services on a per diem basis. Under this method, a hospital will receive reimbursement for an inpatient based on the number of days the patient is hospitalized. Since the first inpatient day is generally the most expensive in terms of the hospital's cost, some per diem structures pay more the first day than subsequent days. Variation also occurs in subsequent days' per diem amounts. This per diem rate can also fluctuate based upon the patient's diagnosis and severity. Other payors can pay based upon other negotiated reimbursement methods, such as a percentage of charges billed, or under a capitation plan, which provides a fixed payment per member per month (PMPM) regardless of the hospital services actually provided.

5.2 Outpatient Visits and Outpatient Reimbursement

An outpatient visit is classified as any medical procedure performed in a hospital setting that does not require an overnight stay. Outpatient visits are the volume driver for a hospital's outpatient revenues, which can often be very profitable.

Outpatient services are generally reimbursed for Medicare patients under the Medicare outpatient prospective payment system (OPPS). Under OPPS, services are classified into ambulatory payment classifications (APCs) based on similar clinical procedures and required resources. Each APC has its own payment rate, which is adjusted based on geographic wage variations.[14]

Reimbursement methods can vary widely from one non-Medicare payor to another (i.e., fee for service, percentage of charges billed, capitation, and so on).

11 Centers for Medicare & Medicaid Services website, Overview of the IPPS.

12 Centers for Medicare & Medicaid Services website, Outlier Payments. www.cms.gov/Medicare/Medicare-Fee-for-Service-Payment/AcuteInpatientPPS/outlier.html.

13 Centers for Medicare & Medicaid Services website, Overview of the IPPS.

14 Centers for Medicare & Medicaid Services website, "Hospital Outpatient Prospective Payment System—Payment System Fact Sheet Series." www.cms.gov/Outreach-and-Education/Medicare-Learning-Network-MLN/MLNProducts/downloads/hospitaloutpaysysfctsht.pdf.

Understanding these value drivers and how they interact with each other is essential when valuing a hospital. It is important for the appraiser to tailor the information request list to the client so that the received data can be useful in identifying trends in these value drivers.

6.0 Valuation Process

The key processes for valuing hospitals are summarized below.

6.1 Information Gathering

The information-gathering process for any valuation is important, and hospitals are certainly no exception. It is important to not only obtain pertinent financial information, but also to get it in a format that allows the appraiser to identify trends and calculate ratios specific to the hospital. With the hospital's value drivers in mind, the appraiser should request information that will identify historical trends and assist with preparing/evaluating cash flow projections. Examples of the types of information typically needed are summarized below.

1. For-profit versus not-for-profit status;
2. Number of patient beds, both licensed and in use;
3. Facility location(s);
4. Ownership information (i.e., community board, physician investors, corporate-owned, and so on);
5. Services provided, key physician relationships (historically and prospectively), and the operating history of the hospital;
6. Payor mix information and the status of key commercial payor contracts, as well as the hospital's in-network or out-of-network status;
7. Certificate of need requirements;
8. Detailed financial statements for the last five years, with revenue segregated by inpatient and outpatient revenue, and any other major service lines;
9. Historical inpatient admissions, inpatient days, and outpatient visits for the last five years;
10. Key operating statistics of the hospital for the last five years, such as adjusted patient days, average length of stay, occupancy rate, and so on;
11. Hospital management's actions and plans regarding the challenges and opportunities related to the ACA;
12. Operating budgets and/or projections; and
13. Prospectuses required for tax-exempt bond financing by exempt hospitals. Federal

law and underwriting standards require far more information in these documents than typically seen in a financial statement or even a Form 990.

Of course, this list is not exhaustive, but will provide the appraiser with a good starting point for recognizing and analyzing various trends present for the hospital being valued.

6.2 Analyzing Financial Ratios and Trends

After obtaining the necessary data, the appraiser must analyze it to identify important trends. Hospitals have unique ratios and statistics that should be calculated and analyzed. This analysis can help identify historical trends for projecting future cash flows; it is also useful in assessing potential risks and normalization adjustments.

Obviously, the appraiser should consider the growth trends in both inpatient and outpatient revenues, inpatient admissions, and outpatient visits. Some of the other important statistics and ratios to consider are as follows:

1. *Patient days*—the number of days the inpatient is in the hospital;
2. *Adjusted patient days (APD)*—patient days plus the calculated outpatient days. The formulation can vary, but may be: (patient days + [outpatient visits × 50%]);
3. *Average length of stay (ALOS)*—calculated as the total inpatient days divided by total inpatient admissions;
4. *Average daily census (ADC)*—calculated as inpatient days divided by 365 days per year;
5. *Occupancy rate*—calculated as the ADC divided by the total number of hospital beds in service;
6. *Gross and net inpatient revenue per day;*
7. *Gross and net outpatient revenue per outpatient visit;*
8. *Total gross and net patient revenue per APD;*
9. *Medical supplies expense per APD;*
10. *Bad debt expense as a percentage of net patient revenue;*
11. *Staff full-time equivalents (FTEs) divided by APD*; and
12. *Salaries, wages, and benefits divided by FTEs.*

Trends in these statistics should be observed and understood, because they will contribute to developing reasonable projections of future cash flows. For example, the ALOS statistic is important in determining how efficiently a hospital is admitting and treating its patients. An increasing ALOS could be negative for a hospital, especially a hospital with a high Medicare patient mix, since Medicare reimburses on a DRG basis, not on a per diem basis. The occupancy rate can give an appraiser an idea of how well the hospital is utilizing its beds and whether it may be facing capacity constraints regarding future growth. The trends in gross and net patient revenues per APD can give some idea of the contracting strength of the hospital. Medical supplies expense per APD can provide insight into how efficiently a hospital is managing its medical supplies. The staffing ratios can also provide insights into how well the hospital is managing its employee costs. The more an appraiser can digest and decipher the reasons for the historical trends, the better basis he or she will have for developing and/or evaluating future cash flow projections.

6.3 Normalization Adjustments

After analyzing the financial trends of the hospital, normalization adjustments may be necessary. The primary purpose of normalization adjustments is to produce a financial picture that will be used as a basis for future cash flow projections. Hospitals generally have more sophisticated accounting systems than other healthcare businesses. Therefore, normalization adjustments for hospitals may entail only eliminating nonrecurring items or adjustments for income taxes. However, historical trends in expenses, especially as a percentage of revenues, should be considered to identify any unusual expenses. Some of the largest expenses for a hospital are salaries and wages, so any abnormal trends in terms of salaries per FTE should be discussed with the client and normalized if necessary. Medical supplies are another large expense item for hospitals. Any significant swings in terms of medical supplies as a percentage of revenue should be understood and normalized if appropriate. Remember that the primary purpose of normalization adjustments is to restate the financials in a manner that will be consistent with expected future operations.

6.4 Income Approach

In preparing the income approach value, the appraiser should review for reasonableness the client's operating budget or financial projections (if available) by comparing the projections to observed financial trends. If, after review and discussion with the client, the projections appear reasonable, then they can probably be used as a guide for projecting future cash flows.

In projecting future revenues, growth factors for both volumes and net revenues should be considered. For inpatient revenues, the volume driver will be inpatient admissions and patient days, while the driver for outpatient revenues will be outpatient visits. Typically for a hospital, inpatient admissions are driven by a number of factors, including, but not limited to, the location and attractiveness of the facility, types of services provided at the hospital, key physicians practicing at the hospital, key insurer payor contracts, competitive environment in the community, population demographics (including growth, affluence, and age), and the strength of the hospital's medical staff. Outpatient visits will typically be driven by the types of surgeries performed at the hospital, any specialized services provided at the hospital (such as imaging services or cancer treatment), key insurance payors, the hospital's relationship with area physicians, and the proximity and prevalence of competing physician-owned outpatient facilities (particularly ASCs). The appraiser should discuss these and any other items affecting volume growth with the client and develop a good understanding of how the hospital is affected by these factors. Historical growth trends in inpatient admissions, inpatient days, and outpatient visits should be analyzed and factored into any volume projections. Also, the occupancy rate should be calculated for each projected period to ensure that projected volume growth does not exceed the hospital's capacity.

For projections of the net charge rates of the hospital, analyzing the hospital's payor mix is crucial. For instance, if a hospital has a high Medicare patient mix, its reimbursement will be greatly affected by any reimbursement changes put forth by CMS. The Medicare reimbursement rates for IPPS and OPPS are updated annually and published on the CMS website. Likewise, a hospital with a large percentage of commercial payors will be more affected by changes in negotiated rates or per diems. An appraiser should consider and discuss in detail with the client the contracting strength of the hospital, as well as expectations of any future changes in rates or commercial insurers.

Operating expenses should be projected based upon whether the expense is generally more fixed or variable in nature. For example, facility rent would typically be projected as a fixed expense, with periodic inflationary adjustments. In contrast, bad debt expense or medical supplies expense should probably be projected as a percentage of projected net patient revenues or as a ratio to APD. However, some expenses contain both variable and fixed components, such as salaries and wages. One way to project salaries and wages could be to discuss with the client what level of FTE staffing would be necessary to support any projected volume growth and multiply the projected FTEs by an average salary per FTE employee, plus inflationary adjustments during the projection period. Whatever method is employed, it is important to ensure that the growth trends in the operating expenses are reasonable compared to the growth trends in the projected volumes and revenues.

Capital expenditures of a hospital can be extremely important in the valuation. The appraiser should discuss with the client any current or planned facility expansions or large equipment purchases, such as highly specialized diagnostic imaging or cancer treatment equipment. The appraiser also should keep in mind that significant capital equipment expenditures can greatly influence the projected inpatient and outpatient volumes. In addition to any planned capital expenditures, the appraiser should make an allowance for the replacement of the hospital's current facility and equipment.

In developing the weighted average cost of capital (WACC), the appraiser should ensure that it corresponds to the risks associated with the projected earnings stream. Specific company risk factors that either increase or decrease risk should be considered. Some of these factors may include the hospital's operating history (volatile versus stable), status of payor contracts, strength of physician relationships, presence of any certificate of need (CON) requirements, management depth, local competitive environment, and the Medicare reimbursement outlook (particularly if the hospital has a high Medicare patient mix).

6.5 Asset Approach

Under the asset approach, the hospital's assets and liabilities should be adjusted to fair market value. Typically, one of the largest assets for a hospital is its real estate and related improvements. As with nonhealthcare valuations, the appraiser should consider the need to have real estate and improvements valued by a qualified real estate appraiser.

The asset approach for a hospital valuation has some unique characteristics that differentiate it from nonhealthcare valuations. Hospitals typically have intangible assets that are different than nonhealthcare entities. One such intangible asset is a CON.

A CON is a state-regulated license to perform certain medical services. The purpose of the CON is to ensure that health providers and services are correctly matched to the needs of those specific health providers and services in a designated area. Not every state has CON requirements, so the appraiser should research whether the hospital being valued is located in a state that has one. Obtaining a CON can be expensive and time-consuming, and in some cases, the granting of a CON can be uncertain or even impossible (due to an excess supply of providers or a moratorium). A CON is generally valued under one of two methods: (1) cost to re-create method, or (2) relief from royalty method.

Another unique intangible asset that the appraiser should consider is favorable or above-market payor contracts. This scenario may be present if the hospital has particular contracting power or exclusive contracts with payors and is experiencing above-market profits. The appraiser should discuss with the client the nature of any above-market payor contracts, the likelihood of their future status, and their potential financial impact on the hospital.

As with other nonhealthcare valuations, intangible assets such as trade name and trained and assembled workforce should be considered. However, in assigning values to the intangible assets, the appraiser must remember that patient activity (and therefore, value) for a hospital is primarily driven by factors such as facility location, services provided, insurance coverage, and medical staff.

Typically, patient files are not valued in a hospital setting, since (unlike a medical practice) the likelihood of the patient returning to the hospital for future care is either unlikely or unknown. Also, the costs of maintaining, retrieving, and overseeing the patient file may outweigh its future economic benefits (if any).

6.6 Market Approach

Like nonhealthcare valuations, the market approach for a hospital is typically performed under two methods: (1) comparable transactions method, and (2) guideline company method.

A source for finding comparable transactions for hospitals is in the Forms 10-K or 10-Q of publicly traded hospital corporations. In addition, Irving Levin Associates Inc. publishes an annual report titled *The Healthcare Acquisition Report,* which compiles transaction information for hospitals and other healthcare providers. The appraiser can compile and sort the data based on a number of factors, including size in terms of revenues and number of beds, geographic location, for-profit versus not-for-profit status, and number of hospital facilities.

The hospital transaction environment has been active, with a major trend in consolidation. According to *The Health Care Acquisition Report 2015,* the total number of hospital transactions for 2010 through 2015 appears in the exhibit.

Total Transactions (Annual for 2010 to 2014)

	2010	2011	2012	2013	2014
Number of Deals	72	90	107	88	100
Number of Hospitals	125	156	244	296	178
Median Price to Revenue	0.60x	0.68x	0.55x	0.49x	0.57x
Median Price to EBITDA	8.3x	10.1x	7.9x	7.5x	7.2x

An interesting trend to note from the above statistics is the increase in the number of deals from 2010, coupled with declining price-to-revenue and price-to-EBITDA multiples. As the ACA provisions have been enacted and financial pressures have been mounting on hospitals, many financially distressed hospitals have sought out acquisitions by larger, more financially stable health systems. The proliferation of these transactions most likely has depressed the hospital pricing multiples in recent years.

The guideline company method can be used as a reasonableness check for the values calculated under the other valuation methods by comparing the pricing multiples (i.e., total invested capital [TIC] to revenue, TIC to EBITDA) for the publicly traded hospitals to the subject hospital's valuation multiples. The reason that this method is generally not the primary indication of value is that the publicly traded hospital corporations generally own dozens of hospitals throughout the United States and even internationally. Therefore, publicly traded hospitals have distinct advantages over smaller hospitals, including contracting power, geographic diversity, access to capital, and the ability to purchase profitable hospitals and divest low-performing hospitals. The guideline company method also can be used to give an appraiser an idea of the hospital industry's growth, EBITDA margin, and capital structure.

Some of the current publicly traded hospital corporations are as follows:

- HCA Holdings Inc. (HCA);
- Tenet Healthcare (THC);
- Community Health Systems (CYH);
- LifePoint Hospital Inc. (LPNT); and
- Universal Health Services (UHS).

6.7 Reconciliation of Values

In reconciling or selecting the final conclusion of value for a subject hospital, the appraiser, based on his or her research, needs to consider the current transaction environment. An important consideration is whether the market is active with numerous participants and abundant capital. In this type of environment, the most likely buyer of a hospital may be another hospital or health system that will continue its operations as a hospital. This fact should be remembered when reconciling the values under each valuation approach.

There could be instances where the asset approach value is higher than the values under the income or market approaches. For example, a hospital could have a large value under the asset approach if its facilities are sizeable complexes that would be costly to replace. For transaction purposes, the probable buyer would be a hospital system that would continue to operate the facility as a hospital with the assets already in place; therefore, more weight may be given to the income approach value, because it encompasses the future cash flows available to an investor from the hospital's operations. While the market approach value is generally not relied upon as a primary indication of value, due to the lack of specific information regarding the transactions (i.e., payor mix, contracting strength, level of competition, and so on), it is important for the appraiser to understand where his or her valuation falls in relation to the observed marketplace transactions.

7.0 Conclusion

Hospital valuations require a thorough understanding of the industry (and specifically, the challenges and opportunities related to the ACA and the current healthcare industry transformation), current hospital trends, and various value drivers. The appraiser should stay abreast of Medicare's reimbursement environment, because it can have a significant impact on the profitability of hospitals. The more an appraiser can develop an understanding of the hospital industry and its value drivers, the more sound opinion of value he or she can render.

8.0 Resource Materials

The following is a listing of some helpful resources to consider when undertaking a hospital valuation:

- American Hospital Association—www.aha.org;
- Centers for Medicare & Medicaid Services—www.cms.gov;
- Optum360—*Almanac of Hospital Financial and Operating Indicators;*
- Irving Levin Associates Inc.—*The Healthcare Acquisition Report;*
- Duff & Phelps, LLC—*2014 Valuation Handbook – Industry Cost of Capital;*
- IRS Form 990 Finder—www.foundationcenter.org/findfunders/990finder; and

- Merritt Hawkins Physician Inpatient/Outpatient Revenue Survey—www.merritthawkins.com/compensation-surveys.aspx.

Chapter 19.
Home Healthcare Services

CONTENTS

Chapter 19.
Home Healthcare Services

By Alan B. Simons, CPA/ABV/CFF, CMPE

The valuation approaches and methods used to value home healthcare businesses are no different than any other business. However, to competently value these businesses, an appraiser must understand the industry and its associated risks. In addition, a number of home healthcare providers are also nonprofit organizations or they may be sold to a nonprofit organization. Valuing transactions involving nonprofit organizations has its own unique issues. As a result, we will focus on what differentiates these businesses from others and what appraisers need to understand to develop a credible business valuation.

1.0 The Industry

Home health and hospice care is a subset of all healthcare providers (such as hospitals, physicians, senior care, and so on) that further breaks down into the following five major service lines:

- Home health—skilled nursing, physical therapy, occupational therapy, speech therapy, aid service, and medical social work provided to patients in their home;
- Home hospice—care provided for terminally (life expectancy of six months or less) ill patients and their families in their homes (can also be provided at other care sites);
- Private duty and staffing services—personal care and supportive services that are primarily provided by a home care aid;
- Home medical and respiratory equipment—durable medical equipment such as walkers, beds, wheelchairs, and oxygen concentrators; and
- Home infusion—intravenous therapies such as parenteral nutrition, antibiotics, and chemotherapy.

The goal of home health care is to provide a continuum of services designed to allow disabled or older individuals to stay in their homes for support and treatment as an alternative to assisted living, nursing homes, and hospital facilities. Proponents of home health care believe it is less expensive and a better care alternative for most people.

These services, when combined, would represent a very comprehensive home healthcare business. But, more often than not, the appraiser will be valuing businesses with fewer service lines, and often the business may be comprised of only one service line.

The profitability and risks associated with each of these service lines is driven by a unique set of variables, making it difficult to make global assumptions about the home healthcare business. The appraiser needs to develop an understanding of each service line and how these service lines interact if the subject business operates in two or more.

In some organizations, each service line can stand on its own as an independent, financially viable business. When this is the case, each business has a broad source of patient referrals independent of the other service lines. Under this scenario, each service line and the business as a whole would have more value than when service lines are interdependent upon each other for referrals.

Acronyms and Abbreviations Used

ACA—Affordable Care Act

ADC—average daily census

ASP—average sales price

AWP—average wholesale price

CAP—community alternative programs

CBSA—core-based statistical area

CIA—corporate integrity agreement

CMS—Centers for Medicare and Medicaid Services

CON—certificate of need

HHA—home health agencies

HHRG—home health resource groups

HIT—home infusion therapy

HME—home medical equipment funding

LUPA—low utilization payment adjustment

MedPAC—Medicare Payment Advisory Commission

OASIS—outcome and assessment information set

OIG—Office of the Inspector General

PPS—prospective payment system

For example, a service line might have no value to a potential buyer if all or most of its business was dependent on a previously related entity. If the service line is sold without the related entity, there is no guarantee that referrals (and therefore, the business) will continue. This can happen when a home health business or service line is a "captive" of a hospital or nursing home. It can also happen when a service line gets most or all of its referrals because of its relationship or proximity to one or more other related service lines. Generally, a home health business is a core business or service line when it has a broad base of referral sources, and other service lines are added to enhance its profitability. In this case, most or all of the value may reside in the core business.

Appraisers need to understand the relationship among the service lines and referral sources to determine where the value resides. This is particularly important when the business is a captive or when not all of the service lines are being sold together.

In addition the Affordable Care Act (ACA) is challenging home health service lines to develop quality measures that will impact future payments. An appraiser needs an understanding of the evolving changes in value-based payment plans that will increase payments for positive performance and decrease payments for negative performance. Another ACA challenge for home health service lines will be the bundling of payments based on an acute episode of care. New bundled payment plans for hip and knee replacements are proposed to start in 2016. The bundled payment would be paid to the acute care hospital and the hospital will be responsible for providing the care needed by the patient for 90 days after discharge.

The appraiser will want to have a discussion with management about the changes that are occurring in the home health provider's community. Are there new entities such as accountable care organizations (ACOs) that are being established to manage the care of individuals in the community? Will these ACOs contract with any willing home healthcare provider or are they going to limit the number of providers? What will be the factors and measurements used to select a home healthcare provider?

2.0 Funding of Home Health Products and Services

Except for private duty services, most home care products and services are funded by government sources, such as Medicare and Medicaid, commercial healthcare insurance, and to a lesser extent, payments from individuals (self-pay or private pay).

Except for reimbursement by Medicare and individuals (because individuals, or "self-pay," would generally pay actual charges), the calculation and method of reimbursement for services can vary for each commercial insurance plan and for each state in the case of Medicaid. As a result, an explanation of each reimbursement system is beyond the scope of this book. However, since Medicare reimbursement is reasonably consistent and is frequently a significant percentage of a provider's total revenue, we will generally explain how Medicare reimbursement works and how it may change as of this writing.

In proposed rules from CMS for the 2016 Medicare home health rates, it was reported that Medicare paid home health agencies approximately $17.9 billion, covering 3.5 million beneficiaries, which means that the average Medicare reimbursement was $5,114 per beneficiary. Medicare home health cost report data for 2013 reflect a median Medicare payment of $2,804 per episode, a cost of $2,534 per episode, and a margin of $270 per episode or 9.6%. According to the 2015 MedPAC report, two factors have contributed to payments exceeding costs: Fewer visits are delivered in an episode than is assumed in Medicare's rates, and cost growth has been lower than the annual payment updates for home healthcare. In 2013 the median volume of visits per episode was 16.42, which includes a mix of all disciplines of services. These are useful benchmarks in evaluating the relative performance of home health agencies.

It is incumbent upon appraisers to develop an understanding of reimbursement for the payors that drive each service line and those that drive the business being valued. While it is generally assumed that home healthcare services are provided to the elderly, it is not always the case. However, most services provided to the elderly and the disabled will be funded either directly by Medicare or through commercial insurance payors that operate Medicare Advantage plans. If and when Medicare coverage runs out, reimbursement may come directly from the individual or from Medicaid for low-income beneficiaries. Younger patients may be funded through commercial insurance, self-pay, or Medicaid if they meet the requirements. Similar to Medicare Advantage Plans, some states may contract with commercial insurance plans to operate a managed care organization (MCO) that assumes all risk for the coverage of the Medicaid population. Examples of commercial insurers that operate Medicaid managed care plans include Blue Cross/Blue Shield, United, CIGNA, and Humana. In some cases, the state retains administrative control of allowed services, fee schedules, and other costs, and a third-party administrator focuses on provider payment processing, claim denials, and other administrative functions. In addition, many insurance plans require some contribution (or payment) from the beneficiary. It should be noted that the health exchanges that have been established under the ACA are offering insurance products from some of these same insurance companies.

A general discussion of how Medicare reimburses home health services and products follows.

2.1 How Home Healthcare Services and Products Are Purchased

Home healthcare treatment plans are prescribed by a patient's physician and provided by a healthcare agency (the provider). Most home healthcare products and services are funded by Medicare, particularly for older or disabled patients. A portion of home health is funded by Medicaid, for lower-income patients; commercial insurance, primarily for patients below Medicare age; and self (or private) pay, for either uninsured patients or for products or services that are not covered by Medicare, Medicaid, or insurance.

During a valuation engagement, appraisers need to understand the mix of payors to evaluate risks and whether normalizing adjustments might be required.

For example, businesses funded primarily by Medicare are at risk for changes in reimbursement (rates and coverage criteria) and age demographics for the market. Businesses funded by commercial insurance may be at risk for the economy and employee layoffs, which would reduce the population covered by commercial insurance. Businesses reliant on payment from individuals (private or self-pay) would also be dependent on the economy. Medicaid rules can be different in every state and are subject to changes in state regulations. Population growth or decline by age and income also need to be considered because it would impact the number of potential patients and how they might pay for these services in the future.

When valuing a controlling interest, the appraiser should consider whether typical normalizing adjustments (for example, owners' compensation and other perquisites or nonrecurring revenues or expenses) need to be made. In addition, normalizing adjustments to revenue might be required if the payor mix being evaluated is not normal for the market, if there are opportunities to add payors, or if the business is not billing properly or is not being reimbursed properly. Assuming these enhancements are available to most buyers in the marketplace, the adjustments would be consistent with the fair market value standard.

3.0 Home Health Funding

3.1 Medicare

Since October 2000, Medicare funds the base payment for home health care under a prospective payment system (PPS). Under PPS, providers are reimbursed a fixed payment for services. Future reimbursement is determined by Congress and is influenced by historical industry results. Medicare pays for home health services in 60-day episodes. Most patients complete their care within 60 days. Additional 60-day episodes may be reimbursed until the patient recovers or moves to an alternative provider, such as a hospital or nursing home, or dies. Often patients are discharged from a "skilled plan of care" and obtain in-home aid, chore, and homemaker services paid for privately (private duty[1]) or possibly using Medicaid funds.

Providers (home health agencies, or HHAs) are paid one fee for each 60-day episode. Medicare adjusts payments to reflect the level of care and services required based on home health resource groups (HHRGs) and local wage differences. It will also increase the payment for the costliest patients (outliers) and reduce the payment for patients needing significantly less than 60 days of services. If there were less than five visits in the 60-day episode, a low utilization payment adjustment (or LUPA) is made. Low utilization care is paid on a per-visit basis using a national standard rate that is wage-adjusted based on the core-based statistical area (CBSA) location of the patient.

Medicare implemented the HHRG-153 system on Jan. 1, 2008, which utilizes 153 resource groups and replaces the prior system that used only 80 resource groups. These resource groups establish different payment rates based on patient need (acuity values) that are derived from a standardized national assessment instrument (called outcome and assessment information set, or OASIS).

Appraisers need to be comfortable that historical and forecasted revenues are reasonable based upon the payment system in effect at the time or proposed changes being considered and the likelihood that they could become law (either Medicare or a state Medicaid program). In addition, historical and forecasted revenues could be too high or too low if the level of care provided to patients is not properly determined. However, few appraisers could make this determination without using a specialist and most appraisers will consider this outside the scope of their work. Nonetheless, appraisers should become familiar enough with the industry to understand changes in reimbursement and the associated risks so that they can evaluate management's

1 It is generally paid by the individual or the individual might get reimbursed through private insurance such as long-term care insurance.

forecast assumptions for reasonableness. Industry surveys and articles that include historical data or assumptions about the impact of future reimbursement changes may be available. Benchmarking the business against similar businesses may help appraisers determine whether historical and forecasted revenue assumptions are reasonable.

4.0 Hospice Funding

4.1 Medicare

Hospice services are available to terminally ill patients with less than six months to live. A physician must certify a patient's terminal illness to qualify for the benefit. Benefits are provided in two 90-day increments and an unlimited number of 60-day increments, but payments are subject to the caps discussed below.

Hospice agencies are paid a CBSA (core-based statistical area) wage-adjusted daily rate based on the level of patient care required, which include:

- Routine home care;
- Continuous home care;
- Inpatient respite care; and
- General inpatient care.

The daily rate includes a labor and nonlabor component and is intended to cover all services required during hospice care. The payment rates are adjusted annually by a congressionally approved market basket inflation rate to account for both inflation and differences in market wage rates. The labor component is adjusted based on the national wage index and the nonlabor component is adjusted based on the inflation factor approved by Congress.

Total payments to a provider are limited by two caps: (1) inpatient care (for example, in a facility such as a hospital or skilled nursing facility—not home hospice) may not exceed 20% of total patient care days; and (2) an aggregate annual payment amount (an amount available to pay all Medicare hospice claims in a given year intended to control increasing Medicare costs) based on the number of patients electing the hospice benefit for the first time within the cap period. The hospice aggregate cap is adjusted annually based on the consumer price index, but the base level of Medicare hospice funding stays constant.

Appraisers should research how these two caps might affect revenue forecasts. Longer average length of stays may cause the aggregate payment to be spread among fewer patients, thereby reducing the benefit available on a per-patient basis. The provider could be liable for a repayment to Medicare for having exceeded the cap limit. A national concern has arisen over inappropriate referrals to hospice, and payment rate reform was called for in the ACA. Starting Oct.

1, 2015, patients that exceed 60 days of coverage will be paid at a lower rate per day. Additional regulatory requirements for more frequent clinical assessments are required for patients that are in care over 180 days. The point is that this is a very tricky area, and revenue forecasts and risk rates need to be evaluated based on the facts known at the time of the valuation.

5.0 Private Duty Funding

Private duty home care services are not funded by Medicare but may be funded through self-pay or government-funded through Medicaid and Medicaid Waiver Community Alternative Programs (CAP) and long-term care insurance.

When valuing a private-duty business, appraisers need to consider patient demographics, particularly wealth factors, to determine the potential for services and profitability. Private-duty businesses are generally more profitable in wealthier communities where patients can fund services through self-pay and long-term care insurance. A provider that is heavily dependent on Medicaid funding for in-home aid services has an increased risk of losses or low margins on this service line.

6.0 Home Medical Equipment Funding[2] (HME)

6.1 Medicare

Medicare reimburses many parts of the country under the Durable Medical Equipment, Prosthetics, Orthotics, and Supplies (DMEPOS) Competitive Bidding Program. Under the DMEPOS Competitive Bidding Program, HME providers located in a competitive bidding area (CBA) are reimbursed the same single payment amount for each item. The reimbursement in each CBA is the result of a bidding process. Medicare regulations allow for the subdivision of CBAs in areas with populations of 8.0 million or more. Most metropolitan statistical areas (MSAs) have one CBA; however, the largest MSAs may have multiple CBAs. The single payment amount in CBAs replaces payments under a fee schedule based on historical supplier charges. The fee schedule was developed in the 1980s and periodically adjusted for inflation. HME providers not located in a CBA are reimbursed based on the adjusted 1980s fee schedule. Numerous studies have determined that payments under the 1980s fee schedule are excessive and that the DMEPOS has save hundreds of millions of dollars.

In addition, Medicare follows a policy referred to as "capped rental." Under a cap rental, many rented items will only be reimbursed for 13 months. The beneficiary must be given a "purchase option" at 10 months. Currently, the capped rental period for oxygen is 36 months; however, there are CMS proposals to lower it to 13 months as with other equipment, such as hospital beds and wheelchairs.

2 Payment basics, Durable Medical Equipment Payment System, Revised: October 2007, published by MedPAC.

There are the following exceptions to the general Medicare payment rule:

- Customized equipment and medications are paid at rates that are determined item by item, by the regional carrier.
- Motorized and special custom wheelchairs now require separate, unique physician certifications as to medical necessity *and* prior approval by Medicare.

Appraisers will need to evaluate the effect competitive bidding has had, on financial forecasts and how it affects risk-adjusted rates of return. Has management adequately incorporated these changes in their forecasts and, if not, how does that affect the appraiser's key assumptions? Also, when using valuation methods under the market approach, consider whether historical transactions reflect HME business that are reimbursed under the fee schedule or the DMEPOS Competitive Bidding Program.

7.0 Home Infusion Therapy (HIT) Funding

This is a very specialized service line and is fraught with regulatory complexities governing coverage and reimbursement. Many infused drugs and biologicals must be "incident to physician services," meaning that the drugs and procedures are administered under the direct supervision of a physician (e.g., drugs administered through implantable pumps). Historically, profit margins in this service line have been the highest of all home care service lines, but payment rates and margins are declining rather dramatically and driving industry consolidation even among large regional and national providers.

Increasingly, hospitals are discharging patients "sicker and quicker." When they return home, some patients will require infused drugs or biologicals. Many treatment regimens are of short duration (three to 10 days) and, as a result, patients are frequently discharged from an acute care hospital to a skilled nursing facility to complete therapy treatments before being sent home.

Home infusion therapy is covered by Medicare under Part B. Unlike home health, hospice, and home medical equipment service lines, however, private insurance (not Medicare) is the major payor of HIT services at this time. Private insurance companies have very competitive pricing and frequently select only a few suppliers in a geographic area for contracting (called "closed panels"). Increasingly, providers must be large in size to compete on rates and many smaller, independent providers have been exiting the market.

7.1 Medicare

A number of HIT therapy regimens and products have been incorporated into CMS's competitive bidding program. Some very specialized therapeutic regimens are paid at rates established by each local Medicare Part B carrier based on a percentage of the average wholesale price for infusion drugs, related administration supplies, and professional pharmacist fees. These services, like HME, are subject to Part B coinsurance and deductibles. The Part B benefit does not reimburse for any associated nursing visits for in-home infusion administration; however, there can be additional funding available for the administration of the drug by a nurse if covered under a home health plan of care by a Medicare-certified home health provider or if covered under a state's Medicaid program or the patient's private insurance policy. If the nursing visits are not reimbursable through any of these sources, then the HIT provider can choose to absorb this cost or attempt to bill and collect it from the patient. However, smaller HIT providers may find that charging the patient for the nursing visits could put them at a competitive disadvantage if larger suppliers (especially national providers) do not charge for this as is their standard practice. Often, HIT providers contract for HIT nursing services from a local home health agency. Alternatively, a patient may elect to complete the required infusion therapy in a skilled nursing facility (SNF) where third-party coverage will pay for both the therapy and the nursing.

Appraisers must be keenly aware of the service area's demographics and median incomes because collection of coinsurances and deductibles is a significant factor in supporting gross margins in this service line. Also the development, or proposed development, of other competing "locations of care" (such as a new outpatient cancer center operated by local oncologists or the development of a hospital-owned (hospital-based) or physician-owned ambulatory infusion center) can dramatically reduce a HIT provider's revenue.

8.0 Home Health Industry Information

It is important for appraisers to compare the subject company being valued to industry benchmarks. The comparison can assist the appraiser in reaching a number of conclusions about the subject company. For example:

- Whether the subject company is being run effectively and efficiently relative to its peers;
- Whether the subject company has too much or too little debt;
- Whether the subject company has a favorable mix of payors or too little fee for service Medicare;
- Whether the subject company has too much or too little working capital; and
- Whether the subject company is growing faster or slower than other companies, and how growth is being financed.

In addition, it is important for appraisers to understand the outlook for the industry to evaluate growth, risks, and other factors that might affect the subject company.

8.1 It's All About Labor

As a service business, labor is the most important resource and cost component for most of the home healthcare service lines (home health, private duty, and hospice). If you understand labor cost and efficiency, you can generally tell how a home healthcare business is performing relative to its peers. First, it's important to know how a company's labor cost per full time equivalent

(FTE) employee compares to other home healthcare businesses. Second, you need to know how productive those employees are relative to their peers. For example, according to the *Homecare Salary & Benefits Report 2014-2015* (published by Hospital & Healthcare Compensation Service, October 2014), a registered nurse should be compensated $30.02 per hour or an average of $37.89 per visit. The report indicates that registered nurses average 5.19 visits in an eight-hour day.

It's also important to know the staffing mix (for example, registered nurses, licensed practical nurses, home care aids, physical therapists, occupational therapists, and social workers). The staffing mix can tell you whether the company is too heavy or too light at various staffing levels and whether it may be missing opportunities to provide additional services.

There can be severe medical personnel labor shortages in many markets. As a result, maintaining low turnover rates is critical and should be carefully assessed during a valuation engagement. Many studies have shown that turnover costs (for example, recruitment, new employee training, and lost productivity) can increase the annual cost of an employee by 33% or more, based on the nature of the position. High turnover rates may result from noncompetitive wages and benefits, poor moral, lack of leadership, and so on.

8.2 Unless They Sell Products

For those service lines that sell products (home medical and respiratory equipment, and home infusion), gross profit margins are the key benchmarks. Gross profit margins can be positively affected by payor mix on the revenue side or by cost of goods sold on the expense side. By understanding what revenue and margins should be, appraisers can evaluate whether or not there are opportunities available to a hypothetical buyer (under the fair market value standard).

8.3 Additional Considerations for Home Hospice

For home hospice services where per diem (or daily) payments frequently represent the total amount available for patient care (that is, there are no separate payments for additional services), it is important to effectively manage the cost of drugs, HME, and continuous care nursing or home health aid expense. Hospice providers with abnormally high costs may be overpaying for these services or providing unnecessary services, and providers that have abnormally low costs may be missing out on necessary services that might attract a better mix of patients for financial success of the service line.

8.4 Data Sources

There are a number of standard industry data sources (such as the Risk Management Association and Integra Information Systems) appraisers use, and there may be industry-specific sources, such as surveys developed through trade associations or industry analyses complied by consultants and financial services companies. In addition, sometimes valuable information can be found in trade magazine articles.

For example, the National Association for Home Care & Hospice (www.nahc.org) and the

National Hospice and Palliative Care Organization (NHPCO) have valuable industry resources but membership is required to access some of the more substantive information.

For highly regulated industries, such as health care, there is a significant amount of information available from government agencies, think tanks, and advocacy groups.

8.5 MedPAC

The Medicare Payment Advisory Commission (MedPAC) is an independent congressional agency established by the Balanced Budget Act of 1997 (P.L. 105-33) to advise the U.S. Congress on issues affecting the Medicare program. The commission's statutory mandate is quite broad: In addition to advising the Congress on payments to private health plans participating in Medicare and providers in Medicare's traditional fee-for-service program, MedPAC is also tasked with analyzing access to care, quality of care, and other issues affecting Medicare.

MedPAC, in numerous reports to Congress has criticized the home health industry for excessive margins above 10%. However, in the 2013 calendar year for Medicare home health cost reports, the median margin for all hospital-owned agencies was a negative (19%), which is significantly lower than margins reported for freestanding providers.[3] However, when CMS selects data for rate setting, all the hospital based providers (there were 1,102 hospital-owned providers in 2013) are excluded. Thus, over 10% of the providers are not included when MedPAC reports that providers should be able to absorb additional cost increases in addition to decreases in base (Medicare) payments. Also, it should be noted that in the 2013 MedPAC data 3,995 of the 8,875 freestanding businesses (not hospital owned) had a margin of less than 10% and 2,394 of these providers had negative margins. In addition, Medicare fee-for-service is the primary revenue source that has historically reimbursed above a provider's cost. As a result, it is important to determine whether the payor mix for the agency reflects a declining percentage of fee-for-service Medicare. If so, the agency could have a major financial challenge.

The negative margins typically found in hospital-owned agencies may relate to the allocation of hospitalwide overhead costs. Hospitals usually do a good job allocating direct costs. However, indirect costs are usually allocated based on a variety of methods such as the relative number of employees or hospital space used. As a result, when valuing a hospital-owned program, appraisers need to consider whether negative margins could be corrected if overhead costs were normalized to reflect a nonhospital agency. This is a critical consideration for the appraiser when valuing a hospital-owned agency. In most cases the appraiser will want to recast the agency as non-hospital-owned to reflect comparable overhead costs.

Under the ACA and recently passed legislation to correct years of inappropriate computations of physician payment rates, CMS plans to continue to reduce Medicare payments to HHAs through 2019.

3 From an analysis developed by CliftonLarsonAllen using a database of Medicare cost reports in the public domain.

A few highlights from 2015 proposed rules from CMS that will affect 2016 fiscal year payments:

Medicare Home Health

- Proposed rules were published July 10 for 2016 Medicare payment rates that call for a reduction in payments by 1.8% from 2015. The rate change would be effective Jan. 1, 2016.
- The rule includes testing of a new home health value-based purchasing (VBP) model to begin January 2016. The model would apply a payment reduction or payment increase to Medicare-certified home health payments, depending on 29 performance measures, for all agencies within nine states. Payment adjustments would be applied annually, beginning with 5% and increasing to 8% in later years. The VBP for these test states in 2018.

Medicare Hospice

- Proposed rules were published May 5 for 2016 Medicare payment rates that provide for 1.3% increase over 2015. The rate change would be effective back to Oct. 1, 2015.
- The rule includes a proposed change in the payment for routine home care services. CMS proposed to establish two different payment rates with a higher base payment for the first 60 days of care and a lower rate for days 61-plus. For hospice patients who are discharged and readmitted to hospice within 60 days of discharge, his or her prior hospice days will continue to follow the patient and count toward their patient days for the receiving hospice upon the original hospice election.
- Service Intensity Add-on (SIA)—CMS proposes to pay an additional amount above the routine home care rate for care provided in the last seven days of life when certain criteria are met. The SIA would not be paid for patients residing in nursing facilities or skilled nursing facilities. The SIA would be based on the continuous home care rate and limited to a certain number of hours and only for care provided in person by a registered nurse or social worker.

Knee and hip surgery with an all-inclusive bundled payment from Medicare ... CMS proposed bundled payments for knee and hip surgeries marks the first time Medicare is making the payment model mandatory for 75 MSA locations across the country. The bundled service covers all related care for a 90-day episode of care for MS-DRG (medical severity-diagnosis-related group) 469 and 470.

- Begins Jan. 1, 2016, for a five-year test period.
- With very few exceptions, all post-acute care is included (intermediate rehab facility, long-term acute care hospital, home health, hospice, outpatient therapy, skilled nursing facility, physicians, etc.).

- Hospitals and post-acute providers would be paid under the usual Medicare fee-for-service model throughout the year. At the end of each year, actual spending for the episodes (total expenditures for related services under Medicare Parts A and B) would be compared to the hospital-specific benchmark for the responsible hospital.
- Hospitals would be paid a bonus or be required to repay Medicare based on the quality and efficiency of the care provided during the episode, as determined by a standard set of quality measures (complications, readmissions, and patient experience). In the first year, there is no risk of payback; only the opportunity for a bonus.
- Patients will continue to have the freedom to choose their post-acute providers.
- Allows for telehealth services, but they cannot be a substitute for in-person home health services provided under the Medicare home health benefit.

9.0 Valuing Home Healthcare Businesses

9.1 The Income Approach

The income approach, and more specifically the discounted cash flow method, is the valuation approach and method preferred by most appraisers to value profitable operating businesses. This method can be difficult to use for marginally profitable or unprofitable businesses if there is inadequate cash flow to provide a reasonable return on the business' assets. In that case, methods under the market or asset approach may be more appropriate.

Under an income approach, it is important to determine whether the forecasted cash flows are reasonable and achievable. If the appraiser thoroughly understands the business and the industry (as previously discussed), he or she should be able to reasonably make this determination and factor it into the development of a discount rate applicable to the cash flows forecasted for the subject company.

When evaluating forecasted cash flow growth rates, the appraiser needs to consider imminent changes and proposed changes to reimbursement, opportunities for the subject company to expand, population growth, age demographics, and age-cohort specific use rates where data might be available.

Looking at the specific operational issues affecting the company, its historical operations, and by making comparisons to industry data, the appraiser should be able to evaluate the reasonableness of future working capital needs and capital expenditure requirements.

Care must be used in developing an equity discount rate that results in a risk-adjusted rate of return necessary to attract buyers to invest in the subject company. Appraisers need to ensure that they understand the operating characteristics (for example, size, growth rates, margins, product, and service mix) of the business or businesses from which discount rates and equity risk premiums are derived and make appropriate company-specific risk adjustments to reflect differences between the subject company and the source of these rates or premiums. In addition, there could be other changes such as new legislation, proposed or enacted, that was unknown when the market-derived discount rates or premiums were published.

Most home healthcare businesses are not capital intensive. (One exception would be a hospice with an inpatient and residential facility.) As a result, they generally do not incur (nor do they have a need to incur) significant long-term debt. The appraiser must consider this and other factors when determining a debt-to-equity ratio for a weighted average cost of capital (WACC) assumption. Caution should be used in automatically using debt-to-equity ratios derived from publicly traded companies because they may not be "pure plays"[4] and the subject company may have significantly different operating characteristics and growth opportunities. Under the fair market value standard, the debt-to-equity ratio, used in the WACC, should be one that is reasonably achievable by the subject company and likely to provide the returns anticipated to debt and equity investors from the anticipated cash flows used in the forecast.

Appraisers need to ensure that risk-adjusted rates of returns used match the earnings stream being valued. It is generally acknowledged that most discount rates are derived from public company transactions on an after-tax basis. When valuing healthcare businesses for regulatory purposes (for example, under the anti-kickback statute and transactions involving nonprofit IRC 501(c)(3) entities), it is generally accepted that controlling interests must be valued on an after-tax basis (including pass-through entities) under the assumption that the most likely buyer is a commercial C corporation. One rationale for this is that, without having to pay taxes, nonprofit organizations could theoretically afford to pay more than a comparable for-profit organization for the same business. Valuing after-tax cash flows also keeps after-tax discount rates derived from public companies consistent with the subject company's earnings stream. Appraisers need to consider adjustments to the discount rate or methodology that might be required for nonregulatory valuation engagements and for engagements involving minority interests in pass-through entities to maintain consistency between the discount rate and the earnings stream.

9.2 The Market Approach

Methods under the market approach can be useful but difficult to use correctly when valuing home healthcare businesses because it is always hard to find publicly traded companies and sales transactions for companies that are truly comparable to the subject company. Unless the comparable company is publicly traded, it is almost impossible to adequately evaluate a comparable company's operating characteristics. Some comparable sales transactions may predate current reimbursement levels, economic changes, or not have anticipated proposed legislation, which might result in an erroneous conclusion about a current transaction. Furthermore, a significant number of comparable sales transactions represent acquisitions by existing healthcare

4 A pure play is a company that is only in one line of business. Many public companies are in multiple lines of business.

companies that may recognize economic synergies resulting in an investment or synergistic standard of value (not fair market value if that is the standard desired).

Despite these limitations, a thorough analysis of publicly traded companies and comparable sales transactions is extremely useful in developing an understanding of the marketplace, value drivers, who the most likely buyers are, and in determining a reasonable range (low to high) to test values indicated under other approaches.

The market approach can also be useful when operating income and cash flows are indeterminable because of poor records or commingled operations, or in the case of the mismanagement of an otherwise sound company. In those cases, market-derived valuation multiples that are not tied to earnings can be useful. Assuming you have reliable revenues and daily census data for the subject company, price-to-revenue multiples, or price-to-average-daily-census multiples from guideline publicly traded companies or comparable sales transactions are useful in estimating an indicated range of potential values.

For example, buyers within the industry will frequently use a multiple of patient average daily census (ADC) data to benchmark the value of these businesses. If the benchmark is $50,000 per ADC and the ADC is 200 patients, the business might be worth $10 million.

However, remember that when choosing a revenue multiple or census multiple, you are implicitly assuming that the subject company has all of the operating characteristics from which the revenue or census multiple was derived. So appraisers must be extremely careful when relying primarily on market multiples.

Developing a significant understanding of the subject company and the industry can go a long way toward overcoming the shortcomings inherent in the market approach. For example, if you can benchmark a company's revenue and direct labor costs relative to its peers, you may become more comfortable in choosing a revenue or daily census multiple.

Methods under the market approach appear simple and intuitive and therefore, have great appeal. But these methods need to be used judiciously and generally in conjunction with other approaches.

Aside from traditional public company research and general sales transaction databases, Irving Levin Associates Inc. (www.levinassociates.com) publishes *The Senior Care Acquisition Report*, which includes information about publicly announced home healthcare transactions.

9.3 The Asset Approach

Methods under the asset approach are rarely used as the primary method to value operating companies such as home health care unless the business is unprofitable or marginally profitable whereby cash flows do not produce an adequate return on assets. However, methods under the asset approach should still be considered to ensure that values under other approaches (primarily the income approach) exceed values that would be developed under an asset approach, which is usually viewed as the lowest or floor value.

Under an income or market approach, the premise of value is almost always a going concern. When using an asset approach, the premise of value is sometimes more difficult to determine but the valuation methods used must be applied consistent with the premise chosen.

10.0 Special Situations Affecting Home Healthcare Value

10.1 Management's Integrity

Health care is arguably the most highly regulated industry in the country. Many of the regulations facing providers today were enacted to address years of providers abusing the system and profiting illegally and unethically under government programs, such as Medicare and Medicaid, and private insurance programs.

Today, there are significant fines, penalties and the possibility of prison for violating federal and state regulations governing the healthcare industry and nonprofit organizations. While enforcement has helped to curb abuses, they still exist.

While appraisers generally are not performing due diligence, it is important for them to do a high level assessment of management's integrity. Appraisers who understand the home healthcare industry and the associated regulations also understand many of the illegal schemes and can evaluate management's integrity fairly effectively through benchmarking the company against its peers (looking for anomalies) and interviewing management (looking for inconsistencies).

The risk associated with management's integrity can impact whether revenue levels and profitability can be maintained by a hypothetical buyer who may not be willing or able to operate the business illegally or unethically. The appraiser should always require that the organization being valued disclose any and all correspondence and external audit findings that have been conducted by state licensure agencies, Medicare-certifying organizations, Medicare and Medicaid fiscal intermediaries, focused medical review audits and findings, and any past or ongoing notifications from the Office of the Inspector General (OIG) including past or current corporate integrity agreements (CIAs). Other useful tools to test the operational integrity of the organization is whether there is a compliance plan in place that is modeled after the OIG's suggested format as well as internal audit committee reports and findings that would be a component of the compliance plan.

The appraiser's assessment of management's integrity may create the need for normalizing adjustments and should have a direct effect on risk-adjusted rates of return used under an income approach as well as judgments made by the appraiser using methods under other approaches.

10.2 Certificate of Need (CON) States

States may restrict or limit new home health businesses though CON legislation. Typically, these states limit CON application to service lines that are "skilled in nature" and heavily dependent on Medicare and Medicaid certification and reimbursement such as home health and hospice. However, some states also have regulations that govern establishment of new "licensed-only" providers that will not be Medicare-certified but will obtain reimbursements from Medicaid.

To start a new home healthcare business in a CON state, you generally need to demonstrate adequate demand and need. Depending on the state, the CON process can be time-consuming and expensive. Generally, home healthcare businesses in CON states will be worth more compared to a similar business in a state without a CON. However, each state's CON rules may be more or less restrictive, and the appraiser should research the state's current plan for home healthcare services to determine whether there is opportunity for new businesses to enter the market. Even if the business is no more profitable in the CON state, the lack of new competition will generally reduce risk compared to businesses in non-CON states.

In states where CONs are very restrictive, the CON alone can be worth a significant amount of money, even without an operating business and, as a result, sometimes CONs are valued independent of the operating business.

Appraisers need to consider the effect on the discount rate when valuing home healthcare businesses in CON states versus non-CON states. When valuing a CON alone (without an operating business), appraisers should generally rely on the income approach (relief from royalty method) or possibly the cost approach, unless comparable transaction data for the CONs in the state are available. If using a relief from royalty method, consider what percentage of the expected operating margin should be allocated to the CON when doing a pretax royalty rate calculation. For example, if agencies are expected to earn 12% in that market, the pretax royalty rate for the CON valuation calculation might be 3% (or 25% of the 12% operating margin, for example) of the forecasted revenues expected if the CON were used in an operating business.

10.3 Valuing Provider-Owned Home Healthcare Businesses

Home healthcare businesses owned by hospitals or nursing homes are unique because they generally will not have their own financial statements or tax returns and will almost never have a balance sheet. They generally only track costs directly applicable to departments or service lines such as home health services (for example, direct supplies, direct compensation, and benefits) but allocate indirect overhead (such as telephone, security, maintenance, rent, utilities, human resource, and information systems) from the parent entity's total overhead. As a result, operations for provider-owned home healthcare businesses are generally not comparable to stand-alone businesses.

Without objective financial statements (and particularly balance sheets), it is usually impossible to develop meaningful financial ratios and analysis. However, a number of operational benchmarks, such as revenue per visit, average daily census, or visits per employee, can still be developed and compared to industry benchmarks to evaluate the quality of operations.

Another potential problem in valuing a provider-owned home healthcare business is that sometimes they are not motivated by profit. In some cases, the lack of profit motivation may be because home health is not a core part of the overall business and may contribute little to overall operations. In other cases, the business may be viewed solely for its contribution to the parent entity's mission or as part of a continuum of care. While lack of profitability is not inconsistent with being a nonprofit organization, management sometimes uses its nonprofit mission to rationalize underperformance. Appraisers need to understand that marginal profitability, or even losses in the hands of management, doesn't necessarily mean these businesses cannot be run profitably in the hands of profit-motivated management.

To value provider-owned businesses, historical and forecasted operations need to be normalized and made comparable to non-provider-owned or stand-alone businesses. Great care must be exercised in doing this to ensure that only controllable costs are adjusted and uncontrollable costs, which may be unique to that marketplace, are not changed. Care must also be exercised to ensure that, under the fair market value standard, adjustments are not unique to a particular buyer.

Appraisers need to develop a reasonable understanding of industry benchmarks for home healthcare businesses to support or evaluate the assumptions that will be necessary to convert the hospital-owned business into a non-hospital-owned business.

Some questions typically asked during these assignments are:

- How much space (square footage) does the business really need?
- Is the rent too high and location too expensive for the needs of the business?
- Is the business sharing management with other departments and how are those costs allocated?
- Are the parent entity's labor costs and benefits comparable to a non-provider-based business?
- Are there costs and other administrative functions that are only required because they are part of the larger entity (for example, Joint Commission accreditation)?
- How are patients referred for home healthcare services?

How referrals are made to a provider-owned business can have a significant impact on its value—and, of course, referrals are a key regulatory risk area. For example, there is less risk of losing referrals if they come from a variety of physicians as opposed to only physicians employed by or on the staff of the parent entity. While this is a typical risk associated with a concentration of customers, it may be more prevalent for provider-owned businesses. In valuing the business under a fair market value standard, the appraiser should evaluate what would change if the business were not part of, or reliant upon, the parent entity.

10.4 Real Estate and Nonoperating Assets

Most home healthcare businesses are not capital-intensive (an exception might be a hospice that has an inpatient or residential facility). As a result, real estate and other nonoperating assets can create special problems in determining value. In particular, cash flows from the operating business often will not provide an adequate return on the real estate and nonoperating assets.

Generally, these assets should be excluded from the value of the operating business and valued separately if they are, in fact, going to be acquired as part of the transaction. These assets should be removed from the balance sheet, and their historical costs should be removed from the income statements. For those assets, such as real estate, that are used in the business, fair market value rent expense (assuming a fair market value standard) should be substituted for the cost of owning and operating the real estate. Fair market value rent for the operating business should be consistent with rents that would be paid by other home care businesses for only the square footage needed to operate a similar business within the subject company's market. Fair market value rent could be more or less than rents paid historically or agreed to prospectively.

If the valuation is being done for regulatory purposes, rent that is below or above fair market value is a potential issue that should be evaluated by a healthcare attorney familiar with applicable regulations.

11.0 Conclusion

Valuing home healthcare businesses is not unlike valuing other businesses except that appraisers should have a significant understanding of their operating characteristics and the industry. Changes in future reimbursement can significantly affect earnings and value. Accountable care organizations and bundled payments may completely change providers' business models and cost structures and the way they are reimbursed. As a result, it is incumbent on appraisers to be familiar with the affect these changes may have on the business. In addition, for any healthcare engagement, appraisers should have a reasonable understanding of regulations affecting healthcare providers and nonprofit organizations and a grasp of the current changes that may be enacted by Congress and state legislatures.

The author would like to thank Ron Clitherow, MPH, and Gary R. Massey, CPA, for their significant contributions to this chapter.

Chapter 20. Valuing Joint Ventures and Other Physician Alignment Initiatives

CONTENTS

Chapter 20. Valuing Joint Ventures and Other Physician Alignment Initiatives

By Carol Carden, CPA, ASA, ABV, CFE

As a starting point for a discussion of the value drivers and typical valuation methodologies for joint ventures, whether equity-based joint ventures or contractual joint ventures, it is important to understand the basic forms these transactions typically take. For ease of reference, any of these collaborations will be referred to as "joint ventures" throughout this chapter. The specific characteristics, benefits and challenges of each structure will be discussed in greater detail later in the chapter, but typically hospital/physician joint ventures come in the form of: (1) equity joint ventures; (2) leases; (3) management agreements; (4) a more comprehensive form of management agreement termed a clinical co-management agreement; and 5) gainsharing/shared savings arrangements. There are certainly other forms of hospital/physician alignment in the current healthcare environment, but this chapter will focus on these most common initiatives.

1.0 Reasons for Valuation

The primary drivers for hospital/physician collaborations are: (1) physicians' desire to identify alternative revenue streams to supplement declining professional revenues; (2) changes in regulations that close old avenues of collaboration or open new ones; and (3) hospital's desire to involve a higher level of clinical expertise in the management of a particular service.

Any collaboration that occurs between a hospital and physicians is subject to regulatory scrutiny. Therefore, as hospital management contemplates one of the forms of joint venture discussed in this chapter, it will often decide to enlist a valuation expert to demonstrate its willingness to transact the joint venture at terms that are both fair market value (as defined by both the IRS and for Stark/OIG purposes) and commercially reasonable (as required for regulatory purposes).

2.0 Regulatory Considerations

The following briefly outlines the five main areas of regulatory compliance consideration in contemplating a joint venture. The appraiser should have at least a basic understanding of these issues to properly assess the risk of any contemplated joint venture. A detailed discussion of these regulations is beyond the scope of this chapter; however, it is critical that the client has competent legal counsel involved if contemplating a hospital/physician joint venture.

2.1 Stark

As discussed previously in this book, the Stark regulations prohibit referrals of designated health services (DHS) from a provider to an entity in which the provider has a financial interest, unless the transaction falls into a safe harbor. More often than not, the contemplated joint venture will involve one of the 11 DHS.[1] Therefore, the Stark implications of a proposed transaction can have a significant impact on the valuation of the venture. It is critical when valuing these types of transactions to ensure the historical or anticipated referrals of business are not factored into the value of the venture. That is not to say that historical volume must be eliminated from the valuation analysis, just that the valuation analysis must be structured in such a way as to not specifically give recognition for previous referral patterns or anticipated referral patterns post-transaction.

For example, if after consummation of the joint venture, it is anticipated that, due to the stronger relationship with the hospital, the physicians will move procedures that they currently refer to competitor facilities to the newly joint-ventured facility, this anticipated volume should not be considered when determining the fair market value of the joint venture during formation. The value of the joint venture should be reflective of the cash flows and risk assessment as it currently exists absent the strengthened relationship that occurs as a result of the joint venture. The analyst must be cognizant of the requirement that the valuation assumptions not reflect the ability of the parties to refer business to one another.

The OIG has expressed some concern about the use of "referrals" in what are otherwise standard valuation methods under the income approach, such as the discounted cash flow method, designed to produce an appropriate measure of fair market value. Appraisers and legal counsel need to consider how best to conform to regulatory requirements while still achieving fair market value. One important consideration in using historical volume as the basis for forecasting future volume is to eliminate from both (historical and future projections) any volume based on a financial incentive to refer or utilize. This can be accomplished by analyzing and comparing referral sources having a financial interest and those not having a financial interest. Additionally, the use of a discount rate derived and based upon the hypothetical willing buyer (not specific to the transaction) adds a level of objectivity and distance from the impact of potential patient

1 Designated health services include clinical laboratory, physical therapy, occupational therapy, outpatient speech-language pathology, radiology, and imaging services; radiation therapy services and supplies; durable medical equipment and supplies; parenteral nutrition, enteral nutrition, prosthetic, and orthotic devices and supplies; home health services; outpatient prescription drugs; and inpatient and outpatient hospital services and the provision of related billable equipment and supplies.

referrals. When addressing this concern over referrals, it is also important for the appraiser to bear in mind that fair market value is a two-way analysis; we must determine the amount that a willing buyer would pay *as well as* the amount for which a willing seller would sell.

Additionally, Stark II Phase III became effective Dec. 5, 2007.[2] Phase III eliminated the safe harbor for compensation arrangements.[3] Now, the parties to the arrangement must be able to demonstrate that the contemplated compensation is stated at fair market value absent authoritative guidance. Phase III does not state that the previous safe harbor methodology cannot be used, just that use of that methodology no longer carries the added benefit of providing safe harbor protection. Compensation comes into play in valuation of management agreements.

Phase III also implemented new rules regarding leases for space and equipment, which will be discussed in greater detail later in this chapter.

2.2 Anti-Kickback Regulations

It is not very likely that the proposed joint venture will fit squarely into one of the 25 AKS safe harbors.[4] Much like the previous discussion above regarding Stark implications, the valuation analyst must have an understanding of the AKS regulations sufficient to assess any undue risk of the contemplated transaction and the related impact on the value. Consideration of the AKS statute was particularly important when a proposed leasing arrangement was stated on a per-procedure or "per-click" basis. CMS eliminated per click leases as discussed in a later section of this chapter.

2.3 Affordable Care Act (ACA)

The ACA legislation was passed in March 2010 and has had far-reaching implications in the healthcare industry. One of the more significant provisions is the broad expansion of the insured population. When appraising a healthcare joint venture, it is important to understand the form this expansion has taken. In many instances, while there are more patients insured, much of this expansion has been in the form of additional Medicaid members and individual policies with high deductibles and resultant bad debt exposure, so the impact on net revenue assumptions will need to be tempered accordingly. Another significant impact of the ACA has been in regard to primary-care-related joint ventures. The ACA's most favorable provisions have been toward primary care. So, when appraising a joint venture that includes primary care services, the analyst should be sure to understand the reimbursement trends. Sources for identifying such reimbursement trend information can be found in Chapter 2 regarding evaluating cost of capital and appropriately forecasting cash flows for healthcare entities.

2 Department of Health and Human Services, Centers for Medicare & Medicaid Services, 42 CFR Parts 411 and 424, (CMS-1810-F), RIN 0938-AK67, *Medicare Program; Physicians' Referrals to Health Care Entities* With *Which They Have Financial Relationships (Phase III).*

3 Including the prescribed use of an average of specifically identified national physician compensation surveys.

4 *Federal Register*/Vol. 79, No. 192/Friday, Oct. 3, 2014, 42 CFR 1001.952 (a) through (y).

2.4 CMS Proposed Fee Schedule Changes

For many years, CMS has proposed significant reductions to physician reimbursement in its proposed Medicare Physician Fee Schedule that typically is issued in late summer each year. The magnitude of these reductions has been 25% and greater, and these reductions have affected certain specialties more than others. Cardiology is one such specialty that has been a particular focus of the reductions. These reductions were a result of CMS attempting to correct the Sustainable Growth Rate (SGR). Historically, Congress would intervene each year in late December right before the reductions were anticipated to occur, eliminating the reductions and, many times, implementing a small reimbursement increase. In April 2015, the Medicare Access and CHIP Reauthorization Act of 2015 took effect, which provided a permanent "fix" to the SGR problem. However, it is important for the valuation analyst to understand and monitor proposed and "final" changes in regulations such as this, in light of a contemplated joint venture.

2.5 Private Inurement/Excess Benefit

If the hospital involved in the joint venture is not-for-profit, the transaction must be consummated at fair market value as defined by the IRS (Revenue Ruling 59-60) to ensure no private inurement or excess benefit implications are triggered. In particular, the IRS is concerned that not-for-profit assets will be transferred in excess amounts to private individuals.[5] If a transaction is determined to contain private inurement or excess benefits, excise taxes can apply to both the hospital as well as the physician, if the latter is a *disqualified person* under the excess benefit transaction regulations.

3.0 Key Features and Typical Valuation Methodologies

It is important to understand the concept of value and, in particular, fair market value as defined by regulatory bodies when determining compensation related to any physician/hospital venture. There are valuation methodologies that are more commonly used for particular types of ventures and having a basic understanding of these will assist you in evaluating the transaction with your client. It is also important to understand the types of information to be considered and the degree to which assumptions should be tested to ensure the valuation will withstand regulatory scrutiny in the event the transaction is selected for review. We will begin our discussion with the simplest form of joint venture and move toward more complex forms.

3.1 Equity Joint Ventures

Equity joint ventures occur when an existing company or, many times a service line of a hospital, is contributed into a new entity and an ownership interest in the new entity is offered to physicians. This type of venture is easily understood and has withstood the test of time. For plain "vanilla" equity joint ventures, an income approach is typically utilized. Generally

5 *Intermediate Sanctions – Excess Benefit Transactions,* Internal Revenue Service at www.irs.gov/charities/charitable/article/0,,id=123303,00.html and *Inurement – Section 501 (c) (4),* Internal Revenue Service at www.irs.gov/charities/nonprofits/article/0,,id=156404,00.html.

speaking, equity joint ventures are chosen solely as an investment vehicle making anticipated cash flows the best indicator of value.

As discussed elsewhere in this Guide, if recent privately held market transactions similar to the entity being joint ventured exist in sufficient number, there are still many hurdles to overcome before a market-based approach can be relied upon for these types of joint ventures. Typically, the value of the entity to be included in the joint venture is determined from the income approach, and the relevant ownership percentage is multiplied by that value. Given the level of ownership contemplated, consideration of discounts related to control and marketability may be warranted.

There are a few challenges to implementing the equity joint venture. Equity joint ventures are prohibited for services comprised of DHS for Stark purposes. The requirement of up-front capital or the incurrence of debt can also make this model less attractive dependent upon the financial goals and risk tolerance of the parties. Finally, equity joint ventures can result in a loss of reimbursement post-transaction due to reimbursement differences between hospital-based reimbursement and free-standing entity reimbursement.

3.2 Leases

Leases typically involve access on a per-block-of-time basis to a piece of equipment or the operations of a service line. Block leases commonly have been used for access to imaging equipment and cardiac catheterization labs. One of the more attractive features of the leasing option is that it gives access to the equipment/service line even if there is not sufficient volume to justify full-time provision of the service.

Typically, a cost-based approach is used for leases. In general terms, total costs to be incurred through the lease are accumulated and a fair market return is added. The resulting total is divided by the hours of operation specific to the block desired to determine the lease rate. The rate of return should be commensurate with the risks being assumed and, generally speaking, ranges from 10% to 15%.

Alternatively, a market-based approach can be used if the analyst has access to lease rates for similar services in the same geographic market. Given that these leases typically occur between unrelated private companies, this type of market information is not usually readily available.

Leasing arrangements are attractive as they do not require up-front capital and allow for the provision of a service when volume is not sufficient to support a full-time offering. However, leases can be tricky to structure from a regulatory standpoint and are fairly easy for competitors to duplicate.

Under the lease, the billing for the technical component of revenue is generally done by the entity purchasing access to the equipment/service line using its provider identification number.

3.3 Management Agreements

Traditionally, management agreements have taken the form of physicians providing a stipulated number of hours per month to actively participate in the management of a service line. Historically, these initiatives have been structured as medical directorships. The physician tracks the hours of service provided and is compensated on an hourly basis for services rendered. In more recent years, management agreements have migrated toward what are termed "co-management agreements" or "clinical co-management agreements." These agreements generally have an administrative component with a fixed fee and a quality incentive that allows a bonus payment if certain goals are met.

Typically, co-management agreements are valued primarily using a blend of cost and market approaches. The administrative component is generally calculated by multiplying an hourly rate by the number of anticipated hours. With the implementation of Stark Phase III, the safe harbor for determining an hourly rate was eliminated. The elimination allows for additional flexibility in determining a fair market hourly rate. The flexibility has always been present (as compliance with the safe harbor was never a requirement), but hospitals that previously would have conservatively complied with the safe harbor methodology can be more creative without stepping outside a comfort zone. The hourly rate analysis will likely incorporate surveys not previously included in the safe harbor calculation as well as geographic-specific compensation data.

The determination of the quality incentive is a more subjective determination with little or no regulatory guidance. Generally, the quality incentive is determined based upon either: (1) other governmental or commercial quality incentive programs that reward providers for good quality or penalizes them for bad outcomes; or (2) the cost the provider would incur absent the quality portion of the agreement. The industry has moved away from paying for reporting of quality outcomes to paying/penalizing for actual clinical outcomes. Therefore, it is important when using an existing quality incentive program criteria as guidance for valuation purposes, that the features of the agreement you are appraising match the features present in the existing quality incentive program.

It is important when assessing the level of compensation attributable to the quality incentive portion of a clinical co-management agreement that the appraiser understands the level of difficulty inherent in the physicians' achievement of the quality outcomes and in earning the associated compensation. All other things being equal, quality outcomes that are more difficult to achieve should warrant higher compensation than metrics that are easily achievable. There is some publicly available information regarding quality outcomes metrics that are typical for particular service categories. This type of information can be found on the CMS website[6] as well as on various industry association websites. Ultimately, the assessment of the rigor of the quality outcomes may require the assistance of a professional with a clinical background.

6 www.cms.gov/Medicare/Quality-Initiatives-Patient-Assessment-Instruments/QualityMeasures/index.html?redirect=/QualityMeasures/03_ElectronicSpecifications.asp.

To illustrate the concept of considering the costs the provider would incur absent the quality incentive, consider that if, in the absence of the quality portion of the agreement, the hospital would have to hire a physician or other professional to administer its quality program, the cost of this hire can be used as one indication for the "value" of the quality incentive program.

The attractive features of a co-management agreement are that no change in ownership occurs and there is no up-front capital required. The original provider of care remains in place and the arrangement is virtually seamless to patients. However, the upside reward available to physicians can often be less than in other types of ventures, and the payment of the quality incentive can be subjective. Additionally, in other industries, fees for management services are typically tied to profitability or performance, but, in the healthcare industry, we must ensure that fees are as disconnected from the referral base and based upon clinical outcomes and direct physician performance to ensure the transaction will withstand regulatory scrutiny.

3.4 'Under Arrangements' Management Agreements

Often touted in prior years, these arrangements were devices to allow a joint venture to provide a hospital with "soup-to-nuts services" (building, equipment, staffing, day-to-day management of a service, etc.) without giving the joint venture an equity stake in the hospital or service line. This type of management agreement is only permitted now for facilities that qualify for a rural exception under the Stark regulations or if the agreement involves nonreferring physicians such as radiologists.

3.5 Gainsharing or Shared Savings Agreements

In Chapter 22, there is a more detailed discussion of these types of alternative payment arrangements. This chapter will address at a high level some of the specific considerations when appraising an affiliation structure such as a gainsharing arrangement. Since the value of the venture is heavily impacted, it is important that some key features of the agreement are understood by the analyst. These include:

- What payors/patient populations will be included under the agreement?
- Are the participating physicians independent or employed by the hospital?
- Is a portion of the savings at risk related to quality metrics?
- Is there a cap to the amount of savings that can be shared?
- Do any of the features of the arrangement overlap with other services the physicians provide, such as management services/medical directorships?
- Is there any regulatory guidance available related to similar arrangements? There have been a number of OIG advisory opinions issued related to gainsharing arrangements. While OIG opinions are not authoritative, they do provide some insight into how a regulator might view such an agreement and what features the OIG felt were important to their decision.

This type of hospital/physician affiliation is highly complex and in the early stages of development in the industry, so there will not be market data or established valuation approaches for some time until the data "catches up to" what is happening in the industry as a result of various healthcare reform initiatives.

4.0 Types of Information Utilized and Testing Assumptions

Many of these ventures are complex to model from a valuation standpoint. The valuation analysis is made more difficult due to the fact that hospitals generally only track direct costs by service line, so determining the total costs associated with a given service offering requires in-depth analysis and working closely with management to ensure all costs are captured. Once historical financial performance is developed, projected financial performance must be determined. Again, it is important to keep the fair market value definitions in mind to ensure that assumptions do not incorporate changes resulting from the transaction.

A thorough understanding of historical and projected volumes must be obtained. Often, volume is tracked by hospitals on a per-procedure basis while the new venture anticipates compensation on a per-case or per-episode-of-care basis. Hospitals typically track volume based on individual charge codes for each procedure performed on a patient. The procedure-based information is transferred electronically to the health information management (HIM) department of a hospital where it is grouped and summarized in a manner that facilitates billing. For outpatient procedures from Medicare and many commercial payors, the hospital receives reimbursement on a per-case basis rather than a per-procedure basis. However, absent the coding and grouping performed by the HIM department, it is difficult for the hospital to bridge the gap between procedures and cases. Therefore, the valuation analyst must work with management to ensure accurate adjustments are made to transition from one volume indicator to another. An analysis of historical collections and reimbursement is necessary to ensure that the impact of potential changes post-transaction are accounted for and understood. This analysis can be quite challenging to perform particularly for inpatient volumes. Hospitals do not track inpatient reimbursement specific to particular departments or service lines as that reimbursement is more traditionally paid to them on a per-admission basis. Therefore, many times outpatient reimbursement is used as a proxy for both inpatient and outpatient volume.

If the Medicare fee schedule is to be used as a proxy under a market-based approach, this will many times require the assistance of outside expertise in coding. To facilitate this analysis, the hospital must be able to produce historical procedure information including diagnosis codes.

When evaluating the thoroughness of the valuation analysis, it is important to understand how the assumptions provided by management are tested. When possible, historical and projected financial performance should be benchmarked against industry sources. The existence of benchmarking will strengthen the results should the transaction be reviewed.

It is also critical that upcoming changes in reimbursement and regulations be given appropriate consideration in the valuation analysis; otherwise the results will be incorrect. The projected rates of return for the venture should be compared to alternative investment opportunities and should make sense relative to the risks being assumed. It is very difficult to balance investment goals, risks assumed, and regulatory guidance, but documenting the thought process as much as possible will pay off if the results have to be supported by a regulatory body.

Chapter 21.
Urgent Care Centers: Valuation Overview

CONTENTS

Chapter 21.
Urgent Care Centers: Valuation Overview

By Aaron Murski and Elliott Jeter, CFA, CPA/ABV

The Urgent Care Association of America (UCAOA) defines urgent care as healthcare provided on a walk-in basis for acute illness or injury that is not life or limb threatening and is either beyond the scope or availability of the typical primary care practice or retail clinic. Urgent care centers (UCCs) differentiate as compared to primary care providers in that: (1) no appointment is required; (2) evening/weekend operating hours are common; and (3) an on-site X-ray is available. By definition, UCCs do not compete against primary care providers and do not treat chronic patient conditions such as hypertension and diabetes.

In addition to the traditional acute condition, many UCCs provide occupational medicine services, travel medicine services, and sports and school physicals. UCCs also provide a variety of ancillary services including radiology services (primarily X-ray/radiology and ultrasound), STD testing, vaccine administration, casting, and wound care. Because of urgent care's wide variety of consumer-friendly services and low cost, the long-term value proposition of urgent care is extremely compelling. Urgent care has become the market-driven solution for many of the healthcare industry's supply and demand, cost, and convenience challenges.

1.0 Retail Healthcare

Unlike the majority of healthcare service segments where a patient or physician referral or managed care plan directs the patient, urgent care is the largest segment of the healthcare services space that mirrors the business dynamics of a nonhealthcare retail business. Location and branding are crucial to business success.

UCCs are concentrated in suburban locations within major metropolitan centers. Typical patient entrapment radius is eight to 10 miles. Beneficially, the entrapment radius corresponds to either the home, place of work, or children's school location. UCCs are more prevalent in areas with large middle-class populations, as patients use UCCs as a tool to help manage their busy lives.

UCCs tend to be positioned in high-visibility, consumer-accessible locations. According to the *Journal of Urgent Care Medicine*, the location of a UCC is an important factor for gaining and retaining patient volume. According to the UCAOA 2014 benchmarking report, approximately 38.0% operate within a shopping center or strip mall while approximately 32.0% operate in a freestanding facility (see Exhibit 1). A smaller percentage are located within a medical office building, where the majority of primary care providers are located. Because UCCs typically operate beyond standard business hours and at night, a high traffic well-lit area is crucial for off-hours patient volume. Patients should feel safe to enter and exit the UCC.

Exhibit 1. Location of UCCs

Type of Location	Percentage of Centers
Freestanding	32.0%
Within a Medical Office Building	20.0%
Within a Shopping Center or Strip Mall	38.0%
Within a Mixed-Use building	9.0%

Source: UCAOA 2014 benchmarking report

2.0 Value Proposition—Patients

UCCs value the most precious asset patients have: their time. Wait times and throughput are, on average, significantly below traditional emergency departments, even those ERs who advertise "fast track" services. As reported by the UCAOA, an extraordinary 70% of wait times for urgent care visits are less than 20 minutes—a stark contrast to emergency rooms (see Exhibit 2).

As the number of emergency room visits has steadily increased, reaching over 135 million patients annually, waiting for treatment has become a central problem of emergency room care. In less than 28% of total emergency room visits is a patient seen in less than 15 minutes. Additionally, only 12% of patients are admitted to hospitals, suggesting that urgent care centers will be able to both effectively and efficiently serve the majority of patients' needs. Consequently, a growing number of patients have begun opting for treatment at urgent care centers as an alternative to the long wait times of emergency departments. Urgent care is popular with households that lie in middle-to-upper-income-bracket areas and young working adults—with or without kids. The majority of urgent care patients are home owners, college educated, and/or have been a resident of the community for more than six years.

3.0 Value Proposition—Payors

While the average cost for a hospital emergency department visit is approximately $582, the

Exhibit 2. Wait Times

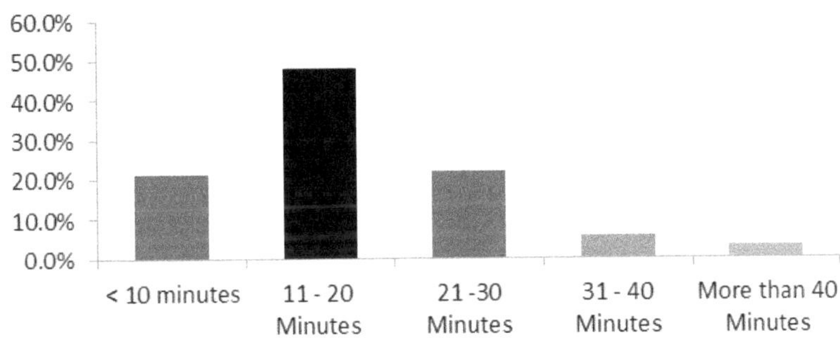

Source: UCAOA 2014 benchmarking report

average cost of an urgent care visit is approximately $140, providing both patients and insurance providers with a lower cost alternative. Managed care companies' increased emphasis on utilizing urgent care clinics as a means of minimizing healthcare costs essentially serves as advertising for UCCs. In addition, copays for UCCs are typically higher than primary care for many insurance plans, ensuring that the patient is partly responsible financially for the convenience of the UCC.

Presented in Exhibit 3 is a summary of the average reimbursement per visit for urgent care centers according to the UCAOA 2014 benchmarking report. According to the report, approximately 95.0% of UCCs report average reimbursement per visit in the range of approximately $75 to $150 per visit. The average reimbursement a UCC receives will vary depending on several factors including payor mix, ancillary services provided (e.g., radiology, laboratory, wound care), negotiated commercial rates, and competitive positioning within the market.

Payors are well educated on what factors drive growth in the urgent care industry, what patients expect, and how top-line revenue is changing. Payors have access to data signifying where costs are high in the system and can redirect to lower-cost sites. Payors also work to strengthen urgent care access in regions where emergency room use is prevalent and overutilized.

Payors can also ensure quality through their relationship with UCCs. Approximately 5% of all UCCs are accredited currently by the UCAOA. Payors are trending to favor accredited UCCs, and in many markets payors will only contract with accredited UCCs, ensuring that their client and market share demand quality and value.

4.0 Payor Mix

Based on the UCAOA 2014 benchmarking report, the payor mix for UCCs is comprised primarily of commercial payors, which accounted for approximately 54.5% of total collections (see Exhibit 4). Medicare and Medicaid accounted for approximately 10.5% and 5.5%, respectively, of the average UCC payor mix. Commercial insurers negotiate contracted rates for service provided

Exhibit 3. Average-Per-Visit Reimbursement (All Visit Types)

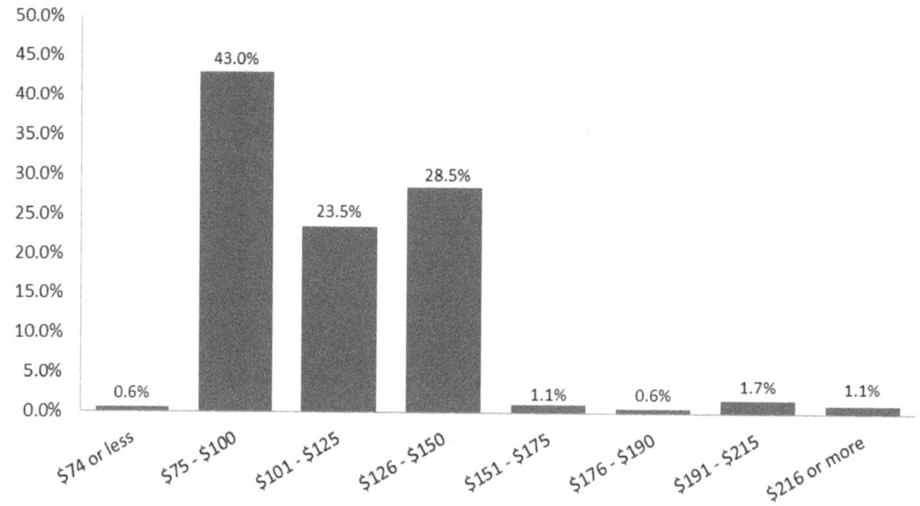

Source: UCAOA 2014 benchmarking report

in a UCC; however, payments from Medicare and Medicaid are the same whether the service is provided in a UCC or a physician office. Approximately 9.5% of the average UCC payor mix are collections from self-pay or uninsured patients. It should be noted that urgent care centers typically offer discounted prices for patients that do not have health insurance.

Exhibit 4. Urgent Care—Payor Mix

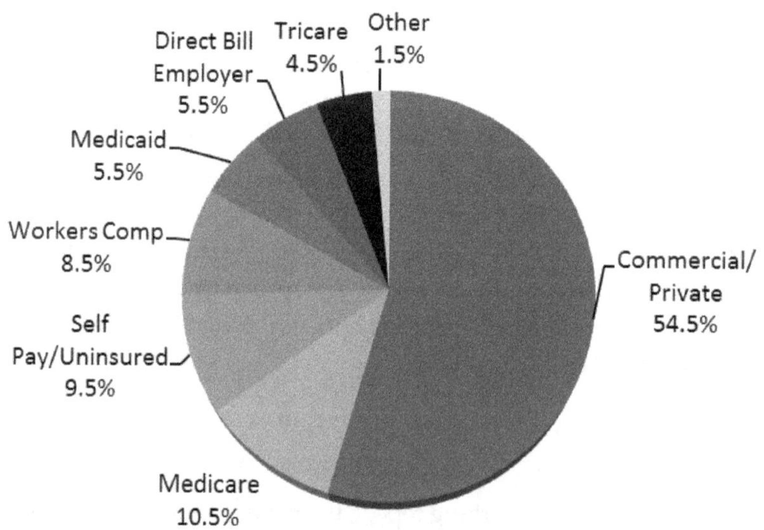

Source: UCAOA 2014 benchmarking report

5.0 Medicare FFS Program

Urgent care centers typically do not have a large Medicare percentage in the payor mix. Medicare patients, due to the large percentage of retired benefactors, often do not have a time rush in their daily lives. In addition, Medicare patients will gravitate toward their primary care physician, who is familiar to them, possesses their chart, and is able to follow and monitor symptoms of chronic conditions. Medicare Part B pays for physician services provided in a UCC based on the Medicare Physician Fee Schedule (MPFS). Under the MPFS, payment rates are established based on relative weights called relative value units (RVUs), which account for the relative costliness of the inputs used to provide physician services. The fee schedule amount is then determined by summing the geographically adjusted RVU components and multiplying the total by the fee schedule conversion factor. For most physician services, Medicare pays the provider 80.0% of the fee schedule amount. The beneficiary is liable for the remaining 20.0% co-insurance.

Payments under the physician fee schedule may also be adjusted upward or downward to reflect other factors. The first potential downward adjustment occurs if certain nonphysician practitioners (e.g. nurse practitioner and physician assistant) furnish services. For example, services provided by nurse practitioners and billed separately are paid at 85.0% of physician's fees. However, it should be noted that practices can receive 100% of reimbursement under the MPFS for services nonphysicians provide if the services are billed as "incident to." "Incident to" is defined as services the nonphysician provider furnishes as an integral part of the physician's personal professional service in the course of diagnosis or treatment of an injury or illness. Services that are provided as "incident to" are billed under the physician's provider number.

6.0 Industry Growth

Due to the compelling convenience and value construct of the urgent care industry and the response of patient demand and preference, the number of UCCs has grown substantially. As illustrated in Exhibit 5, industry growth, in the form of new net UCCs opening, has been impressive.

Exhibit 5. Number of Urgent Care Centers

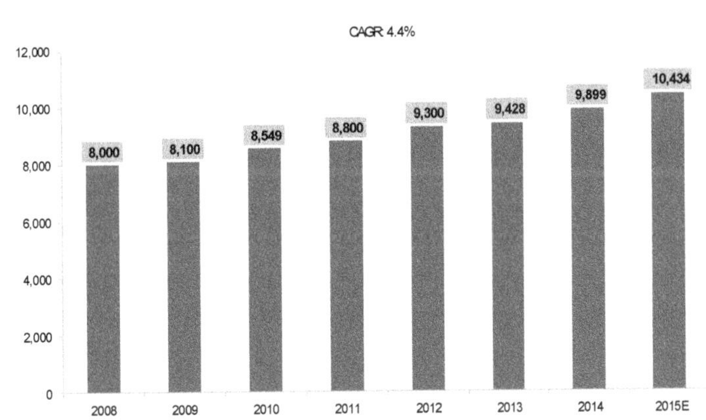

Source: UCAOA 2014 benchmarking report

Since 2008, the industry has added UCCs at a compounded annual growth rate of 4.4%. Urgent care center growth is causing significant disruption for traditional hospitals and medical groups. Although the industry has begun consolidating, there is still a tremendous amount of de novo UCC activity. Corporate and hospital operators have captured desirable locations. Also, unsophisticated "mom and pop" operators continue to infiltrate the market and capture same store growth. Although there is significant patient volume growth industrywide, same-store growth is challenging in certain markets as the addition of new centers affects per-center demand. Demand for urgent care services will continue to increase during the next decade, driven by middle-class population growth. These people have no choice, due to high demands on their time, but to seek Medicaid care for themselves and their family quickly.

7.0 Market Participants

According to the UCAOA, approximately one-third of UCCs are owned by or affiliated with a hospital system, with the remaining facilities either being physician owned or owned by a corporate operator (see Exhibit 6). There are no federal registration requirements for UCCs, and most states do not have licensure requirements specific to UCCs, therefore UCCs are licensed in the same way as a typical physician practice. Urgent care centers may also provide other healthcare services in addition to treating common and acute illness and injury.

Exhibit 6. Ownership Type

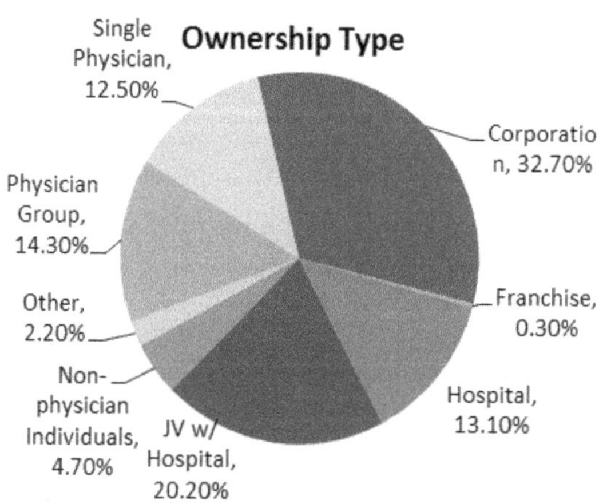

Source: UCAOA 2014 benchmarking report

Presented in Exhibit 7 is the number of UCCs operated by the nine largest UCC management companies. As of September 2015, Concentra and US Healthworks were the largest operators with 300 and 200 centers, respectively.

Exhibit 7. Number of UCCs Operated by the Nine Largest UCC Management Companies

Company Name	Number of Clinics
Concentra	300
Dignity/USHealthworks	200
MedExpress	150
American Family Care	160
NextCare	116
FastMed	91
CareSpot	52
Patient First	57
Doctors Care	51
Total	**1,177**

Source: VMG Research and Merchant Medicine Newsletter as of September 1, 2015

Recent growth in the urgent care market came primarily from the pure-play segment and, more specifically, from the independent operators as compared to hospital-owned urgent care operators. Many of the top-tier companies have private equity sponsors. MedExpress, NextCare, Fastmed, and CareSelect grew considerable over the last few years thanks to private equity sponsorship. The largest pure-play urgent care operator (not focused on occupation health) is MedExpress, with 150 clinics in 11 states. MedExpress had net growth of 20 clinics in 2014 and early 2015. NextCare has 116 clinics in 11 states. NextCare grew by 20 clinics in 2014 and early 2015. Despite the private equity-driven expansion in the top companies, the industry remains highly fragmented, with the top companies representing 11% of the total.

8.0 Private Equity and Urgent Care

Key aspects of private equity investment criteria include the presence of cash flow to feed growth, a business that is value priced to grow, and a well-funded universe of strategic purchasers for an exit. Using the operating cash flow and outside capital for growth, PE firms can achieve scale with the addition of new centers or clusters of centers in adjacent markets. With scale, the business becomes very attractive to a strategic acquirer, such as a hospital, an insurance company, or a larger urgent care company. The successful private equity investment transforms a cluster of UCCs in a market, with very little to nothing in common but ownership, into a thriving company with real infrastructure, capable of growing the network of centers and adapting to any future payment changes.

9.0 Hospitals and Urgent Care

As a first point of triage for many patients, urgent care physicians represent a valuable referral source for other healthcare providers. Some of the downstream providers UCCs refer to include: orthopedic surgery, ENT, and primary care. Hospitals were the first owner operators in the urgent care space. Historically, urgent care centers operated by hospitals were not run effectively. Although they were established to relieve emergency-room lower acuity volume, they often brought expenses and inefficiencies that caused initial UCCs to operate unprofitably. Subsequently, private operators and physician entrepreneurs illustrated that UCCs could be operated profitably, causing UCCs to proliferate. Once volume started trending away from hospital-owned physician practices to UCCs, hospitals once again became interested in owning or joint venturing UCCs. Usually, hospitals are joint venturing with for-profit urgent care companies and relying on third-party operators to operate the UCCs efficiently.

UCCs are expected to gain increased importance in the healthcare delivery system as healthcare reform seeks to reduce hospital admissions, but they can also help a hospital system gain market share. As an inexpensive means of gaining access to markets where they have no presence, UCCs become an integral part of a health system's outreach efforts to patients and to gain intelligence on the markets in which it operates.

10.0 Physician Entrepreneurs

Physician entrepreneurs will continue to open and operate urgent care centers. Physician owners may originate from working the hospital emergency room or a primary care setting. The lure of opening an UCC may be an improvement in lifestyle or independence or an increase in compensation. Physician entrepreneurs typically work all or most of the allotted weekly hours at a UCC that they own, blurring the line between equity and professional income. When valuing a physician-owned UCC, the valuation professional should differentiate the level of profits derived from ownership as opposed to labor. The value of the UCC is only correlated to profit attributable to ownership.

11.0 Typical Urgent Care Income Statements

An example five-year urgent care income statement is illustrated in Exhibit 8.

This income statement is typical in that it has some defining characteristics of an urgent care center. First, physician salary is the largest expense component. After the physician is compensated, the second largest expense is nonphysician staff salary. Theses salaries include midlevel, clinical professionals, technical staff, and administrative salaries.

Next, as revenue and volume grow, variable costs follow. Variable costs include administrative and nonphysician personnel. Finally, as revenue and volume grow, physician salaries as a percentage of revenue are relatively fixed. Although the costs may increase slightly, physician costs, paid on an hourly basis, are not correlated to volume but to time. A positive value characteristic of a UCC's financial performance is that, if the UCC is able to grow volume and revenue, profits—in the form of operating leverage—should increase disproportionately.

Most UCCs utilize a "physician-based" model whereby the physician is the primary provider of medical services to the UCC's patients. The most common physician specialties employed by

Exhibit 8. Five-Year Urgent Care Income Statement

	2010	2011	2012	2013	2014	2010	2011	2012	2013	2014
Revenue:										
Total Net Operating Revenue	1,718,216	1,769,763	1,822,856	1,877,541	1,933,868	100.0%	100.0%	100.0%	100.0%	100.0%
Operating Expenses:										
Non-Physician Salary	354,050	362,901	371,974	381,273	390,805	20.6%	20.5%	20.4%	20.3%	20.2%
Physician Salary	414,960	425,334	435,967	446,867	458,038	24.2%	24.0%	23.9%	23.8%	23.7%
Employee Benefits	153,802	157,647	161,588	165,628	169,769	9.0%	8.9%	8.9%	8.8%	8.8%
Occupancy Costs	81,341	83,375	85,459	87,595	89,785	4.7%	4.7%	4.7%	4.7%	4.6%
Drugs & Medical Supplies	70,321	73,134	76,059	79,102	82,266	4.1%	4.1%	4.2%	4.2%	4.3%
Ancillary Services & Supplies	15,829	16,146	16,468	16,798	17,134	0.9%	0.9%	0.9%	0.9%	0.9%
Insurance	32,293	33,262	34,260	35,288	36,346	1.9%	1.9%	1.9%	1.9%	1.9%
General & Administrative	225,069	229,570	234,162	238,845	243,622	13.1%	13.0%	12.8%	12.7%	12.6%
Total Operating Expenses	1,347,665	1,381,369	1,415,938	1,451,395	1,487,764	78.4%	78.1%	77.7%	77.3%	76.9%
EBITDA	370,551	388,394	406,918	426,146	446,103	21.6%	21.9%	22.3%	22.7%	23.1%
Depreciation & Amortization Expense	15,487	15,797	16,113	16,435	16,764	0.9%	0.9%	0.9%	0.9%	0.9%
Earnings Before Income Taxes	355,064	372,597	390,805	409,711	429,340	20.7%	21.1%	21.4%	21.8%	22.2%
Federal & State Income Tax Expense	124,272	130,409	136,782	143,399	150,269	7.2%	7.4%	7.5%	7.6%	7.8%
Earnings After Income Taxes	230,792	242,188	254,023	266,312	279,071	13.4%	13.7%	13.9%	14.2%	14.4%

Source: VMG internal database

UCCs include family medicine, emergency medicine, internal medicine, and pediatrics. UCCs typically employ physicians at a base hourly rate plus bonus based on various production metrics (e.g., wRVUs, patients, net collections, etc.) Based on the UCAOA benchmarking report and illustrated in Exhibit 9, the average hourly rate for employed physicians was $95, with approximately 74.4% of respondents reporting an average hourly rate in the range of $80 to $110.

In addition to the physician and midlevel providers, UCCs employ a mix of medical assistants, X-ray technicians, and occasionally registered nurses.

Exhibit 9. Hourly Rate: Physicians

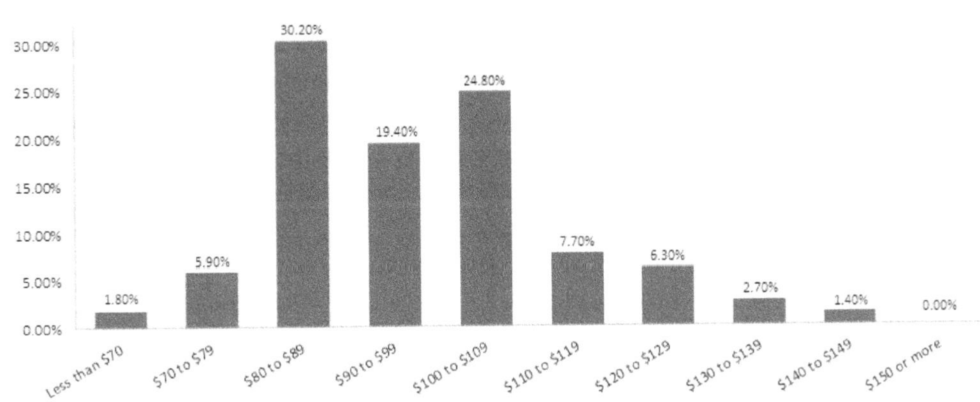

Source: UCAA 2014 Benchmarking Report

According to the UCAOA benchmarking report, 97.8% of UCCs report having physicians on staff at all times. However, an increasing number of UCCs are utilizing midlevel providers (physician assistants and nurse practitioners) for additional patient capacity particularly in areas where there is a shortage of primary care physicians. According to the UCAOA benchmarking report, the average hourly salary for physician assistants and nurse practitioners was $54 and $52, respectively, or approximately 57% and 55%, respectively, of the average physician hourly salary.

12.0 Transaction Market Defined

Prior to discussing the transaction market and resulting valuations applied to urgent care centers and urgent care chains, one must first consider precisely what types of businesses are included in the urgent care transaction market and where these businesses fit in the continuum of care. For example, a business's signage and marketing may be branded as an urgent care center but operationally functions as a primary care clinic that leaves unscheduled time available to accommodate walk-in patients, or perhaps stays open after hours in order to serve walk-in patients. Additionally, lab and X-ray services may not be provided on-site. While this business may appear to fit the description of an urgent care center to some extent, it would not necessarily meet the definition of an urgent care center, strictly speaking.[1] However, it may be valued the same as an urgent care center, as it may be more similar to a physician's professional practice from a valuation perspective (see "Physician Practice Valuation" section).

Urgent care in its purest form fits squarely in the continuum of care between primary care and emergency room services. Services are provided on a walk-in basis, and diagnostic and ancillary services are provided on-site, during all hours of operation. An urgent care center may find itself competing with local primary care physicians and local emergency departments for lower acuity services, especially during startup.

Due to the retail nature and the consumer-centric customer service model of urgent care centers, many types of buyers are active in the transaction market, including urgent care chains, local tax-exempt hospitals and regional tax-exempt health systems, large publicly traded hospital operators, as well as private equity investors. More recently, hospitals and health systems are entering the transaction market for urgent care, as evidenced by the many large health systems that are joint venturing and co-branding both existing and de novo urgent care centers across the country with urgent care chains. The added nuance for health systems, and perhaps helping to explain why health systems have been relatively slow to adopt the urgent care model, is that health systems do not want to compete with their own physician groups. Most health systems have spent and will continue to spend considerable time and financial resources building and integrating employed physicians. Adding an urgent care model to the mix, which has a completely different physician compensation and operational model from primary care, can rightly or wrongly be seen by primary care physicians as competitive behavior. Navigating these local political realties is never easy.

1 See UCAOA certification and accreditation criteria at www.ucaoa.org.

13.0 Valuation Characteristics and Methodology

UCC buyers most commonly analyze and price controlling equity interest transactions in a straight-forward manner, using a multiple of EBITDA less interest-bearing debt. UCC owner-operators often prefer to own a controlling equity interest in order to enhance the ability to achieve economies of scale and enhance negotiating influence and leverage across a platform.

Unlike UCC owner-operators who typically price controlling equity interest transactions using a range of multiples of EBITDA, most hospital systems rely on the fair market value opinion provided by an independent appraiser to ensure that they meet Stark and fraud and abuse statute requirements and private inurement concerns. Various professional standards require that business appraisers consider all relevant approaches and methods in developing an opinion of value. These other approaches and, in particular, the income approach or discounted cash flow method may provide a superior framework for measuring the impact of the individual facts and circumstances surrounding a subject UCC. Like all fair market value analysis, the cost approach, market approach, and income approach should be considered when valuing an urgent care center or chain under the fair market value standard. Important to understanding the value of UCCs is the size and scale of the operations, which has implications for the market and income approaches to value.

14.0 Cost Approach

Many smaller urgent care chains or single-site operations owned by physician entrepreneurs are either breakeven or not expected to provide a return greater than the required return on the working capital and fixed assets employed in the operation of the UCC. These UCCs may be generating sufficient cash flow to pay physician compensation but generate no profit for the owners. In these cases, the asset approach provides a "floor," or lowest minimum value, related to a controlling interest in a UCC. This may be the appropriate approach when the market and income approaches produce lower values.

In a transaction for a controlling interest in the context of marginal or zero earnings, a UCC owner-operator is not likely to pay for all, or maybe even any, of the intangible value created through the ownership and management of a UCC. However, in the context of a make-or-buy decision typical of this type of transaction, the buyer may pay for the assembly of all tangible and some intangible assets under the premise of value in continued use, as part of a mass assemblage of assets.

From the perspective of a single-site or small urgent care chain, UCCs can appear to be an asset-intensive business (e.g., to a physician starting a UCC). The average gross property and equipment plus working capital per location hovers around $750,000. The UCCs may be overbuilt relative to the realized average daily visit volume. This type of circumstance can lead to transaction and, often, the application of the cost approach.

15.0 Market Approach

The two common market approach methodologies include the guideline public company method and the merger and acquisition method. The guideline public company method relies on valuation metrics from publicly traded companies, while the merger and acquisition method relies on valuation metrics from transactions involving comparable UCCs. Given the lack of publicly traded pure-play urgent care concerns and lack of comparability between other publicly traded healthcare services companies and UCCs, the guideline public company method is not typically considered applicable to derive a value indication for UCCs.

Given the number of transactions that occur in the UCC space, the merger and acquisition method is considered applicable. Virtually all buyers use a multiple of EBITDA less interest-bearing debt in pricing a controlling equity interest in a UCC. While UCC operators often reference and use these general-market-guideline multiples, many factors may lead to an adjustment of the historical EBITDA or an ultimate transaction price that resides outside of this typical range.

In the discussion of the primary UCC value drivers, we detailed the need to consider changes in Medicare and commercial payor reimbursement when analyzing historical information and developing future projections. Based on our experience, the acquisition multiple used to price the purchase of a controlling interest is often applied to prospective or adjusted, rather than historically reported, EBITDA. A UCC company may have one or more startup UCCs. In fact, an aggressive growth strategy could substantially depress reported EBITDA for a growing UCC platform. These startup losses from existing recently opened sites should be normalized before applying a multiple in order to understand a reasonable EBITDA run rate after operations stabilize. UCC developers and operators also often adjust for startup losses and changes in reimbursement, as well as service mix, to estimate the EBITDA to which the multiple is applied. Typical UCC multiples, varying with the size of the platform, are displayed in Exhibit 10.

Exhibit 10. TIC/EBITDA Multiple Ranges

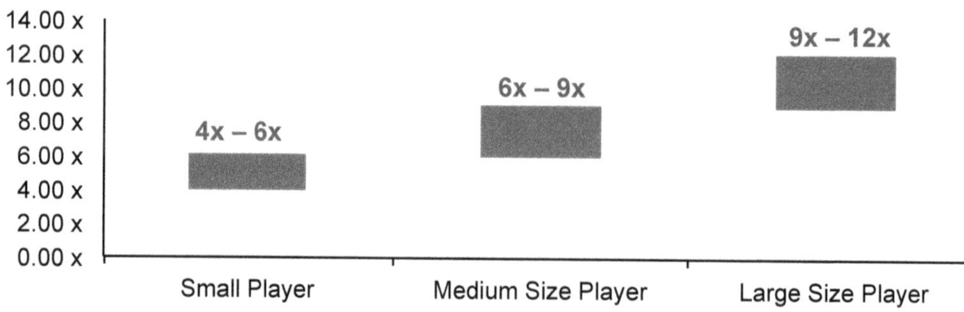

Source: VMG internal database

16.0 Income Approach

Two general income approach methods may be utilized in the application of the income approach, which include capitalizing a single-period cash flow, as well as discounting multiperiod cash flows. Due to the ever-changing healthcare landscape, changes in local competition, and growth prospects, the single-period cash flow capitalization approach is not considered applicable. The multiperiod discounted cash flow is considered applicable, as many variables may be incorporated into the cash flow projections, which can affect value. In this method, the revenues, earnings, and resulting cash flows of the UCC are projected over typically five years. These cash flows are then discounted to present value utilizing an appropriate discount rate.

The terminal value is most often calculated using the Gordon growth model, which is then discounted to present value as well. In practice, certain types of buyers, primarily private equity buyers, may use an exit multiple approach to calculate a terminal value, as an exit is actually expected at some point at or near the end of their forecast period. The exit multiple approach may imply a cost of capital or growth rate that is inconsistent with the forecast period or may assume market conditions that are inconsistent with past or current conditions experienced. Considering these factors, the Gordon growth model is the preferred approach. The total enterprise value or equity value, depending on the benefit stream that was used in the forecast, may then be calculated as the sum of the discounted cash flows from both the discrete period and terminal period. For a growing UCC chain, UCC management may be very bullish on the prospects of the enterprise. Whether the appraiser projects a number of scenarios with a range of applicable discount rates or develops a single most likely case scenario with a single appropriate discount rate, the mechanics of the projections should be similar.

Patient volume is a primary determinant of financial performance for an urgent care center. Volume is typically analyzed and projected in terms of number of patient visits. Given the seasonality of urgent care businesses, average daily patient volume by month should be trended and considered when forecasting patient volume. Reimbursement levels are the second and equally as important determinant of financial performance. Shifts in payor mix and service mix can have a dramatic impact on overall average net revenue per visit, and trends should be analyzed and factored into the reimbursement forecast.

UCC cost structures are somewhat fixed in nature and can exhibit a high degree of operating leverage. Assuming an efficient staffing model given overall volume levels, incremental volumes over the breakeven level create significantly higher margin. Physician and staff costs are the largest two expenses for the typical UCC, making the staffing model a primary area of scrutiny when forecasting expenses.

Capital expenditures (CapEx) are also significant to the discounted cash flow method for UCCs. A UCC is typically an asset-intensive business. While the dangers of following rules of thumb have been subject to lively debate throughout the history of the valuation profession, annual amounts ranging from \$20,000 to \$40,000 per year can be considered typical amounts. In addition to considering the age and condition of the existing furniture and equipment and the potential maintenance required, CapEx assumptions should also consider possible growth in volume.

For UCC chains and larger operators, the consolidated back-office and administrative functions are typically fixed for a given number of sites. As the platform grows, these expenses are a step function based on the number of sites. When forecasting the revenue and expenses of larger UCC chains, bifurcating the forecast between the "four-wall" revenue and expenses associated with the actual UCC sites and the back-office and shared administrative functions is crucial. For growing UCC chains, this enables the valuation professional to understand the ramp-up timeline for specific UCC sites.

Consistent with the tendencies of UCC owner-operators, we typically perform a discounted cash flow analysis whereby the market value of invested capital (MVIC) is calculated using debt-free cash flows and book value of debt is deducted from MVIC to arrive at a total equity value. While most UCCs typically use long-term debt to fund initial operations, many UCCs fund subsequent furniture and equipment purchases out of cash flows.

Prior to opening, the selection of the location of an urgent care center's facility is crucial to ensuring the success of the UCC. Virtually all UCCs lease their facilities. If not, the UCC's valuation may be impacted. If the UCC does own the real estate as well, the business appraiser should consider the potential difference in required returns on the real estate versus the UCC operations. The preferred solution is to engage a real estate appraiser to value the land and building separately and impute the implied market rental rate as an expense of the UCC. Then the values of the real estate and the UCC operations may be combined to arrive at an overall value.

If a separate real estate appraisal cannot be obtained, adjust the discount rate utilized in the discount cash flows to reflect the generally lower expected returns associated with the real estate. An adjustment to account for real estate may be considered when using the market approach (discussed earlier) and is applicable in the valuation of either a controlling interest or noncontrolling interest.

The valuation of a controlling equity interest approaching 100% requires an additional consideration. Under the income and market approaches, the pricing of most controlling interest transactions is for 51% to 60% interest. The same market multiples and rates of return may not apply to the incremental 40% to 49% interest of a 100% equity purchase.

17.0 Conclusion

The UCC industry has grown significantly because of its popularity with patients. To continue to grow, the industry must survive challenges to the business model. These include the proliferation of lower-cost access points such as telemedicine and retail health centers. Threats to growth will also occur from higher-cost, higher-service models such as freestanding emergency rooms. For now, UCCs are well positioned to become a key player in the changing healthcare landscape. To ensure viability, UCCs must understand their position in their local market and how they can be differentiated from a patient's other options in that market.

As health systems continue to pursue urgent care strategies through acquisition and development, the question remains as to where urgent care centers fit within alternative payment model methodologies. This is not likely to be answered anytime soon; however, until that time comes, urgent care centers are well positioned relative to the "triple aim," as UCCs provide low-cost, quality care in local communities they serve.

Chapter 22.
Valuing CINs, ACOs, PHOs, and IPAs

CONTENTS

Chapter 22.
Valuing CINs, ACOs, PHOs, and IPAs

By Karin Chernoff Kaplan, MBA, CVA; Stuart J. Schaff, CVA, CHFP; and Jessica E. Stack, MBA

1.0 Shifting Focus From Volume to Value

Healthcare spending, which accounted for just 5.0% of gross domestic product (GDP) in 1960, rose dramatically over the following 50 years, reaching 17.4% of GDP in 2010. This trend, shown in Exhibit 1, received widespread attention and became a national priority as expenditures continued to rise and an increasing share of the burden was placed on federal, state, and local governments.

Exhibit 1. National Health Expenditures as a Percentage of GDP (1960-2013)

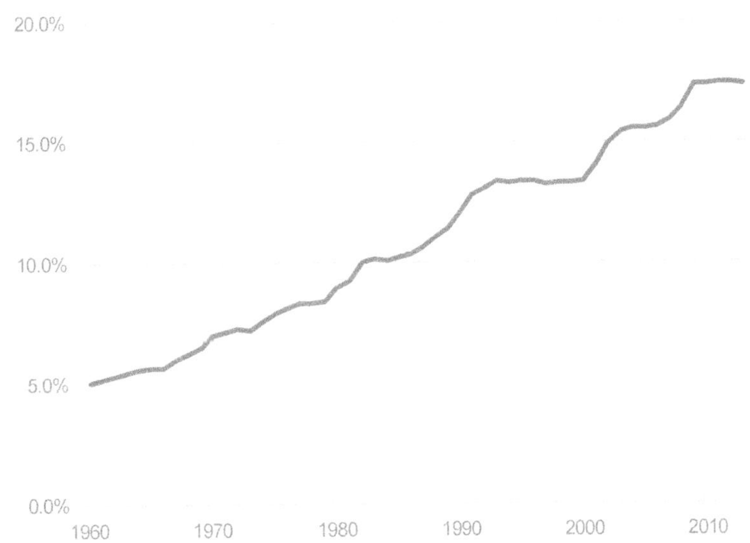

In response to this and other related issues, Congress passed the Affordable Care Act (ACA) in 2010. ACA seeks to:

- Increase the number of citizens who receive healthcare coverage through either public-sector insurance programs or private-sector insurance companies;
- Expand the array of healthcare providers that consumers may choose among;
- Improve the access to healthcare specialists;
- Improve the quality of healthcare; and
- Decrease the cost of healthcare.

ACA addresses these goals through a combination of new regulations as well as fundamental changes to the way healthcare is financed (and, to some extent, the way it is delivered). As the federal government is the largest payor in the United States, ACA leverages Medicare to drive this shift toward value, primarily through a variety of new payment and service delivery models developed by the Center for Medicare & Medicaid Innovation (CMMI). These new payment arrangements focus on rewarding value (i.e., higher quality at lower cost) instead of volume, as has been the norm under traditional fee-for-service models. Examples of these initiatives include:[1]

- *Accountable care organizations* (ACOs) and similar care models designed to bring together healthcare providers to collectively assume responsibility to manage the health and total cost of care for a given population. Medicare's ACO models include the Medicare Shared Savings Program, the Pioneer ACO Model, and the Next Generation ACO Model for general Medicare populations, the Comprehensive ESRD Care Initiative for dialysis patients, and the ACO Investment Model and Advanced Payment ACO Model for organizations that require upfront financing for infrastructure investments.
- *Episode-based payment initiatives,* under which participating providers are held accountable for the cost and quality of care beneficiaries receive during an episode of care, which usually begins with a hospitalization or some other triggering event. The best known of these initiatives is the Bundled Payments for Care Improvement (BPCI). There are currently four BPCI models, which vary in when the payment is made and which portion of the episode is covered (e.g., acute care hospital stay only, post-acute care only, or a combination of the two). CMMI has also announced models specific to joint replacement and oncology.
- *Primary care transformation initiatives,* such as "medical homes" in which primary care providers—the gateway to healthcare for many patients—utilize a team-based

1 CMMI, "Innovation Models." Accessed on Sept. 15, 2015, at innovation.cms.gov/initiatives/index.html#views=models.

approach that emphasizes prevention, health information technology, care coordination, and shared decision making among patients and their providers.

- *Initiatives focused on the Medicaid and Children's Health Insurance Population (CHIP).*
- *Initiatives focused on the Medicare-Medicaid enrollees* (i.e., those who are designated as "dual eligible").
- *Initiatives to accelerate the development and testing of new payment and service delivery models.*
- *Initiatives to speed the adoption of best practices.*

These initiatives are numerous, diverse, and constantly changing. It is critical for a valuator in this space to stay on top of the nuances and frequent updates and to adjust his or her models accordingly.

Commercial payors have followed the federal government's lead in implementing new payment methodologies, developing their own ACO, bundled payment, medical home, and other value-based payment models with the same goal: provide appropriate incentives to support the delivery of high-quality care and lower total costs.

Healthcare spending remained at approximately 17.4% of GDP between 2009 and 2013.[2] However, as the population continues to age and utilize more healthcare services, the rate of spending growth is expected to increase faster than GDP, eventually reaching 19.6% by 2024.[3]

Given the imperative to "bend the cost curve," the momentum toward value-based payment models has shown little signs of slowing. In January 2015, the Department of Health and Human Services (HHS) announced its goal to have 30% of Medicare provider payments in these new models by 2016 and 50% by 2018.[4] Shortly thereafter, a group consisting of "several of the nation's largest health systems and insurers" announced the intention to shift 75% of their business to value-based contracts.[5]

2 CMS, "National Health Expenditures 2013 Highlights." Accessed Sept. 15, 2015, at www.cms.gov/Research-Statistics-Data-and-Systems/Statistics-Trends-and-Reports/NationalHealthExpendData/Downloads/highlights.pdf.

3 CMS, "National Health Expenditure Projections 2014-2024." Accessed Sept. 15, 2015, at www.cms.gov/Research-Statistics-Data-and-Systems/Statistics-Trends-and-Reports/NationalHealthExpendData/Downloads/proj2014.pdf.

4 HHS, "Progress Towards Achieving Better Care, Smarter Spending, Healthier People." Accessed on Sept. 16, 2015, at www.hhs.gov/blog/2015/01/26/progress-towards-better-care-smarter-spending-healthier-people.html.

5 Modern Healthcare, "Major providers, insurers plan aggressive push to new payment models." Accessed on Sept. 16, 2015, at www.modernhealthcare.com/article/20150128/NEWS/301289934.

2.0 Bringing Providers Together

As payors continue to turn toward new payment models, many healthcare providers have embraced some form of accountable care, bundled payments, or other types of shared savings/shared risk arrangements. The first step often involves the development of an entity through which physicians in a community can contract together with governmental and commercial payors, often (but not always) alongside a health system and its employed physicians. Like the payment arrangements themselves, there are several types of these entities including the aforementioned ACOs as well as clinically integrated networks (CINs), physician-hospital organization (PHOs), or independent practice associations (IPAs). A brief description of each of these entities follows:

- An *IPA* is an organization created and owned by independently practicing physicians who come together for the purposes of contracting with payors. The IPA obtains contracts from an HMO, negotiates the terms and conditions of the contract, and often processes the claims for services.
- A *PHO* is similar to an IPA, but it is jointly owned by a hospital and members of its medical staff.
- In addition to being a type of contract, an *ACO* is an entity in which physicians (and sometimes a hospital or health system) come together to accept collective accountability for the cost and quality of care delivered to a defined population of patients. In other words, an ACO is a PHO taken to the next level.
- The term *"CIN"* can refer to a specific type of legal arrangement that allows hospitals and physicians to collaborate on improving quality and efficiency, while remaining independent entities, in exchange for the ability to negotiate collectively with insurers for better payment rates. While this collective bargaining would otherwise be illegal under antitrust rules, the Federal Trade Commission (FTC) issues waivers to certain organizations that meet specific requirements. The term is also used to describe ACO-like networks that negotiate with both governmental and commercial payors.

In this chapter, we will refer to the types of entities described above more broadly, as multi-provider networks (MPNs). The general idea underlying MPNs is that otherwise independent parties can work together, in a manner that complies with antitrust regulations, to reduce the total cost of care for a designated patient population, improve the quality of care delivered to that population, and be rewarded by a payor for doing so.

Therefore, MPNs work to ensure that patients get the right care at the right time, avoiding unnecessary duplication of services, preventing medical errors, and using costly specialty care and higher-level services appropriately. This generally requires investment in sophisticated information systems and evidence-based care management protocols to meet the challenges of providing improved quality in a cost-effective manner.

One of the advantages of MPNs is that they seek to redesign the care delivery model on more of a "macro" basis for all patients before entering into population management contracts with payors, which allows the physicians to treat each patient in the same manner, regardless of his or her insurance plan. This concept is illustrated in Exhibit 2.

Exhibit 2. Illustrative MPN Population Management Contracts

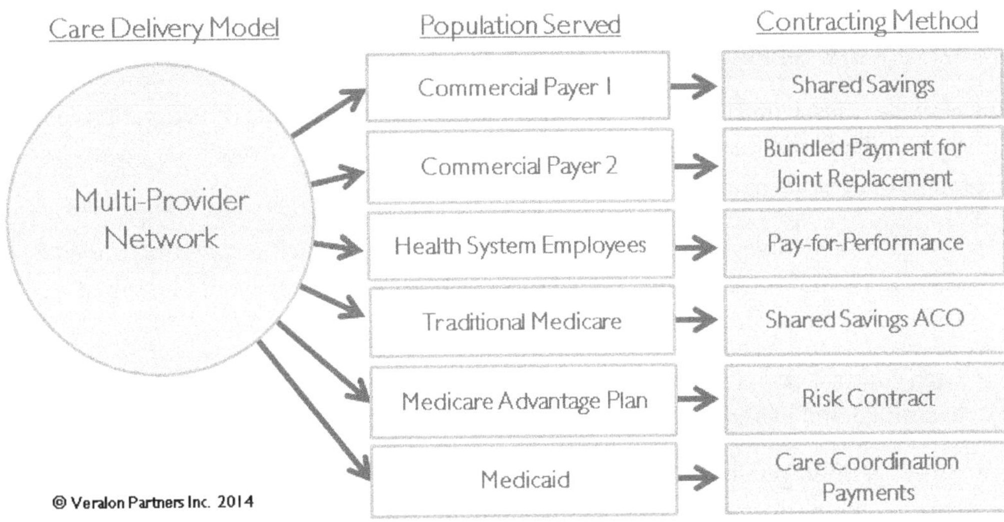

3.0 Transactions Involving MPNs

Much attention has been given in the literature to the strategic imperative to create MPNs and to the mechanics for doing so.[6] Over the past five years, hundreds of MPNs have sprung up in markets across the country. As one might expect in a rapidly consolidating market, transactions involving MPNs are becoming increasingly common.

Valuators are asked to render opinions on a wide variety of transactions in this space. At the advent of MPNs, conventional wisdom suggested that a valuation would primarily be required for purposes of determining the equity investment of the respective owners of an MPN or to determine a fair market value payment of the services delivered by the various members of the MPN (e.g., hospital, physicians, and ancillary service providers).

As the market continues to evolve, we are faced with these as well as many other business situations where we are requested to opine on the FMV of a particular transaction. Consider the following typical examples:

6 See, for example, John Harris, and Stu Schaff, "Mergers and Real Competition," hfm Healthcare Finance blog, December 2014.

- A hospital decides to acquire all or part of the ownership interest in an existing MPN instead of developing its own entity;
- A health system seeks to expand an existing CIN by acquiring or partnering with another MPN;
- One of two health systems that have decided to merge holds ownership interest in an MPN; and
- A hospital or provider group contracts with an MPN for care management, leadership, and analytic support services to achieve shared savings goals.

In any of these cases, it is critical that valuators understand the unique considerations and drivers that affect the economics of MPNs. The following themes run throughout any assessment of the fair market value of an MPN:

- An MPN's revenues are produced, at least in part, by reducing spending under shared savings contracts rather than through patient service fees, as would be the case in a typical fee-for-service contract;
- Each contract an MPN holds has a specific risk/reward profile and must be thoroughly examined and evaluated accordingly;
- An MPN often generates no cash in its early stages because shared savings revenue is based upon performance and calculated by the payor or payors at the *end* of specified periods (although certain payment models provide for an advance of expected savings); and
- It is not always clear who is responsible for the significant infrastructure investments required to successfully execute an MPN's contracts.

Further, as stated in this book's prior edition:

> One of the lessons of the tax court decision in *Derby*—involving an integration transaction from the 1990s—is that appraisers must value the actual transaction; fair market value contemplates the price that would take place between a hypothetical buyer and seller of a specific interest or item of property. The transaction itself is not a "hypothetical," and failure to recognize that point makes many valuations inaccurate. Thus, contrary to the view held by many appraisers who are not familiar with the regulatory structure of the healthcare industry, any valuation requires the appraiser to be intimately familiar with the transaction documents. If those documents change after the valuation is completed, the valuation should be reconciled to the final version of the documents.[7]

7 Carol Carden and Mark Dietrich, "A Valuation Model for the Formation of ACOs," *BVR's Guide to Healthcare Valuation,* 3rd edition enhanced, page 899.

Together, these issues make for a number of unique challenges in the financial value of an MPN, including evaluating revenue and expense projections, assessing shared savings revenue risk, determining how profits are to be distributed, and understanding the cost structure and working capital requirements. In all of these transactions, the three valuation approaches (income, market, and cost) are applicable to varying degrees. In this section, we present two examples drawn from actual transactions. The cases illustrate the actual application of various valuation methodologies and the associated challenges the valuator faces.

4.0 Example 1: Income Approach

4.1 Background

In this example, a regional health system is interested in acquiring a 75% equity interest in an MPN formed in 2012 by seven independent physicians and nonphysician administrators. After speaking with the management of both entities, the valuator has gathered the following information:

- The MPN has a Medicare Shared Savings Program (MSSP) ACO arrangement with an initial three-year term through 2015 and one three-year renewal term through 2018 as well as evergreen value-based payment arrangements with two separate commercial payors;
- Each primary care physician (PCP) in the network pays a $3,000 annual membership fee, and each specialist in the network pays a $5,500 annual membership fee;
- As an incentive to participate, providers share in the surplus or revenues of the various contracts:
    - Twenty percent of MSSP surplus (revenue less allocated expenses) is distributed to providers who participate in that contract; and
    - A small portion of the capitated revenue received from the commercial payors is distributed to providers who participate in the respective contracts.
- The MPN's assets include:
    - A workforce-in-place consisting of approximately 25 full-time equivalent staff members who provide executive leadership, data analytics, provider relations, and care management services;
    - Basic furniture, fixtures, and equipment;
    - A network of over 250 independent physicians have joined the MPN in order to participate in those contracts;
    - The payor contracts; and
    - Proprietary data analytics and care management systems.

Though the valuator will consider all three approaches to value, this example will focus on the income approach.

5.0 Income Approach Analysis

5.1 Estimating Size of Physician Network and Number of Beneficiaries

To date, the MPN has demonstrated success in recruiting primary care physicians and specialists to its network. The MPN's management has assumed that this success will continue over the five-year projection period, though the rate of physician additions will slow over time.

Each new physician brings along beneficiaries (also known as "covered lives") who will be attributed to the MPN under its payor contracts. Based on its track record and published benchmarks, the MPN's management projected the number of network physicians that will participate in the MSSP ACO and each commercial contract each year, as well as how many beneficiaries will be attributed to each PCP or specialist under each contract.[8] In the interest of network growth, any given physician is not compelled to sign onto a contract with a payor with which that physician does not already participate. Though the MPN recruits new physicians throughout the year, the attribution models under its three contracts specify that new beneficiaries are only added beginning on the following January 1.

The MPN's beneficiary projections are shown in Exhibit 3.

Exhibit 3. Network Providers and Beneficiaries by Contract

	2013	2014	2015	2016	2017	2018
Network Providers by Contract						
Total Network Providers	*270*	*443*	*663*	*859*	*987*	*1,086*
Total Est. Beneficiaries	*35,840*	*58,738*	*92,766*	*124,250*	*142,887*	*157,176*
MSSP Contract						
Total Providers Participating in MSSP		398	597	773	889	978
Avg. Beneficiaries per PCP		135	135	135	135	135
Avg. Beneficiaries per Specialist		30	30	30	30	30
Beneficiaries Attributed to MSSP		36,754	57,591	76,764	88,278	97,106
First Commercial Payer Contract						
Total Providers Participating in First Payer Care Mng Contract		144	231	312	359	394
Avg. Beneficiaries per PCP		125	125	125	125	125
Beneficiaries Attributable to First Payer Care Mng Contract		18,047	28,875	38,981	44,828	49,311
Second Commercial Payer Contract						
Total Providers Participating in Second Payer Care Mng Contract		79	126	170	196	215
Avg. Beneficiaries per PCP		50	50	50	50	50
Beneficiaries Attributable to Second Payer Care Mng Contract		3,938	6,300	8,505	9,781	10,759

8 Under most payors' models, a beneficiary is more likely to be attributed to a primary care physician than a specialist. Patients are first attributable to their predominant primary care physician. Patients without any recent visits to primary care physicians are attributed to the specialist, nurse practitioner, physician assistant, or clinical nurse specialist who provided the plurality of the patient's outpatient evaluation and management care.

The MPN had demonstrated success in recruiting physicians during its short operating history. The MPN assumed continued physician recruitment wherein physicians would be added during each of the five years—at a faster rate in the initial years and growth at slower rates in the outer years. We reviewed the projected provider growth. Considering the provider and beneficiary population in the MPN's target region and the lack of significant competition, we determined the provider projections to be reasonable.

5.2 Estimating MSSP Revenue

If the MPN's total Medicare expenditures are below a certain level each year (determined using attributed Medicare beneficiaries, historical expenditures per beneficiary,[9] and a savings benchmark rate), Medicare will share a portion of the savings with the MPN. The level of shared savings the MPN ultimately receives depends on the MSSP ACO's specific contract model as well as the MPN's aggregate score across a series of defined quality measures.

During its initial term (2013-2015), the MSSP ACO contract is a "Track 1, Upside Only" model, which means that the MPN is eligible to receive up to 50% of the savings generated without any risk should expenditures end up exceeding historical levels per beneficiary. In the renewal term, the contract will convert to a "Track 2" model, where the MPN accepts downside risk in exchange for a higher portion of the potential savings (60%).

Management expects quality scores to be strong in 2014 and then decline slightly before rebounding in 2017. This trend relates to the staged roll-out of quality metrics by CMS, combined with the MPN's ability to improve on quality over time.

Because the MPN's MSSP ACO contract began in 2012, the valuator is able to review initial CMS benchmark reports and interim performance reports to gain confidence that management's projection, which is shown in Exhibit 4, is reasonable.

Exhibit 4. MSSP Shared Savings Revenues

	2014	2015	2016	2017	2018
Beneficiaries at Beginning of Period	36,754	57,591	76,764	88,278	97,106
Benchmark Expenditures per Beneficiary*	$ 9,270	$ 9,548	$ 9,262	$ 9,540	$ 9,826
Annual Change in Benchmark	3.0%	3.0%	NA	3.0%	3.0%
Total Exp.	$ 340,707,263	$ 549,884,627	$ 710,982,492	$ 842,158,761	$ 954,165,877
Projected Savings Rate - per Client	3.00%	3.25%	2.50%	2.75%	3.00%
Savings Benchmark Rate - per MSSP Regs	2.33%	2.15%	2.00%	2.00%	2.00%
Shared Savings Achieved	Yes	Yes	Yes	Yes	Yes
Total Savings Generated	$ 10,221,218	$ 17,871,250	$ 17,774,562	$ 23,159,366	$ 28,624,976
ACO share with CMS	50%	50%	60%	60%	60%
Available to ACO	$ 5,110,609	$ 8,935,625	$ 10,664,737	$ 13,895,620	$ 17,174,986
Quality Score	90%	85%	85%	90%	90%
Net to ACO	**$ 4,599,548**	**$ 7,595,281**	**$ 9,065,027**	**$ 12,506,058**	**$ 15,457,487**

*Benchmark re-established for second ACO contract period starting in 2016 depending on MSSP regulations and historical ACO performance.

9 This figure includes both Medicare Part A and Medicare Part B expenditures, is calculated by Medicare using three-year trends for attributed beneficiaries, and will be reset in 2016 after the initial term using the experience over the prior three years. If the MPN is successful in reducing health expenditures over that time, as projected, the "bar will be lowered" accordingly.

5.3 Estimating Revenue From Membership Fees and Commercial Contracts

Management's projection for Commercial Contract 1 and Commercial Contract 2, as well as the annual membership fees the MPN's physician participants pay ($3,000 per PCP and $5,500 per specialist through 2018 and $2,000 per PCP and $4,000 per specialist thereafter), are shown in Exhibit 5. In addition to the access to potential shared savings distributions, membership fees afford physicians with access to the network and its population health management infrastructure. In other words, there are both financial *and* strategic reasons why a physician would participate in the MPN.

Under the MPN's two commercial contracts, the MPN is paid a fixed care coordination fee each month for each attributed beneficiary. The care coordination fee is $4 per member per month (PMPM) for Commercial Contract 1 and $3 PMPM for Commercial Contract 2. As both contracts are focused on care management, each commercial payor has chosen to only attribute beneficiaries to their PCPs.

Exhibit 5. Membership and Care Management Revenues

	2014	2015	2016	2017	2018
Membership Fee Revenues					
Network PCPs	263	420	567	652	717
Fee per PCP	$ 3,000	$ 3,000	$ 3,000	$ 3,000	$ 3,000
Membership Fee Revenue from PCP	$ 787,500	$ 1,260,000	$ 1,701,000	$ 1,956,150	$ 2,151,765
Network Specialists	180	243	292	335	369
Fee per Specialist	$ 5,500	$ 5,500	$ 5,500	$ 5,500	$ 5,500
Membership Fee Revenue from Specialists	$ 990,000	$ 1,336,500	$ 1,603,800	$ 1,844,370	$ 2,028,807
Total First Payer Membership Fee Revenue	$ 1,777,500	$ 2,596,500	$ 3,304,800	$ 3,800,520	$ 4,180,572
First Payer - Care Management Revenues					
Estimated number of lives	18,047	28,875	38,981	44,828	49,311
Annual Fee per Member	$ 48.00	$ 48.00	$ 48.00	$ 48.00	$ 48.00
Total Care Management Revenue	$ 866,250	$ 1,386,000	$ 1,871,100	$ 2,151,765	$ 2,366,942
Second Payer - Care Management Revenues					
Estimates number of lives	3,938	6,300	8,505	9,781	10,759
Annual Fee per Member	$ 36.00	$ 36.00	$ 36.00	$ 36.00	$ 36.00
Total Care Management Revenue	$ 141,750	$ 226,800	$ 306,180	$ 352,107	$ 387,318

5.4 Estimating Distributions of Shared Savings to Participating Providers

Just as each MPN has its own expense profile, so does it choose its own surplus distribution model for participating physicians.[10]

Revenues generated under the MPN's MSSP ACO contract are assumed to first cover expenses used to generate those revenues. The MPN allocates 75% of the total operating expenses for this purpose. Then, 70% of any remaining MSSP ACO earnings are distributed to the physicians.

10 Each MPN should consult with legal counsel and other experts who understand the implications of various distribution methodologies from the legal and regulatory perspectives; a thorough discussion of same is well beyond the scope of this chapter.

Using the same rationale, the MPN distributes $1.50 PMPM for Commercial Contract 1 and $1 PMPM for Commercial Contract 2 to participating physicians.

The distribution calculations are shown in Exhibit 6.

Exhibit 6. Physician Distributions

		2014	2015	2016	2017	2018
MSSP Distributions						
MSSP Revenue		$ 4,599,548	$ 7,595,281	$ 9,065,027	$12,506,058	$15,457,487
ACO Overhead Allocated to MSSP @	75%	1,523,847	1,589,183	3,027,918	3,912,047	4,502,700
MSSP Revenue Less Expenses		$ 3,075,701	$ 6,006,098	$ 6,037,109	$ 8,594,011	$10,954,787
Percent Distributed to Physicians		70%	70%	70%	70%	70%
Distribution to Physicians		$ 2,152,991	$ 4,204,269	$ 4,225,976	$ 6,015,808	$ 7,668,351
First Payer - Care Management Distributions						
Estimated number of lives		18,047	28,875	38,981	44,828	49,311
Annual PMPM Distribution per Beneficiary Life		$ 18.00	$ 18.00	$ 18.00	$ 18.00	$ 18.00
Distributions to Physicians		$ 324,844	$ 519,750	$ 701,663	$ 806,912	$ 887,603
Second Payer - Care Management Distributions						
Estimates number of lives		3,938	6,300	8,505	9,781	10,759
Annual PMPM Distribution per Beneficiary Life		$ 12.00	$ 12.00	$ 12.00	$ 12.00	$ 12.00
Distributions to Physicians		$ 47,250	$ 75,600	$ 102,060	$ 117,369	$ 129,106

5.5 Estimating MPN Operating Expenses

Generally, the costs required to generate savings include:

- IT infrastructure and ongoing analytic support;
- Staffing, including management, analytics, IT, administration, and care coordinators;
- Office space, utilities and maintenance, and other miscellaneous operating expenses necessary for provision of the services; and
- Financial and performance reporting.

The MPN's management developed detailed budgets and expense projections, based on current plans and what will be needed as the network and beneficiary population grows. Care management staff, for example, is estimated using ratios of staff positions per covered life for the attributed members.[11] As the MPN's attributed beneficiaries grow, its care management staff grows. Other expenses included professional fees, purchased services, information technology, marketing, and physician recruitment activities.

Management assumed that when the MSSP ACO contract terminated at the end of 2018, the cost to manage the remaining population would reduce along with the remaining number of beneficiaries.

11 We reviewed management's projection of one care manager per 4,000 Medicare beneficiaries and per 8,000 commercial beneficiaries. Given the profile of the MPN's patient population and our experience with other MPNs, we determined these ratios to be reasonable.

No single MPN is exactly like the next. Each entity may have unique complexities; some may outsource a number of core services. In a new market, it can be difficult to determine the levels of activities and costs required to achieve the targeted results, especially given that the targeted results of each MPN can differ significantly. Since proper financial analysis and valuation require an assessment of the reasonableness of the projected expenses of the MPN (and appropriate corresponding adjustments to the discount rate applied to expected cash flows), it is useful for valuators to be familiar with the various strategies and effective costs structures being developed by similarly structured healthcare organizations and other MPNs.

6.0 Working Capital and Cash Flows

The cash flows associated with value-based contracts are unique. This is particularly true of MSSP ACO revenues; the MPN's MSSP ACO revenue is assumed to be distributed by Medicare in July following the performance year-end in December. In effect, this is a 365-day receivable as illustrated in Exhibit 7. It is important not to understate the average days in accounts receivable, as this would artificially inflate cash flows by making it appear that the MPN will generate cash to cover expenses significantly earlier than it actually can, which will ultimately result in an overstated valuation.

Exhibit 7. MSSP Contract Receivables

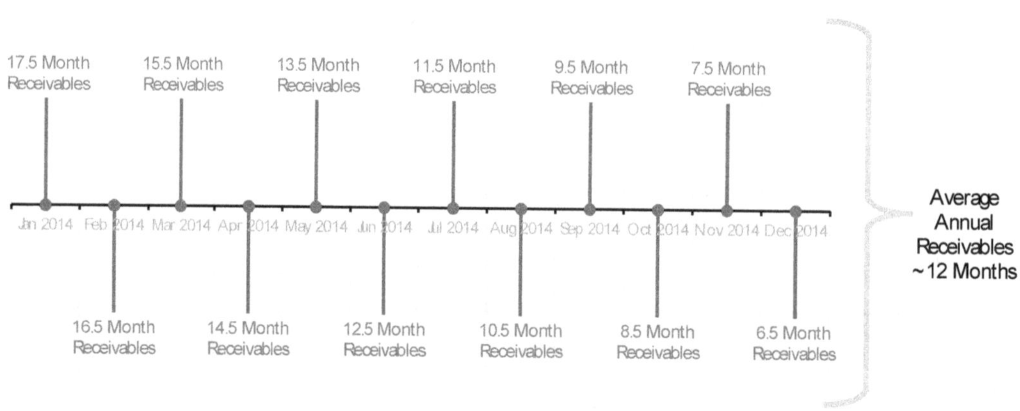

Further, if a perpetual cash flow model (i.e., no exit event) is used, it is important that the projections be made for the number of periods required until cash flows are stable.

7.0 Summary Financials

Given the unique timing of the MPN's MSSP ACO contract receivables, we projected cash flows for a total of seven years, two years beyond that contract's termination. The trailing receivables for the MSSP ACO will be converted into cash in 2019. In the following year, 2020, there will be no collection of cash related to MSSP ACO revenue. Therefore, the cash flows in 2020 represent the steady state cash flows into perpetuity generated by the other membership and care management programs.

The seven-year projections shown in Exhibit 8, Exhibit 9, and Exhibit 10 reflect the economics of the MPN on a stand-alone basis.

Exhibit 8. Projected Income Statements for 2014-2020

	2014	2015	2016	2017	2018	2019	2020
Revenue							
MSSP Contract	$ 4,599,548	$ 7,595,281	$ 9,065,027	$ 12,506,058	$ 15,457,487	$ -	$ -
Other Contracts							
Membership Fees	$ 1,777,500	$ 2,596,500	$ 3,304,800	$ 3,800,520	$ 4,180,572	$ 2,965,296	$ 3,021,637
First Payer - Care Mng.	866,250	1,386,000	1,871,100	2,151,765	2,366,942	2,411,913	2,457,740
Second Payer - Care Mng.	141,750	226,800	306,180	352,107	387,318	394,677	402,176
Total Revenue	$ 7,385,048	$ 11,804,581	$ 14,547,107	$ 18,810,450	$ 22,392,318	$ 5,771,886	$ 5,881,552
Expenses							
Physician Distributions	$ 2,525,084	$ 4,799,619	$ 5,029,699	$ 6,940,089	$ 8,685,060	$ 1,036,026	$ 1,055,711
Direct Operating Costs	2,171,796	2,263,111	4,185,750	5,369,044	6,161,171	3,405,559	3,542,120
Total Expenses	$ 4,696,881	$ 7,062,730	$ 9,215,448	$ 12,309,133	$ 14,846,231	$ 4,441,586	$ 4,597,831
Depreciation and Amortization	79,333	80,213	81,120	82,053	83,015	84,005	85,026
Total Expenses	$ 4,776,214	$ 7,142,943	$ 9,296,568	$ 12,391,186	$ 14,929,246	$ 4,525,591	$ 4,682,857
Net Income Before Taxes	$ 2,608,834	$ 4,661,638	$ 5,250,539	$ 6,419,264	$ 7,463,072	$ 1,246,295	$ 1,198,695
Total Taxes	$ 1,012,697	$ 1,809,555	$ 2,038,154	$ 2,491,830	$ 2,897,015	$ 483,787	$ 465,310
Net Income	$ 1,596,137	$ 2,852,084	$ 3,212,384	$ 3,927,434	$ 4,566,057	$ 762,508	$ 733,386

Exhibit 9. Projected Balance Sheets for 2014-2020

	2014	2015	2016	2017	2018	2019	2020
Assets							
Current Assets							
Checking/Savings (CASH)	$ 450,000	$ 450,000	$ 450,000	$ 450,000	$ 450,000	$ 450,000	$ 450,000
A/R - MSSP Contract	4,599,548	7,595,281	9,065,027	12,506,058	15,457,487	-	-
A/R - Other Contracts	465,522	703,472	916,183	1,053,611	1,158,972	964,617	982,944
Total Current Assets	$ 5,515,070	$ 8,748,753	$ 10,431,210	$ 14,009,668	$ 17,066,459	$ 1,414,617	$ 1,432,944
Net Fixed Assets	$ 223,444	$ 227,320	$ 231,653	$ 236,470	$ 241,800	$ 247,674	$ 254,123
Total Other Assets	$ 654,545	$ 604,545	$ 554,545	$ 504,545	$ 454,545	$ 404,545	$ 354,545
Total Assets	$ 6,393,060	$ 9,580,619	$ 11,217,408	$ 14,750,684	$ 17,762,805	$ 2,066,836	$ 2,041,613
Liabilities and Equity							
Current Liabilities							
A/P - MSSP Shared Savings Dist.	$ 2,152,991	$ 4,204,269	$ 4,225,976	$ 6,015,808	$ 7,668,351	$ -	$ -
A/P - Care Mng. Dist.	92,769	148,430	200,380	230,437	253,481	258,297	263,205
A/P - Operating Expenses	95,005	98,931	178,121	226,933	259,674	146,624	152,436
Total Current Liabilities	$ 2,340,765	$ 4,451,629	$ 4,604,477	$ 6,473,177	$ 8,181,506	$ 404,921	$ 415,641
Members' Equity							
Member Capital	$ 1,374,545	$ 1,374,545	$ 1,374,545	$ 1,374,545	$ 1,374,545	$ 1,374,545	$ 1,374,545
Retained Earnings	2,677,750	3,754,444	5,238,385	6,902,961	8,206,753	287,369	251,426
Total Members' Equity	$ 4,052,295	$ 5,128,990	$ 6,612,931	$ 8,277,506	$ 9,581,298	$ 1,661,915	$ 1,625,972
Total Liabilities and Equity	$ 6,393,060	$ 9,580,619	$ 11,217,408	$ 14,750,684	$ 17,762,805	$ 2,066,836	$ 2,041,613

Exhibit 10. Projected Cash Flow Statements for 2014-2020

	2014	2015	2016	2017	2018	2019	2020
Net Income	$ 1,596,137	$ 2,852,084	$ 3,212,384	$ 3,927,434	$ 4,566,057	$ 762,508	$ 733,386
Plus Depreciation	29,333	30,213	31,120	32,053	33,015	34,005	35,026
Plus Amortization	50,000	50,000	50,000	50,000	50,000	50,000	50,000
Cash Flow From Operations	$ 1,675,470	$ 2,932,297	$ 3,293,504	$ 4,009,487	$ 4,649,072	$ 846,514	$ 818,411
Changes In Working Capital							
Dec (Inc) in A/R - MSSP Contract	$ (4,599,548)	$ (2,995,733)	$ (1,469,745)	$ (3,441,031)	$ (2,951,430)	$ 15,457,487	$ -
Dec (Inc) in A/R - Other Contracts	(465,522)	(237,950)	(212,711)	(137,427)	(105,361)	194,355	(18,328)
Inc (Dec) in A/P - MSSP Shared Savings Dist.	2,152,991	2,051,278	21,708	1,789,831	1,652,543	(7,668,351)	-
Inc (Dec) in A/P - Care Mng Dist.	92,769	55,661	51,950	30,057	23,044	4,816	4,908
Inc (Dec) in A/P - Operating Expenses	95,005	3,925	79,190	48,812	32,742	(113,050)	5,812
Total Change in Working Capital	$ (2,724,305)	$ (1,122,819)	$ (1,529,608)	$ (1,709,758)	$ (1,348,462)	$ 7,875,257	$ (7,608)
Capital Expenditures	$ (32,778)	$ (34,089)	$ (35,452)	$ (36,871)	$ (38,345)	$ (39,879)	$ (41,474)
Net Cash Increase (Decrease)	$ (1,081,613)	$ 1,775,389	$ 1,728,444	$ 2,262,858	$ 3,262,265	$ 8,681,892	$ 769,329

8.0 Accounting for the Risk of Shared Savings Revenue

Even though the MPN's largest potential source of revenue, its MSSP ACO contract, is upside-only for the first half of the projection period, there is still a risk that it will generate no *revenue* from that project if it fails to meet the required minimum savings ratio (MSR) and/or quality thresholds.

In the MPN's case, achieving these thresholds is critical to achieving positive cash flows. A unique challenge in valuing cash flows from shared savings contracts is determining the most likely scenario and the associated risk. The valuator may be familiar with different methods for handling projections with high potential variance. For example, he or she may increase the discount rate to account for the increased variance (i.e., riskiness) of shared savings contract revenue. Alternatively, the valuator may develop multiple projected cash flows scenarios (i.e., most likely case, pessimistic, and optimistic scenarios).

Only One-Quarter of MSSP ACOs Generated Shared Savings Revenue in 2014

- Of the 333 MSSP ACOs that started in 2012, 2013, and 2014, about half (181 ACOs) generated savings in 2014.
- Of these 181, approximately half (92 ACOs) generated sufficient savings to hit the MSR threshold necessary to share in savings. However, six of these 92 ACOs failed to report quality measures.
- In other words, approximately one-quarter (86 ACOs) of the MSSP ACOs ended up sharing in savings in the 2014 performance year.

These results are similar to those in the 2013 performance year.

9.0 Residual Value

While the MPN's commercial contracts and associated revenues were anticipated to continue after 2018 into perpetuity, the MSSP ACO revenue and related care management expense was not expected to continue past 2018. If one assumes that the entity was designed primarily for holding and executing the MSSP ACO contract, it is reasonable to ask what will happen to the assets the MPN holds when shared savings revenue is no longer generated.

In this case, the most likely scenario was that the health system would continue to leverage its assets for other population health strategies and new value-based payment models. Either the health system would acquire the remaining portion of the MPN and assume the assets or enter into a management services contract through which the health system would compensate the MPN for its population health management expertise.

However, given the fair market value standard, we did not consider this strategic interest of the health system. Instead, we assumed that the cost of population health management would be reduced in line with the reduction in managed beneficiaries as reflected in the cash flows.

The following discussion addresses three related considerations introduced above:

- Developing multiple projected cash flows scenarios (i.e., best case, pessimistic, and optimistic scenarios);
- Applying a higher discount rate to account for the increased variance (i.e., riskiness) of shared savings contract revenue (referencing venture capital research); and
- Assuming an exit event occurs in which the health system will acquire the net assets of the entity.

The subject transaction involved a 75% interest in the MPN. For the sake of simplicity, we present calculations of 100% enterprise value below.

10.0 Sensitivity Analysis—Multiple Cash Flow Scenarios

The anticipated earnings stream is typically capitalized by using a factor reflecting the weighted average cost of capital (WACC). Traditional cost of capital estimates are derived using the capital asset pricing model or "buildup" to determine the cost of equity. The WACC combines the equity cost of capital and the cost of debt capital based on an assumed capital structure.

We selected a high company-specific risk premium given the unique risks associated with the MPN that are not typical of general healthcare entities. We considered the following company-specific risk factors:

- Retention of existing physician network following any major transactions in which controlling ownership is transferred;

- Achievement of physician network growth projections;
- Achievement of minimum cost savings to generate MSSP ACO contract revenue;
- Renewal of commercial payor care management contracts; and
- Additional operational risk of an early-stage company.

The cost of equity buildup is shown in Exhibit 11.

Exhibit 11. Cost of Equity Detail

Systematic Risk:	
Risk Free Rate (20-year U.S. Treasury bond yield as of 12/31/2013)	3.7%
Equity Risk Premium – Long-Horizon S&P 500 Market Benchmark (Ibbotson, SBBI 2013 Yearbook)	6.7%
Industry Premium – Accident and Health Insurance and Medical Service Plans (Ibbotson, SBBI 2013 Yearbook)	2.2%
Impact of Size Effect on Risk – Expected 10 decile Capitalization Equity Size Premium, S&P 500 Market Benchmark (Ibbotson, SBBI 2013 Yearbook)	6.0%
Subtotal Systematic Risk	18.6%
Unsystematic Risk Premium:	
Business Specific Risk	7.0%
Subtotal Unsystematic Risk Premium	7.0%
Total Cost of Equity Capital – Business Specific	25.6%

Typically, the capital structure assumption employed in the WACC determination is derived from databases of publicly traded companies engaged in businesses similar to the valuation subject whose assets are considered similar to that of the subject company. The availability of capital structure information that is reflective of comparable businesses to that of the MPN was limited at best. The capital structure employed in the determination of a WACC reflects the anticipated ability of the MPN to obtain debt financing. MPN assets that would have value as collateral for financing would include fixed equipment and working capital. Assets that would support debt financing are estimated to total approximately 10% of total capitalization. The WACC calculation is shown in Exhibit 12.

Exhibit 12. Weighted Average Cost of Capital

	Capital Structure	After Tax Cost of Capital	Weighted Average Cost of Capital
Debt	10.0%	3.00%	0.30%
Equity	90.0%	25.60%	23.04%
Total	100.0%		23.30%

The WACC applied in the probability weighted cash flow model was 23.3%. Discounted cash flows for the base case scenario (using the projections presented earlier in this discussion) are presented in Exhibit 13.

Exhibit 13. Discounted Cash Flows

		2014	2015	2016	2017	2018	2019	2020
Cash Distributions to Owners (Addnt'l Paid in Capital Req.)		$ (1,081,613)	$ 1,775,389	$ 1,728,444	$ 2,262,858	$ 3,262,265	$ 8,681,892	$ 769,329
Time Factor (Midpoint)		0.5	1.5	2.5	3.5	4.5	5.5	6.5
Discount Factor Based on Discount rate @	23.3%	0.9006	0.7304	0.5924	0.4804	0.3896	0.3160	0.2563
Present Value of Forecasted Cash Flows		$ (974,101)	$ 1,296,744	$ 1,023,930	$ 1,087,077	$ 1,270,978	$ 2,743,478	$ 197,179
Total Present Value of Discreet Period Cash Flows		**$ 6,645,286**						
Residual Period Cash Flows								
Year 1 of Residual Period	$ 783,946							
Capitalization Rate @	21.4%							
Value of Residual Cash Flows at 12/31/2021	$ 3,663,301							
Time Factor	6.5							
Discount Factor	0.2563							
Total Present Value of Residual Period Cash Flows		**$ 938,904**						
Total Present Value of Residual Period Cash Flows		**$ 7,584,190**						

We then considered the primary value drivers for this particular MPN: network growth and achieved cost savings. We developed the following pessimistic and optimistic scenarios to test the sensitivity of the projection model:

- In the pessimistic scenario, we reduced total provider network growth trends 50% in the five years 2014 through 2018 and reduced achieved savings rates in the first three years such that no shared savings revenue would be generated; and
- In the optimistic scenario, we increased the achieved cost savings by 2.0% in each MSSP contract year.

Exhibit 14 presents the calculated values under each scenario using the discount rate presented above.

Exhibit 14. Perpetual Business Model Value Driver Sensitivity Analysis

Scenario	Assumptions	WACC	Calculated Enterprise Value
Base Case	As presented herein	23.30%	$ 7,584,190
Pessimistic Scenario	Network growth trend decreased 50% in 2014 through 2018 and MSSP revenues achieved in Years 2017 and 2018 only.	23.30%	$ 827,263
Optimistic Scenario	2% Greater cost savings achieved in each year	23.30%	$ 9,975,298

Given the significant variability of value outcomes, contingent on the MPN being able to achieve multiple key performance goals and the lack of market history to rely upon for developing a sound WACC, we considered applying a higher discount rate, consistent with venture capital rates.

11.0 Venture Capital Discount Rate

We have observed transactions involving a number of MPNs that are in very early stages of development (as described below), in which case venture capital discount rates might be considered (see Exhibit 15).

Exhibit 15. Early Stages of Development

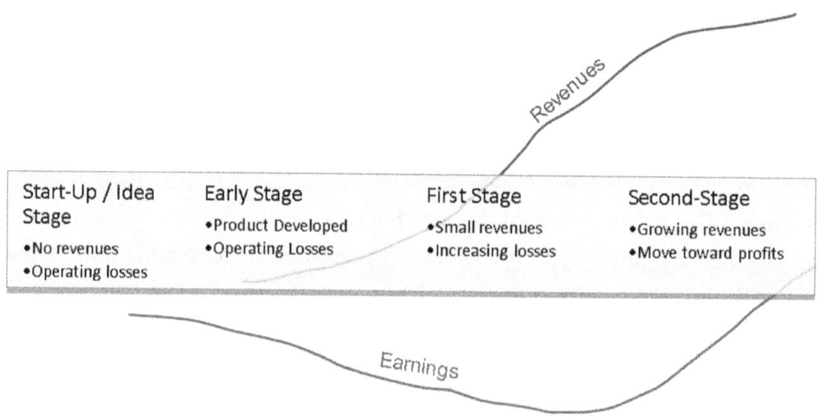

Several publications provide rates of return venture capital investors used at various stages of an enterprise's development. A number of these publications are presented in Exhibit 16. Venture capital rates incorporate the risk of equity investors and include the likelihood that the business would fail. Venture capital required rates of return are generally much higher than discount rates applied to publicly traded companies and mature private entities.

Exhibit 16. Venture Capital Target Rates of Return

Stage of Development	Characteristics	Plummer[1]	Scherlis and Sahlman[2]	HVA Study Actual Returns[3]	Babson College Mass[4]	Frei & Leleux[5]	Seiffer Software[6]
Start-up	Pre-prototype	50%-70%	50%-70%	100%-125%	60%-80%	70%-100%	60%-80%
Early – Development	Pre-commercialization	40%-60%	40%-60%	60%	50%	50%-70%	50%-60%
First Stage	Commercialization	[40%-60%]	[40%-60%]	[60%]	[50%]	40%-60%	40%-50%
Second Stage/Expansion	Shipping Product	35%-50%	30%-50%	50%	40%	35%-50%	30%-40%
Mezzanine/IPO	Profitable	25%-35%	20%-35%	30%-40%	25%-30%	25%-40%	25%-30%

[1]Plummer, James L., QED *Report on Venture Capital Financial Analysis* (Palo Alto: QED Research, Inc. 1987).

[2]Scherlis, Daniel R. and William A. Sahlman, *A Method for Valuing High-Risk, Long Term, Investments: The Venture Capital Method* (Boston: Harvard Business School Publishing, 1987).

[3]Houlihan Valuation Advisors and Venture One study on pricing of venture capital investments in Technology and Life Sciences Companies in the United States, January 1993 to June 1996. Note that only successful VC backed companies were included in this study.

[4]William Bygrave, Babson College Mass., as quoted in the Expert's Report by PricewaterhouseCoopers, Aotea Bio Limited Prospectus and Investment Statement, November 14, 2002.

[5]Frei, P. & Leleux, B. *Valuating the Company. Starting a Business in the Life Sciences – from Idea to Market.* (Luessen, H. (ed).) 455 (Edition Cantor Verlag, Aulendorf, Germany, 2003).

[6]John Seiffer, "The Business of Software: The Venture Capital Rate of Return." November 21, 2005.

The MPN had minimal operational history but had secured payor contracts and competed a year of operations in which revenues were collected. Positive cash flows are expected to be achieved in Year 2 of the projection period. Given these factors and the need for additional funding to sustain current operations, and the reasons previously stated, we concluded the MPN could be categorized as a second-stage company.

We considered that the research supporting the venture capital rates is not industry specific. In general, healthcare as an industry demonstrates less risk to investors (based on a review of industry beta factors) than other industries. In terms of startup entities, health services have the highest survival rate as illustrated in Exhibit 17. Therefore, we concluded a discount rate at 35%, at the low end of the second-stage-company range.

The discount rate of 35% is applied to the cash flows presented above (base case scenario) in Exhibit 18.

12.0 Exit Event Assumed on Dec. 31, 2018

If the valuator determines that such an exit event is the likely path for most hypothetical buyers, he or she may consider developing a two-stage model, discounting cash flows for a discreet period, and determining the value of the assets upon the exit event.

The value of the discreet cash flows for the five years ending Dec. 31, 2018, would be consistent with the approach presented above. The net assets with value as of Dec. 31, 2018, would include:

- Minimal fixed assets;
- Accounts receivable (significant MSSP contract receivable);
- Contracts in-place:
    - The IPA network participation contracts (membership); and
    - Commercial payor care management contracts.
- Workforce in-place.

The concluded value of the asset transaction would then be discounted to present value and added to the present value of the projected cash flows.

In determining the value of the MPN, we did not prepare a valuation model that simulated an exit event. It is more likely that the MPN would utilize its population management expertise to assist other healthcare providers under a services contract with those providers.

13.0 Other Considerations

Financial statements do not always capture the whole picture. There are often debt obligations that are not obvious on the balance sheet or unique cash transfers between related companies to support working capital. MPNs may receive services or operational support from a related company for which no expense is recorded on the income statements.

Startup companies, or entities that are developed as part of two related organizations or more can be especially challenging. It is critical to understand the contractual and other relationships between the related entities.

14.0 Example 2: Market and Cost Approaches

14.1 Background

In this example, a community hospital is interested in acquiring a 50% equity interest in an MPN formed on Jan. 1, 2013, by a 400-physician independent multispecialty group for the sole purpose of entering into an MSSP ACO contract. After speaking with the management of both entities, the valuator has gathered the following information:

- The three-year MSSP contract launched on Jan. 1, 2013. The MPN plans to renew for an additional three years upon expiration of the current contract, on Dec. 31, 2015.
- The MPN's 13,000 assigned Medicare beneficiaries in its MSSP contract are all attributed to a group practice of primary care physicians.
- Beyond the MSSP ACO contract, the MPN does not own any assets. Instead, all services, space, and resources required for the MPN's operations are provided under contract with a management services organization (MSO) or by partnering organizations.
- The hospital intends to cause its employed physician group to join the MPN once the transaction closes, which would add approximately 5,000 Medicare beneficiaries.

The MPN retains no shared savings bonus payments; any shared savings achieved from MSSP participation flow directly to MPN members and participants. Therefore, the valuator will rely upon the cost approach and market approach.

14.2 Cost Approach Analysis

Generally, the conclusions of the cost approach are reflective of the costs to establish the functional utility of the tangible and identifiable intangible assets that support business operations. In this case, the MPN holds no tangible assets; instead, all furniture, equipment, computer hardware and software, facilities, and inventory necessary for the MPN's operations are contracted from the MSO. Additionally, the MPN has no workforce-in-place or other owned infrastructure. The MPN's only identifiable asset is its MSSP ACO contract, which is considered to be an

Exhibit 17. Proportion of Firms That Were Started in 1998 That Survived

	Survival Rate						
Industry	Year 1	Year 2	Year 3	Year 4	Year 5	Year 6	Year 7
Health Services	**85.59%**	**72.83%**	**63.73%**	**55.37%**	**50.09%**	**46.47%**	**43.71%**
Natural Resources	82.33%	69.54%	59.41%	49.56%	43.43%	39.96%	36.68%
Construction	80.69%	65.73%	53.56%	42.59%	36.96%	33.36%	29.96%
Manufacturing	84.19%	68.67%	56.98%	47.41%	40.88%	37.03%	33.91%
Transportation	82.58%	66.82%	54.70%	44.68%	38.21%	34.12%	31.02%
Information	80.75%	62.85%	49.49%	37.70%	31.24%	28.29%	24.78%
Financial Activities	84.09%	69.57%	58.56%	49.24%	43.93%	40.34%	36.90%
Business Services	82.32%	66.82%	55.13%	44.28%	38.11%	34.46%	31.08%
Leisure	81.15%	64.99%	53.61%	43.76%	38.11%	34.54%	31.40%
Other Services	80.72%	64.81%	53.32%	43.88%	37.05%	32.33%	28.77%
All Firms	81.24%	65.77%	54.29%	44.36%	38.29%	34.44%	31.18%

Source: Knaup, Amy E, May 2005, "Survival and longevity in the Business Employment Dynamics data," Monthly Labor Review, pp. 50–56; Knaup, Amy E and MC. Piazza, September 2007, Business Employment Dynamics Data: Survival and Longevity, Monthly Labor Review, pp 3-10.

Exhibit 18. Perpetual Business Model Discounted Cash Flow Summary—Venture Capital Discount Rate

	Cash Flows	Time Factor	Discount Factor @ 35% WACC	Discounted Cash Flows
12 Mos. Ending - Dec. 31, 2014	$(1,081,613)	0.5	0.8607	$ (930,944)
12 Mos. Ending - Dec. 31, 2015	1,775,389	1.5	0.6375	1,131,811
12 Mos. Ending - Dec. 31, 2016	1,728,444	2.5	0.4722	816,171
12 Mos. Ending - Dec. 31, 2017	2,262,858	3.5	0.3498	791,548
12 Mos. Ending - Dec. 31, 2018	3,262,265	4.5	0.2591	845,253
12 Mos. Ending - Dec. 31, 2019	8,681,892	5.5	0.1919	1,666,055
12 Mos. Ending - Dec. 31, 2020	769,329	6.5	0.1422	109,399
Residual Value	3,663,301	6.5	0.1422	520,921
Total Enterprise Value				$ 4,950,213

identifiable intangible asset. As such, the cost approach analysis involves the determination of the replacement cost of the MSSP ACO contract.

Because the MSSP ACO contract is already in place and would otherwise have to be applied for and secured by a hypothetical buyer, it is considered to be an asset in a going-concern valuation. To determine the value of the contract, a valuator must consider what it would cost a hypothetical buyer to acquire a contract with the same characteristics, utility, and terms. Relevant costs would include costs associated with the establishment of an entity capable of delivering on the contract as well as the costs associated with developing and completing the contract application.

14.3 Estimating Startup and Development Costs

The *actual* startup and application development costs can be used as a proxy for the value under the cost approach. These costs can be divided into three categories:

1. *Startup expenses:* Startup expenses included legal, accounting, consulting, and certain management expenses. A functional obsolescence discount was applied to reflect the

fact that, of the assumed total amortizable asset life of 15 years, 13 years remain at the date of valuation.

2. *Consulting costs:* Commonly, organizations such as the MPN hire outside professionals, such as consultants, to develop and complete the MSSP ACO application. The MPN utilized a healthcare management consulting firm to develop its accountable care strategy and to complete the MSSP ACO application at a cost of $500,000. A functional obsolescence factor was applied to this cost as well, to reflect the fact that, given the assumed total asset life of six years, four years remain at the date of valuation.

3. *Management and physician time:* Development of the entity and applying for/attaining the MSSP contract required a significant time commitment from participating physicians and management. A value can be determined based on the estimated hours related to meetings, number of attendees, in relation to the development and creation of the MPN. Similar to the obsolescence applied to the general startup expenses, a functional obsolescence discount was applied to the calculated meeting expense. The discount reflects the fact that, of the assumed total amortizable asset life of 15 years, 13 years remain at the date of valuation.

An analysis of these expenses is shown in Exhibit 19.

Exhibit 19. Expense Analysis

Target Start-Up - General Expense (Recorded on Target Tax Return)		
Recorded Start-Up Expenses	$	397,000
Contract Start Date		1/1/2013
Standard Amortizable Life (Years)		15
Remaining Amortizable Life as of 1/1/2015		13
Assumed Obsolescence (%)*		13%
Assumed Obsolescence ($)	$	(52,933)
Estimated Value ACO Application	**$**	**344,067**
ACO Application Consulting Costs		
Estimated Cost of MSSP ACO Completion	$	500,000
Contract Start Date		1/1/2013
Life of Contract (Years)		6
Years Left in Contract as of 1/1/2015		4
Assumed Obsolescence (%)**		33%
Assumed Obsolescence ($)	$	(166,667)
Estimated Value ACO Application	**$**	**333,333**
Target Start-Up - Meeting Expense		
Participant Hours		600
Average Hourly Rate	$	125
Estimated Meeting Expense	$	75,000
Assumed Obsolescence (%)*		13%
Assumed Obsolescence ($)	$	(9,750)
Estimated Value - Meetings Expense	**$**	**65,250**

*Applied obsolescence adjustment considers amortizable life of start-up costs of 15 years; 13 years remaining.

**Applied obsolescence adjustment considers asset life of 6 years; 4 years remaining.

As shown in Exhibit 20, the value conclusion for 100% equity, under the cost approach, is approximately $740,000. Therefore, the value of 50% equity is approximately $370,000.

Exhibit 20. Cost Approach Summary

	Estimated FMV	
	100% Equity	50% Equity
Start-Up Expense Recorded on Tax Return	$ 344,067	
Consulting Fees	333,333	
Meeting Expense	65,250	
Total	$ 742,650	$ 371,325

14.4 Market Approach Analysis

On the surface, use of a market approach (i.e., evaluating the costs others have incurred to develop a comparable set of assets) is an appealing methodology. However, given the nature of the programs being developed, the lack of standardized processes related to developing ACOs and ACO-like organizations, the available information, while informative, is not robust enough to rely on in determining a valuation conclusion. As the sector develops over the next few years, more relevant data will become available. That said, it is useful to review reports, surveys, and white papers about similar ACO entities, as a reasonableness test for the cost approach findings. Two key available studies are:

1. American Hospital Association's (AHA) "The Work Ahead: Activities and Costs to Develop an Accountable Care Organization" was published in April 2011. This white paper examined the steps and associated costs of four organizations that were actively developing programs or organizations poised to be "accountable for care." The white paper identified 23 activity areas and estimated the costs of the activities, both for startup and ongoing operations, for two prototype organizations, based on the studied organizations. Much variation exists among entities of this nature, and there are many ways to develop, structure, and operate these entities, making identification of true comparable organizations challenging. As the AHA white paper indicated, "neither the nature of ACOs nor the process of developing them has become standardized"; and

2. Modern Healthcare's 2013 and 2014 "ACO Survey," which reports a variety of self-reported data from established ACOs, including startup costs. Between the 2013 and 2014 survey, a total of 32 established ACOs provided an estimate of their organization's startup costs.

Application of the market approach first involved analysis of the data provided in the AHA study related to the categories and amount of startup expenses subject organizations incurred. This process involved the following steps:

- Review of total startup costs incurred by typical startups, broken down by source of cost, as reported in AHA's study;

- Identify the categories of startup costs deemed to be applicable to the MPN, including engaging legal and consulting support, providing management and staff, developing and managing relationships with specialists, and compensating physician leaders; and
- Estimate the portion of the total AHA reported costs that were applicable to MPN-specific startup expenses (which were assumed to include the legal, consulting, meeting, and travel expenses required to establish the entity and secure its MSSP contract).

The startup costs that were relevant to the MPN being valued included:

- Engaging legal and consulting support;
- Providing MPN management and staff;
- Developing and managing relationships with specialists; and
- Compensating physician leaders.

Based on the AHA study, these costs represent 12% to 21% of total typical ACO startup costs (see Exhibit 21).[12]

Exhibit 21. Buildup of ACO Startup Expenses Applicable to Target

	AHA Prototype A*	AHA Prototype B*
Estimated Costs Applicable to Target		
Engaging legal and consulting support	$ 350,000	$ 500,000
Providing ACO management and staff	550,000	600,000
Developing contracting capabilities	150,000	150,000
Compensating physician leaders	75,000	190,000
Total Estimated Applicable Start-Up Costs	$ 1,125,000	$ 1,440,000
Total Full-scale ACO Start-Up Costs	$ 5,315,000	$ 12,000,000
Target Applicable Start-Up Costs as a % Total	21%	12%

*Prototype A figures based on an ACO composed of a single free-standing hospital with 80 PCPs and 250 specialists. Prototype B figures based on an ACO composed of a five hospital system with 250 PCPs and 500 specialists. Prototype figures based on data from actual ACOs.

12 Analysis of AHA's 2011 "The Work Ahead: Activities and Costs to Develop an Accountable Care Organization."

Applying the findings from the analysis of the AHA study to total ACO startup expenses market data (as self-reported by ACOs) from Modern Healthcare's 2013 and 2014 "ACO Survey" provided a range of estimated total startup expenses for ACOs incurring similar startup expenses as the MPN. This is shown in Exhibit 22.

Exhibit 22. ACO Startup Cost Market Data

	Total Start-Up Costs	12% of Total Start-Up Costs*	21% of Total Start-Up Costs*
25th Percentile	$ 1,450,000	$ 174,000	$ 304,500
50th Percentile	$ 2,126,000	$ 255,120	$ 446,460
75th Percentile	$ 3,651,250	$ 438,150	$ 766,763
95th Percentile	$ 10,000,000	$ 1,200,000	$ 2,100,000

*Prototype A figures based on an ACO composed of a single free-standing hospital with 80 PCPs and 250 specialists. Prototype B figures based on an ACO composed of a five hospital system with 250 PCPs and 500 specialists. Prototype figures based on data from actual ACOs.

The equity value of the MPN indicated by the cost approach, $740,000, falls within the observed range of startup costs indicated by the market approach of $174,000 at the 25th percentile to $2.1 million at the 95th percentile. Thus, the results of the market approach are used as a reasonableness test for the cost approach findings.

15.0 Conclusion

Business valuation in the MPN space is not for the light of heart.

As CMS and commercial payors change their value-based contracting programs and offer new options, business models will continue to adapt accordingly. The change in market conditions and business models may cause different value drivers to be more (or less) critical. The case studies presented here are drawn from actual valuation engagements. They are based on specific transactions and specific market conditions, which can have a significant impact on the valuation of an MPN. For example, the extent to which value-based contracts exist in a given market will be a critical driver in a valuation. While many hospitals and health systems continue to evaluate value-based payment models, such as accountable care, bundled payments, or shared savings/shared risk, the level of adoption varies significantly across different markets. The degree and speed of transformation toward value-based competition will drive the level of risk associated with the financial projections. In addition, actual results from MPNs tell us that achieving shared savings may not be an automatic result, as not everyone will win under this strategy. The valuator can reflect these risks in the valuation via a rigorous evaluation of the various risk factors associated with the transaction and the entity.

As discussed, the unique economic drivers of MPNs will significantly impact a valuation analysis. In particular, MPN revenues are produced, at least in part, by reducing spending under shared savings contracts rather than through patient service fees. Second, often no cash is generated in the early stages of an MPN because shared savings revenue is based upon performance and calculated by the payor or payors at the end of specified periods. And, finally, it is not always clear who is responsible for the significant infrastructure investments required to successfully execute an MPN's contracts.

To successfully value transactions related to integrated networks or shared savings contracts, it is critical to understand the business model, the structure of the actual transaction, what drives value to owners rather than participants, and the areas where an MPN is most exposed to risk. Healthcare is a continually changing marketplace, but this corner of the market is, quite possibly, evolving the quickest.

www.ingramcontent.com/pod-product-compliance
Lightning Source LLC
LaVergne TN
LVHW080644210926
848485LV00003B/325